ALSO BY KEVIN D. McCANN

The Kitty League (with Joshua Maxwell)
The Jackson Generals: Minor League Baseball in Jackson, Tennessee
Jackson Diamonds: Professional Baseball in Jackson, Tennessee
The Peg Leg Politician: Adam Huntsman of Tennessee
Hurst's Wurst: Colonel Fielding Hurst and the Sixth Tennessee Cavalry U.S.A.

KEN BOYER

KEN BOYER

ALL-STAR, MVP, CAPTAIN

KEVIN D. McCANN

BRAYBREE
Publishing

Copyright © 2016 Kevin D. McCann
All rights reserved

Published by BrayBree Publishing Company LLC
FIRST EDITION

No part of this book may be reproduced, stored in or introduced into a retrieval system or transmitted in any form or by any means (electronic, mechanical, photocopying, recording, or otherwise) without the prior written permission of the publisher and copyright owner.

The scanning, uploading, and distribution of this book on the Internet or through any other means is not permitted without permission from the publisher and copyright owner.

ISBN-13: 978-1-940127-14-9

Printed in the United States of America

BrayBree Publishing Company LLC
P.O. Box 1204
Dickson, Tennessee 37056-1204

Visit our website at www.braybreepublishing.com
and the book's website at www.kenboyerbook.com

Frontispiece: JTooley SportsArt (www.JTsportsart.com)
Front cover: John Rogers Archive
Back cover: National Baseball Hall of Fame Library, Cooperstown NY
St. Louis Mercantile Library Collection
Griva Family Collection

For my Dad, Jerry McCann, who shared with me his passion for the Cardinals.

CONTENTS

Prologue   xi

1. A Boy Who Always Delights in Sports   3
2. A Cardinal Takes Flight   18
3. Omaha and Overseas   39
4. Houston and Havana   53
5. Great Expectations   79
6. The Reluctant Dragon   102
7. The Captain   128
8. All This Integration   156
9. All-Star Infield   182
10. A Pennant Winner   209
11. A World Championship   231
12. All Mixed Up   253
13. But the Mets Are In Last Place   265
14. A Final Challenge   281
15. West Coast Finale   291
16. Back to the Minors   303
17. Cardinals Manager   321
18. Heading for Home   349
19. An Exceptional Ballplayer   362

Statistics   369
Acknowledgements   371
Notes   379
Bibliography   439
Index   445

Prologue

All Ken Boyer ever wanted to do was play baseball.

He grew up in an America where children spent their free time outdoors and had adventures away from the supervision of their parents. It was a world without the modern distractions of hand-held devices, video games, and streaming entertainment. This culture of the 1930s and '40s produced some of the best players in the game's history, a time when baseball was truly the National Pastime.

Ken's love for the game started in the backyard of his home in the prairie of southwest Missouri. His father, exhausted from working all day to provide for his large family in the midst of the Great Depression, played catch with him and his older brothers. The youngster trailed them to the ball field a half mile away where he competed in pick-up games and honed his skills against other local boys.

He dreamed of playing for his favorite team, the St. Louis Cardinals, and he realized that dream. A fifteen-year major-league career produced eleven All-Star Game appearances, five Gold Glove Awards, a Most Valuable Player Award, and a World championship. He was one of the best overall third basemen in the game, a durable athlete in the field and a model of consistent production at the plate. On a team that included one of the greatest hitters of all time, Ken was the Captain, a leader whose firm but reassuring demeanor earned the admiration and respect of his teammates.

He never forgot the dreams that began in his backyard. With his playing career behind him, he received a letter from a mother seeking advice for her young son who aspired to become a big-leaguer himself. Ken tapped into his own childhood ambitions when he took the time to write him a letter that read in part:

> I know if you are like most boys that like to play baseball, and like we were when we were youngsters growing up, you probably have some notion about making professional baseball your career. Assuming this to be so, please allow me to assure you of what you are in for, and up against.
>
> Baseball is probably one of the most gratifying of all vocations. It allows us to do the one thing we always dreamed of as children, playing Baseball every day—and getting paid to do it. Secondly, the competitive spirit learned in Sports will be with you the rest of your life, no matter what business you eventually wind up in.
>
> But, don't ever try to kid yourself about one simple fact. It requires an awfully lot of work on your part, first to develop your skills well enough to be offered a contract, and secondly, to become one of the very best in the whole United States to reach the Major leagues. So if the Lord gave you athletic ability, let me be one to encourage you to concentrate on improving these very precious skills.[1]

He who makes no mistakes never makes anything.

—Proverb posted in Ken Boyer's locker at Busch Stadium

KEN BOYER

Chapter One

A Boy Who Always Delights in Sports

Kenton Lloyd Boyer was born on Wednesday, May 20, 1931, in a rented home on Lincoln Street in Liberty, Missouri, fifteen miles northeast of Kansas City. Except for the fact that his paternal grandparents lived one street over, there were nothing else that bound his family to the small town.[1] His father, Chester Vern Boyer, brought his wife Mabel and two young children to Clay County three years earlier seeking steady work and higher wages in the midst of the Great Depression.

Vern and Mabel's roots were actually 160 miles south in Jasper County, located in the southwest corner of the state. The Boyer family's ancestry went back to Germany. Vern's great-grandfather, Andrew Boyer, was a Maryland native who came to Missouri from Ohio in the late 1850s or early 1860s. He settled in Scotland County in the northeast part of the state.[2] Though born in the village of Arbela in Scotland County in 1903, Vern moved with his parents Lewis Winfield Boyer and Pansy (Powell) Boyer and younger brother Clarence to Jasper County when he was six years old. He was raised on a farm in the Preston township, southwest of the town of Jasper, where he remembered plowing the fields from four o'clock in the morning to eight at night. Vern earned enough money to buy a brand-new buggy when he was 16. Apparently, it was a newsworthy purchase—part gossip, part advertisement. The local paper, *The Jasper News*, wrote: "Vern Boyer joined that happy and increasing number that are driving new Hercules buggies, the good kind Webb Bros. sell."[3]

In 1922, Vern met fifteen-year-old Mabel Agnes Means, the sixth child and third daughter of Willace Frederick Means and his wife Carrie (Dunlap) Means. She was a Jasper County native who was born near the Cossville community in 1907. Because they were under the legal age of twenty-one, the couple needed their parents' consent to wed. Once given, they traveled to Webb City in the southwest part of the county and were married in the home of a local minister, Thomas L. Harris, on April 7, 1923.[4] The newlyweds made their home in the Duval community and started a family that year with the birth of their first child, a daughter named Juanita LaVerne. A second daughter, Lila Thelma, was born in 1926. Unfortunately, she passed away at seventeen months old. The possible cause was roseola, a viral infection common with young children. Their first son, Cloyd Victor, was born a year later.[5]

Vern moved his family to Clay County in 1928, settling first in Washington township and finding work as a farm laborer, a house builder, and a railroad worker. They relocated to Liberty a year later, where two more sons, Milton Wayne and Kenton Lloyd, were born. Mabel named her third son after a friend of one of her nephews. "I always was one to think of unusual names," she said.[6]

The couple grew homesick and returned to Jasper County in 1934. They rented a small house—"It was kind of a shack," son Cloyd remembered—about seven miles north of the town of Alba. Vern provided for his growing family as best he could, working primarily on government-funded Works Progress Administration projects in the area. According to the 1940 Census, he was employed as a stock clerk for a WPA road project. He also worked at a blacksmith shop and garage in nearby Cossville. Mabel supplemented the family income by washing and ironing clothes for other families. In 1936, the Boyers moved a few miles south of Cossville to a small house the children remembered as the "poor farm." "Mom said she called it the 'poor farm' because nothing would grow on the land," recalls sister

Delores (Boyer) Webb. It had no electricity and no indoor plumbing. Mabel cooked on a wood stove that heated the house in the winter. Spaces between the floor boards let enough cold inside to freeze the mop that stood behind the stove.[7]

Life was difficult in the Depression, and the hardships impacted the lives of the Boyer children. Asked about childhood memories Kenton may have shared over twenty-five years of marriage, his wife Kathleen Boyer recalled only his family's poverty and the cold winter winds that blew through the cracks of his home. He reflected on the adversity many years later: "A thing that helps make a family close is the problems you have growing up. We didn't have things, but nobody else did either." Despite their financial circumstances, Vern and Mabel made sure the children never wanted for food. They grew their own vegetables in the family garden and canned much of them for the winter. Chickens were raised for their eggs and a cow produced milk. Mabel was a wonderful cook who baked bread, cakes, and pies and made homemade jellies.[8]

The children did what they could to help make ends meet, often working on neighboring farms baling hay, harvesting wheat, or milking cows. To earn spending money for themselves, they mowed yards and went door-to-door selling magazines, tubes of salve that promised to cure skin irritations, or issues of *Grit*, a popular weekly family newspaper. "When I was selling that paper, I'd walk ten miles out into the country to make a couple of nickels," recalled Kenton. Cloyd believed their parents' perseverance and strong work ethic influenced them all. "My dad and mom were honest, hard-working people. I think that rubbed off on all of the kids. All of our kids were hard workers and honest, which you don't find that all too much today. Especially the hard-working part."[9]

Kenton and his brothers got along as well as siblings often do. "We didn't tangle much, just every day," he quipped. The stakes were raised when Cloyd and Wayne used their earnings to purchase a bicycle, the first one in the family. "The bike caused all the fights," Kenton remembered. "We were always fighting for it."[10]

Vern's sons grew taller than his 5-foot-8 stature and each inherited his deep chest, broad shoulders, and thick legs. Years of farming and manual labor gave him "arms (that) were like two clubs," his daughter

Pansy (Boyer) Schell remembers. The stresses of life coupled with a large household and his own upbringing made him a strict disciplinarian. Cloyd remembered one instance when he, Wayne, and Kenton were caught by a neighbor smoking corn shucks and their father punished them. "When he got home, we had a little smoke shed. He got his razor strap and called us out there and we took turns, the three of us."[11]

"Dad was real strong, but he was very short-tempered in those days," remembered Kenton. "He had no patience. After all, raising a lot of children in times like the Thirties wasn't easy, and you can see how it would make a man short-tempered. Dad demanded a lot of respect and got it." In contrast, Mabel was remembered for her sweet temperament and sense of humor. "Kenton got his disposition from Mom," said Pansy. "I never saw her unhappy."[12]

Fortunately, life wasn't always hard work for the Boyer siblings. A favorite pastime on Saturday afternoons was going to the movies. The closest venue was the air-conditioned Civic Theater in Webb City, advertised as the "Coolest Spot in Town." The children would leave home early in the morning and walk nine miles—or possibly catch a ride with someone along the way—to be there in time for the afternoon matinee. Another diversion was swimming in a collapsed mine shaft filled with over a hundred feet of water. One time, Wayne was playing around and pushed Kenton, barefoot but still wearing his clothes, down the twenty-foot embankment toward the water. He managed to stay on his feet, but sliding on the rocks sliced the bottom of his foot. Wayne jumped into the water and laughed. Kenton angrily threw rocks at him but missed. Eventually, one skimmed off the surface and smacked Wayne on the head, sending him down for a few moments. Kenton wouldn't go in after his brother. "No, two other kids did—I still had my clothes on."[13]

Their favorite recreation was baseball. No matter how tired he may have been at the end of the day, Vern Boyer made time to play catch and hit grounders and fly balls to his boys. "My dad loved the game and he started working with us when we were old enough to stand up, I guess," Kenton remembered. Fifty-cent baseball gloves were typical gifts on Christmas Day. Spring couldn't come soon enough to use them and they often ran outside to play catch in the snow. When authentic baseballs were scarce, they threw homemade ones made of string and put together by their mother or simply hit corncobs with a bat. Being the youngest of the three boys, Kenton was always the last to hit.[14]

The oldest children—Juanita, Cloyd, Wayne, and Kenton—attended Rosebank School about a mile from home. The rock-walled, one-room country schoolhouse had twenty-five students and a baseball team. Cloyd, Wayne, and even nine-year-old Kenton played on it. Instead of uniforms, the boys played in their overalls. Five of Kenton's teammates—including his brothers—later played pro ball. The coach was a first-year teacher named Carl Parker, who remembered the team and the smallest kid on the roster. "Even as a second grader, Ken could run real well and he could place his hits. He usually hit right over second base."[15]

The Rosebank team was almost unbeatable in 1938 and finished their season with a record of 24-1. An ill-timed case of curiosity by the star pitcher stopped their winning streak. To spare his wife the drudgery of washing the family's laundry by hand, Vern Boyer purchased a motorized washing machine. The mechanical marvel on the back porch soon became the focus of the children's attention. Despite a warning from his mother to leave it alone, Cloyd dared point his finger too close and caught it in the spinning rollers. He panicked and pulled it out forcefully, resulting in a deep cut that left him unavailable to pitch in the team's next game, which Rosebank lost.[16]

When Kenton was ten years old, the family moved a few miles southeast to Alba.[17] They rented a small five-room frame house at 512 North Orchard Street. Like all their previous homes, it lacked electricity and indoor plumbing. By this time, the Boyer clan had grown to nine children with the additions of Delores Lorraine in 1933, Lewis Lynn in 1935, Cletis Leroy in 1937, Pansy Jean in 1939, and Shirley Mae in 1940.[18] The house had three bedrooms—the boys slept together in one room, the girls in another, and Vern and Mabel had their own. "We had a room with two double beds and three [children] were in each bed," recalls Cloyd. "Six were sleeping in that one room, and the room was just about big enough for the beds."[19]

Across the street was a large cornfield. Vern and other neighborhood fathers rented the lot for a few dollars and turned it into a baseball field. The fathers and sons planted Bermuda grass, graded base paths, and measured foul lines. "In summertime, whenever a ball was hit real hard to left, the fielder out there would have to go into the rows of corn growing on the field next to ours to hold it to a double or triple," remembered Kenton. "We never had any trouble getting enough kids together for a game, and we played it until dark all summer." It was such a well-maintained field that the high school team later played on it and installed lights for night games. Another team would play there as well, one that would help Kenton Boyer achieve his lifelong ambition to play pro baseball.[20]

THE ALBA ACES were coached and sponsored by Buford Cooper, who owned two grocery stores in Jasper County, including the one on North Main Street in Alba that Vern Boyer managed.[21] The thirty-four-year-old Cooper loved baseball and because there were no organized teams for young boys in the area, he helped create the Cardinal Junior League in 1941. It fielded teams representing several small communities in the northwest section of the county. His successful businesses enabled him to provide the Aces with bats, balls, uniforms (advertising Cooper Grocery on the back), and other equipment at a time when most parents had no extra money for such luxuries.

"He was a guy that everybody liked, and we played hard for him and went all out," remembers Cloyd Boyer. "He never got on anybody. He was pretty easy-going. He just liked baseball, and we happened to have a pretty good team most every year. I think he really enjoyed managing about as much as we did playing. If it hadn't been for him, we probably wouldn't have had a team because he kind of financed it. He was the only one around who had a little bit of money." Cooper later explained why he did so much for the boys in the community. "There weren't a lot of opportunities around Alba. One way to get ahead was to get into professional ball, and I was going to make sure the boys got every chance to develop any talents they might have."[22]

The Cardinal Junior League played an important role in the development of many young men in the tri-state region of Missouri, Kansas, and Oklahoma—including Kenton—who went on to play professional baseball. It gave them the opportunity to compete against the best young players in the region and showcase their skills for area scouts.

Between 1941 and 1948, at least nineteen players graduated from the league and signed pro contracts.[23]

Each season began after local high school baseball ended. A split-season schedule was adopted with winners of the first and second halves meeting in a championship series. The winning team received a paid trip to St. Louis to watch a Cardinals or Browns game at Sportsman's Park or to Kansas City to see the minor-league Blues of the American Association. For the first six years, league games were held only on Sunday afternoons. The schedule was expanded to 30 games played twice a week in 1946, and night games were introduced in towns like Alba, Baxter Springs, and Columbus, Kansas. Local volunteers served as umpires until the league realized unbiased arbiters were needed and paid for their services beginning in 1945.[24]

The league was first organized on June 4, 1941, with teams in Alba, Belmont, Cossville, Medoc, Neck City, and Webb City. Cooper served as the first president. They played every Sunday for ten weeks beginning June 8. The Alba Aces won the inaugural championship and were rewarded with a trip to St. Louis to watch a Cardinals game. Cloyd and Wayne made the team that first season. Even though other teams had players upwards of fifteen years old, ten-year-old Kenton impressed Cooper enough to be added to the roster. Much of his first season with the Aces was spent on the bench, though he sometimes played in right field and batted .280.[25]

Over the next seven years, the Cardinal Junior League added teams from larger towns like Carl Junction, Carthage, and Joplin, and grew beyond the boundaries of Jasper County to include ones from southeast Kansas. The age limit was increased from fifteen to nineteen years old and eligibility restrictions were implemented to ensure that players lived within a twenty-five-mile radius of their team.[26]

Because he played against his brothers and their friends growing up, Kenton wasn't intimidated by the older players. In fact, he enjoyed the challenge. One memorable game against the Pittsburg, Kansas, Elks in 1942 demonstrated Cooper's confidence in his abilities. With Kenton on deck and the go-ahead run at the plate, the Elks coach instructed his young pitcher to intentionally walk the batter and load the bases, anticipating a force out by the smallest player for the Aces. Instead, Kenton tripled to clear them, giving Alba the lead and eventual win. Cooper said with admiration, "He thought he could play ball, and he could."²⁷

In 1944, Vern Boyer heard the St. Louis Cardinals were holding a tryout camp nine miles away at Carthage and tracked down his seventeen-year-old son Cloyd, who was baling hay for a local farmer. "We needed the money, but my father came and took me off the hay baler and carried me to the tryout camp," recalled Cloyd. The Cardinals liked his arm and signed him as a right-handed pitcher the following spring. They sent him to their Lynchburg, Virginia, club to await the start of the season with their Class D club in Johnson City, Tennessee, in June 1945.²⁸

Cloyd Boyer became one of six players from the 1944 Cardinal Junior League to sign a professional contract. "This is a remarkable record for an amateur league," noted the *Joplin Globe* on March 11, 1945, "and gives a boost to the youngsters who have displayed their ability and ambition once a week, on Sundays, for the pleasure they got out of it and for the opportunity to catch a scout's eye and a chance in professional baseball. It also shows plainly the caliber of play in the league, which was close to Class D quality."²⁹

It was a poignant moment for the Boyer family when Cloyd left home. Kenton went with his parents and siblings to the train station at Carthage to see him off. There were tears on their faces as they watched him leave. "Don't worry," Cloyd told his brothers, "some day there will be three or four of us catching this train." From that moment, fourteen-year-old Kenton was determined to fulfill his brother's prophecy and become a professional ballplayer.³⁰

A little older and more experienced, he received more consistent playing time in the 1945 season. His name first appeared in the *Joplin Globe* newspaper after smacking a bases-loaded triple that put Alba ahead by a run in a 9-4 comeback victory over the undefeated Columbus (Kansas) Lions on June 10. The Aces were knotted in a three-way tie with Columbus and Joplin for the first-half title on July 2. A playoff doubleheader was scheduled in Columbus on the fifteenth, with Alba facing the Joplin Sunny Jims and the winner taking on the Lions for the title. The Sunny Jims held the Aces to two hits and beat them in the first game, 4–2, but lost the second contest and the first-half title to Columbus, 11–2.³¹ Before joining the Navy, Cloyd returned home and pitched five games for the Aces in July and August. Kenton's two-run double in the bottom of the ninth inning on August 13 beat Joplin, 4-3. He was Cloyd's catcher two days later in a 5–3 victory at Galena, Kansas. Despite back-to-back victories over Joplin and Cloyd striking out 12 batters in each contest, Alba fell short and lost the second-half title to the Sunny Jims.[32]

"When Kenny was a kid, he was strictly a pull hitter," recalled brother Wayne Boyer. "Nobody taught him. We were just country kids. We didn't have professional coaches. The guy who coached us the most [Buford Cooper] owned the grocery store. He spent most of his time in the store, not at the baseball field. So Kenny would kick that left leg up in the air and he was a pull hitter, a power hitter, from the time he was an early teenager."[33]

The Opening Day lineup for the Alba Aces in 1946 found fifteen-year-old Kenton playing second base and batting seventh while Wayne was in left field and hitting cleanup. It was a disappointing season that saw Alba lose seven in a row and finish with a losing record. Before it was over, Wayne became the second Boyer brother to embark on a professional baseball career. The Cardinals signed him as a left-handed pitcher and sent him to their Opelika, Alabama, club in the Class D Georgia-Alabama League. But Cooper felt Kenton had overtaken his older brothers with his natural talent and abilities. "By the time he was fourteen or fifteen, I thought he was the best kid ballplayer I'd ever seen."[34]

At sixteen, Kenton came into his own with the Aces. He played shortstop with such a strong right arm that some teammates wouldn't take his throws at second base. "Kenny had a heck of an arm, but he could be a little wild," recalled a friend. "He scared other high school kids to death." Cooper knew he had potential to be truly special. "But I decided I'd never try to get him to ease up. As young as he was, I knew he had possibilities. I didn't want to do anything that might ruin that arm."[35]

His hitting was equally robust. After he and teammate George Hosp homered on Opening Day of the 1947 season, spectators showed their appreciation by "passing the hat" and rewarding them with $16.87. A .364 average at mid-season earned him a starting berth on the Cardinal Junior League All-Star team. They faced the first-half champion

Whiz Kids from Baxter Springs, Kansas, in the All-Star Game on August 1, 1947. The All-Stars were victorious, 10-9, on a bases-loaded walk in the ninth inning. The opposing shortstop was a fifteen-year-old from Commerce, Oklahoma, named Mickey Mantle.[36]

Alba battled Baxter Springs for the league lead in the season's second-half, but fell short and ended in a third-place tie with Carl Junction. In 116 at-bats, Kenton finished with a .310 average (tenth-best in the league), 36 runs, 36 hits, five doubles, one triple, five home runs (tied for first), 36 RBIs, and 10 stolen bases. Hosting night games for the first time, Alba ended the season with attendance of more than 11,000 for exhibition and league games, a remarkable figure for a town of 300 residents.[37]

The Aces endured a losing season in 1948 in what proved to be their last one in the Cardinal Junior League. Kenton's final average isn't known, but he batted below .300. No doubt his performance was affected by a frightening at-bat in a game against the Whiz Kids. He was struck on the temple by a fastball from right-hander Ben Craig and became timid at the plate as a result. The season finale featured a reunion of the Boyer brothers as Cloyd and Wayne, back home from their minor-league seasons, joined Kenton for an exhibition contest with a team from nearby Purcell. To retain their rosters of older teen-aged players, Alba and Baxter Springs switched to the Ban Johnson League of Southeastern Kansas for the 1949 season.[38]

KENTON'S ATHLETIC DEVELOPMENT continued at Alba High School, where he became a star baseball and basketball player. He was a popular student and elected class president in his freshman, sophomore, and senior years. In addition, he was class business manager as a sophomore and senior, worked on the *Chatters* newspaper staff, and acted in the freshman, junior, and senior class plays. "He usually wore jeans that were too short, and his shirts were hand-me-downs from his older brothers, but it never distracted from his charm," recalls former girlfriend Zena (Allison) Williams, whose father was the principal. It wasn't until high school that he owned a new shirt of his own. She remembered him as "a lot of fun to be around" and would entertain his friends with a trick he learned. "Kenton could fall straight down on his face and catch himself, and we tried to get him to do it over and over."³⁹

Because he was so popular in school, it wasn't easy for his younger siblings to follow in his footsteps. "I can't say there was a person who didn't like him," said his younger sister, Delores (Boyer) Webb. At the same time, she admitted, "Sometimes, I hated being his sister because we had teachers who just loved Kenton, and I had to follow him two years later."⁴⁰

Like most small towns, there wasn't a lot for teenagers to do. Alba sat at the crossroads of two highways in the middle of the Jasper County prairie with only a gas station, Cooper's Grocery, and a café. Sports was often the only source of entertainment. "Few of us had cars, so we spent our evenings running around Alba if there wasn't a basketball game or baseball game," says Zena (Allison) Williams. "I don't know what we did to have so much fun, but I remember laughing." Joe Cook, a childhood friend of the Boyer brothers, recalled, "Back in those days, there were only two things to do in Alba. You either played baseball, or you went and watched somebody else play baseball. There was no pool hall, no television, nothing else to do."⁴¹

Kenton was a quiet and respectful student who made good grades, though he "wasn't quite as interested in his honor roll as he was his sports," his mother remembered.⁴² His love of sports was reflected in the school yearbook, *The Albamo*. In the last will and testament of the 1949 senior class, he bequeathed "his everlasting love for all sports" to a friend in the junior class. The yearbook prophesied that he would hit "his fifty-fourth homer of the year for the Cardinals" in the 1958 World Series. His senior picture included the following epithet:

> *A boy who always delights in sports,*
> *always a friendly, likable sort.*⁴³

In addition to baseball, Kenton became an excellent basketball player. He was captain of the high school team in his senior year when they won 17 games in a row, captured the Tri-County League championship, and finished with a record of 24-7. In 18 out of 31 games reported in the *Joplin Globe*, he consistently led the squad with an average of 15 points per game, mostly as a forward. Recalled teammate

Melvin Rector: "He was the best high school athlete I ever saw. The rest of us just went along for the ride." Porter Wittich of the *Globe* wrote, "Kenton Boyer...has been referred to this department by more than a few coaches as the smoothest piece of basketball material in the district."[44]

Before a game with Alba, coach Russ Kaminsky asked his Joplin High School team, "Who's going to guard Boyer tonight?" One player volunteered and Kenton scored 17 points in the first half. Back in the dressing room before the third quarter, the coach told him, "Okay, you've had your half. Which one of you two guys want him? We're gonna put two guys on him for the rest of it."[45]

"He was just outstanding in basketball," recalls Cloyd Boyer, who had the opportunity both to watch his younger brother in high school and play alongside him in independent games.

> I always compared him to Larry Bird. Of course, I don't know if he could have been as good as Larry Bird, but he was a similar style player. He could do anything. He could pass and he could get rebounds. When he got his hands on the ball, it was his. I know I played with him after he got out of school, and I could score 20 points when he was there because he'd give you the ball when you were breaking for the basket. He just had an instinct. And he wasn't a selfish guy. He'd get the game where they would win, 80-40. He might not score 10 points. He'd let the other guys do the scoring. But you get into a nut-cut game and he'd do all the scoring. He took control of the game like Michael Jordan did in high school. He was that good.[46]

It wasn't until Kenton's senior year in 1948 that Alba High School had its first football team. Though he had never played the sport before, it didn't stop him from trying out and making the team as a fullback. Wayne Boyer was impressed with his younger brother when he had the opportunity to watch him. "He was the best athlete on the team. When he kicked off, he kicked it clear through the end zone. A lot of guys who are professionals don't do that. I marveled at that at the time. He was a seventeen-year-old kid with only that year in the sport. He could boot the ball sixty-five or seventy-five yards in the air." The all-rookie squad started with five straight losses, including a 60-0 drubbing to El Dorado Springs, Missouri, before earning their first victory over Mulberry, Kansas, 7-6, on October 22. A 56-0 trouncing by Greenwood followed a week later, but Alba rebounded with consecutive wins over Weir, 7-6, and Mindenmines, 20-6. The Wildcats finished with a 3-7 record in their inaugural season.[47]

Kenton's athleticism drew attention from several college recruiters, particularly Missouri and Arkansas. They offered him scholarships for both baseball and basketball, but he was determined to pursue his ambition of playing professional baseball. And there was already someone willing to give him that opportunity.[48]

Clifton Ambrose "Runt" Marr scouted in a nine-state region of the Midwest for the St. Louis Cardinals. Nicknamed for his diminutive 5-foot-5 stature, Marr was a third baseman in the minors from 1912 to 1932. He became a minor-league manager, team owner, and eventually a scout with the Cardinals, Detroit Tigers, Cleveland Indians, Kansas City Athletics, New York Mets, and Baltimore Orioles in a career that stretched over sixty years. The fifty-seven-year-old scout had signed Cloyd and Wayne to their first pro contracts. After being told about Kenton by Buford Cooper, who acted as a "bird dog" or associate scout for the Cardinals, Marr's eyes were now on him.[49] He lived just sixty-five miles away in Grove, Oklahoma, so he was able to keep track of Kenton's games and stay in touch with him and his parents. Marr practically became a fixture in the Boyer household over the next twenty years, signing all but two of the seven brothers to professional contracts. "I've always felt if I had signed all of them, I really would have went down in baseball history," he lamented years later.[50]

Runt Marr wasn't the only person interested in Kenton. Johnny Sturm, one-time big leaguer and player-manager of the New York Yankees' Class C farm club in nearby Joplin, had also seen him in action. Sturm had given Mickey Mantle a tryout that spring and was willing to do the same for the young Boyer. But Kenton had his heart set on playing for the Cardinals and told him emphatically, "I don't want to be a Yankee." Not even Sturm's assurance of a higher bonus offer could dissuade him. "The Yankees wanted to sign me pretty bad," Boyer later recalled, "but being from Missouri and having followed the Cardinals so long, I naturally leaned to the Redbirds."[51]

Kenton attended a Cardinals tryout with many other area players in Carthage and was among a select few invited to a second tryout at Sportsman's Park on May 27.[52] A day after his high school graduation, Kenton, his father, and Buford Cooper drove 300 miles to St. Louis for the special workout. Cardinals minor-league director Joe Mathes and scouts Joe Monahan, Walter Shannon, and George Silvey watched Boyer take batting and infield practice, then asked him to pitch. He didn't understand why—he had never seriously pitched before—but he took the mound anyway. "I must have made twenty pitches and thrown only one strike," he remembered. "I could hardly stand on the rubber." But it was his velocity that made the biggest impression.[53]

The Cardinals saw potential in his strong right arm and offered him a contract as a pitcher instead of a shortstop and a $5,000 signing bonus, plus an additional $1,000 at the end of the season. He became the first of the Boyer brothers to be offered a bonus. A thousand dollars more would have classified him as a "bonus baby" and required him to spend two seasons sitting on the bench in St. Louis. His father advised against that route and Kenton signed his first professional contract.[54] Most of his bonus paid off medical bills his father had accumulated over the past few years for a non-existent heart condition that turned out to be simply an ulcer. "Well, they say worry causes ulcers," laughed Kenton, "and after raising our big family, our dad had more than his share of worries." What was left over he used to purchase his first car, a brand-new 1949 Kaiser Fraser.[55]

Kenton played in only two regular-season games with the Aces before leaving home. He traveled with the team to Baxter Springs for Opening Day on May 29 and homered in a 6-4 defeat.[56] Back in Alba the next evening, he hit another one in a slugfest with the Parsons, Kansas, club. The Aces trailed in the bottom of the ninth inning when he smashed a dramatic walk-off home run to give them the 16-15 victory, writing a storybook ending to his amateur career.[57]

In light of his obvious offensive attributes, it was a curious decision for the Cardinals to convert Kenton into a pitcher when "his hitting is the most impressive thing about his ball playing," noted

Porter Wittich of the *Joplin Globe*. Cooper remembered him pitching on occasion "just for the fun of it," but he was too wild to be effective. "I never put him into a game to pitch if were were trying to win it," he laughed. Regardless what position he would play, it would be in professional baseball. St. Louis assigned his contract to the Rochester Red Wings, one of their Triple-A teams. On May 31, 1949, it was Kenton's turn to climb on the train, say good-bye to his family, and pursue his own major-league dream.[58]

Chapter Two

A Cardinal Takes Flight

The Cardinals sent eighteen-year-old Kenton Boyer to Rochester, New York, until a spot opened with one of the eight rookie-level Class D clubs in the organization. He didn't pitched an inning or have an official at-bat with the club, though he was there long enough to be included in the official team photograph. Rochester was only a temporary stop before his professional career started, but it gave him the opportunity to watch the game played one step below the major leagues.[1]

Kenton was teammates once again with his brother Cloyd, who had made his major-league debut with the Cardinals at the start of the 1949 season but was sent back down to the Red Wings. He also met two men in Rochester who would impact his future major-league career—the team's general manager, Bing Devine, who would hold the same position in St. Louis, and manager Johnny Keane, who would become skipper of the Cardinals in 1961. Almost thirty years later, Kenton himself would return to Rochester and manage the Red Wings.

The Cardinals made room for him on the roster of the Lebanon Chix, a Class D club in the North Atlantic League. The local newspaper, the *Lebanon Daily News*, referred to him as "Kent" Boyer, a name that stayed with him during his first two minor-league seasons. Because his contract was still held by Rochester, his $200 a month salary was split between that club and Lebanon, with the Red Wings contributing $125 and the Chix $75.[2]

Boyer arrived in Lebanon, Pennsylvania, on July 25, 1949, and reported to his new manager, Harold "Hal" Contini. The thirty-year-old, whom Boyer later remembered fondly as "the little skipper" for his short, slender stature, had managed in the Cardinals organization for the past three years. Like most in the minor leagues at that time, he was a playing manager—Contini was the everyday shortstop and pitched as needed.[3]

When Kent joined the Chix, they were tied with the Mahanoy City Brewers for second place in the eight-team North Atlantic League. The first-place Stroudsburg Poconos, a farm club of the Cleveland Indians, held an insurmountable 13 ½ game lead at the time, so Lebanon and the rest of the league were competing for three postseason playoff berths instead.

Though the team represented the city of Lebanon and the players rented rooms there from local residents, the ballpark was actually nine miles north in neighboring Fredericksburg. Cole E. Grimes Stadium was named for the man who had financed its construction, while the Chix nickname alluded to his local poultry business. Boyer later described the ballpark as "one of the best I ever saw during my several years in the lower minors, and even compared favorably with some I played in on the way up in higher leagues."[4]

Kent worked out with his new teammates before the July 25 game and watched from the bench as they beat the Carbondale Pioneers that night, 8-4. Afterward, the players boarded their new team bus—a luxury, especially in the lower minor leagues—and traveled to Stroudsburg, Pennsylvania, for a two-game series against the league-leading Poconos. In the first game on July 26, Lebanon pitcher Dick Umberger gave up three runs in the first inning, another in the second, and had the bases loaded with two outs when Contini walked in from his shortstop position and took him out of the game.

This was the moment that the manager decided to see what his new pitcher could do. It would be a baptism by fire: Kent Boyer—having never pitched in a professional game—walked to the mound, stood awkwardly on the rubber, and faced his first batter, Stroudsburg third baseman Stan Pawloski. The future big-leaguer smashed one of his offerings for a base-clearing triple and increased their lead, 7-0. Boyer pitched the last six and two-third innings, striking out four batters but yielding six runs on six hits, seven walks, three wild pitches, and a balk. Umberger was credited with the 13-1 loss. Kent was hitless in his first three professional at-bats against right-hander Albert "Mike" Coma, who won 17 games for the Poconos that season. In the clubhouse afterward, Contini gave his rookie pitcher a reassuring smile. "He didn't say anything to me," Boyer later recalled. "He knew I hadn't pitched ever."[5]

Coming off Umberger's rain-shortened, five-inning no-hitter the night before, Kent received his first professional start in the second game of a doubleheader at Peekskill, New York, on July 31. It was another rough outing as the fifth-place Highlanders smashed 12 hits and took advantage of four walks to give Boyer his first loss by the score of 9-1. Having already lost the first game of the twin bill, the Chix found themselves in third place, a game-and-a-half behind second-place Mahanoy City.[6]

In August, Contini decided to use Kent strictly as a reliever to build his confidence. The wildness was still evident on occasion but with each appearance, he showed improvement and better control. W.W. "Tiny" Parr, sports editor for the *Lebanon Daily News*, writing about the Chix pitching staff as a whole, reminded local fans that the minor leagues were proving grounds for young, inexperienced players who needed to learn perseverance when faced with adversity.

> [I]t may be well for some fans who want pitching switches immediately to keep in mind that these youngsters…are making their first bids for baseball careers, and are definitely not experienced major league flingers. In Class D ball, even the wild lads must take their turns and must be kept in there to gain the experience they need, and a glance at minor league records throughout the nation will show that it is common and accepted practice. They can't all be no-hit hurlers every day, that's for sure.[7]

Boyer's first professional hit was a bunt single in the seventh inning of a 9-4 triumph over the Hazelton Mountaineers on August 7.[8] Five days later, he pitched exceptionally in relief and earned his first professional victory against the Nazareth Barons. Called into the game with two outs in the third inning and the Barons threatening to add to their 3-2 lead, he got the third out and pitched no-hit ball the remainder of the game. He struck out seven batters and allowed only three base runners on a walk and two errors. His teammates rallied for 15 hits and Boyer contributed an RBI triple of his own to win, 13-3.[9]

Having lost a three-game set at home to the league-leading Stroudsburg Poconos, the Lebanon Chix embarked on an arduous six-game road trip (including two doubleheaders) in the middle of August. It was at this point that Kent began to show his hitting prowess in addition to his improved pitching. He was the starting pitcher for only the second time during the season in the opener of a doubleheader at Carbondale, Pennsylvania, on August 15. He scattered seven hits, hit a batter, and struck out two while giving up only two runs in the 14-2 victory over the Pioneers. At the plate, he went 2-for-3 with his first professional home run, a grand slam in the fifth inning and the first by a Lebanon player that season. The blast gave him a comfortable lead, which was increased in the same inning by a two-run homer by Contini. Boyer's victory sparked a six-game sweep at Carbondale and Mahanoy City, the longest win streak of the season for the Chix.[10]

Contini utilized Kent as both a starter and a reliever as well as an occasional pinch-hitter and pinch-runner the remainder of the season. On August 24, Boyer shut out the fifth-place Carbondale Pioneers over five innings before yielding a run in the sixth and two in the eighth. He rallied his teammates with a leadoff single in the bottom of the fifth and scored Lebanon's first run on a sacrifice fly by Pep Baselici. The game was tied in the bottom of the ninth, 3-3, and the winning run on second base for the Chix. "The youthful moundsman provided the story-book finish to a tense contest," wrote Parr, as Boyer singled to left field to score his catcher, Bill Whitaker, with the game-winning run and earn his third victory of the season.[11]

Kent's best pitching and hitting performances came in the last game of the regular season. At Hazelton, Pennsylvania, on September 3, he held the Mountaineers to one run and two hits and won his fifth game, 13-1. At the plate, he went 3-for-4 with two homers and three RBIs.[12]

The Lebanon Chix ended the regular season with a record of 80-56, 20½ games behind the North Atlantic League champion Stroudsburg Poconos. Their second-place finish qualified them for the postseason playoffs against the fourth-place Peekskill Highlanders. The first two games of the best-of-five series were played at Grimes Stadium. Before the start of the first contest on September 7, the Lebanon County Chamber of Commerce and Chix fans rewarded manager Contini and his players with gifts from local businesses and cash purses raised through advance ticket sales. In addition, Contini was given a wristwatch and each player was presented with a wallet.[13]

Lebanon dropped the series opener to Peekskill, 4-2. The next evening, Kent entered the game after a three-run rally by the Highlanders in the third inning. Giving up an initial run-scoring single, he allowed only one more tally on four hits the remainder of the game and struck out six batters. He came to bat in the bottom of the eighth with the score tied, 5-5, and smashed a 350-foot home run over the left field wall to give himself a one-run lead. His teammates followed with two more tallies for the 8-5 victory.[14]

With the series tied at one game apiece, the Chix traveled to Peekskill, where the third game was played in frigid, windy conditions. Kent struck out as a pinch hitter in Lebanon's 12-4 loss to the Highlanders. A 14-inning contest that went past midnight the next evening resulted in a 5-4 defeat. Facing elimination on September 11, the Chix held a 5-0 lead until three walks allowed Peekskill to score. Boyer pitched in relief despite a sore arm and walked in a run himself. He yielded two hits, including one coupled with an error that scored three runs, before being taken out. Lebanon lost the fifth game and the series to the Highlanders, 7-6.[15]

Kent finished the regular season with a 5-1 record and a 3.42 earned-run average in 71 innings pitched. He struck out 32 batters and walked 34. He attributed his won-loss record more to the second-best offense in the North Atlantic League (led by batting champion J.C. Dunn, who hit .384) than his own pitching ability. "All those .300 hitters we had on the team just gave me a lot of runs to work with," he remembered. He was among that same class of hitters on the club—albeit with fewer plate appearances—batting .455 with 15 hits (including three home runs) in 33 at-bats.[16]

Ten years later, sports editor Tiny Parr of the *Lebanon Daily News* visited him in spring training and talked with him about his first professional season with the Chix. Boyer remembered the 1949 club as "a good hitting team" and was surprised that he was the only player who made it to the major leagues. "Looking back now and recalling my impressions in that first pro experience, I can't help but wonder how come at least a couple of them never made it all the way," he told Parr. "To me, as a kid, they looked great as young ball players and at the time certainly seemed to have much better chances that I did of moving up. I guess I was just lucky, that's all."

As Parr left the clubhouse, Boyer told him, "Don't forget to give my regards to the fans up Lebanon way."[17]

KENT RETURNED HOME to Alba in the off-season and stayed in shape playing basketball with his brothers. At a YMCA tournament in Joplin in February 1950, he was introduced to eighteen-year-old Kathleen Belle Oliver. She was there with her older brother to watch a cousin, who was one of Boyer's teammates and graduated with him at Alba High School. Kent was immediately taken with the attractive brunette and asked her for a date that night. In fact, he asked her out every night but one before leaving for spring training. "He was good-looking and tall and he had a great sense of humor," she remembers.[18]

Kathleen was born in Joplin in 1932, the fourth child and oldest daughter of Clarence and Viola (Clark) Oliver. She had graduated from high school the previous spring and was working as an operator for the local telephone company. Her father, the pastor of a local Assembly of God church, was protective and disapproved of her dating a ballplayer. "[H]e didn't care much for me at first," recalled Kent. "He didn't go much for baseball, especially because we played it on Sunday."[19]

Boyer reported to his first spring training at the St. Louis Cardinals minor-league camp in Albany, Georgia, on March 5. The 75-acre complex had six practice diamonds, a nearby minor-league ballpark, and a spacious clubhouse that accommodated 400 players. Two hundred rookies reported early to receive special instructional work before the more experienced players arrived three weeks later. There were so many players in camp that many went about their workouts with triple-digit numbers on their jerseys. "We did a lot of running, a great deal of batting practice, practiced cut-off plays, backing up bases and base running, and played pepper," recalled farmhand and future big-leaguer Ed Mickelson.[20]

Kent was still perplexed at the organization's insistence on making him a pitcher. His .455 average at Lebanon may have raised eyebrows, but it did nothing to deter them. "They just felt someone my size couldn't be fast enough to be a fielder," he said years later. "Even in 1949, it still was that old story—the biggest guy became the pitcher on a team. They wisely got away from that idea soon after." It would take another season before the Cardinals would come to that realization.[21]

The minor-league personnel met on April 13 to determine player assignments for the twenty-one farm clubs. Hal Contini lobbied for Boyer to return to Lebanon, but instead he was assigned to Hamilton, Ontario, Canada, in the faster Class D Pennsylvania-Ontario-New York League. It would be hard to imagine he ever thought his dream of playing professional baseball would take him to another country. Kent received a small salary increase to $250 a month for the 1950 season. He was considered the most promising pitcher on a team that included future big-league right-hander Stu Miller. The Hamilton Cardinals were led by thirty-three-year-old Avitus "Vedie" Himsl, a veteran minor-league pitcher in his first season as a manager. The soft-spoken Montana native was well-liked by his young players and later managed the Chicago Cubs as the first of their experimental "College of Coaches" rotation in 1961.[22]

KENT WAS THE STARTING PITCHER on Opening Day for Hamilton as they hosted the Batavia Clippers, a farm club of the Cleveland Indians, on April 29. He must have been excited putting on his uniform prior to the game and wearing the iconic birds-on-the-bat across his chest for the first time—with the number 15 on his back—as the Hamilton club wore hand-me-down jerseys from the parent club. Three thousand fans endured the cold Canadian spring weather for the afternoon game at Civic Stadium. The eighteen-year-old struggled with wildness and defensive lapses behind him in the back-and-forth affair. Looking back on his pitching abilities, Boyer remembered, "I had no control, no curve, and not much of a fastball." He allowed 10 hits, walked seven, hit a batter, and committed a balk, though he pitched a complete game in the 9-8 defeat. In his next start against the Hornell Dodgers six days later, he lasted only six innings, giving up seven runs on six hits, six walks, and three hit batsmen as the Redbirds lost, 8-1.[23]

According to teammate Stu Miller, Himsl offered his young players very little instruction on the art of pitching. "[A]ll he did was tell the pitchers that we should come up with a change of pace," he recalled. "He said, 'You throw it to make it look like a fastball.' He didn't show us. He just told us that we had to make it look like a fastball." In fairness to Himsl, a minor-league manager at this time was a one-man coaching staff responsible for all aspects of the game.[24]

In the middle of May, Hamilton won eight straight and climbed to second place, just a half-game behind the Olean Oilers. They outslugged the Wellsville Senators, 20-16, on May 16 in a contest that lasted over three hours and featured 34 hits and 21 walks. Boyer was moved to the bullpen where his performance was often inconsistent. Himsl brought him into an eighth-inning, bases-loaded situation and he escaped unscathed; a week later, he gave up three runs in an inning's work. Kent returned to the starting rotation a few weeks later, but lost his first three decisions. Against the Jamestown Falcons on May 25, he pitched shutout ball with the exception of an unearned run in the second inning in a duel with future big-leaguer Duke Maas. He allowed only two hits through the first seven frames. Kent seized the lead with a two-run triple to right field in the seventh. The local sportswriter felt the sprint around the bases "took too much out of him," however, and Boyer weakened on the mound the last half of the game. With the score tied in the ninth, 3-3, he gave up a two-run double and a bases-loaded single that plated two more and was lifted in an eventual 7-3 defeat.[25]

Following a humiliating 21-3 loss to the Bradford Phillies, the Cardinals rebounded with an 8-4 victory that put them a game out of first place on May 29. But six losses in a row the first week of June during which they were outscored 36 runs to 13 dropped them six games back to fifth place. Frustrated with the lack of timely hitting, the team's business manager announced facetiously that he would get help from the parent club "if he has to walk on his hands and knees all the way to St. Louis to put the bite on the powers-that-be!"[26]

Kent almost ended the skid himself at Bradford on June 5. He pitched no-hit ball for three innings before the Phillies tied the game with two runs in the fourth. He held them scoreless from that point until his teammates gave him a 3-1 lead in the sixth. Two singles, a hit batsman, an infield error, and a 400-foot triple by Rudy Paparella put the Phils ahead in the eighth, 5-3. Boyer came to the plate in the ninth with a runner on first, two outs, and the chance to tie the score. Facing future big-leaguer Roy Face, he belted a high fly ball that soared toward right field. Center fielder Sam McCain caught it just before crashing into the wall, then right fielder Phil Guiliano collided into him and both players fell to the ground. As the umpire rushed to the scene, Guiliano took the ball from the glove of McCain—who was knocked out for a few seconds—and showed it to the umpire, who called Boyer out to end the game.[27]

The Cardinals snapped the losing streak three days later with a 14-6 victory over the cellar-dwelling Lockport Reds and moved past Bradford into fourth place. Kent pitched five scoreless innings the next day before weakening in the late frames, yet held on and beat them, 10-6, earning his first victory of the season. In the series finale on June 10, third baseman Hank Greifzu objected too strongly to a called third strike and was ejected from the game in the fourth inning.

Coming off a 3-for-4 performance the previous day, Boyer played third in Greifzu's stead. He smashed a drive in his first at-bat that went past the center fielder. Kent charged around the bases, almost overtaking the two runners that scored ahead of him. Himsl waved for him to stop at third, but instead he rounded the bag "like a hungry nag headed for the barn," wrote the *Hamilton Spectator*. Boyer collided with Lockport catcher Eugene Fleming and was called out at the plate, narrowly missing an inside-the-park home run. Kent got payback in the sixth when Fleming popped up with the bases loaded and Boyer made a one-handed catch at the edge of the Cardinals dugout. "It was a remarkable defensive effort, and it rounded out a great night for Boyer," wrote the *Spectator*. The fact that Kent was a pitcher and the younger brother of St. Louis Cardinals hurler Cloyd

Boyer made it especially newsworthy. The story was carried on the wire services, the first time his performance earned such widespread media attention.[28]

The offense fizzled once again and Hamilton dropped nine of its next 10 games through mid-June to fall back to fifth place. With no help on the way from St. Louis, Himsl was desperate for a spark. He began playing his hard-hitting young hurler in right field between starts and relief appearances to take advantage of his bat. Boyer's ascending .297 average began appearing in the weekly list of top PONY League batters. The losing skid ended thanks to Miller's masterful four-hitter and a stray dog at Batavia on June 19. With a 3-2 count and the Cardinals clinging to a one-run lead in the seventh, first baseman Dick Barnhart watched a third strike go past, but the base umpire ruled that time had already been called because a dog wandered into right field. Given a second chance, Barnhart smacked the next pitch over that fence and ignited a three-run outburst, giving Hamilton the 4-0 triumph.[29]

The streaky Redbirds won the next five games and Kent factored in most of them. Brought into a bases-loaded predicament with one out in the ninth inning against the Bradford Phillies on June 21, he struck out the first batter he faced and enticed the next one to ground into the final out. He saved the 8-5 victory that started the win streak. Boyer pitched three innings of relief the next evening, striking out three, to preserve another win, 4-3. On June 23, he contributed with his bat playing in right field. He singled and doubled twice and knocked in three runs in Hamilton's 7-2 victory over the Batavia Clippers. Two more wins against the Cleveland Indians farm club elevated them to fourth place and two games over .500. But the Cards ended the month losing three of the last four games—including 20-10 and 18-14 slugfests at Bradford—and the Phils tied them for fourth.[30]

The extra playing time enabled Boyer to show off his hitting ability. In the series at Bradford, he had three safeties and two RBIs in one game and smacked a three-run single and scored two in the next. Unfortunately, he also showed his lack of experience in right field with two costly errors, including a high throw to third base. With Barnhart sidelined by a leg injury the first week of July, Himsl out of necessity shifted Kent to first base. One player's misfortune can sometimes be another's opportunity. So it was with Boyer.[31] Batting fifth in the lineup, he smashed a two-run home run over the left-center field fence in the second game of a July 1 twin bill. But he also dropped a perfect throw from shortstop Claude Robert that led to an unearned run in a 8-7 loss to the first-place Olean Oilers.[32]

At the same time, third baseman Greifzu was released and catcher Hal Smith filled in at the position. But when Smith's replacement, Joe Ossala, was hurt in a home-plate collision during the Fourth of July doubleheader, Boyer was moved across the infield to third and the injured Barnhart put back at first base. Hamilton dropped the opener to Hornell, but clouted six round-trippers in the second game and won, 14-11. Coupled with three more blasts by the Dodgers—including one by future major-league player and manager Don Zimmer—both clubs broke the PONY League record for home runs in a single contest. Kent belted a two-run shot as part of his 4-for-5 performance.[33]

Two days later, Hamilton slipped to fifth place after four of their hurlers were pummeled by the second-place Dodgers on 22 hits and lost, 16-6. St. Louis finally sent help to the beleaguered Hamilton club when first baseman/outfielder Prentice "Pidge" Brown arrived from Class B Allentown, Pennsylvania, and batted .338 with nine homers and 64 RBIs. Smith took over at third base and Kent returned to the mound the rest of July.

Despite a two-week layoff, he earned a save against Hornell on July 7 and tossed six shutout innings four days later to beat Wellsville in the first game of a doubleheader, 2-1. Miller's five-hitter over Lockport on the thirteenth lifted the Redbirds into a three-way tie with Batavia and Braford for third place. Three straight victories gave them sole possession, including one at Lockport won by Boyer on July 16. With Hamilton trailing in the eighth inning, 3-2, he smashed a pinch-hit triple and drove in two runs to put them ahead. The Reds tied it in the ninth and Kent answered with another extra-base hit in the tenth that plated two more for the 8-4 triumph. He missed a second triple after being called out for not stepping on first base.[34]

Boyer continued to be used as a pinch-hitter with occasional starts in right field and at third base. Coming off the bench, he drove in the winning run in the second game of a twin bill against Hornell on July 8 and homered in a loss to Wellsville on the twentieth. Hamilton knocked Olean out of first place with Kent on the mound. He overcame 10 hits, four walks, and two hit batsmen to beat the Oilers, 6-5, on July 28. Barnhart provided him ample support with three safeties and four RBIs. The next day, Boyer started at third base and knocked in three runs. He was batting .340 with 36 hits in 106 at-bats by the end of the month.[35]

A 1-for-11 slump the first week of August brought his average down twenty-four points to .316. Yet he enjoyed one of his best pitching performances in a 6-1 win over Bradford on the fifth. He walked eight batters but struck out seven, holding the Phillies to four hits and shutting them out the last eight innings to earn his sixth victory against eight losses for the season. At the plate, he broke out of his slump with three safeties and was rewarded with a start at first base in the second game of the doubleheader.[36]

Never again would Kent Boyer pitch in a professional game. Beginning August 7, Himsl penciled him in at third base and sent Dave Johnson back to the outfield.[37] Except for back-to-back starts in right field that month, the hot corner became his position. A player later considered one of the finest defensive third basemen of his generation wasn't enthused to be there. "I didn't like third base at first and I was terrible, too," he later admitted. But it was offensive results more than defense that concerned his manager at this point in the season. Kent rapped three hits in that game and never let up the last month of the season. He hit safely in his next 10 games at a robust .605 clip. Hamilton won five straight in the middle of August, then dropped seven of the next eight and fell to fourth place. Four wins in a row lifted them back to third, with Boyer contributing four safeties and three RBIs in an 8-5 victory at Olean. Moving from fifth in the lineup to cleanup, he had four hits—including a double and two home runs—and three RBIs in Tom Keating's two-hit, 12-0 shutout victory over Batavia on August 30.[38]

The Cardinals maintained their hold on third place, but were unable to close the double-digit gap between them and the front-running Hornell Dodgers and second-place Olean Oilers. They won 10 of the last 12 games, however, and clinched a playoff spot, finishing the season with a 68-57 record, 13 ½ games behind the Dodgers.

Hamilton faced the second-place Oilers in the opening round of the PONY League Governor's Cup series. They lost the first two games at Olean, New York—including the opener after a six-run lead disintegrated in the ninth inning—but returned home and took the third on Miller's six-hit, 9-1 victory on September 8. After a disheartening 16-1 setback the next evening and facing elimination in the fifth game, Kent swatted a pitch over the left-field fence to give his team a 6-4 lead in the tenth inning. Olean tied it again in their half, but the Cardinals tallied five times in the twelfth for the 11-6 triumph.[39]

With no fresh arms available, Himsl pitched the sixth game himself on September 11. The veteran right-hander dueled with Bill Gazdik of the Oilers, both allowing only three hits through the first eight frames of a 1-1 tie. After a leadoff single in the ninth, the next Olean batter sacrificed to third base. Boyer fielded the ball and tried hurriedly to get the runner out at second. Instead, his throw sailed into right field, a costly error that plated the go-ahead run and sent the other runner to third. The 3-1 loss ended Hamilton's season. Kent had a disappointing series with no hits in three of the contests—including the finale—and only three safeties overall in 25 at-bats.[40]

Nevertheless, the 1950 season was an important turning point in his fledgling career. He proved a more promising prospect as a hitter than a pitcher, reflected in his .342 batting average, 17 doubles, six triples, nine homers, and 61 RBIs in 80 games. As a pitcher, he walked 71 batters, struck out 43, hit 15, and finished with a 6-9 record and 4.39 ERA in 121 innings pitched.

World events would impact Ken and his teammates. On June 25, 1950, Communist forces in North Korea, with backing from the Soviet Union, crossed the 38th Parallel into neighboring South Korea to forcefully reunify the two countries. The invasion resulted in a joint military action led by the United States to aid the South Koreans. China provided the same assistance to the North Koreans. The first peacetime draft had been enacted two years earlier as tensions grew between the U.S. and the Soviet Union. With the Korean War now an active extension of the existing Cold War between them, all qualified men between the ages of eighteen-and-a-half and twenty-six were required to register for selective military service and the possibility of twenty-four months of active duty.[41]

Vern and Mabel Boyer surrounded by 13 of their 14 children (daughter Lila passed away at 17 months old). Left to right (top row): Cloyd, Wayne, Kenton, Lynn, Cletis. (Seated) Shirley, Delores, father Vern, mother Mabel, Juanita, Pansy. (Bottom row) Marcy, Bobbie, Lenny, Ron. (*Boyer Family Collection*)

Kenton Boyer graduated from Alba High School on May 26, 1949. The next day, he was at Sportsman's Park for a special tryout with his favorite major-league team, the St. Louis Cardinals. (*Boyer Family Collection*)

The 1939 Rosebank School team. Left to right (bottom row): Kenton Boyer, Ray Coss, Lynn Brown, Wayne Boyer, Leonard Brown, Harold Martin, Royden L. Coss. (Top row) Carl Parker (coach), Buford Coss, Cloyd Boyer, Dale Moore, Walter Comstock (*John Hall and Jane Boyer*)

Wayne, Cloyd, and Kenton Boyer with the Alba Aces (*Cloyd Boyer*)

A CARDINAL TAKES FLIGHT   33

The Alba Aces, champions of the inaugural 1941 Cardinal Junior League. Left to right: (Front row) Kenton Boyer, Max Rose, Wayne Boyer, Stanley "Bud" Betebenner, Ramon Cooper. (Back row) Vernon Joseph Decker, Cecil Cooper, Dan Rose, Cloyd Boyer, Buford Cooper (manager), Tommy Maples (batboy), Keith "Ping" Patterson, Bob Barkley. (*John Hall and Jane Boyer*)

The Alba Aces, circa 1948. Kenton Boyer is in the back row, fourth from the left. Notice Alba's water tower in the background. (*Nate Rider*)

(**Above**) The Boyer family moved to this small five-room frame house at 512 North Orchard Street in Alba, Missouri, in 1940. Across the street (**below**) was a cornfield that the neighborhood fathers and sons converted into a baseball field. (*Photos by the author*)

(**Above**) Main Street in Alba looking north toward the crossing with Highway D. The Boyer home is located in a neighborhood beyond the trees on the right. The water tower (**below**) is a distinctive landmark in town. No doubt Kenton and his brothers climbed up the ladder and sat at the top on many occasions. "Most kids just know their parents shouldn't be told some things," said their mother, Mabel Boyer. (*Photos by the author*)

Proud father Vern Boyer with his four of his first five sons to sign professional baseball contracts. Left to right: Cloyd, Kenton, Cletis, and Lynn. (*John Rogers Archive*)

A CARDINAL TAKES FLIGHT 37

The St. Louis Cardinals sent 18-year-old "Kent" Boyer to the Triple-A Rochester Red Wings to await an open roster spot with a Class D club. He stayed long enough to be in the team photo (**right**) (*Author's Collection*). He spent the last month-and-a-half of the 1949 season with the Lebanon Chix in the North Atlantic League. Kent is second from the left in the top row (**above**). He crosses home plate (**below**) and accepts the hand of his manager, Hal Contini, after blasting a home run that put the Lebanon Chix ahead in a Game 2 victory in the PONY League playoffs. (*Lebanon Daily News*).

"Kent" Boyer with the Hamilton Cardinals in 1950. He finally convinced St. Louis that his bat would be more productive than his right arm on the mound. (*Hamilton Spectator*)

Chapter Three

Omaha and Overseas

After Ken Boyer's hitting performance at Hamilton, the Cardinals were finally convinced his conversion to pitching should be abandoned. He became a full-time hitter and third baseman instead. At the end of the season, his contract was transferred from the Rochester club to the Pocatello (Idaho) Cardinals of the Class C Pioneer League. But when he reported to spring training at Albany, Georgia, on March 19, 1951, he joined players from five Class A and B-level farm clubs.[1]

Initially, Boyer worked out with players assigned to Omaha, Nebraska, a Class A team. He shared time at third base with veterans Bob Rausch and Joe Aliperto. The left-hand hitting Rausch was twenty-seven years old and the incumbent, having spent the past two seasons at Omaha. Twenty-three-year-old Aliperto was a right-handed batter who had played six seasons in the Boston Braves, Pittsburgh Pirates, and Philadelphia Athletics' organizations from 1944 to 1948.[2] Boyer had some standout spring performances in his favor, including two doubles and five RBIs in one game and a grand slam in another.

The consensus among the minor-league personnel was that Boyer needed more experience in the lower minors. If he went to Omaha, he would jump three levels from Class D to Class A and face tougher pitching while playing every day and adjusting to a new position. There was also concern about him being subject to the military draft. He passed his physical on April 26 and awaited word from the draft board when he would be required to report. It was inevitable—perhaps during the season—that he would be inducted into the Army.[3]

Ultimately, it was decided Ken would leave camp with the Omaha Cardinals. Their manager was thirty-year-old George Kissell, a bespectacled, diminutive third baseman who had played eight seasons in the organization. He was beginning his sixth season as a minor-league skipper and his first at the Class A level. Future Hall of Fame manager Earl Weaver considered him "one of the sharpest men I ever played for."[4] Kissell was also an innovator, implementing an early version of the designated hitter when he and Boyer batted in the pitcher's spot in an exhibition game against the Winston-Salem Cardinals.[5]

According to Kissell, minor-league director Joe Mathes told him, "I want you to take that pitcher from Hamilton and make him a third baseman." Kissell was impressed with Boyer's hitting, speed, and throwing arm, but he already had a third baseman in camp batting .320. "Well, you're going to take Ken Boyer," insisted Mathes. "OK, you say take him, I'll take him," relented Kissell.[6]

OMAHA WAS ABOUT 200 miles northwest of Ken's birthplace in Liberty, Missouri. When the season began on April 18, the older and more experienced Joe Aliperto started at third base and Boyer sat on the bench. When he was in the lineup, Ken took advantage of every opportunity to show what he could do. He went 2-for-4 with a triple and knocked in four of Omaha's runs in a 6-4 victory over the Des Moines Bruins on April 23. Five days later, with St. Louis Cardinals owner Fred Saigh in the stands, he tripled again and scored twice against the Sioux City Soos. By month's end, Aliperto had been promoted to Triple-A Columbus and Boyer installed as the starting third baseman the remainder of the season.[7]

Losing five of their first nine games in April, the sixth-place Omaha club began a steady climb out of the second division in May. Dropping two games to the Lincoln Athletics, a farm club of the Philadelphia American League team, the Cardinals embarked on a twelve-game road trip and broke even at Des Moines, Colorado Springs, Pueblo, and Wichita, including a three-game sweep against the sixth-place Colorado Springs Sky Sox May 6–8. They returned home to Municipal Stadium on May 15, where right-hander Willard Schmidt struck out nine and scattered nine hits against the fourth-place Denver Bears for a 3-1 victory, surpassing the Boston Braves farm club in the standings. Omaha won two out of three games from Denver and the fourth game—tied 6-6 after 10 innings—was called in order for the Bears to catch a train back home. They took two of three from the Wichita Indians and moved to third place with their 2-1 victory on May 20. Boyer, who had only two hits in 19 at-bats during the homestand, contributed a single and two doubles in the game.[8]

Afterward, the Cardinals made a 600-mile trek to Pueblo, Colorado, to begin a 10-game circuit through the western cities of the league. Omaha divided a four-game series with the Dodgers and helped knock the Brooklyn farm club from their first-place berth. They won both games of a doubleheader on May 22, in which Ken had three hits, including a two-run home run, as part of the team's 13 hits in the first contest behind Schmidt. Teammate Russell Rac blasted a grand slam in the second game for George Eyrich's seventh win against two losses during the season.[9] In the second game of a twin bill the next night, Boyer chased a popup into foul territory and crashed into the Pueblo dugout, momentarily knocking himself unconscious.[10]

He showed no aftereffects from the collision when he returned to the lineup at Colorado Springs two days later. The Cardinals belted 18 hits off three Sky Sox hurlers and Ken contributed a single and a triple and scored a run. Schmidt gave up 13 hits by himself, but his teammates' bats enabled him to hold on for the 16-11 victory. Three subsequent losses at Denver dropped them back to fourth place.[11]

Omaha split the Memorial Day doubleheader at home against the league-leading Pueblo Dodgers, with Schmidt pitching a three-hit shutout in the opener. Heavy rain postponed the next three games and high water delayed their trip to Wichita. They split a four-game series with the last-place Cleveland Indians farm club and Eyrich and Harlan "Hal" Coffman pitched back-to-back shutouts. The Cardinals won seven of their next nine games and reclaimed third place on June 6. Schmidt overcame five errors by his catcher and infielders (including

Boyer) and held Colorado Springs to the same number of hits for the 6-5 victory. Ken made up for his error with a single and two RBIs.[12]

The Redbirds maintained their third-place position throughout the month of June. They even managed a momentary tie for second with the Sioux City Soos after an extra-inning victory against league-leading Pueblo on June 11. Ken had two doubles and started at third base, but shifted to center field when manager Kissell entered the game. Through the first week of the month, Boyer was batting .299 (second on the team) with 46 hits and 18 RBIs. In a heated three-hour contest at Denver on June 15 that almost saw Eyrich—who wasn't even pitching for Omaha that night—come to blows with Bears right fielder Danny Holden, Ken doubled and homered and drove in two runs behind Schmidt, who gave up five unearned runs to lose, 6-5. A loss the next night dropped them back to fourth place, but the Cardinals rallied with 15 hits off two Denver hurlers led by left fielder Rac, who fell short of the cycle by a triple, and Earl Weaver, who drove in four runs. Boyer had two singles and scored a run and Coffman took the victory, 14-6, to reclaim third place.[13]

The Cardinals returned home and split two-game series against Wichita and Sioux City and took two out of three from Des Moines. On the night of June 25, the third-place St. Louis Cardinals came to town for an off-day exhibition game against their Class A affiliate. At the time, they were eight games behind the Brooklyn Dodgers with a 32-30 record in the National League race.

A record-breaking crowd of 17,083 packed Muny Stadium and overflowed onto the field for the contest, eager to see Cardinals stars such as Enos Slaughter, player-manager Marty Marion, and Stan Musial. The only player missing from the major-league lineup was second baseman Red Schoendienst, who had injured his leg two days earlier in a game against the Boston Braves. The main attraction was Musial, the reigning NL batting champion, who tried to make a good showing but managed only two pop flies and a fly ball to right field in three at-bats. With St. Louis leading in the third inning, 1-0, Stan attempted a shoestring catch in left field, but instead booted the ball over the head of center fielder Harry "Peanuts" Lowrey, who was backing him up. The misplay allowed Omaha to score two runs and take the lead. St. Louis regained the momentum in the fifth with two of their own, but the kid Cardinals took it back with three tallies in their half on three singles, a double, and two errors. Despite giving up 10 hits to the big-leaguers, Coffman prevailed for the 5-3 victory. Cloyd Boyer pitched for St. Louis and held his younger brother Ken hitless in three at-bats. Though he lost the game on the mound, Cloyd did much better at the plate with a double and scored a run.[14]

Ken was still adjusting to playing third base. "I have heavy legs," he said. "They're strong enough for running but not too good for the quick stops and starts of a shortstop. I was making the big plays at third but the 33 errors I made [that tied the league lead for third basemen] were embarrassing." As the season progressed, he became more comfortable at the position and exhibited the defensive qualities that would later make him exceptional in the major leagues. Robert Phipps of the *Omaha World-Herald*, watching him play every day, marveled at "his wonderful gracefulness" in the field for a man of his size. The strong arm that led the St. Louis minor-league personnel to think him better suited for pitching was put to good use throwing runners out across the diamond. "Ken has one of those million-dollar arms," wrote Phipps. "I can't recall anything in the Western League in the last few years to compare with a Boyer bullet throw to first base to catch a fast runner." Years later, Kissell recalled, "That year, I had Boyer at third and Earl Weaver at second. What a combination that was. Boyer turned out to be an excellent third baseman."[15]

The nineteen-year old Weaver joined the club two weeks into the season. A few days after his debut, Phipps wrote, "Weaver has already drawn the nickname of Stanky [for the equally small and scrappy second baseman Eddie Stanky of the New York Giants] from the admiring fans." The St. Louis native and future Hall of Fame manager of the Baltimore Orioles batted leadoff and hit .279 with 35 doubles (second-best in the Western League) and 52 RBIs, enjoying the best season of his fourteen-year minor-league career.[16]

Following the exhibition victory against St. Louis, the Omaha Cardinals traveled fifty miles southwest to Lincoln and swept a June 27 doubleheader against the Athletics. Ken homered and Schmidt tossed a two-hitter with eight strikeouts to win the first game, 3-1. In the nightcap, Boyer doubled, hit another home run, and had four RBIs in the 5-2 victory. The next night at Sioux City, Omaha right-hander Joe Chuka and Soos right-hander David Sayers dueled for five innings until Boyer homered in his third straight game in the sixth to give Omaha a 2-0 lead. But the New York Giants farm club rallied for a run in the seventh and four in the eighth to take the second game, 5-2. After being shut out on three hits by Sioux City right-hander Sam Brewer, the Redbirds won the next game, 10-6. They drove back to Omaha where a hometown crowd of 4,647 saw them win both games of a July 1 doubleheader against the Soos. The victories enabled Omaha to take second place, while the Denver Bears displaced the Pueblo Dodgers once again from the league lead and sent them into third place.[17]

The climb to second place was short-lived, however, as the Redbirds dropped a twin bill to Sioux City and split a Fourth of July doubleheader with Lincoln to fall back to third. Four victories against the seventh-place Athletics and two rainouts at Des Moines returned them to second place momentarily, only to fall back to third after splitting a four-game series against the Bruins. After Omaha lost the opener of the July 9 doubleheader to Des Moines, 2-1, Ken belted a two-run home run in the top of the twelfth inning to win the second game, 9-4. Two subsequent rainouts at Lincoln played havoc with the Western League standings on July 12, when second-division clubs Wichita and Colorado Springs beat the top two teams Denver and Pueblo and enabled the idle Redbirds to inch into the league lead by five percentage points.[18]

Prior to the team's doubleheader against Des Moines the next day, the Cardinals players were honored with a parade through downtown Omaha and recognized at City Hall by councilman Johnny Rosenblatt, who organized the event. They won both games and another against the Bruins to strengthen their first-place lead by a game-and-a-half over the Denver Bears. Traveling to Colorado Springs, the Redbirds took two out of three from the last-place Sky Sox, highlighted by a 20-hit barrage in the second game of a July 15 doubleheader. Ken hit two doubles, knocked in three runs, and scored three in the 15-8 victory. After splitting two games with the Bears at Denver and dropping a three-game series at home against second-place Wichita, the Omaha club enjoyed its longest winning streak of the season July 26–29 that resulted in a 4½-game lead over Denver and Wichita.[19]

At the end of July, Ken was batting .288 with 45 runs scored and 50 driven in, almost half of which came in the month. But writer Robert Phipps believed the twenty-year-old had unrealized potential at the plate, describing him as someone "who will be a whale of a ball player as soon as he finds out how good he actually is." During a 15-0 rout over Pueblo at Muny Stadium on July 24, he drove a pitch into the far right-field corner known as "Dickey's Corner," an impressive feat according to Phipps. "Right-handed hitters rarely reach this area and it's an unusual direction for Boyer," he wrote about the bases-loaded, opposite-field triple. "But the big, loose infielder, it is freely predicted, will be breaking down the fences in almost any competition as soon as he gains confidence."[20]

The Cardinals started the month of August winning nine of fifteen games on the road against Pueblo and Colorado Springs and their closest rivals, first-division clubs Denver and Wichita. When either the flu or food poisoning kept some of his teammates out of a doubleheader at Colorado Springs on August 6, Ken shifted over to shortstop. He had two hits and scored two runs in the 8-3 victory in the opener and three safeties (including a home run) and three RBIs in an 18-0 romp in the second. The next night, his three-run blast off future St. Louis teammate Barney Schultz proved the difference in the Cardinals' 7-4 win at Denver. After winning two of three against the second-place Bears, Omaha held a 5 ½-game lead over them.[21]

The story was different two weeks later when Denver came to Muny Stadium for an important five-game series. After the Redbirds dropped the first game of the August 22 doubleheader, Schmidt won his 18th of the season in the nightcap. Boyer helped turn three double plays at third base and contributed three hits, including a double and a home run, in the 6-0 shutout. Two more losses, however, and a 3-3 tie with two outs going into the bottom of the ninth inning left the Cardinals in danger of being tied for the league lead. Instead, Ken—who had knocked in two runs to tie the game in the seventh—stroked a pitch to left field that scored pinch-hitter Kissell from second base to win the fifth game of the series and give Omaha a two-game lead in the standings.[22]

In July, the team had announced an exhibition game for August 20 with the Kansas City Blues of the American Association, the Triple-A club of the World champion New York Yankees. The Blues' roster featured outfielder and prize prospect Mickey Mantle, whom Boyer hadn't faced since both played shortstop in the Ban Johnson League two years earlier. But the contest never materialized and the Redbirds instead shut out the Wichita Indians that night, 6-0.[23]

Omaha went 23-14 in the month of August, including a five-game win streak sparked by Ken's two-out, game-winning, 365-foot home run at Sioux City on August 27. In fact, his batting proficiency was evident throughout the month and raised his average to .298, seven points behind teammate Rac for the club lead. Boyer paced the Cardinals with 150 hits and was second behind Rac with 86 RBIs. His 400-foot solo homer on August 30 broke up a scoreless contest in the sixth inning and gave Omaha right-hander Coffman the lead in his four-hit, 2-0 shutout over the Lincoln Athletics. "The ball cleared the fence between the scoreboard and a light tower in left-center," wrote Robert Phipps of the *World-Herald*, "and it was still good for plenty of roll when last seen." The victory gave the Redbirds a three-game lead over Denver with less than two weeks left in the season.[24]

Phipps was enamored with the offensive and defensive improvements made by Boyer over the course of the season. He considered him "one of the finest prospects in the country" who "has the power to hit the ball a mile and does, more often as time goes by, makes hard chances [at third base] look easy, and has speed to burn." He described him as the "big, graceful third baseman. Only 20, he's a priceless prospect."[25]

But the temperatures and many of Omaha's bats grew colder the first week of September, making the pennant race more tense than loyal Cardinals fans wanted. Their lead was cut to a single game over the Denver Bears as the Western League season drew into its final week. Having lost six of their last 10 games, the Redbirds swept a doubleheader from the last-place Lincoln Athletics on September 8, 18-2 and 8-0. Ken went 4-for-5 with an RBI and three runs scored in the first game and scored twice in the second.

The next day, 2,224 fans welcomed the team home as they hosted another doubleheader against Lincoln. Left-hander Victor Gohl, who lost 18 games for the Athletics, pitched a four-hit gem and beat Omaha, 2-1. The Cardinals trailed in the second game, 4-1, but loaded the bases in the seventh inning with Boyer at the plate. He smashed a line drive to the outfield fence, but umpire John Rice ruled that he had passed the runner ahead of him and called him out. A 4-3 defeat and Denver's victory over Colorado Springs knotted them for first place with only two games left.[26]

Omaha hosted the fourth-place Des Moines Bruins on September 10 and 11. Eleven-game winner Coffman pitched well the first four innings and held a 5-1 lead. But in the fifth, Des Moines knocked four straight hits and plated three runs, reducing Omaha's lead to a single tally. Jack Shirley relieved Coffman and held the Bruins to three hits the remainder of the game. The Cardinals tacked on another run in the eighth and held on for the 6-4 win. Ken had two safeties, including a double, and scored two runs. Meanwhile, Andy Skurski of Colorado Springs played the role of spoiler with an tenth-inning, two-out home run that muzzled the Denver Bears, 10-8. Omaha's win coupled with Denver's loss once again gave the Redbirds a one-game lead.[27]

Sensing a pennant-clincher, 5,327 fans packed Muny Stadium to overflowing capacity on the last day of the regular season to watch the Cardinals capture the Western League title. Des Moines took a 5-3 lead in the first four innings off three Omaha hurlers. The Redbirds tied the contest in the seventh on a two-run homer by Rac and clinched it an inning later with an inside-the-park homer by Harvey Zernia (which should have been held to a single if not for a muffed shoestring catch) that made it 8-5. Ken had only a single in four at-bats but scored two runs. The victory gave the Omaha Cardinals their second consecutive pennant and Boyer his first professional championship.[28]

The first round of the Western League playoffs against the Sioux City Soos proved anticlimactic. Omaha dropped the first two games at home, 5-3 and 3-2. Before the second game, the players presented Kissell with a movie projector as a gift. Despite a forty-five degree nighttime temperature at Sioux City, the Cardinals took advantage of six errors and won the third game, 9-4. Ken contributed two safeties and scored twice in the contest. But the Soos clinched the best-of-five series the next evening with a commanding 10-3 victory. Boyer made a poor showing in the series, batting .200 with a double and RBI, though he scored four runs in five games.[29]

Ken was selected by the Omaha media as the team's rookie of the year. He finished second to Weaver for most popular player, but still received a new suit of clothes from a local clothing manufacturer. "He was a silent hustler," recalled Kissell about his young third baseman. "He was the opposite of Earl Weaver, who would hoot and holler." George Freese, batting champion of the Western League, was chosen over Boyer as third baseman on the postseason All-Star team. Ken tied with Weaver and Des Moines second baseman Vern Morgan at two votes each for utility player honors.[30]

Playing at his highest level of competition in two-and-a-half seasons of pro ball, Ken met the challenge. He played in all but four games (151) and led his club with a .306 average (fourth-best in the Western League) and hit 14 home runs with 90 RBIs and 11 stolen bases. "He's the best two-strike hitter on the club and a good long ball hitter," praised Kissell. Almost forty years later, he remembered, "The first month he hit everything to right field, the second month he hit it to right center, the third month he hit it to left center, and the fourth month he hit it in the bleachers."[31]

Robert Phipps of the *Omaha World-Herald*, reflecting on the 1951 season, wrote: "Kissell made a brave decision early in the year. He picked a rookie, Ken Boyer, over two experienced third basemen. It was a dangerous gamble in that a bad guess would have hurt George's standing badly in the organization. Boyer came through like a champion, although he was jumping a long way up the ladder. One scout (outside the St. Louis chain) termed the lad one of the two best prospects in the Western League at season's end."[32]

While teammates were returning to their hometowns, Ken Boyer and Willard Schmidt (who finished second in victories behind Elroy Face of the Pueblo Dodgers with a 19-14 record and led the Western League with 202 strikeouts and a 2.11 earned-run average) drove 550 miles to St. Louis and joined the parent club for the last week-and-a-half of the major-league season. Cardinals officials wanted them to work out under the watchful eyes of manager Marty Marion and his coaching staff—Terry Moore, Ray Blades, Mike Ryba, and Clyde "Buzy" Wares—to determine where they would be assigned the following year. Ken had the opportunity to be around players he had idolized as a kid like Marion, Enos Slaughter, Red Schoendienst, and

Stan Musial. He also reunited with his brother Cloyd, who was on the roster but had recently been sidelined with a sore arm. As Boyer and Schmidt watched from the bench, the Cardinals finished in third place in the National League race behind the second-place Brooklyn Dodgers and the league-leading New York Giants.[33]

TWO WEEKS AFTER WORKING OUT in St. Louis, the Omaha Cardinals sold Ken's contract to the Houston Buffaloes of the Double-A Texas League in anticipation of him climbing the organizational ladder to the big leagues.[34] But Houston would have to wait two years—Uncle Sam required his services first. Private Kenton Boyer was inducted into the Army at Kansas City, Missouri, on October 30, 1951, becoming one of 140 Cardinals minor-leaguers in military service by the spring of 1952. After completing eight weeks of basic training in California, he returned home to Alba in April before reporting to Fort Bliss in El Paso, Texas.[35]

Ken had maintained a long-distance relationship with Kathleen Oliver through letters and telephone calls ever since he left for spring training in 1951. Before leaving for Texas, he asked her to marry him. Because Kathleen's father still objected to his baseball career, they decided to elope and traveled 123 miles southeast to Huntsville, Arkansas, where they were married on Good Friday, April 11, 1952. His brother Wayne and his sister-in-law were witnesses. The newlyweds drove to El Paso shortly after and started their new life together.[36]

"We had no money whatsoever," says Kathleen. "We had our wedding dinner at his sister Juanita's house and we had pancakes. Then we drove to Springfield, Missouri, and that's where we spent our wedding night. We spent a few days with his brother Cloyd and headed to El Paso with no money. We drove straight through. We did pull over on the side of the road and sleep for a little bit."[37]

Once they reached Fort Bliss, the newlyweds found a small apartment off post, but didn't have enough money for the first month's rent. Fortunately, the landlady allowed them to move in and pay her when Ken received his first Army paycheck. A similar arrangement was made with a local grocer who happened to be a Cardinals fan. The small apartment had few amenities and no air conditioning. "It had a little water cooler type thing in the window," remembers Kathleen. "The wind and the sand blew in El Paso and it would blow right through that water cooler all over the living room floor." To help with the bills, she arranged a transfer to a local telephone company and continued working as an operator.[38]

Ken attended the Antiaircraft and Guided Missiles Branch of The Artillery School at Fort Bliss in April and May. His studies and other military responsibilities occupied much of his time. He and his new bride spent only ten days together over the first two months he was stationed there. What leisure time they had was spent at the post's swimming pool on Sundays or venturing with friends across the border to Juarez, Mexico. "We would not dare go by ourselves," recalls Kathleen. "We went there a couple of times and that was quite an experience."[39]

Being a professional ballplayer, Ken was an obvious recruit for baseball teams on post. He played for the 4054th ASU (Army Service Unit) squad, competing against other units in the Fort Bliss Baseball League. In August, he joined the post's official team, the Fort Bliss Falcons, and took part in tournaments and all-star contests against other post clubs.[40]

That summer, Kathleen became pregnant with their first child and returned to Missouri. She lived with Ken's parents in Alba; both she and her mother-in-law were expecting at the same time.[41] A few months later, Ken returned home, but only for a short while. He was deployed overseas in October and assigned to Battery D of the 899th Anti Aircraft Artillery AW Battalion, a Pennsylvania National Guard unit attached to the 28th Division Artillery stationed at Stuttgart, Germany.[42]

Like most professionals, Ken played a lot of baseball while in the service. In the spring and summer of 1953, he was a shortstop and third baseman for his unit's team, the 28th Division Artillery Redlegs. In a three-game exhibition series against the 172nd Regiment Indians, he went 5-for-6 in the opener and had nine safeties in 16 at-bats overall.[43] The Redlegs struggled with a 6-9 record in the Southern Conference the first-half of the season. They rebounded and took the second-half championship, winning 15 out of 18 games and beating the rival 28th Division Special Troops Troopers in the playoffs. The deciding game was clinched after the Redlegs scored four runs in the bottom of the ninth inning for the 14-13 triumph.

"The big Div[ision] Art[iller]y gun at bat, in the field, on the mound, and just about every place else is Ken Boyer," wrote Leo Levine of the *European Stars and Stripes* newspaper. "Boyer is the finest fielding shortstop in the zone. He is big, fast, covers lots of ground and has an excellent arm." He batted .342 in the regular season and led the Redlegs with five home runs and seven doubles. In addition to playing the infield, he was asked to pitch in the second-half and finished with a perfect 5-0 record in five games. His team advanced to the U.S. Army in Europe (USAEUR) tournament quarterfinals at Bad Kreuznach, Germany, but were shut out in both games of the best-of-three series by the 2nd Armored Division Travellers.[44]

KEN RETURNED TO THE STATES that fall and was transferred from active duty to reserve status on October 12, 1953. Two days later, he was back home in Alba. It wasn't until February 20, 1960, that he was honorably discharged from military service. He reunited with Kathleen and saw his seven-month-old daughter Dewana Sueann (Suzie) for the first time.[45]

It didn't take long for him to return to baseball as well. On October 18, he played in an exhibition game at Joplin to benefit the family of Joe "Red" Crowder, a pitcher in the New York Yankees minor-league system from nearby Seneca, Missouri, who drowned two weeks earlier. Both Ken and Mickey Mantle played against him in the Cardinal Junior League when he pitched for the Seneca Indians. The contest between the Joplin All-Stars and the Tri-State Miners showcased the baseball talent of the region. In addition to Ken and brother Cloyd, other current or future big leaguers included Cliff Mapes, Tom Sturdivant, Gale Wade, and All-Stars manager Ferrell "Andy" Anderson.

The featured attraction was Mantle, fresh from his World Series victory over the Brooklyn Dodgers. Mickey managed the Miners and pitched shutout ball for the first four innings, throwing mostly knuckleballs. In typical Mantle fashion, he also blasted a 345-foot home run that landed well beyond the left field fence. Ken hit one that went even further—376 feet to left-center—and the All-Stars won, 7-3. The game drew 2,300 spectators and raised almost $2,000 for the Crowder family.[46]

Ken and Cloyd played ball locally for the Joplin and Cassville All-Stars the rest of October. They were joined for at least one game by their eighteen-year old brother Lynn, who Runt Marr had just signed for the St. Louis Cardinals. "After all, baseball runs in the family," mother Mabel Boyer proudly told the *Joplin Globe*. Ken and Cloyd earned extra money that winter officiating regional basketball games.[47]

Now that his military obligations were fulfilled, Ken was ready to pick up where he left off in his baseball career. He would advance to Double-A ball with the Houston Buffaloes in the Texas League for the upcoming 1954 season.[48]

Chapter Four

Houston and Havana

The Houston Buffaloes anticipated the debut of Ken Boyer for six years. It began in September 1948, when the Cardinals Double-A club was in the Texas League playoffs. The entire Boyer clan traveled to Tulsa, Oklahoma, to watch Cloyd pitch for the Buffs. He pointed out his seventeen-year-old brother to anyone who would listen and told them he was the most promising prospect in the family: "You watch, he'll be the best." Word of Ken's promise as a hard-hitting, slick-fielding third baseman filtered down to Houston three years later from scouts who had seen him in Omaha. His contract was sold to Houston at the end of the 1951 season, but military service postponed his arrival three years longer until 1954.[1]

Ownership of the St. Louis Cardinals had changed while Ken was in the Army. Fred Saigh, indicted for income tax evasion and sentenced to fifteen months in a federal prison, had sold the club on February 20, 1953, to the Anheuser-Busch Brewery for $3.75 million, despite more lucrative offers from groups in Milwaukee and Houston. Brewery president August Anheuser Busch Jr. became the new president of the Cardinals as well. "Gussie" Busch knew little about the game, but he knew beer and baseball went well together and that owning the team would be a financial and advertising boon for his company. While projecting the image of a civic-minded individual who saved the team from leaving St. Louis with no desire to exploit it to sell his product, Busch told the brewery's board of directors a much different story. "Development of the Cardinals will have untold value for our company," he said behind closed doors. "This is one of the finest moves in the history of Anheuser-Busch."[2]

Before reporting for spring training with Houston, Boyer was invited to a special advance camp for the Cardinals' top minor-league prospects and returning servicemen in DeLand, Florida. Over seventy players took part in instruction and conditioning led by St. Louis manager Eddie Stanky, his coaching staff, the organization's minor-league managers, and club scouts. "If it weren't for this camp, it would have been impossible for me personally to see many of these youngsters perform," said Stanky. The workouts attracted several team officials, including Busch, who was impressed with the young players. "After seeing what I have, there doesn't appear to be any doubt that some potentially great baseball talent is being developed in our minor league system."[3]

The Cardinals' Double-A and two Triple-A clubs trained 24 miles northeast at Daytona Beach. Players worked out downtown at City Island Park—a ballpark located on an island in the Halifax River—and played sixteen exhibition games against the Rochester Red Wings and Columbus Red Birds (both St. Louis farm clubs) as well as the Triple-A Louisville Colonels and Indianapolis Indians. The normal program was disrupted when someone broke into the clubhouse while the Buffs was on the road and stole the players' wallets, watches, rings, and other personal items, as well as $1,368 in cash and $700 in expense checks.[4]

That spring, Ken was able to spend time in camp with Cloyd, who had been assigned to Rochester when St. Louis acquired pitcher Vic Raschi from the New York Yankees. The oldest Boyer brother had pitched parts of four seasons for the Cardinals from 1949 to 1952, and compiled an overall record of 15-18 and a 4.24 earned-run average. He developed a sore right shoulder near the end of the 1950 season—likely damaging his rotator cuff—but the mentality of managers and pitching coaches at the time was to pitch through the pain and it would eventually subside. A winter of rest improved it somewhat the next season, but the pain returned after repeated dives into first base and landing on his right arm while practicing to be a pinch-runner during spring training in 1952. He spent the next year back in the minors in Houston trying to work his way back to St. Louis.[5]

One day, Houston manager Dixie Walker took Cloyd aside and told him Ken might need to return to Class A Omaha, where he had played before leaving for the service. Bad habits at the plate picked up while playing ball in the Army and a sweeping swing caused him to struggle early in camp. Mornings were often spent on instructional work with little time for batting practice, preventing him from working out his problems. Cloyd asked Walker to hold off making a final decision for a few days and was allowed to work with Ken away from the rest of the team. The brothers spent several days together as Ken batted against Cloyd and they discussed what he was doing right and wrong while retrieving the balls. Both benefited from the extra work: Ken hit a home run against Rochester on March 17 and a week later, Cloyd pitched four innings against Houston, allowing only one run and three hits in a Rochester victory.

Ken kept his spot on the Houston roster, though the Cardinals added infielder-outfielder Emanuel "Sonny" Senerchia, who had a brief stint with the Pittsburgh Pirates two years earlier and hit 16 home runs in the minors in 1953, as insurance at third base. "I figured the Lord sent me there, the timing and everything," recalls Cloyd. "He straightened himself out. But I just figured that happened for a reason." Ken gave his older brother much more credit for his improvement. "Cloyd made the big difference," he said.[6]

AT THE END OF SPRING TRAINING, the Buffs traveled to Houston and hosted the St. Louis Cardinals for an exhibition game in front of 3,643 fans on April 3 before the start of the Texas League season. With the score tied, 3-3, Ken slapped an infield hit to third base to lead off the eighth inning and sparked a bases-loaded opportunity for the Buffs. A ground ball to first baseman Steve Bilko forced Boyer out at the plate, but another went through his legs and allowed two runs to score. A grounder hit by Hal Smith, Ken's former teammate with Hamilton four years earlier, took a bad hop and deflected off the glove of third baseman "Peanuts" Lowrey, pushing across another run to beat the parent club, 6-3. Cardinals stars Enos Slaughter and Red Schoendienst pinch-hit and Stan Musial was hitless in three at-bats.[7]

Kathleen and one-year-old Suzie were driven by Ken's sixteen-year-old brother Cletis 600 miles from their home in Webb City to join him in Houston. The family shared a duplex with teammate Willard Schmidt and his wife Margaret. They rented furniture for their summer home, but had no air conditioning to offer comfort against the oppressive Texas heat and humidity. Many days were spent going to the movies in an air-conditioned theater or outdoors watching Suzie play in her small plastic swimming pool. That summer, Boyer received a salary of $600 a month and the Cardinals raised it an additional $100 on August 19.[8]

The Buffs won the season opener against the Fort Worth Cats on April 10, but lost nine of their first eleven games and fell to last place. Injuries to Senerchia, second baseman Don Blasingame, catcher Dick Rand, and others played a big part in the team's subpar performance. Three errors committed by Boyer at third base in a 15-13 loss at Oklahoma City on April 19 were attributed in part to a back sprain he suffered while sliding into second base the night before. Three of the last four seasons—with the exception of a pennant winner in 1951—had been disappointing second-division finishes for the Buffs, including two spent in the Texas League cellar. Clark Nealon, who covered the team for the *Houston Post*, felt the upcoming campaign would be a make-or-break one for the St. Louis Double-A club. "They say the Cards are embarked on a youth program. Youth is OK if it produces, but Cardinal youth has failed here before."[9]

Wearing the collar in the opener, Ken hit safely in the next seven games and batted .303, though he had only four extra-base hits (with no home runs) in 33 at-bats through April 18. His manager was still concerned about the sweeping swing he had at the plate, one similar to Cloyd when he played for Houston. "We've got to get him out of that," said Walker. "That's the only question about Boyer: Will he hit?" He felt the swing impeded him from generating the consistent power that the 6-foot-2, 190-pounder was capable of producing.

During a three-game series at Oklahoma City beginning on the nineteenth, Walker—who won the National League batting title with a .357 average for the Brooklyn Dodgers in 1944 and led the league in RBIs a year later—encouraged him to start breaking his wrists at the end of his swing rather than sweep at the ball. Boyer worked at it and extended his hit streak with a pair of doubles and singles that weekend. He returned home and doubled twice with two RBIs on April 23. Before the next evening's game with the Tulsa Oilers, Houston general manager Art Routzong told the writers in the press box, "Dixie says Boyer is going to start hitting the ball out of the park. He's starting to break his wrists." That night, Ken increased his streak to thirteen games—longest in the Texas League to date—and knocked in all four runs for the Buffs, smashing his first home run of the season in the sixth inning to break a 1-1 deadlock in the 4-3 victory. "They'd been getting me out on inside pitches," Ken smiled afterward. "I hit one out of the park this time."[10]

Houston won four straight and climbed to sixth place, then dropped two of the next three games to end the month in seventh place, 4½ out of first but also a half-game out of the cellar. Boyer's improved stroke paid dividends. On the twenty-sixth, he had three safeties, including a double and a round-tripper, and scored three runs in a 7-4 victory over Tulsa. He narrowly missed a grand slam the next evening against the Oklahoma City Indians that bounced off the top of the left-field fence and back into play for a long single. There was no doubt about a pitch he smacked over the left-field scoreboard in an 8-4 victory on April 30. Ken ended the month of April with a .333 average, 13 extra-base hits (counting three homers), and 16 RBIs.[11]

The Buffs lost 20 of 34 games in May and fell back to last place with a 22-32 record, 8½ games behind the San Antonio Missions, a farm club of the Baltimore Orioles. Schmidt's two-hit, 5-0 shutout over the Beaumont Explorers on the eleventh highlighted an otherwise disappointing month. Boyer crushed his first Texas League grand slam in the contest, giving him four homers and 25 RBIs. Batting as high as .348 through the first month of the season, a prolonged 9-for-58 slump dropped his average sixty-six points to .282 on May 25. He was benched and relegated to pinch-hitting duties as Houston lost three of the first four in a five-game set at Beaumont. Ken's frustration was evident when he returned to the lineup for the series finale on May 24. With the Buffs trailing 2-0, he was called out trying to steal home and protested too strongly to the home-plate umpire. He was ejected from the game along with Rand (the on-deck batter) and skipper Walker. An RBI double two nights later against the Shreveport Sports and four multi-hit games in a row ended the slide and Walker promoted him from seventh in the order to the cleanup spot. Boyer smashed a bases-loaded triple in the 11-4 victory on May 27 that also featured the debut of Bob Boyd, the first African American player in Houston professional baseball history. The twenty-seven-year-old first baseman's contract was purchased from the Chicago White Sox. He became a valued member of the team, batting .321 with 22 doubles, seven home runs, and 63 RBIs in 94 games.[12]

Houston won nine of ten games beginning May 31—including five straight, the team's best streak in two seasons—and climbed out of the Texas League cellar for the last time. Four victories came in back-to-back doubleheaders over Fort Worth June 1–2. Schmidt twirled a one-hitter in the finale on June 1, yielding one unearned run and retiring the last 15 batters he faced. The score was knotted, 1-1, with two outs in the eleventh when Ken doubled home the winning tally for the 2-1 triumph. Right-hander George Condrick duplicated Schmidt's one-hit mastery of the Cats and Boyer contributed an RBI two-bagger and homered in a seven-inning, 5-2 win in the June 2 opener. Losing 4-1 in the finale, Fort Worth manager Al Vincent went into the box seats in the eighth inning and punched a Houston fan repeatedly who had taunted him throughout the contest before his own players intervened. Buffs second baseman George Lerchen came to blows with Cats catcher Al Ronning on the field at the same time. In his game coverage in the *Houston Post*, Nealon referred to Boyer as "Kenny"—the first time a reporter ever called him by that nickname—and continued doing so the remainder of the season.[13]

A four-game losing skid put the Buffs a half-game short of eighth place, but they recovered and took 15 of the last 22 games to close the month. They won two of three over the fifth-place Tulsa Oilers, a farm club of the Cincinnati Redlegs, and leapfrogged over them in the standings. Ken had five hits in the series, including two RBIs, three runs scored, and a 400-foot triple to the center-field fence off former major-league hurler Clyde King in the 10-2 rout on June 16.

It raised his average to .308 with eight homers and a team-best 59 runs batted in.

The Buffs swept three in a row from the cellar-dwelling Dallas Eagles, then traveled to Fort Worth with the opportunity to crack the first division in a three-game set against the fourth-place Cats. Houston took the opener, 7-2, and returned to the .500 plateau at 41-41 for the first time since April 11. Hard-throwing but erratic Fort Worth left-hander Karl Spooner walked 14 batters the next evening (two short of the league record), but the Buffs stranded 12 runners in the 7-2 defeat. Hitless in his last 18 at-bats, Boyer managed only a double down the left-field line in three at-bats against the future big-leaguer. Spooner would finish with a 21-9 record and 262 strikeouts and pitch for the Brooklyn Dodgers at the end of the season. Ken paced the team with three safeties and two RBIs the next night and Schmidt struck out eight to win his tenth game, 10-2. Returning to Buff Stadium, a crowd of 6,148 fans—the largest attendance thus far—watched the home team smack 14 hits and beat Beaumont, 6-3, moving ahead of the Cats to fourth place and 5 ½ out of first on June 26.[14]

Houston split four-game series with first-place Shreveport and second-place San Antonio the first week of July to climb within two games of the league leaders. Boyer singled twice in the opener with the Sports to give him 101 hits for the season and his sacrifice fly in the eleventh inning plated Blasingame for Houston's second straight extra-inning victory over them on July 2. Ken tripled and homered to the upper left-field deck off future big-league right-hander Ryne Duren, then tripled again and knocked in a season-high five runs in a 12-3 thrashing of the Missions the next evening.

The San Antonio series concluded with losses in both games of a July 5 doubleheader that drew 11,631 fans, the most since World War II ended. Boyer had two safeties in the first and one in the second, but his involvement in a fight at second base resulted in his ejection from that contest. In the fifth inning, he stole second and Missions shortstop Patricio "Witty" Quintana started swinging at him. Boyer grabbed him and didn't retaliate at first, but eventually landed a few blows of his own. Both benches converged around them while they wrestled on the ground. Each group tried restraining their respective teammates, but the two broke loose and traded punches again.

The umpires concluded both men were at fault and removed them from the game.[15]

Houston climbed to third place momentarily and 3 ½ games back with a 10-inning, 4-3 victory over first-place Shreveport on July 10. Ken singled to center in the ninth to break an 0-for-8 slide, stole second on a controversial call, and scored the tying run on Fred McAlister's fourth hit of the night. A two-out RBI single by Blasingame won it in the tenth. Boyer's hit that night sparked a personal 30-game consecutive hit streak, the fifth longest in Texas League history up to that time. (The record of 37 was set by Ike Boone of the San Antonio Bears in 1923 and later tied by Bobby Trevino of the El Paso Sun Kings in 1969.) A subsequent five-game losing skein against the Sports and Missions—including three straight on game-ending homers in San Antonio—knocked the Buffs back to fourth, a game under .500 at 52-53, and seven games out.[16]

Left-hander Luis Arroyo, promoted a few days earlier from the Cardinals' Single-A club in Columbus, Georgia, subdued the Missions' bats on July 14. Pitching on two days' rest, the twenty-seven-year-old Cuban native held San Antonio to four hits, struck out eight, and only Ken's error with two outs and a runner on third in the ninth inning prevented a shutout in the 11-1 victory. Houston won seven of the next nine games leading to the one-day All-Star break. Boyer contributed two doubles and his 10th home run of the season to a 15-hit outburst—including five homers, rare for a club ranked last in the league in round-trippers—in an 18-4 romp over Fort Worth on the sixteenth. Three nights later, Arroyo used his screwball with efficiency and struck out 15 to beat Dallas, 5-2. Ken homered with two outs in the eleventh inning for his third hit of the July 21 contest with the Eagles, enabling Lerchen to win it with a walk-off homer in the next frame, 8-7. Boyd's three-run blast made him the hero the next evening in the 7-6 victory over Dallas.[17]

THE BUFFS WERE SECOND only to the last-place Dallas Eagles in representatives chosen for the Texas League All-Star Game at Fort Worth's La Grave Field on July 23. Boyer was named along with Blasingame, Schmidt, Rand, second baseman Howie Phillips, and pitcher Hugh Sooter. They played on the South team, consisting of players from the Beaumont, Houston, San Antonio, and Shreveport clubs and were managed by Don Heffner of San Antonio. The North squad, representing Dallas, Fort Worth, Oklahoma City, and Tulsa, was led by Tommy Tatum of Oklahoma City. Before the contest, players received custom Elgin watches with "Texas League All-Stars" inscribed on the face. The All-Stars put on a show for the crowd of 6,177 as both teams combined for 29 hits, 18 by the South squad. Boyer singled in his only plate appearance and drove in Phillips to give the South a 6-4 lead in the sixth inning. The North tallied three runs in its half, 7-6, but Ken started a 5-2-3 double play with the bases loaded to end the frame.[18] The South squad stranded 13 runners, but two homers by James "Buzz" Clarkson of Dallas prevailed in the North's 9-8 victory.[19]

A come-from-behind victory in twelve innings at Oklahoma City on July 29 enabled Houston to climb to third place, a game-and-a-half behind front-running San Antonio. To bolster their pursuit of the Texas League pennant the last five weeks of the season, the Buffs invested in power-hitting right fielder Willard Brown, purchasing his contract from the cellar-dwelling Dallas Eagles for $7,500. The thirty-nine-year-old had been a formidable home run hitter in the Negro Leagues and proved a potent addition to the Buffs lineup. Batting cleanup ahead of Boyer for 36 games, the future Baseball Hall of Famer contributed six round-trippers down the stretch. Overall, he hit .314 for both clubs with 35 homers and 120 RBIs. His addition—along with Blasingame, Boyd, and Boyer—added a quartet of "Killer B's" to the Houston offense.[20]

It wasn't until Ken's 3-for-3 performance against the Tulsa Oilers on August 4 that Clark Nealon of the *Houston Post* took notice of his extensive hitting streak, which stood at 27 games. In that contest, he smashed a home run, drove in three runs, and scored three in the Buffs' 13-2 victory. An unproductive string of four plate appearances threatened to break it as he batted in the bottom of the eighth inning on August 6. The 8,274 fans at Buff Stadium—sensing the importance of the moment—cheered for him and the organist played "It's Been A Long, Long Time" as he stepped to the plate. With two strikes, Boyer stroked a single to left field, extending his streak to 30 games, and received an ovation from the crowd. Houston lost the contest in eleven innings, 6-5, and slipped to fourth place by a percentage point behind Oklahoma City. They regained their third-place footing with a 4-2 victory the next evening. In his first three plate appearances, Ken struck out, fouled out, and grounded out. A ground ball in his last at-bat went through Indians shortstop Joe Damato's legs—a discernible error—and the streak ended seven games short of the Texas League record. Over the 30-game span, Boyer had multiple hits in sixteen games and a trio of three-hit performances. He batted .377 with 10 doubles, five homers, 26 RBIs, and 16 runs scored.[21]

The Buffs won five in a row and with a 10-4 victory over the hapless Dallas Eagles on August 10, they moved past the San Antonio Missions into second place—their highest position in the standings all season—and 5 ½ back of the Shreveport Sports. Arroyo capped the winning streak with a no-hitter at Dallas two nights later. General manager Art Routzong rewarded the team with steak dinners at a local restaurant. On the thirteenth, Ken had three safeties and knocked in three tallies, including his 15th home run of the season, in a 7-2 victory over Fort Worth. A stiff neck resulting from a cold kept him out of the lineup for two games. Boyer returned on the twentieth and rapped two hits but committed one of five costly infield errors in a 10-7 defeat to the Beaumont Explorers. Sliding home safely with what proved to be the winning run in the 7-6 triumph over San Antonio on August 21, he alarmed Houston fans when he lay prone on the ground while the Missions argued with the home-plate umpire about the call. Ken injured his right ankle, but limped back to the dugout and stoically returned to his position the next frame.[22]

A mediocre string of lose one, win one games over twelve days allowed Oklahoma City to outpace them and Houston fell back to third place on the twenty-third. The Buffs recovered during the last week of August, taking two of three at Shreveport and three of four at Beaumont to close within a game of the Indians and five behind the league-leading Sports.[23]

A sensational series against Shreveport—seven hits, two home runs, two doubles, and seven runs scored—prompted John Hollis of the *Post* to call him "That Man Boyer." Ken ripped three singles and knocked in four tallies as part of a 16-hit assault in a 10-3 romp over the Explorers on the twenty-eighth. He and the Buffs duplicated their hit totals two nights later and Blasingame had five safeties to beat Beaumont, 8-4.[24]

Houston hosted Shreveport in the final home stand of the season at Buff Stadium beginning August 31. With eight games left, pennant hopes were fading though a berth in the postseason playoffs was all but certain. Houston dropped the opener, but won three in a row to outdistance Oklahoma City for second place and reduce their margin to three games behind the Sports. Arroyo twirled a five-hitter on the first of September and Boyer scored the go-ahead run on Boyd's single the next evening in the eventual 7-4 win that officially clinched a playoff spot. A 7-3 triumph on September 3 finished off Shreveport, highlighted by Brown's three-run home run and Schmidt's 10 strikeouts and 18th victory. The four-game set drew 32,412 fans for a total attendance of 310,531, best in the Texas League.[25]

The Buffs ended the season with four games at San Antonio. There was still a remote chance for the flag as the fifth-place Missions had lost their last nine games and the Sports were on the road facing the eighth-place Beaumont Explorers. Ken made up for a lackluster showing in the Shreveport series with seven safeties against San Antonio pitching. He doubled and homered in the September 4 opener but made two errors at third base, one of which resulted in an unearned run. Fighting for their own playoff chance, the Missions pummeled three Houston hurlers with 13 hits and a four-run outburst in the seventh inning put the game out of the Buffs' reach. The 8-3 defeat enabled Shreveport to clinch the Texas League championship and third-place Oklahoma City inched one game closer behind Houston.

In danger of losing second place and not hosting the first game of the playoffs, Houston overcame a pair of home runs by power-hitting first baseman Frank Kellert to beat San Antonio the next evening, 8-4. Two round-trippers and four RBIs by Russell Rac and 17 strikeouts by Arroyo knocked the Missions out of playoff contention. Ken shined in the season-ending twi-night doubleheader on September 6 with five hits in both contests—raising his season total to 202—a game-tying home run in the opener, and his 21st of the season an inning later. The 9-7 and 10-5 victories solidified Houston's second-place finish with a record of 89-72, one game behind Shreveport.[26]

"Will he hit?" was the question manager Dixie Walker asked about Ken Boyer at the beginning of the 1954 season. He proved that he could indeed—a .319 average that was fifth-best in the Texas League, 42 doubles, seven triples, 21 home runs, 119 RBIs, and 116 runs scored. He finished second to Kellert of San Antonio for Player of the Year honors.[27] Matching power with speed as no other player that season, he stole 29 bases and finished second to teammate Don Blasingame's league-leading 34. The twenty-three-year-old competed in an eight-club circuit that featured more experienced players, many of whom already had major-league experience. Among the top 10 hitters, only Blasingame was younger. Asked later if he was intimidated by the competition in the Texas League, Ken replied, "I might have been a little scared going up to Houston, but when I got there and saw the players, I said to myself, 'Hell, I played with fellows like this in the Army.'"[28]

THE BUFFS' SEASON wasn't over yet. The first round of the best-of-seven Texas League playoffs between Houston and Oklahoma City opened in front of 9,281 fans at Buff Stadium on September 8. Twenty-eight hits—including 15 by the home team—highlighted the contest. Three home runs by Indians left fielder Howie Boles accounted for five of his club's tallies. Four errors and hitting into four double plays contributed to the Buffs' 9-8 defeat. Ken had four safeties with three RBIs and two runs scored. With two outs and trailing 9-5 in the ninth inning, Blasingame hit his second homer of the game, Phillips singled, and Boyer homered to make it 9-8. The rally ended on Brown's subsequent ground out.[29]

The next evening saw another close contest that ended with local police escorting the umpires from the ballpark. Two-run homers by Boyer and Brown and an RBI single by Lerchen gave the Buffs a 5-0 lead. Arroyo dominated the Indians, allowing only two hits through six innings until Boles crashed the shutout with a two-run blast in the seventh. Oklahoma City threatened to add more following a dropped pop foul by Boyer in front of home plate, but he atoned for the miscue by starting an inning-ending double play. The Indians rallied again in the ninth, scoring two more runs off reliever Bob Tiefenauer. With one out and a runner on first base, second baseman Phillips fielded a ground ball and threw to Blasingame to start a double play. Even though the ball came out of his glove, umpire Sam Carrigan ruled that he had possession long enough for the force out. Indians manager Tommy Tatum charged onto the field and argued the decision to no avail. Another grounder ended the game in Houston's favor, 5-4. Things became heated when Tatum and two of his players continued arguing with Carrigan and wouldn't let him leave the field. Eventually, the police intervened and escorted the umpire and his partner Ken Burkhart away from the fray. As Tatum and his players returned to the dugout, fans threw seat cushions and scorecards at them, hitting one of the players and making for an ugly end to the contest.[30]

The Buffs boarded a plane for Oklahoma City, where the series resumed in front of 4,040 fans at Holland Park on September 10. Giving up three tallies in the first three innings, Houston right-hander Dick Atkinson handcuffed the Indians the rest of the way and benefited from three double plays behind him. Cuban right-hander Vicente Amore, an 18-game winner during the regular season and a future major-leaguer with the Chicago Cubs, was equally dominant and held Houston to one run in the first six innings. The Buffs finally broke through in the seventh on a home run, a triple, and a single that plated two runs to tie the contest, 3-3, and sent it into extra innings. In the tenth, Ken doubled to left field, Boyd and Lerchen both walked, and Rand doubled home Boyer and Boyd for the 6-3 victory.[31]

George Condrick held Oklahoma City to six hits and catcher Hal Smith hit an eighth-inning grand slam for the 7-2 win on September 12. The Buffs took a 9-2 lead with a six-run sixth inning the next evening and Schmidt pitched well before tiring in the ninth, giving up a run and leaving two Indians on base with two outs. Tiefenauer pitched in relief and though he gave up a two-run double, his knuckleball resulted in a tap back to the mound to win, 9-5, and clinch the series. Second baseman and team captain Phillips led the Houston offense with a .476 average in the five-game series. Ken batted .391 with two doubles, a home run, and five RBIs.[32]

THE FINALS of the Texas League postseason championship series began at Buff Stadium on September 14 against the Fort Worth Cats, who had defeated the league champion Shreveport Sports four games to one.

A crowd of 11,648 saw the Buffs win in dramatic fashion when Blasingame, who had five home runs during the regular season, smashed his third of the week for the 4-3 victory in eleven innings.[33] The Cats took the second game, 7-1, before the series shifted to Fort Worth on September 16. With two outs in the initial frame, Ken dropped a single into short left field, advanced to second base on a wild throw to first, and scored on Brown's double to give the Buffs the early lead. Condrick of Houston and Spooner of Fort Worth pitched themselves out of difficulties throughout the contest. The Cats tied the score with a home run by Cal Felix in the seventh and the contest went into extra innings. The Buffs went ahead in the eleventh, 2-1, but Fort Worth tied it once again in their half. Tiefenauer scored the go-ahead run in the seventeenth on a double by Phillips. He returned to the mound and slipped a knuckleball past former big-leaguer Ray Coleman to end the four-hour, twenty-nine minute contest with a 3-2 victory.[34]

The Buffs dominated the next two games. The Killer B's—Boyer, Brown, and Boyd—stung Fort Worth pitchers with home runs on September 17. Ken's sixth-inning blast sparked a four-run outburst that put the Buffs comfortably ahead in the 11-2 win. In the fifth game, Houston had 15 hits and bunched most of their runs in the second and fourth innings, highlighted by a grand slam in the fourth by Lerchen. Ken singled twice, scored two runs, and drove in another in the game. Houston starting pitcher Hugh Sooter, returning after several weeks out of action with a sore shoulder, held the Cats to one run and three hits before a blister on his thumb forced him from the game in the fifth. Jim Atchley finished in relief with five shutout innings and allowed only one hit the rest of the way. The Buffs' 13-1 victory clinched the postseason series, four games to one. They would represent the Texas League in the annual Dixie Series, facing the winner of the Southern Association playoffs.[35]

THE JUBILANT BUFFS boarded a flight for Atlanta, Georgia, where the Crackers, a farm club of the Milwaukee Braves, awaited them after beating the New Orleans Pelicans four games to one. The players sang songs, shared stories, and laughed at imitations made by trainer Doc Foley. Thirty-one-year-old George Lerchen, who had played briefly with the Detroit Tigers and Cincinnati Redlegs the last two seasons, enjoyed being part of the team. "I've been on a lot of clubs, but this is the best gang of guys I've run into yet," he said. "I've never had as much fun playing ball on a team before in my life."[36]

Houston won the first two games of the Dixie Series in Atlanta. Their bats lifted Arroyo, who walked five but struck out seven, and crumbled six Crackers pitchers for the 10-4 victory on September 21. Ken had an RBI double and scored two runs. The next evening, Schmidt pitched a masterful two-hitter to win, 7-2, his only mistake being a two-run home run by Atlanta second baseman Frank Diprima in the second inning. Houston drove 24-game winner Leo Cristante from the mound in the fourth, the final straws being Boyer's double and Brown's single that scored him for their seventh run. The editorial staff of the *Houston Post* had fun with the team's first two victories, posting headlines such as "Buffs Salt Atlanta's Crackers" and "Schmidt's Nifty 2-Hitter Crumbles Crackers."[37]

The Dixie Series shifted west to Houston with the Buffs poised to take a commanding three games to none lead on September 23. Among the Texas League and Southern Association officials and 11,572 fans in attendance were former St. Louis Cardinals manager Eddie Dyer and Johnny Keane, skipper of the Cardinals' Triple-A Rochester club. The Buffs and the Crackers matched run for run through the first seven frames. Ken had three safeties, a stolen base, and an RBI, but his teammates failed to capitalize on opportunities and left 13 runners stranded. In the eighth, Atlanta pummeled reliever Atchley with four hits (including a home run by Bob Montag) and a sacrifice fly for four tallies to beat Houston, 7-4.[38]

With the score tied the next evening, 2-2, Ken doubled to left field off Crackers reliever Don McMahon in the sixth inning and plated Blasingame from second base with the go-ahead run. Brown singled to drive in Boyer, then the big man stole second and scored on Rac's double over the head of the Crackers center fielder to make it 5-2. After yielding two runs in the third, Sooter pitched shutout ball the rest of the way for the Buffs. Atlanta threatened in the ninth, but Ken snagged a line drive away from future major-leaguer Frank Torre and used it to turn a double play. Sooter struck out the next batter, Montag, for the final out.[39]

The 5-2 victory gave Houston a three-to-one advantage and the chance to clinch the Dixie Series in front of 10,876 hometown fans on September 25. The team was confident with Arroyo on the mound and the knowledge that a three-game series had not been lost at Buffs Stadium since the first week of April. On the verge of elimination, the Crackers pounced on the Cuban left-hander in the first inning with back-to-back singles and an RBI single by Pete Whinsenant. A one-run lead was all 6-foot-5 Atlanta right-hander Glenn Thompson needed against Houston's bats, hurling a three-hit shutout and striking out 11. Two walks gave the Buffs hope for a game-winning rally in the eighth, but Thompson struck out Blasingame, Phillips, and Boyer in succession on 3-2 counts to end the threat. Ken's streak of hitting safety in 14 consecutive playoff games ended with an 0-for-4 night in the 1-0 defeat.[40]

The Dixie Series returned to Atlanta's Ponce de Leon Park for Game 6 on September 27. Walker was so confident his team would win that he didn't bother reserving hotel rooms. Schmidt, winner of Game 2 for the Buffs, and Dick Donovan, Game 3 winner for the Crackers, each pitched shutout ball over the first three frames for their respective clubs. Rac's sacrifice fly scored Phillips in the fourth to give Houston a 1-0 lead, but Atlanta answered with five runs in their half that forced Schmidt's early exit. Donovan scattered seven hits over nine innings and struck out eight to beat the Buffs, 6-2. Boyer managed only a single in four at-bats. The Crackers' victory tied the series at three games apiece and forced a seventh game.[41]

Houston struck first in Game 7 against Thompson, winner of Game 5 who was pitching on two day's rest. Leadoff hitter Blasingame tripled and scored on Phillips' sacrifice fly to give the Buffs the early lead. Sooter, winning pitcher in Game 4, pitched out of jams thanks to the defense behind him through the first three frames. But three runs in the fourth and an RBI double by Torre in the fifth led to his early departure. Arroyo was summoned from the bullpen. He walked Chuck Tanner intentionally to load the bases in order to face Montag, who didn't hit left-handed pitchers well. Atlanta skipper Whitlow Wyatt countered with a pinch-hitter, Jim Solt, who belted Arroyo's first pitch over the left-field fence for a decisive grand slam that thrilled the packed crowd of 13,293 fans. The deflated Buffs never mounted a comeback. As they came to bat in the top of the ninth, the ballpark organist played, "I'm Heading for the Last Roundup." Thompson retired the last 20 batters he faced to complete the 7-1 victory and clinch the Dixie Series for the Southern Association. Ken had a pair of singles in the finale and batted .357 in the Series with three doubles and four runs batted in. Overall, he hit .325 in 17 postseason games with seven doubles, three homers, 11 RBIs, and 15 runs scored.[42]

Ken's successful season at Houston brought him newfound attention. Buffs general manager Art Routzong called him "the best prospect I've seen in my 17 years in baseball." Of all the position players in the organization, Cardinals minor-league scout Gus Mancuso was most excited about Ken's potential. "Boyer is No. 1," he proclaimed in early September. "He's got great hands, a great arm, power and tremendous speed. I don't know a third baseman he couldn't be as good as with experience and practice on slow-hit balls, the only play that bothers him."[43] The Cardinals weren't the only major-league club interested in him. When general manager Dick Meyer approached the New York Yankees about a trade for catching prospect and St. Louis native Elston Howard, he offered one of several young minor-league shortstops in exchange. The Yankees asked for Boyer instead. Scouts from other clubs knew what the Cardinals already did—Ken was versatile enough to play either third base or short. Meyer remarked, "If the Yankees believe Boyer can play shortstop, I'd say they're right."[44]

BEFORE THE THIRD GAME of the Dixie Series, Ken agreed to play winter ball in Cuba. With barely any rest between the end of the postseason series and the beginning of the Cuban Winter League season, he, Kathleen, and daughter Suzie boarded a plane for the island nation in the Caribbean. In addition to Houston teammates Blasingame and Rand, he was joined by Cardinals minor-league shortstop Dick Schofield, pitcher Floyd Wooldridge, and outfielder and 1954 International League batting champion Bill Virdon.[45]

The young minor-leaguers played for the Habana Leones (Lions), a club owned by former Cardinals catcher and coach Miguel Angel "Mike" Gonzáles. The manager was sixty-four-year-old Dolph Luque, a legend in Cuban baseball who had pitched twenty seasons in the major leagues, mostly for the Cincinnati Reds from 1914 to 1935. The

Leones competed against clubs from Almendares, Cienfuegos, and Marianao, each a district (or suburb) of the capital city of Havana. The Cuban Winter League played a 72-game schedule with four games a week including a Sunday doubleheader. All games were played in Havana at the Gran Stadium de La Habana.[46]

The team arranged for the American players and their families to live at the Club Náutico, a gated residential complex on the beach. Ken and many of his teammates brought their cars with them on a boat from Miami. "They only played about three games a week, so it was like a vacation," remembers Kathleen Boyer. "We really had a great time there. It was a lot of fun." She and Ken spent time at the Club with another married couple, Bill and Shirley Virdon.[47]

Yet there was an unmistakable military presence in the city and at the games. The dictator Fulgencio Batista ruled over Cuba, having led a successful coup two years earlier. Machine gun nests could be seen on the way to the ballpark and armed soldiers were stationed on the roof and around the stadium. Virdon recalled one instance when Club Náutico was locked down and games were canceled because of a threat from Communist rebels led by Fidel Castro.[48]

The Leones endured a terrible start to the season. After losing the opening game to the Tigres de Marianao (Marianao Tigers) on October 8, they dropped 20 of the first 30 games and plunged into last place. Their performance was attributed to bad luck and being one of the youngest clubs in the league. Habana's struggles continued through the mid-season mark and the Leones remained in the cellar with a record of 13-20, 10 games behind the league-leading Almendares Blues.[49]

Though he wasn't among the league's top hitters, Ken still had his moments at the plate. He smashed a tenth-inning home run to beat the Elefantes de Cienfuegos (Cienfuegoes Elephants), 4-3, on November 16. Three days later, he and teammates Blasingame and Sandy Amoros each had four hits in a victory over second-place Marianao. Pedro Galiana of *The Sporting News* observed early in the season: "Boyer has been whaling the ball, only to have sensational catches at the wall rob him of many hits to cut down his average."[50]

Habana broke a string of 24 consecutive scoreless innings with a 9-3 victory over Cienfuegoes on December 4. But in the top of the ninth, Ken was struck over the left ear with a fastball thrown by Elephants right-hander Alfredo Ibanez. "I was very careless and never even saw the pitch," Boyer later recalled. "I didn't freeze or anything, but I got caught right smack in the ear. But I don't feel that the kid was throwing at me. He was a young Cuban kid, and he was out there before a lot of his own people. I think he was probably scared to death to even be out there pitching, and the last thing he would have been thinking about would have been hitting anybody." Ken was carried off the field and taken to a local hospital, where he was unconscious for at least two days. He suffered a concussion, but X-rays revealed his skull had not been fractured. "He didn't die, but he thought he had," remembered Virdon.[51]

Kathleen was not at the game, but she remembers it as "a very horrible time." After about a week, he grew restless and left the hospital without being officially released, wanting to recover at his apartment instead. "He was just tired of being in there, I guess," she says. "Of course in the hospital, hardly anyone spoke English. He probably couldn't understand anybody." It wasn't until February 1955 that he was completely free from spells of dizziness and vertigo.[52]

While Ken recuperated in Havana, moves were being made in St. Louis that would impact his future with the Cardinals. The triumvirate of general manager Dick Meyer, vice president Bill Wasingham, and manager Eddie Stanky decided the club needed help in the bullpen and that Boyer was ready to take over at third base. On December 8, they dealt power-hitting third baseman Ray Jablonski—who led the team with 104 RBIs in 1954—and pitcher Gerry Staley, an 18-game winner just two years earlier, to the Cincinnati Redlegs for right-handed reliever Frank Smith. Stanky defended the club's decision to trade Jablonki, whose bat in the lineup had been protection for Stan Musial. "[I]f all reports we have received on Ken Boyer were true, Boyer—and not Jablonski—would have been my 1955 Cardinal third baseman." The trade made a clear path for Boyer to claim the position the following spring.[53]

In Ken's absence, the Habana Leones won six straight and climbed out of the cellar and into third place. He rejoined the club two weeks after the beaning and batted .283 with 16 RBIs and 39 hits in 138 at-bats. The Leones surpassed the struggling Cienfuegos Elephants and took over second place on December 19. At this time, the Cardinals dispatched scout Gus Mancuso to Havana to check on Boyer's progress. Mancuso reinforced the team's confidence in him:

> Boyer [is] a good left field hitter, plays third base with the smoothness of an old hand at the job. He has a fine arm and has a knack for learning fast. All experienced observers who have seen him appear united in the opinion that young Ken is ready.[54]

The Leones won 15 out of 18 games toward the end of the season and looked poised to challenge first-place Almendares, who had enjoyed a sizable lead. Showing no ill effects from the beaning, Ken was fielding well and hitting just below .300. For a short time, he even challenged Virdon's .331 average that was third-best in the Cuban Winter League. The Leones' winning ways continued into the New Year as they took 24 of their last 30 games by the end of January. A seven-game winning streak brought them within four games of the Blues with nine left to play. Ken raised his average to .306 (sixth-best in the league) with 63 hits in 206 at-bats and 28 RBIs.[55]

Branch Rickey, former Cardinals general manager now with the Pittsburgh Pirates, traveled to Cuba to scout players. He spent two days in Havana watching the Leones and the Cienfuegos. Rickey was very impressed with Ken and made special note of his strengths and abilities.

> At third base, I saw the best ballplayer on first impression that I have seen in many a day. Boyer by name. He can run with very deceptive speed, and he does run. Never loafs. He has big hands and knows what to do with them. He has a quick arm and a fine arm from his elbow on down. Every body muscle is under control. He could play shortstop and certainly would be a corking second baseman. Indeed, I think Boyer could play anywhere, and I mean anywhere. He drives the ball with great power and he is a line drive hitter deluxe. The newspapermen down here are raving about the outfielder [Bill] Virdon, saying, in effect, unanimously, that

Virdon is the greatest player ever to be in Cuba etc. etc. I will take Boyer. He must be 6' tall and weigh 185 pounds. I was not close enough to him to risk positive accuracy of his vital statistics, but every inch of him and every pound of him is a professional player of great promise.[56]

With two weeks left in the season, Habana's offense that had averaged 10 runs and 12 hits per game during their win streak vanished. The team was shut out in consecutive games by second-division clubs Marianao and Cienfuegos on January 25 and 26, and Almendares clinched the Cuban Winter League championship against the Leones four days later. Trailing in the ninth inning, 4-1, Boyer and teammate Pedro Almendares hit back-to-back home runs for Habana to come within a run of trying the game against Almendares. But Blues left-hander and future big-leaguer Joe Hatten buckled down to retire the side, clinch the title, and secure a trip for his team to Venezuela for the Caribbean Series.[57]

The Cuban Winter League held its All-Star Game in front of 10,000 fans at the Gran Stadium de La Habana on February 1. Fans selected the teams of American and Cuban players that competed in the contest. Boyer was the offensive star, crashing a game-tying homer in the eighth inning and winning it for the Americans with a bases-loaded double in the ninth, 6-4.[58] A few days later, Kathleen learned her mother had passed away back in Joplin, Missouri. Team owner Mike Gonzáles made arrangements for her and Suzie to return home for the funeral.[59] Ken stayed behind to finish the season as the Habana Leones clinched second place with a record of 36-33.

LOOKING BACK, Boyer was grateful for the four years he spent in the minor leagues. They developed him into a more polished and experienced professional athlete. "That minor-league experience is invaluable. You find out…there are good days and bad days and that you can come back. It must be awfully hard for an eighteen-year-old boy to fight back up here [in the majors] if he gets off to a bad start playing after he has been given a big bonus."[60] He added to that experience with his successful five-month stint in the Cuban Winter League. Overcoming a potential career-threatening beaning, he finished with a .304 average in 62 games and 234 at-bats. He had 71 hits, 10 doubles, one triple, six home runs, 30 RBIs, 48 runs scored, and two stolen bases. His whirlwind baseball season would continue back in the States with spring training in the big-league camp and a position waiting for him with the St. Louis Cardinals.[61]

Ken Boyer with the Omaha Cardinals in his first full season as a third baseman, 1951. (*Cloyd Boyer*)

Earl Weaver (left), a scrappy 21-year-old second baseman, was a teammate of Boyer's at Omaha. The future Hall of Fame manager of the Baltimore Orioles was voted the most popular player on the team. Ken came in second. (*Author's Collection*)

Ken met 18-year-old Kathleen Oliver before leaving for spring training in 1950. They were married two years later. (*Boyer Family Collection*)

Ken spent two years in the Army, 1952–53, including service in Germany. There he played shortstop and pitched for the 28th Division Artillery Redlegs baseball team. (*Boyer Family Collection/ Stars and Stripes*)

After returning from the Army, Ken played for the Houston Buffaloes in the Double-A Texas League in 1954. (*Houston Metropolitan Research Center Photo Archives*)

Boyer and Don Blasingame (left) were teammates at Houston and St. Louis. (*Houston Metropolitan Research Center Photo Archives*)

Twenty-three-year-old Ken Boyer with the Houston Buffaloes in 1954. A year later, he would be playing third base for the St. Louis Cardinals, his childhood team. (*Houston Metropolitan Research Center Photo Archives*)

Chapter Five

Great Expectations

Ken Boyer was a phenom in the spring of 1955. Expectations were high that the twenty-three-year-old not only would be a defensive upgrade at third base and a productive addition to the batting order, but potentially one of the greatest players in franchise history. Without having stepped onto a major-league diamond, he was heralded as "the Cardinals' first complete infielder since Red Schoendienst" by *St. Louis Post-Dispatch* sports editor J. Roy Stockton. Scouts touted him as "the next Pie Traynor," comparing Boyer to the Pittsburgh Pirates star considered the finest defensive third baseman ever. Redbirds chief scout Joe Mathes believed he "could become the greatest third baseman in Cardinal history."[1]

St. Louis made a bold move over the winter, trading their All-Star third baseman and cleanup hitter Ray Jablonski to Cincinnati. A durable power-hitter with back-to-back 100-RBI seasons, his 104 mark in 1954 was second only to Musial on the club. He also tied with Willie Mays for tenth in the National League with 33 doubles. But Jablonski's fielding at third base had worsened from 27 errors in his rookie season to a league-worst 34 (by a wide margin) in 1954. Before he was traded, manager Eddie Stanky had already decided there would be a competition for the position in spring training. Now there was no doubt that Boyer would be the starting third baseman on Opening Day.[2]

There were expectations for the Cardinals as well in 1955. It was the second year of a youth movement that pushed promising minor-league prospects onto the major-league stage—"force feeding" as Bob Broeg of the *Post-Dispatch* labeled it. Team vice president Bill Walsingham touted the club's renewed emphasis on scouting in recent years and pointed to the speed and versatility of players like Boyer, Bill Virdon, Alex Grammas, Don Blasingame, and Wally Moon, the league's reigning Rookie of the Year, as reasons for optimism. With veterans Stan Musial and Red Schoendienst entering their thirties, these would be the players to eventually take their places. "[T]hey're not flashes in the pan," said Walsingham, "but sound, durable players who will be Cardinal mainstays for a long time."[3]

Ken flew from Joplin to St. Louis to sign his first major-league contract in late February. After a short press conference, he called his brother Wayne, who was studying dentistry at Washington University in St. Louis, before returning home the same day.[4] A few weeks later, he reported to his first spring training with the major-league club at Al Lang Field in St. Petersburg, Florida. The players stayed a few blocks away at the Bainbridge Hotel, the official lodging for the Cardinals since 1938. Boyer recalled the railroad tracks for the Atlantic Coast Line ran parallel to the hotel and made it sound like "the train [was] coming through the hotel room" every morning.[5] Lingering concerns about his health as a result of the beaning in Cuba were put to rest when team physician Dr. I.C. Middleman determined Ken had no symptoms of vertigo or permanent damage to his left ear and cleared him to play. Because he had the same physical stature as departed pitcher Gerry Staley (who was part of the Jablonski trade), equipment manager Butch Yatkeman gave him Staley's jersey and uniform number 14. Though intended as a temporary assignment for the duration of the spring workouts, Boyer kept the number for most of his major-league career.[6]

Ken's hustle made a positive impact with Stanky, who called him, "My No. 1 boy." He told Broeg, "He's not colorful, but he's deadly efficient, and with no apparent weakness. He's got exceptional body control, he's versatile and he has almost as good an appreciation of the strike zone as Moon had when he came up."[7] Stanky tested his versatility by putting him at shortstop in the initial spring exhibitions and was impressed with his range. "I found out what wanted to know," he told columnist Arthur Daley of the *New York Times*. "Boyer is good enough to play shortstop in the big leagues and I won't hesitate to use him there if I need him."[8] Veteran sportswriter Red Byrd compared his performance at both positions:

> There was a natural tendency for the young infielder to stop, look and measure his throws from short, whereas at third he had the reputation of getting the ball away from any necessary angle. But the throws were strong and accurate, and on double plays, the relays were so sharp that spectators applauded. There's no doubt about it, Boyer has the best throwing arm that any Cardinal infielder has displayed in many a year.[9]

His potential drew sportswriters to him for interviews and opposing players and managers who wanted to see for themselves if the hype was real. "Ken is a pleasant but uncommunicative youngster," surmised Daley. "He lets his actions do the talking." Broeg noted his maturity when asked about the lack of competition at third base without Jablonski in camp. "There's no doubt that there's bound to be less pressure than trying to beat out a man who drives in 100 runs in the big leagues," Ken conceded. Both Boyer and Virdon had slow starts at the plate in the exhibitions, with Ken going 2-for-14 in the initial contests. Stanky reassured both players they would make the team. "Just do what's asked of you," he told them. "Don't worry about a thing—you guys will start when the season opens." To Boyer, he remarked, "I don't care if you hit .125 down here, you're going to be my third baseman."[10]

Ken's former manager at Houston, Dixie Walker, now a coach on Stanky's staff, liked his chances in the big leagues. "Boyer does everything well. He has a wonderful arm, is fast, strong, and has the proper attitude, and besides, he's intelligent with it…I think he'll go far with the St. Louis Cardinals." Now he was teammates with players whom he had watched at Sportsman's Park as a kid. "I was star-struck," he recalled. "I idolized Stan and Red. I read about everything they did. I saved all their bubble-gum cards." A poll of contributors to *The Sporting News* predicted Boyer would win the National League Rookie of the Year award at season's end.[11]

THE CARDINALS OPENED THE SEASON on a "gray, cool day" at Wrigley Field in Chicago on April 12. Like any rookie, Ken was nervous before his first major-league game in front of 26,153 boisterous fans. Sensing his apprehension, the 5-foot-8 Stanky put his arm around the shoulders of the 6-foot-2 Boyer and pointed to the right-field wall. "I hit one out of there"—then pointed to left field—"and I hit one out there too." If he could do it, so could Boyer.[12]

Ken played third base and batted sixth in the order. In the field, he made two putouts and three assists. He almost fell into the Cubs dugout in pursuit of a foul ball off the bat of first baseman Dee Fondy in the second inning. Boyer caught the ball, but dropped it when he lost his balance at the top step. He had to grab the edge of the concrete roof with both hands to keep from falling in while his body stretched across precariously. The moment was captured in a photograph and appeared on the front sports page of the *Chicago Tribune* the next day.[13]

St. Louis was behind, 5-1, when Ken led off the second inning in his first major-league plate appearance. He faced veteran left-hander Paul Minner, an imposing figure on the mound at 6-foot-5. Minner enjoyed great success against the Redbirds with a lifetime 21-8 record. In their first encounter, Boyer flew out to right field. He struck out swinging with the bases loaded in the fourth and again in the sixth with one on. St. Louis trailed in the eighth, 14-2, when Schoendienst singled with two outs. Ken came to the plate for the fourth time with Minner still on the hill. This time, he connected for his first major-league hit, a two-run home run over the left-field wall, in the 14-4 defeat. Interestingly, Minner had given up teammate Wally Moon's first major-league homer the previous season and a year later would do the same to future Hall of Famer Frank Robinson.[14]

The Cardinals returned to St. Louis for their home opener on April 14. The ballpark had changed since Ken watched games there as a young boy and worked out on the field before signing his first pro contract. Sportsman's Park was now called Busch Stadium, renamed in memory of Gussie Busch's late father, grandfather, and brother. (Busch originally wanted it to be Budweiser Stadium until Baseball Commissioner Ford Frick convinced him the name was blatantly commercial in nature.) The brewery also invested in extensive renovations to the aging ballpark, installing new drainage and sprinkler systems, repainting or replacing box seats, remodeling the clubhouses, dugouts, restrooms, and concession areas, upgrading the lighting system, and replacing the bleachers seats in center field with shrubbery and green space to serve as a batter's eye. The colorful advertising signs on the concrete outfield walls were concealed by a coat of green paint. The large scoreboard above the left-center field bleachers now featured both an animated neon Anheuser-Busch eagle that flapped its wings and a redbird that swatted a ball for every home run.

In his home debut against the Milwaukee Braves, Boyer had two hits in five at-bats. After a second-inning homer by Schoendienst tied the score, 1-1, Ken followed with a triple but was later thrown out at the plate trying to score on a ground ball to short. The Braves enjoyed a 7-3 lead before he singled and scored as part of a three-run rally in the eighth that made it 7-6. Musial tied the game with a home run in the ninth. The Cardinals should have won the game the next inning, but a base-running gaffe caused Moon's apparent single to be a force out, ending the frame. Virdon finally won it with a round-tripper in the eleventh to beat Milwaukee, 8-7. Boyer started his rookie season with nine safeties in his first 28 at-bats for a .321 average.[15]

After winning the opener of a doubleheader at Pittsburgh on May 1, the second-place Cardinals had an 8-5 record and were five games behind the first-place Brooklyn Dodgers. Seven losses in a row on the road dropped them to fifth and 11 ½ games out of first. "We've lost some games on mistakes, the physical and mental ones you've got to expect particularly of a young club, and we've wasted a lot of scoring chances too," lamented Stanky. Ken was one of the culprits when he was caught flat-footed at first base on what should have been a double steal. "That'll cost you five dollars, kid," chastised his manager.[16]

After starting the season batting sixth in the order, Boyer was moved to leadoff as St. Louis faced left-hander Johnny Podres at

Ebbets Field on May 4. Stanky knew Ken was deceptively fast for a man of his solid 6-foot-2, 190-pound stature. He had demonstrated his speed in a preseason exhibition in St. Louis on April 10, stealing three bases in a row off pitcher Ray Herbert of the Detroit Tigers.[17] Stanky was so confident in Ken's quickness that he staged a 100-meter race between Boyer, Moon, and Virdon and took bets on the winner. "I won the race and he must have won $80," recalled Ken. "He came over and shoved $40 in my lap and said, 'Here's your half.' In those days, $40 was like a half-week's pay." Boyer batted leadoff more than any other spot in the lineup his rookie season and hit .269 with a .300 on-base percentage.[18]

The Redbirds bounced back from their seven-game funk and won seven of their next eight at Busch Stadium. Five consecutive victories over Pittsburgh and Brooklyn May 14–18 raised their record two games over .500 at 15-13. A first-pitch, two-run home run off Brooklyn reliever Jim Hughes, who led the league with 24 saves the year before, lifted Ken's average to .267 on the seventeenth. But a seven-game road trip proved to be the Cardinals'—and Stanky's—undoing. They lost the first three of a four-game set at Cincinnati beginning May 20, then dropped three in a row in Chicago to fall three games below .500, never to reach the mark the remainder of the season. While chasing a foul ball at Crosley Field, Boyer tore a finger on the mesh fence and missed the next game. He returned for the Sunday doubleheader on the twenty-second and he and Schoendienst homered in the second game for the 5-2 win, their only success on the trip.[19]

Even with a 7-4 victory over the Redlegs back home on May 27, Stanky was fired the next day. A publicized outburst of temper in the visitors' clubhouse at Cincinnati following their defeat in the first game of the twin bill five days earlier proved to be the last straw. Stanky, nicknamed "The Brat," was never popular with Cardinals fans, who viewed him as an outsider and remembered him as a combative second baseman with the rival Brooklyn Dodgers. After the announcement was made, Stanky went into the clubhouse and quietly told his players goodbye. "I would have managed this club for nothing in 1956, that's how good I think it'll be with experience and with [pitcher Wilmer] Mizell back from service," he told Broeg. Stanky intended to shift

Boyer to shortstop and promote Ken's former minor-league teammate Don Blasingame from Triple-A Omaha to play third base.[20]

Boyer was grateful to Stanky for the patience and confidence he showed in him. He considered him "an excellent tactician" and the best teacher of fundamentals he ever had. "I'm glad I broke in under a manager as smart as Stanky," he recalled as an aspiring manager himself fifteen years later. "I'm fortunate I learned so many little things from him, including how to run the bases." Several years later, Stanky became part of the Cardinals' administration within the Player Personnel and Development Department of the ballclub.[21]

St. Louis was in fifth place with a 17-19 record when former Cardinals outfielder and current Triple-A Rochester, New York, skipper Harry "The Hat" Walker was named manager for the remainder of the season. The change failed to make an immediate impact, however, as the team dropped 18 of their next 31 games. A 3-for-31 slide dropped Ken's average forty points to .227 on May 28, though he broke out with three doubles and two RBIs in a 7-2 victory over Cincinnati the next day. He enjoyed the first multi-home run game of his major-league career in the opener of the Memorial Day doubleheader against the Chicago Cubs. He homered in the second inning to give the Redbirds a 1-0 lead and hit a two-run shot with two outs in the bottom of the ninth to tie the game, 5-5. Both blasts came off Minner, the victim of Boyer's first major-league homer on Opening Day. The bullpen failed to hold off the Cubs, however, who scored four runs during the next frame to win in 10 innings, 9-5.

A 3-for-4 day at Pittsburgh on June 1 raised his average fourteen points to .259. In the first of a twin bill at Ebbets Field on the fifth, he tied the score with a ninth-inning solo homer to the upper deck in left field and a two-run shot in the tenth contributed to a five-run rally that beat the Dodgers, 9-4. Both homers came on the first pitch from reliever Jim Hughes, against whom Boyer also homered on the first pitch three weeks earlier.[22]

Despite his success against Hughes, Ken struggled through his worst month of the season, hitting .227 in June. Broeg still considered him a promising rookie who at times exhibited "raw power," but Boyer still had "much to learn at the plate." He was moved to shortstop for twelve games to replace a slumping Grammas and Solly Hemus came off the bench to play third base. St. Louis lost 15 of 28 in June, dropping to sixth place and 19 ½ games out of first.[23]

Ken's warmup throws helped spark a fistfight between Walker and Cincinnati Redlegs manager Birdie Tebbetts during a July 5 game at Crosley Field. After Cincinnati tied the score, 4-4, in the bottom of the ninth inning on misplays by third baseman Hemus and right-fielder Joe Frazier, Walker took both players out and replaced them with Boyer and Pete Whisenant, respectively. The substitutes threw warmup tosses with teammates while catcher Bill Sarni talked with reliever Paul LaPalme on the mound. Irritated with what he felt were stalling tactics by the Cardinals, Tebbetts protested the game to home-plate umpire Jocko Conlan, claiming Boyer and Whisenant weren't allowed to warm up. Walker joined the conversation and obscenities were exchanged between the managers. Tebbetts swung at the Redbirds skipper and missed, but Walker landed his blow. Both men wrestled to the ground as the benches emptied around them. The fracas occurred in front of National League president Warren Giles, who was at the game. Tebbetts, Walker, and Sarni were ejected and later fined by the league office.[24]

St. Louis was back in fifth place at the All-Star break, having won 11 of their last 17. Though 18 games behind Brooklyn, they were only four games below .500 and 2 ½ out of the first division. Ken led the league with 13 stolen bases and showed his power potential with 12 home runs thus far, but his batting average was mediocre at .244. He finished sixth among NL third basemen in the All-Star vote.[25] When the regular season resumed on July 14, the Cardinals won five of eight to start a 14-game road trip and benefited from superb pitching by veteran Harvey Haddix and rookies Larry Jackson and Luis Arroyo, along with recently recalled Willard Schmidt. On the twentieth, Boyer had three safeties and drove in two runs, including an RBI single off knuckleball reliever Hoyt Wilhelm. Musial doubled and homered with three RBIs in a 15-hit attack that pummeled the third-place New York Giants, 9-2.

After that, the Redbirds went into a tailspin the rest of the season. Dropping five of the last six games of the road trip, they returned home and lost all but three of a 13-game homestand primarily to first-division clubs Brooklyn, New York, and Philadelphia through

August 7. Pitching had been problematic since early in the season, but now the offense struggled with a collective .242 team average and .294 on-base percentage in August. The result was a horrendous 9-22 record for the month that plunged them into seventh place and 29 ½ games out of first. A seven-game losing streak that carried over into the first two days of September left them 2 ½ games out of the National League basement.[26]

It was expected that rookies Boyer and Virdon would have their troubles, but even the second-year players and veterans failed to live up to expectations. Starting catcher Bill Sarni, who batted .300 with 70 RBIs in 1954, had slumped to .255 with 34 RBIs. Schoendienst's average fell forty-seven points from the previous season to .268. Musial led the club with 35 homers and 108 RBIs, but his .319 average was the lowest in eight years. With so many young players on the club, Walker felt he needed to instruct them on fundamentals, work normally done in spring training. He held clubhouse strategy sessions and workouts on mornings and afternoons before games in the heat of summer. As the Cardinals failed to make improvements, Walker admitted he may have overworked and confused them more than he helped. "But I considered it an investment toward making 'em full-fledged big leaguers."[27]

Throughout his rookie season, Ken's hitting was sporadic with bursts of offensive production intermittent with spells of futility. He attributed it to making adjustments to major-league pitching and his manager's efforts to tinker with his approach at the plate. A natural pull hitter since childhood, he was encouraged to try hitting to the opposite field. As a result, he chased outside pitches and "got all fouled up." A year later, Boyer said of Walker's instruction, "That's all right if you're a punch hitter like he was. I don't believe you should try to make a singles hitter out of a free-swinger like I am."[28]

In mid to late August, Ken was benched for a few games against right-handed pitching in favor of Hemus or used for late-inning defense. Before a game at the Polo Grounds on August 23, Walker asked Giants shortstop and team captain Alvin Dark if he would talk with Ken about his own approach at the plate—hitting behind the runner, to the opposite field, and for power. Dark's tutelage had immediate but short-lived results, as Boyer, Musial, and Schoendienst each had three safeties. Ken doubled and scored the tying run in a 2-1 comeback victory.[29]

Boyer also resisted Walker's suggestion to stride into the ball. Memories of the beanball in Cuba made him uncomfortable doing it. Writer Bob Broeg prompted the superb hitter Rogers Hornsby to work with him on the technique, but Boyer politely declined the offer. "I can't go into the ball," he told Broeg. "I was almost killed with a pitch." Over the course of his fifteen-year major-league career, he tried putting it out of his mind. "[Y]ou have to overcome fear of the ball," he later said. "And the more hitters discuss this among themselves, the more they're liable to get thinking about it and be afraid of the ball." It was a fear he never completely overcame; he always stood deep in the box and waited for the pitch to come to him.[30]

Boyer ended his rookie season on a positive note, batting .301 in 83 at-bats for the month of September. He enjoyed the first 4-for-4 performance of his career on September 2 at Wrigley Field. Batting leadoff, he doubled to start the game, stroked three singles, and scored the Redbirds' first tally when Musial grounded into a double play. Despite his best game of the season, the Cubs beat the Cardinals, 12-2. All his blows were off Minner, who was 5-0 in eight starts versus St. Louis in 1955 but against whom he batted .414 for the season. Three days later, Ken had three safeties (two off current 15-game winner Joe Nuxhall) and scored the winning run on Rip Repulski's RBI single in the tenth inning in a 3-2 triumph over Cincinnati. A modest eight-game hitting streak in mid September raised his average to .269, but a subsequent 4-for-24 slide the final eight games of the season brought it down to .264.[31]

St. Louis ended the 1955 campaign with 13 victories in their last 21 games, including a three-game sweep of the pennant-winning Dodgers. They set a club record of 143 home runs led by Musial's 33 and Repulski's 23. But it wasn't enough to salvage a season that ended with a seventh-place finish, 30½ games behind Brooklyn, and a record of 68-86, their lowest finish since 1919 and the most losses since 1924. It was little consolation when Dodgers owner Walter O'Malley called them the "best seventh-place club in baseball."[32]

Ken led the Redbirds and finished third in the National League with 22 stolen bases (though he was also caught stealing 17 times).

He was third on the club with 78 runs scored, fourth with 18 home runs, and fifth with 62 RBIs. Boyer placed in the top three in the NL Rookie of the Year balloting as Virdon became the second straight Cardinals player to win the award. (Moon won it in 1954.) Ken was voted third baseman on *The Sporting News* All-Rookie Team, of which Broeg wrote, "Boyer...gives promise of becoming an outstanding defensive third baseman—he's strong-armed and far-ranging—and, in addition, he has great power if he'll use it more often."[33]

When the season was over, Boyer joined teammate Willard Schmidt and Richie Ashburn of the Philadelphia Phillies for a barnstorming tour in Missouri, Kansas, and Nebraska in October. They played against local teams and hosted baseball clinics for young fans. Ken also earned extra money during the off-season making public appearances. He traveled with Moon and Schoendienst on weekends to meat markets and grocery stores on behalf of the Independent Meat Company, talking with fans, signing autographs, and posing for pictures. In December, Kathleen gave birth to their second child and first son, David Victor Boyer, who shared his uncle Cloyd's middle name.[34]

Ken earned the major-league minimum salary of $6,000, enough to fulfill a promise to himself that his parents would have a larger home before he and Kathleen purchased their own. Vern and Mabel Boyer still lived in the same small three-bedroom house across from the baseball field in Alba. Together, he and younger brother Clete, who received a $35,000 bonus that year to sign with the Kansas City Athletics, purchased older brother Cloyd's larger home for their parents and remaining siblings. "He was very, very giving to his family," says Kathleen. She and Ken purchased a new ranch-style home on a corner lot that same year at 8469 Bayberry Drive in Berkeley in north St. Louis County. "I had colored sheets hung in the windows for a year because we couldn't afford to buy the window treatments," she recalls.[35]

"PROBABLY THE MOST EXCITING CHAPTER in the history of St. Louis baseball is about to be enacted."

J.G. Taylor Spink, editor of *The Sporting News*, made this bold and optimistic declaration when it was announced that Frank Lane would be the new general manager of the Cardinals in 1956.[36] Spink endorsed

Lane to Gussie Busch after the end of a successful but tumultuous tenure with the Chicago White Sox. Lane's enthusiasm for making trades—241 of them involving 353 players over seven years—helped transformed the White Sox from a club that lost 101 games and languished in the American League cellar in 1948 to one with back-to-back 90-win seasons that finished five games out of first in 1955. Busch was impressed with his track record and what he could potentially do to shake up his club and make them pennant contenders.[37]

Lane hired an equally competitive man, former major-league pitcher and Detroit Tigers skipper Fred Hutchinson, as his manager. Afterward, he spent a quiet winter evaluating his current roster. One player he took particular interest in was Ken Boyer. In December, he signed him to "a substantial pay increase" over his rookie salary to about $10,000 a year and proclaimed, "I have just signed the youngster destined to become the best all-around third baseman in baseball." He felt Boyer should've been the NL Rookie of the Year and envisioned him as a rising young superstar with "a tremendous natural potential," both on the field and at the turnstiles.[38]

Having experienced his first major-league season, Ken arrived for spring training with more confidence and higher expectations. "My goal is a pennant first and a world championship," he told Broeg of the *Post-Dispatch*. "If the club wins, so do I." His personal goals for his sophomore season were a .300 average and 85 RBIs if he hit in the middle of the order. Twenty home runs was a possibility, but he had reason not to focus on the long ball. "Our ball park isn't the best for a right-handed hitter to become home-run conscious," he surmised.[39] Asked whether he was afraid of falling victim to the so-called "sophomore jinx" that sometimes affected players after successful rookie seasons, he replied, "No, I'm not afraid of it. But just what is it?"[40]

Boyer got off to a slow start in the early spring exhibition games and was batting .240 in the first nine contests. As a young player with tremendous potential, he was scrutinized more than others in camp. Pundits saw his even-keeled demeanor and misinterpreted it as a lack of desire. Red Byrd of *The Sporting News* felt he lacked confidence and remarked, "Observers would like to see more fire and aggressiveness in the sturdy Missouri boy, in the field and especially at the plate." Lane saw complacency and had a frank discussion with him one day during batting practice. "You can become a great star and one of the highest paid players in history," the general manager told him. Rather than take offense at the criticism, Lane said Boyer "thought I'd gotten him wrong." The two talked for several minutes and Lane seemed satisfied for the moment. "He's a fine boy and he'll be a great star."[41]

The Cardinals left Florida with the best record in the Grapefruit League at 16-8. Ken's hitting improved to .380, second only to Wally Moon's .392, thanks in part to a 13-game hit streak.[42] The club traveled north to Cincinnati and enjoyed their first Opening Day victory in four years on April 17. Boyer singled in his first plate appearance of the season and Musial hit the game-winning home run with two outs in the ninth inning for a 4-2 win over the Redlegs.

In the home opener three days later at Busch Stadium, Ken had three hits off left-hander Warren Spahn, including his first home run of the season, in a 5-4 loss to Milwaukee. The crowd of 23,984 fans saw the Cardinals for the first time in their redesigned uniforms. Lane had replaced the traditional birds-on-the-bat insignia on the front of the home and road jerseys—a distinctive feature since 1922—with the team's nickname in script type and an underline flourish below. The new general manager explained it was done for the comfort of the players. The old insignia had a canvas backing, making the jerseys heavier with perspiration and St. Louis was notorious for its oppressively hot summers. Needless to say, the familiar birds-on-the-bat returned in 1957. "To me...tradition meant the men who wore the uniform, not the uniform," insisted Lane. It wouldn't be the last unpopular decision he would make during his two-year tenure in St. Louis.[43]

The Cardinals were in the thick of a five-team scramble with Milwaukee, Cincinnati, Brooklyn, and Pittsburgh for first place the first three months of the season. Ken was the hottest hitter in the league through May 18. He ranked first in batting average (.406), slugging (.723), hits (41), RBIs (27), and runs scored (23), and second in home runs (nine) and on-base percentage (.455). His exceptional start earned praise from Hutchinson:

> This is the kind of a player you wish you had 12 of them, so you could play nine and have three on the bench just to stir things up. He's the kind of guy you dream about:

terrific speed, brute strength, a great arm. There's nothing he can't do. He's the best base runner on the team. I think he has the greatest future of any young player in the league.[44]

The skipper moved Boyer up in the batting order from sixth to cleanup against the Redlegs on April 24 and he responded with a three-run homer in the 5-3 victory. After going 0-for-3 against Chicago the next day, he hit safely in nine consecutive games and belted two homers, including his first major-league grand slam off Roger Craig of the Brooklyn Dodgers on May 5. Along with Tom Poholsky's three-hitter, they won the game for St. Louis, 4-1. The Redbirds took two out of three from Brooklyn and were only a half-game and 24 percentage points behind the first-place Milwaukee Braves.

Lane announced that five players on the Cardinals roster were untouchable: Musial, Schoendienst, Rip Repulski, Moon, and Boyer. Everyone else was fair game.[45] Despite the club's advantageous position in the standings, he lived up to the nicknames of Frantic Frank and Trader Frank with a flurry of deals beginning the first of May. In a little over two weeks, he dispatched reigning NL Rookie of the Year Bill Virdon, three starting pitchers (Harvey Haddix, Stu Miller, and Ben Flowers), two left-handed relievers (Luis Arroyo and Paul LaPalme), and three bench players (infielders Alex Grammas and Solly Hemus and outfielder Joe Frazier). Among the players obtained in return were center fielder Bobby Del Greco, right-handed starters Murry Dickson and Herman Wehmeier (who had an 0-14 record against St. Louis over 11 seasons), reserve outfielder-first baseman Chuck Harmon, and infielder Bobby Morgan.

Neal Russo of the *Post-Dispatch* was perplexed by all the transactions. "It must be quite a rarity—this wholesale turnover in personnel on a team in a virtual tie for first place after nearly one month of play, especially when the club looked so good so often in winning." Lane in turn was surprised by the negative reactions to his deals. "Why, I really think they would rather finish seventh with names they know than try to get up a few pegs with new faces."[46]

The Cardinals kept pace with the first-division clubs in May, at times coming within percentage points of the league lead but never taking it. Ken's hot streak continued as he batted .344 and drove in 33 runs for the month. He enjoyed his first multi-home run game of the season in the second of a May 13 doubleheader at Wrigley Field. A two-run homer disrupted Cubs right-hander Sam Jones's no-hitter in the fourth inning. He followed with a three-run blast in the next frame off reliever Vito Valentinetti that put the Redbirds ahead, 7-5, and contributed to a comeback 14-7 victory. At Philadelphia four days later, he collected four safeties, including a round-tripper off former teammate Harvey Haddix, in the 5-4 win over the Phillies.

In a virtual tie for first place (42 percentage points behind Milwaukee), St. Louis had the opportunity to gain ground in the National League race with a 20-game homestand May 25–June 12. Ken hit safely in the first 10 games and smashed three homers. Against the Giants on June 4, he doubled twice, scored three runs, knocked in five, and smashed a first inning homer to give them a lead they never relinquished in the 11-5 victory. A 10-10 record during the homestand dropped them to fourth place but still a game back of the league-leading Pirates.

The homestand revealed significant weaknesses in the St. Louis infield at shortstop and first base. Hutchinson had tried converting outfielder Moon into a first baseman, but he had trouble catching low throws from the other infielders. Second baseman Don Blasingame was moved to short, but it was obvious his arm wasn't strong enough for the position.

With these needs in mind, Lane made his most controversial trade yet. On June 14, he dealt Red Schoendienst, highly-regarded outfield prospect Jackie Brandt, catcher Bill Sarni, shortstop Bobby Stephenson, and pitcher Dick Littlefield to the New York Giants for veteran shortstop Alvin Dark, outfielder Whitey Lockman, catcher Ray Katt, and pitcher Don Liddle. (Lockman was obtained with the idea of playing him at first base; the experiment lasted only one game and he returned to the outfield. Musial was moved to first for the rest of the season.) Fans were outraged at the trade of the popular Schoendienst and bombarded the team's telephone lines expressing their frustration. Lane defended his decision. "We let Schoendienst go with great reluctance, naturally, but to get a star like Dark you've got to give a star."[47]

The reaction to the Schoendienst deal would have paled in comparison to one he had in the works before the June 15 trading deadline. In an effort to add a top-flight pitcher to the starting rotation, Lane offered Musial, thirty-five years old and at the time hitting a little below .300 with eight homers, to the Philadelphia Phillies in exchange for struggling right-hander Robin Roberts, a six-time 20-game winner with a 5-8 record and 5.00 earned-run average. After confirming the rumor was true, Musial's business partner Biggie Garagnani told an Anheuser-Busch official that Stan the Man would retire rather than report to Philadelphia. It would be a public relations mess for the Cardinals and the brewery. Busch emphatically told Lane that Musial would not be traded. Moreover, he took away the general manager's autonomy to make trades without his approval.[48]

The Cardinals went back on the road and divided a four-game series at Pittsburgh, lost two of three at Brooklyn and three of four at Philadelphia, and split a two-game set at New York to end the month of June. In their lone victory against the Phillies in the opener of a June 24 doubleheader, Ken singled, tripled, and hit two home runs in the 8-4 win. The second homer tied him with Dale Long of Pittsburgh for the league lead and his three RBIs tied him with Musial in that category. Boyer had another two-homer game three days later at the Polo Grounds as Tom Poholsky threw a five-hit shutout to beat the Giants, 6-0. At the end of the trip, St. Louis was still in fourth place but now four games behind front-running Milwaukee.[49]

The Redbirds returned home the last week of June and split a four-game set with Cincinnati, then lost six of their next seven on the road. At the All-Star break, they were two games below .500 for the first time since mid-April and eight back of the first-place Redlegs. Even though his torrid bat had cooled somewhat, Ken was still hitting .321 with 96 hits, 20 homers, and 60 RBIs. "Boyer's got enough power, enough good hitting technique that when he meets the ball right, he's going to hit it well to right or left center," said Hutchinson. "When he meets the ball a little better than just right, he'll pull it naturally. That's what he's been doing."[50]

Ken was surprised to learn he was on pace to become the first Cardinals right-handed hitter in 17 years with 200 or more hits and break Johnny Mize's club record of 43 home runs. "I just worry about the next hit, not the 200th, and shucks, I didn't even know what the high for homers in St. Louis was," he said modestly.⁵¹

BOYER'S BREAKOUT SEASON WAS REWARDED by fans across the country. They voted him to start at third base for the National League in the All-Star Game to be played in the nation's capital on July 10. He, Musial, and Pittsburgh first baseman Dale Long were the only players selected who were not from the league-leading Redlegs. The day before the contest in Washington, D.C., Ken attended a luncheon at the Washington Touchdown Club with Frank Lane, Fred Hutchinson, and other baseball notables where Musial was honored by *The Sporting News* as the Player of the Decade.⁵²

The 23rd major-league All-Star Game was played in front of 28,843 fans at Griffith Stadium. Prior to the contest, NL president Warren Giles visited his team's clubhouse and stressed to the players its importance and not to treat it as simply "a parade of stars. We're out to win and not to use every player we have on the squad."⁵³

Ken took his words to heart and made an immediate impact defensively in the bottom of the first inning. The American League's leadoff batter, Harvey Kuenn of the Detroit Tigers, smacked Pittsburgh Pirates right-hander Bob Friend's first offering. Boyer dived to his left, making a sensational catch of what looked to be a sure hit to left field. He robbed Kuenn again in the fifth on a smash inside the third-base line, lunging to his right and backhanding it across the foul line. Then he jumped to his feet and fired across to first base for the out. "These two infield plays were among the best ever seen in All-Star competition," remarked Fred Lieb, a well-respected baseball writer who covered 30 All-Star contests in his career. Ken made another impressive play in the seventh, leaping to snare a line drive off the bat of Kuenn's Detroit teammate, Ray Boone.⁵⁴

Boyer was the brightest star of the All-Star Game. He played the entire contest and led the NL squad with three straight safeties in five plate appearances. Thrown out by catcher Yogi Berra trying to steal second in the second inning, he later scored on a home run by Willie Mays in the fourth and drove in Johnny Temple of the Redlegs with two outs in the fifth to give the National League a 4-0 lead.

Musial's homer in the seventh and an RBI double by Ted Kluszewski of the Redlegs plated the final tallies.

There was a frightening moment in the eighth when Ted Williams hit a fly ball to short left field and both Boyer and Musial chased it. Stan made a sliding catch to his right and Ken moved in the opposite direction to avoid a collision. But as Musial fell to the ground, Boyer accidentally kicked him on the left thigh with his spikes. Musial was taken out of the game as a precaution and Hank Aaron replaced him. "That Boyer was all over the place today, wasn't he?" Stan smiled afterward. "He seemed to want to handle every ball—and he did quite a job of it, too."[55]

Berra and Nellie Fox led the American League with two hits each and Mickey Mantle and Williams both homered, but the National League prevailed, 7-3. It was the senior circuit's sixth win in the last seven contests. Both managers complimented Ken's performance. "I'd say that in addition to Willie Mays' hit that Boyer's fine play at third and the strong pitching throughout were the key factors in the game," said Walter Alston of the Dodgers. Never good at remembering the names of players, the AL skipper, Casey Stengel of the New York Yankees, remarked, "Very good boy, very good. That third base fellow cut us out of a rally or two."[56] Asked later if he was excited about playing in his first All-Star Game, Ken replied, "More than a little at first." He looked forward to batting against Herb Score of the Cleveland Indians, who pitched in the eighth inning, but Boyer didn't have a turn at bat. His "biggest thrill" was "watching [Ted] Williams for the first time."[57]

THE SEASON'S SECOND-HALF GOT OFF TO A PROMISING START as St. Louis won the first four games of a 12-game homestand, including a three-game sweep of Schoendienst's New York Giants. Boyer hit safely in the first 10 games, including a 4-for-4 performance with a double, three singles, two runs scored, and two RBIs as he and his teammates collected 20 hits in a 13-6 win over the Dodgers on July 21.

The next afternoon, he received his first major-league ejection in the second game of a doubleheader with Brooklyn. In the fourth inning, with Musial on first, he hit a ground ball to third baseman Pee Wee Reese. Reese's throw to second was too late to catch Musial and second baseman Junior Gilliam threw to first, where umpire Frank Secory called the speedy Boyer out. He and first-base coach Terry Moore protested that Gilliam's throw was late and Gil Hodges's foot had been pulled off the bag. Ken's protests led Secory to toss him from the game. According to Bob Broeg, Ken "told the umpire he'd missed it and then used an impersonal vulgarism, though he did not question the umpire's ancestry."

The ejection raised the ire of Lane, who complained to league president Giles about the arbiter's conduct. At the same time, he liked the flash of temper from Ken: "We've been trying to make an aggressive player of Boyer all year." He later added, "Secory put out our hottest hitter in the fourth inning of a close game. Some fans, many of whom had driven 300 miles, told me they weren't going to come that far again to see some quick-thumb umpire show off." The Redbirds lost both games of the twin bill and six of the last eight of the homestand (with one tie), falling 12 games out of first place.[58]

The Cardinals embarked on a successful 23-game road trip that netted 13 victories, though they were still in fourth place and 11 games behind Milwaukee. Ken continued his modest hitting streak and raised his average to .324 at the end of July. He hit his 21st home run of the season—his first since the Fourth of July—in a 14-9 comeback victory at Philadelphia. But over the next two weeks, Boyer experienced a power outage at the plate. What started as a sudden inability to produce extra-base hits degenerated into his first real slump of the season that brought his average down seventeen points to .307. After going 1-for-14 in four games, he was benched for the next eight beginning August 10. Bobby Morgan took over at third base and Moon batted cleanup.[59]

Ken returned to the lineup against the Cubs on August 17, though he had been demoted from the cleanup spot he held since April 24. He rotated between fifth and sixth in the order the rest of the season. His struggles continued the next few weeks and his average dipped below .300 for the first time. Boyer's desire to succeed was scrutinized by his general manager, his manager, and the press. Lane was especially exasperated with him. Some of it could be attributed to the team's poor showing, but that frustration found a target in his underachieving young superstar. "He hasn't swung hard in two months," grumbled Lane, who often screamed profanely at him from the press box, "Swing the bat!"[60]

The slump once again brought into question Ken's quiet, laid-back disposition and what was perceived to be his lackadaisical attitude toward his talents and competitiveness, issues that were first brought up in spring training. Hutchinson was competitive and combative just like Lane. Though intimidating with his strong physical stature and fiery temper, he was patient with young players and earned their respect. Still, the young third baseman's disposition went against Hutchinson's nature. He bluntly felt Ken lacked "that everyday, fierce, competitive instinct" needed to be successful at the major-league level. "Boyer has everything he needs to be a great player except one thing," he decided. "He has to develop more drive, more aggressiveness. He doesn't push enough." It was a stigma Boyer would never completely shake with critics for the rest of his career in St. Louis.[61]

One anonymous writer believed "he was born with so much ability [and] never had to try hard." In an article for *Sports Illustrated* entitled "Brilliant Enigma," Robert Creamer speculated that "he does not have that innate compulsion to succeed, to win, at all costs." Ken attributed the slump to a natural regression after a fantastic start rather than some flaw in his attitude or the way he played the game. "I don't know if I am a .330 hitter," he suggested. Sharing a conversation he had with the Cardinals general manager, Boyer recalled Lane "talked about drive and aggressiveness. I don't think I really know what he means. I know that I try, that I give everything I have. I don't loaf. I know that all my life people have been saying that to me, that I don't look as if I'm trying. I guess I don't look as if I'm putting out. But I am."[62]

The Redbirds couldn't get traction the last two months of the season to rise more than a few games above or below the .500 plateau, much less challenge front-runners Milwaukee, Cincinnati, and Brooklyn. They won five home games in a row toward the end of August. Ken showed signs of breaking out of his slump with a double, single, and two RBIs against Pittsburgh on August 25. But a seven-game losing skein followed, including four to league-leading Milwaukee, that knocked them 17 ½ games out of first. They still clung to fourth place by a game-and-a-half over Philadelphia.

Hopelessly out of contention in September, St. Louis nonetheless influenced the outcome of the close pennant race between Milwaukee, Cincinnati, and Brooklyn. They won 10 of their next 13 games, including a three-game sweep of the second-place Redlegs, each decided by two runs or less. Wilmer "Vinegar Bend" Mizell pitched a two-hit shutout in the opener on September 7 and Boyer homered off Joe Nuxhall—his first since July 26—for the 1-0 victory. He contributed RBI singles in the second and third games, the finale won in 13 innings, 6-5. The Redlegs came into the series a game-and-a-half behind the Braves and left in third place and three games out.[63]

Having regained his power stroke, Ken started hitting home runs again with increased frequency. He smacked one off Curt Simmons on September 11 to give St. Louis an early lead at Philadelphia in a 5-3 victory. He clubbed two more at the Polo Grounds as they won two out of three from the Giants. Trailing the front-running Dodgers, 5-4, with two outs in the ninth inning at Ebbets Field on September 18, Boyer hit his 26th homer off right-handed reliever Carl Erskine with Musial on base to win, 6-5. Their defeat of Brooklyn enabled Milwaukee to climb within one percentage point of the league lead.

After an embarrassing 17-2 defeat to the Dodgers the next day, the Cardinals traveled to Cincinnati where the Redlegs returned the favor from two weeks earlier and beat them four straight. St. Louis lost two of three to the last-place Cubs at Wrigley Field before returning home for the final three games of the season against the first-place Braves.

Milwaukee entered the series leading the National League by one game over Brooklyn. A victory over the Redbirds in the opener on September 28 and a Dodgers loss to Pittsburgh would assure them of at least a tie for the pennant. In the first inning, Ken doubled to left with the bases loaded to force the early exit of right-hander Bob Buhl. The Braves tied it in the fifth, but he singled and scored the go-ahead run on Bobby Del Greco's hit to retake the lead in the sixth. After pitcher Lindy McDaniel singled to load the bases, Blasingame grounded to first baseman Joe Adcock, who forced Repulski at the plate for the first out. Catcher Del Crandall threw back to first, hoping for the double play, but the ball went a few feet past Adcock, who watched intently to ensure Del Greco stopped at third base as he retrieved the ball. Instead, Del Greco sprinted for the plate and added to the lead, 5-3.

Milwaukee scored on an RBI single by Hank Aaron in the eighth, but reliever Larry Jackson retired the last five batters to give St. Louis the 5-4 victory. Because Brooklyn's game with Pittsburgh was rained out, the Braves still held a half-game lead. "These Cardinals have no place to go, but they're still fighting us to the end," lamented Warren Spahn afterward.[64]

Milwaukee's pennant hopes rested on the left arm of Spahn in the second game. After giving up a home run to the number-two hitter, Bill Bruton, in the first inning, St. Louis right-hander Herm Wehmeier yielded nine hits—five of them in the first three frames—but pitched scoreless ball the rest of the game. Spahn was even more effective, giving up only five hits, though back-to-back doubles by Blasingame and Dark tied it in the sixth. The pitching duel extended into extra innings, thanks to two sensational catches by Del Greco in center that robbed the Braves of extra bases in the ninth. With one out in the twelfth, Musial doubled and Boyer was walked intentionally. Repulski hit a sinker ball that glanced off the glove of third baseman Eddie Mathews for a double that scored Musial with the winning run. The Braves beat them in the finale, 4-2, but the twin losses and the Dodgers' three-game sweep over Pittsburgh crushed Milwaukee's World Series aspirations.[65]

The Cardinals finished the season in fourth place with a record of 76-78. Though it looked much better than their seventh-place finish the year before, they actually won only eight games more than in 1955.[66] Despite an awful August slump in which he batted .219 for the month, Ken rebounded and finished a successful sophomore season with a .306 average and 182 hits, both fifth-best in the National League. His 26 homers were one short of the club record for third basemen set by Whitey Kurowski in 1947. In addition, he had 30 doubles, 91 runs scored, and 98 RBIs (fifth in the NL). Members of the Baseball Writers Association of America named him the best third baseman in both leagues on *The Sporting News* postseason All-Star team. He finished three points behind Cincinnati's Ed Bailey for sophomore player of the year honors in the NL.[67]

A .306 average would have marked an exceptional year for most players, especially one in his second major-league season. Any self-respecting general manager would have been pleased with it, but Frank Lane had higher expectations for his twenty-five-year-old superstar—he wanted Boyer to be the next Mickey Mantle. Upon signing him in December to a new $18,000 contract for the 1957 season, Lane asserted, "Ken hasn't approached his peak performance yet. He has a tremendous natural potential."[68]

Chapter Six

The Reluctant Dragon

His free-wheeling nature restrained by Gussie Busch, Frank Lane made fewer but smarter deals in the off-season that addressed specific needs. He sent outfielder Rip Repulski and infielder Bobby Morgan to the Philadelphia Phillies for power-hitting outfielder Del Ennis to give Stan Musial additional protection in the lineup. An eight-player deal with the Chicago Cubs brought Sam Jones to the starting rotation and Lane bolstered a problematic bullpen by acquiring knuckleballer Hoyt Wilhelm from the New York Giants. The future Hall of Famer became the third member of the pitching staff along with veteran Murry Dickson and Jim Davis who utilized the baffling pitch.[1]

Busch had high hopes for the Cardinals in 1957. Speaking at a Knights of the Cauliflower Ear event before the team left for spring training, he told attendees, "I expect the Cardinals to scare the daylights out of a lot of clubs this year." He was confident they would win the pennant this season or next. "If we don't, Frank Lane will be out on his ass." Lane, who was in attendance, quickly responded, "Mr. Busch, if I don't produce that winner by the end of 1958, I'll believe that I have failed and I'll leave the ball club." In hindsight, he wasn't sure whether his boss was joking or not.²

Over the winter, Ken attended banquets and made paid appearances at grocery stores representing the Independent Packing Company of St. Louis with former teammates Red Schoendienst and Tom Poholsky. He finished a distant second to J.G. Taylor Spink, publisher of *The Sporting News*, for the "Outstanding St. Louis Sports Figure for 1956" award selected by local sportswriters and broadcasters and sponsored by the Benevolent & Protective Order of Elks No. 9 of St. Louis.³ His successful sophomore season resulted in commercial endorsements in 1957, including one for the A.B.C. Cap, one of the earliest protective batting helmets. It was manufactured by the American Baseball Cap Company, owned by former Cardinals general manager Branch Rickey and his son-in-law.⁴

When the Cardinals began their workouts in St. Petersburg, Boyer was shagging fly balls in center field instead of fielding grounders at third base. The idea of utilizing his strong throwing arm there began late in 1956 as Hutchinson searched for a capable hitter and defender to take over the position after the trade of Bill Virdon. Lane initially dismissed such a move. "It would be silly to try to make an outfielder out of a player who is potentially the best third baseman the Cardinals have ever had and one of the greatest, again potentially, in National League history."⁵ The team had hoped to give rookie Charlie Peete, winner of the American Association batting title with Omaha in 1956, the opportunity to take the position in spring training. But the twenty-seven-year-old African American was killed with his wife and three children in a plane crash in Venezuela as he prepared to play winter ball there.⁶ When the exhibition games began, Ken was back at third base and incumbent Bobby Del Greco, Chuck Harmon, and rookie Bobby Gene Smith were competing for the center field job. Boyer batted .304 that spring with eight extra-base hits.

THE CARDINALS OPENED the 1957 season at Cincinnati on April 16 and won, 13-4. Because of position shifts and Lane's deals, Boyer was the only player in the lineup still at the same position on Opening Day the year before. Wally Moon and Smith both homered and Musial had two doubles as part of his 4-for-4 performance. Ken was hitless in five plate appearances, but his sacrifice fly in the eighth inning scored Alvin Dark and added to the Redbirds' sizable lead.

Boyer got off to a terrible start at the plate and was hitting as low as .193 with only three extra-base hits—including his first home run of the season against Cincinnati on April 22—entering the first week of May. He improved somewhat over the next few weeks, smashing his fifth homer off Robin Roberts of the Philadelphia Phillies at Busch Stadium on May 17. Three safeties with three runs scored the next day raised his average briefly to .273, but a 1-for-12 slide dropped it nineteen points to .254. His struggles carried over onto the field as he committed 12 errors at third base in the first 29 games. Two of those miscues contributed to three unearned runs and a 5-3 loss against the New York Giants on May 14. "I wish I knew what the trouble was," Ken later recalled, looking back on his fielding woes. "All I know is, if a ball had taken six big hops, I wouldn't have caught it." Normally supportive Cardinals fans even started booing him.[7]

Boyer wasn't the only player fumbling the ball. The whole team committed 32 errors in the first 23 games. Former Cardinals manager Frankie Frisch caused a stir when he blamed Lane's trade threats for the defensive lapses. "Lane is a nice guy, but he may not realize that he is giving his club the jitters with all that talk about trades, because his men have to wonder where they'll be playing next week." Frisch wanted the general manager to meet with the players and reassure them that no trades would be made. Lane bristled at the criticism. "What he failed to consider is the fact that Ken Boyer, who committed 11 of our first 33 errors, is less likely to be traded than anyone on the club," he fumed. "So his argument dies right there." Still, Lane was dissatisfied with the young third baseman's performance thus far and referred to him as the "reluctant dragon."[8]

Fellow infielder Dark defended Boyer. "That kid is a great ball player with a tremendous future and, contrary to some notions, he is not jittery. He has had to contend with some bad hops and bad breaks." He later remarked, "Never in my life did I see an infielder get so many discouraging hops and tricky chances. There was a whole string of little things, but they all added up to enough to throw him off stride."[9]

After losing eight of 11 home games May 10–20, the Cardinals were in fifth place with a 13-16 record and 7 ½ games behind the Redlegs. Before the team embarked on a road trip to Cincinnati, Busch met with Lane and other club officials to discuss the situation. It was officially decided that no trades would be made to improve the team. Instead, rookies Eddie Kasko, Dick Schofield, Joe Cunningham, and Tom Alston would receive more playing time and young center fielder Bobby Gene Smith, a good defender who was hitting only .225, would be benched. It was allegedly Busch who endorsed Ken's long-contemplated move to center field—dubbed by Jack Herman of the *St. Louis Globe-Democrat* as the "Ken Boyer Experiment"—to fill the troublesome position. Shortstop Kasko, batting .333 at the time, became the starting third baseman.[10] Lane claimed it was Boyer's wish to move from third base in spring training and that Hutchinson was eager to make the change. Because he was coming off an All-Star season at the position, it had been decided to hold off on the conversion.[11]

Regardless with whom the notion originated, when Hutchinson wrote out the lineup card in Cincinnati on May 23, Ken was in center field and back in the cleanup spot for the first time since mid-August 1956. Boyer called the move to center "a blessing" and later admitted, "They had to get me out of the infield for my own protection."[12] Both Hutchinson and coach Terry Moore felt Boyer had the athleticism to make a successful transition. "He can run, throw, and cover ground," said the manager. "The hardest part will be for Kenny to charge low liners and go back for drives," suggested Moore. Ken credited the former All-Star center fielder with helping him make the adjustment to the new position over the course of the season.[13] Hutchinson was impressed with his willingness to make the change. "He showed me something with that. He didn't have to accept the switch, but he did it for the good of the ball club."[14]

The revamped lineup and improved pitching were the catalysts for the Cardinals' resurgence. Boyer responded well initially at the plate with six hits in 14 at-bats as the team split the four-game series with the Redlegs. But after returning home for four games against Chicago and Cincinnati followed by one at Milwaukee and going 0-for-18, Hutchinson benched him for five games and Smith went back to center field. Ken returned to the lineup on June 7 as the Redbirds were in their third contest of an eight-game winning streak on the road at Pittsburgh, New York, and Philadelphia. Larry Jackson's 4-0 shutout over the Phillies on the twelfth tied them with that club for third place and only a game behind front-running Cincinnati. The Cardinals subsequently took three of four from the Dodgers at Ebbets Field, then returned to St. Louis and did the same against Pittsburgh. Their 7-4 victory over the Pirates on June 20 gave them first place by a half-game over Milwaukee with a 34-24 record.

Though Boyer had raised his average to .259 in mid-June, the hits were often not for extra bases. Fortunately, when he did launch the ball out of the park, it was at an opportune moment. His sixth home run of the season—the first since May 17—was the only run the Cardinals had off Brooklyn right-hander Don Newcombe in an extra-inning, 2-1 loss at Ebbets Field on June 14. Two days later, in the first game of a doubleheader and the Redbirds trailing by three runs, Musial smashed a game-tying homer in the sixth and Ken followed with a solo shot in the seventh to give eighteen-year-old rookie reliever Von McDaniel his first major-league victory over the Dodgers, 7-6.

With Lane's reputation for making deals, the June 15 trading deadline brought angst to the Cardinals clubhouse. There were trade rumors despite the public declaration that none would be made. The Pirates, seeking a power hitter, had reportedly offered Roberto Clemente and right-handed starting pitcher Ron Kline for Boyer. It wouldn't be the last time his name would be linked to Pittsburgh that year.[15]

After losing the first three of a four-game set with the Giants, St. Louis bounced back and won nine of their next 10 games leading into the All-Star break. They held a 2½ game lead over Milwaukee and 3½ over Philadelphia and Cincinnati. In the opener of the Fourth of July doubleheader against the Cubs at Wrigley Field, Boyer and Schofield each had three safeties in five at-bats and Ken blasted his ninth home run in the 7-6 loss. He hit another two days later against second-place Cincinnati, who at the time were only a half-game behind them, and the Cardinals won, 13-3. St. Louis hosted the All-Star Game at Busch Stadium on July 9. Musial, Moon, Jackson, and Hal Smith represented the home team. Boyer wasn't selected for the National League squad. An errant batting practice pitch two days earlier left him with a swollen left elbow and the All-Star break gave him time to rest it.[16]

THE SECOND-HALF OF THE SEASON began on July 11 with a 1-0 loss on a five-hit shutout by Johnny Antonelli and the Giants. Sam Jones of the Cardinals responded with a two-hit victory the next day, 5-1. They lost five of their next seven road games, including a 10-9 heartbreaker to the Dodgers at Ebbets Field on the eighteenth that dropped them to second place behind Milwaukee. Despite winning three of four at Pittsburgh July 19–21, they still bounced between second and third place.

Boyer had nine hits in the series as part of a personal hitting resurgence in July in which he batted .309 with five doubles, four homers, and 15 RBIs. On the twentieth, he doubled, singled twice, and stole second in a 9-4 victory and had four safeties in the second game of a twin bill the next day. His leadoff homer sparked a four-run rally in the second inning that put the Cardinals ahead, 4-2, then he doubled to score Moon in the sixth. A seven o'clock curfew by Pennsylvania state law forced play to stop with one out in the top of the ninth and St. Louis leading, 11-2. (The suspended game was completed on August 27.) [17]

The Cardinals were next scheduled to play the Chicago White Sox in the annual Hall of Fame exhibition game as part of the induction ceremonies at Cooperstown, New York, on July 22. Because a chartered flight couldn't land at the Utica airport forty miles away, the team had to catch a train at 10:40 P.M. following the doubleheader at Pittsburgh. They made an almost twelve-hour trek to Utica, where buses drove them and the White Sox to Cooperstown. The teams arrived too late to witness the inductions of Joe McCarthy and Sam Crawford or visit the Hall of Fame and Museum. An eight-run third inning by the White Sox put the game out of reach as the Redbirds dropped the exhibition, 13-4. Ken singled in five at-bats and scored twice. After dinner at the Hotel Otesaga, the players made a seventy-five mile bus trip to Syracuse and boarded a twin-engine plane bound for St. Louis. Delayed by bad weather and two fuel stops, they landed at Lambert Field more than five hours later at 2:40 A.M. on the morning of July 23.[18]

The road-weary Cardinals—now in third place—returned home for a 21-game homestand beginning that evening against second-place Brooklyn, who were just a half-game ahead of them. They lost the opener, 1-0, despite a three-hitter by Jones. Jackson countered with an identical performance the next evening and benefited from two triples by Dark and RBIs from Musial and Ennis to win, 3-0. Having broken the spell of twelve consecutive losses to Newcombe a week earlier, the Redbirds beat him in the third game on the twenty-fifth. With one out in the fourth inning, Moon and Ennis both singled and Ken plated Moon with a hit to center field for the first run of the game. An inning later, Blasingame doubled and scored on an error to give the Cards a 2-0 lead, but the Dodgers tied it in their half of the sixth. Moon's sacrifice fly in the eighth won it, 3-2. St. Louis moved into second place, only a half-game behind Milwaukee.

Boyer enjoyed another productive series against the Pirates as the Cardinals took four of five from the seventh-place club. Trailing 3-0 in the opener on July 26, he homered off Roy Face to put them on the board in the fifth inning. Blasingame's two-run blast tied it in the same frame. A single by Dark with the bases loaded won it in the tenth, 4-3. Ken had two safeties in each of the next four games and raised his average to a season-high .279. Superb pitching performances were made by rookie sensation Von McDaniel, who threw a one-hitter in the first game of the July 28 doubleheader, and inconsistent veteran Mizell, who tossed a two-hit shutout the next evening. Cunningham won the second game of the twin bill with a walk-off homer in the eleventh inning. Despite a successful series, the Redbirds were still a half-game behind the league-leading Braves.

The Pittsburgh series sparked an eight-game win streak—their second of the season—as St. Louis swept three games from the sixth-place Giants and took two from the fifth-place Phillies. In addition to McDaniel and Mizell's performances, Cunningham, in a pinch-hit role, provided more pennant drama. He hit his second game-winning home run in three days, this one a grand slam that beat the Giants, 7-3, on July 30. An 8-0 victory the next evening returned the Cardinals to first place and Willard Schmidt won his tenth consecutive game with four innings of relief against the Phillies on August 2. Von

McDaniel's sixth victory of the season the next afternoon gave St. Louis eight in a row and a 1 ½ game edge over Milwaukee.

The Redbirds almost made it nine straight in the opener of the August 4 doubleheader against Philadelphia. Coming back from a 3-1 deficit, Ken's double advanced Moon to third, who scored on Hobie Landrith's sacrifice fly in the fourth. Musial's two-bagger tied it in the next frame. They went ahead by a run in the sixth, but reliever Jackson gave up a two-out home run to pinch-hitter Harry Anderson in the ninth that sent the game into extra innings. With two outs in the twelfth, Jackson gave up a pair of singles, threw a wild pitch, and allowed two walks to give the Phillies the lead. Having already struck out twice in the game, Boyer objected strongly to a called third strike in the Redbirds' half and was quickly ejected by home-plate umpire Bill Baker, who had already run two Phillies players and manager Mayo Smith earlier. According to Cardinals broadcaster Joe Garagiola, he kicked a few batting helmets in frustration before leaving the field. "Boyer made some beautiful boots but fell short about ten yards of the National League record," he quipped. St. Louis lost, 5-4, to end the streak.[19]

A victory in the second game of the twin bill gave the Cardinals a slim half-game edge over the Braves. With seventh-place Chicago and Milwaukee coming to town to finish the homestand, there was the opportunity to pad their lead before embarking on a lengthy 21-game road trek. Instead, St. Louis lost the next nine games—and their hold on first place—in their longest skid of the season. The Cubs beat them three times at Busch Stadium and three at Wrigley Field. The Braves swept their series August 9–11 and won 10 straight games, giving them a 7 ½ game lead over the Redbirds and the Dodgers on August 16. St. Louis went into a collective batting slump, scoring only 13 runs in the losing skein and batting .245 overall in the month of August. A personal highlight for Ken was three hits against Milwaukee, including his 13th home run of the season—the first since July 26—in the 5-1 loss on August 11.

Hutchinson tried reshuffling the batting order, moving Boyer from sixth to leadoff and Moon from cleanup to second, while dropping Blasingame from leadoff to seventh and Dark from second to fifth. The team emerged from their funk in a four-game set at Milwaukee

August 16–18, winning three and reducing the Braves' lead to 6½ games. The usually stone-faced skipper, trying to break the tension before the August 16 contest, canceled the club's midnight curfew and posted a mock lineup on game day that featured the team's coaches, Stan's son Dick Musial, and equipment manager Butch Yatkeman instead of the regulars. The players enjoyed a good laugh and beat the Braves that night, 6-2. Ken did well in the leadoff spot, swatting four safeties, walking four times, and scoring five runs in the set.

In their final series at the Polo Grounds before the Giants' move to San Francisco in 1958, the Redbirds took three of four but remained 6½ behind Milwaukee with Brooklyn just one percentage point behind them. Boyer hit better at the horseshoe-shaped ballpark than anywhere else in the National League that season—.341 with 15 safeties (including three home runs) in 11 games—and capped it off with a 2-for-4 day in his finale on August 21. He clubbed his 15th homer, drove in two runs, and scored two in a 13-6 loss.[20]

The next evening, the Cardinals lost Musial, who was leading the league with a .340 average. He suffered a torn muscle and chipped shoulder blade on an awkward swing at Philadelphia on August 22. The injury kept him out of the lineup for almost two weeks, ending his consecutive games played streak at 895. Without their best hitter and power threat, the club dropped four of the next five games to Philadelphia, Brooklyn, and Pittsburgh, despite good pitching by starters Mizell, Jones, Von McDaniel, and Jackson. St. Louis fell to third place, a half-game behind the Dodgers, and were 7½ back of Milwaukee. Unbeknownst to the Cardinals at the time, they played their final game at Ebbets Field on August 25, as the Dodgers would later announce their move to Los Angeles to join the Giants on the West Coast. In that contest, Ken was hitless in four at-bats and struck out three times, including the ninth inning with the bases loaded and two outs to end the game.[21]

The Redbirds traveled to Chicago and returned the favor from a month earlier, taking three games from the Cubs August 30–September 1. The hard-fought sweep elevated them to second place and 6½ games behind the Braves. But they subsequently lost two of three at Cincinnati and fell two games further back. Boyer homered off Hal Jeffcoat to start the opener of the Labor Day doubleheader at Crosley

Field on September 2, then struck out four times in the second game against left-hander Don Gross. Displaying uncharacteristic anger, he kicked a water bucket in the visiting dugout after fanning the third time, spraying a few fans nearby.[22]

With 23 games left in the season and the team's offense unproductive since Musial's injury, pennant hopes had faded for the Cardinals. They were still in second place but 8 ½ games out and the third-place Dodgers trailing them by a half-game. Yet in the last game of the Cincinnati series, they erupted for eight runs on 10 hits in the first two innings off starter Joe Nuxhall and reliever Raul Sanchez. Dark, Cunningham, and Hal Smith each had three safeties in the contest. Smith drove in four runs and cleanup hitter Ennis blasted a homer and knocked in three. Even starting pitcher Mizell got into the act with three RBIs of his own. Now batting fifth in the order, Ken singled to drive in two runs in the first inning and scored on a hit by Smith, then walked, stole second, and scored again on Smith's double in the second. Another walk to Boyer in the eighth led to his third run scored on a bases-loaded hit by Smith that sparked a five-run frame. When the game was over, they had bludgeoned the Redlegs, 14-4.

The Cardinals returned to St. Louis for a two-game set with Milwaukee beginning September 4. They picked up where they left off in Cincinnati, starting off with four runs in the first inning on a single by Ennis, a double by Moon, and an error by Eddie Mathews at third base. The uprising forced Braves starter Juan Pizarro's early exit after facing only four batters. Former Redbird Del Rice's three-run home run off Herm Wehmeier in the second and a solo blast by Mathews in the fifth tied it up, 4-4, as Wehmeier and Braves reliever Gene Conley otherwise pitched scoreless ball into extra innings. In the twelfth, Conley was relieved by Don McMahon, who gave up a double and a stolen base to Blasingame. With one out and "The Blazer" on third, the next two batters were walked intentionally to set up an inning-ending double play. But Ennis' sacrifice fly to right field was dropped by Bob Hazle and Blasingame scored the winning run, 5-4.

St. Louis took the second game in more dominating fashion with a 10-1 decision as they knocked 14-game winner Lew Burdette from the mound after four-and-a-third innings. Having worn the collar in the first game, Boyer didn't start but pinch-ran for Ennis in the eighth. He scored on a fielder's choice by Eddie Kasko as part of a five-run outburst. The victories brought them two games closer to first place, 6½ games back.[23]

With the Braves losing to the Cubs the next night, the Cardinals had the chance to pick up another game against the visiting Redlegs. Trailing 2-0 in the second, Ken smashed his 18th home run to put them on the board, then singled and scored on Kasko's hit in the fourth to put them ahead, 3-2. Ennis doubled in the fifth to add to their lead, but Cincinnati pinch-hitter Jerry Lynch blasted the first pitch from reliever Schmidt in the sixth for a two-run homer to put them ahead. At a time when every game was crucial, the 5-4 defeat when they were ahead was especially disappointing. The loss also ended Schmidt's 10-game consecutive win streak.[24]

Over the next two weeks, the Redbirds won eight of their next nine games while the Braves went 5-5 in the same stretch, cutting the deficit between them to three games with 10 left in the season. On September 8, St. Louis came back to beat Cincinnati, 4-3, tallying in the last two frames. In the ninth, Boyer and Moon both singled to score pinch-runner Wehmeier with the tying run. Ken then scored the game-winning run on a hit to right by Dark.

After splitting time between center field and third base in the Cincinnati series, Boyer returned to third base in the next six games as Bobby Gene Smith came off the bench to play center. St. Louis took two from the Phillies, winning the opener on Ken's bases-loaded single in the fourteenth inning off Robin Roberts in relief, 4-3, and beating them the next evening, 14-6. They split a two-game set with New York as Boyer smashed a triple and scored in the 6-1 victory on September 14. The Redbirds swept a doubleheader against Pittsburgh the next day to climb within 2½ games of Milwaukee. In the first game, Ken belted his 19th homer and scored two runs. Musial returned to the lineup and contributed a single and two doubles in the twin bill. With a 12-5 victory over Brooklyn on September 17, St. Louis had won four in a row.[25]

The next evening, the Cardinals had 11 hits off young right-hander Don Drysdale but still lost, 6-1. Though Moon homered for their only tally, the game might have ended differently had the wind not hindered a first-inning drive off his bat with two runners on base that center fielder Duke Snider caught at the wall. The Redbirds took two of three from Cincinnati and would have swept the series except for another pinch-hit homer by Lynch in the ninth and a two-out, two-run blast by Roy McMillan—his only one of the season—in the tenth.

The Cardinals couldn't afford to lose close games. Now five games out of first and facing elimination with a single loss, they traveled north to Milwaukee's County Stadium for a crucial three-game series with the Braves, who had won their last six. In the opener on September 23, three singles and an error in the second inning by center fielder Moon gave the Braves an early 1-0 lead. Burdette pitched five scoreless innings for Milwaukee before Dark's two-out single plated Moon and Musial to give St. Louis the lead. Jackson did equally well for seven innings of relief, but gave up a double to Mathews in the seventh that scored Red Schoendienst with the tying run. Hitless in his last 12 at bats, Ken wasn't in the starting lineup but pinch ran for catcher Hobie Landrith in the ninth inning. With the score tied 2-2, he stole second base to put himself in scoring position, but two ground outs and a fly ball to center ended a potential rally.

Reliever Billy Muffett held Milwaukee to one hit over two innings. He had not allowed a home run in 44 innings during his rookie season. With two outs in the eleventh and a runner on first, Hank Aaron smashed Muffett's offering over the center-field fence. The 4-2 decision clinched the National League pennant for the Braves, the first for the franchise in Milwaukee, and ended St. Louis' quest for its ninth championship. "I guess it's justifiable retribution," bemoaned Frank Lane. "We took the pennant away from them last year and they beat us to win it this year."[26]

The Cardinals were crushed. It didn't help that the entire city of Milwaukee had a raucous celebration with cheers, shouts, and car horns honking into the early-morning hours. Because the kitchen staff at the team's hotel was among the revelers, the players had to settle for a postgame meal of stale sandwiches from a nearby bus station vending machine. Lane and Hutchinson both praised them for what they had accomplished, rebounding from a nine-game losing streak to average seven-and-a-half runs per game and challenge the Braves into the final week of the season. "I was never so proud of a team in my life," Lane told Bob Broeg of the *Post-Dispatch*. "Win or lose, they battled all the way." He added, "Milwaukee won more games than we did, but the Redbirds are my champions. They never gave up. They went down fighting, right to the end." Hutchinson remarked, "They gave me all they had and I'm real proud of 'em."[27]

Aaron thwarted the Cardinals once again the next evening with his first major-league grand slam and left-hander Warren Spahn held them to five hits with six strikeouts for his 21st victory of the season, 6-1. St. Louis rallied for four runs in the eighth inning to take the final game with Milwaukee, 4-1, and clinch second place on September 25. With the pennant race decided, Hutchinson rested several players—including batting champion Musial, who finished at .351—and started rookies in their places for the final series of the season against the Chicago Cubs. Mired in a late-season batting slump, Ken was relegated to the bench as Kasko played third base and Moon and former Cub Jim King shared time in center field.[28]

St. Louis ended the 1957 campaign in second place with a record of 87-67, an 11-game improvement over the previous season. It was their highest finish in the standings since 1949. They drew their third-highest attendance in franchise history as 1,183,575 fans came to Busch Stadium, second-best in the National League and a mark that would not be surpassed for eight years. Fred Hutchinson was honored as the National League Manager of the Year by *The Sporting News* and United Press International and received a new contract to lead the Redbirds in 1958. *The Sporting News* named Frank Lane as its Major League Executive of the Year.[29]

Though it had been successful season for the team, it was a discouraging one for Ken personally. His batting average fell forty-one points from the previous season to .265, only a point higher than his rookie campaign. He hit only .241 at home. His offensive numbers—144 hits, 18 doubles, 19 homers, 62 RBIs, and 79 runs scored—dropped in almost every category; his on-base percentage was twenty-nine points lower and his slugging percentage fell eighty points. He proved ineffective in clutch situations, batting .180 in 133 at-bats with runners in scoring position. A performance similar to 1956 could have been the difference between a second-place finish and a pennant.

Boyer attributed his downturn not to Lane's criticisms but to overthinking. "I think that at bat, I have been too conscious of where I stand, how I hold my hands, whether my right elbow is out from the body instead of close to it, instead of just going up there to take my cuts as I did in the minor leagues. But I've got no excuse."[30]

"That was the only year I've seen him feeling low," Kathleen Boyer recalled. "He wouldn't speak up. I knew he was depressed. He exercises pretty good control usually, whether he's had a good night or a bad night."[31]

Boyer's transition to center field, however, had been a success. He led the majors in fielding percentage at the position (.993) while committing only two errors in 278 chances. Notwithstanding his decreased production, he combined with Del Ennis and Wally Moon to become the most productive outfield in club history with 66 home runs and 240 RBIs. Still, he had not given up on returning to the infield and proving his defensive abilities there. "If I lose confidence, I've lost everything. I still believe I can play third base and through experience can play a better center field."[32]

KEN REALIZED FRANK LANE was frustrated with his performance and would likely trade him over the winter. Indeed, at least five clubs approached the Cardinals general manager about a possible deal. Lane publicly extolled Boyer's promise while working behind the scenes to trade him for a center fielder or a third baseman. "Several clubs have sounded me out on the availability of Boyer in a big trade," he confirmed in early October. "But how in the world can I trade a young star like Boyer? The potentialities of this young man are so great that I shudder at the mere mention of his name in connection with possible deals. If some other club in the National League landed Kenny, I'm sure he'd come back to haunt the Cardinals with his slick fielding and heavy hitting for years to come." A month later, he added to this line of thinking: "[A]ctually because of his natural ability Ken ought to be an untouchable. He can do everything, but will he?"[33]

Throughout October, Lane and Pirates general manager Joe L. Brown discussed a trade that would send Boyer to Pittsburgh for first baseman-outfielder Frank Thomas and infielder Gene Freese. Manager Danny Murtaugh was reportedly intrigued about the possibility. Though Thomas (.290, 23 homers, and 89 RBIs) spent more time at first base and only five innings in center field in 1957, Lane believed he could be a solution to the center field predicament. Murtaugh intended on using him at third base in 1958, which could have been another possibility for him in St. Louis. Conversations were serious enough that Boyer was reportedly told of its likelihood.[34]

The autonomy to make trades had been taken from Lane after he dispatched Red Schoendienst and tried to do the same to Stan Musial. Now Gussie Busch demanded final approval of all player transactions. The Boyer deal was presented to Busch and club executive vice-president Dick Meyer for approval on November 8, but they rejected it. For the wheeler-dealer Lane, it was the ultimate indignity. Coupled with the beer baron's earlier refusal to extend his contract, he sought employment elsewhere. He quickly negotiated a three-year deal with the Cleveland Indians for their vacant general manager's position and left behind the uncompleted deal to send Boyer to Pittsburgh.[35]

"There are some other people there (in St. Louis) who think they know baseball," said Lane. "The situation limited me to do certain things. I'm smart—or stupid—enough to want to win or lose on my own judgment." He continued relying on his own judgment and living up to his "Trader Frank" moniker with the Indians. Over the next three years, he dealt away fan favorites Early Wynn, Herb Score, and Rocky Colavito, and future stars Norm Cash and Roger Maris.[36]

Lane's departure was a welcome reprieve for Ken, ending a captious two-year relationship with the turbulent general manager. "I usually don't pay much attention to trade stories," said Boyer. "But after the season I had, I had made up [my] mind that I was going to be traded by Lane. Now I think there's a chance I might stick it out here this winter, at any rate."

Lane had been Ken's biggest supporter and harshest critic. He expected much from him and felt he should be as good as—or even better than—New York Yankees slugger Mickey Mantle. He wasn't timid about publicly chastising what he perceived to be Ken's lack of competitive hustle and aggressiveness. "Boyer always had everything too easy. He never had to extend himself. Even when he hit .306 [in 1956], he should have hit .360." Because Lane received a bonus for increased attendance in St. Louis, Ken felt he was trying to turn him into a marketable superstar. "He wanted to make something out of me that I wasn't—a colorful gate attraction," he later said. "It's fine to have color and be able to electrify a crowd like Willie Mays does, but that's Willie's nature and everybody can't have it."[37]

Ken took the criticism and never challenged Lane in the press. "I think Lane was the only man in baseball who ever bothered Ken," recalled his friend and road roommate Larry Jackson. It wasn't until a few years later that Boyer admitted Lane's barbs did indeed affect him in 1957. "Everything went wrong," he said, looking back on that season. "I knew the club was disappointed in me and I was getting down on myself. It didn't help reading in the papers that Lane was going to get rid of me that winter. St. Louis was my home and I didn't want to leave it."[38] It wasn't until the following spring that he finally broke his silence and spoke his mind. While complimenting the job he did as general manager and claiming he "never had any difficulties with Lane," Boyer added:

> Don't think I wasn't aware of all the uncomplimentary things Lane said about me. In fact, he came to me one day and repeated all the things he had said to the press about me. He said he wanted me to hear it from his own lips rather than from the newspapermen. I can't say I like what he said but what I resented most was his insinuation that I didn't hustle and go all out. That wasn't true, of course. I realize he is an erratic baseball fan who sometimes can't control his feelings but that doesn't give him any right to make such irresponsible accusations. How can a guy look like he's hustling when he's having a bad year? Was I expected to do handsprings when I was hitting .250? I was having troubles enough of my own.[39]

The Cardinals immediately named Lane's assistant, Vaughan P. "Bing" Devine, as his successor. The forty-year-old St. Louis native had served in the organization for eighteen years and apprenticed for the position as general manager of the Cardinals' Triple-A Rochester club for six seasons. It was there he first met Ken after he had signed with the organization in 1949 and awaited assignment to a Class D club. Asked at his introductory press conference if Boyer would still be traded, Devine expressed his desire to keep him. "Stan Musial is the only player not tradeable, but Boyer comes close to it," he said. "We'd need a very attractive deal to give him up. I never had Ken in the minors, but he's a natural athlete with great potential. I'd like to see him realize that potential with the Cardinals." Though willing to play him in center field again, Hutchinson remained skeptical of his desire and felt inclined to trade him. "Boyer has potential, all right, but I don't know whether he's determined enough to achieve that potential."[40]

Even though Devine wasn't seeking to deal him, it didn't stop other clubs from making proposals. Philadelphia Phillies general manager Mayo Smith offered center fielder Richie Ashburn and former St. Louis left-hander Harvey Haddix. "I told my wife that if I'd have been the Cardinals, I'd have made that trade," remarked Ken. Reflecting on the offer forty years later, Devine wished he could have had both Ashburn and Boyer on the same roster. Ashburn stayed in Philadelphia and won the National League batting title the following season with a .350 average, leading the league with an on-base percentage of .440. "But in a sense, I had grown up with Boyer," said Devine. "I was general manager of his first pro club he ever reported to, the Rochester Red Wings. I guess I looked upon him, as I looked upon myself, as someone who hopefully had a future in this game. I just had a feeling about Kenny. I didn't want to lose him."[41]

The interest from other teams only reinforced Devine's determination to keep him. After returning from the winter meetings, he met with Boyer on December 17 and offered him a contract for about $15,000, a slight increase from the previous season. Ken made no excuses for his poor performance, which impressed Devine. "Actually his figures were about average for a big leaguer," he said. "They were poor only because of Ken's tremendous potential, which we still believe he'll achieve with the Cardinals."[42]

That winter, Devine made a bold pronouncement: "I'll stake what little baseball reputation I might have that Boyer, out of position this year in center field, will become a standout third baseman, maybe the best the Cardinals ever had, and the kind of player on whom we can build for the future."[43]

WHEN KEN TOOK OFF HIS UNIFORM at the end of the 1957 season, he believed his days with the St. Louis Cardinals were numbered. Given a second chance, he arrived for spring training in 1958 determined to reward Devine and the Cardinals for their confidence in him. "I'm going to put out to the best of my ability. I always have and always will…A guy feels better when he knows he's wanted."[44]

He worked with coach Terry Moore to refine his defensive skills in center field. "Kenny still has a lot to learn," the former All-Star center fielder said. "But he'll be much better, naturally, than last year, when the job was brand new to him. He still has to learn how to go back on fly balls, but we're working on that." Throwing proved to be another challenge. "You throw differently from the outfield and I had always played the infield except for my pitching," he recalled. "Now I had to anticipate not only how to get set for the long throw, but where to throw the ball if I caught it." Though slated for the outfield once the season started, he also worked out at third base. He made enough strides defensively that Bob Broeg of the *Post-Dispatch* lamented the fact that Boyer didn't have a twin for them to play both positions.[45]

Ken also worked to improve his hitting. Hutchinson had suggested he take practice swings over the winter using a 50-ounce, lead-weighted bat. Repetitions of 25 swings 200–300 times a day helped strengthen his arms and back muscles and made his normal weight bat seem lighter during the season. He carried the lead bat with him everywhere in Florida. "I felt a little silly carrying it on the beach, but after the season I'd had the year before, I was willing to try anything."[46]

Boyer was upbeat and more relaxed than the previous spring. It showed especially at the plate where he batted .375 in the exhibitions. His improved approach and hitting prowess impressed Hutchinson. "He had his elbows locked too close to his body (last season), but now he's got more freedom in his swing again and is a pleasure to watch." To cap off his great spring, Ken smashed two homers and drove in five runs against the Chicago White Sox at his minor-league stomping ground, Buffs Stadium in Houston, on April 5.[47]

Fans in St. Louis were optimistic the Cardinals would improve on their second-place finish in 1957. A throng of 26,246 greeted them at Busch Stadium on April 15, the largest Opening Day attendance in club history to date. The visiting Chicago Cubs ruined the evening, scoring in the first inning and building a 4-0 lead on 10 hits while the Redbirds were held to seven and stranded 14 runners. Instead of playing center field, Ken started at third base in place of veteran Alvin Dark, whom Hutchinson tried unsuccessfully to move from shortstop in spring training. Bobby Gene Smith went to center. Boyer played at third for eight games before returning to the outfield the last weekend of April.

Losing four straight to start the season—all to the Cubs—and in last place, St. Louis finally won on April 20 at Wrigley Field, 9-4. Afterward, the players embarked on their first-ever flight to the West Coast to play the relocated Giants and Dodgers. The Cardinals took the opener at San Francisco's former minor-league ballpark, Seals Stadium, but dropped the next three, including their first at Los Angeles Memorial Coliseum. On the twenty-sixth, Ken scored on rookie right fielder Gene Green's home run as the Redbirds tied and later beat the Dodgers, 6-4. Despite matching them with 10 hits the next day, St. Louis ended their first West Coast trip with a 10-3 loss.

Smashing his first home run of the season off Johnny Podres in that game, Boyer endured a subsequent stretch of 21 consecutive plate appearances without a hit. His terrible start was reminiscent of what happened to him the previous season. After 16 games, his average plunged to .145 with only one extra-base hit and five RBIs. Hutchinson first dropped him from fifth to seventh in the order, then benched him for three games and tried rookies Curt Flood in center field and Benny Valenzuela at third base as well as Dark. A seven-game losing skid forced him to choose defense over offense. He stabilized the left side of the infield with Dick Schofield replacing Dark at short and Boyer returning to third base despite his batting slump. Wally Moon shared time with Flood in center field and hard-hitting Green took over in right. Except for a two-inning appearance two days later, the "Ken Boyer Experiment" in center field was over.[48]

A 3-2 triumph over the Cubs on May 9 ended the skein. It led to an identical winning one that lifted the Cardinals out of the cellar and into fifth place. Ken tried opening his stance slightly to see the ball better and was rewarded with a seventh-inning home run in a 3-1 victory the next day. "Don't know whether that did any good, but you have to try something," he said. "I do think I got to be a little more relaxed hitter before the season ended."⁴⁹

In that stretch, Stan Musial reached his career milestone 3,000th hit at Wrigley Field on May 13. Hutchinson intended to save the historic base hit for fans back in St. Louis. But with Green on second base and the Cardinals trailing in the sixth inning, 3-1, he called upon the thirty-seven-year-old Musial to pinch-hit for pitcher Sam Jones. As Ken and his teammates watched from the dugout, Stan rapped a double into the left-field corner for number 3,000, driving in Green and sparking a four-run rally that continued the win streak with a 5-3 victory. On an occasion that also marked the Redbirds' final road trip on the rails, the celebration continued as the train made its way to St. Louis. Fans acknowledged Stan's feat at stops along the way. It was close to midnight before the team finally arrived at Union Station, where a thousand St. Louis fans were packed inside waiting for Musial. "No school tomorrow, kids," he laughed.⁵⁰

Back at third base, Ken regained his confidence and showed none of the defensive lapses that plagued him at the position the previous season. His fielding was excellent, wrote Bob Broeg of the *Post-Dispatch*, "[c]harging under the gun for bunts and getting force outs at second through powerful pegs, diving for backhanded catches to his right and lunging for good stops to his left."⁵¹ His batting drought had ended, but he was still hitting a paltry .165 before the opener of a May 18 doubleheader with the cellar-dwelling Dodgers. With the bases loaded and two out in the first inning, he fouled off eight pitches before smashing a grand slam in an eventual 6-5 victory. Boyer went 3-for-4—his first multi-hit game in almost a month—and added two more safeties in the finale.

The hitting spree raised his average forty-two points to .207, the highest it had been since Opening Day. After dropping five of eight on the road in late May, the Cardinals returned home and won seven of their next 10 games, knocking San Francisco out of first place with three victories. Boyer was the catalyst with eight hits, three home runs, and eight RBIs in the four-game set. In the second game of the Memorial Day doubleheader, he belted two round-trippers and knocked in four runs batting cleanup for the first time all season as part of a 3-for-4 performance. The next day, he equaled his number of hits with three RBIs and crushed a game-winning homer in the twelfth inning, 10-9. He batted .341 for the month and saw his power return with six homers in the last two weeks of May. A nine-game consecutive hit streak elevated his average even further to a more respectable .277. "I'm batting the same as I always have," he said. "The hits are just dropping in now. It's a funny game."[52]

An 18-10 record in June propelled St. Louis into the first division. With the additions of Jim Brosnan and Sal Maglie, the pitching staff performed yeomen work with a collective 3.39 ERA, compensating for a lackluster offensive team effort of .256. Boyer himself batted only .241 for the month but contributed six homers and 16 RBIs. With their 2-1 victory over the front-running Braves at Milwaukee on June 21, the fifth-place Cardinals started a six-game win streak that leapfrogged them over the Redlegs, Pirates, and Giants to second place on the twenty-fourth. Ken's two-run double was the difference in a 2-1 triumph over the Braves on the twenty-second and he surpassed Musial for the club lead in RBIs.[53] In a four-game sweep at Pittsburgh, he had another RBI double that pulled the Cardinals within a score on June 23 and then crossed the plate with the tying run in their subsequent 7-5 victory. Trailing 2-0 on the twenty-sixth, St. Louis rallied for three runs in the seventh inning. Boyer smashed a triple that plated Musial with the first tally and later scored to tie the game on Green's single in an eventual 6-2 victory. They were now only a game-and-a-half behind Milwaukee in the National League race.

The plateau was fleeting, however, as the Redbirds lost six of their last 10 games before the All-Star break and slid to third place, though only 2 ½ back of the Braves. A twin bill with the last-place Dodgers on July 3 drew 66,485 fans to LA Memorial Coliseum, the largest crowd ever to watch a night game in the league up to that time. The opener, a 4-2 victory, was the first televised regular-season game ever broadcast across the Rocky Mountains back to St. Louis. In the historic contest, Ken walked, singled, and stole two bases. His 15th home run of the season came in a losing effort in the second game, 3-2. The Cardinals subsequently dropped two straight at San Francisco—each decided with the bases loaded and the game tied in the bottom of the ninth—and relinquished second place to the Giants. Summoned from the bullpen in both contests, Ken's road roommate,

Larry Jackson, walked pinch-hitter Willie Kirkland on a 3-2 count on July 5, then the next day hit rookie Jim Davenport with a pitch.[54]

OMITTED FROM THE ALL-STAR BALLOTING, Boyer enjoyed a resurgence at the plate that carried him through the second-half of the season. He continued an on-base string of 23 games and hit safely in 13 of them, raising his average to .283 on July 20.[55] The Cardinals halted their four-game losing skein with victories at home over Philadelphia and Pittsburgh. In their 6-2 win over the Phillies on the eleventh, Moon homered and Boyer and Don Blasingame each had three safeties, with Ken smacking a double and two triples, scoring three runs, and driving in a run. On the sixteenth, he smashed a grand slam off Warren Spahn, his second of the season, in a 6-5 defeat to Milwaukee. But the team plunged into its second seven-game losing skid of the season in mid July, falling into a fifth place tie with Cincinnati. They dropped four games below .500 at 39-43 and were seven games out of first on July 18.

That evening, Ken and Larry Jackson stayed out until two o'clock in the morning and were caught arriving at the team's hotel by Hutchinson and Devine. Fortunately, Jackson pitched a six-hit shutout the next afternoon and Boyer crushed Redlegs left-hander Alex Kellner's first pitch in the tenth inning for a 1-0 victory at Crosley Field. "It wasn't a question of win or lose," recalled Jackson, "but whether we lived or died."[56]

St. Louis took six of their next 10 games, including a four-game split against the league-leading Braves. In the first game at Milwaukee on July 21, Ken suffered a pulled leg muscle running out a ground ball that forced him out of the lineup. He returned three days later and singled, scored a run, and drove in another with a sacrifice fly as Jones tossed a four-hit shutout with six strikeouts to beat the Braves, 4-0. Starting with a 10-1 defeat in the finale of the July 27 doubleheader with Cincinnati, the Cardinals lost a season-high eight in a row. They plunged 12½ games out of first and into the National League basement by August 3.[57]

Six straight victories enabled them to climb back to fifth place, then overtake Philadelphia for fourth on August 10. A 7-3 comeback victory at San Francisco on the twelfth gave them a 54-56 record,

8 ½ back and two games below .500, a mark they had not reached in almost a month. But the Redbirds lost five of seven on their last West Coast trip, including three at Los Angeles, allowing the Dodgers to tie them for fourth. Ken had seven hits in the twin doubleheaders, including his 20th home run—his first in about a month—on the fifteenth, raising his average to .295. They slipped down to sixth place by the end of August before regaining fifth on September 1, where they stayed the last month of the season.

Boyer had made a remarkable turnaround at the plate. Overcoming a dreadful start that saw his average stay below .200 and only five extra-base hits in the first 27 games (all but two home runs), he batted .325 thereafter and swatted at a .343 clip the last three months of the season. He hit safely in 12 straight games in early September, a 3-for-5 performance at Wrigley Field on September 4 enabling him to cross the .300 threshold for the first time in 1958.

With almost two weeks left in a discouraging season, manager Fred Hutchinson was fired on September 17. Theirs was an uneasy relationship at times, but Ken respected his leadership and considered him "a man's man" who would "fight you or fight for you, whichever was necessary." He influenced Boyer's own managerial career later in life. "But, man, Hutch had a temper. He could chew you out in front of anybody, but a half hour later, he'd forget it."[58] Coach Stan Hack took over as interim manager the last 10 games of the season. The Cardinals lost seven of them and finished in a fifth-place tie with the Chicago Cubs with a record of 72-82, 20 games behind the Milwaukee Braves.[59]

Ken was one of the bright spots on a club that finished third from last in the league in batting average and last in runs scored, proving his poor showing in 1957 was an aberration. He ended the season with a .307 average (second only to Musial's .337 among the regulars and eighth overall in the league) and led the team in hits (175), home runs (23), RBIs (90), and runs scored (101). "Boyer is now an established star," declared his first major-league manager, Eddie Stanky. "He's here to stay. I'd like to see him blossom out as a .330 or .340 hitter!"[60]

Defensively, Boyer led National League third basemen in putouts (164) and double plays (41) and finished one below Eddie Mathews in assists (350). His exceptional fielding was recognized by his peers who named him to *The Sporting News* All-Star Fielding Team for 1958 and sporting goods manufacturer Rawlings awarded him its first National League Gold Glove Award for the position. *The Sporting News* considered him "the unquestioned master of the hot corner...A daring performer with quick hands and instantaneous reflexes, Ken was a defensive standout in game after game with diving catches of line drives and stops of hot grounders."[61]

THE CARDINALS ACQUIRED a new manager when they traded for former Redbirds infielder Solly Hemus from the Philadelphia Phillies on September 29. The thirty-five-year-old veteran had made a lasting impression on Gussie Busch after being traded from St. Louis in 1956. He wrote a letter to him expressing his appreciation for his time spent there and hoping he might have the chance to return some day. He lacked coaching or managerial experience, however, and would be the last playing manager for the Redbirds.[62]

Hemus had the unique opportunity for on-the-job training before the 1959 season began. The Cardinals were invited to Japan for a series of exhibition contests against that country's leading players from late October through mid-November 1958. His most discussed move was shifting Musial back to the outfield and giving more playing time at first base to Joe Cunningham, which he intended to carry over into the 1959 season. Hemus was confident his ball club would win every game on the trip. "I know I'm reflecting the attitude of my whole team when I tell you that we'll play as hard here as we do during the regular season. We didn't come this far to lose."[63]

Kathleen Boyer was among the wives who joined their husbands on the overseas trip. She remembers:

> It was a lot of fun. We just had Suzie and David and Ken's Aunt Grace [Heston] came up to stay with them. It was six weeks we were gone. We were in Hawaii for maybe three days. We played there before we went to Japan. We landed on the little island of Wake—it looked like the plane wasn't going to be able to land on that little bitty island. Then we were in Manila for three days and the wives couldn't get out by themselves because it just wasn't real safe there.

But when we were in Japan, the guys would go to different cities and some of the places they went, the wives couldn't go. It was too dangerous. We had a man and a woman as our guides who stayed with us the whole time. We got to tour a lot of the countryside by train and we went to Osaka, Nagoya, Kyoto. It was lots of fun to see all the rice paddies. We actually got to see more of the countryside than the guys did.[64]

The exhibitions began with two victories in Hawaii and one in the Philippines. The Redbirds beat the Armed Services All-Star team in Okinawa, 12-2, thanks to two home runs by Boyer and one each by Green and Moon. The players arrived in Tokyo on October 20 and were welcomed with a 10-mile ticker tape parade from the airport to their hotel. After winning at Seoul, South Korea, the club returned to Japan and took 14 of the next 16 exhibitions. Their Japanese opponents were impressed with the team's hustle and competitiveness. "The Cardinals came to Japan as a fifth-place team," said All-Star manager Nobuyasu Mizuhara, "but they showed us more than any previous American major league club to visit our country."

Ken finished the tour with the second-highest average on the club at .364. He had seven hits in two games November 2–3, tying the latter with a ninth-inning home run and winning it with a hit in the tenth. When they weren't on the field, the players and their wives attended receptions with the Japanese prime minister and the U.S. Ambassador to Japan as well as parties and sightseeing tours. A more somber moment was their visit to the memorial at Hiroshima where the first atomic bomb had been dropped during World War II.[65]

Asked by a sportswriter what he would do during the off-season, Ken replied, "I'll just hunt." He and roommate Larry Jackson got a head start, leaving the rest of the team when they returned to the States and traveling to Jackson's home state of Idaho to hunt elk. Hunting was Boyer's favorite pastime, particularly quail hunting. His enjoyment took away from alternative pursuits like golf, in which he scored in the low nineties. ("I'm just a hacker, good drives but bad approach shots.") Often he went hunting with family, friends, or teammates like Bill Virdon, Red Schoendienst, and Stan Musial. "He was very much of an outdoorsman," recalls his daughter Suzie (Boyer) Hartwig. Ken remembered one particular hunt with Schoendienst when one of his dogs flushed a chukar out of hiding and it flew directly towards him. "I started to shoot it, but the dog was in the way. The stupid bird flew right over the plate, about letter high, and I swung at it with the gun barrel. I clobbered it."[66]

Chapter Seven

The Captain

Ken Boyer was honored at the St. Louis baseball writers dinner in January 1959 with the first-ever J.G. Taylor Spink Award recognizing him as the city's player of the year. In his acceptance speech, he thanked Bing Devine for his confidence in him and former skipper Fred Hutchinson, "whose faith in me restored my faith in myself." He also acknowledged trainer Bob "Doc" Bauman, "who kept me in the lineup" and enabled him to play in all but five games. Boyer took the occasion to announce that he had signed a one-year contract that afternoon for an estimated $25,000. Ray Gillespie of *The Sporting News* wrote that the twenty-seven-year-old had become "the logical successor to Stan Musial as the No. 1 man with the bat and the paycheck."[1]

It took a few seasons for Boyer to earn Hutchinson's respect, but he had no trouble convincing his new manager of his abilities or worth to the club. "Boyer's one of the top five players in the National League," Hemus declared shortly after his hiring. Early in the season, he placed his worth at a million dollars—"But I doubt if I would let him go even at that price."[2] In its season preview, *Sports Illustrated* opined that Ken was "probably the best all-round third baseman in the majors. He can hit with real power, ranges all over the left side of the infield, throws with a shotgun arm and runs like a greyhound on the bases. Milwaukee likes Mathews, but everybody else will take Boyer."[3]

The Cardinals left spring training having lost 17 of 25 exhibition games and didn't fare much better once the regular season began. They opened at Busch Stadium on April 10 and dropped the initial three-game series to the San Francisco Giants. Hemus's plan to move thirty-eight-year-old Stan Musial to left field ended after two games and two collisions with the unpadded concrete wall. He returned to the infield, further exacerbating the logjam at first base and sending Joe Cunningham and Bill White to the outfield. White had been acquired two weeks before the season began from the Giants in exchange for starting pitcher Sam Jones, a popular player in St. Louis. The veteran right-hander would win a league-leading 21 games with a 2.83 ERA for the contending Giants. Many Cardinals fans felt San Francisco received the better end of the deal. Rebuilding with young players, the Redbirds were a few years removed from serious contention. The twenty-five-year-old White held promise as a potential power bat in their lineup for years to come.

St. Louis lost 15 of the first 20 games of the season. Trailing 2-0 at Los Angeles on April 15, they rallied with two outs on consecutive singles by Musial, Boyer, and Cunningham in the sixth inning. Musial was called out at the plate to end the frame and flashed uncharacteristic anger at umpire Dusty Boggess's call. In the subsequent row, Hemus was ejected for the first time as manager. A more important milestone in the contest was the major-league debut of twenty-three-year-old right-hander Bob Gibson as a reliever in the seventh. After giving up a home run to the first batter he faced, Gibson retired six of the next seven in the 5-0 loss. Hemus tried lineup and position changes to spur the team's anemic offense, even shifting Boyer to shortstop for four games and lifting the team curfew. He played his entire 25-man roster on April 16, setting a league record. By the twenty-fourth, the Cardinals were in last place.[4]

After going without a hit in his first five plate appearances against San Francisco, Ken started a modest six-game hit streak that raised his average to .333. His first home run came off Sandy Koufax on April 16, then he hit another off the left-hander ten days later. He had three hits in the 17-11 defeat before twisting his neck on a swing and leaving the game. He returned to the lineup in Milwaukee three days later.⁵

Hemus tried motivating his players by instigating a confrontation at Pittsburgh on May 3 with unfortunate racial overtones. After the Cardinals dropped the opener of a twin bill, he inserted himself into the lineup for the second game. Facing right-hander Bennie Daniels in the first inning, he was hit on the leg by a pitch. Hemus trotted to first base and called the African-American pitcher a "black bastard." Both players exchanged words as teammates rushed onto the field without further incident. Hemus doubled in his next at-bat and gave St. Louis a 2-0 lead. When he batted in the sixth, Daniels threw the first pitch close to his chin. Hemus swung at the next offering and the bat flew out of his hands toward the mound. Daniels suspected it was done intentionally and stepped toward the St. Louis manager at home plate. Both benches cleared again with players shouting, shoving, and punching for five minutes until order was restored. Neither Hemus nor Daniels was ejected.⁶

Shortly after, Hemus held a team meeting and purportedly referred to Daniels with a racial slur. For African American players George Crowe, Curt Flood, and Gibson, it confirmed suspicions of what he really thought of them. "Either it didn't occur to him or he didn't care that guys like me and Flood and White and Crowe—not to mention Musial and Boyer and Alex Grammas and other white players—would be personally offended," Gibson later recalled. "It was hard to believe our manager could be so thickheaded, and it was even harder to play for a guy who unapologetically regarded black players as niggers."⁷

After an awful start to the season, the Cardinals took their first back-to-back games at Philadelphia and over Chicago May 6-7, winning 10 of the next 14. In a five-game weekend set with the Cubs at Busch Stadium, Ken had six hits, two homers, and eight RBIs—including a grand slam as part of a seven-run outburst on May 9—and the Redbirds clinched their first series. An 8-2 victory over Philadelphia on the sixteenth enabled St. Louis to climb out of the National League cellar and winning three out of four against Pittsburgh and Chicago lifted their record to 17-21, just four games under .500 and seven games back of the Milwaukee Braves.

But the Cardinals couldn't sustain the momentum. They dropped 10 of their next 11 and fell 12 games under .500 and back to last place. Boyer's ninth-inning, inside-the-park home run could have stopped a seven-game losing streak before it started in Los Angeles on May 30, but back-to-back clouts by Ron Fairley and Gil Hodges won it for the Dodgers, 7-6. Boyer cut his hand sliding home and only played defense the last two innings the next day when his teammates struck out 14 times, nine against Koufax, in a 5-3 loss.[8]

In that stretch, Ken smashed a two-run triple at Pittsburgh on June 3 to spark a personal 13-game consecutive hit streak. Three days later, he homered off Robin Roberts to tie the game at Philadelphia, but St. Louis lost in the ninth, 4-3. A five-hit shutout by Wilmer Mizell over the Phillies in the second game of a June 7 twin bill finally ended the team's losing skid. The Redbirds subsequently took 11 of 14, including two victories over first-place Milwaukee. On June 9, Boyer went 3-for-5 with a double and four RBIs against the Braves and homered off Warren Spahn in the 12-3 victory. Beginning in a four-game series with Cincinnati on the twelfth, he started an unusual streak within his streak of two safeties in each of his next five games. It enabled him to raise his average thirty-one points to .313, the highest in almost two months. In the opener of the June 14 doubleheader with the Redlegs, Boyer smashed a pitch to deep left field off Joe Nuxhall with a runner on second and two outs in the first inning. He circled the bases for an inside-the-park home run, giving St. Louis a 2-0 lead in an eventual comeback victory, 5-4. It was the 100th round-tripper of his major-league career.[9]

Among the moves made by Devine to bolster the pitching staff near the June 15 trading deadline was exchanging right-handed relievers with Cincinnati, Jim Brosnan for Hal Jeffcoat. After a successful season with the team in the second-half of 1958, Brosnan had struggled as a long reliever. Unbeknownst to his former teammates, he had been keeping a daily journal since spring training in preparation for a book he was writing. *The Long Season*, published in 1960, was a groundbreaking work that offered readers a unique glimpse into the everyday life of a major-league player. Some teammates were upset that he broke the respected rule of keeping clubhouse matters behind closed doors. Ken was among them. Brosnan was perplexed that Boyer told him, "I shouldn't have written what I did because I hadn't pitched well enough to deserve the right to say it."[10]

A pulled leg muscle suffered while chasing a foul ball forced Boyer out of the second game of a twin bill with Philadelphia on June 16. He missed the next four games, but was called out on strikes as a pinch-hitter in the second of a Father's Day doubleheader with Pittsburgh on the twenty-first. Before the game, an errant grounder struck his right eye during infield practice as he tested his injured leg.[11]

In his absence, the Cardinals climbed to sixth place and 7 ½ back of the Braves. The pinch-hit strikeout snapped his hitting streak, but Ken resumed the pace upon his return at Milwaukee on June 23, reeling off a new eight-game string. He crushed a two-run homer that tied the game in the third inning, but the Braves rallied to beat them, 9-5. Two days later, he singled to center and plated Cunningham for the 3-2 victory. Cunningham, Boyer, and Musial each homered to give St. Louis a four-run cushion at Cincinnati on the twenty-sixth, but the Redlegs pummeled two Cards relievers to tie it in their half and beat them in the tenth, 7-6. St. Louis finished the month of June as the best hitting club in the National League and won four straight, including a two-hit shutout by right-hander Ernie Broglio over the Redlegs on the twenty-seventh.

July started with four losses in six games leading to the All-Star break. After going hitless in 20 at-bats, Ken rebounded with a single and an RBI double in the second game of a July 5 doubleheader against San Francisco. The Cardinals had six representatives for the All-Star Game held at Forbes Field in Pittsburgh on July 7, including Boyer as a reserve. It was his first All-Star selection since his debut in 1956. Despite his ninth-place position in the NL batting race (.315) and season-best .381 average in June, he finished second in the voting to third baseman Eddie Mathews of the league-leading Braves, 165 to 47. The National League trailed, 4-3, when Boyer entered the game as a pinch-hitter to start the eighth inning. He singled off New York Yankees right-hander Whitey Ford, was sacrificed to second base by Dick Groat of the Pirates, and scored the tying run on Hank Aaron's double to center field. An RBI triple by Willie Mays drove in Aaron with the go-ahead tally. Boyer stayed in the game at third base and caught Harvey Kuenn's pop foul to end the contest, 5-4.[12]

KEN CONTINUED his 15-game hit streak when the regular season resumed. After the Cardinals dropped the first of a July 9 twin bill at Philadelphia, 11-0, he singled and scored their first run on Gino Cimoni's double in the second tilt, then homered in the 6-2 victory. They won nine of the next 12, tying them with the Chicago Cubs for fifth place and trailing first-place San Francisco by 6½ games. On the nineteenth, Boyer's home run broke up a scoreless game with Milwaukee that ended in a 9-5 win; he did the same with an RBI single the next evening to beat the Cubs, 2-0.

A 5-for-31 funk coincided with a seven-game road trip to the West Coast and Cincinnati, dropping his average to .296. Three safeties off left-hander Jim O'Toole of the Redlegs on July 30 proved a temporary remedy. He scored the team's only run on Cunningham's single in the second inning and Gibson earned his first major-league victory with an eight-hit, 1-0 shutout. Boyer was hitless in his next two games at Milwaukee, however, including a rare three-strikeout showing against lefty Juan Pizarro of the Braves on August 1. Perhaps his mind was back home where his wife Kathleen gave birth that day to their third child, Dan Lloyd Boyer. His focus was sharper for the next day's doubleheader: four straight hits in five at-bats in the opener and a two-run homer in the finale as they split the twin bill with the Braves.[13]

Beginning in 1959, a second All-Star Game was held each season through 1962 with gate receipts contributing to the major-league players pension fund. Boyer, Musial, Cunningham, Mizell, and Hal Smith flew from Milwaukee to Los Angeles for the contest held at the Coliseum on August 3. Ken started at third base and batted second in the order, but he was hitless in two at-bats and walked in the fifth inning as the National League lost, 5-3.

Boyer and his All-Star teammates rejoined the Redbirds the next day in St. Louis, where his hitting streak continued in nine straight games against Pittsburgh and Philadelphia. On August 7, he smashed his 20th home run to put them on the board against the Phillies and Musial won it with a two-run shot in the ninth, 3-1. The Cardinals took both games of a Saturday doubleheader the next day. In the opener, Ken had three safeties off Robin Roberts and rookie right-hander Bob Miller won his own game with an RBI single in the seventh inning, 4-3. Gibson allowed only two earned runs in the second tilt and struck out eight batters (though he walked eight) in 10 innings. Back-to-back doubles by White and Boyer won it in the eleventh, 5-4.

The victories gave St. Louis the opportunity to climb to the first division with another twin bill sweep the next day. But the Phillies beat them in both contests, highlighted by first baseman Ed Bouchee's two-out, ninth-inning grand slam in the opener. Ken doubled in that game, but right-hander Jim Owens blanked him in the second to break his nine-game hit streak. The losses started a five-game losing spell for the Redbirds and dropped them to seventh place, four games out of the cellar.

Boyer regrouped the next evening and started the longest hit streak of his major-league career. He singled in a 3-2 loss to San Francisco and had two safeties in each of the next four games against the Giants and Dodgers. On the fifteenth, back-to-back home runs by White and Boyer in the first inning—Ken's blast landing on the right-field pavilion roof at Busch Stadium—gave the Cardinals a three-run lead and knocked Johnny Podres out of the game. Homers by reliever Larry Sherry and Duke Snider won it for the Dodgers, 4-3. "The Cardinals could use more slugging Boyers in their hour of need," opined Jack Herman of the *Globe-Democrat*.

The next day, he singled and scored the Redbirds' first run in the second inning. It was a contentious game between them and the umpires. Don Blasingame was ejected in the initial frame for yelling at the first-base arbiter after grounding out, quickly followed by Hemus when he asked why Blasingame had been tossed. Even a remark from Snider about the umpires continuing the game in a light rain led to his ejection. After White homered to give them a 5-1 lead in the fifth, Ken was called out on strikes to end the frame. He questioned the pitch location and home-plate umpire Clem Labine threw him out for making what he considered a "'show up' gesture." St. Louis avoided further ejections and held on for the 5-3 victory.[14]

Splitting a two-game set at Philadelphia, the Cardinals lost seven straight at Pittsburgh and Cincinnati and back home against Milwaukee and were entrenched in seventh place, trailing San Francisco by 13 ½ games toward the end of August. There wasn't much for fans at Busch Stadium to cheer except Ken's hit streak, which stood at 14 games—his longest of the season—on August 25. St. Louis beat Milwaukee the next evening and won four in a row against the Braves and the Redlegs, their longest string in over a month. On the twenty-seventh, he smashed a three-run homer off Bob Buhl of the Braves and plated Cunningham with a sacrifice fly for the 5-4 victory.

DURING THE HOME STAND, Hemus invited Boyer to dinner and asked him to be the team captain, a role last held by Red Schoendienst in 1953. The manager "wanted somebody on the field to get his messages across to the players," said Ken. "Sometimes that's easier for a player to do than for a manager." It was recognition of his influence on the field and in the clubhouse. The added responsibilities also came with a modest $500 addition to his salary. Asked if he thought his teammates would object to the new role, Boyer replied, "Well, as far as I'm concerned, nobody should be resentful if you're trying to be constructively critical."[15]

"I could see the leadership in him," recalls Hemus about his decision. "I needed somebody that everybody looked up to, and I felt that he was that person. I think that I was correct in doing so, too, because everybody just thought he was a person that they could go to if they had a problem at all. If they couldn't come to me, they could go to him and get everything corrected."[16]

Now in his fifth season with the Cardinals, Ken was more comfortable in the role of team leader, exhibiting qualities that made a positive impact on his younger teammates. They admired him and found him approachable and willing to help. "He was the guy everyone asked—and not just about baseball," said teammate Mike Shannon. "They went to him when their wife was sick or they had trouble with the car or they needed a couple of bucks. He was the captain." He spent time with them off the field; young catcher Tim McCarver remembers being invited to his home for a barbecue. It wasn't Boyer's style to admonish them for mental mistakes or loss of temper detrimental to themselves and the team. A subtle rebuke or a discerning look got the message across more effectively. His consistent performance year after year added to his credibility and allowed him to emerge from Musial's imposing shadow.[17]

Ken's personality and demeanor were compared to the quintessential lawman depicted in Western movies of the period—handsome, tough, and principled. One writer likened him to the "sheriff of a tough western town who cows all the gunslingers with dirty looks at 20 paces." "He's the strong, silent type, like Gary Cooper in *High Noon*," observed Cardinals radio broadcaster Joe Garagiola. "He was "a real good-looking guy, kind of a John Wayne character in his presence and command for respect," says McCarver. "He would have a way of telling you when you did something or he would look at you. I got a couple of looks when I came in (the dugout) and slammed my bat down. Believe me, you didn't want to get one of those looks."[18]

"Although he was shy off the field, shy in conversations, Ken had the poise of a leader in the infield," recalled pitcher Jim Brosnan. Even with the veteran Musial playing first base, it was Boyer who went to the mound and offered encouragement or advice for getting a particular batter out. "It means a lot to a pitcher to hear from a guy who seemed to know exactly what he was talking about," Brosnan added. "Ken had been through it, and although he might be pointing out something you might not want to hear, you knew damn well you should hear it…That's the kind of leader he was. He said the right thing with a few words."[19]

"He was not a rah-rah guy," says pitcher Tommy John, a later teammate with the Chicago White Sox. "He just played the game hard. Maybe it wasn't what he said, but it was what he *didn't* say. There was something about him. It's hard to explain, but something about him (showed) that he was a leader."[20]

McCarver played with the Cardinals for parts of six seasons from 1959 to 1965. He saw Musial and Boyer as two distinct figures on the team.

> Musial was the star, but Kenny was the leader, no doubt about it. Kenny, all he had to do was be there. It's that certain leadership quality that some guys have and other guys don't have a clue about. Not that Kenny had a clue about it because it was just by his very nature—showing up, being there. He had such a countenance to him. It was regal in many ways. I can't stress that enough either. Regal

countenance are two words that I would use for Kenny. More than Stan, because Stan had an *iconic* kind of countenance. There was only one Musial; nobody ever tried to be Stan Musial. And nobody ever tried to be Kenny Boyer either. But Kenny had those engrained leadership qualities. You can't develop those; it's just there. Certain people have them and Kenny did.[21]

Boyer's leadership transcended the field. He acted as an intermediary between the players and management and served as the club's official player representative with the fledgling Major League Baseball Players Association from 1960 to 1965. "Obviously, the players didn't have the clout in those days that they have now," says McCarver. "So Kenny was a very, very important man between management and the players."[22]

His teammates held such esteem for him that his lead was followed without question. Left fielder Lou Brock, who joined the club in 1964, paid close attention to him at third base. He would see Ken wiggle his glove behind his back and Brock would shift himself with each movement, believing the veteran was helping position him better. When he learned Brock was following his directions, Boyer admitted the glove wiggling was nothing more than "a crazy habit I have."[23]

During a frustrating 1965 season, an entertaining clubhouse kangaroo court session involving relief pitcher Barney Schultz was interrupted by coach Mickey Vernon. He relayed orders from manager Red Schoendienst that infield practice would start in fifteen minutes. "Nuts to Red," one player said. Another laughed at the remark. Though said in jest, it was an uncomfortable and rebellious moment for the coach. Up to this point, the team captain had been silent and unnoticed by writer George Vecsey. Boyer then "stood up and stretched, very casually, and moved toward the door. 'Come on,' he said, in a very soft voice. 'We can get Barney tonight on the plane to LA.' The clubhouse was empty in two minutes. Ken Boyer was the leader of the Cardinals."[24]

Indeed, even after he was traded six years later, his character and leadership left an indelible impression on his teammates. McCarver says:

The most endearing thing about Kenny was that years after we left and went to other teams…everyone to a man kept referring to him, even after his playing days were over, as Captain. In baseball, it's a nebulous term. It doesn't mean a lot. It does in football, but it doesn't in baseball. But it did with Ken Boyer. It has the impact, I think. And I still refer to him as Captain. Those on the Cardinals team know exactly to whom I'm referring. That's in an age where Musial was the most iconic names in the game or one of the top five. To be referred to as Captain for such a long period of time after that Musial era I think is really a trememdous sign of respect. And it was certainly that way when it pertained to Kenny.[25]

THE CARDINALS WON TWO OF THREE at Los Angeles as Ken's hit streak reached 20 games with a home run on the first of September. Two nights later, he blasted a three-run shot off Don Drysdale, his 27th of the season—eclipsing his major-league high in 1956—to beat the second-place Dodgers, 5-3. He singled in his last plate appearance at San Francisco to extend it 25 games as St. Louis dropped two of three to the league leaders on Labor Day. The club flew to Milwaukee where the Braves, having tied the Dodgers for second place, hoped to gain more ground in the pennant race. Boyer had two safeties in each game of the series, including a two-run single in the finale on September 10 that tied it in the seventh inning. Cunningham, chasing Aaron for the batting title in the final weeks of the season, followed with an RBI single to put St. Louis ahead. Aaron responded in Milwaukee's half with a double that plated two runs and Johnny Logan singled in another to rally, 7-4. With two outs in the ninth, seventeen-year-old bonus baby Tim McCarver, a recent call-up from the minors, pinch-hit and flew out to right field in his major-league debut.

The Redbirds concluded their last road series of the season at Chicago beginning September 11. Cubs right-hander Bob Anderson held them to one hit through eight innings before Cunningham singled, pinch-runner White stole second, and Boyer singled to left for their only run in the 2-1 loss. The next afternoon, Ken smashed his 28th home run off lefty Art Ceccarelli to give the Cardinals a two-run lead. He tallied again with a triple to right and scored on an error. Gibson struck out 10 and allowed six hits for his second major-league victory, 6-4.

The 29-game consecutive hit streak was now the longest in the majors since Musial had a 30-game stretch in 1950. In that span, Ken batted .350 in 126 plate appearances with eight homers and 23 RBIs, slugging .607 with an OPS of .996.[26] He had the opportunity to match The Man's mark against Glen Hobbie, who was seeking his 15th win on September 13. But the Chicago right-hander scattered three singles in the first four innings while his teammates pounded rookie starter Tom Hughes and three relievers with two home runs and 10 more hits to subdue the Redbirds, 8-0. Ken flied out, grounded out, and hit into two force outs, including the final at-bat of the game. The streak fell four games short of the club record set by Rogers Hornsby in 1922. A more extensive 46-game streak for reaching base safely also ended that stretched back to July 26. It ranks as the ninth-longest in franchise history through the 2015 season.[27] Once again, Boyer picked up where he left off the next day and hit safely in six straight games through September 22.

If not for wearing the collar in the second game of the August 9 doubleheader with Philadelphia and Hobbie's masterful performance, perhaps Ken could have hit safely in 46 straight games. It would have surpassed the National League record of 45 set by Wee Willie Keeler of the Baltimore Orioles in the 1896 and 1897 seasons and ranked second to the historic 56-game major-league record established in 1941 by Joe DiMaggio.[28]

The stalwart Musial was unable to contribute to the team's offense as he had in past seasons. A combination of age, the off-season goodwill trip to Japan, and prescribed inactivity in spring training left him out of shape when the 1959 campaign began. He struggled early with his timing at the plate and Hemus rested him for extended periods, further complicating his ability to break out of the slide with more consistent play. Musial's average fell to .245 the first week of June, his worst slump in 12 years. He hinted it might be his last season. "If I can't play regularly, hit well over .300, and not help the club, I don't want to embarrass the Cardinals or myself." His playing time further diminished in early August and rumors persisted of his imminent retirement or even his trade. In a hastily arranged press conference, it was announced that Musial would indeed return in 1960. But it was evident that Hemus preferred the youth movement instituted by ownership and the front office; perhaps he had lost confidence in Musial as well. Stan was limited to occasional starts and pinch-hitting duties the remainder of the season. He finished at .255 with 14 home runs and 44 RBIs, all career lows.[29]

Playing the last five games of the season against two of the best clubs in the National League, the Cardinals were in an excellent position to affect the outcome of the tight race. The Dodgers were tied with Milwaukee for the league lead and the Giants were just a game behind as St. Louis hosted Los Angeles on September 22. It was a slugfest from the start with both teams clubbing 14 hits each in the contest. St. Louis led, 4-3, after both starters—Jackson for the Redbirds and Koufax for the Dodgers—were knocked out in the first inning. Hemus was ejected for the eighth time during the season and Hal Smith blasted a grand slam in the frame. The Dodgers took the lead in the third, but the Cardinals responded with singles by Boyer and Musial and a three-run homer by Flood in their half to reclaim it. A three-run shot by Gil Hodges in the ninth made it close, but Lindy McDaniel recovered for the save in the 11-10 victory. With Milwaukee's win at Pittsburgh and Chicago's comeback over San Francisco, the Braves took sole possession of first place and the Giants fell two games out.

St. Louis was shut out on five hits by Roger Craig the next evening, 3-0, and LA regained its first-place tie with Milwaukee. Ken struck out three times against the tall right-hander. Next came the Giants, still two games behind, to close the season in a three-game set at Busch Stadium beginning September 26. With his club's pennant chances on the line, former Redbird Sam Jones handcuffed the Cardinals' bats through seven innings without allowing a hit. Threatening winds and torrential rain halted the game in the top of the eighth and San Francisco earned a 4-0 victory. But the next afternoon, St. Louis beat them in a doubleheader sweep, coming from behind to take the opener, 2-1, and bludgeoning the Giants with 14 hits in the finale, 14-8. The Dodgers advanced to the one-game playoff and defeated Milwaukee to clinch the pennant.[30]

Ken was collared in his last 10 plate appearances and sat out the final game of the season. The slump dropped him out of the top five National League batters and he finished with a .309 average, eighth-best in the circuit. He, Cunningham (.345, second-best in the NL), and White (.302) gave the Cardinals a trio of .300 hitters for the first time since 1954. Boyer's 28 home runs and 94 RBIs led the team and he finished tenth in the voting for the league's Most Valuable Player. Defensively, he won his second Gold Glove and led NL third basemen in turning the most double plays and was third in putouts and assists. "He can do everything," insisted Hemus. "He can run, throw, field, and hit for distance and average. What more do you want?"[31]

St. Louis finished in seventh place and 16 games out of first with a record of 71-83, almost identical to their mark the previous season. While the offense was the second-best in the league (.269), third in on-base percentage (.333), and fourth in slugging (.400), it was near the bottom in home runs. "We won't stand pat with this club," Hemus declared toward the end of the season. "We need someone else to back up Boyer next year."

A pitching staff that finished last in earned-run average (4.34) was another concern. Jackson and McDaniel led the club with 14 victories each, though McDaniel spent most of the season in the bullpen where he saved 15 games, best in the league. Promising young starters Broglio and Gary Blaylock and veteran Mizell failed to live up to expectations. Though it had been a disappointing season, the pieces of a future championship team were slowly being put into place with the additions of White and Gibson.[32]

KEN WAS NOW A RISING STAR in the National League. He took an early interest in his endorsement potential when he signed a two-year contract with Frank Scott Associates during his second big-league season in August 1956. A former traveling secretary for the New York Yankees, Scott knew players could earn more than just token items like wristwatches for product endorsements, personal appearances, and speaking engagements. During the 1950s and 1960s, he built a clientele of 91 players, including Joe DiMaggio, Mickey Mantle, Willie Mays, Hank Aaron, and Yogi Berra. Scott pursued opportunities for his clients and took a ten percent cut for his services.[33]

Boyer became a member of the Baseball Advisory Board for the St. Louis-based Rawlings Sporting Goods Company in 1959 and remained one through 1966. Rawlings produced the Ken Boyer TG 15 Trap-Eze model infielder's glove (and later the Ken Boyer TT20) and used his name and image for promotional photos and advertisements in *The Sporting News, Boy's Life,* and other publications. In 1962, he became a vice-president and spokesman for the Yoo-Hoo chocolate drink company when it first came to Missouri. After agreeing to endorse Vitalis hair tonic, his crewcut gave way to thicker hair during the winter of 1962–63. "You remember Samson," he said of the Biblical character whose source of incredible strength was the length of his hair. "I don't want to lose any power."[34]

Ken had a busy off-season. He joined teammate Hal Smith for a radio fundraiser on KMOX to benefit the United Fund of Greater St. Louis on October 1. A week later, he barnstormed with a team of NL stars featuring Mays, Aaron, Hodges, Bill Mazeroski and Roy Face of the Pirates, Johnny Antonelli and Hobie Landrith of the Giants, and Don Newcombe of the Redlegs. They faced an American League team that included Mantle, Harvey Kuenn of the Detroit Tigers, Bob Shaw of the Chicago White Sox, and Hoyt Wilhelm and Bob Nieman of the Baltimore Orioles in exhibitions at Philadelphia, Syracuse, and Rochester, New York. On October 18, Ken returned to Buffs Stadium in Houston (now called Busch Stadium) and hit a grand slam over the right-center field fence in a 6-0 victory over another team of AL players.[35] He joined the banquet circuit a month later, accepting the Good Sportsmanship Award from the YMCA Industrial Athletic Association and the "Outstanding Sports Figure of 1959" award at the tenth annual Sports Celebrity Night Dinner held by The Benevolent and Protective Order of Elks Lodge No. 9 in St. Louis.[36]

Ken flew to Los Angeles for the taping of a new television show called *Home Run Derby*. Each thirty-minute episode featured two home run hitters competing for the chance to win $2,000. The contest lasted nine innings and each batter was given three outs. A called or swinging strike or any ball not hit out of the park—including a foul—was considered an out. The player with the most round-trippers was the winner and returned to face a new challenger in the next episode. The show was filmed at Wrigley Field, former home of the Los Angeles

Angels, a minor-league club in the Pacific Coast League. The host and show creator was Mark Scott, a former broadcaster in the PCL and one-time voice of the Cincinnati Redlegs. While one player batted, the other sat beside Scott, who would ask questions or engage in brief conversations between his play-by-play commentary.[37]

Boyer appeared in the sixth episode opposite returning contestant Harmon Killebrew of the Washington Senators, who had won two in a row over Mickey Mantle and Rocky Colavito. "I only hope I can hit one more than Harm here today," he told Scott during the introductions. Batting in the bottom of the first inning, the Senators slugger cracked a home run on the first pitch he saw. "Mantle told me that when he hits one, it just keeps going," said Ken. "He's a strong boy." In the top of the fourth, the host complemented Killebrew on his one-run lead. "Well, of course, that one run doesn't look too sure there," he replied. "I'm afraid Ken's gonna break out any minute here." Sure enough he did, smashing one over the ivy-covered left-field wall to tie it. Killebrew went ahead in the fifth, but Boyer countered in the sixth to knot it once again.

The score remained tied until the ninth inning when Ken drove a pitch over the left-field corner to go ahead, 3-2. With Killebrew at the plate and one out, Boyer turned to Scott and asked, "You don't mind if I sit here with my fingers crossed?" After Killebrew popped up on the next pitch, he added, "If you don't mind, I think I'll cross a few more fingers." Killebrew grounded foul for the final out, giving Boyer the victory and a check for $2,000. He became the first National League player to win *Home Run Derby*.

Ken provided Scott with a few interesting and delightful comments over the course of the episode. The host asked if he patterned his batting style after anyone. "No, I've tried not to. I've altered my stance quite a bit since I first come up, but I haven't tried to copy anybody in particular, no." After Boyer hit the go-ahead homer that won the contest, Scott asked if he was thinking it might be a foul ball instead. He replied honestly, "No, to tell you the truth, a man gets a little nervous in these things and I really don't know what I was thinking about. I guess I'm human." When Killebrew missed a pitch and grounded out in the sixth, Boyer remarked, "Missing those kind make you say words you're not supposed to say."[38]

Ken returned for the seventh episode against Hank Aaron of the Braves. The future home run king homered twice in the top of the first inning, leading Boyer to say in admiration, "He's mean." With two outs in his half, Ken responded with back-to-back clouts that tied the score. Aaron smiled and shook his head. "It's gonna be real tough, I can see that." Boyer took the lead with round-trippers in the third, fourth, and fifth innings to give himself a 6-3 cushion. Still, he knew it wasn't enough against his opponent. "I tell you, I just don't feel secure until I hit about 12 or 15." Aaron came back even with him in the seventh and went ahead with three homers, including back-to-back blasts in the eighth. Boyer flied out and grounded out twice in the ninth to lose, 9-6. Though he came out on the losing end, he still received a consolation prize of $1,000 and took home a total of $3,000 for two days in sunny California.[39]

Twenty-six episodes of *Home Run Derby* were produced during the winter of 1959–60. The show debuted in April 1960 and featured 302 home runs by 19 contestants, who received a total of $84,500 in prize money. Though it was popular, *Home Run Derby* was canceled following the untimely death of its creator and host, Mark Scott, who had a sudden and fatal heart attack three months later at the age of forty-five.[40]

Between his regular hunting trips, Ken kept busy with other off-season activities. He and teammates Hal Smith and Wilmer Mizell held a two-day, indoor baseball clinic in St. Louis, instructing youngsters and teens while it snowed outside. They helped Joe Cunningham christen his new bowling alley south of the city with a game against staff members of the KMOX radio station.[41] He also served as chief instructor at the year-round Ken Boyer Baseball School in Tampa, Florida, operated by the National Baseball Placement Bureau. He typically worked with students in January and February before the start of spring training.[42] That winter, he supervised construction of his family's new $50,000 two-acre, ranch-style house at 4 Nob Hill Drive in the Spanish Lake community in north St. Louis County.[43]

An opportunity presented itself in November 1959 for him to take part in a worthy cause. As a young athlete, he was recommended to serve as chairman for the St. Louis Area Chapter of the National Multiple Sclerosis Society's annual fundraising campaign. Multiple

Sclerosis is a disease that affects the central nervous system, disrupting the transmission of signals within the brain and to other parts of the body. Ken saw young men in the Veterans Hospital at Jefferson Barracks in St. Louis who were confined to wheelchairs and unable to do for themselves. It made him consider what would happen to his wife and children should something ever happened to him. He accepted the role of fundraising chairman and learned as much as he could about the disease from patients and physicians.

Boyer became an active leader, attending luncheons, banquets, and other fundraising gatherings throughout the St. Louis area, eastern Missouri, and southern Illinois. He made radio and television appearances to recruit volunteers and asked teammates and local sports personalities to help bring awareness of the disease and solicit funds for research and treatment. His involvement was more than he originally intended. "But after you see the people afflicted with this disease and meet their families and learn how nice they are, how dedicated the relatives of MS victims are, you can't lose interest," he explained. Ken served as campaign chairman for at least eight years, even after his trade from St. Louis. Once asked if the hardships of the patients and their families were disheartening to him personally, he disagreed and replied thoughtfully, "I'd say it enlightens you."[44]

MEANWHILE, THE CARDINALS improved themselves and added more punch to the lineup for the 1960 season with the acquisition of outfielder Bob Nieman from the Baltimore Orioles for outfielder Gene Green and minor-leaguer Chuck Staniland. They also obtained outfielder Leon Wagner and infielder Daryl Spencer from the San Francisco Giants. The bullpen was strengthened by trading outfielder Gino Cimoli and pitcher Tom Cheney for veteran hurler Ron Kline of the Pittsburgh Pirates. At the baseball winter meetings, overtures were reportedly made to the New York Yankees to acquire shortstop Clete Boyer and unite the brothers on the left side of the St. Louis infield. Manager Casey Stengel proposed a counteroffer—"Why don't they give me Ken so he can play with his brother for us?"[45]

The 1959 Cardinals led the National League with 1,166 runners left on base, an average of nearly eight players stranded per game. Reflecting on the club's past failures, Boyer remarked, "We beat ourselves a lot last year. We left too many men on base. With the extra power, we've got to do better next year than we did in 1959 when we were pretty bad at times." Solly Hemus was certain his team captain would provide much of that power. "I expect Boyer to have his best season. He'll hit at least 35 home runs for us and drive in more than 100 runs. I'm confident of that."[46]

Ken signed a new contract in early February 1960 estimated at about $35,000. During the press conference, he played it up for the photographers, confidently leaning back in Bing Devine's chair, feet crossed and propped on top of his desk with a cigar in his mouth, admiring his contract. Devine reiterated that Boyer was "one of the five best players in the National League in all-around ability" and with his second straight productive season, "he has turned the corner as a mature, top-drawer player and will stay among the best in the league for a long time."[47]

Musial's future with the club, however, remained uncertain. He worked hard over the winter to report for spring training in better physical shape than the previous spring. But many—including his manager—had already written him off and considered his best days behind him. "An era of sorts has ended for the Cardinals," wrote John P. Carmichael of the *Chicago Daily News*. "Stan Musial no longer carries them; they carry him. Obviously this is not from choice, but the 1960 team has been fashioned to win, if possible, without the Musial of yesterday." Hemus himself acknowledged that "the man on our club now is Ken Boyer. A lot of teams would like him, but if I ever traded him, I might just as well take Highway 66 right out of St. Louis...and run, not walk."[48]

The Cardinals were the best club in the Grapefruit League with an 18-8 record, but things went badly once the regular season started. They dropped the first five games in San Francisco and Los Angeles and found themselves in last place. Ken went without a hit in his first eight plate appearances until he clubbed a home run off Johnny Podres of the Dodgers on April 14, then hit safely in eight straight games. The Redbirds snapped the losing streak in their home opener on the nineteenth when Musial doubled home two runs and White homered in a 5-2 triumph. They won nine out of 12 in the inaugural homestand and climbed to the first division, 3 ½ games behind the league-leading Pittsburgh Pirates. Against the Dodgers on the twenty-third, Boyer, White, and Spencer each had three safeties and Ken smashed two round-trippers and drove in five runs. Two more blasts against Los Angeles and San Francisco put him in the National League lead for home runs, giving him 11 RBIs in four days and raising his average to a season-high .343.[49]

Though successful at home, the team struggled away from St. Louis in April and May, losing 16 of their first 19 road games. The next trip had a foreboding start when it took a push from the Philadelphia Phillies' team bus to get their own bus going to the airport, then one of the plane's engines caught fire after landing in Cincinnati. An eight-game skid dropped them to seventh place and eight back of San Francisco. Hemus was under scrutiny for questionable decisions like putting first baseman Bill White in center field and benching Curt Flood, taking his closer Lindy McDaniel out of the bullpen and putting him back in the starting rotation, and shortstop Daryl Spencer and second baseman Alex Grammas switching positions.

Though Hemus was reportedly in danger of being fired, Ken could offer him little support. A 2-for-32 slide had plunged his average 129 points to a season-low .214. The slump, coupled with Kathleen's fourth pregnancy and wanting to live up to his higher salary, weighed on his mind, according to teammate Larry Jackson. "It was the first time I've ever seen him show his concern. When he came out of that slump, though, he was terrific."[50]

A lineup move from cleanup to leadoff offered a temporary fix in the opener of a doubleheader at Wrigley Field on May 15. Boyer smashed two home runs and drove in three runs in a 6-1 victory that ended the losing streak and possibly saved Hemus's job. But St. Louis lost the second game when right-hander Don Cardwell tossed a no-hitter—the first thrown against the team in forty-one years—to beat them, 4-0.

In the middle of May, Devine reshuffled the pitching staff, demoting Bob Gibson to the minors and promoting nineteen-year-old bonus baby left-hander Ray Sadecki, then signing veteran lefty Curt Simmons, who had been released by Philadelphia.[51] Slowly, Boyer built momentum starting with a weekend series against the third-place Cincinnati Reds back at Busch Stadium that steadily raised his average. After wearing the collar in the opener and making an error that allowed the eventual tying run on base the next day, he came to the plate in the ninth inning with the bases loaded and the score tied on May 21. He rapped a grounder that bounced off the glove of third baseman Willie "Puddin' Head" Jones and plated the winning run in the 6-5 victory.

In the first game of a Sunday twin bill the next day, he tripled and scored the Redbirds' first run while Musial tied it with an eighth-inning home run and Spencer won it on a blast of his own in the ninth, 5-4. Ken homered twice off Warren Spahn to beat the Braves, 5-3, on May 25. In that same game, thirty-nine-year-old pinch-hitter George Crowe hit his first home run of the season—and the 11th pinch-hit homer of his eight-year major-league career—off reliever Don McMahon. It set a new record for pinch-hit blasts in the majors.[52] Two days later, Boyer smashed a leadoff triple, tallied their first run, and clouted a two-run shot to edge the league-leading Giants, 5-4.[53]

A key acquisition on May 28 allowed Hemus to settle on a consistent lineup. Minor-league second baseman Julian Javier was obtained from Pittsburgh for Mizell and started at that position for the Cardinals. This four-player deal also included minor-league pitcher Ed Bauta leaving the Pirates organization with utilityman Dick Gray transferring from the St. Louis roster. Spencer moved back to short, White to first base, and Flood to center field, giving the club a better defensive alignment. Nieman's offensive outburst enabled him to take over left field when both Musial and Wagner faltered.

The Redbirds flew to the West Coast and took two of three from the Dodgers and split a four-game set with the Giants. On Memorial Day, they pounded 16 hits off Don Drysdale and four relievers led by White, who hit two homers and drove in six runs, as they bludgeoned the Dodgers, 15-3. St. Louis moved into fifth place with a 9-4 victory in the finale of the Giants series on June 5. Boyer had three safeties and scored three runs, raising his average to .253.

While in San Francisco, Ken and teammates Smith, Grammas, and Simmons had the opportunity to visit the infamous federal penitentiary at Alcatraz Island in the Bay. They spent a few hours touring the prison and talking with inmates who were baseball fans. Before leaving on the trip, Boyer left behind a note for Jim Toomey, the

Cardinals traveling secretary, that deadpanned: "Hal Smith, Grammas, and Boyer are going to Alcatraz."⁵⁴

Ken had a dry sense of humor. During a game with the Philadelphia Phillies on May 19, 1965, the ticket window outside Busch Stadium was robbed. One of the robbers fired his gun and the bullet deflected off a steel girder, shot across the diamond, and grazed the neck of a thirteen-year-old girl sitting along the third-base line. Someone asked Boyer if the spent bullet went past him at third base. Having struck out three times that day against future Hall of Fame pitcher Jim Bunning, he replied, "I haven't even seen Bunning's curve yet."⁵⁵

Boyer enjoyed teasing his friends and teammates. "Kenny was one of the great agitators," says Tim McCarver, who remembered Boyer kidding him about the size of his head and calling him "Goathead." "If he knew you were thin-skinned, you could be in a lot of trouble," recalls friend and former minor-league trainer Lee Landers. He recalled one spring training when Ken's former teammate and fellow minor-league manager Joe Cunningham asked him to tell the young players what type of outfielder he was in the majors. "Kenny looked at him, and he says, 'Guys, he was the worst excuse for an outfielder I've ever seen in my life. Why they put him out there...' It just deflated Joe. Then he says, 'But he was the fanciest fielding first baseman I've ever seen.' Joe lightened up. That was Kenny."⁵⁶

Not even Stan Musial was spared Boyer's biting wit. While Ken was getting a rubdown on the trainer's table, Musial told Doc Bauman that he needed one too and was in a hurry. Because Musial was the veteran, Ken crawled off the table and sat on a stool to wait for his turn again. Musial was on the table again a few days later when Gussie Busch walked in complaining about his bad back. Bauman quickly called for Boyer in the clubhouse, who walked in to see Musial getting off the table for the team owner. "Well, well," said Ken. "I've finally seen the day when somebody ran Stan the Man off the table." He grabbed the stool and placed it beside the table. "Here you are, Stanley. You just sit right here. That's where I had to sit the other day."⁵⁷

He was also a pratical joker, though his victims rarely suspected him as the culprit. "You never knew what you were going to find in your glass if you went to the restroom," says Landers. "That's why you made sure to (pour it) down the hatch before you left it there."

When Ken later managed the Cardinals' Triple-A club, he moved home plate a few feet out of line before the start of a game. It wasn't until the first pitch was thrown that future American League umpire Dale Ford realized what had been done. It took over forty years before he figured out Boyer had pulled the prank. "That was funny," recalls Landers. "Ken was always doing something."[58]

Boyer put together a seven-game hitting streak that included home runs in back-to-back victories over the league-leading Pittsburgh Pirates. The Cardinals beat them three out of four, then traveled to Cincinnati and swept a three-game set over the Reds in mid-June to climb to fourth place. He smashed a two-run homer that gave St. Louis an early lead in the opener and had a two-RBI single in the finale. Before the trading deadline on June 15, they acquired veteran outfielder Walt "Moose" Moryn from the Cubs and demoted the slumping Wagner to the minors.[59] The Redbirds lost eight of their next 12 games and dropped back to fifth place.

Ken struggled the last half of June with only seven safeties in 50 at-bats, bringing his average down twenty-seven points to .249. He did hit home runs in successive games at Philadelphia on the twenty-fourth and twenty-fifth. The latter was a blast in the ninth inning that enabled Simmons to shut out his former teammates, 1-0, and win his first game since September 1, 1958. Hemus tried a move that worked a month-and-a-half earlier when Boyer was in a slump, batting him leadoff instead of cleanup. It worked once again. After Cincinnati pummeled St. Louis, 10-4, Ken singled twice and drove in a run the next night to beat them, 5-2, on June 29. He collected six hits in a July 1 doubleheader with second-place Milwaukee and knocked in four runs, three of them in the opener. Broglio won both games in relief. A 7-1 victory over Spahn and the Braves the next evening gave them four in a row and raised them to fourth place and a game above .500.[60]

A leg injury sidelined the hot-hitting Nieman in the middle of June. Languishing on the bench for a month, Musial finally returned to the starting lineup after Hemus's efforts to find any other replacement over the next week failed. Stan's forced exile had been the subject of heated debate in the St. Louis press and revived rumors of his impending trade or retirement. Playing in left field every day, the thirty-nine-year-old Musial soon flourished, raising his average fifty-eight points to .300 before the All-Star break.[61]

Just when Ken started hitting again, an abdominal muscle tear threatened to stall him. He made it through both games of the Fourth of July doubleheader with the Dodgers despite the pain and had an RBI single and tallied two runs to win the opener, 6-2. But he sat out a subsequent two-game series at Chicago as the Redbirds lost the finale, 10-1, and fell back to fifth place with a record of 38-38. It would be the last time they would fall that far the remainder of the season. They took the first three of a four-game West Coast trip highlighted by Boyer's ninth-inning home run off Dodgers reliever Larry Sherry—his 20th of the season, third-best in the league—in a come-from-behind, 4-3 triumph on July 9. St. Louis entered the five-day All-Star break tied with San Francisco for fourth place, only a half-game out of third, and 8½ behind the league-leading Pittsburgh Pirates.[62]

The Cardinals' success surprised many pre-season pundits who thought they would be mired in the second division. Though the offense wasn't as potent as the club hoped, the pitching had exceeded expectations. Both were fourth-best in the National League with a .256 batting average and 3.89 earned-run average, respectively, and the offense ranked fifth in home runs with 70. Ken's home run prowess was credited for the turnaround, but there was still concern it wouldn't be enough to carry them the rest of the season. "The big man now is Kenny Boyer," wrote Dick Young in *The Sporting News*. "When he hits, the Cards jump, but the pitching is too thin for them to jump high."[63]

KEN WAS SELECTED as a reserve on the All-Star team along with Jackson, White, McDaniel, and Hemus as third-base coach. Musial was a sentimental choice for the final roster spot. The first contest was held at Municipal Stadium in Kansas City on July 11. During the festivities, Yogi Berra of the Yankees joked with Boyer that his younger brother Clete said to call him the next time he was in New York. Alluding to Ken's recent hitting woes, Berra teased, "He wants to give you some batting tips." (At the time, Ken was batting .262 and Clete .241.) With the National League ahead, 5-1, Boyer replaced Eddie Mathews at third base in the bottom of the seventh inning.

The American League made it a close game with a two-run homer by Al Kaline of the Detroit Tigers in the eighth. Ken walked with two outs in the ninth and sprinted to third on an errant pick-off attempt, but was sent back to second after a fan interfered with the play. A lineout by Roberto Clemente made the extra score irrelevant and the NL won, 5-3.

The muscle tear continued to trouble Boyer. Prior to the second All-Star Game at Yankee Stadium two days later, he told National League skipper Walter Alston he was available as a defensive replacement, though he might be ineffective at the plate. Once again, he substituted for Mathews in the seventh inning and batted in the ninth. The NL led, 4-0, and he added to it with a two-run blast off Cleveland Indians right-hander Gary Bell, his first home run in 11 All-Star plate appearances. All six runs were tallied on homers, including Musial's as a pinch-hitter in the seventh, tying an All-Star Game record. McDaniel came in and finished the 6-0 shutout victory.[64]

Enjoying a breakout season for the Cardinals, Broglio started the second-half with a one-hitter and 14 strikeouts over the Chicago Cubs on July 15. Ken singled and doubled and had an RBI in the 6-0 triumph. The worsening pain from his injury finally forced him to the bench for a week and limited him to pinch-hitting and late-inning defense. The Redbirds won eight of the next 10 games and were four behind Pittsburgh and Milwaukee, who were tied for first. A 3-7 record led to starting pitcher Ron Kline's demotion to the bullpen and the fireballing Gibson's return from the minors as both a fifth starter and a long reliever.[65] With the chance to gain even more ground, St. Louis instead was swept by the Pirates in three games at Busch Stadium and fell seven games back. Returning to the starting lineup but hitless in the finale of the Pittsburgh series, Boyer led the club with three safeties and three RBIs against the Philadelphia Phillies on July 29. Broglio dominated with a five-hit effort and 12 strikeouts in the 3-0 shutout.[66]

The victory sparked a seven-game winning streak—their longest of the season—and propelled the Cardinals to their best month of the season in August. After completing a four-game sweep over the Phillies that featured a 2-for-4 performance from Boyer and his first home run since the All-Star Game, they picked up 3 ½ games in the standings. Next came the second-place Milwaukee Braves for a three-game set. Medication eased the inflammation in his abdomen and his bat caught fire. He smacked six hits, including a two-run homer off Spahn as part of his 3-for-5 evening, and plated three runs in the 13-8 win on August 3. As his wife Kathleen delivered their fourth child, Ken had an RBI single in Sadecki's six-hit, 4-2 victory the next evening. He rushed to the hospital afterward to see his new daughter, Jane Rene Boyer. St. Louis swept the series, took second place from Milwaukee, and were 3 ½ back of Pittsburgh.[67]

Splitting a four-game series with Cincinnati and taking four straight over the Reds and Phillies, the Redbirds traveled to Pittsburgh for an important five-game series with the league leaders beginning August 11. Now five games out of first, a sweep was unlikely, but there was hope for chipping away at their formidable lead. "We're here with the idea of beating the Pirates and tightening the race," said Hemus. "We know we have to do something about it before we leave town." In the opener, right-hander Bob Friend was anything but to Boyer in his first three plate appearances. He finally stroked a two-out single in the ninth with the score tied, 1-1. Musial doubled to right field and Ken tried scoring the go-ahead run, but was thrown out at the plate. Stan later won it with a two-run homer in the twelfth, 3-2. The next night, Boyer smashed a three-run homer—his 25th of the season—to give his club a lead it never relinquished in a 9-2 victory.

The Cardinals were now three games behind the Pirates. But Pittsburgh recovered and won the next three, including a Sunday doubleheader in which Ken had a 3-for-5 performance and two doubles in an 11-inning, 3-2 loss in the finale. The fact that the team left the Steel City six games back and a half-game away from third place was almost irrelevant when one of the plane's propellers stopped working in flight, forcing them to land and wait three hours for a substitute plane to carry them back to St. Louis.[68]

The Cardinals returned home and lost four of their next five games, dropping to fourth place. Ken extended his personal hit streak to 12 games and raised his average to .295 until Podres of the Dodgers held them to three hits in a pitching duel with Jackson on August 19. Jackson prevailed when Gibson scored as a pinch-runner with two outs in the bottom of the ninth and snapped the six-game losing skid.

Boyer experienced a 5-for-32 slump the last two weeks of August that brought his average down to .282. During the course of two games, he struck out in five consecutive plate appearances against Los Angeles—two short of the major-league record at that time—before rapping an RBI double to left field in the Redbirds' 2-0 victory on August 21. They beat Pittsburgh in a weekend series at home three straight to come within 5 ½ games of the league leaders and trail second-place Milwaukee by one percentage point.[69]

The Cardinals and Braves exchanged second place seven times in September. Beginning with two hits off Spahn in a 10-0 loss on August 30, Ken broke out of his funk and started pounding the ball once again, doubling twice and scoring in a 2-1 win at Cincinnati the next evening. It was his best month of the season with 40 hits at a .385 clip, earning him National League Player of the Month honors. He homered in successive games against the Chicago Cubs and smashed his 29th at Wrigley Field on September 5, a new career high, as St. Louis won five straight (with one tie) and reclaimed second place. Boyer hit safely in his next 14 games, his longest streak of the season. A 6-2 defeat to San Francisco on the sixteenth dropped the Redbirds back to third. Despite fouling a pitch off his instep, he had three of their five hits off right-hander Jack Sanford—including his 30th home run—to beat the Giants, 4-1, the next afternoon. The Cardinals reclaimed second place and were 5 ½ back of Pittsburgh. Two doubles and two runs scored by Boyer helped Broglio win his 20th game on September 18. Two more safeties the next evening against the Dodgers brought his average over .300 for the first time since May 2.[70]

The Cardinals' four-game win streak coincided with the Pirates' six-game string, countering their efforts to make up ground in the standings. Drysdale and Podres silenced Ken's bat in an extra-inning, 5-3 loss, ending both his and the club's streaks. Pittsburgh dropped three straight at Milwaukee toward the end of September. Despite Boyer's two triples and two runs scored, the Redbirds couldn't take advantage and lost at Chicago, 5-4. Facing elimination, a six-hit shutout by Glen Hobbie of the Cubs on September 25 enabled the Pirates to clinch the National League title.[71]

The 5-0 defeat also knocked St. Louis out of second place. The free fall continued as the club lost five of the last six games. They finished third with a record of 86-68, two games behind Milwaukee and nine back of Pittsburgh. Ken ended the season hitting safely in eight of his last nine games and batting .304 with 26 doubles, 10 triples, and 97 runs batted in. While he didn't hit 35 home runs as Hemus predicted, he come close, swatting his career-high 32nd round-tripper on September 28. Boyer was among the league leaders in most offensive categories and finished third in slugging (.562), fourth in homers, and fifth in batting average and RBIs. He also won his third straight Gold Glove at third base and placed sixth in the balloting for Most Valuable Player.[72]

Chapter Eight

All This Integration

Ken Boyer was coming into his own as leader of the St. Louis Cardinals. Over the past three seasons, he averaged 28 home runs, 94 RBIs, and 94 runs scored at a .307 clip. He was seeking a raise to $55,000 a year when general manager Bing Devine countered with a two-year, $100,000 contract offer for the 1961–62 seasons. This was an era when multi-year deals were rare—even for star players—but Devine felt an exception was warranted in Boyer's case and received Gussie Busch's reluctant approval. It was a unique way to acknowledge his production and value to the club. "We recognize this is an unusual procedure," said Devine, "but Ken, like Musial, is an unusual ballplayer." Boyer appeared for the press conference with a noticeable bruise under his right eye. He was evasive about the cause when questioned by the writers, first attributing it to "a bad hop" and then running into a door. Eventually, he confessed it came from playing with his eighteen-month-old son Danny.[1]

Ken's financial success enabled him to pursue opportunities outside baseball. He became a part-owner in Ken Boyer's Travel Inn, a 52-room motel on Route 66 in Springfield, Missouri, sixty-seven miles east of his hometown of Alba.[2] In 1961, he invested in a real estate company called Consolidated Investment Associates that purchased twenty-two apartment buildings on the south side of Chicago. Among its investors were eighty major-league players, six of whom served on the board of directors, including Boyer. "Each building is a separate corporation," he explained. "This year alone, we've added three buildings. It looks good. I've also had about half a dozen other stocks and never had a loser."³

His confident outlook changed a year later. Building, housing, and fire prevention code violations were discovered in several buildings. As a result, the city withheld rent payments to welfare recipients. Under investigation by the state of Illinois, CIA founder Patrick Wagner admitted that unregistered stock certificates had been sold to investors, a violation of state and federal laws. Ken was unaware of the company's dealings and never attended a board meeting. "I've always been led to believe that the operation is on the up and up and that the property was in good repair," he said. By October 1962, the twenty-two buildings—most of them slums—had been taken over either by court-ordered receiverships, repossession, or foreclosure. Wagner fled the state and Boyer's investment (as well as the other players) was "a total loss."⁴

HOPES WERE HIGH for greater success going into spring training in 1961 following the club's third-place finish the previous season. Progress depended on the young pitching staff led by 21-game winner Ernie Broglio, 18-game winner Larry Jackson, promising southpaw Ray Sadecki, and closer Lindy McDaniel, who led the majors with 27 saves. The Cardinals brought back Red Schoendienst, who had recovered from tuberculosis and been released by the Milwaukee Braves, to serve as a part-time second baseman, pinch-hitter, and coach. Expectations were crushed when Duke Snider's splintered bat head struck Jackson's face and fractured his jaw two weeks before Opening Day. Asked by Bob Broeg of the *Post-Dispatch* what he thought of the Cardinals' chances to win the National League pennant, Ken replied, "You want my opinion with or without Jackson?"⁵

The Redbirds split the two-game opening series at Milwaukee and lost to Cincinnati in the home opener. They won the next two over the Reds, then flew to the West Coast and beat the Dodgers to claim a momentary tie for first place. Boyer's first hit of the season was a home run off Lew Burdette of the Braves on April 13. It was the only safety in his first 17 plate appearances until a game-tying triple and RBI single three days later helped beat Cincinnati, 5-3. On the eighteenth, he homered twice off right-hander Roger Craig of the Dodgers to raise his average to .217. St. Louis hammered Los Angeles with 17 hits in the finale—including four by Julian Javier, three by Joe Cunningham, two homers by Daryl Spencer, and one round-tripper by Boyer—in an 11-2 victory. The blast off Dodgers right-hander Stan Williams was his 17th career home run at the LA Coliseum, which would tie with Frank Thomas at season's end for the most hit by opposing players there.[6]

After dividing series with the Dodgers and Giants, the second-place Cardinals returned to Busch Stadium and lost five of six, falling to seventh place on May 2. Ken made strides to steadily bring up his average, but pitchers started feeding him outside pitches to avoid his power stroke. He responded by taking them to right field, a practice he resisted earlier in his major-league career. Thirteen hits in 36 at-bats raised his average to .290 despite a nagging sore shoulder. One was a ninth-inning home run that tied the game against the Philadelphia Phillies on April 30. A sore neck kept him out of the lineup on May 2 and he managed just two singles in his next 10 plate appearances. Boyer rebounded in the middle of May with five safeties in a three-game set at Philadelphia and climbed to .300 for the first time.[7]

The sixth-place Redbirds took the first of a four-game series over the Phillies and returned to .500 on May 12. Despite better pitching, the offense struggled with only five extra-base hits and nine runs scored, losing six straight on the road. Busch reaffirmed Hemus's job status and was confident the team would improve. "I still think we have a fair team," he said. "I don't think we'll win the pennant, but we ought to finish in the first division. I certainly hope so." A twin-bill sweep at Chicago halted the streak and they won five of their next seven after returning to St. Louis. Ken rapped three hits against the league-leading San Francisco Giants on May 22 and repeated it four days later with two home runs (his first in almost a month), six RBIs, and four tallies in a 12-2 drubbing of the second-place Pittsburgh Pirates. It ended a drought of no RBIs in his last 14 games.[8]

Road trips continued to be a detriment to the Cardinals. Three wins in a row at home were followed by the same number of defeats on the West Coast in late May. Boyer contributed two hits and two RBIs in a 7-6 victory at San Francisco on the first of June that knocked the Giants out of the league lead. A win at Milwaukee the next evening put St. Louis in fifth place and 5 ½ games behind the front-running Cincinnati Reds. Losing twice to the Braves and falling back to sixth, they returned home and took three from the Cubs (with one tie). Ken collected eight hits in the series and added two more with three RBIs over the Reds on June 9. The 8-4 triumph put the Cards back in fifth place and five games behind the Dodgers, who were now in first. Boyer raised his average to .321, the highest it had been all season, and cracked the top 10 in the National League batting race.[9]

By the Fourth of July, St. Louis had dropped three out of four at Cincinnati and 13 of 21 since June 15, falling to sixth place and 14 ½ games out of first. The second-best hitting club in the league relied heavily on Boyer, White, and Musial for extra-base production; when they weren't hitting, the team wasn't scoring. All three weren't hitting the long ball as frequently as they had the previous season. While Ken was consistent at the plate with seven and 10-game hit streaks, he went for extended periods without driving in a run. When he did, it was often in bunches as happened in a 6-4 loss to San Francisco on June 25. During the first game of a doubleheader, he drove in three runs with a triple and a home run.

Slumps, injuries, and unforeseen circumstances also thwarted the club. Cunningham slumped to .269 after hitting well over .300 earlier in the season. Second baseman Julian Javier went on the disabled list with a sore right thigh while White kept playing on sore ankles. Catcher Hal Smith was lost in early June to an apparent career-ending heart ailment. The pitching staff, a strength in 1960, had faltered by mid-season. Broglio had a 6-9 record and 4.12 earned-run average. Jackson, weakened from a liquid diet after having his jaw wired shut for several weeks, had won only three games with an inflated 5.47 ERA after his return in late April. McDaniel was ineffective with just four saves and a 5.84 ERA.[10]

Despite a 9-1 victory at Los Angeles that featured a new team record of three home runs by White on July 5, the Cardinals decided a change needed to be made. The next morning, it was announced that Solly Hemus had been fired and replaced by third-base coach Johnny Keane. "We feel a change is called for before an extended losing pattern becomes fixed," explained Devine.[11]

Hemus wanted to win a pennant for Busch and justify his decision to hire him two years earlier despite his lack of experience as a manager. "When you lose, you expect to get fired," he said at the time. "I hold no animosity. I appreciated the opportunity to manage the club." His feelings were unchanged over fifty years later. "We didn't get off to a very good start. We lost a lot of ball games and had too many injuries. It's just one of those things. If you don't win, they're going to fire you. That's part of life." Looking back on his team captain, he says, "Ken Boyer—I can't say enough about him because he gave me everything he had. I'd say that he still is the best third baseman that I've ever seen."[12]

Despite an inability to "leave the umpires alone," Boyer felt Hemus communicated well with his players. He disagreed with his approach of rewarding a successful player with two hundred dollars for dinner. Instead, Ken believed the same tactic could motivate someone struggling who needed the positive reinforcement even more.[13]

Keane had been a member of Hemus's coaching staff and managed him in the minors at Houston. He brought experience and a winning record at the minor-league level to the position. He was also a longtime friend of Devine when both were at Triple-A Rochester. The St. Louis native grew up as a member of the Knothole Gang and spent eight seasons as an infielder in the Cardinals farm system. Keane supported the team's advancement of young players and had managed many of them in ten seasons as the Triple-A skipper. He was Ken's first pro manager—albeit briefly—when Boyer was sent to Rochester awaiting assignment to a Class D club in 1949.[14]

When he took over, Keane felt there was "a morale problem" on the club, but "nothing that winning a few games won't cure." The Redbirds lost the first game under their new manager in a 10-1 drubbing to the Dodgers on July 6, then won three in a row in San Francisco to take their first road series of the season. Ken had three safeties, scored three runs, and knocked in three on July 8. Trailing by five runs in the fourth inning, he smashed a two-run homer to put them on the board in that game. He broke a 7-7 tie when he scored on a double by Charlie James in the eighth inning of a 9-7 victory. Boyer went 4-for-5 in the first game of a doubleheader the next day and clouted another eighth-inning comeback blast to help take the series with a 6-3 win. Losing the second tilt, St. Louis entered the All-Star break with a 36-43 record, 15 ½ games behind the league-leading Reds. They were only a half-game away from falling to seventh place.[15]

THE 30TH ALL-STAR GAME was held at Candlestick Park in San Francisco on July 11. For the third year in a row, Ken was a reserve on the National League team along with Musial, while White was elected the starting first baseman. Kathleen Boyer and Lillian Musial joined their husbands for the festivities. Ken entered the game for defense in the fourth inning and had his worst All-Star performance, striking out twice in three at-bats and committing two pivotal errors at third base. Strong, gusty winds off San Francisco Bay late in the afternoon game played havoc with other fielders as well and resulted in a record seven errors—five by the NL—in the contest.[16]

The National League was ahead in the ninth, 3-2, when former Cardinal Stu Miller of the Giants relieved Sandy Koufax with runners at first and second and one out. Facing Rocky Colavito of the Cleveland Indians, Miller went into his stretch and a strong wind gust pushed his shoulder, he recalled, "and I waved like a tree." He completed his first pitch and caught Colavito out in front swinging and missing, but the home-plate umpire belatedly called a balk and the runners advanced. (It became known as the "wind-blown balk," an exaggeration Miller declared years later: "Sounds like I got pinned against the center-field fence, for crying out loud.") Boyer botched Colavito's grounder and Al Kaline of the Detroit Tigers scored from second with the tying run.[17]

Ken tried to redeem himself with a two-out walk in the bottom of the ninth, but was stranded at second as the contest went into extra innings. In the tenth, Kaline bounced the potential third out to Boyer. The wind carried his throw to right field instead of first base, enabling Nellie Fox of the Chicago White Sox to score from first with the go-ahead run. Thankfully, his teammates rallied in their half with an RBI double by Willie Mays and a game-winning single by Roberto Clemente that plated Mays for the 5-4 victory. "I'm glad we won so I didn't have to tell you guys about that boo-boo," Ken told the writers afterward.

Keane made three significant changes going into the second-half of the season. He took struggling right-hander Jackson out of the bullpen and put him back in the starting rotation, where he excelled the rest of the way with an 11-3 record. Curt Flood was eventually installed as the starting center fielder and blossomed into a .322 hitter. Keane showed confidence and patience in hard-throwing Bob Gibson and kept him in the rotation as the young right-hander struggled to sharpen his control. In addition, he assured Musial that he was wanted—and needed—in the lineup every day.

The Cardinals began the second-half of the season with seven victories in the first nine games. They distanced themselves from the seventh-place Chicago Cubs with a four-game sweep over them during back-to-back twi-night doubleheaders in mid-July. In the opener of the July 18 doubleheader, Boyer, Cunningham, and White each had three safeties and one home run apiece to account for all but four of St. Louis' 13 hits in an 8-3 win. Another 3-for-4 night wasn't as productive for Ken two nights later as the Redbirds lost to San Francisco, 10-6. His leadoff single off Don Drysdale in the second inning helped spark a three-run uprising—and a season-high, personal 13-game hitting streak—in an eventual 10-1 victory over the second-place Dodgers on July 21. St. Louis maintained its hold on sixth place despite losing six one-run games the last week of July. Boyer's first-inning grand slam (his 15th home run of the season) and a solo shot by Charlie James in the sixth resulted in a 6-5 win at Chicago on the twenty-fifth.

The second All-Star Game was held at Fenway Park in Boston on July 31. This time, Ken sat on the bench the entire contest and watched as Colavito homered in the first inning for the American League and White tied it with an RBI single for the National League in the sixth. Musial struck out as a pinch-hitter in the fifth. After a thirty-minute rain delay, the game ended in a 1-1 tie after nine innings, the first All-Star Game to end in a deadlock.

The month of August started badly when St. Louis suffered a lopsided and embarrassing 19-0 defeat at home to Pittsburgh that tied a modern National League record for shutout losses. The Pirates plundered 24 hits from three Redbird hurlers and tallied all their runs in the first six innings. Boyer had one of four hits allowed by left-hander Harvey Haddix. It proved to be a momentary setback as the Cardinals rose to fifth place with an eight-game winning streak—their longest since 1957—that included two against the Reds, who came in just a percentage point behind the league-leading Dodgers. St. Louis took the first game on August 7 thanks to home runs by Carl Sawatski and Musial. Jackson pitched eight shutout innings to even his record at 8-8 with the 5-1 triumph.

The next evening, Ken faced 13-game winner Bob Purkey, against whom he was hitless in his last 12 plate appearances dating back exactly a year earlier. He tried a different strategy—laying off fastballs inside and off the plate—and enjoyed a 4-for-5 performance as a result. An RBI single broke a 1-1 tie in the first inning, then he followed a leadoff home run by White in the third with one of his own. He crushed a hanging curveball off the left-field scoreboard to give the Redbirds a three-run lead. After a single in the fifth and a force out in the seventh (though he scored to break a 4-4 tie), Boyer stepped to the plate in the bottom of the ninth with the game knotted once again, 5-5. Purkey's first pitch was a curveball below the knees and Ken swatted it for the game-winning homer in the 6-5 victory. "Purkey's been impossible for me more than six years," he said afterward. "I don't think I ever got four hits off him in a whole season before this."[18]

A West Coast trip in mid-August proved less successful. The Cardinals dropped three-game series to the Dodgers and Giants, then flew to Cincinnati and lost another, enabling the Reds to increase their league lead over the Dodgers to two games. St. Louis took the finale on August 20 and started another eight-game win streak. They finished the month with a 20-9 record and 10 games out of first. After a 1-for-12 slide on the trip, Boyer hit safely in his next 12 games and raised his average to .321, fifth-best in the National League. His two sacrifice flies in the late innings cushioned the 7-4 victory at Cincinnati that broke the losing skein. A week later, he blasted his 20th home run and knocked in three runs as Jackson shut out the third-place San Francisco Giants, 6-0, and won his 10th game of the season on August 27.[19]

Ken enjoyed his best month in September when he batted .406 and slugged .615 in 96 at-bats. He started off by singling twice and scoring two runs against Pittsburgh in the Cardinals' 13th consecutive home victory on September 1. After splitting a four-game set with the Pirates, they dropped four of five to the front-running Reds in back-to-back series at Busch Stadium and Crosley Field, including two one-run losses in extra innings. Boyer had three safeties in their 11-5 victory in St. Louis on September 6 and did the same in Cincinnati two nights later in a ten-inning, 3-2 defeat. The four losses knocked them back 13 games but they were still in fifth place, three games ahead of Pittsburgh.

The Redbirds returned home and took four in a row over Milwaukee and Chicago the second week of September. Ken enjoyed multiple-hit games in each contest. He singled three times and scored twice in their 4-1 win over the Braves on the eleventh. In a doubleheader with Chicago on the fourteenth, he cracked seven hits in 11 at-bats, including a 5-for-6 performance in the second tilt alone, the first five-hit game of his major-league career. His feat consisted of a single to left field in the first inning, another to right in the third, a ground out to short in the fifth, a triple to left in the seventh, then a double to right that scored White and tied the game in the ninth, 5-5. The Cubs brought in right-handed reliever Don Elston to pitch in the eleventh and Ken promptly hit a walk-off home run to win the game, 6-5, and complete his first major-league cycle. It marked the first time in major-league history that a cycle was completed with a game-ending homer. It also boosted his average to a season-high .333, placing him third in the National League batting race behind Roberto Clemente of the Pirates (.359) and Vada Pinson of the Reds (.344). Catching Clemente in the last 13 games was improbable; Boyer was content simply having the highest batting average of his career so late in the season. "Just let me enjoy this fresh air," he told the writers.[20]

After taking the first two of a three-game set at Pittsburgh, St. Louis and Milwaukee were tied for fourth place with less than two-and-a-half weeks remaining in the season. Fourth was a financially more rewarding position for the players than fifth place, enabling them to share a portion of the gate receipts from the first four games of the World Series. A 3-0 shutout by veteran Simmons over Philadelphia on

September 19 edged them past the Braves and put them three-and-a-half games back of the third-place San Francisco Giants. "Maybe we can waltz into third place, and a $1,200 slice wouldn't be a bad Christmas present," pondered Ken. Instead, the Redbirds lost six of their final nine games—including two at Milwaukee—and tumbled back to fifth. He hit safely in eight of those games and his 23rd home run was the only St. Louis highlight during a 9-2 loss in Milwaukee on September 26. Four days later, he belted a two-run homer and smashed a bases-clearing double in a 12-2 rout of the cellar-dwelling Phillies.

Musial always felt if Boyer could avoid prolonged slumps, he had an excellent chance of winning a batting title. "The ballplayers know he's a good one but nobody else does." In 1961, the longest stretch Ken went without a hit was eleven at-bats September 17–19. Otherwise, he maintained a level of consistency that resulted in the highest batting average of his 15-year major league career. An 0 for 4 showing in the season finale dropped it three points to .329, still third-best in the National League behind Clemente's .351 and Pinson's .343. He missed only one game all season and led the Redbirds with 194 hits, 24 homers, 95 RBIs, and 109 runs scored.[21]

For the fourth straight season, his major-league peers chose him as the best defensive third baseman in the league and recipient of the Gold Glove Award. "Of this year's NL fielding all-stars," wrote *The Sporting News*, "Boyer probably comes closest to [Willie] Mays in the matter of matching offensive prowess with fielding finesse over a period of years. In his four-year reign as a hot-corner fielding standout, Kenny also has ranked among the top ten hitters each season."[22]

St. Louis finished in fifth place with a record of 80-74, 13 games behind former Cardinals skipper Fred Hutchinson's Reds. It was a disappointing season for fans expecting the club to contend after its third-place finish in 1960. Attendance fell to 855,305, the lowest in six years. For the second year in a row, the team had a terrible first-half (36-43) and a losing record on the road (32-45). The offense relied heavily on Boyer and White (.286, 20 homers, 90 RBIs) though Musial contributed 15 homers and 70 RBIs. The pitching staff had the lowest earned-run average in the league at 3.74, despite sub-par performances from starters Broglio (9-12, 4.12 ERA) and Jackson (14-11, 3.75 ERA) and closer McDaniel (nine saves, 4.87 ERA). Still, there were signs of future promise and success with the improvement of young hurlers Gibson (who won 13 games) and Sadecki (a 14-game winner) and the added production of center fielder Flood.[23]

KEN BOYER PRIDED HIMSELF on playing every single game and enduring minor injuries to stay in the lineup. His durability would be tested with a new 162-game schedule in the National League after expansion clubs were added in New York and Houston in 1962. In addition, he started the New Year in a St. Louis hospital being treated for a mild case of pneumonia. Though he wouldn't admit it, he hadn't fully recovered from the illness when spring training began a month later.[24]

The Cardinals were confident of their roster and few changes were made over the winter. The exception was the need for another bat to help Boyer and White drive in runs. For this purpose, Joe Cunningham was dealt to the Chicago White Sox for veteran outfielder Minnie Minoso, a career .304 hitter with 180 homers and 978 RBIs the past 12 seasons in the American League. It was believed the thirty-nine-year-old Cuban native could still bolster the team's offense in spite of his age. "We're going to surprise a lot of people," manager Johnny Keane said prior to spring training.[25]

But there were underlying social issues affecting players on his roster each spring in St. Petersburg. Along with local laws that segregated restaurants, restrooms, drinking fountains, and other public facilities, blacks and whites were prohibited from staying in the same hotels. Ever since the Cardinals signed their first African American player (first baseman Tom Alston in 1954) and those who followed, the club made arrangements for them to stay at private homes in the black community. The players felt isolated from the rest of the team and inferior to their teammates. Because of the living arrangements, they couldn't bring their families with them to enjoy the vacation atmosphere like the white players. Veteran George Crowe, who was respected by men of both races, lamented the situation in 1960:

> Our position down here, living away from the other players in their hotel on the beach, is not the fault of our club, or of baseball. I cannot say that I am pleased, or happy about it, but that is a social, and not a baseball, problem. We've

got to accept it, make it the best of it, and trust that in time there will be a change.[26]

The movement for integrated housing started a year later with an invitation for the Cardinals and New York Yankees to attend a "Salute to Baseball" breakfast event sponsored by the St. Petersburg Chamber of Commerce. Even rookies who had not made the club were invited, yet every African American player on the Cardinals roster was excluded, a slight that infuriated Bill White. Their exclusion turned out to be a misunderstanding, even though the St. Petersburg Yacht Club where the event was being held remained segregated through 1985. But it gave White the opportunity to express the grievances of himself and other black players about the team's separate accommodations and other forms of segregation in the city. "How much longer must we accept this without saying a word in our behalf?" he told Joe Reichler, a reporter for the Associated Press. "This thing keeps gnawing away at my heart. I think about this every minute of the day. I'm a member of the ball club, but I can't stay at the same hotel with the white players...These players are my friends, yet I can't go swimming with them. I can't even go to the movies with them."[27]

The story drew nationwide attention. An African-American newspaper in East St. Louis urged a boycott of Anheuser-Busch products. The Cardinals' hotel refused to allow black and white players to stay together and Busch threatened to pull his club out of St. Petersburg. Having already lost the Yankees, who left for Fort Lauderdale the year before, the business community was eager to accommodate his wishes.[28]

A local businessman purchased the Skyline Motel and the adjacent Outrigger Inn on Tampa Bay and leased them to the club in 1962. The entire team (except for three players who had relatives in the area), as well as Keane, his coaching staff, Devine and other front-office personnel, writers, and all of their families—137 people in all, including 30 children—stayed at the complex. One benefit of veteran status was having accommodations away from the rest of the team. Like Musial, Ken would rent a beachfront house outside St. Petersburg and spend time with his family on Reddington Beach or Treasure Island. Both players gave up those accommodations and joined their teammates. White said the gesture "lent a large measure of credibility to what we were doing."[29]

The children were entertained during the day with games, costume parties, fishing trips, a day at Busch Gardens, and other activities. Busch's public relations man Al Fleishman arranged for movies to be shown every night and Musial passed out popcorn to the kids. There was even a newsletter distributed to everyone called "Red Bird Chirps" that gave the daily itinerary. Barbecues were preferred over the restaurant's Polynesian-themed offerings, with Boyer and Jackson buying the meat and grilling, Gibson and White cooking, and pitching coach Howie Pollet making salad. The adults socialized as the children played and swam together in the pool. "All this integration was so unheard of in Florida that people would drive by the motel all day just to gawk and stare," wrote White in his autobiography.[30]

That spring, the Cardinals came together as never before. A true sense of camaraderie was forged both on and off the field that remained throughout the decade. Ken was a chief proponent, especially on the road. He made sure teammates spent time together, whether it was having dinner together or going to the movies. "Kenny was such an understanding guy," recalls Tim McCarver. "He was a friend to everybody. And the black players knew that (he) was respectful of them as anybody...Kenny did a lot toward soothing relationships."[31] In later years, Boyer and White would play bridge against Gibson and Dick Groat ("In fact, I might add, nobody beat us," says Groat). Gibson remembered Boyer and Musial being "as adamant against segregation as the black players were." David Halberstam wrote in his book *October 1964*:

> The Cardinals not only dealt with the white-black issue better than most teams, they did it, Tim McCarver noted years later, before the team had won a pennant, whereas most teams tended to come together on the question of race only after winning. The mutual respect Cardinal players had for each other cut across racial lines.[32]

There were aspects of race that made Ken uncomfortable, but his honesty did nothing to deter from the admiration his teammates held for him. "We enjoyed each other's company," remembered Gibson. "We didn't all see eye-to-eye on every social issue—there were plenty of opinions represented in our clubhouse—but we agreed not to let the differences drive us apart. Boyer had some strict thoughts on interracial marriage, for example, and yet he and I could sit down calmly and exchange our views on the subject." Not everything was serious. With a blinding Florida sun overhead in camp, Ken applied charcoal beneath his eyes to ward off the glare. Flood stared at him and remarked, "You're taking this integration pretty seriously, aren't you?"[33]

THE CARDINALS ENJOYED the best record in the spring exhibitions at 18-8. Ken batted .306, fourth-best on the club, despite fouling a ball off the instep of his left foot that kept him out of the lineup for a few days. With a potentially robust pitching staff, the bats of Boyer, White, Musial, and Minoso, and the potential home run power of catcher Gene Oliver, the team was picked by *The Sporting News* to win the National League pennant.[34]

St. Louis won the first seven games of the season—including five straight on the road—for the team's best start since 1944. In their first series at the old Polo Grounds against the New York Mets, Ken had five safeties, three home runs, and scored six times in two games. Two more hits the next day raised his average to a season-high .367. The winning streak only elevated them to second place, however, as Pittsburgh enjoyed an even better 10-game skein to begin their season. Three straight losses broke St. Louis's streak, including their first major-league contest in Houston, Texas, the club's longtime minor-league affiliate. On April 25, the Redbirds and Colt .45s battled to a 17-inning, 5-5 tie that ended after five hours and 13 minutes, a major-league record at the time. Boyer's RBI single tied the game in the ninth inning.[35]

The Cardinals led the league in hitting and pitching through the end of April. A 5-4 victory over Cincinnati on the twenty-eighth put them in a virtual tie with the Pirates and San Francisco Giants at the top of the standings. The next day, Boyer enjoyed a five-hit afternoon in a twin bill against the Reds, along with a double, two triples, and five RBIs in the opener. That performance placed him third in the

National League with 20 RBIs in his first 16 games and a .338 average. He attributed the great start to warmer than usual spring weather that prevented stiffness in his neck, arms, and back.[36]

The team held close to league-leading San Francisco in early May but fell back steadily as the month progressed. After winning three in a row over the Colt .45s, they lost nine of their next 12 and slid to fourth place, seven games behind the Giants. The offense was dealt a serious blow when Minoso collided with the unpadded concrete wall at Busch Stadium on May 11. Tracking a line drive in left field, he suffered a broken wrist and a fractured skull. Having already been sidelined much of April with a pulled rib muscle and hitting only .194, the Cardinals believed Minoso would eventually rebound and provide much-needed run support. Instead, he was out of action for over two months. Two weeks after his return in August, he suffered a cracked bone in his forearm when he was hit by a pitch that ended his season. Overall, Minoso batted .196 with one home run and 10 RBIs in 39 games.[37]

A 4-for-27 slump the second week of May—including three strikeouts in a 15-inning triumph over the Dodgers on the twelfth—dropped Ken's average to .291. At San Francisco on May 15, he had three safeties and two more off Juan Marichal the next day. Gibson closed the series with a pitching duel against left-hander Billy O'Dell, each throwing eight shutout innings and giving up six hits. The Redbirds prevailed in the ninth after pinch-runner Julian Javier stole second, went to third on a bad throw by the Giants catcher, and scored the winning run on a single by Charlie James. The victory sparked a six-game winning streak that elevated the club to second place and put them 2½ back of San Francisco. But the climb was short-lived: eleven losses to Milwaukee and Pittsburgh in the next twelve contests plunged them back 12 games to fifth place and a .500 record (24-24) on June 3.

One of the month's highlights was Musial's pursuit of the National League career hit record of 3,430 held by Honus Wagner. He had endured a week-long drought trying to force the tying hit in St. Louis—a home run, no less—prior to the team's West Coast trip. In the dugout before Musial batted for the third time at Candlestick Park on the afternoon of May 16, Ken performed the ritual of rubbing his teammate's arm and "massaging a hit" into it. "This is going to be it," he told Stan. Indeed, Musial lined a single to right-center off Marichal to tie the record. He broke it three nights later at Dodger Stadium with a single to right field in the ninth inning for No. 3,431. "I never worked so hard for two hits," he said. After the game, Boyer joined Musial and Red Schoendienst for a late-night celebratory dinner in Los Angeles.[38]

The Cardinals enjoyed their best full month of the season with a 19-12 record in June. They broke an eight-game losing skid with an extra-inning, come-from-behind triumph over Cincinnati on the fifth. The Reds knocked Simmons and Sadecki out of the box and held a 9-1 lead after batting in the sixth inning. In St. Louis's half, Boyer—who had slumped to a season-low .274—doubled and scored in the three-run frame, then knotted it with a two-run homer in the seventh. Musial won it, 10-9, with a round-tripper of his own in the eleventh, the 450th of his major-league career. The thrilling comeback propelled the Redbirds to win 10 of the next 11 and put them a game behind the third-place Pirates. They took five victories over the second-place Giants, with Boyer getting three hits in an 8-4 win and smashing a home run 460 feet to the farthest part of the left-center field bleachers off Marichal at Busch Stadium on June 8. "I never hit one that far in that area," he said.[39]

Adhering to their streaky nature, the Cardinals subsequently dropped four in a row, including two one-run losses to the league-leading Dodgers. They fell 9½ back to fifth place. Ken enjoyed an eight-game hit streak in late June and had two safeties in three straight, boosting his average sixteen points to .291. He batted twice in a nine-run eighth inning at Wrigley Field on June 26, first walking and scoring, then blasting his 10th home run of the season in a 15-3 blowout over the Cubs.

Boyer's round-tripper in a 7-2 defeat on the twenty-eighth tied him with Jim Bottomley for third-most on the Cardinals career home-run list. On June 30, he drove in the first three tallies for St. Louis with a homer off Vern Law—surpassing Bottomley—and a two-run single in a 17-7 loss to Pittsburgh. The hit streak coincided with five straight victories (including back-to-back shutouts by Jackson and Sadecki in the June 27 doubleheader over the Cubs) that elevated them a half-game out of third and 5 ½ games behind first-place San Francisco. They dropped five of the next eight before splitting a four-game series with the New York Mets leading to the All-Star break. The long ball won it for the Redbirds in the second game of a July 7 twin bill at the Polo Grounds. Boyer's two-run shot—his 15th of the season—gave them a 2-1 lead in the fourth and Musial's round-tripper won it in the eighth. Rookie Ray Washburn and McDaniel held on for the 3-2 win. The next day, St. Louis pummeled three Mets hurlers, including former Cardinal Bob Miller, for 16 hits and six home runs, three off the bat of the forty-one-year-old Musial.

Ken was overwhelmingly chosen to start at third base in the two All-Star Games for the first time since 1959. He received 171 votes to 63 for Jim Davenport of the San Francisco Giants. The first contest was held on July 10 at the new District of Columbia Stadium in Washington, D.C. President John F. Kennedy threw out the first pitch from his box seat location. The National League manager and Boyer's former skipper, Fred Hutchinson of the Reds, batted him sixth in the order. In two plate appearances, he struck out against Jim Bunning of the Detroit Tigers in the second inning and grounded out to short off Camilo Pascual of the Minnesota Twins in the fifth. After five scoreless innings, the NL took a two-run lead in the sixth and the American League tallied once in their half. Davenport took over for Ken at third base in the bottom of the sixth. A sacrifice fly by Felipe Alou plated Maury Wills for the final run in the eighth and the NL held on for the 3-1 victory.[40]

When the regular season resumed on July 12, the Cardinals were in fifth place with a 47-38 record and trailed the front-running Los Angeles Dodgers by nine games. Their poor showing in the standings was attributed to a lack of timely home-run production despite their consistent position among the league leaders in team batting, pitching, and fielding throughout the first-half of the season.[41] About this time, Boyer and Musial became the last Cardinals to give up the fitted plastic liners worn inside their caps and began wearing batting helmets instead. Keane thought it was a good idea considering the influx of inexperienced young pitchers in the league.[42]

Ken inched his average back over .300 after the first All-Star break and hit safely in 11 of his next 13 games. In the opener of a twin bill at Pittsburgh on July 15, he singled twice before being ejected in the seventh inning for arguing with umpire Tony Venzon about a runner called safe at third. (Venzon had also ejected him from a game two years earlier.) Boyer came back in the second game with another single and a two-run homer that tied it in the ninth inning. Six days later, he had five safeties—including two homers—in a sweltering day-night doubleheader at Houston. A 3-for-18 slump, however, prompted Keane to move him temporarily from the middle of the order down to seventh for the second game of a doubleheader with the New York Mets on July 27.[43]

In the second All-Star Game at Wrigley Field on July 30, the National League loaded the bases in the first inning off rookie right-hander Dave Stenhouse of the Washington Senators. With two outs, Ken hit what appeared to be a low line drive, but White Sox shortstop Luis Aparicio moved to his left and speared it a few inches off the ground to end the threat. The AL tied it up one-all on a home run by Pete Runnels of the Boston Red Sox in the third. With two outs in the frame, Tommy Davis of the Dodgers dropped a line drive off the bat of Detroit's Rocky Colavito against the left-field wall. Billy Moran of the Los Angeles Angels rounded third heading for home. Boyer took Davis's relay throw and fired to catcher Del Crandall, nailing Moran at the plate for the third out. Ken ended a personal 0-for-5 string dating back to the 1961 All-Star Game when he singled off Ray Herbert of the White Sox to lead off the fourth. Each team had 10 hits, but three home runs proved the difference for the American League and they prevailed, 9-4.[44]

In the midst of a disappointing season, some St. Louis fans began directing their frustrations at Boyer like never before. They booed him regardless whether he failed or succeeded. He had five hits in a Sunday afternoon doubleheader split against Houston on August 5, yet there were enough vocal fans booing him that he said it "was noticeable." The boos became a frequent and unfortunate occurrence that marked his last four seasons with the Cardinals. Initially, he said the amount of booing in 1962 "was exaggerated," but took it in stride in later seasons as part of being a professional athlete. "I never understood it, but it never bothered me much. If they wanted to boo, well, it was their right. They paid for the ticket. I just tried to do my best."

He wouldn't allow himself to think about the few disgruntled fans and let them affect his performance. "If you do, you could start to lose your confidence and that's the worst thing that could happen."[45]

Often Ken resorted to self-deprecating humor among teammates or when speaking at banquets and writers' dinners to deflect the criticism. He reassured a new player worried about the reception he would receive from the home crowd, "Oh, you don't have to worry here—I've got all the wolves to myself." At one postseason function, he remarked that Gibson "wanted to boo tonight to make me feel at home." Boyer called himself the "Del Ennis of St. Louis," referring to his former teammate who was often a target of boos while playing in Philadelphia.[46]

Ken responded once to a particularly vocal fan sitting behind the home dugout. Despite having a good day at the plate with a pair of safeties in a doubleheader, the man heckled him relentlessly throughout both contests. Boyer dropped a pop fly close to him and the fan told him to sit down and let him play. "Mister," he answered, "you could probably do a better job because all I got here is this little glove and you got that great big mouth."[47]

Blame for the treatment he received at Busch Stadium was attributed to Cardinals broadcaster Harry Caray. Brash, colorful, and opinionated, Caray described his play-by-play style as that of any other fan with the opportunity to express his sentiments on the air. The St. Louis native's enthusiasm rose and fell with the team's fortunes and it came across to his listeners. They enjoyed his spirited descriptions of the action and his trademark phrases such as "Holy cow!" and "It might be...it could be...it *is*...a home run!" He could be tough on his beloved Redbirds and wasn't afraid to criticize players when they failed to live up to expectations. During the late innings when he was clamoring for the "long one," but instead the St. Louis batter produced a weak fly ball, Harry would lament, "Popped it up...that wouldn't be a home run in a phone booth!" He took such offenses personally and his criticisms could be especially biting and sarcastic. "I'm so tough on my guys because I want them to win so much," he explained.[48]

Caray had been the voice of the Cardinals for seventeen years in 1962, and his microphone wielded great influence over the far-reaching airwaves of the 50,000-watt radio station KMOX. For a fan base that stretched throughout the Midwest and the South, his commentary carried great weight. "Harry ruled St. Louis in those days," recalled Bob Uecker, who played two seasons with the Cardinals. "As a player, you tried to stay on his good side. If he got down on you, look out."[49]

Boyer reportedly got on Caray's bad side in 1960 or 1961. He and his broadcast partner, Jack Buck, were calling a game from behind home plate at the Los Angeles Coliseum. The circumstances vary with each recollection. Buck remembered Ken making a fine defensive play and Caray calling him over for a quick interview as he returned to the dugout. "Harry, the ballgame's going on," he told him. "I can't stop and talk to you on the radio." Another version claimed while broadcasting from a field box beside the Cardinals dugout, Harry tried speaking to him when he was on deck but was brushed off. Tim McCarver, who was Boyer's teammate for six seasons, attributed it to an interview request from Caray between games of a twi-night doubleheader that was declined.[50]

Regardless of the particulars, Ken's refusal "ticked Caray off," recalled Buck, "and thereafter when Harry got a chance to say something critical about Boyer, he blasted him." He would praise Eddie Mathews of the Braves as a better defensive third baseman and disparage Boyer. "Eddie Mathews is the best third baseman in the National League. Look at that range—do you think Boyer could make that play? No way!" He injected cutting remarks routinely into his play-by-play:

> *I don't believe it. Here's Boyer, he struck out three times tonight, and the Cardinals still without a run.*

> *It's the last of the ninth. The Cardinals have the tying run on second. Two out. Boyer's the hitter. We'll be back in one minute for the wrap-up.*[51]

Wrote Myron Cope in *Sports Illustrated*: "Caray's detractors insist that he can damn a ballplayer in his broadcasts without misstating a single fact but merely by employing the inflection of disgust. It is said, for example, that simply by repeating time and again the number of base runners…Ken Boyer left stranded, Caray planted St. Louis fans squarely on Boyer's back."[52]

Harry was "merciless" in his criticism, according to Bob Broeg. "Boyer would come up in the ninth inning, the game on the line, and you could just tell from his voice, he expected, he was *certain*, Boyer would make an out." And that pessimism resonated with fans because he was the voice of the Cardinals. Though Caray never addressed his criticism of Boyer specifically, he was unapologetic about his commentary in general. "Listen, I don't believe any ballplayer ever put on a Cardinal uniform who shouldn't have known I wanted his success as much as he did. But I refuse to fool the audience."[53]

Harry's critiques became fodder for the players. Uecker did the best impersonations of him on the team bus, much to the delight of his teammates and the displeasure of Caray. "Well, here's the Captain, Ken Boyer. Boyer haaaaaaasn't had an RBI in his last fifty-two games...I don't understand why they continue to boo him here at Busch Stadium...Striiiiiike one, he doesn't eeeeven take the bat off his shoulder...here's striiiiiike two...and strike three...He *nevvvvvver* even took the bat *offffff* his shoulder. I don't know why they're booing him."[54]

Though they made fun of him and didn't appreciate his treatment of Boyer, the players rarely challenged Caray publicly. One exception was pitcher Tracy Stallard, who had enough of the second-guessing against himself and his teammates in the midst of a difficult 1965 season. "All some fans know is what they hear from Caray. He gives the impression he (Boyer) goes up to the plate and isn't trying." Buck agreed with this assessment. "Harry constantly criticized Ken Boyer, who did everything that some people thought he was not giving 100 percent. It appeared he was loafing, but he wasn't; but Harry used to pick on him relentlessly."[55]

At one point, Caray allegedly threatened him: "Do you know that I can make you or break you with my microphone?"

Ken wasn't intimidated. "You can stick that mic right up your ass."[56]

Kathleen Boyer would listen to the games on the radio when she wasn't at the ballpark. "During those times, Harry Caray really was on his case," she recalls. "It was bad, but what could you do? He did have the microphone. Everybody thought he was God and whatever he said was the gospel." Boyer never publicly responded to Caray's criticisms, though at one time he purportedly challenged him in the

Cardinals clubhouse. It's been suggested the broadcaster influenced the club's decision to trade him after the 1965 season. "He was instrumental in getting Kenny out of St. Louis," says Tommy John, a teammate later with the Chicago White Sox. "Kenny told me that." The sentiment is shared by members of Ken's family.[57]

Caray's play-by-play wasn't always negative towards Boyer. When he drove in a run, made a great play at third, or hit a home run, Harry celebrated those moments as he would any other player on the club. "Harry didn't necessarily hammer him when he was up, but when he was down, he did, which everybody thought was unfair," says McCarver. "But that was Harry." Uecker, who later became a Hall of Fame broadcaster himself, felt Caray's comments weren't malicious. "I remember things he said about Kenny Boyer. He loved Kenny Boyer. Harry never said anything because he disliked somebody. He said it because he thought they could do a better job."[58]

Kathleen attended three games a week with her children Suzie and David. The younger ones, Danny and Jane, went to their first games in 1964. Like her husband, she understood the boos directed at him were "all part of the game. You just have to accept it." Still, she added, "I guess some people expect a player to produce every time and, believe me, no one wants to more than Ken, even though he looks so easy-going." But Kathleen wasn't always silent. She recalls one particular incident:

> We used to sit in Section P at Sportsman's Park—the wives all did—and of course during a doubleheader on a Sunday in the summertime, it gets hot and the beer gets to flowing. One guy was booing and saying all kinds of things about Ken. He had no idea who I was. I turned around and said, "You know, I've really enjoyed all the nice things you've been saying about my husband."[59]

During another Sunday doubleheader, a fan nearby was giving him an especially rough time. Suzie looked at her mother and said, "I wish that man wouldn't say those things about daddy."[60]

THE CARDINALS WON four straight games in early August 1962, including back-to-back shutouts by Broglio and Gibson over the Pirates, and climbed back to fourth place in the standings. Boyer missed the next three games against Philadelphia with a bruised right elbow, ending a personal string of 175 consecutive games played.[61]

Following an 11-3 debacle to the seventh-place Philadelphia Phillies on August 11, St. Louis went into a tailspin, losing 25 of their next 37 games and falling to sixth place, 21 ½ games out of first. A lack of clutch hitting in close games, an ineffective bullpen, and a failure to dominate the second-division clubs—particularly the expansion Colt .45s and Mets—proved their undoing. The team's struggles provoked the wrath of club president Gussie Busch, who threatened salary cuts for ineffective players and an overhaul of the front office in the off-season. At one time, he thought a third-place finish was realistic. "But now, I think we'll be lucky to finish fifth or even sixth." The only players he saw being with the team in 1963 were Gibson, Flood, and Musial. Asked for his thoughts on Busch's remarks, Boyer replied, "It's his ball club. He had a lot of money invested in it. He has a right to say anything he wants."[62]

Ken enjoyed a nine-game hitting streak, his longest of the season, beginning August 15. Trailing the Mets, 4-2, in the opener of a twin bill at the Polo Grounds on the eighteenth, he rocketed a three-run homer in the fifth inning to give St. Louis the lead and eventual 7-4 victory. Two singles and a double with two RBIs the next day raised his average to .300 for the first time since July 24. He did the same in the first game of a twin bill against Pittsburgh on the twenty-fifth. Hitless in the finale, he had three more safeties and scored three runs to beat the Pirates in a come-from-behind, 6-5 victory.

After hitting his 20th home run and stroking an RBI single in a 10-5 win over the Mets on the first of September, Boyer endured an 0-for-19 slump. As a result, he fell behind Bill White in the club lead for RBIs and finished the season with 98. "I tailed off on RBIs in the second half of the season through my own fault," said Ken. "I certainly had enough opportunities, especially with Curt Flood on base so much. What I really felt bad about was leaving so many men on third." His average also dropped ten points from .304 to .293, the last time it would be at that plateau the rest of the season. Still, he reached and surpassed a significant milestone the second week of September. On the eleventh, he tied Hall of Famer Rogers Hornsby's mark of 191 home runs for second on the club's all-time list when he homered off Bob Purkey of the Cincinnati Reds. His fifth-inning blast over the left-center field wall at Philadelphia against rookie Jack Hamilton on September 15—the 182nd of his major-league career—clinched the mark. At the same time, he became the leading right-handed home-run hitter in St. Louis Cardinals history.[63]

Though officially eliminated from the pennant race, the Redbirds nonetheless played the role of spoiler the last week-and-a-half of the season. Second-place San Francisco trailed Los Angeles by four games when they visited Busch Stadium on September 19. The Giants split the two-game series with St. Louis and Ken factored in both contests. He had three hits in the opener—including his 24th homer—and drove in the game-winning run with the bases loaded off Don Larsen in the ninth inning of the finale. Next, the Cardinals hosted the Dodgers and took two out of three, both blowout victories. On the twenty-first, a grand-slam by Charlie James knocked Koufax out of the box in the first inning and Simmons pitched a masterful five-hitter to win, 11-2. Gibson had been scheduled to start that evening, but he fractured his right ankle during batting practice and prematurely ended his season. Two days later, Jackson overcame 12 hits allowed and threw eight scoreless innings to beat Drysdale. Boyer had another three-hit performance in the 12-2 win.

St. Louis closed the season on the road with three-game series at Candlestick Park and Dodger Stadium. The Giants beat them in the first two and climbed two games back of Los Angeles while the Redbirds fell to seventh place. Musial's five safeties and Gene Oliver's three-run homer proved the difference in the third contest, 7-4. But the Cardinals made it up to San Francisco by sweeping the Dodgers while the Giants won two of three over Houston, forcing a tie for the National League pennant on the last day of the season. On September 28, Jackson pitched a complete game for his 16th victory as James singled home the winning run in the tenth inning, 3-2. A masterful two-hit, 2-0 shutout by Broglio—his 12th win of the season—bested 25-game winner Drysdale the next evening. Simmons pitched nine shutout innings of five-hit ball on September 30 that were matched by veteran Johnny Podres through seven-and-a-third. Oliver clouted the deciding blow for St. Louis over the fence in the eighth for the 1-0 triumph. San Francisco clinched the pennant after taking a best-of-three playoff from the reeling Dodgers but lost the World Series to the New York Yankees in seven games.[64]

Winning their last four games of the season, the Cardinals finished in sixth place with a record of 84-78 (and one tie), 17 ½ games behind the Giants. The pitching staff lead the majors in shutouts with 17. Jackson paced the club with 16 victories, but Gibson (15-13) stepped up for his first All-Star season with a team-best 2.85 earned-run average, 208 strikeouts, 15 complete games, and five shutouts. In his first full season, the highly-touted Washburn won 12 games and rookie Sadecki had a 6-8 mark. Veteran closer McDaniel saved 14 games, but had a 3-10 record and 4.12 ERA.

A 4-for-25 skid in the final six games, capped by three consecutive strikeouts and a triple against Podres in the finale, brought Ken's final average down to .291. It marked the first time in five seasons that he failed to hit better than .300. He paced the club with 24 home runs but finished second to White with 98 RBIs. His 26 doubles remained consistent, but his five triples were half of what he had accumulated the previous two seasons. He did flash more speed on the base paths with 12 stolen bases, the first time since 1959 that he reached double-digits in that category. His 104 strikeouts were a career high.

"I feel I had a good year in '62, but I was somewhat disappointed in myself as well as in the club's showing in general," Boyer assessed. "I had a shot at a really big year, what with Curt Flood and the others on base so often, but I just left too many runners on base, especially third."[65]

It wasn't until the off-season that Ken confessed to feeling fatigued for the first time in his career. He was still recovering from his bout with pneumonia when the season began. Coupled with a more demanding travel schedule and eight additional games on the schedule (including 12 in sweltering Houston), his stamina diminished over the course of the season. Nevertheless, he still upheld his standard of iron man endurance and played in all but two games of the 162-game schedule.[66]

Ken Boyer at Busch Stadium.
(*National Baseball Hall of Fame Library, Cooperstown NY*)

Chapter Nine

All-Star Infield

The need for a productive shortstop and a power bat in the outfield were imperative if the St. Louis Cardinals were to contend in 1963. There was even a rumor speculating that Ken could be traded to the Detroit Tigers for slugging outfielder Rocky Colavito. "The boo-birds probably would shed few tears if Ken Boyer were dealt," suggested Neal Russo in *The Sporting News*.[1]

General manager Bing Devine wasted little time after the 1962 season ended. In October, he acquired outfielder George Altman from the Cubs—who had just produced back-to-back seasons of hitting over .300 with more than 20 home runs—along with pitcher Don Cardwell and catcher Moe Thacker in exchange for pitchers Larry Jackson and Lindy McDaniel and catcher Jimmie Schaffer. He turned around a month later and dealt Cardwell and Julio Gotay, who had been the Opening Day shortstop in 1962, to Pittsburgh for veteran shortstop Dick Groat and reliever Diomedes Olivo. "These two deals have remade our club," said Devine.[2]

But the Groat deal almost didn't happen. A power struggle had developed in the front office in late October when Gussie Busch—desperate for a pennant after ten years of ownership—brought eighty-year-old Branch Rickey back to St. Louis as a "special personnel consultant" to Devine. Rickey had been the team's general manager from 1917 to 1942, creating the farm system that brought talented young players to the major-league roster and winning six National League pennants and four World championships. He served in the same capacity with the Brooklyn Dodgers and the Pittsburgh Pirates. His most enduring achievement was integrating the majors leagues with the signing of Jackie Robinson.

Busch intended for the vastly experienced Rickey to advise Devine on potential trades and other roster decisions if he was unavailable on brewery business. It became evident at the press conference, however, that Rickey saw himself as the decision-maker instead. He declared the Cardinals had to be strengthened from within and "cannot be traded into a pennant." In his opinion, Musial was "keeping a young player out of the lineup" and should retire. Naturally, Devine felt Rickey was undermining his authority as general manager. He had no choice but to make the awkward arrangement work for the next year-and-a-half.[3]

Rickey was opposed to swapping a young shortstop for one almost ten years older. Devine realized Gotay wouldn't live up to his potential and insisted the club needed a veteran presence at the position, one that had been absent since Marty Marion's departure 13 years earlier. Unable to persuade him over several weeks, Devine finally arranged a meeting with like-minded team personnel, invited Rickey, and once again proposed the trade. Realizing he was outnumbered, Rickey grudgingly agreed to advise Busch that the deal should be made. A month later, Devine sent another young prospect, power-hitting first baseman Fred Whitfield, to the Cleveland Indians for right-handed reliever Ron Taylor and infielder Jack Kubiszyn.[4]

The Groat deal turned out to be a crucial piece to the success enjoyed by the Cardinals over the next two seasons. The thirty-two-year- old veteran was a outstanding contact hitter who employed the hit-and-run proficiently, batting .290 in nine seasons in Pittsburgh. He was well-respected and Devine hoped he could mentor Julian Javier and help improve his development at second base.[5]

Groat also had something to prove. The Pittsburgh native was hurt that his hometown team traded him but pleased with his destination.

Devine made him feel needed and his new teammates made him feel welcome. Three years removed from his MVP season and World championship, he wanted to show the Pirates that he could still help a contending team. Says Groat, "It worked out to be three wonderful years in the Cardinal uniform."[6]

Ken felt the addition of Groat would improve the team's defense. "Dick can add a lot with all his experience, especially on such things as pickoff plays at second base. He should help keep everyone alert." He later added, "He'll make us even tougher defensively because he knows the hitters and he's on top of every play. He doesn't drag his feet."[7] Boyer and Groat knew each other through a mutual friend, Bill Virdon, who played for both the Cardinals and Pirates. The pair was inseparable in spring training as Groat became acclimated to his new club. They grew closer over the course of the season. Ken helped him find a home near his own in Spanish Lake north of St. Louis. They drove to the ballpark together and were roommates on the road. "Kenny was a great, great person," recalls Groat. "He was always fun to be with. Our families went places [and] the kids all kind of grew up together those three years. Ken Boyer made my move to St. Louis just a joy."[8]

As a result of the team's disappointing finish in 1962 and a decline in his own statistics, Boyer accepted a $5,000 pay cut and signed a one-year deal reportedly for $45,000. Still, he enjoyed the second-highest salary on the team and understood the expectations of Cardinals fans because of it. "I can't change the fans' opinion. All I can do is play as best I can every day. Fortunately, once the new season begins, all of last year is forgotten."[9]

Rickey continued to generate controversy, predicting St. Louis would finish in fifth place owing to its young pitching staff of Bob Gibson, Ray Sadecki, and Ray Washburn. Devine was more optimistic and responded tactfully that the team had "an outside chance" at the pennant. He would be "greatly disappointed, in myself and in the club, if we don't show a marked improvement over 1962. And I always have said the National League is so closely balanced that all you have to do is stay somewhere close and you have a chance to compete." For his part, Ken expected a first-division finish.

Though pessimistic about the Redbirds' pennant chances, Rickey was confident in its future with Boyer on the club. "His age, his character, and his ability make him one of the great players of the game today. This boy can run, he can throw, he can hit and he has power. What more could you ask? The next three or four years ought to be his best."[10]

THE CARDINALS STARTED the 1963 campaign with three consecutive shutout victories by Ernie Broglio, Washburn, and Curt Simmons. Coupled with five scoreless frames against Philadelphia on April 14, it gave the pitching staff 53 consecutive scoreless innings dating back to the last two games of the 1962 season. Thirteen of their first 20 games were on the road, yet St. Louis lost only three, splitting two at San Francisco and sweeping three games in Los Angeles to close the month. An RBI double by Bill White and a solo home run off the bat of Javier gave them a 2-1 victory over the Milwaukee Braves, the best record in the majors at 14-6, and first place on April 30.

Ken enjoyed a productive spring training and finished second on the club with a .341 average. He drove in two runs on Opening Day in New York, but it was part of a 3-for-18 start that lowered his average to .167. He rebounded briefly with two safeties and five RBIs in each of the next three games, raising it to .321. But after hitting his first home run of the season against Pittsburgh on April 18, he slumped again over the next five games to .250. A two-game set in Houston heated his bat for two hits in each contest, including a four-RBI performance on the twenty-third that placed him in the league lead in that category. He had a trio of safeties in back-to-back games at San Francisco and Los Angeles, then belted two homers at Dodger Stadium to raise his average fifty-eight points to .308 on April 28.

St. Louis began the month of May with three undefeated starters in Broglio, Washburn, and Simmons, who combined for 12 victories and a 1.50 earned-run average in their first five games. The Cardinals hosted the Chicago Cubs on the second with former teammate Jackson on the mound. "What's going to be interesting is when Kenny Boyer comes up to face me," the right-hander said prior to the showdown. "We used to kid each other all the time about the possibility. He'd say he wished the Cards would trade me so he could knock me out of the park, and I'd tell him he'd hit nothing but air." In that initial contest, Ken grounded out and struck out in his first two at-bats, but later walked to load the bases and force Jackson's exit in the seventh inning of a 4-3 Redbirds victory. Jackson would hold the upper hand the remainder of their careers—Boyer had only 10 hits in 61 at-bats (.164) against him.[11]

The Cardinals lost 13 of the first 19 games in May and fell to fourth place, four behind the league-leading San Francisco Giants. In a 6-0 loss at Cincinnati on May 3, Ken was spiked above the right knee when Johnny Edwards of the Reds made a late slide into third base on a fielder's choice tag play to end the fourth inning. The wound required thirteen stitches and kept him out of the lineup the next three days. Initially, it slowed him in the field as he protected the knee from tearing open. The injury had repercussions, robbing him of speed on the bases the rest of his career. As a result, he said, "a lot of my triples became doubles and doubles became singles." His bat came alive upon his return and he enjoyed his best month of the season, swatting at a .361 clip and hitting safely in eight consecutive games May 8–15. In the opener of a twin bill with Pittsburgh on the twelfth, he singled off Roy Face in the twelfth inning to drive in Flood from second and beat them, 2-1.[12]

The club finished the month with nine victories in their last 11 games. Broglio's five-hit shutout and Gene Oliver's homer at Chicago on May 23 enabled the Redbirds to move into third place. Boyer had a perfect day at the plate three days later in the opener of a doubleheader against the New York Mets. In the first inning, he smashed an RBI double for St. Louis' first run, then singled in the third to knock in another, doubled in the fifth, singled in the seventh, and tied the game with another hit in the eighth, 4-4. Charlie James followed with a three-run homer that beat the Mets, 7-4. The second 5-for-5 performance of his major-league career raised his average twenty points to .339. He ended the month hitting at a .333 clip, third-best in the league. The top three hit leaders were all Cardinals—Groat, White, and Boyer. St. Louis took two out of three over the front-running Giants to put them in second place and two games back on June 2.[13]

The National League race became tighter in June. At Philadelphia on the sixth, Ken singled and scored an insurance run on Altman's pinch-hit double, giving the Redbirds a two-run lead in the eighth inning. It proved more important after the Phillies tallied in their half and St. Louis held on to beat them, 5-4. The victory put them in a three-way tie for the league lead with San Francisco and Chicago. In a 3-2 walk-off loss to the Mets the next evening, Boyer smashed the 200th home run of his career off left-hander Al Jackson. The Cardinals had first place to themselves on June 11 after Gibson threw a six-hitter at Pittsburgh, striking out eight and driving in the go-ahead run himself in the 3-1 win. Splitting a doubleheader with the Pirates and falling a half-game behind San Francisco, they beat the New York Mets, 8-1, to reclaim the league lead for their own on the seventeenth. Broglio allowed only one unearned run and five hits. Boyer and Flood each had three safeties and White homered in the contest.[14]

Eight victories over the next two weeks—half of them decided by one run—enabled the Cardinals to hold off the Dodgers and the Giants through the first of July. Broglio and Gibson each won two games and veteran right-hander Lew Burdette (acquired from the Milwaukee Braves for catcher Gene Oliver and minor-league pitcher Bob Sadowski a half-hour before the June 15 trading deadline) clinched his first victory with the Redbirds on the eighteenth. Ken struggled at the plate in the first week but rebounded with six hits in a three-game series with San Francisco at Busch Stadium. He singled and doubled off Juan Marichal on the twenty-fourth, belted home runs in back-to-back games, and went 3-for-3 with four RBIs in the finale. After learning they had been chosen to play in the All-Star Game together, Boyer, Groat, and White combined five hits and beat Houston, 2-1.[15]

Holding a precarious game-and-a-half lead over the Dodgers, St. Louis dropped their next eight at Houston, Los Angeles, and San Francisco, and tumbled 4½ back to fourth place. Failure to overcome one-run deficits in five of those losses cost them the league lead. Ken had three safeties and an RBI on the Fourth of July, but the Dodgers prevailed, 10-7. A misplayed ground ball at third base with the bases loaded in the fifteenth inning enabled the Giants to score the winning run in the opener of a July 7 doubleheader. Red Schoendienst pinch-hit for Burdette in the fourteenth and grounded to first base in the final at-bat of his major-league career. The forty-year-old started the season as a coach, but was reactivated as a pinch-hitter on June

24. He was hitless in six plate appearances. Gibson's 5-0 shutout and eight strikeouts salvaged the finale going into the All-Star break.[16]

OVER THE NEXT TWO SEASONS, the infield of White, Javier, Groat, and Boyer earned praise for its offensive and defensive prowess. Longtime St. Louis baseball writer J. Roy Stockton felt it was one of the "best ever" for the Cardinals. Branch Rickey deemed it "the greatest hitting infield I have ever seen," supplanting in his mind Gil Hodges, Jackie Robinson, Pee Wee Reese, and Billy Cox of the 1948–1952 Brooklyn Dodgers. "I'd still give that Brooklyn infield the edge defensively," he said, "but this Cardinal infield has more offensively and might even get to be better." At mid-season, Groat was second in the NL batting race with a .326 average, while White was fifth at .320, Boyer hitting .305, and Javier .270. Groat and White were tied for the league lead with 111 safeties, White was third in slugging at .527, Groat and Javier were one-two in doubles with 23 and 22, respectively, and White and Boyer were three-four in RBIs with 59 and 52.

The addition of Groat made a good defensive infield even better. An intelligent ballplayer, he compensated for a lack of speed and range at shortstop with quickness and a thorough knowledge of pitchers on his own team. He knew where to position himself based on their pitch selection. "They were a bunch of individuals until [Groat] came along," one San Francisco Giants player remarked. "Defensively, they were loose. Now they're the best." Ken believed Groat was just as valuable for his defense as he was his offense. "It adds to your confidence to have a player of Dick's stature standing next to you."[17]

It was a durable infield that missed only eight games collectively in 1963 and 10 in '64. "It was a good infield, the best infield that I was on," recalled White, "but I'm not sure it was the best ever. It might have been the best Cardinals infield." Groat was grateful to be part of the exceptional quartet. "I've said before I thought I was the luckiest shortstop in the history of baseball because I got to play between Don Hoak and [Bill] Mazeroski in Pittsburgh and between Boyer and Javier in St. Louis. You can't play with better people than those four guys."[18] Though statistically not the greatest infield, modern-day baseball analyst and author Bill James still ranked the 1963 Cardinals infield as "in the top 1% of all teams" in history. Keane said proudly, "I wouldn't trade my infield for any other in the league."[19]

When Javier replaced injured Pittsburgh second baseman Bill Mazeroski on the National League roster, he completed an exclusive Cardinals infield in the starting lineup for the All-Star Game at Cleveland's Municipal Stadium on July 9. "When you've got an infield that starts with Bill White at first base and runs through Javier, Dick Groat, and Ken Boyer, you've got power and class," remarked San Francisco manager and NL All-Star skipper Alvin Dark. It was White's seventh, Javier's first, and Ken's ninth appearance in the contest, tying him with Eddie Mathews for most by a third baseman. Groat saw his seventh selection as vindication. "I was very proud of that year," he says, "because [Pittsburgh general manager] Joe Brown had made this statement when he traded me that I couldn't play shortstop on a pennant winner anymore and I got more votes than any player in either league for the All-Star Game. It meant so much more to make the All-Star team when your peers voted. Much more of an accomplishment than today, when the fans vote."[20]

The National League took a one-run lead in the second inning, but the American League tied it in their half when a grounder bounded off Ken's glove into left field, scoring Leon Wagner of the Los Angeles Angels from second. With the game knotted in the fifth, 3-3, a groundout by Willie Mays drove in the Dodgers' Tommy Davis with the go-ahead run. Ron Santo of the Cubs singled home White in the eighth for the final tally, 5-3. Former Redbird Jackson was the winner with three strikeouts in two innings. Boyer was hitless in three at-bats, popping up twice and flying out to left. White, Javier, and Groat played the entire contest while Santo replaced Boyer in the sixth inning. For the first time since 1959, there was only one All-Star Game instead of two.[21]

The regular season resumed on July 11. Ken started a modest eight-game hit streak with two singles and a home run in the second game of a twi-night doubleheader with the Milwaukee Braves. Three days later, he smashed a three-run homer in a 10-3 drubbing of the Cubs during the first game of a twin bill. The Redbirds took two out of three at Cincinnati and won nine of their next 11 games through late July. They climbed back to second place and four games back of the front-running Dodgers. Gibson contributed three victories, part of a personal five-game win streak, and Simmons two, including a three-hitter at Chicago.

Groat hit safely in 14 consecutive games to lead the league with a .340 batting average, .401 on-base percentage, 144 safeties, and 31 doubles through July 30. He attributed his offensive resurgence in St. Louis to hitting in front of a future Hall of Famer. "Think how lucky I could be...to hit in front of Stan Musial for a whole year? I never had so many good balls to hit in my life. Who's going to walk *me* to get to Stan Musial?"[22] Boyer drove in 11 runs in that span for 69 RBIs, tying him for third-most in the league. He was belatedly honored at Busch Stadium prior to the July 21 game with Houston for hitting his 200th career home run on June 7. That evening, he capped off a successful three-hit series against the Colt .45s with three more safeties. He raised his average to .309 and added home run number 206.[23]

After taking the first two of a four-game set at Chicago, St. Louis dropped both games of a July 28 doubleheader. The Cubs walloped three Redbird hurlers for 14 hits and left-hander Dick Ellsworth struck out 10 for his 15th victory of the season in the opener, 5-1. The Cardinals put up more of a fight in the second game, pounding 15 hits—including five round-trippers—as Flood went 4-for-4, White, Altman, Javier, and Carl Sawatski each had two hits, and Boyer smacked a two-run homer that broke a 4-4 tie in the fifth inning. But the Cubs answered with 16 hits (counting four homers) off six pitchers—including Sadecki, who threw in relief after losing the first game—and beat the Redbirds, 16-11. Two of the three players St. Louis dealt to Chicago in the Altman trade factored in the decision: catcher Jimmie Schaffer homered and knocked in three runs in the eighth and McDaniel was the winning pitcher with one-hit relief over the last three frames. The main culprit in the Cubs' offensive attack was Lou Brock, who was in his second full season in the big leagues and hitting .239 entering the twin bill. The twenty-four-year-old left fielder had a hit in the opener and went 3-for-4 with a triple and two homers, drove in five runs, and scored three in the finale.

The Cardinals started August with three straight victories over Cincinnati and Philadelphia, then dropped six of their next eight to the second-division Phillies, Mets, and Braves. They fell back to third place and six games out. Despite back-to-back games with double-digit hit totals, they tallied only a handful of runs. Two losses to the cellar-dwelling Mets August 7–8 and stranding 17 runners total were especially infuriating to Keane. As a result, he cracked down with a mandatory midnight curfew. He ordered an off-day morning workout at Busch Stadium prior to a team picnic at Gussie Busch's estate on August 12.[24]

Ken endured a terrible slide from late July through the second weekend of August with only 12 hits in 77 at-bats. His average dwindled twenty-seven points to .282. There were a few intervals when he produced, driving in what proved to be the game-winning run at New York on August 6 and stroking a two-run single that beat Milwaukee four days later. But he went 48 plate appearances without an extra-base hit. "I've been pulling the ball too much and I've been taking my eye off the ball," he said. "I'm going to try a straightaway stroke again."[25]

Rain on the morning of the twelfth canceled the mandatory workout. That afternoon, the players took their families to Grant's Farm, the Busch family estate southwest of St. Louis, for the team picnic. Ken, Kathleen, and the children enjoyed themselves despite the rainy, humid weather. It was an appropriate forecast considering the news Stan Musial would share that day. "All of a sudden, we looked up and here came all these television stations," recalls Groat. "Their trucks were pulling in there quickly. We knew something was up but didn't know for sure. That's when Musial announced his retirement." After 22 seasons with the Cardinals, this would be his last. It was a decision he first considered after signing his contract over the winter, but one he finally reached a few days earlier on the road. He wanted to wait and tell his teammates and the local sportswriters when they returned to St. Louis.[26]

It was an emotional day for Stan and his wife Lillian. As the team captain, Ken spoke on behalf of the players, who were stunned at the news. Musial is "an inspiration," he said, "the leader who's won for us. We'll be sorry to see Stan go. The thing that stands out in my mind is that, when he broke records, it was for the modern-day player, not just for himself." Then he turned to Stan and congratulated him as "the greatest player who ever put on a uniform."[27]

Musial wanted his announcement to motivate his teammates the last six weeks of the season. "I'd like nothing more than to go out a winner. Our 1942 club was farther behind and won. We still have a chance." Speaking for them, Groat remarked, "Looking over the past week makes you sort of sick the way we played. But maybe Stan's retiring will have an effect on us. It would be wonderful to let him finish a great career in a World Series."[28]

Initially, the Redbirds responded by taking two of three from the Houston Colt .45s and sweeping a three-game series from the San Francisco Giants in the homestand. During the first week-and-a-half of the month, Ken established a new major-league record, going eight consecutive games August 4–11 without a putout at third base. The string ended when he caught a pop foul for the last out of the Cardinals' 4-2 victory over Houston on the thirteenth.[29]

Trying to escape his hitting slump, he switched from his 34-ounce bat to one that was two ounces heavier with a larger barrel to keep him from being out in front of the pitch. Choking up on the thicker handle, Boyer had better results. He hit safely in each contest and raised his average nine points to .291. He had two singles and three RBIs against Houston on August 13 and a 4-for-6 showing three days later with two homers, four RBIs, and four runs scored. Yet the second-place Redbirds gained only a half-game on the league-leading Dodgers. The last western trip of the season beginning at Dodger Stadium on August 20 offered the chance to cut further into their lead. Instead, St. Louis dropped the first two games—including a 16-inning, 2-1 loss in the second contest despite three safeties by Boyer—before salvaging a 3-2 victory when Ken doubled and scored the winning run in the sixth. The Cardinals subsequently lost two out of three in series at Houston and San Francisco. With 30 games left in the season, they were now in third place, 6½ back of the Dodgers and only a half-game ahead of the fourth-place Philadelphia Phillies.[30]

A cross-country flight took them to Philadelphia for a series with the Phillies, who had won 12 of their last 16. The Redbirds swept the series and Ken homered in three consecutive games August 30–September 1. He blasted a two-run shot in the ninth inning of an 11-6 victory, a game-winning round-tripper in 11 innings, 7-5, and hit his 20th of the season in a 7-3 win. "I'm sure I never hit home runs in three successive games before, even in the minors," he said. (In fact, he did with the Omaha Cardinals in both games of a twin bill on June 27, 1951, and one the following day.) The sweep dropped the Phillies to fifth place. With the Giants losing two of three to the Dodgers, St. Louis reclaimed second place and trailed Los Angeles by six games.[31]

IT WAS THE START of an incredible run of 19 victories in 20 games to challenge Los Angeles for the pennant. Musial described the stretch as "the most incredible of my 22 years in the majors." "When he announced his retirement, it's like he woke everybody up on that ball club," recalled Groat, though it took almost three weeks to energize them. The pitching staff combined for a 1.94 ERA and six shutouts, three by Simmons, two by Sadecki, and one by Gibson. They received plenty of firepower—92 runs scored, 21 home runs, and a team batting average of .314. "For three unbelievable weeks, we kept winning and winning and winning," remembered Gibson. The offense had double-digit hit totals in all but four games. During the stretch, Ken swatted .347 with six homers and 18 RBIs. The youngest starting player on the club, catcher Tim McCarver, looked to the veterans for guidance to perform under the pressure. "Boyer was a terrific guy and our steadying influence as we got involved in our first pennant race."[32] A good-luck charm from the team's last championship season in 1946 was tracked down, a folksy song recorded by Spike Jones entitled "Pass the Biscuits, Mirandy." The hillbilly melody was played in the clubhouse after every victory by trainer Doc Bauman to the bemusement of the younger players.[33]

Ken finally reached the pinnacle of 100 RBIs that eluded him in his first nine major-league seasons. He singled off reliever Galen Cisco in the seventh inning and drove in pinch-runner Gary Kolb with the winning run in a 6-5 victory over the Mets on September 4. The Cardinals won nine straight over the Phillies, Pirates, and Mets before being shut out by hard-throwing left-hander Bob Veale at Pittsburgh, 5-0, during the second game of a doubleheader on September 6. Trailing by two runs the next day, Boyer tied the game on McCarver's sacrifice fly in the eighth inning. Flood singled to knock in Gibson, who was pinch-running for Musial, with the winning run in the ninth, 6-5. It started a 10-game winning streak that brought them within a game of the league-leading Dodgers with 10 games left in the season. "It was such a fun drive," says Groat. "We didn't make any mistakes whatsoever. We were playing so well."[34]

Taking three of four from the Pirates, the Redbirds returned to Busch Stadium for an 11-game homestand beginning September 9. Simmons, Gibson, and Sadecki pitched consecutive shutouts over the seventh-place Chicago Cubs. On September 13, Ken homered off Warren Spahn and Simmons pitched a five-hit, 7-0 shutout against the Milwaukee Braves. St. Louis was now 2 ½ games behind LA. "Sure we're closing in on them, but we all realize we're still behind," said Keane after the game. "We can't afford to lose any more. We're just hoping that somebody hangs a couple of defeats on them." Gibson won his 18th of the season the next day. In the first game of a doubleheader on the fifteenth, Boyer doubled and scored on White's homer and smashed one of his own in the 3-2 victory. Sadecki held the Braves to five safeties and shut them out, 5-0. During his final plate appearance of the series, Eddie Mathews looked down at McCarver catching and told him, "You guys are going to win with everything you've got going for you." Meanwhile, Los Angeles split a four-game set at Philadelphia that reduced their lead to one game over the Cardinals.[35]

Pennant excitement was rampant in St. Louis for the first time in six years as the Dodgers came to town. Fans packed Busch Stadium for the pivotal three-game showdown. Keane was confident: "We couldn't be more ready for this series."

"We were playing so well," recalls Groat. "We thought we were really going to win it. But Podres and Koufax had different ideas."[36]

In the opener on September 16, Broglio and Johnny Podres both pitched scoreless ball through the first five innings. In the sixth, Broglio yielded two hits and a walk that scored Maury Wills. Musial tied it in the seventh with his 475th and final home run of his major-league career. It wasn't until Broglio was lifted for reliever Bobby Shantz in the ninth that the Dodgers scored two runs to beat them, 3-1, and snap St. Louis's 10-game winning streak. The Cardinals managed only three hits off Podres and reliever Ron Perranoski. Boyer flied out three times and struck out to end the game.

The task was even more difficult the next evening. Sandy Koufax pitched a brilliant four-hit, 4-0 shutout to beat Simmons and Ken suffered another 0-for-4 showing. He almost put St. Louis ahead when they trailed in the seventh, 1-0. After Musial led off with a single and was lifted for pinch-runner Gary Kolb, Boyer drove a high fastball to right field. "When I hit the ball, I thought it had a chance to go out, and that at least it would hit the fence," he recalled. "I hit the ball good." But 6-foot-7 Frank Howard caught it against the wall and ended the rally.[37]

St. Louis fought back in the finale and scored early in support of Gibson. Already leading, 3-1, Boyer forced Musial at second base in the third inning, advanced to second on White's single, went to third on a wild pitch, and both scored on Curt Flood's double to make it 5-1. Ken was hitless for the third game in a row, but made some outstanding defensive plays, including a backhanded grab on a hard-hit ball in the seventh.[38] Gibson held the lead until the eighth when he gave up three singles and a walk that plated two runs for the Dodgers. He was relieved by Shantz, who gave up another tally. Still, the Redbirds held a one-run lead until Dick Nen—in only his second major-league plate appearance—blasted a game-tying home run with one out in the ninth that sent the contest into extra innings. Groat led off with a triple in the tenth and Boyer and White were walked intentionally to load the bases with one out. Ground outs by Flood (to force Groat out at home) and rookie Mike Shannon ended the Cardinals' only serious extra-inning threat. Los Angeles had a more productive ground-out with the bases loaded in the thirteenth to score the deciding run, 6-5.

WITH A DECISIVE three-game sweep, the Dodgers knocked off their closest competitor and flew back to the West Coast with a four-game lead and the National League pennant all but clinched. The demoralized Redbirds dropped their next three at Cincinnati and Chicago and fell 2 ½ games further back. "You could sense something like this happening after the LA series," lamented Boyer. Mired in an 0-for-22 slide, he crashed a two-hit shutout by Glen Hobbie of the Cubs with a two-run triple and scored the tying run. But Chicago rallied to beat them, 6-3, extending St. Louis' losing streak to six games and officially eliminating them from the race. "I hate to see them finish this way," Keane said afterward. "They just haven't been hitting the ball since the hot streak, but we went as far as we could go."[39]

St. Louis halted the losing skid with a 5-2 victory on September 25. They returned to Busch Stadium for the last series of the season against the Cincinnati Reds, but dropped the first two games leading up to the finale—Musial's last game—on Sunday, September 29. The weather was fitting for the occasion and Cincinnati's Jim Maloney, seeking his 24th victory of the season, was on the mound. Reds infielder and former Cardinals teammate Eddie Kasko remarked, "After the tremendous career he's had, you knew it had to end on a day like this. Sunny, with a gale blowing to right and a hard-throwing right-hander pitching."[40]

Players from both clubs stood on the baselines as Musial was honored in a pregame ceremony filled with accolades and tributes. His uniform number was officially retired and plans were unveiled for a statue of him to be erected at the new downtown stadium. As team captain, Ken presented him a ring on behalf of his teammates with six diamonds shaped like Stan's No. 6, a gift Musial said he cherished more than any other. Stan had two singles in his last three at-bats to finish his 22-year major-league career with an even 3,630 hits. Batting behind The Man for the last time, Boyer struck out twice and singled. He had three more safeties before the Cardinals finally beat the Reds in the fourteenth, 3-2.[41]

Not only was Boyer losing a teammate, but a memorable part of his childhood as well. It would be the last time he and St. Louis fans would see his broad smile and unique corkscrew batting stance on a major-league diamond. Said Ken, "The big thrill I got today was having my son (David) at the ballpark to watch Stan with binoculars the way I watched him 15 years ago."[42]

Boyer never felt slighted playing in Musial's shadow because he never sought the spotlight for himself. He insisted his role as team captain in no way supplanted Musial's leadership on the club. Their relationship was one of mutual respect and admiration. Even though they hunted together on occasion during the off-season, they weren't close friends away from the ballpark, perhaps because of the eleven-year age difference between them. Still, Ken drew closer to his idol after the departure of Stan's friend Red Schoendienst in 1956 and took the locker next to him. "Just being around him had to make you a better player," he said. Both men were pillars for a team that changed around them over the next seven years. When Schoendienst returned to St. Louis in 1961, he and Boyer's lockers flanked that of Musial.[43]

Ken learned many valuable lessons from Stan—how not to be discouraged in the midst of slumps, learning to trust the media, and what to say (and not say) about teammates or opposing players. "Stan had probably as much influence on my career as anyone," he remarked. "He said so many things to me that you knew were right and made sense." The respect he held for Musial was best reflected in the following statement: "Stan ought to be an inspiration to anyone in baseball. He's living proof that nice guys don't have to finish last."[44]

The Cardinals closed the season in second place with a 93-69 record, six games behind the Dodgers, who swept the New York Yankees in four straight games during the World Series. St. Louis led the majors in team batting average at .271, with Flood, Groat, and White each attaining the 200-hit plateau for the season. Keane conceded that "the better team won. But they knew they were in a fight. All we need are a couple of more key men and we won't have to apologize next year." Still, it was their best finish in six years with the highest number of victories since 1949 and a nice consolation prize of $2,278.09 per player.[45]

Keane intended to rest Boyer over the course of the season, but as usual, he played in all but three games. In the midst of the pennant race in August, the manager said, "I just haven't been able to rest the regulars because it's been such a dog-eat-dog race." Ken batted .285 with 24 home runs, three behind White's team-leading total. He paced the club with 111 RBIs and finished second in the National League in that category behind Hank Aaron and two ahead of White.[46]

The acquisition of Altman, intended to add a power-hitting outfielder to the order alongside Boyer and White, was a major disappointment. He started the season hitting .370 through the end of April, but never recovered from an 18-for-98 slide a month later and lost his starting right-field berth in the second-half. Weakened eyesight and pulling the ball to launch home runs over the enticing short right-field porch at Busch Stadium resulted in only 34 extra-base hits (nine of those round-trippers) in 464 at-bats. Altman had a decent

.274 average, but the results were literally night and day: he struggled under the lights, batting .221 in 69 night games, and hit exceptionally in the daytime at a .322 clip in 66 games.[47]

After the season, Altman was traded with minor-league pitcher Bill Wakefield to the New York Mets for right-handed reliever and spot starter Roger Craig. Two of the players dealt to the Cubs for him enjoyed productive careers in Chicago and beyond. Ken's friend Larry Jackson won 14 games in 1963, reached 21 victories a year later (tied for the NL lead), and had double-digit win totals over the next four seasons. McDaniel led the majors with 48 games finished and 21 saves in '63 and remained a valuable reliever for 12 more years.[48]

Though it didn't end as well as the Cardinals had hoped, the late-season pennant chase in 1963 nonetheless was a precursor of championship seasons to come in the decade. All the pieces were now in place—except for a base-stealing, offensive catalyst near the top of the batting order. After the abysmal Altman deal, the Chicago Cubs owed them one.

Ken Boyer during his rookie season with the St. Louis Cardinals in 1955.
(*St. Louis Mercantile Library Collection*)

Ready for the major leagues, 1955. (*Author's Collection*)

Boyer's 1955 Topps rookie baseball card. (*Topps trading card courtesy of The Topps Company, Inc.*)

Boyer crosses the plate after smashing his 19th home run, best in the National League at the time, in 1956. The iconic birds-on-the-bat disappeared from the Cardinals jerseys that season before a public outcry forced new St. Louis general manager Frank Lane to bring it back a year later. (*St. Louis Mercantile Library Collection*)

Boyer receives the second of his five Gold Glove Awards for defensive excellence at third base, 1959. (*National Baseball Hall of Fame Library, Cooperstown NY*) His 1959 Gold Glove Award remains with the Boyer family today (**right**).

(**Above**) Boyer was a leader on the field and in the clubhouse. In 1959, Cardinals manager Solly Hemus (left) made him team captain, a role he held until he was traded after the 1965 season. Also pictured are pitcher Hal Smith and pitcher Gary Blaylock (right).
(*Hal Smith Family Collection*)

Boyer poses with two of his hunting dogs. Quail hunting with family, friends, and teammates during the off-season was a favorite pastime.
(*Boyer Family Collection*)

Ken at home with daughter Suzie and son David.
(*Boyer Family Collection*)

Kathleen and Ken Boyer.
(*Boyer Family Collection*)

Ken poses with Kathleen and their family at Busch Stadium.
(Left to right) Suzie, David, Danny, and Jane.
(*Boyer Family Collection*)

(**Above**) Daughter Jane Boyer kisses her father good-bye as he prepares to leave. (Left to right) David, Danny, Suzie, and mother Kathleen look on. (*St. Louis Mercantile Library Collection*)

(**Left**) Ken and son Danny Boyer at Busch Stadium. (*Boyer Family Collection*)

Ken, Kathleen, and Suzie Boyer (right) pose with Stan Musial, wife Lillian, and his daughters on the day Musial announced his retirement following the 1963 season.
(*Boyer Family Collection*)

No. 14 smacks a hit to left field. (*Kevin Noland*)

Boyer's home for eleven major-league seasons: Busch Stadium in St. Louis. (*St. Louis Mercantile Library Collection*)

Boyer had two baseball instructional schools, one in Tampa, Florida, and another in Montauk, Missouri. Boys spent three weeks working with former and current major-leaguers on all aspects of the game. (*Author's Collection*)

Chapter Ten

A Pennant Winner

On the last day of the 1963 season, Ken Boyer echoed what manager Johnny Keane said about Stan Musial's retirement: "[W]e won't miss Stan until next year."

Musial wasn't really gone. He was now a vice president in the front office and still worked out with his former teammates in spring training. But his bat was no longer in the lineup and his iconic presence was missing from the team. There was even a physical absence in the clubhouse as his locker between those of Boyer and Schoendienst had been removed and donated to the National Baseball Hall of Fame in Cooperstown, New York. At his retirement party, Musial smiled at Boyer and told him, "You're on your own now."[1]

Ken's leadership was more valuable than ever as the Cardinals attempted to build on a surprising finish the previous season. Musial's absence placed greater responsibility on his shoulders. He felt an obligation to mentor his young teammates and help them develop into major-league players. "They come to the older players for advice and an older player can help by giving the younger player compliments, pats on the back, to help him gain confidence. Another player can reach a ballplayer better than a coach or a manager and help him with some points on hitting and base running, for instance."[2]

Boyer was confident St. Louis would win the pennant in 1964. "We have the best team in the National League. We had the best team last year, but we made our own mistakes. This time we'll win." His playing career would be incomplete without reaching the pinnacle of his sport—the World Series. "If I am as good as people say, I should have been able to help my team win a pennant." In February, while on a Cardinals Caravan promotional tour in Joplin, Missouri, near his hometown, he agreed to a new contract that raised his salary back to $50,000.[3]

Ken had a terrific spring training, finishing second to rookie outfielder Johnny Lewis with a .321 average in 24 exhibition games. The Redbirds began the campaign with a western swing through Los Angeles, San Francisco, and Houston, winning four of their first seven games. Boyer doubled and stroked two safeties, including a two-run single, off Dodgers right-hander Don Drysdale on April 15. Three days later, he smashed his first home run of the season in a 3-2 win at Candlestick Park.

The team returned to St. Louis for their evening home opener against the Dodgers on April 22. Before a crowd of 31,410—the largest ever at Busch Stadium for a home opener—the Cardinals debuted their new red caps for home games. They faced Sandy Koufax, who had shut them out on six hits on Opening Day at Dodger Stadium on April 14, but the left-hander was less effective in this game. Bill White's strikeout that should have ended the first inning instead became a wild pitch, allowing him to reach base. Ken followed with a walk and both scored on Charlie James's home run. St. Louis added to their 3-0 lead once Koufax exited with a stiff elbow as Boyer doubled and came home on a blast by Carl Warwick in the second. Another homer by White proved the difference in the 7-6 victory.[4]

After a dismal 3-for-15 start in the first four home games, Ken caught fire with a nine-game consecutive hit streak that raised his average to .372 the first week of May. All but two were multi-hit games and he drove in 11 runs in that span. He playfully attributed his success to wearing a red undershirt that belonged to Musial. "The balls are falling in for me. Others are hitting the ball harder, but right at somebody. I've been satisfied just to meet the ball and stroke it."[5]

After splitting the May 31 doubleheader with Cincinnati, the Cardinals were in third place, 2 ½ games behind the front-running Philadelphia Phillies. Ken was having his best start to the season yet, batting .343 with 38 RBIs, second behind Willie Mays's 43 in the National League. Musial was pleased with his former teammate's offensive outburst. "The important thing about Boyer is that he's not trying to slug with these pitchers. He's just meeting the ball and hitting to all fields. He's hit this way before, but mostly he's done it in spurts."[6]

When the Redbirds were winning, Ken wore the same plaid sport jacket for good luck. "I'm not superstitious," he claimed, "but I'm sticking with this coat." The sweltering St. Louis summers, however, created a dilemma for his teammates. "Because he was our captain, no one had the courage to tell Ken when he thought it had to be cleaned," says Tim McCarver. "Consequently, from a personal hygiene standpoint, rooting for a winning streak had its perils."[7]

But over the next two-and-a-half weeks, the offense sparked by the bats of Boyer, Flood, and Javier fizzled. After a 7-5 win at Chicago on June 3, St. Louis scored only 20 runs in their next 12 games and were shut out in four of them. Ken made a crucial fielding error in the ninth inning at Cincinnati, allowing the Reds to rally from a 4-1 deficit. Harry Caray lamented to his listeners, "I don't know how we lose some of these ballgames, but we do! So it's all over! Almost unbelievable—the Reds score four runs in the ninth inning and beat the Cardinals, 5-4." St. Louis lost 11 out of 16 on the road, tumbling to eighth place and seven games out on June 15. Boyer was hitless in 19 at-bats and saw his average fall to .304.[8]

On the team's flight to Houston two days before the trading deadline on the fifteenth, Bing Devine told Keane he could make a deal for twenty-four-year-old outfielder Lou Brock. He had been talking with the Chicago Cubs about acquiring him since the off-season. But their Midwest rivals were committed to a youth movement and hesitant to trade a promising player, even though starting pitching was a commodity they desperately needed to contend. In sixth place but only 5 ½ games behind Philadelphia and with Brock batting .251, they were ready to deal. Devine didn't want to give up any of his young pitchers.

Instead, he offered experienced starter Ernie Broglio, a 20-game winner in 1960 who was coming off an 18-win season. The right-hander had struggled up to this point in the season with a 3-5 record and a 3.50 ERA in 11 starts and had fallen out of favor with his manager.

Keane told Devine, "What are we waiting for?"[9]

The trade was finalized fifteen hours before the deadline, sending Broglio, veteran left-handed reliever Bobby Shantz, and reserve outfielder Doug Clemons to the Cubs for Brock and minor-league pitchers Jack Spring and Paul Toth. "If Brock was hitting .300, you couldn't get him," Devine explained to *The Sporting News*. "But he hasn't fulfilled his potential. I was not thinking it would be a popular deal. Brock never played that well against the Cardinals and Broglio is considered a front-line pitcher."[10]

The initial reactions to the deal were unbridled excitement in Chicago and complete skepticism in St. Louis. The Cubs believed the addition of Broglio to their starting rotation would make them a pennant contender. *Chicago Daily News* columnist Bob Smith was jubilant: "Thank you, thank you, oh, you lovely St. Louis Cardinals. Nice doing business with you. Please call again anytime." Brock's new teammates questioned giving up a quality starting pitcher for a promising but unproven player who had already been in the majors three seasons. "We all thought it was nuts," recalled White frankly. "Lou was a raw talent. At that point, he didn't really understand baseball. He might try to steal while 10 runs up or 10 runs down." Bob Gibson was even more blunt: "I thought it was one of the dumbest trades in the world." The unpopularity of the Broglio trade was so bad in the Cardinals clubhouse that Keane called a pre-game meeting in Houston to remind his squad that it was he and Devine's prerogative how the roster would be altered. Prophetically, the general manager said, "You never know how these things work out."[11]

For the Cardinals, the trade worked out very well. After striking out as a pinch-hitter in a 9-3 loss at Houston on June 15, Keane put Brock in the starting lineup the next evening in right field, batting second behind Flood. He walked in his first at-bat, singled and scored from second on Ken's triple to center in the fifth inning, and smashed a three-bagger of his own in the sixth. In the 7-1 win, Boyer collected four safeties, including his 10th home run of the season, and knocked in three runs. He became the 19th major-league player to hit for the cycle twice in his career. Not only was he the first Cardinal ever with two, but he became the first Cardinal and only the fifth player in major-league history to have a "natural" cycle—single, double, triple, and home run—in sequential order.[12]

The month of June was the worst of the season for the Redbirds, losing 18 of 29 games. When it was over, they were in seventh place, two games under .500 and 9½ behind the San Francisco Giants. They did influence the top of the standings, however, splitting a four-game home series with the league-leading Phillies the last week of the month. Their 8-2 victory in the second game of a June 28 doubleheader helped the Giants briefly knock Philadelphia out of first place.

It was no coincidence that the downturn occurred while Ken was experiencing his own worst month of the season. Three times in two weeks, he hurt his back diving for ground balls before he "finally decided to quit diving for a while." Still, he made no excuses and stayed in the lineup regardless of the pain. "I thought I could do the job defensively and swing the bat good enough too," he recalled at the end of the season. "I figured if I was wrong, Johnny would take me out." An eight-game hit streak toward the end of June helped somewhat, but his average still dipped below .300 for the first time since the middle of April. During the streak, he took over the NL RBI lead for the first time when he doubled home Dick Groat against Milwaukee for his 54th RBI on June 29. (Mays reclaimed it a few games later.) The Cardinals finished the first-half of the season on July 5 with a 39-40 record in fifth place and 10 games out of first.[13]

Three-fourths of the St. Louis infield—Boyer, Groat, and White—returned to the National League roster and Flood made his first appearance in the All-Star Game.[14] Ken enjoyed a commanding lead over Ron Santo of the Chicago Cubs in the voting to start at third base, 172 to 84. In the closest vote for a starting berth, Groat edged Leo Cardenas of the Cincinnati Reds by just five votes. The St. Louis shortstop was hitting .290 at the break and his 19 doubles were tied for third-best in the circuit. White finished second to San Francisco's Orlando Cepeda to start at first base. That he finished so high on the ballot was surprising. White had a terrible month of May and early June, hitting as low as .224 on June 10. He managed to raise his average to .263 by the All-Star break. Flood—fourth in the NL with 95 safeties and hitting .296—came in second to perennial All-Star Willie Mays in center field, but still made the roster as a reserve.[15]

The game was held at New York's Shea Stadium in front of 50,850 fans on July 7. Groat and Boyer were in the starting lineup batting second and sixth, respectively. In the second inning, Ken had the National League's first hit, a two-out single in his first at-bat, but was forced out on a ground ball to short by Joe Torre of the Braves. The NL tied the score in the fourth, 1-1, on a home run by Billy Williams of the Cubs off Kansas City Athletics right-hander John Wyatt. Three batters later, Wyatt threw a first-pitch fastball to Boyer, who drove it over the left-field fence to put them ahead. "It was the first pitch he threw me, but I didn't figure to get a better one," he said. Ken shook the extended hand of All-Star coach and Cincinnati Reds manager Fred Hutchinson as he rounded third base. "I've always had great respect for Hutch as a manager," he later remarked about his old skipper. Hutchinson had been diagnosed with lung cancer and would pass away four months later at the age of forty-five.[16]

The National League tallied again in the fifth on Groat's RBI double that scored former Pittsburgh teammate Roberto Clemente to make it 3-1. The AL came right back in the sixth and tied it on a triple by Brooks Robinson of the Baltimore Orioles that scored Mickey Mantle and Harmon Killebrew, then went ahead in the seventh when Fregosi flied out and Elston Howard of the Yankees scored.[17]

The Boston Red Sox's hard-throwing reliever Dick Radatz blanked the NL for two innings and struck out five before yielding a walk on 11 pitches to Mays to lead off the bottom of the ninth. Mays stole second, then scored the tying run on Giants teammate Cepeda's single and a wild throw home by first baseman Joe Pepitone of the Yankees. Flood entered the game as a pinch-runner for Cepeda before Boyer popped up to Robinson at third base for what proved to be his final All-Star plate appearance. Johnny Edwards of the Cincinnati Reds was walked intentionally and pinch-hitter Hank Aaron struck out. One out away from extra innings and the score tied, 4-4, Radatz threw a fastball inside to Johnny Callison of the Phillies, who smashed it to deep right field for the walk-off, three-run homer. The 7-4 victory evened the midsummer classic between the two leagues at 17 wins apiece and one tie.[18]

WHEN THE CARDINALS resumed the regular season on July 9, they faced what seemed an impossible task in an increasingly tight pennant chase. There were three teams between them and the first-place Philadelphia Phillies—San Francisco, Cincinnati, and Pittsburgh—with three games separating them from the Pirates, four from the Reds, and 8½ from the Giants. They were tied with Los Angeles for fifth place and Milwaukee and Chicago were just a half-game behind. "It's a longshot—there's a steep road ahead," Devine candidly admitted about his club's chances in the second-half. "There are several clubs besides the Phillies and Giants ahead of us and they're not all going to be beaten every night." He added, "When you're in a position like ours, you've got to have a long winning streak, something like eight out of nine or nine out of 10. We haven't done that yet. We haven't shown signs of doing it."[19]

The Redbirds made strides in that direction, winning eight of their first 11 games, including five straight July 10–14. They took both games of a twi-night doubleheader at Pittsburgh on the thirteenth that brought them within a half-game of the fourth-place Pirates. In the second game, a three-hour affair that lasted until one o'clock in the morning, Ken had three safeties and scored three runs and White and Brock both homered. The 12-5 victory was the first major-league victory for twenty-seven-year-old, left-handed rookie and future Cy Young Award winner Mike Cuellar.

Hitless in his last 11 at-bats going into and coming out of the All-Star break, Boyer caught fire with a blistering 18-for-38 outburst in eight straight games beginning July 11—all but one were multiple-hit games—and raised his average to .303. With St. Louis trailing the Mets, 4-3, on July 17, he was caught stealing second in the fifth inning. Boos rained down from the stands until fans realized he had stayed in the rundown long enough for Brock to steal home and tie the score. St. Louis eventually won, 9-8. Ken smashed a grand slam the next afternoon, the first of three successive blasts by White and McCarver in an 11-run eighth inning of a 15-7 rout over New York.[20]

A three-game home series against the Pirates afforded the opportunity to move past their closest competitors in the standings. Instead, the Cardinals were swept, much to the disgust of Gussie Busch, who made a rare appearance at the ballpark for the series. "I'm not satisfied at all the way we're going," he grumbled after the 8-5 loss on July 23. "I'm not happy with the morale of the club—the players look listless on the field." Despite improving over the past few weeks, Busch was pessimistic about his club's second-half chances. "I've got my fingers crossed that we'll do better—but I don't know."[21]

With a 9-1 defeat to open a four-game series at Philadelphia the next evening—their fourth loss in a row—St. Louis had a record of 47-48. They were tied with the Dodgers for seventh place and 10 games behind the front-running Phillies. The next day, both teams had 14 hits with White and recent call-up Mike Shannon getting three safeties each. Boyer blasted a grand slam (his second in a week) and a solo homer in back-to-back plate appearances—his only multi-home run game of the season—to help the Redbirds build a ninth-inning, 10-2 lead. A seven-run outburst by Philadelphia with none out in the ninth almost cost them the game, but Cuellar preserved the 10-9 victory. It was the last time the Redbirds would fall below .500 or lose more than two games in a row the rest of the season.

St. Louis reeled off six straight wins on the road, including three at Philadelphia. After returning home and losing two of three to the third-place Reds, they took the next three series against the Cubs, Colt .45s, and Giants the first two weeks of August. A season-best 11-game hit streak July 23–August 2 raised Boyer's average to .311, the highest it had been since June 11.

In August, the Cardinals were the best hitting club in the league, thanks to Boyer, White, Flood, Brock, and Groat. They had fought their way back into the pennant race and were in fifth place and seven games over .500 on August 12. At the plate, Ken and fellow infielders White and Groat began wearing golf gloves to give them a better grip on their bats.[22]

Unfortunately, it wasn't enough to save Devine's job. Not only did an 8½-game deficit between them and the Phillies seem insurmountable with less than eight weeks in the season, but Busch felt Devine and Keane tried to hide internal strife in the Cardinals clubhouse from him. A month earlier, Keane had taken away Groat's authority to call the hit-and-run on his own and the veteran complained to his friend Eddie Mathews of the Braves, who was dating (and would later marry) Busch's daughter. Learning about the incident from someone other than his manager or general manager did not sit well with the beer baron. It had already been resolved on July 9 with Groat's apology to the entire team during an uncomfortable pre-game tirade by Keane. The controversy was settled when Busch questioned Devine whether there was anything he needed to know. Busch took Devine's denial as disloyalty and fired him and long-time business manager Art Routzong on August 17.

Echoing Branch Rickey's sentiments, Busch felt a contender should be built from within and not through trades. He was also displeased with the quality of prospects in the minor-league system under Devine's six-year watch. "I've worried about the Cardinals for a long time. The club has not been making any progress. I felt it was time to make a change before we moved into the new stadium in 1966." A Cardinals fan since childhood, Devine was disappointed at his dismissal. "I hope they'll win soon—for old times' sake—because, if they do, they'll win with my players."[23]

The players liked and respected Devine and were stunned at the news. Ken's reaction was indicative of what others felt in the clubhouse. "The whole thing came as a surprise to me—and a lot of the players." Keane held a clubhouse meeting and gave everyone the opportunity to express his feelings about the firing. Many believed it was the final act in a front-office power struggle between Devine and Rickey that went back to the former general manager's hiring as a "special consultant" in 1962. It was a charge Busch denied, but the fact that he named Rickey's protégé, Bob Howsam, as Devine's replacement did little to dissuade it. In retrospect, Boyer believed the gathering may have given the Cardinals a renewed purpose. "That meeting didn't start out as a pep rally, but maybe subconsciously it had something to do with our coming back to win the pennant." Among the last moves Devine made were promoting outfielder and St. Louis native Mike Shannon and thirty-seven-year-old veteran reliever and knuckleball pitcher Barney Schultz. Both would be key additions to an improbable pennant chase for the Cardinals.[24]

Splitting the last 10-game western road trip of the season, St. Louis returned home and won 12 out of 15 games August 24–September 7. Ken was fighting a stomach virus before the September 4 contest against the Cubs and considered not coming to the ballpark. He changed his mind, but was hitless in his first four plate appearances. With runners at first and second and two outs in the bottom of the ninth, Boyer cracked the first pitch from rookie reliever Freddie Burdette onto the right-field pavilion roof for a game-winning home run, 8-5. When he stepped on home plate, he recorded his 100th RBI, the second year in a row he passed the century mark in that category. "Before the season, I said getting 100 RBIs in our league would be tough with all the good pitching," he remarked. "But I've had a lot of good horses on base ahead of me, and I've been getting a lot of RBI mileage out of my extra-base hits." The win moved them into third place, a game-and-a-half behind second-place Cincinnati.[25]

St. Louis rallied to beat Chicago again two days later in extra innings despite strong pitching from ex-teammates Ernie Broglio and Lindy McDaniel. They took both games of a Labor Day doubleheader with the Reds in walk-off fashion to move into a second-place tie, 6½ behind Philadelphia. In the opener, Ken broke up a scoreless pitching duel between Gibson and Jim O'Toole with a two-run homer in the third inning. The Reds tied it in the ninth; in the Cardinals' half, Boyer led off with a walk, advanced to third on two passed balls by catcher Don Pavletich (who had just entered the game), and scored the winning run on McCarver's single.[26]

The Cardinals hit the road for their next 18 games, the longest trip of the season. At Philadelphia on September 9, Ken singled in the first inning off Jim Bunning, who had a record of 16-4 coming into the contest, to score Brock. The Phillies tied it in their half, went up by one in the second, and knocked ex-Phillie Simmons (and now their nemesis) from the game with two runs in the fourth to take a 4-1 lead. Brock and Boyer both homered in the fifth, but the Phils added another run in the eighth to make it 5-3 when their relief pitcher delivered a two-out RBI double. A ground out by White in the ninth scored Flood and Ken drove in Brock—who had five hits and scored four times—with a two-out, game-tying single off closer Jack Baldschun to send it into extra innings. Boyer had bludgeoned

Philadelphia pitching the entire season, especially at Connie Mack Stadium, where he batted .361 in nine games with three homers, 10 RBIs, and slugged .722. Phillies manager Gene Mauch later told him about that ninth-inning blow: "You've had a big year, but the one hit that was the biggest and hurt us the most was the one in Philly that turned the whole thing around and got the Cardinals going."[27]

Two innings of perfect relief by Gordon Richardson and Bob Humphreys enabled the Cardinals to make it to the eleventh. They scored five runs in that frame and beat Philadelphia, 10-5, taking sole possession of second place and putting themselves five games out of first. "I've got a feeling they might be peeking back at us now," said Ken afterward. "If they had won this one, they might have broken this thing wide open with a seven-game lead."[28]

Said reserve outfielder Bob Skinner, "Both teams are driving the same kind of car, wide-open, and both are floor-boarding, but the Phillies had the head start." And St. Louis was fighting hard to catch up.[29]

The Redbirds took two out of three at Chicago, including a historic 15-2 triumph on September 13. They scored in all nine innings, only the second time such a feat had occurred since 1923. It was achieved when Boyer crossed the plate on Shannon's sacrifice fly in the ninth. He also contributed two safeties, knocked in two runs, and scored twice as part of St. Louis' 18-hit attack.[30]

Winning two of three at Milwaukee, the Cardinals traveled to Cincinnati to face the third-place Reds. A Friday night rainout necessitated a Saturday evening twin bill on September 19. They scored five runs on six hits, all but one for extra bases, including homers by Shannon and Boyer. His two-run blast gave him a career-high 112 RBIs for the season. Gibson hurled five shutout innings before giving up a three-run shot to Deron Johnson to make it 5-3 after Ken misplayed a grounder by Frank Robinson. Marty Keough's two-out solo home run made it a one-run game in the eighth. In the ninth, Gibson had the Redbirds a strike away from another win when Robinson connected for a three-run walk-off blast to hand St. Louis a crushing 7-5 defeat. In the second game, Ray Sadecki pitched eight shutout innings and knuckleballer Schultz closed it for the 2-0 win.

The next day, the Cardinals took a commanding 6-0 lead in the first four frames thanks to home runs by Brock, Groat, and Shannon, and Ken's two-run triple. But the Reds rallied with a hotly-disputed hit by pitch and 12 safeties, tying it in the sixth on Johnny Edwards' two-run single and scoring three unearned runs off Schultz in the eighth to beat them, 9-6. The loss enabled Cincinnati to tie St. Louis for second place; both clubs were 83-66 and still 6½ out of first with 13 games left to play.

With the Cardinals idle before a two-game series with the Mets at Shea Stadium, the front-running Phillies had a magic number of seven as they hosted Cincinnati on September 21. Philadelphia stranded two runners in scoring position in the first two frames before Cuban rookie Chico Ruiz of the Reds unexpectedly stole home with two outs in the sixth and cleanup hitter Frank Robinson at the plate for what proved to be the only run of the game. The 1-0 defeat seemed meaningless at the time—the Phillies front office began selling World Series tickets the next day—but it was actually the beginning of a historic collapse that would change the course of the pennant race.[31]

On September 22, the Mets scored in the first inning and the Redbirds countered in the fourth on Boyer's RBI triple (his 10th of the season) and Groat's sacrifice fly that drove him in for the 2-1 victory. New York came back the following day to beat St. Louis by the same score. Meanwhile, Cincinnati completed a three-game sweep over Philadelphia that dropped St. Louis into third place and five games back.

The Redbirds traveled to Pittsburgh for a crucial five-game series with the Pirates. In the first match of the September 24 twi-night doubleheader, they scored on a balk in the first and a sacrifice fly by Gibson in support of himself in the second. Two more tallies were added in the fifth on a two-run single by White. Gibson struck out 11 and pitched eight scoreless innings, giving up Donn Clendenon's two-run homer in the seventh, for the 4-2 victory. Sadecki fanned 10 and scattered five hits in the second contest for the 4-0 shutout. Homers by Brock and Shannon and an RBI double by White provided support. The next evening, the Cards tallied three in the first inning and added two more in the seventh on only four hits to beat the Pirates, 5-3. Pittsburgh scored first on September 26, but St. Louis countered with four runs in the fourth. After Groat doubled and Boyer and Javier walked to load the bases with one out, Shannon singled to short right field and Groat scored. Rounding third, Ken missed coach Vern Benson's stop sign and upended catcher Jerry May as he crossed the plate. Right fielder Roberto Clemente's throw bounced past the sprawled May to the backstop screen, allowing Javier to score on the error. McCarver then singled and drove in Shannon with the fourth run. The Redbirds added two more tallies and Boyer finally broke out of his batting slump with a seventh-inning single in the 6-3 win.[32]

Keane spoke for himself and his players when asked about the thrill of the pennant chase. "Yes, it is exciting. But it isn't much fun." The stress took a toll on all of them, even the veteran Boyer. "The truth of the matter is, you're living on Scotch and soda and coffee and cigarettes, coming down a stretch like that," recalls Groat. Despite the team's success in the Pittsburgh series, Ken was fighting a personal 0-for-12 slide in the first four games and frustrated with himself for his lack of production. He had struck out an uncharacteristic three times—twice looking—in the second game of the September 24 twin bill. Still, Pittsburgh respected his bat enough to walk him four times, twice intentionally to load the bases. Boyer remembered being unable to sleep at night and playing cards and drinking beer with teammates into the early morning hours to try and relax. Cigarettes were a habit he had given up eleven years earlier after returning home from the military, but the stress of the race led him to start again. "Some of us were smoking two or three packs of cigarettes a day," he told *Post-Dispatch* writer Neal Russo.[33]

At the same time, the adversity strengthened their friendship. Groat was a member of four contending teams in his major-league career—two with Pittsburgh in 1958 and '60 and two in St. Louis in '63 and '64—and life-long bonds were forged in those seasons. "If you ever experience playing in a pennant race as tight as those four were, that's a friendship and a relationship you have with those guys that never, ever, ever goes away," he says. "You have a closeness, a unity to this day. We were the same way when we went to St. Louis [for the 50th anniversary reunion of the '64 Cardinals]. It's like we'd never been apart."[34]

The Cardinals completed the five-game sweep of the Pirates with Roger Craig's 5-0 shutout on September 27. Meanwhile, Philadelphia had lost seven in a row, including three to Cincinnati, and relinquished its hold on first place to the Reds. Cincinnati matched St. Louis win for win that week and kept them from making headway in the standings. The Redbirds remained in third place but only a game-and-a-half back. "We had to win all five against the Pirates to stay in the fight—and we did it," said Groat. "Now we must win all three with the Phils. We can't even afford the luxury of one defeat. If we can win all three from the Phils, then we can hope the Pirates might bounce back and stop the Reds."[35]

Over 5,000 diehard Cardinals fans cheered the players at Lambert Airport as they returned home to face the demoralized Phillies for three games. In the opener on September 28, Gibson dominated with five scattered hits and seven scoreless innings before yielding Philadelphia's only run in the eighth. Ken doubled twice, drove in two runs, and scored twice. White had three safeties and Shannon plated three RBIs in the 5-1 victory. With the Reds idle, St. Louis moved ahead of Philadelphia into second place, one game back of Cincinnati. "We're still looking up at another club," said Boyer afterward. "Our best shot is to beat these guys twice more and hope they beat Cincy twice."[36]

Despite falling to third place, the Phils tried to flash bravado for the writers after the loss. "We ain't through yet. Don't count us out too soon," insisted MVP candidate Johnny Callison. Teammate Wes Covington remarked, "I don't see the Cardinals winning it." But the Redbirds saw shaken confidence in their opponent's eyes, crushed under the weight of the losing streak and faded pennant hopes. Regardless of Philadelphia's state of mind, the Redbirds still had a job to finish. "We've got to win them all," urged Keane about the importance of the next five games. "If we lose one, we're in trouble. If we lose two, we're out of it."[37]

Staked to an early three-run lead in the second game of the series on the twenty-ninth, Sadecki allowed only three hits through the first three innings before giving up two runs in the fourth. White's homer provided insurance in the sixth. With runners on first and third and eventual 1964 NL Rookie of the Year Richie "Dick" Allen coming to bat in the seventh, Keane called on his reliable stopper, Schultz, who got Allen to pop up for the third out and pitched two-and-a-third scoreless innings of relief. The knuckleballer earned his 13th save and preserved Sadecki's 20th win of the season, 4-2, when

Boyer threw out Cookie Rojas to end the game. As the Redbirds congratulated one another on the field, the Busch Stadium crowd suddenly cheered even louder as the scoreboard showed Pittsburgh had just beaten Cincinnati, 2-0. Broadcaster Harry Caray burst back on the air: *"Pittsburgh has won!* Pittsburgh won its ballgame! Two to nothing, it's over! Pittsburgh has just beat the Reds two to nothing! The National League race is in a tie! *Hoooo-ly* Cow! Never has it been a more thrilling moment!" St. Louis's victory coupled with Cincinnati's loss tied both clubs for first place, a game-and-a-half ahead of Philadelphia.[38]

Back in the clubhouse, Ken sat in front of his locker and put his face in his hands. "This is the closest I've been to playing in a World Series," he whispered. "I'd give ten years of my life to play in one."[39]

Before the third game of the series on September 30, he shared the team's confidence going into the final four of the regular season. "We couldn't be in better shape at a better time. The schedule is in our favor. Simmons has worn out the Phillies, so we've got to like our chances." Indeed, the former Phillie beat the current ace Jim Bunning and handed his old club its 10th consecutive defeat, completing the sweep and winning the Redbirds their eighth in a row. Simmons pitched no-hit ball for the first six and two-thirds innings as his teammates built an 8-0 lead on 14 hits, including three safeties by Boyer, Flood, and Groat, a double by White, and McCarver's two-run home run. Philadelphia mounted a comeback in the late innings, but Gordon Richardson saved it in the ninth for the 8-5 triumph. "We just wouldn't quit," recalled Groat fifty years later. "It felt like we won every big game down the stretch when we had to."[40]

The victory elevated the Cardinals to first place by a half-game pending the result of the scoreless Cincinnati-Pittsburgh contest that went to extra innings. The players stayed in the clubhouse and listened on transistor radios to the play-by-play being relayed from Pittsburgh over KMOX. "I'd rather play anytime than watch or listen," said Boyer. "I'm more nervous than I was on the field." As the game remained deadlocked into the night, some players left and kept track of it elsewhere. Ken left after the twelfth inning and took Kathleen out for dinner, but no one in the restaurant was being served—the waitresses and cooks were too distracted listening to the broadcast. He later joined several of his teammates who were staying at the Bel Air Motel on Lindell Boulevard and still listening to the game. Finally, in the top of the sixteenth, Donn Clendenon led off with a double for Pittsburgh and advanced to third on Bill Mazeroski's sacrifice bunt. The next batter, Jerry May, placed a perfect suicide squeeze bunt that went for an infield single down the third-base line. Clendenon broke for the plate and scored the go-ahead run. Ground outs by Pete Rose, Chico Ruiz, and Vada Pinson extended the Reds' scoreless streak to 33 innings.[41]

Cincinnati's 1-0 defeat gave St. Louis sole possession of first place. "I like our position," Keane cautiously remarked. "We've got great pitching and a good defense now—and that's an awfully tough combination," said Boyer in evaluating his club. "Look at the great plays we've been getting, from Julian Javier, Curt Flood, Lou Brock and the others. What I like best at this stage is that we're not fouling up and putting our pitchers in bad situations."[42]

October 1 was an off day for St. Louis and Philadelphia. Cincinnati won the last game of the series at Pittsburgh, 5-4, to slice a half-game off the Cardinals' first-place lead. The New York Mets arrived in town for the final three games of the season entrenched in the National League cellar with a 51-108 record, having lost eight consecutive games and 21 of their last 28. The Redbirds were the hottest team in baseball since the All-Star break, riding an eight-game win streak with a magic number of three—any combination of wins and Reds losses—to clinch the pennant.

Gibson started the first match, seeking his career-high 19th victory of the season. Facing him was Al Jackson, who had lost 16 games and was hoping to win his 11th. As expected, the Cardinals right-hander produced another quality start by striking out seven while scattering eight hits, the only blemish being a two-out RBI single by Ed Kranepool in the third inning. It was one run more than Gibson received, however, as Ken and his teammates couldn't do much with Jackson's sinker. The young left-hander had great control the entire game and held the Redbirds to four singles and a double to win, 1-0. "Jackson was just too good," said Keane afterward. Gibson later recalled, "I have never known a loss that was harder to take than that one against the Mets that Friday night." Luckily for the Cardinals, Philadelphia scored four runs in the top of the eighth to beat the Reds, 4-3, keeping them a half-game behind. The Phillies were now a game-and-a-half back. The fourth-place San Francisco Giants, two games out of first after winning nine of their last 12 games, further complicated matters with the possibility of a four-way tie for the pennant.[43]

The second game was a disaster for the Redbirds from the start. Two errors, four hits, and a wild pitch led to four runs for the Mets off Sadecki in the first inning. St. Louis responded with three tallies in their half as Brock walked and White and Boyer clouted back-to-back home runs. But New York blasted five of their own and 17 hits total off Sadecki and seven relievers to whip them, 15-5. The lowly Mets did what the Phillies and Reds could not—extinguish the red-hot Redbirds.

The clubhouse was somber after the game. Players sat facing their lockers with their heads down. The twin losses brought back painful memories of the 1963 season when three straight defeats to the Dodgers crushed their pennant aspirations. Keane walked into the silence with a message. "Johnny doesn't give pep talks," recounted reserve outfielder Carl Warwick. "His pep talk is no louder than his mad talks.

> He just said, "Guys, let me tell you something. If you want to pout about this and if you want to keep your heads down and just call this a season, that's fine. I can't do anything about it because I can't play for you.' But he said, 'I want to tell you something. We have come from 11 games back. No one thought we could. We've been given every chance that could be given to an athletic club. The rest of the season is in the past. It's over with. We have [one game] left to be in the World Series. Which would you rather do: Be in the World Series or go home? If you want to go home, pack your gear. If not, let's go out there and win, and we won't have to worry about packing."

"I'd rather play in the World Series," answered Ken. "We'll get them tomorrow," Gibson added.[44]

WITH CINCINNATI AND PHILADELPHIA both idle, the Cardinals and Reds were now tied for first place leading into the final game of the regular season. The Phillies were lurking a game behind. The possibility of a four-way deadlock was eliminated when the Giants fell to the Cubs the day before, 10-7. A St. Louis victory and a Cincinnati defeat would give the Cardinals the pennant, while a St. Louis loss and a Cincinnati win would give it to the Reds. If both teams won, there would be a best-of-three playoff beginning in Cincinnati on October 5. If both teams lost, there would be a more complicated and lengthy three-team playoff with Philadelphia for the National League title.[45]

A bruised left hip put Javier out of commission for the most important game of the season. After the 15-5 loss to the Mets, Keane told light-hitting infielder Dal Maxvill that he would start at second base the next day. It would be just his second appearance in the starting lineup all season, having gone 4-for-22 and batted .182 in 36 games thus far.[46]

A crowd of 30,146 frenzied Cardinals fans packed Busch Stadium on Sunday afternoon, October 4, anticipating the team's first pennant in 18 seasons. Before the game, Ken noticed a few forlorn beat writers in the clubhouse. "You guys look as if you're going to a funeral," he told them. "We're still in first place."[47]

It was a back-and-forth battle through the first six innings. After two scoreless frames to start the game, Simmons gave up three runs on seven hits and was relieved by Gibson with one out in the fifth. Pitching on one day's rest, the hard-throwing right-hander ended the threat with the score 3-2 in favor of the Mets. Gussie Busch angrily left his box seat and marched upstairs to his luxury box, the Redbird Roost. There he paced the floor before finally kicking a hole in one of the walls in frustration.[48]

Brock walked to lead off the fifth, then White singled and Boyer slashed a double to left, scoring Brock with the tying run. A ground out by Groat brought in White and Ken came across on Maxvill's second RBI single of the game to put the Redbirds ahead, 5-3. Gibson yielded a bases-loaded walk in the sixth to reduce their lead by one run, but his teammates backed him with another three-run outburst and widened the margin. After Flood grounded out to start the sixth, Brock doubled and scored on White's home run. Boyer then walked and came home on McCarver's double, even though he pulled his left hamstring rounding third. He went into the clubhouse, took a cortisone shot from the team physician, and returned stoically to the field. Asked why he didn't come out of the game, he replied, "Oh, I thought they might need me, so I just asked the Doc for a shot."[49]

The Cardinals now led, 8-4. When they looked at the scoreboard and saw the Phillies were ahead of the Reds, 9-0, Ken said it "took the pressure off us. After that, we figured we've got only one game to worry about. Most of us thought we could do it all after we won that fifth game in a row in Pittsburgh." Philadelphia scored once more to beat Cincinnati, 10-0.[50]

The Redbirds tallied three more times in the eighth on Flood's home run and McCarver's two-run single up the middle that scored Boyer and Groat. At that point, some fans began lining up at the ticket booths outside Busch Stadium to purchase World Series tickets the next morning.[51]

Despite pitching a complete game just two days earlier, a tiring Gibson kept the pesky Mets at bay. "He was pitching with more heart than stuff," recalled radio broadcaster Jack Buck.[52] The right-hander allowed only two hits over four innings, but his weariness began to show after walking two batters with one out in the ninth. Keane lifted him and brought in Schultz to close the door on the pennant clincher. A knuckleball got past McCarver and moved the runners to second and third. Charley Smith struck out, but pinch-hitter Rod Kanehl singled to drive in Roy McMillan from third and made it 11-5.

The Cardinals were tense, even with two outs and a six-run lead in the ninth. Kanehl remembered walking to the plate and congratulating McCarver on his team's inevitable pennant. "We haven't won yet," the catcher told him. Then after his RBI single, Kanehl stood at first base and offered the same congratulations to Bill White. "We haven't got the last out yet," he replied.[53]

The next batter, Kranepool, popped up weakly in foul territory between home plate and third base. Ken sprinted toward the Cardinals on-deck circle, looking up and pounding his glove. McCarver flipped off his catcher's mask in pursuit as well. Both converged underneath it, passing in front of each other near the home dugout. Boyer raced past McCarver and looked back over his shoulder to see the ball drop into the young catcher's mitt for the final out. On October 4 at 4:37 P.M., the arduous and nerve-wracking two-week chase for the pennant finally ended with a St. Louis victory and the team's 10th National League championship. Harry Caray, perched in a field box beside Busch and the home dugout, exclaimed to Redbird fans everywhere: "The Cardinals win the pennant! The Cardinals win the pennant! The Cardinals win the pennant!"[54]

As Ed Wilks of the *Post-Dispatch* put it, "The tension of the three-hour game—of the last few weeks of the season, in fact—drained away in a moment of exultation." After making the catch, McCarver excitedly jumped up and down and leaped toward Schultz, wrapping his arms around the pitcher's shoulders. Teammates ran from their positions and out of the dugout to swarm around them in celebration. Fans surged onto the field to join them. Outside Busch Stadium, car horns blared at the corner of Grand Boulevard and Dodier Street and throughout the city of St. Louis. To cynics who attributed the Cardinals' pennant only to the collapse of the Phillies, Ken was quick to point out, "Hell, we won it just as much as they lost it."[55]

"It's been a hectic thing, but it's all worth it," smiled Keane. Asked when the turning point of the pennant drive was, he replied, "When? Today."[56]

The players made their way to the clubhouse where iced champagne bottles awaited them. Corks were popped, toasts were exchanged, and contents were poured profusely over each other's heads as the media and members of the Cardinals organization watched. Youngsters McCarver, Sadecki, and Shannon cavorted around in monster masks and poured champagne through the mouthpieces. Long deprived of a winner, Busch was ecstatic. "I'm the happiest guy in the world, and we're going to win the World Series for our loyal fans—in four games," he declared. Fittingly, Bing Devine was also there, but in his new role as assistant to the president of the Mets. He was welcomed into the clubhouse by Gibson, who told him, "I'm sorry you're not in this. You deserve it more than anyone else." Asked his thoughts on the championship team he built, Devine confessed, "I had a conflict of emotions. I was glad to see the Mets win a couple of games and I was glad to see the Cardinals win the pennant."[57]

Hundreds of fans packed the area beneath the catwalk leading to the clubhouse, chanting for particular players—"We want Boyer!"—to come outside and be cheered. Kathleen Boyer gathered with the other player wives and girlfriends beyond the crowd at the bottom of the clubhouse stairs. A security guard brought them a bottle of champagne and glasses so they could have their own celebration. When the team battled the Dodgers in 1963, Kathleen had developed a rash from the anxiety and tension of the race. This time, with the suddenness of the Cardinals' surge and the Phillies' timely collapse, she didn't have time to worry.[58]

As their teammates celebrated in the clubhouse, veterans Boyer and Groat sat together on a table back in the trainer's room. "Fourteen years of baseball, that's how long I've waited for this glass of champagne," Boyer told him. "Thank you, Philadelphia. Thank you, Pittsburgh. Thank you, Cincinnati. Thank you, Cardinals."[59]

The raucous party lasted as long as the pennant-clinching game itself. When it finally subsided three hours later, Ken was alone in the clubhouse, stepping over empty bottles, overturned locker stools, and discarded uniforms. He still wore his own except for his jersey and spikes, not wanting the moment to end. He was proud of his teammates and the accomplishment they all shared. "Winning the pennant is everything," he told Neal Russo of the *Post-Dispatch* a few years later. "If my career had ended that day, I wouldn't have had to go through the rest of my life wondering like a lot of players who never were on a pennant winner. That's one thing those players hated: the thought of never being on a winner."[60]

He had experienced nine seasons of futility in his major-league career, watching other winning teams go to the World Series. His younger brother Clete, third baseman for the New York Yankees, had been there the last four postseasons. Eighteen years since their last appearance in the Fall Classic, now it was the St. Louis Cardinals' turn. It was *Ken's* turn.

Boyer smiled with satisfaction and said to himself, "This ball club can really play ball, can't it?" Reluctantly, he took off his own uniform and literally soaked in the moment, settling into the warm, soothing waters of the clubhouse whirlpool with a cigarette in one hand and a bottle of champagne in the other.[61]

The Captain: Ken Boyer at Busch Stadium in 1965.
(*Griva Family Collection*)

Chapter Eleven

A World Championship

In the midst of the clubhouse celebration after clinching the 1964 National League pennant, Ken Boyer looked forward to the World Series and the opportunity to play against the New York Yankees. "This is the greatest thing that ever happened to me. And I'm glad it's the Yankees we're playing. My brother Clete has been wanting to play against me for a long time. He never made the All-Star team, so we've never played against each other."

Cletis Boyer was twelve years old when Kenton left home to pursue his major-league dream. A talented high school baseball and basketball player like his brothers, he accepted a $35,000 signing bonus from the Kansas City Athletics after graduation in 1955. The large bonus required him to spend two seasons on the big-league roster, impeding his development but giving him the chance to be teammates with his older brother Cloyd, pitching in his final major-league season. After three years with Kansas City, he was traded to New York, where he became one of the finest defensive third basemen in the American League, despite not making the All-Star team or winning a Gold Glove Award. Because they were in separate leagues, Clete had never played against Ken except in spring training. His older brother attended World Series games when the Yankees opposed Pittsburgh in 1960 and San Francisco in 1962. Now it was his chance to experience postseason baseball as Clete had the last five seasons. "I've wanted Ken to get in every year," he said. "This is really a big thrill for me, as much as our winning it. He's 33 and he hasn't been in one yet. I'm really happy for him."[1]

Not since Emil and Bob Meusel, members of the New York Giants and New York Yankees, respectively, played in three straight from 1921–23 had brothers opposed each other in a World Series. The Meusels each played left field, just as the Boyers each played third base. The brothers had contrasting personalities. While Ken was serious and reserved, Clete was boisterous and liked to have a good time. New York was the perfect environment for him. "Cloyd and I are more alike," said Ken of his older brother. "Clete has the same kind of personality as Wayne, who's a dentist now. They express themselves more and, as a result, are more controversial."[2]

The "sibling rivalry" made for good newspaper copy and the writers played it up for their readers. There was no animosity, yet the brothers were competitive and aimed to outdo the other. Bragging rights in the family were also at stake. Ken's rallying cry for his teammates was "Let's Beat Clete." His little brother countered, "If he hits a hard ground ball down the line, it would be quite a thrill to take a double away from him." After Ken made a great fielding play to take a sure hit away from him during the Series, he compared the look on his younger brother's face to "the way he used to when I took his candy when we were kids." They teased each other daily in passing. "It was like I'm trying to show my big brother, my idol, how good I am, and he's trying to show me how good he is," remembered Clete. "To me, that is the way baseball is supposed to be."[3]

The brothers enjoyed the experience and looked out for each another. They had dinner together after the games but never discussed them. Messages were exchanged giving advice about their respective ballparks. Prior to the first game at Busch Stadium, Clete received a note: "Dear No. 6. Watch that infield. It's harder than concrete. You're liable to get a bad bounce. Signed, No. 14."[4] When the Series shifted to Yankee Stadium, Ken received similar guidance after dropping a pop fly: "Watch this air, you get a lot of bad hops."[5]

Ken and Clete posed for photographers together and with their parents, who attended the games played in St. Louis.⁶ To the inquisitive national media, Vern and Mabel Boyer maintained a neutral position throughout the Series. "Oh gosh, we couldn't favor one team over the other," insisted Vern. When writers asked their mother who she would support, she replied tactfully, "The third baseman." But Clete knew his parents were die-hard Cardinals fans and always listened to the games on the radio. "So I'm sure that Mom and Pop rooted for Kenton and the Cardinals when we got together in the 1964 World Series. After all, he'd never been in the Series." Ken thought the same thing. "My parents showed poise. They claimed throughout the World Series that they weren't prejudiced...But if my parents were really truthful, I think they'd admit they were pulling for the Cardinals. After all, Clete is in the Series annually."⁷ Mabel confessed the same—somewhat—to a Joplin sportswriter the day before the Series began.⁸

Back in Alba, where Vern was now the mayor⁹ and Mabel the city collector, family and friends listened to the games on radio station KFSB based fifteen miles away in Joplin. Classes at the high school were interrupted so the students—including Ken and Clete's younger sisters Barbara and Marcy—could watch each game on a small television in the auditorium. The only gas station in town became a minor tourist attraction with a display of photographs and autographed baseballs. A sign outside Jones's Food Center wished both brothers good luck and proclaimed: "Alba has a winner in the World Series."¹⁰

Experts predicted another championship for the storied New York franchise. They had won a fifth consecutive American League pennant, though it took a late-season push to overtake the Baltimore Orioles and Chicago White Sox in September, winning fifteen of their last nineteen games (eleven in a row) to clinch on October 3. Not the dominant club it had once been, nevertheless the Yankees were still a formidable opponent powered by Mantle (.303, 35 home runs, 111 RBIs), Roger Maris (26 homers, 71 RBIs), and Joe Pepitone (28 homers, 100 RBIs). Right-hander Jim Bouton led the pitching staff with 18 victories, young left-hander Al Downing contributed a 13-8 record with a club-best 217 strikeouts, and rookie sinkerballer Mel Stottlemyre won nine games after his promotion in mid-August. The old workhorse, thirty-five-year-old Whitey Ford, won 17 with a sparking 2.13 earned-run average over 244 innings.

The Cardinals were confident. Much of it stemmed from the frenzied pennant race they had endured over the last few weeks of the regular season. "If we'd won the pennant earlier," suggested Ken, "maybe we would have more time to think and stew or to steam ourselves up for the Series, but actually I think this is better." They weren't intimidated by the postseason mystique surrounding the Yankees. Having played against them during spring training, they were very familiar with the team. Boyer predicted the showdown would last six or seven games. "Nobody on the team is nervous as far as I know."[11]

There were concerns whether Ken and second baseman Julian Javier would even be ready to start the Series. Both were injured in the final weekend of the regular season, Boyer tearing his left hamstring and Javier bruising his hip. Ken was also dealing with a cold. After extensive whirlpool and diathermy treatments, massages, and exercise, trainer Doc Bauman was guardedly optimistic that Boyer's injury was "a little better" but "could possibly get worse," especially when running the bases. Having waited his entire life for this moment, nothing was going to keep him out of the lineup. "I'll play unless they cut off a leg," he joked, though he played the entire Series with his left leg taped prior to every game. Javier tried some swings during batting practice, but experienced too much pain in the process. Keane inserted Dal Maxvill into the starting lineup at second base. Maxvill would bat eighth, with McCarver and Shannon moving up in the St. Louis batting order.[12]

A CROWD OF 30,805 ENTHUSIASTIC FANS packed Busch Stadium for the opening game of the World Series on the afternoon of Wednesday, October 7, as the postseason classic returned to St. Louis for the first time since 1946. There was a definite local flavor to the Fall Classic. Managers Johnny Keane and Yogi Berra were both natives of the Mound City, as well as New York catcher Elston Howard. Mickey Mantle grew up a Cardinals fan living in northeast Oklahoma.

Shortstop Phil Linz led off the top of the first inning for New York and grounded to third. Ken bobbled it for a moment, but recovered for the first out of the Series. He gave the Cardinals the initial lead in their half with a sacrifice fly to Mantle in right field that scored Brock. The Yankees went ahead on a two-run home run by left fielder Tom Tresh and a single and stolen base by Clete Boyer, who later raced home on an RBI single by Ford in the second frame. A smart play by Ken with runners at first and third and one out helped put an end to the scoring. With Ford on second and Linz on first, Bobby Richardson singled to left. When Ford rounded third, Ken noticed he wasn't running well. Brock fielded the ball and threw to Boyer as the cut-off man. Ken eyed Linz at second to ensure he wouldn't try for third and allowed the throw to go through to the plate, where McCarver tagged Ford for the second out. A called third strike to Maris ended the frame with the Yankees leading, 3-1.[13]

In St. Louis' half, Sadecki drove in Shannon to make it a one-run deficit. A fine defensive effort by Ken snuffed a potential rally for New York in the fourth inning. With a runner on first base and two outs, he ranged to his right and deflected a smash down the third-base line off the bat of Linz into foul territory. He made a strong throw to first and umpire Bill McKinley ruled Linz out on a close, disputed call. A double by Tresh in the fifth scored Mantle and increased New York's lead, 4-2.

Ford, the postseason veteran, allowed only five hits through the first five innings. But in the sixth, Ken led off with a single and went to second on a passed ball. After Bill White struck out, Shannon crashed a slider high over the left-field bleachers and against the top of the seventy-foot high scoreboard, striking the U in the Budweiser sign and tying the game. Shannon's blast was followed by McCarver's double that rolled to the right-center power alley and ended Ford's day. It was the final World Series appearance of his Hall of Fame career. The Redbirds tallied again in the frame on pinch-hitter Carl Warwick's RBI single and Curt Flood's triple that Tresh misjudged and lost in the wind and sun, scoring pinch-runner Javier to move ahead, 6-4.

Barney Schultz was on the mound in the seventh to finish out the contest. Javier was pressed into action at second base, but he aggravated his injury attempting to field an eighth-inning infield hit by Maris. He was later lifted for a pinch-hitter, marking his last appearance in this World Series. New York scored once in the eighth, but

St. Louis added three more runs in their half to win the first game of the Series, 9-5.[14]

New York evened the Series behind Stottlemyre the next day, 8-3. Gibson struck out nine but gave up seven hits and four earned runs in eight innings. The Yankee right-hander yielded eight safeties himself, but used his sinker effectively and induced 18 ground balls. Hitless in four plate appearances, Boyer thought it was the best sinker he had seen in years and complimented the rookie's poise and effectiveness. "He never wavered. The few times he was in a jam, he just worked a little harder and kept hitting the corners. He was great."[15]

The Series moved to New York for Game 3 on October 10. A pitcher's duel between a pair of 18-game winners, Curt Simmons and Bouton, highlighted the contest. After Clete Boyer's RBI double in the second inning, Simmons retired 10 of 11 batters over the next three-and-a third innings. Bouton was equally dominant with a one-hitter through four until McCarver singled, advanced to second on Mantle's error in right field, and moved over to third on a ground out. Simmons singled sharply past a diving Clete Boyer to knock him in and tie it in the fifth. The game stayed knotted into the ninth. The Redbirds looked to score again when McCarver reached on shortstop Linz's error, Shannon sacrificed him to second, and pinch-hitter Warwick walked. With a chance to take the lead, manager Johnny Keane lifted Simmons for a pinch-hitter, but the gamble failed when Bob Skinner flew out and Flood lined out to end the rally.

Reliable stopper Schultz entered the game with Mantle leading off the bottom of the ninth. He smashed the first pitch into the third tier of seats in right field for the game-winning blow and 2-1 victory. "Mickey Mantle was a dead low-ball, left-handed hitter," remembers Groat. "That knuckler did nothing and Mickey just killed it. He hit it so far, it seemed like it was in the air forever." Ken crossed the third-base line in front of Mantle, looking back to make sure he touched the bag, then put his head down and walked toward the dugout.[16]

It was crucial that the Cardinals win Game 4. A third straight defeat would be difficult to overcome and ensure a potential Series clincher at Yankee Stadium the next day. The contest didn't have a promising start when Sadecki failed to retire a batter in the first inning. Linz led off with a double. An aborted hit-and-run by Richardson left

Linz stranded between second and third. Trying to toss over Linz's head in the rundown, Ken instead threw it in the dirt, enabling Linz to reach third safely and score on Richardson's subsequent double to left. A hit by Maris put runners on second and third, then Mantle singled to drive in Richardson and move Maris to third before being thrown out trying to stretch out a double. Keane was forced to take out Sadecki and call on reliever and spot starter Roger Craig to halt the rally. Even though Elston Howard drove in Maris to give the Yankees a 3-0 lead, Craig struck out Tresh and Pepitone flew out to right to end the frame.

Pitching for the injured Ford, left-hander Al Downing held the Cardinals to a single through the first five innings. Craig matched his effectiveness, yielding two hits himself, pairing with Groat to pick Mantle off second base, and striking out eight with an assortment of curveballs. The pitcher's spot led off the top of the sixth for St. Louis and pinch-hitter Warwick delivered a single to left, their first hit since the third inning. It also tied the individual record for pinch-hits in a World Series. Next, Flood singled to right, but Brock flied to center for the first out. Groat grounded to the right of second baseman Richardson for what seemed a certain inning-ending double play. However, the ball stuck in the webbing of his glove and resulted in a low toss to shortstop Linz, who was unable to secure the baseball. Flood upended him with a slide into second base.

With the bases loaded and one out, Ken stepped to the plate. He had only one hit in 13 plate appearances thus far in the Series and struck out looking in the second inning and flied out in the fourth. Downing's first pitch was a slider low and outside taken for a ball. Catcher Elston Howard next signaled for a fastball, but the young hurler shook him off. He thought Boyer would be expecting it; he wanted to throw a changeup instead. It was the same pitch that he struck him out on in the second inning.

"The change was my strikeout pitch," Downing later recounted. "It was an important part of my repertoire. I didn't have a good curve. My plan of attack against right-handed hitters was a fastball and a straight change. I thought Boyer was looking for a fastball, and I didn't want him to get his bat out in front and hit a homer right inside the foul pole. I had two balls hit the foul pole that year. I thought I could either lead him off with a strike or get him to get out on front and pop up. It didn't happen."[17]

"I saw him [Howard] wiggle his finger," recalled Linz at shortstop. "I couldn't believe it. I wanted to call timeout and run to the mound, but I didn't do it. They hadn't hit a fastball all day, and it was hard to see at the plate, because of the haze and the shadows that come late in the season…God, I should have called that timeout."[18]

Ken was looking for the fastball, but also remembered the two changeups Downing had thrown him in Game 1. The Yankee left-hander reared back, came toward the plate with his over-the-top motion, and threw the changeup. Prepared for the fastball, Boyer was slightly out in front when he swung. "He got the ball up in my eyes, and that's where any hitter likes to swing," he said. "If Downing had gotten the ball down, I probably would have hit into a double play." Ken managed to hold his weight back, turn his hips, and connect, driving the pitch to left field.

"I wasn't trying for a homer. I just wanted to swing through the ball and get a piece of it."[19]

The only question was whether it would stay fair or not. Sprinting toward first base, Boyer watched intently as the ball sailed through the October air and descended into the seats in Box 378-D fifteen rows back, about five feet inside the left-field foul pole. A brisk 10-mile-per-hour wind helped keep it fair. Umpire Frank Secory, standing along the third-base line, ensured it was fair before signaling a home run. At first base, Groat had no doubt. "When he hit it, it was gone."[20]

Fittingly, Ken's biggest detractor, Harry Caray, who shared the World Series radio broadcast duties with Curt Gowdy, made the call: "There's a drive! Way back! It might be…it could be…it *is*! A *home run*! Listen to the crowd! Kenny Boyer…long time due in this World Series…just became the ninth player [in World Series history] to hit a grand slammer."[21]

The ball was caught in the outstretched glove of a young accountant from Lowell, Massachusetts, named Eddie Hession—a Cardinals fan, no less, whose favorite player was Boyer. It was knocked out of his glove in the ensuing scramble, but he jumped on top of it and secured it, notwithstanding a ripped pants leg. Hession happened to be staying at the Commodore Hotel, the same as the Cardinals, and it was later arranged for him to meet Ken and his wife Kathleen. The couple posed with the ball for photographers and Boyer signed it, but the prize went home with Hession.[22]

The Cardinals were anxious to see what would happen when Ken passed Clete at third base. Tim McCarver remembers everyone moving to the other end of the visitor's dugout to watch. As Ken rounded third, he was surprised Clete said nothing to him. "I looked right at him, and he had a puzzled look on his face. I guess he felt a little put out." McCarver recalls a different response. "(Clete) patted him on the rear end and they both smiled that Boyer smile."[23] He was very proud of his older brother, even though his blast potentially tied the Series. "When he hit that homer, I loved it," remembered Clete. "In my heart, I think I was pulling for him that year because it was his first Series."[24]

Heading home, Ken clapped his hands together and took the extended hands of Groat and Flood as he crossed the plate. Warwick, the bat boy, and White, the next batter, gave him congratulatory handshakes and back slaps. He sprinted back to the dugout where Keane said something to him, but he couldn't understand because of the boisterous crowd. Boyer couldn't ask him to repeat it because his own mouth was too dry to speak from the excitement of the moment. "It's an emotional feeling you simply can't describe," he said.[25]

"That one swing changed the entire complexion of the series," wrote Leonard Koppett of the *New York Times*. Groat agreed. "It was the turning point of the Series. Ken got the big hit for us."[26]

Said Boyer years later, "I can remember as I ran around the bases that the uppermost thought [I had] was that this might square the series." Indeed, his grand slam turned out to be the pivotal blow of the game and inspired confidence in his teammates. "We were on the ropes at the time," recalled Gibson in his autobiography, "and as Boyer's ball slipped over the left-field fence, I had the distinct feeling that we were going to win the Series."[27]

To start the bottom of the sixth, Keane summoned Ron Taylor from the bullpen to hold the precarious one-run lead. Ken went to the mound and suggested he "keep 'em fast and low" and no changeups. The right-hander listened and retired 12 of the 13 batters he faced without a hit over four innings and saved the 4-3 victory.[28]

With his grand slam, Boyer became the first player ever to account for all runs in a Cardinals postseason win. Afterward, he saw team vice-president Stan Musial walk into the visitor's clubhouse and joked, "Bring the VP over here. By the way, where were you yesterday after we lost?" Musial hugged him and laughed, "That's the way I used to hit 'em." St. Louis mayor Raymond R. Tucker passed by and remarked, "Now everybody in St. Louis is happy." The media surrounding Ken at his locker were surprised at his modesty following such a dramatic hit on the national stage. He didn't consider himself a slugger, he told them. "Maybe when I first came up to the Cardinals I pulled the ball a lot and thought I was a home run hitter, but no more." Asked if it was the most memorable moment of his career, he replied, "No, it wasn't. Our winning the pennant was. I'll never recapture that. But the homer helped a lot. I'll certainly take it." Then he redirected the spotlight to the stellar work of Craig and Taylor, posing for photographers with his arms around them saying, "These are the guys who won the game."[29]

With the Series now tied at two games apiece, the fifth game featured a rematch of the Game 2 showdown between Gibson and Stottlemyre. Each allowed only one hit going into the fifth inning before Gibson looped a one-out single to short left field just in front of Tom Tresh. Flood's potential double play grounder was muffed by Richardson and Linz with no out being recorded. Brock lined a single to right that scored Gibson and a force out by White plated Flood to make it 2-0. Gibson dominated with nine shutout frames and 13 strikeouts, two short of tying Sandy Koufax's World Series record set the year before.[30] Clete Boyer had the opportunity to match his brother's feat with the bases loaded in the second inning, but he struck out instead. He did make two great defensive plays on hard-hit grounders from Ken in the third and eighth innings. The elder brother remarked, "If I'm going to be robbed, it'd best be by him. He can have the plays, so long as we get the runs."[31]

The Yankees capitalized on an error by Groat when Tresh belted a two-out, two-run homer in the bottom of the ninth to tie the game. Fortunately, Gibson kept the go-ahead run off base one batter earlier. Pepitone's hard grounder up the middle went off the right-hander's hip and ricocheted toward the third base line. Gibson recovered quickly enough with a throw across his body to barely get him out at first base. After a leadoff walk by White in the tenth, Ken was given the sign to sacrifice him to second. Not only did he advance the runner, but he bunted so well to the right side of the mound that he beat the throw to first. "That bunt was a big play for us," said Keane. "Boyer can do anything you ask him to do. And he can run, too."

Ken was forced out at second by Groat, but the next batter, McCarver, smashed a fastball into the right-field seats and gave St. Louis a three-run lead. With two outs and a runner on first in the bottom of the tenth, Maris popped up into foul territory behind the third-base line. Boyer sprinted under the ball and reached into the field box occupied by National League president Warren Giles to make the game-ending catch for the 5-2 win.[32]

That evening, the Cardinals were welcomed back to St. Louis as conquering heroes just one victory away from a World championship. Local dignitaries and ten thousand enthusiastic fans waving homemade signs and pennants greeted them at Lambert Airport as a band played "Meet Me in St. Louis" and other upbeat tunes. Manager Keane and a few players, including Boyer, addressed the crowd and thanked them for their support. Ken told them, "With old pro Curt Simmons pitching Wednesday, we can hope we'll wrap it up."[33]

But the Yankees reasserted themselves as the Bronx Bombers in Game 6. The veteran Simmons was effective early with six strikeouts and scattered seven hits in a 1-1 tie pitching against Game 3 winner Bouton. Back-to-back home runs by Maris and Mantle in the sixth, however, forced an early exit an inning later trailing, 3-1. Pepitone's grand-slam in the eighth capped off their 8-3 win and tied the Series at three games apiece. Accustomed to his club fighting with its back against the wall, Keane shrugged, "This is normal for us."[34]

The mental strain of the tense pennant race continued into the postseason. "I've been smoking a lot since," confessed Ken. He was finally able to relax the night before Game 7, having fulfilled all requests to family and friends seeking tickets and other obligations. He didn't take batting practice before the seventh game and rested in the clubhouse instead.[35]

Vern and Mabel Boyer were at Busch Stadium on Thursday, October 15, courtesy of a television station that paid their travel expenses.

"We couldn't stay in Alba," said Vern. "The excitement was too much." Mabel watched the game with a feeling of sadness: "One of my boys had to lose."[36]

Gibson and Stottlemyre, starters in the second and fifth games, returned on two day's rest. The Cardinals right-hander withstood a bases-loaded threat in the second inning and held the Yankees scoreless through four. Having already struck out in his first plate appearance, Ken led off the fourth inning. He had struggled throughout the Series, batting only .131 with three safeties, the grand slam in Game 4 being his only extra-base hit. This time, he singled to center off Stottlemyre and advanced to second on Groat's walk. McCarver bounced a grounder to first baseman Pepitone, who threw to second to get Groat out. But shortstop Linz's wild throw to Stottlemyre covering first base failed to complete the double play and McCarver was safe. Meanwhile, Boyer came around and scored the first run for the Redbirds. Shannon singled to right and McCarver advanced to third, then both pulled off a double steal for a second run. Maxvill slapped an opposite-field single to right and Shannon slid home safely under the tag to make it 3-0.

The Cardinals staged another three-run assault in the fifth after Stottlemyre was taken out of the game. Facing Downing, who had not pitched since Boyer's grand slam in Game 4, Brock drove the first offering high and deep to right-center field where his blast bounced on the pavilion roof and onto Grand Boulevard. The next batter, White, singled to center and Ken followed with a double to the right-center field wall. Boyer called time and went to the dugout for a fresh cap and instructions. J. Roy Stockton of the *Post-Dispatch* told his fellow writers in the press box, "He just went to make sure they had the champagne iced up." After Downing was relieved by Rollie Sheldon, White scored on Groat's ground out to second and McCarver flied to right field. Ken challenged Mantle's throwing arm and slid safely into home on an off-line throw to make it 6-0.[37]

The Yankees struck back in the sixth and cut the Cardinals' lead in half on Mantle's three-run homer, his third of the Series and 18th overall in 12 postseason appearances, establishing a new record. St. Louis took one back in the seventh when Ken crashed a two-out solo blast into the left-field bleachers off left-handed reliever Steve

Hamilton to make it 7-3. It was his second round-tripper of the postseason, making him the first player in franchise history with multiple home runs in the same World Series. Ken nudged Clete playfully on the arm as he trotted past him near third base.

Pitching on adrenaline and pure determination, Gibson took the mound in the ninth. Throwing nothing but fastballs, he struck out Tresh for the first out. Clete Boyer belted a 3-2 pitch over the left-field wall, making the Boyers the first siblings to hit home runs in the same Series. Ken stood with hands on his hips at third base and watched as his little brother trotted in front of him with a grin on his face. Pinch-hitter Johnny Blanchard fanned for the second out on Gibson's ninth strikeout of the game and 31st overall in the Series, setting a new postseason mark. But Linz followed with another homer to cut St. Louis's lead to two runs. Though Sadecki and Craig were warming up in the bullpen, Keane stayed with Gibson. The crowd of 30,346 watched nervously as Richardson—who was 13-for-31 (.419) in the Series—came to the plate. If he reached base, Maris and possibly Mantle would follow. Instead, on a 1-1 count, Richardson popped up to second base where Maxvill camped underneath, watching and waiting. Groat shouted to him, "Now don't get hit on the coconut, Maxie." The ball dropped into Maxvill's glove at 3:41 in the afternoon for the final out of the 7-5 triumph.[38]

Ken ran to the mound and hugged Gibson, who practically collapsed into his arms from exhilaration and exhaustion. The Captain turned around and McCarver was there to shake his hand. It was a special moment the three stalwarts of the Series shared before teammates swarmed around them in celebration. Boyer patted McCarver repeatedly on the backside as fellow infielders Groat and Maxvill raced toward them. Soon they were engulfed in a red and white tide from all directions as the entire club converged around them. Fans from the left-field bleachers scaled down the eleven-and-a-half foot tall outfield wall and rushed onto the field to take part. Uniformed guards tried in vain to keep them away from the players, but there were too many. The jubilant Cardinals ran into the dugout with fans in pursuit, the guards forming a human wall to prevent them from following. In the bedlam, someone grabbed Ken's cap for a souvenir, a bit of friendly thievery that happened to other players as well.[39]

The clubhouse celebration was no less subdued than the pennant-clincher a few weeks earlier and carried over that evening to Musial's restaurant, Stan & Biggie's, in southwest St. Louis. The players were rewarded financially with a winner's share of $8,622.19 each. Boyer's three safeties in the seventh game enabled him to finish the Series with six overall and a .222 average. He was one hit better than Clete, who batted .208 with one homer and three RBIs. Ken's six RBIs tied him with Les Bell (1926), Jack Rothrock (1934), and Harry Walker (1946) for the franchise postseason record.[40]

There was more drama after the last out was made. Gussie Busch scheduled a press conference the next morning to announce that he was rewarding Johnny Keane with a three-year contract. But the dismissal of his good friend Bing Devine, as well as Art Routzong and Eddie Stanky, and rumors that he would be replaced as manager by Los Angeles Dodgers coach Leo Durocher led Keane to tender his resignation instead. It was a decision he made as early as September 28, when the club was still in third place and a game-and-a-half back of Philadelphia with six left to play. It was effective at the end of the regular season or the World Series. A week earlier, Busch offered no comment when asked if Keane would return in 1965. But with the team on the cusp of the pennant, he suddenly wanted to talk contract on the first of October for a "substantial increase" in salary. Keane rebuffed him, however, saying he wanted to focus on the race instead.[41]

Asked why he was stepping down after thirty-four years in the organization and achieving a long-sought championship, Keane's response was ambiguous. "It was an accumulation of a lot of little things," he intimated. That afternoon, in an equally shocking announcement, the Yankees fired Yogi Berra and said Keane was one of four candidates for the position. He was officially given the job three days later, though reportedly it had been his since the end of September. "It's hard to leave the players," said Keane afterward. "During the last 30 days, during the stretch run, we have become a closely knit unit. I have become closer to the players than with any other ball club I've been with before. I've been one of the boys and liked it."[42]

The postseason awards for Keane as Manager of the Year and Devine as Executive of the Year (for the second year in a row) were reminders of Busch's mistakes. Their absence took some of the sparkle from the club's World championship splendor. To restore the faith of Cardinals fans, the popular Red Schoendienst was named Keane's successor on October 20, even though he had coached only one full season and lacked managerial experience. Branch Rickey—considered the source of discontent in the front office for the past two seasons—was dismissed as special consultant.[43]

THE EXCITING PENNANT RACE with the Philadelphia Phillies and Cincinnati Reds followed by the World Series victory against the New York Yankees meant everything to Ken. It was the culmination of his childhood dreams when he and his brothers would play on the homemade diamond back in Alba, Missouri, times when he dreamed of playing for the Cardinals "forever." "The season couldn't have been more satisfying," he said. "I think I did just about everything I had hoped to do." That he was able to share the experience with Clete made it much more special.[44]

Boyer's offensive production and team leadership during the regular season were finally recognized by the baseball world. In addition to *The Sporting News* naming him its Major League Player of the Year, the writers honored him as the National League's Most Valuable Player. He was on a quail hunting trip sixty miles from home near Hermann, Missouri, when Kathleen received the telephone call on November 23 that he had won the award. He received 243 points in the voting—including fourteen first-place votes—and finished ahead of Johnny Callison of the Philadelphia Phillies, who had 187 points. Teammate Bill White was third with 106.5 points. "I guess 14 must be my lucky number," said Ken about his first-place vote total. "That's my uniform number and that's how many birds we shot today." Kathleen seemed more excited about the award than her husband. "It's one of those things you hope for deep down. This is the greatest honor he could get."[45]

The MVP award was the pinnacle of Ken's major-league career and the crowning achievement of an amazing season. In the heat of the pennant race with Philadelphia, former All-Star outfielder and broadcaster Richie Ashburn of the Phillies insisted, "If the Cardinals win, Ken Boyer has to be the most valuable player." Groat felt his teammate deserved recognition for his leadership. "Kenny Boyer never swung the bat better," he said in mid-September. "Without him this year, we're a second-division club—easily. If we finish first or second, he should be given strong consideration." Devine was pleased his contributions to the team were finally being acknowledged. "After Stan Musial left, it was up to Boyer to tie the club together. Now the public, the fans, can realize how good this player is."[46]

"Ken deserved the award," remarked Musial. "He had a great and steady season and kept us in the race all year long. He's an easy-going guy and he deserved the victory." Boyer modestly disagreed. "I don't know about deserving it. There are so many great players. Just say it's a great honor. That's the most important thing—the honor." He acknowledged the contributions of his teammates that made it possible and accepted the award on their behalf. He credited Brock's base stealing and White's hitting in particular with his league-leading RBI totals at the end of the season. "This is an honor every baseball player dreams of winning. To get it, you have to get a lot of breaks and have a fairly consistent year. But most important, you have to have teammates like I had—and they should feel they share it."[47]

The Cardinals tied with Milwaukee for the best average in the National League (.272), leading in safeties and runs batted in. White batted .303 with 21 home runs and 102 RBIs and paced the club with 37 doubles. Groat slumped somewhat from the year before, but still had 35 doubles and 70 RBIs while hitting .292. Flood led the league with 211 hits at a .311 clip. After his arrival in St. Louis, Brock was sensational with a .348 average, 12 homers, and 44 RBIs, and stole 33 bases. His full 1964 season line showed a .315 average, 200 hits, 14 home runs, 111 runs scored, 58 RBIs, and 43 stolen bases. Shannon contributed 53 RBIs in 88 games. On the mound, the three main starting pitchers posted new career-highs in victories as Sadecki won 20 games, Gibson 19 (with a club-best 3.01 ERA and 245 strikeouts), and the veteran lefty Simmons 18.

Boyer played in all 162 games of the regular season and batted .295, a ten-point increase from the previous year, with a fourth straight season of 24 home runs, and scored 100 runs for the first time since 1961. He became the first Cardinal since Enos Slaughter in 1946 to lead the league in RBIs with 119, a career high. He enjoyed remarkable consistency throughout the season, whether it was his performance in the first-half (.288) and the second-half (.301), day games (.291) and night games (.297), or facing right-handed (.296) and left-handed pitching (.291). He hit well against first-division clubs Philadelphia (.351), Cincinnati (.309), and Milwaukee (.309), with the exception of San Francisco, whose pitching held him to a .185 average in 75 plate appearances. Boyer also displayed a penchant for late-inning production, hitting .347 during the last three innings of games.[48]

"He always made the big plays," said Gibson about his teammate that season. "Whenever we were in a tight spot, Ken came up with what we needed. I think he personally won ten of my nineteen games for me with either a run batted in or a big fielding play."[49]

Longtime St. Louis sportswriter Bob Broeg epitomized the 1964 Cardinals as a team that "never won a game they could afford to lose and never lost one they had to win." At its core were veterans Boyer, White, and Groat, who guided a new generation of leaders in Gibson and McCarver and influenced the promising careers of young players like Javier, Sadecki, Shannon, and Maxvill. It was a close-knit group of men from different races and nationalities who overcame racial prejudices of the era and genuinely enjoyed being in each other's company, on and off the field. White attributed their harmony to the integration of spring training housing two years earlier.

The two-week stretch drive in September, characterized by the team's perseverance, tenacity, and competitiveness, became one of the greatest comebacks in baseball history. Reflecting on that memorable season, Gibson wrote:

> [W]e knew that our triumph was not a product of hitting and fielding and pitching skills alone, but, in an almost tangible sense, of the mental, social, and spiritual qualities that made the Cardinals unique—of intelligence, courage, brotherhood, and faith...I can't honestly explain the '64 Cardinals any other way. That's what and who we were.[50]

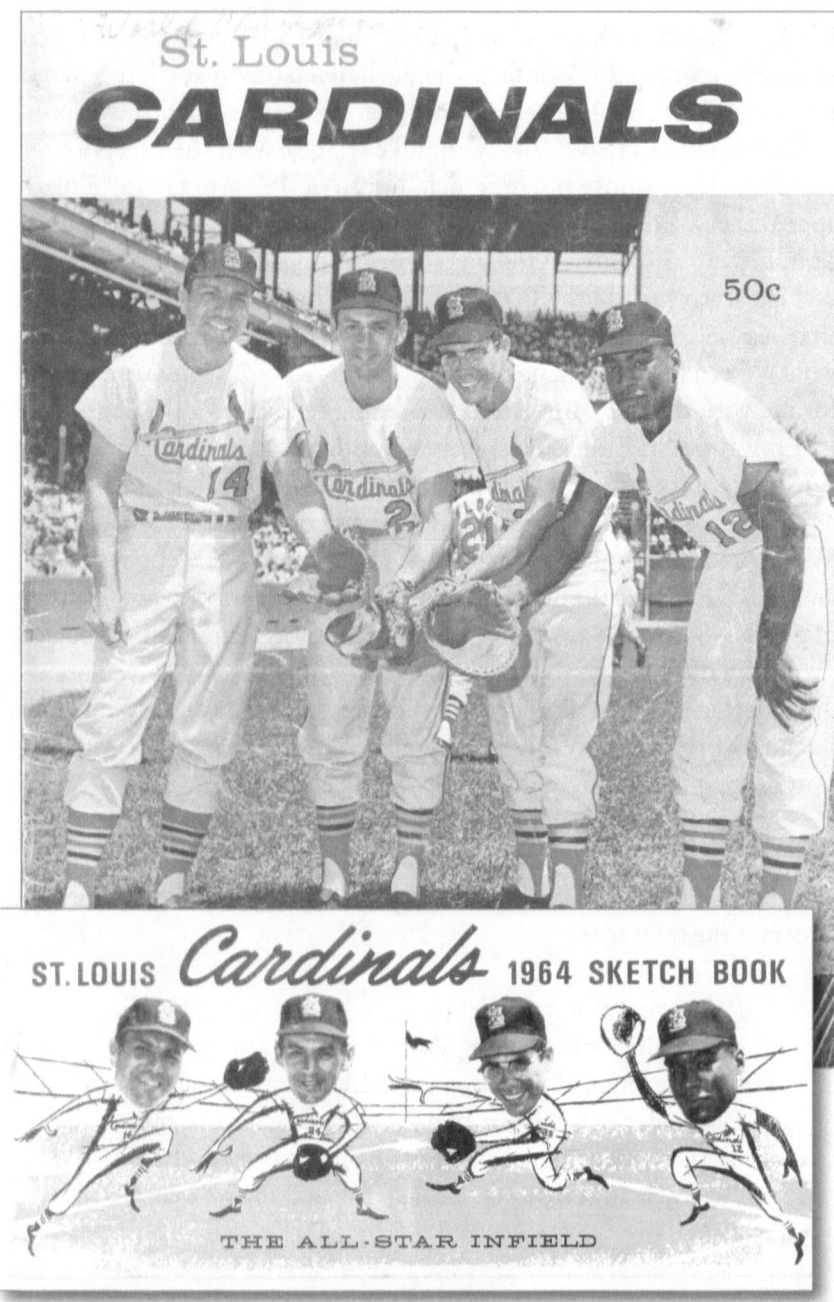

The 1963–64 Cardinals infield of Ken Boyer at third, Dick Groat at shortstop, Julian Javier at second, and Bill White at first was considered the greatest offensive quartet in team history. (*Author's Collection*)

A long way from the Ban Johnson League:
Mickey Mantle (formerly of the Baxter Springs Whiz Kids) and Ken Boyer (of the Alba Aces) meet in the 1964 World Series. (*St. Louis Mercantile Library Collection*)

(**Top**) Boyer's grand slam not only changed the outcome of Game 4, but the Series as well. *(Topps trading card courtesy of The Topps Company, Inc.)*
(**Bottom**) Boyer is greeted at home plate by (left to right) Bill White, Carl Warwick, Dick Groat, and Curt Flood. (*St. Louis Mercantile Library Collection*).

The three stalwarts of the 1964 World champion Cardinals—Tim McCarver, Ken Boyer, and Bob Gibson—congratulate one another after the final out in Game 7. (*St. Louis Mercantile Library Collection*).

Ken's parents Vern and Mabel Boyer (right) attend a game at Busch Stadium.
(*Griva Family Collection*)

The reigning National League Most Valuable Player during spring training, 1965.
(*St. Louis Mercantile Library Collection*)

Chapter Twelve

All Mixed Up

Being the Most Valuable Player is not going to change my life in any way. I'm still going to be the same person I was before."

Ken Boyer was still the same modest person in the winter of 1964–65, but the award did change his life. From the last out of the World Series to the beginning of spring training, he was in constant demand. He estimated that he traveled some 20,000 miles to sports banquets across the country—New York, Chicago, Detroit, Kansas City, Memphis, Nashville, and smaller cities—where he received accolades and even more awards to add to his growing collection. In Tulsa, Oklahoma, he was presented with the inaugural Pepper Martin Award by its namesake. Of the famous Gashouse Gang member, Boyer remarked, "He is one of the reasons I am proud to wear a Cardinal uniform." The Houston baseball writers honored him with the Tris Speaker Award. Back in St. Louis, he received the Outstanding Sports Figure award from the local Elks Lodge No. 9 for the second time in his career, tying him with Stan Musial, who presented him the award. Asked if his children still remembered him after all his travels, Boyer joked, "As long as they have their television, they don't miss me."[1]

Ken's endeavors for the St. Louis community were recognized as well. He was the recipient of the 10th annual Lou Gehrig Memorial Award as chosen by Phi Delta Theta, the fraternity of the Hall of Fame first baseman at Columbia University. The prestigious award took into account his contributions both on and off the field. "In the Gehrig tradition," the fraternity stated, "Boyer has reflected credit on major league baseball to an extraordinary degree..."[2] The Multiple Sclerosis Society honored his volunteer efforts on behalf of its St. Louis area chapter with the organization's Bronze Hope Chest award presented to him by the society's founder, Sylvia Lawry. When he accepting it, Ken remarked, "The Most Valuable Player award is most gratifying but it feeds the ego. The Hope Chest award feeds the soul..."[3]

Ego was one thing missing from Boyer's character. Despite his fame, he remained a humble, unpretentious person. "He was the most down-to-earth star I ever met," recalled Los Angeles Dodgers pitcher Claude Osteen. During a game when Ken ranged almost to shortstop for a hard-hit grounder, umpire Dusty Boggess told young catcher Tim McCarver, "Take a good look, son, because you're not going to see anyone like him again." McCarver relayed the compliment to Boyer, but Ken said simply, "Never get caught up in stuff like that."[4] Fans remember him taking time to sign autographs and talk with them in the player's parking lot outside Busch Stadium or away from the ballpark. One fan recalled him signing autographs at a St. Louis store. "I was tongue-tied and didn't say much, but I remember him asking me if I had been to the game that day and encouraging me to come out soon and see him play," he said. "He could have just quickly signed everything and left, but he took time to connect, if only briefly, with every little kid in line."[5]

Daughter Suzie (Boyer) Hartwig remembers her father as a "compassionate, caring, loving person, whether it was to his family or anybody else." In 1964, he received a telephone call about a ten-year-old fan dying of cystic fibrosis. A family member recalled, "In the middle of a hot summer night that was in the middle of a pennant race, and with absolutely no publicity, Mr. Boyer drove to the hospital, spent a couple of hours at Steve's bedside, chatted with him and left an autographed picture...Sometimes small deeds do make a difference." The little boy passed away a few months later, but lived long enough to watch the World Series on television and see his favorite player hit a grand slam.⁶

Suzie would read the fan mail her father received. "She's a Beatles fan and she gets a kick out of teenagers who write idolizing Ken 'as the greatest,'" her mother Kathleen said at the time. Suzie remembers her friends being in awe of him too. "But he'd be dressed in jeans and just be somebody's dad, no big deal or anything like that," she says. "I guess our friends were impressed, but my dad never put on. He never had an attitude. If somebody wanted an autograph, he'd give them an autograph. It was just a different era back then, too, not at all like it is today."⁷

Ken's modesty carried over into his private life and became a life lesson for his children. "He was a very down-to-earth person (who) didn't want to make a big deal out of what he was," says son Dan Boyer. "Subsequently, that's how we were raised, not to make a big deal of it. Our dad happened to play baseball, but at the end of the day he's a human being. That's probably the one thing, looking back now, I have as much respect for that he did was say, 'You're no different than anyone else. Whatever it is that you do in life, whatever your accomplishments are, so be it. Don't make a big deal of it because really you're no better than anybody else.'"⁸

At the eighth annual St. Louis baseball writers dinner in January, Ken and teammate Bill White shared the J.G. Taylor Spink Award as the city's Baseball Men of the Year. "Receiving all these awards has been rewarding," he said, "but not financially—yet." He glanced at Cardinals general manager Bob Howsam, who chuckled at the remark. "He's laughing on the outside, but forget it. The contract talks may be just as good competition as the competition on the field."⁹

Indeed, after competitive negotiations, Howsam signed Boyer to a one-year contract a few weeks later estimated at $65,000, making him second only to Stan Musial as the highest-paid Cardinal ever. He was pleased with the new deal. "When I was in the minors, I hoped to play ten years in the majors at $10,000. After I was up for a while, I shot for $25,000 and made it. I still didn't see anybody scaring me so I went for $50,000. Then, after last season, I decided to shoot for the moon." But he never saw himself as a superstar like Musial, Willie

Mays, or Mickey Mantle. "The $100,000 ball player is the kind who can put people in the park by himself. No, I'm not kidding myself, I'm not in that category."[10]

In the wake of his MVP season, Ken and the Cardinals had no reason to believe he wouldn't be productive for the next few seasons. He continued working out every winter with Walter C. "Doc" Eberhardt, physical education director at St. Louis University, and stayed in peak physical condition. "I think he's got at least three more good years ahead of him, maybe five," said his new manager and former teammate Red Schoendienst. "He's one of those players who gets better as he gets older. He's a better hitter every year. He knows how to adjust at bat, how to hit to all fields. He knows when to take the extra base. And he has the balance that makes him such a good glove man." Entering the 1965 season, Boyer ranked second on the Cardinals' all-time career home run list with 242 round-trippers to Musial's 475. Catching him was improbable, but the prospect of reaching 300 was a possibility if Ken stayed healthy. "I think I can play three or four more years—if I can keep from getting hurt," he said.[11]

AFTER A WHIRLWIND OFF-SEASON, Ken made up for his absence over the winter with an early family vacation to St. Petersburg before the start of spring training. The Cardinals won their first two exhibitions, then lost nine in a row. He struggled with a .200 average in his first 30 at-bats. He played in all but one of the 28 exhibition games and eventually raised his average to .276 with nine doubles and 13 RBIs. The Redbirds rebounded the last half of the Grapefruit League schedule and won eight of their last nine. Before the club went north for an exhibition series in Kansas City with the Athletics, Boyer "twisted something" in his back sliding into second base and further aggravated it with more sliding.[12]

The Cardinals opened their defense of the World championship in Chicago on April 12. They burst out of the gate with a five-run assault against former Redbird Larry Jackson and reliever Ted Abernathy in the first inning. Overcoming 17 hits against them, the Cubs chipped away at Bob Gibson and five relievers while the Cards tried rebuilding the breaches. Chicago finally tied it with two outs in the ninth when Barney Schultz gave up a three-run homer to Ernie Banks to make it 10-10. The score remained knotted until the bottom of the eleventh when the game was stopped for darkness. The Cubs took the next two games, the lone highlight for the Cardinals being Ken's 4-for-4 showing against left-hander Dick Ellsworth on April 14.

The Redbirds returned to St. Louis in last place for the home opener the next evening against the Cincinnati Reds. After a festive downtown parade and Opening Day ceremonies, a crowd of 24,364 left the ballpark disappointed after a 10-4 loss. Ken and his teammates were presented with their World championship rings by Commissioner Ford Frick on April 17 and took their first victory of the season, 8-0, thanks to Gibson's 11 strikeouts and Boyer's three safeties and four runs batted in. On Easter Sunday, the championship pennant was hoisted over Busch Stadium, but St. Louis capped off a discouraging inaugural home series with an 8-2 defeat. White, Boyer, and Groat each struck out with the bases loaded in the bottom of the ninth.[13]

It was indicative of the frustration the Cardinals and their fans would experience in 1965. The team finished the month of April losing eight of 13 games (with one tie) and positioning themselves in ninth place, just a half-game behind the cellar-dwelling New York Mets. Ken was batting .286 but playing through painful muscle inflammation in his lower back. Resistant to taking himself out of the lineup, he finally relented for two games at Cincinnati April 23–24. He had been the active major-league leader with 306 consecutive games, a streak that started after his return from a spike wound on May 7, 1963. Testing his back against club vice president (and former pitcher) Stan Musial in St. Louis—"I've got the highest-priced batting practice pitcher in baseball," joked Boyer—he rejoined the team at Milwaukee on the twenty-seventh. It would be the unfortunate start of a rash of lower body injuries that would afflict him throughout the season.[14]

Ken's award-winning 1964 season was recognized in a ceremony held between games of the May 2 doubleheader with the Pittsburgh Pirates. He was officially presented with the Player of the Year Award by *The Sporting News*, the Lou Gehrig Memorial Award, and the National League's Most Valuable Player Award. "Better than 15 years ago," he told the crowd of 23,630 fans at Busch Stadium, "I watched great stars like Stan Musial and Marty Marion get awards like this, and I hoped that some day I'd get one, too. And now that dream has been realized." He added, "I certainly appreciate these awards, and I want to thank my teammates because I wouldn't be here without their support. They played good baseball last year, and I know that we can do it again." Boyer belted his first home run of the season in the second game as St. Louis swept the twin bill.[15]

The team started the month of May with four straight victories at home over Pittsburgh and took the first of a three-game set with the San Francisco Giants. The first significant win streak of the season enabled them to climb to fourth place, three games behind the league-leading Reds. Warmer spring weather helped loosen Ken's back and his average rose to a season-high .313. After losing four of six on the road, a four-game series at Pittsburgh in mid-May proved the perfect remedy. The Cardinals swept the last-place Pirates, then won seven straight May 18–24 to climb above .500 for the first time and claim third place, trailing the front-running Dodgers by a game-and-a-half. Losing to the Mets, 7-0, on the twenty-third, McCarver smashed a two-run homer in the eighth and Ken contributed an RBI single as part of a five-run rally that tied it in the ninth. The Redbirds eventually won in the twelfth, 8-7. Curt Flood led the club with a torrid .396 average during the streak, setting the table with Lou Brock that enabled Bill White, Boyer, and Dick Groat to drive them in. Gibson led the mound corps with five victories in the month.[16]

On May 27, the Cardinals made their initial visit to the new Astrodome in Houston. The first domed stadium in major-league history had a seating capacity of 46,217 and specially grown Bermuda grass that eventually died without sunlight over the course of the season. It also featured a large exploding scoreboard, prompting Ken to relate what other players had told him: "You've never had so much fun losing in your whole life!"[17]

Five straight losses at the end of May and an 11-20 free fall in June dropped St. Louis back to the second division for the remainder of the season. "Just as everything went right for us in the second half of 1964, everything went wrong for us all through 1965," wrote Gibson in his autobiography.[18] Injuries and subpar performances bedeviled the club. McCarver broke a finger three games into the spring exhibitions, then his backup Bob Uecker smashed his knee against the brick backstop at Wrigley Field on Opening Day. Injuries to Boyer,

Flood, Brock, White, and Julian Javier thwarted the offense. Twenty-game winner Ray Sadecki and veteran Curt Simmons, who won 18 a year earlier, both struggled and finished with records of 6-15 and 9-15, respectively. Schultz, who saved 14 games down the stretch in 1964, saw his earned-run average swell from 1.64 to 3.83 and was sent back to the minors in August. Mike Shannon slumped to .221 with three home runs in 124 games after batting .261 with nine homers in 88 games a year earlier.[19]

Despite being the Cardinals' top run producer, Ken's shrinking .261 average led Schoendienst to take him out of the starting lineup before the second game of the June 13 doubleheader with the Milwaukee Braves. "Boyer isn't 100 per cent," the manager explained. "I wanted to give him a rest because he hasn't been feeling too good." He returned two days later and had three safeties and two RBIs against Pittsburgh. In that game, the Redbirds' streak of 17 consecutive victories over the Pirates (including nine in 1965) ended with a 10-6 defeat at home.

Losing six of their next eight (four by two runs or less), Schoendienst had the players meet without the coaches present in the visitor's clubhouse before the game at Cincinnati on June 24. Ken led the conversation as they took turns discussing the reasons—both personal and as a team—for the frustrating string of close defeats. One problem addressed was a lack of concentration in the field and at the plate. Fines were implemented to help remind them about its importance. "We were feeling sorry for ourselves," said Boyer. "We were looking back at the losses instead of ahead. We were waiting for things to happen to beat us. We got in a lull, we made base-running blunders." Howsam felt they weren't playing as aggressively as the year before and wanted Schoendienst to be tougher on them.[20]

The players had no respect for Howsam as they had Bing Devine. Howsam stayed away from the clubhouse celebrations in October 1964, but when he tried taking credit for the late-season success, a few players let him know publicly that it wasn't his to claim. He was tightfisted in contract negotiations and seemed more concerned about the appearance of the field and the players than the game itself. Even though the new downtown stadium was under construction, thirty thousand dollars was spent to resod the grass at the current ballpark.

He instructed the players not to stand outside the on-deck circle because it wore out the new turf, even though doing so enabled them to sneak a quick glance at the opposing catcher's signs and relay them to the batter. "Howsam felt compelled to assert complete control over the ballclub," wrote Gibson in his autobiography. "He imposed rules about such petty things as how high we were supposed to pull up our baseball pants. If he looked down from the press level and saw one of our guys slouching in the dugout, he would fire down a memo ordering him to sit up straight."[21]

The Redbirds started the month of July with a seven-game win streak and took 17 of 27 to bring themselves back to .500. Ken's two singles and two runs scored at Pittsburgh helped break a three-game losing skid and spark the win streak with a 7-1 victory on June 30. At the All-Star break, he was batting .258 with eight homers and 42 RBIs and for the first time since 1958, he wasn't elected to the All-Star Game. Richie "Dick" Allen, hitting .328 with 12 homers and 52 RBIs for the fourth-place Phillies, was chosen to start at third base for the National League instead. The lone representative for the seventh-place Cardinals was Gibson, the first time since Joe Medwick in 1938 that the club had so few players in the contest.[22]

When the season resumed, Boyer missed three games with a stiff right hip that felt "like I've got a bottle cap in there." It hindered him for several games and brought his average down to a season-low .256. Trainer Doc Bauman prescribed an athletic girdle to help stabilize his lower back and right hip and it seemed to help. "I feel fine, girdle and all," quipped Ken.[23]

In August, Boyer "looked more like himself," thought Neal Russo of the *Post-Dispatch*, and his bat showed it. He enjoyed his best month of the season, batting .286 with five homers and 26 RBIs. A 13-game consecutive hit streak July 31–August 12 was his longest of the season. In that span, he swatted .360 with two doubles, two home runs, and 11 runs batted in. It started with a come-from-behind victory over the first-place Dodgers in which Ken singled and scored on Brock's two-run single that won it in the bottom of the ninth, 4-3. In the second game of a twin bill with Houston on August 3, he and White each had three hits, the first time since June 16 he had collected that many in a game: a two-run double in the first inning, an RBI single in the third, and a solo home run in the fifth. His four RBIs was his highest total since April 17. On the twenty-sixth, Ken hit his 13th home run, a three-run blast in the first inning at Busch Stadium that led to a 7-4 win over the Cubs. It was the 255th of his major-league career and the last he would hit for the Cardinals. He lifted his average to .272, the highest since the end of May.[24]

It was late August when the Cardinals started their improbable comeback in 1964. At the time, they were in fourth place and 7½ out on the thirty-first of that year. An even more miraculous surge was needed to make a pennant challenge this time. Exactly a year later, they were in sixth place and 9½ back with five teams separating them from the league-leading Dodgers. "We had virtually the same lineup that had won the World Series," recalled reserve catcher Bob Uecker. "Yet at the point where we had begun our pennant drive the year before, our tank was empty." In early September, Boyer conceded that the Redbirds couldn't come back this time and took his share of the blame for the downturn. "There is no way to make this a good year now. I'm the first to realize it—even if I drive in 80, 90, or 100 runs. The only way to feel happy about a year is to be consistent. I've had some good spurts at bat this season, but I haven't been consistent, and it's when you're consistent that your club wins."[25]

As the highest paid player on the club, St. Louis fans took out their frustrations on Ken even more than in seasons past. Gibson blamed their reactions on critical remarks made by Harry Caray during his radio broadcasts. He recalled, "The Cardinals' field announcer, Charlie Jones, would call Boyer's name, and in the dugout I'd count 'one, two, three…' On three, the boos would start heaping down from the upper deck. And this was the man who had been the MVP of the league only a year before." Boyer would laugh at his teammate's ribbing, but the abuse took a toll on his family. Kathleen no longer enjoyed going to Busch Stadium and subjecting the children to the boos and jeers hurled at their father. As the difficult season wore on, Ken questioned whether it was worth staying in the game. "Why should I stay in a business she's not happy about? It's a torment for her and the kids listening to some of the remarks about me at the park."[26]

Recurring back trouble and a sore shoulder forced him from the lineup for five home games with the Dodgers and Astros beginning

September 17. Before the opener, right-hander Don Drysdale noticed he wasn't in the lineup. "Well, I'll be," he told him. "First time in ten years that you missed a game I was pitching."

"Don't worry, Double D," replied Boyer. "Every time you come side-arm tonight, I'll be flinching."[27]

Drysdale won his 20th of the season that night and Koufax and Claude Osteen each pitched shutouts to sweep the series. After taking two over Houston, the Redbirds flew to Los Angeles for the final road trip of the season. Ken was back at third base and batting cleanup in the opening game on September 24. St. Louis dropped three more to the Dodgers, including back-to-back shutouts by Koufax and Drysdale, the final loss placing LA in a first-place tie with the Giants.

The Redbirds did better in San Francisco, winning two out of three and helping the Dodgers take the league lead. In the second game on September 28, Ken had two safeties and drove in Flood in the ninth for his 1,000 major-league RBI. The milestone came off veteran lefty Warren Spahn in the next-to-last appearance of Spahn's Hall of Fame career. The next evening, Boyer stroked a two-out single in the fifth and knocked in another run. Though the Giants came back and tallied six times in their half, the Redbirds prevailed, 8-6.[28]

In that game, Ken flew out to center fielder Willie Mays to lead off the ninth inning in what proved to be his last plate appearance of the season—and his final one with the St. Louis Cardinals. Schoendienst rested the former All-Star infield of White, Javier, Groat, and Boyer the last four games of the season at Houston. Ken watched from the bench as his teammates took two out of three to finish in seventh place, a game below .500 at 80-81 and 16½ behind the National League champion Dodgers. Gibson won his 20th of the season in the finale, the first such milestone of his Hall of Fame career.

THE CARDINALS SEARCHED for answers to the farthest fall a World championship club had ever suffered. Ken felt they never overcame the mental mistakes that were brought up during the players-only meeting at Cincinnati in late June. "It wasn't complacency or lack of desire that killed us," he said in retrospect. "The best way I could put it was we seemed to lack concentration. We made a lot of errors of the mental type. Not just me, but everybody. All of us were guilty. When we'd lose a game we'd go back into the clubhouse and look at one another and ask ourselves what was wrong. The things that worked the year before just didn't work last year. We were all mixed up."[29]

"We got old," says Groat unequivocally. "There comes a time, and that was the beginning of the end for Bill White, Ken Boyer, and myself. It's just that simple. We were just bad that year. You're just kidding yourself when you're hitting the way we did. I hate to even look back on that year, because I was treated so well by the Cardinals. To me, that was the worst season I had in baseball without a doubt."[30]

Defensively, the club tied for the second-best fielding percentage in the NL and had the second fewest errors. But the starting lineup couldn't stay healthy and its best players—Boyer, White, and Groat—failed to produce as they had before. Ken prided himself on his durability and consistency but for the first time since 1957, he failed to appear in at least 149 games, hit over 20 homers, and drive in 90 runs or more. A hectic off-season schedule of banquets and speaking engagements precluded him from working out as often as he normally did, which could have made him more susceptible to injuries. His back ailment forced him to take shorter swings and prevented him from driving the ball.

The effects were evident in his final statistics: a .260 batting average with 13 home runs (third best on the club behind White's 24 and Brock's 16), 18 doubles (fourth-best), and 75 RBIs (second to Flood's 83) in 144 games. It was only the second time in ten seasons he didn't lead the team or share the lead in homers and RBIs. His .374 slugging percentage was 111 points below his career average of .485. The effectiveness he enjoyed against lefties diminished from .291 in his MVP season to .235, a loss of fifty-six points. Where he excelled with runners on base in 1964, he faltered a year later. His average dropped seventy-nine points with runners in scoring position and 178 points with the bases loaded, even though he had more opportunities than the previous season. He enjoyed one of his finest seasons at third base, leading the National League in fielding percentage for the first time in his career, but the Gold Glove was awarded to Ron Santo of the Cubs.[31]

It was a difficult season both for the team and Ken personally. His teammates were frustrated and morale was low. He admitted, "There were times I had to kick myself in the tail just to make myself go to the ball park." Still, the adversity made him more determined to do better in 1966 and show that age wasn't a factor in his performance. Otherwise, he reportedly contemplated retirement. Having Kathleen and the children endure another season of the boos and heckling was another consideration. "I have something to prove to myself next year. If I have a decent year in '66, I'd try again. If not, it could be my last year. I'd do a hell of a lot of thinking about it before deciding."[32]

Howsam met with individual players and the whole team before the season ended to gauge their thoughts about the disappointing season. He also shared with them what might happen over the winter. Boyer came away from his meeting with the impression that the general manager was "not in favor of wholesale changes." Gussie Busch had already decided that Schoendienst would return to manage in 1966. A trade might be made and players brought up from the minor leagues to help. "I'm not so sure that we need major changes to contend next year," believed Ken. "I suppose we'll make some changes though."[33]

Chapter Thirteen

But the Mets Are In Last Place

On the afternoon of Wednesday, October 20, two-and-a-half weeks after the 1965 season ended, the telephone rang at the Boyer home in Spanish Lake. It was Jack Herman, writer for the *St. Louis Globe-Democrat*. He asked Ken for his reaction to the news that he had been traded to the New York Mets for left-handed pitcher Al Jackson and third baseman Charley Smith.

"You're kidding," Boyer replied, dumbfounded. "I'll be damned. That's really something."[1]

The fans' reaction to the trade in St. Louis was immediate. Despite the fact he had been "booed more than any Redbird star in recent memory" according to Bob Broeg of the *Post-Dispatch*, they were livid. Protests were made to the city's media outlets and the Cardinals front office, threatening to cancel season tickets. Callers bombarded the telephone switchboard at KMOX to vocalize their outrage on Jack Buck's afternoon radio program, "At Your Service." One eleven-year-old fan started a petition to reverse the trade.[2]

They were even more upset to learn the Cardinals had not notified him. Team officials claimed they tried unsuccessfully to contact him before the announcement was made at 4:30 in the afternoon.

Attending baseball meetings in Chicago where the trade was made, Bob Howsam did not give his team's captain and longest tenured player the courtesy of a telephone call from him. The only acknowledgment Boyer ever received was a slip of paper in the mail stating his contract had been terminated.[3]

Howsam sought pitching and a right-handed power bat. He believed Jackson was a better pitcher than his 40-73 record in New York indicated and the twenty-seven-year-old Smith a capable replacement for Boyer's production, coming off a season with 16 homers and a career-high 62 RBIs. The Mets asked specifically for Boyer in exchange. At the time, no other clubs but New York and Los Angeles were seeking a third baseman. The St. Louis general manager claimed reluctance to trade "such an asset to the Cardinals," but "to strengthen your club in a position, sometimes you have to give up a player you think highly of." Red Schoendienst felt the trade had to be made. "We hate to see a player of Ken's caliber go because he has been great in his 11 years with the club. But in Smith we obtained a power hitter and a good fielder. In Jackson, we got a fine starting pitcher. We just couldn't pass up the deal."[4]

The senior baseball writers in St. Louis, Broeg of the *Post-Dispatch* and Bob Burnes of the *Globe-Democrat*, both understood the reasoning for the deal, but questioned whether the Cardinals received enough in return for Boyer. Jackson was the Mets' best starting pitcher, but he was still a two-time 20-game loser; Smith was a journeyman who hit 32 home runs in the last two seasons, but whose power would likely diminish in the team's capacious new stadium. "It has to be stated," concluded Burnes, "that at their best, Smith and Jackson would never approach even on a cumulative basis, the best of Ken Boyer."[5]

Ken's reaction was one of shock and disappointment. "I realize it's part of baseball and I've always said I wouldn't worry about being traded. But it really shook me up." He expected it at the end of the 1957 season when Frank Lane was in charge, but this was a complete surprise. In conversations at the end of the season, Howsam led the players to believe that the team would begin 1966 intact. "They do what they feel is for the best future of the club, right or wrong," said Boyer. "You go along with it." The so-called reserve clause in every major-league contract that tied a player to his team—which teammate

Curt Flood would fight all the way to the Supreme Court seven years later—left him no recourse except retirement. He had looked forward to playing in the Cardinals' new downtown stadium; now it would have to be as an opposing player.

After receiving the news, without thinking, he exclaimed to Kathleen and the children that he had been traded to New York. Twelve-year-old Suzie burst into tears. "But the Mets are in last place," she cried.[6]

Ken wasn't thrilled to play for a perennial second-division club either. But being the professional that he was, he set aside his personal loyalties—with a tinge of hurt—and looked forward to a better season in New York in 1966. "I'll put my whole heart and soul for the Mets...like I did for the Cardinals. I think I'll be able to help the Mets. The sentiment is gone for the Cardinals...it'll strictly be on a business basis now."[7]

Having been traded himself after twelve seasons in St. Louis, Schoendienst understood Boyer's feelings almost fifty years later. "You don't want to leave. You want to stay...but the time comes when you're going to get traded. That's the way it was when they traded me. I hated like hell to go because I came up through the organization, but there are times when you're going to go."[8]

Ken soon learned there was more to being traded than simply adjusting to life in a new city with a new team. "My family is my first consideration. I have a wife and four kids—five lives I'm responsible for. You can't help being a little upset when you know this trade affects them as much as it does you. Ballplayers all know they face the possibility of being traded someday...But how can you prepare for something like that? You can't, especially with a family, so when it comes, you just have to make do." Rather than uproot them, Ken decided to keep his home outside St. Louis. He would find an apartment in New York where Kathleen and the children would join him when school was out for the summer. He knew he had to find one with open space for the kids to play, an especially challenging stipulation in the Big Apple.[9]

A week later, the Cardinals dealt Bill White, Dick Groat, and Bob Uecker to the Philadelphia Phillies for outfielder Alex Johnson, right-handed reliever Art Mahaffey, and catcher Pat Corrales. White had been in St. Louis for seven seasons; like Ken, he received no call from the front office informing him of the trade. "It was the sort of petty, unclassy behavior I had come to expect from Howsam," White wrote in his autobiography. He believed their higher salaries were part of the decision. Boyer questioned the wisdom of dismantling the former All-Star infield with no proven players to replace them, particularly at first base. "The others may be younger, but we're not ancient; we're not finished. I think they could have kept the infield together for another two years."[10]

Howsam discussed the trades in his own autobiography thirty-four years later. "My player moves were mostly youth oriented," he explained. "You have to do that to keep a team competitive. Mr. Rickey used to say that it's better to trade a player one year too early than one year too late. I think that makes sense, although I realize the wrench of the fans['] hearts when a longtime favorite is traded or released[,] but often it's necessary for the continued success of the team."[11]

Both trades effectively gutted the veteran leadership of the club. Only Julian Javier remained from what had arguably been the best infield in Cardinals history. Asked if he had more deals in the works, the general manager laughed, "Haven't I done enough already?"[12]

Ken was hurt and disappointed, but not bitter. Still, he told it like he saw it and shared his personal appraisal of what had been done to the team he loved. "We were Devine's team," he said after a winter of reflection, "and when Howsam came in, especially when we dropped in seventh place last season, he had to rebuild his own team. Howsam was Branch Rickey's man, and he probably was following Rickey's old idea of trading players while they still had some market value. I have this consolation: It's not the same Cardinal organization I played for 17 years."[13]

THE NEW YORK METS were the laughingstock of the National League. Since their inception as one of two expansion franchises in 1962 (the other being the Houston Colt 45's, later renamed the Astros), they consistently lost over 100 games and finished in last place. A roster of inexperienced young players, castoffs from other teams, and big-name veterans well past their prime managed to find new and comical ways to lose time and again. Yet fans in New York eager for National

League baseball after the departure of the Giants and the Dodgers took the lovable lovers to their hearts. In 1965, the Mets drew over a half million more fans than the Yankees.

After four seasons being the league's doormat, Mets president George Weiss (and his assistant Bing Devine) wanted the club to be respected instead of ridiculed. It was one of the reasons Ken Boyer was brought to New York. Unlike veterans such as Duke Snider, Richie Ashburn, and Warren Spahn, who were essentially gate attractions, Ken was still considered in his prime and only a season removed from being the Most Valuable Player. He was an elite third baseman who could greatly improve the Mets defense and bring veteran leadership to a club still building with young, home-grown talent. Weiss hoped Boyer could regain his power stroke and be productive for a few more seasons until those prospects were ready. With seventy-four-year-old Casey Stengel stepping down and forty-three-year-old Wes Westrum taking over as manager, there was the chance for a fresh start in 1966.[14]

Westrum was excited about Boyer in his lineup. "Just having him on the ball club means from five to ten games to us. That's not counting what he'll do with the bat and glove." He added, "I'm aware that Kenny is 34 years old, but I'm sure he can come back and have one or two more good years. He didn't exactly flop last year. He still had 75 RBIs and a .260 batting average."[15]

Ken went to New York in mid-November for a physical. While there, he made a series of television commercials with brother Clete and spent a day meeting fans and signing autographs on the "Hot Stove League Express," a two-car train that traveled through Long Island promoting the team. Back home, he continued working out at St. Louis University just as he had in past off-seasons with other players who lived in the area, including new teammates Ron Hunt and Dennis Musgraves.[16]

After a five-minute telephone conversation with Weiss in late January 1966, Ken agreed to a new contract for the same salary he had the previous season. "I don't believe a player of his caliber should be cut after one poor season," the Mets president asserted. During a press conference with the team's highest-paid player over the phone, the New York writers were more interested in the revelation that a horse had kicked him below his left knee a few weeks earlier. Ken reassured them that he was all right, even though the wound required eight stitches. "I was riding my own horse when another horse reared up and struck me," he told them. "I was fortunate that the horse was unshod. My first concern was the possibility of a bone fracture. But it's all right, just a little tender. The cut is healed." He also assured his new manager that despite reports to the contrary, he was not considering retirement at the end of the season.[17]

THERE WAS A FAMILIARITY to spring training in 1966, even with a new team. Boyer made the same journey he had for the past eleven years to St. Petersburg, Florida. He still wore the same No. 14 on his jersey, compliments of his new teammate Ron Swoboda. The only difference was instead of working out with the Cardinals at Al Lang Field, he was now six miles north with the Mets at Huggins-Stengel Field. Where Stan Musial made visits after his retirement and sometimes worked out with his former teammates, now there was former manager Casey Stengel in a suit and tie entertaining Ken and the rest of the Mets with stories from his fifty-three-year baseball career.[18]

Westrum wanted to instill a positive attitude in a team accustomed to losing every season. He posted signs with motivational statements around the clubhouse and hoped Ken's professionalism and past successes would resonate with his younger teammates. Even before the season began, he made that impression on first baseman Ed Kranepool. "He has a winning attitude. He has no use for losers," he said after meeting Boyer over the winter. "No matter what he does with his bat or his glove, he should help us just by his presence."[19]

Ken was an early arrival at camp and took extra batting practice after everyone else left for the day, working to improve his swing. He took it easy in the exhibitions out of concern for his troublesome back, not wanting to injure himself like the previous spring. He played in all but one of the 25 games, batting .169 with three home runs and 10 RBIs. His best performance was against the Detroit Tigers on April 5 when he had three safeties with a homer and three RBIs. "I don't even worry about that down here," he told the New York writers unfamiliar with his typical spring production. "I figure what I don't get down here, I'll get up North. I've never hit in the spring, never."[20]

Westrum asked Ken to take a leadership role on the club, something entirely in his nature anyway. He took the initiative and approached his new teammates first, getting to know them, and making them feel comfortable enough to come to him, especially rookies in camp. "I think that's the responsibility of any veteran ballplayer. Heck, it's for the good of the club. Maybe they can show me something." Never imposing himself on them, he offered advice only when asked. The exception was when he saw someone not doing his best for the team. "If somebody doesn't tell a man he's made a mistake, he'll keep on doing it. I couldn't jump all over a guy, but I'll ask him why he did something and if he has no reason, I'll have to tell him."[21]

His teammates were watching him as well. "He's a steady man," remarked Swoboda. "He doesn't kick things and throw things when he makes [an] out. He doesn't get excited when he gets a hit." They noticed how his mind was always in the game and the encouragement he offered them even from the bench. "It's an intangible thing," explained pitcher Jack Fisher. "I can't put it into words and I'll bet you can't put it down on paper. All I can tell you is that he's a pro. What does that mean? It means that everything he does is for one thing: to win."[22]

The Mets opened the season at Shea Stadium on April 15 against the Braves, who had relocated from Milwaukee to Atlanta. They dropped the first game, 3-2, but won the next two and climbed to a game above .500 for the first time in franchise history.

Boyer batted third in the order as protection for cleanup hitter Kranepool. He quickly dispelled any concerns about his health, hitting safely in 11 of the first 12 games at a .391 clip, third-best in the National League. He doubled three times on April 17, the last one driving in two runs in the eighth inning off knuckleball reliever Phil Niekro, who had just entered the game. Ken watched him warm up and saw all three of his pitches, including his fastball. With two strikes Niekro tried sneaking one past him, but Boyer ripped it to left field for the game-tying hit. "Giving me a ball high inside is pitching to my strength," he said afterward. "That's the ball I hit out of the park. When you throw to a guy's strength, the bat swings by itself. It sort of goes after the ball automatically. That's what happened on this one." The three doubles tied him for the club record with Ron Hunt and Charley Smith, for whom he had been traded.[23]

The thrill of a winning record was fleeting, however, as New York dropped their next five in a row and fell below .500, a plateau they wouldn't reach again the remainder of the season. Two of those losses came against the Cardinals, with Ken homering off rookie left-hander Larry Jaster, his first of the season, in a 5-2 loss on April 19. The Mets' tradition of ineptitude seemed to wear off on him—at least for one game—when he committed three uncharacteristic errors (the most in his major-league career) in an 8-4 loss on April 2. On a rain-soaked field, he made a wild throw trying to start a double play, was called for obstructing a runner at third base, and threw another ball in the dirt to first base, enabling the Braves to win their first home game in Atlanta. "This was a most unusual game for Ken," said Braves manager Bobby Bragan, whose club tallied three times on the misplays.[24]

Boyer played his first game in St. Louis as a Met on May 3. When he walked to the plate in the first inning and his name was announced, the fans greeted him with "many cheers—but a few familiar boos," wrote the *St. Louis Post-Dispatch*. He was hitless in the 5-2 defeat, but he had an RBI single in the Mets' 8-0 victory the next evening. Jack Hamilton pitched a one-hitter for New York, yielding only a bunt single to third against opposing hurler Ray Sadecki with two outs in the third inning. "If he's got a no-hitter going in the late innings, I might have guarded the line," explained Boyer, whose throw was too late to get the left-hand hitting Sadecki at first base. "But a bunt was the furthest thing from my mind in the third inning." Ken's hit proved to be his final one at the first Busch Stadium. Five days later, the Cardinals played their last game at the former Sportsman's Park—where he made trips from Alba to watch Stan Musial, Marty Marion, and other players of his childhood—and officially moved to their new downtown home, Busch Memorial Stadium, on May 12.[25]

Having been fired as manager of the crosstown Yankees, Ken's old skipper Johnny Keane and his wife watched the last half of the Mets' 7-4 win over the Astros at Shea Stadium on May 10 before flying home to Houston. He missed Boyer's game-tying home run in the first inning. "I'm glad to see he's doing so well over here," said Keane. Over the winter, he was hired as a special assignment scout with the

California Angels, but died of a heart attack on January 6, 1967, at the age of fifty-five. Ken fondly remembered him as a "family man, the type you would be proud to have for a brother or father." He added, "As a manager, he demanded respect and got it. He expected a lot of his ball players, and rightly so. He was not an easy man on players, but he was a good manager."[26]

With a crowd of 56,658 at Shea Stadium for the San Francisco Giants' first appearance of the season on May 13, Ken scored his 1,000th career run in the fourth inning when rookie center fielder Billy Murphy blasted his first major-league hit—a three-run homer—to put the Mets ahead in an eventual 17-inning, 5-4 loss. Boyer missed the next eight games with an inflamed right elbow.[27] Four days after his return, a scoreless pitcher's duel between Hamilton and Claude Osteen at Dodger Stadium on the twenty-seventh unraveled for the Mets when a leadoff double and three errors, including Boyer's errant throw to first on a bunt, allowed the Dodgers to score four runs in the sixth inning. Injury was added to insult when he charged a popped-up bunt, tumbled to the ground, and landed on his left wrist. The worst was feared, but X-rays came back negative and the jammed wrist didn't keep him out of the lineup the next day. In fact, he hit safely in the next four games and smashed his first triple of the season in the second game of a twin bill with Philadelphia on the thirtieth.[28]

The balky elbow limited him to a dismal .208 average in the month of May, however, but he rebounded with 34 hits, five home runs, and 14 RBIs for a .266 clip in June. Ken singled twice and knocked Don Drysdale out of the box with a two-run homer to beat the Dodgers, 6-2, on June 3. He hit safely in 10 of his next 11 games, cracking a home run with three RBIs over the Braves on the ninth and four days later having another 3-for-4 performance, this time against the Cardinals.

For a team seeking respectability, every positive milestone was noteworthy. The Mets had their most successful road trip in franchise history when they won eight out of fourteen games June 15–26. Splitting a two-game series at Atlanta, they dropped three of five at Cincinnati. Boyer and Hunt each had three safeties in the third game against the Reds on June 18. Ken had two doubles, one of which momentarily put the Mets ahead in the seventh. But with the tying run on third and two outs in the ninth, he grounded out to end the game, 5-4. With those hits, he raised his average to .293, the highest it would be the rest of the season. Next, they traveled to St. Louis for their first series at the new Busch Memorial Stadium and won two of three. Ken's first hit there was a single off Tracy Stallard in the fourth inning on June 21, and he scored what proved to be the game-winning run on Swoboda's single in a 2-1 victory. The trip concluded with New York taking three of four at Chicago, Boyer contributing an RBI double that knocked in the first run in a 4-2 victory on the twenty-fourth.[29]

Kathleen traveled to New York in June when the children were out of school for summer vacation. Ken had subleased a sixth-floor apartment from Dan Jenkins, a writer for *Sports Illustrated*, on East Eighty-Sixth Street in Manhattan. It was located across from Central Park, but Ken and Kathleen felt it was unsafe for the children to play there. After two weeks of boredom and with Ken about to leave on a road trip, he thought it best for them to return home. He then shared an apartment with his brother Clete and his Yankee teammate Roger Maris and Mets third-base coach Whitey Herzog. When the Yankees were on the road, Ken and Herzog had the place to themselves and vice versa. Before the arrangements were made, Clete in all seriousness felt his older brother should pay the entire rent. "Sure, why not? He beat us in the World Series and there is a difference in our salaries."[30]

The Mets enjoyed their best month ever with an 18-14 record in July, including ten victories on the road. After losing seven straight before and after the All-Star break, they set a new franchise mark by winning seven in a row over the Astros, Giants, and Dodgers July 17–22. The streak was broken when Sandy Koufax beat them on the twenty-third, 6-2. Despite striking out seven and holding the Mets to two runs, Koufax later complained about his inability to command his trademark curve during the complete-game victory. (Losing sensation in his fingertips coupled with arm pain would lead Koufax to retire at the end of the season.) Ken quipped, "I'll probably lie awake for hours worrying because Sandy has temporarily mislaid his curve ball." He added, "He threw one pitch that was impossible. No ball can get up to the plate that quick. Then he threw it again."[31]

Westrum attributed the team's success to "togetherness" between young players like rookie outfielder Cleon Jones and second baseman Ron Hunt and veterans like Boyer, Ed Bressoud, Roy McMillan, and Chuck Hiller, all having the drive to win. "In previous seasons after they lost, they would cut up a bit," he recalled. "Losing was a habit and it didn't matter. But it's no longer a habit." On July 15 and 16, Ken made his first-ever appearance and start at first base, respectively, when a pulled hamstring in his right thigh hindered his mobility at third. The injury wasn't severe, however, and he soon returned to his customary position.[32]

Unfortunately, togetherness didn't lead to many more victories the last two months of the season. The Mets did manage to stay in ninth place and steer clear of the cellar-dwelling Chicago Cubs. Ken enjoyed his best month in August, batting .286 with eight home runs and 12 RBIs. He had a trio of three-hit games and smashed a three-run homer against his old club on August 6. Four days later at Pittsburgh, he collected four safeties against a Pirates club he batted .320 against for the season. He hit a pair of doubles and drove in two runs at Philadelphia on the nineteenth. In an abbreviated two-game set at Los Angeles, Boyer collected five hits—three of them doubles—and helped knock Koufax out of the box in the fourth inning of a 10-4 victory on August 30.

A ten-game hit streak highlighted the end of his first season in New York. It started with three safeties (including his 14th home run) and two runs scored in the second game of a doubleheader with Cincinnati on September 5. He had eight singles and a double in the next nine games before going hitless in the first of a twin bill at Houston on the eighteenth. In that game, a hard-throwing, nineteen-year-old right-hander just called up from the minors named Nolan Ryan made his major-league debut for New York in a 9-2 defeat. While fielding a slow-rolling grounder at third, Ken's spikes caught in the new synthetic AstroTurf and he twisted his back, tearing a muscle. It forced him to miss the final nine games of the season, though he insisted he could have played if needed.[33]

The Mets didn't win 70 games or break out of the second division as Westrum optimistically predicted in the spring. Nonetheless, they avoided the National League cellar and another 100-loss season. New team records were set for winning achievements instead of futility. There were no 20-game losers on the pitching staff. The club finished in ninth place with a record of 66-95, the best in franchise history and an improvement of sixteen games above their win total in 1965. Westrum rewarded his players on the final day of the season with a champagne celebration fit for a championship club. "I wanted to show the boys that I appreciated their play. Maybe ninth place is no great shakes for other teams, but for us it's the first time we didn't finish last."[34]

Ken believed he could still contribute to the Mets in 1967. He led the club with 61 RBIs and 28 doubles, and his 14 home runs were two short of Kranepool's club lead. But for the second year in a row, injuries affected his durability and performance. Even though he played in eight fewer games than the year before, he felt 136 games was a good number for a thirty-five-year-old. He drove in fourteen less runs than in 1965, but he had a higher slugging percentage (.415, forty-one points better than his '65 mark) and raised his batting average to .266. "I was satisfied with my hitting," he concluded. "I tailed off in the second half, but I thought I had a real good first-half. Early in the season, I was swinging about as good as I ever have."[35]

After Christmas, Ken agreed to a new one-year contract reportedly for $58,000. He told Bing Devine, who was now the Mets president and general manager after two seasons as George Weiss's assistant, that he would sign for any amount offered. "Kenny and I have negotiated contracts nearly every year for more than 10 years," Devine told reporters in New York in a telephone press conference from his St. Louis home. "We've never had a debate or an argument over salary, and the contracts have always been on a mutually agreeable basis." Boyer accepted a pay cut of about eight thousand dollars because he felt he didn't deserve a higher salary.[36]

KEN WOULD TURN thirty-six years old during the upcoming 1967 season. He conceded he had "lost a step or two to first base" and needed to rest more often to stay fresh, perhaps a day at a time, and sit out a game in doubleheaders. "[A]s long as I can get the bat around on the fastball, I'll play major league ball." Though prepared to play anywhere he was needed, it wasn't fair to promising young players like

Ed Kranepool and Ron Swoboda for him to shuffle between third and first base. "The future of this club lies with youngsters, not with fellows like me," he said. At the same time, he needed consistent playing time and not be rested for as long as a week at a time like Westrum did the previous season. "I lose my timing when I sit down that long and find it tough to get back."[37]

Boyer considered his future after baseball when he acquired a Ford-Mercury car dealership seventy miles west of St. Louis in the small town of Hermann, Missouri, a favorite hunting spot. His business partner Raymond Chancellor ran the day-to-day operations during the baseball season while Ken continued his playing career and later managed in the minor leagues. "Business keeps me busy," he said in 1966. "I haven't even hunted much this winter." Ken Boyer Ford (later renamed Boyer-Chancellor Ford) operated from 1966 until it was sold about 1978.[38]

No longer tied to St. Louis, he purchased a 1,600-acre horse farm outside Hermann and built a single-story home on a hilltop overlooking the picturesque German settlement and the Frene Valley. It was a home designed for entertaining guests with a spacious living room and large windows that offered a beautiful view. "You would come in from hunting and they would pour you a big glass of that German wine," recalls former teammate Tommy John. "You would sit there with floor to ceiling windows overlooking the valley. They had a fire going in the fireplace to your back and you would look out the windows. It was beautiful; it was absolutely beautiful."[39]

Boyer made a good showing in spring training, batting .279 in 61 at-bats, though he committed five errors at third base. Normally an average spring hitter, he attributed his improved performance to pleasant Florida weather and using his normal weight bat instead of a heavier one as he did most every spring. One memorable exhibition was a wild scoring affair at Al Lang Field in St. Petersburg. Thirty to forty mile per hour winds coming off Tampa Bay contributed to the Mets' 18-13 lead over the Boston Red Sox on March 16. Ken had a single, a double, and an RBI. The Red Sox came back and scored 10 runs in the ninth inning to beat them, 23-18.[40]

The Mets began the season with four wins and four losses, the best start in franchise history. They were tied with the Chicago Cubs for fifth place and 2 ½ games behind the league-leading Cardinals. After going 1-for-8 in his first three games, Ken doubled off his old roommate Larry Jackson at Philadelphia on April 16 and hit safely in six straight, raising his average to .290. Four days later, his RBI single broke a 1-1 tie and he scored two runs in a 6-1 win over the Cubs, the first major-league victory for twenty-two-year-old Tom Seaver, the eventual NL Rookie of the Year and Hall of Fame pitcher.[41]

New York lost nine of their next 13 and fell to ninth place, just a half-game out of the National League cellar. The pitching held up with a 3.24 ERA in April, but the offense slumped with an anemic .201 average. After his streak was broken, Ken had only two hits in his next 30 at-bats and saw his own average fall to .164 by May 4. His luck was so bad that against the San Francisco Giants two days earlier, with runners on first and second and no outs, he smashed a ball off Gaylord Perry that looked like a sure hit. Instead, Perry snagged it and started an inning-ending triple play, the first ever executed against the Mets. "It was the hardest ball I've hit in a month," lamented Boyer.[42]

He was rested for a game with Houston the next day, followed by Saturday and Sunday rainouts, then returned to the lineup on May 9 against the Cincinnati Reds. The next evening at Shea Stadium, he singled in the second inning and did the same in the fourth off veteran right-hander Milt Pappas of the Reds for the 2,000th hit of his major-league career. Afterward, he asked Pappas to sign the ball for him, a ritual he had done with other milestone balls, including his 1,000th hit, his 200th home run, and his 1,000th RBI. "I don't know how it started, but when I got my first one, I asked the pitcher I got the hit off to sign it and I've been doing it ever since."[43]

Unfortunately, it proved to be the highlight of his season in New York. Ed Charles was acquired from the Kansas City Athletics that evening and installed at third base two days later, leaving Ken on the bench for much of May. Charles was only two years younger and like Boyer, his production had diminished the past two seasons. Devine reassured Ken that he was still the Mets third baseman, but implied he had "reached the stage where he no longer can play every day." After a week, Boyer told Westrum he felt rested, but the manager stayed with Charles, who was hitting well though not for much power. Ken returned to the lineup for a two-game series with St. Louis beginning

May 19. He had two safeties and scored a run in each contest, including a triple off Bob Gibson in the first game and an RBI double on his thirty-sixth birthday on the twentieth—the 300th double of his major-league career—that put the Mets ahead in the second contest. Even though he went 2-for-2 with a walk in that game and raised his average to .230, Westrum lifted him for a pinch-runner in the sixth inning and kept him out the next five games.[44]

Ken played more often in June with an occasional start at first base and pinch-hitting appearances. Perhaps the increased playing time was intended to showcase him for a possible trade, as the team had already placed him on waivers. It did little to help solve his batting troubles, however, and his average sunk to .212. A modest five-game hit streak in the middle of June brought it back up twenty-one points. In one of those games, he led the club with two hits against Cincinnati, including an RBI double, and scored with Kranepool on a double by Tommy Davis in the 4-0 victory. "I'm not trying to kid myself. I'm not the player I was three or four years ago," he conceded. "I know it, the manager knows it. I come to the park every day hoping to play. If I don't start, well maybe I can help in the seventh or eighth innings. I have to act like a Boy Scout—be prepared. I feel fortunate I'm with a club that can use me 40 to 60 percent of the time."[45]

He cracked his first home run of the season on June 26, a two-run shot that tied the game with two outs in the eighth. Charles's pinch-hit RBI single won it in the ninth over Pittsburgh, 3-2. Before the next day's game with the Pirates, Paramount Pictures filmed a scene at Shea Stadium for the movie adaptation of Neil Simon's play *The Odd Couple* starring Walter Matthau and Jack Lemmon. In the scene, Matthau played a baseball writer watching a game from the press box sitting beside long-time New York sportswriter Heywood Hale Broun. Trailing the Mets by a run with no outs, the Pirates had the bases loaded in the ninth inning and Bill Mazeroski at the plate. Matthau's character, Oscar Madison, received an "emergency" telephone call from his roommate describing what Felix (Lemmon) would be fixing for dinner that evening. He turned his back on the field, missing the game-ending triple play started by Boyer at third. The movie crew had only thirty-five minutes to film the mock triple play before the actual game started, which the Mets won, 5-2. Even though he appeared in the film version, Ken didn't play in the actual game.[46]

A dramatic eighth-inning blast by Boyer off reliever Joe Hoerner tied the score during the first game of a doubleheader on July 2 and the Mets rallied to beat the first-place Cardinals, 5-4. The next evening against the San Francisco Giants, he hit another to put his team on the board and contribute to a 5-3 win. The two victories enabled New York to climb out of the cellar and into ninth place. Ken now had three home runs and 12 RBIs for the season. He may have been dealing with shoulder pain for much of the season in New York, as well as an injured finger. "I don't recall ever going into the All-Star break with less than 40 RBI," he said. "Usually it was around 60. But I can't put my head between my legs and quit. I've just got to keep swinging."[47]

The home run on July 3 and a pair of singles two days later were his last hits with the Mets. After the All-Star break, Westrum settled on Charles as the regular third baseman and Kranepool at first. It wasn't until a week later that Ken appeared as a pinch-hitter in back-to-back games. He struck out looking in his final plate appearance against the Dodgers on July 21. "Boyer looked more and more like a man who'd be scouting, coaching or managing somewhere, and soon," wrote George Vecsey of the *New York Times*. In fact, there was speculation that Devine might fire Westrum and hire Boyer to take over as manager. Instead, Ken was traded to the Chicago White Sox the next day for Bill Southworth, a Double-A infielder/outfielder, and an undisclosed cash payment.[48] Both clubs agreed to exchange players to be named at the end of the season to complete the deal.[49]

It was the second time in less than two years that Ken had been traded. This time, he had an inkling it would happen. The Mets had placed him on waivers in May, hoping another team would claim him and make a deal. Negotiations were serious enough with the Chicago White Sox in early June that Devine told him to take all his belongings with him on a road trip to the Windy City. It took another month before an agreement could be worked out.[50]

Chapter Fourteen

A Final Challenge

Ken's fortunes improved dramatically. He was immediately thrust into a pennant race for the first time in three seasons. Instead of sitting on the bench for a ninth-place club, now there was the possibility of playing every day for a first-place team in the American League. Devine felt the deal would benefit both Boyer and the White Sox. "They're slipping right now and they could use help. I think Kenny might get a chance to play. This could really be a challenge for him." Ken agreed, considering it "more of a challenge than a dramatic change."[1]

The White Sox needed a productive bat. They had lost seven out of 11 games since the All-Star break and were clinging to a half-game lead over the Boston Red Sox. The California Angels, Detroit Tigers, and Minnesota Twins were close behind. Speed, defense, and the best pitching staff in the league had sustained them to this point, but a weak offense with the second fewest home runs and a collective .234 average was no match for the more powerful contenders. After finishing seven straight seasons in the first division without a pennant, expectations were high on the South Side of Chicago for their first American League title since 1959.[2]

Despite his paltry statistics with the Mets, the White Sox expected much from him. "Getting Boyer might give us the push we need," remarked center fielder Tommie Agee. General manager Ed Short compared him to Ted Kluszewski, another mid-season acquisition from the National League in the team's last championship season. "Big Klu" batted .297 in the pennant drive with two homers in 31 games. "Boyer will help us with his bat, but I look for more than that," said Short. "He'll help us personally, too. I remember Klu did more for our morale than anything else."[3]

When Ken joined the club in Kansas City on July 23, they had a record of 51-40. His new manager was actually his first one—Eddie Stanky, who gave him the opportunity to play for the Cardinals in 1955. After meeting Stanky and his coaching staff, Boyer went to the ballpark two hours early for an afternoon doubleheader with the Athletics. He was anxious as a rookie, pacing the clubhouse floor, trying to contain his pregame jitters. "I was trying to keep from getting too nervous, but I couldn't shake it," he recalled. "I hadn't played in ten or twelve games in New York. I tried on four or five pairs of trousers before I found one that fit me. Then I had to borrow underwear." His new teammates teased him playfully as "The National Leaguer" and called him "Clete." Ken started in the first game, batting third in the order and playing third base. In his first plate appearance, he singled to drive in rookie Walt "No-Neck" Williams with the White Sox's first run in an eventual 8-4 victory. One teammate remarked, "Maybe we didn't get the wrong Boyer after all."[4]

Stanky had a good defensive infield with Tom McCraw at first, Wayne Causey at second, Ron Hansen at short, and Don Buford at third. What he lacked was someone vocal enough to offer leadership and direction in certain situations, not only to the infielders but the pitchers as well. "All I want is someone to take charge of things in the infield—go to the pitcher and remind him to keep that ball down, calm him down when he's wild," Stanky said earlier in the season. "But you really can't change a fellow's personality. He either has that gift of leadership or he doesn't." Now he had that take-charge personality in Ken Boyer. "Run my infield," he told him.[5]

"The thing about Kenny is when he came in, he blended in as if he had been on the ball club all year," recalls Tommy John. "He was just one of us." Boyer and the twenty-four-year-old left-handed pitcher struck up a quick friendship. John grew up in Terre Haute, Indiana, and listened to Cardinals games on KMOX radio when Ken starred on the team. Both listened to county and western music and enjoyed hunting. "He would take me with him on the road," remembers John. "Because he had been around, he had a lot of friends in a lot of cities. We would go out and have dinner with them after a game and sit around and talk and laugh. He took me under his wing and didn't say anything but more or less, 'This is how you act as a major-league ballplayer.'"[6]

A four-game win streak enabled Chicago to pad their lead over Boston by two games and 2½ over California. Ken played in both games of a July 25 doubleheader with the Cleveland Indians—his first appearance at White Sox Park—and had five safeties, including a 3-for-3 performance in the second contest when he didn't even start. He entered the game as a pinch-hitter in the ninth with the score tied, 4-4. He led off with a single, but was stranded at first base and the game went to extra innings. In the bottom of the sixteenth, he singled again and scored on Ken Berry's game-winning home run for the 6-4 victory. Afterward, Stanky praised Boyer's humility among his new teammates. "Ken was leading the parade to congratulate the other players. He didn't say, 'I'm Ken Boyer, you got the pennant won.' He was one of 25…"[7]

The White Sox split a four-game series with the third-place Tigers, maintaining a 3½ game lead over them and the Red Sox still in second place two games back. Ken contributed to both victories. He hit his first American League home run on July 29 to give them a two-run lead in the first inning and veteran reliever Don McMahon saved it in the ninth, 4-3. In the opener of a twin bill the next day, he singled and scored with Williams on Pete Ward's double in the 4-1 win.

The excitement of a pennant race rejuvenated him. He was sensational in his first eight games with Chicago, batting .385 with 10 hits in 26 at-bats in July. The thirty-six-year-old even flashed hustle when he hit an infield dribbler in one game and dived head-first into first base to avoid the tag. "[S]ince I've been with the Sox, I've been hitting the ball good and they've been dropping in," he said. "I suppose you could say there's luck in it, but when you hit the ball, it might drop in." He did his best to encourage his new teammates, much to the appreciation of Stanky. "Why, the first day he joined us, he was in the dugout patting guys on the back, cheering and trying to boost them. You'd think he'd been with us four or five years." Back in the National League, the Atlanta Braves were in third place and 3 ½ games behind the front-running St. Louis Cardinals on July 22. Little brother Clete Boyer was enjoying a career year in Atlanta's bandbox ballpark, having been traded from the New York Yankees over the winter. He ended the season with 26 home runs and 96 RBIs.[8]

The White Sox added another discarded star seeking redemption in former home run slugger Rocky Colavito from the Indians on July 29. From 1956 through 1966 with Cleveland (twice), Detroit, and Kansas City, Colavito had averaged a .270 mark, 33 home runs, and 99 RBIs. "Having those two in the lineup makes a difference," remarked pitcher Joe Horlen. Two days later, Stanky held a meeting in the visitors clubhouse in Cleveland. "You put us in first place," he told his young players. Turning to his two veterans sitting together, he added, "Colavito and Boyer have to keep us there."[9]

Both men lived up to expectations, at least initially. That evening, on July 31, the White Sox were one out away from losing to the Indians in the ninth inning. Ken came to the plate as a pinch-hitter and singled with runners on first and second, driving in Buford with the tying run. Facing the team that had just traded him, Colavito smashed a two-run homer to win it in the tenth, 4-2. The writers gathered around him after the game, but he pointed to Boyer instead. "Here's the guy who saved the game. Without his single, we lose 2-1 in nine innings."[10]

Winning two of three at Cleveland, the White Sox lost two straight at Baltimore but took two of four at Detroit to stay two games ahead of second-place Boston and 2 ½ over Minnesota. Ken started a triple play in the second game of the August 6 doubleheader when Brooks Robinson of the Orioles slapped a grounder to him at third with runners on first and second in the fifth inning. In the finale at Tiger Stadium on the tenth, he hit what proved to be the game-winning home run on a slider from rookie reliever Mike Marshall in the eighth inning of the 2-1 victory. "It was a bad pitch," lamented Detroit manager Mayo Smith. "Inside, to Boyer's power." Though Colavito had slumped to

.216 after a strong start, Ken was still productive. He played in 14 of the team's 17 games since joining the club and was batting .377 with 20 hits in 53 at-bats.[11]

The team traveled to Bloomington, Minnesota, for an important series beginning August 11 with the third-place Twins, who were 2 ½ games back. Fielding a ground ball at third by the first batter in the opener, Boyer pulled a muscle in his left leg and had to leave the game. He could barely get out of bed the next morning and went to the ballpark early for the trainer to work on him. Asked by pitcher Gary Peters how he felt, Ken told him his leg hurt. "That's what happens when you get old," said Peters playfully. "That's right, Gary," Ken replied slyly, "that's what happens when you get old." He missed the second game and tied the third as a pinch-hitter with a sacrifice fly in the seventh inning, but the Twins came back and won, 3-2. Minnesota swept the series and knocked Chicago out of first place for the first time in sixty-three days.[12]

The White Sox enjoyed a rare offensive outburst of 17 hits against the cellar-dwelling Kansas City Athletics on August 16 and beat them, 14-1. Ward led the way with two home runs and four RBIs as part of his 4-for-4 performance. Jerry McNertney also homered and Williams had three safeties. Reduced to pinch-hitting duties, Ken crushed a pitch over the head of left fielder Danny Cater with the bases loaded and two outs in the fourth inning. As each runner crossed the plate to increase their lead 9-0, it was all Boyer could do simply to limp to first base. After taking the series with the Athletics, Chicago won three of four from Baltimore and three of five from New York to claim a virtual first-place tie with Boston (though one percentage point ahead) on August 24. Ken made his first start in eleven games on August 22 against the Yankees, playing first base in the second game of a doubleheader, but was hitless in three at-bats.[13]

The White Sox hosted Boston for a five-game weekend series with first place at stake beginning August 25. The clubs split the Friday doubleheader, enabling the third-place Minnesota Twins to leapfrog into first with a half-game advantage. Boyer started the second game of the twin bill and had two safeties in the 2-1 walk-off win. He singled and drove in a run the next day, but Horlen gave up 10 hits and five earned runs and Chicago lost the third game, 6-2, falling to third place. After dropping the first half of the Sunday doubleheader on two home runs by Carl Yastrzemski, the White Sox won the second with a gutsy performance by Peters. The left-hander held the Red Sox to four hits over 11 scoreless innings while the opposing hurler, Jose Santiago, allowed one less safety in nearly ten frames. Four walks by Boston reliever Bucky Brandon—one intentional—enabled them to win in the eleventh, 1-0. Chicago finished the series in third place, one game behind Minnesota, with Boston one percentage point behind.

As the season entered September, the race became much tighter between the Twins, Red Sox, Tigers, and White Sox. "It was nerve-wracking, pulsating fun," wrote Tommy John in his autobiography. Chicago took three of four from Boston at Fenway Park and two of three at Yankee Stadium. A thirteen-inning, 3-2 walk-off victory over the California Angels on September 6 tied them with Minnesota for first place while both Boston and Detroit were only a percentage point behind. They lost two straight to the Tigers and dropped back to fourth place and two games behind Detroit, who now led the league. Thanks to two stellar pitching performances, the White Sox bounced back in the September 10 doubleheader and knocked the Tigers out of first and into a tie with them for third place. Horlen pitched a 6-0 no-hitter in the opener for his 16th victory, with a hit batter in the third inning, and a bobbled ground ball at first base by Ken in the fifth keeping him from a perfect game. Rookie right-hander Cisco Carlos, pitching in his fourth major-league game, combined with relievers Hoyt Wilhelm and Bob Locker to hurl a five-hit shutout to win the second game, 4-0. Boyer had four hits during the first three games of the series, including an RBI triple, and raised his average to .292.[14]

Boyer started in all but two of the last 18 games of the season as the pressure of the incredible four-team pennant race intensified going into the final stretch. "In all fairness to the rest of the team who put us in first place," Stanky later confessed, "I didn't think we could contend for the pennant without Ken and Rocky." Chicago lost three in a row after the Detroit series, two of them against the seventh-place Cleveland Indians in a twi-night doubleheader. They persevered over the Tribe in a four-hour, 32-minute marathon on September 13. With one out in the seventeenth inning, Boyer singled and was lifted for a pinch-runner, Buddy Bradford. A passed ball advanced Bradford to second and McCraw was given an intentional walk. The next batter, Colavito, singled to right and plated Bradford for the 1-0 victory. Buford's grand slam—the first for the White Sox all season—won another extra-inning affair the next evening.[15]

After two exciting come-from-behind victories, the White Sox knocked the Minnesota Twins out of a tie for the league lead with three straight wins and moved up to second place, just a half-game behind Detroit. Ken's average had dipped to .269, but in the opener on September 15, he doubled and hit two singles, scored two runs, and shined defensively at third base in the 7-3 victory. Leading Chicago by three runs in the ninth inning the next evening, the Twins unraveled as the White Sox rallied to win, 5-4. Peters extended his scoreless streak to 20 innings on September 17 and his 4-0 shutout completed the sweep.[16]

Boyer carried a modest hit streak through the next week. With four clubs jockeying for position and just two weeks left in the season, every game counted. Unfortunately, Chicago managed to lose the most crucial ones. They dropped a ninth-inning heart-breaker to the California Angels, 3-2, on September 18. Boston beat Detroit and Minnesota won over Kansas City, resulting in a three-way tie between the Red Sox, Tigers, and Twins for the league lead. Meanwhile, the Cardinals clinched the National League championship that evening for the first time since 1964. Winning the American League flag meant Boyer would have the chance to face his old team in the World Series.

But first they had to overtake the Red Sox, Tigers, and Twins. Chicago beat California in the next two games—including Horlen's 18th victory with a six-hit, 3-0 shutout on the nineteenth—but remained stuck in third place and a half-game out. Flying back east to Cleveland for an important contest on the twenty-second, they found themselves on the losing end of another one-run game when Tony Horton of the Indians crushed a home run in the thirteenth inning to beat them, 2-1. Because Boston split a doubleheader, Detroit swept a doubleheader, and Minnesota won their game, Chicago slipped to fourth place and trailed Minnesota by two games. Ken contributed to their next two victories over Cleveland, doubling home two runs in a three-hit, 8-0 shutout for Horlen's 19th victory followed by a 2-for-4 showing with a home run to win the rubber game, 3-1. All it gained them, however, was third place and one game back of the Twins with five left to play.

Stanky was correct in his early August prediction that the American League pennant would not be decided until the final week of the season. His club traveled to Kansas City a day early before the start of a two-game series on September 26. "We never played well after an off day [and] Stanky called a workout. We had a full-fledged workout game," recalls Tommy John. It didn't help because just as batting practice started the next day, a downpour forced a doubleheader the next evening. On the twenty-seventh, the Red Sox and Twins lost their games and Detroit was idle. This gave Chicago the opportunity to reclaim first place with a sweep of the twin bill.[17]

But the offense vanished in both games and the last-place Athletics played the role of spoiler at the most inopportune time. Kansas City built a five-run lead off Peters in the opener and a ninth-inning rally by the Sox fell short, 5-2. Going for his 20th victory, Horlen dueled with twenty-one-year-old Jim "Catfish" Hunter in the second contest, each allowing only two hits through five scoreless innings. Horlen flinched in the sixth, giving up five hits and three earned runs, then an error and a passed ball allowed another run to score after he was taken out. Hunter dominated the remainder of the contest and the Sox managed only one more hit in the 4-0 defeat. Ken was hitless in both games. "I remember the silence in our locker room after those games," recalled Peters. "I've gotten over that over the years… but I know some of the guys on the team are still bothered by what happened." South Side fans called this pair of crushing losses "Black Wednesday."[18]

The White Sox were in trouble. They needed to win their last three games of the season to ensure a tie for first place with either Boston or Minnesota—who would oppose each other in a two-game series at Fenway Park—or Detroit. A loss would mathematically eliminate them from the race. They returned to Chicago to face the eighth-place Washington Senators on September 29 with Tommy John on the mound. The game started badly when first baseman McCraw dropped Boyer's throw from third and leadoff hitter Tim Cullen reached safely. The next batter, Hank Allen, forced Cullen at second. Trying for a double play, second baseman Buford threw the ball out of McCraw's reach and Allen was able to advance to second base. After Frank Howard walked, Fred Valentine hit a pop foul behind first base, but a temporary enclosure built for postseason NBC television cameras kept the ball out of McCraw's reach. Valentine singled on the next pitch and plated Allen with what proved to be the only run of the game. Ken had a chance to tie it with McCraw on third and two outs in Chicago's half, but he forced Colavito at second to end the frame. John followed with eight shutout innings, but his teammates couldn't move further than second base the remainder of the game. "I just wish we hadn't lost it this way," lamented Stanky afterward. "I hate errors. A good clean base hit is not bad, but to lose on an error is hard to take." He met with the players in the clubhouse afterward and blamed himself for their failure to win the pennant. Some believed he was right.[19]

The 1-0 defeat ended the 1967 pennant chase for the White Sox. "We were beat," recalled Horlen. "We knew it. It was simply a question of playing the final two games. It was our lowest point mentally in the season." The offense once again failed to score against Washington on the twenty-ninth and they lost, 4-0. Their mark for futility stretched to 28 consecutive innings before Horlen—a pitcher—singled and knocked in two runs in the 4-3 defeat on the first of October. The Detroit Tigers split their last four games during back-to-back doubleheaders with California and the Boston Red Sox won two straight over Minnesota to clinch their "Impossible Dream" pennant on the final day of the season.[20]

KEN BOYER AND ROCKY COLAVITO brought experience and leadership to a young contending club. Their teammates voted them full shares of the players pool for the club's fourth-place finish at $428.51 each. But they weren't the saviors that the White Sox hoped for or the power hitters they desperately needed. Neither did well in September—Boyer hit .211 and Colavito .202. Overall, Ken batted .261 with five doubles, one triple, four home runs, and 21 RBIs in 57 games with the White Sox. Colavito hit .221 with four doubles, one triple, three homers, and 29 RBIs in 60 games. "Both of them helped us to some degree," remarked general manager Ed Short when the season was over. "But I wish they'd have helped more."[21]

Chicago finished tied for eighth in the American League in batting average (.225) and ninth in on-base percentage (.291) and slugging (.320). Among the regulars, third baseman Don Buford and right fielder Ken Berry tied to lead the club in batting at .241. Boyer defended the much-criticized offense and attributed the lack of production to the playing conditions at White Sox Park. "From the White Sox owner on down to the casual fan, everybody keeps rapping the players for not hitting, but everything is done to help the pitcher." In addition to the large field dimensions and the wind that blew in off Lake Michigan, the grounds crew were instructed to let the infield grass grow tall and water it in front of home plate to give Chicago's sinkerball pitchers a better advantage at the expense of the home team's hitters. Ken believed it took twenty to twenty-five points off their batting averages. "You need a cannon to drive a ground ball through that infield," he claimed, "because first the sting is taken out of it by the soggy turf in front of the plate and then the grass slows the ball down even more. Only a lame infielder could miss those." For the season, the White Sox hit just .208 at home while their nine American League opponents managed a combined .205 mark in Chicago.[22]

During the off-season, Ken invited teammate Tommy John to hunt quail and stay for several days at a time at his family's home in Hermann. He also introduced his young friend to homemade wine produced from the local vineyards. "I was not a drinker—and still am not—but that wine would knock you right on your keister," says John. "That's what Kenny said. He laughed and said, 'The stuff won't hurt you. It'll kill you, but it won't hurt you.'" He spent many enjoyable winter evenings in the company of Ken and his family.

"I really liked Ken," he says. "There was something about him that was a magnet."[23]

Chapter Fifteen

West Coast Finale

The White Sox brought Ken back in 1968 and he reported a week early to spring training at Sarasota, Florida. At thirty-six, he was the oldest position player in camp. "Ken Boyer is seasoned and he's the type who tries to give the kids the benefit of his experience," said his ex-Mets and now White Sox teammate Tommy Davis, himself a veteran of eight full major-league seasons. Starting in only 12 of the team's 25 exhibition games, he hoped for more playing time, but Eddie Stanky wanted to give Pete Ward a few starts at third base as he tried to decide on a regular position for him. Boyer had a decent spring and batted .286 in 49 at-bats, though he had only one extra base hit.[1]

Opening Day around the major leagues was delayed two days out of respect for slain civil rights leader Dr. Martin Luther King Jr., who was assassinated in Memphis, Tennessee, on April 4. When the season began, the White Sox lost their first 10 games and fell into the American League cellar with a 2-12 record by the end of April. Disappointed after the team's disastrous finish the year before, fans at White Sox Park booed what they were seeing on the field. Ken was expected to provide more offense and was 24 home runs away from 300 for his career. But he started in only five games and struggled with a .125 average, no extra base hits, and no runs batted in. "It takes more time to get in shape at my age," he said. "Then, too, if you're playing regularly once the season starts, that helps you get in shape. But at my age, you kinda get lost in the shuffle."

Ken's slow start coupled with the team's dismal start and his expensive contract led the White Sox to place him on waivers on May 2. Twenty-two-year-old minor-leaguer Bill Melton replaced him at third base. "When we brought him up here, we hoped he'd give the club a little extra spirit," remarked general manager Ed Short about Boyer. "We did well last season, but we didn't win the pennant. This year we decided dropping Boyer would be the best thing." If no other team claimed him, he would receive his unconditional release. Ken understood the decision. "If I were in their position, I'd probably do the same thing." Quickly, he left Chicago and returned home to Hermann, anticipating calls from interested teams. "There are a few clubs I know I can help," he said while awaiting the outcome. "And there's going to be expansion next year. I'd prefer to get back to the National League."

Almost thirty-seven years old, it was possible his playing career could be over. He acknowledged having "thought some about a future in baseball" in some capacity, "but as long as you're a player, you can't really talk too much about it."[2]

When no team claimed him, Boyer became an unrestricted free agent able to negotiate his own deal. A few days later, he received a one-year, $47,000 offer from the Los Angeles Dodgers, who had reportedly been interested in him as far back as 1960. They had also purchased the contract of his former White Sox teammate Rocky Colavito just before the end of spring training to add veteran experience to their young club. "Both Boyer and Colavito are old pros, especially when it comes to swinging the bat," said one team official. Ken made arrangements with former Dodgers pitcher Stan Williams of the Cleveland Indians to rent his home in Long Beach south of Los Angeles during the season. His familiar No. 14 was already worn by outfielder Len Gabrielson; for the first time in fourteen years, he took a different number: 45.[3]

The Dodgers had a 13-14 record and were tied with the Cincinnati Reds for sixth place in the National League, 4½ games behind the front-running St. Louis Cardinals. Ken flew to Atlanta to meet the team before the second of a three-game series with the Braves on May 11. Manager Walter Alston was a longtime admirer of Boyer ever since his rookie season and had managed him previously in four All-Star Games. Ken understood his role as a right-handed pinch-hitter, but Alston had other ideas. In his debut at Dodger Stadium two days later, he started at first base and batted fifth behind Colavito. He singled twice and drove in the Dodgers' only run in the first inning of a 5-1 loss to the Cubs. "I hadn't batted for 10 days aside from a few cuts at the ball," he said afterward. "But I feel that in this more temperate climate [in southern California], I should be able to play every day if the club wants to use me." He started in his first seven games with the Dodgers, mostly at third, and batted .304. "Boyer did a good job for us," said Alston. "We want to give him every chance to get back his batting form because we feel he can help us at the plate."[4]

In Ken's second game on May 14, veteran Dodgers starting pitcher Don Drysdale, who had lost his last three decisions, tossed a two-hit shutout over the Cubs, 1-0. Four days later, he prevailed against the Houston Astros, 1-0; Boyer reached on a two-out error to score the only run of the game. Drysdale beat Bob Gibson and the Cardinals with five-hit, 2-0 shutout at Busch Memorial Stadium on May 22. Ken was out of the lineup for Drysdale's next start at Houston, his fourth shutout in a row. He had not allowed a run in 36 innings.[5]

The long-armed, 6-foot-5 right-hander's dominance threatened the National League record of 45 $1/3$ scoreless innings set by Carl Hubbell of the New York Giants in 1933 and Walter Johnson's major-league mark of 55 $2/3$ innings for the Washington Senators in 1913. From that point forward, Alston wanted Boyer to start at third base when Drysdale was on the mound. "I took that as a tribute to my fielding ability and it made me feel good," said Ken years later. He took extra fielding practice and worked with Gabrielson on relays from left field. "[W]hen the streak was alive, it really fired the team up," he recalled. "Everybody worked a little harder to keep it going."[6]

Boyer was back in the lineup for Drysdale's next start against the rival San Francisco Giants on May 31. He contributed a sacrifice fly to center in the eighth inning to bolster a 3-0 lead at Dodger Stadium. The streak was in jeopardy when Drysdale walked the lead-off batter, then gave up a single and another base on balls to load the bases with none out in the ninth. On a 2-2 count, he hit Dick Dietz on the elbow with a slider. Home-plate umpire Harry Wendelstedt ruled the batter had not made an effort to avoid the pitch and called it a ball instead. For several minutes, Dietz, Giants manager Herman Franks and third-base coach Peanuts Lowrey argued with the umpire as Ken and his teammates tossed the ball around the infield to stay warm. When the game finally resumed after Franks was ejected by Wendelstedt, Drysdale retired the side to preserve the streak with his fifth consecutive shutout. Now he had 45 scoreless innings, just a third of an inning short of Hubbell's National League mark.[7]

On June 4, the Dodgers backed Drysdale with five runs against the Pittsburgh Pirates, tying for the biggest lead he enjoyed during the streak. Boyer had an RBI single in a three-run fourth inning and was walked intentionally in the sixth. The big right-hander struck out eight and held the Pirates to three hits for his sixth straight shutout. After Willie Stargell grounded out to second to end the game, Ken was the first infielder to reach Drysdale and shake his hand as he walked toward the dugout. His 54 consecutive scoreless innings gave him the NL record and was only an inning and two-thirds short of the major-league mark. Democratic presidential candidate Robert F. Kennedy congratulated Drysdale during his victory speech after winning the California primary that evening. Minutes later, he was assassinated while walking through the kitchen area of the Ambassador Hotel in Los Angeles.[8]

A Ladies' Night crowd of 50,060 packed Dodger Stadium for the historic evening on June 8. Ken put LA on the board in the first with an RBI single against his old friend Larry Jackson, now with the Philadelphia Phillies. Drysdale's moment came in the third—Roberto Pena hit a grounder to Boyer at third and he threw across to first baseman Wes Parker for the record-breaking putout. Two innings later, the scoreless streak ended at 58 $2/3$ innings when Tony Taylor scored on a sacrifice fly by pinch-hitter Howie Bedell. It was Bedell's only RBI that season. "I wanted the record so bad, but I'm glad it's over," said Drysdale afterward. "I could feel myself go 'blah' when the run scored. I just let down emotionally. I'm sure it was the mental strain."

Ken remembered his contribution to the historic streak being "one of the most satisfying parts of my career."[9]

When the streak began, the Dodgers were in fifth place. Winning nine of their last 10 since the end of May, they had positioned themselves in second place, 2 ½ games behind the league-leading Cardinals on June 8. Ken was playing regularly with some rest and one of the few Dodgers hitting above .300. But St. Louis caught fire and took 11 of their next 15 games while the Dodgers lost the same number, falling back to fifth place and nine games behind on June 25. In that time, Ken enjoyed his best month of the season, batting .328 with 14 RBIs in 58 at-bats. At San Francisco on June 27, he stroked a two-out, pinch-hit single in the sixth to score the tying run from second during an eventual 11-inning, 6-5 victory. He smashed his first home run as a Dodger—and his first since September 24, 1967—the next scheduled game on the evening of June 29 at Dodger Stadium against the Atlanta Braves. When he rounded third, brother Clete playfully tossed dirt on him. Ken laughed, "He was just getting even. I did that to him when he hit one against us in that '64 Series."[10]

Kathleen and the children joined him in southern California that summer. It was first time since their abbreviated stay in New York two years earlier that the family had been together during the season. The Boyers enjoyed the swimming pool at the rented home in Long Beach and thirteen-year-old David and nine-year-old Danny spent time with their father on the field before games at Dodger Stadium.[11]

A horrible 7-20 record in July highlighted by five and six-game losing skids left them two games out of last place. Ken's average fell below .300, but he was still one of the top hitters on the club. Injuries, however, limited him to only 12 games during the month. He returned to the lineup at Houston on July 29, but was hurt again on a play at first base in the fourth inning. A wide throw from third baseman Bob Bailey forced him into the baseline where the runner, Bob Watson of the Astros, collided with him. Boyer was knocked backward to the ground and taken out of the game for X-rays. He was out of action for almost two weeks as a result.[12]

August wasn't much better for the Dodgers. A season-high eight-game losing skein landed them in the National League basement for over two weeks toward the end of the month. Regardless, Ken enjoyed his best performance of the season against Philadelphia on August 10. He collected four safeties in seven at-bats despite playing hurt with a stiff neck and delivered the game-winning hit in the fourteenth to give Los Angeles the 3-2 walk-off win. "With it hurting, maybe it makes me keep my head straight," he quipped.[13]

The Dodgers rallied in September and finished the season strong, taking 18 of their last 27 games. Batting cleanup at Philadelphia on September 3, he crashed a two-run home run in the sixth that wrecked Grant Jackson's three-hit scoreless hurling and cut his lead in half. The Phillies added three more tallies before the Dodgers countered in the eighth with a five-run outburst highlighted by back-to-back homers by Bill Sudakis and Boyer. Three more runs in the ninth enabled Los Angeles to edge Philadelphia, 10-9.

Ken's playing time diminished as the season closed. Still, there was a special moment in St. Louis on September 21 when the past and future of the Cardinals met. In the fifth inning, Ted Simmons singled to right field. Playing first base, Boyer asked the nineteen-year-old rookie catcher if it was his first major-league hit. Simmons nodded. Ken replied, "I hope it's the first of 2,500." Simmons finished his major-league career 20 years later with 2,472 hits, just 28 hits short of Ken's prediction.[14]

Boyer's thoughts turned to his old team as the season neared its end. Four days before St. Louis clinched the National League pennant for the third time in five years, *Post-Dispatch* sports editor Bob Broeg talked with him about the World Series matchup between the Cardinals and the Detroit Tigers. Having played against the Tigers in 1967, Ken felt both teams were comparable but gave St. Louis the edge with speed at the top of the order and right-handed hitters who could take advantage of the short right-center fence at Tiger Stadium. The 1968 Cardinals were similar to his '64 club—the young players from that time were now more experienced and Orlando Cepeda, Roger Maris, and Dal Maxvill had assumed the roles once held by himself, Bill White, and Dick Groat. Boyer praised Mike Shannon's transition from the outfield to third base and "proved what a good, natural athlete can do. He had done some job over there." He ranked Bob Gibson's '68 season with a phenomenal 1.12 earned-run average as the greatest pitching performance he had ever seen, even more remarkable because he had to pitch over half of his games in St. Louis. "[W]ith due respect to Koufax, Drysdale, and Marichal, they haven't had to pitch in the heat the way Gibby has. I've seen them come in to St. Louis in hot weather and pull their cork in five or six innings. Gibson's stamina is incredible."[15]

The Dodgers finished in seventh place with a record of 76-86, 21 games behind the pennant-winning Cardinals. It was only the fourth losing season in Alston's twenty-three seasons as manager and the team's first back-to-back losing seasons in thirty years. In the Year of the Pitcher, only the New York Mets had a worse team batting average than the Dodgers' anemic .230 mark in the National League. Ken adapted well to his new part-time role with six game-winning hits and 11 RBIs off the bench. In his first season in LA, he batted .271 in 83 games and started at either first or third base in more than half of them. "I'd like to play again," he said toward the end of the season. "Anyone who couldn't play for Walter Alston isn't trying."[16]

THE DODGERS REPORTEDLY left Boyer unprotected in the October 14 expansion draft for the newest NL franchises, the Montreal Expos and the San Diego Padres, but he wasn't selected. Regardless, he felt he could still be productive for "two or three more" seasons. Alston hoped he would return to Los Angeles in 1969. "He's a handy guy to have around and gives you a good feeling when you see him walking up to the plate."[17]

Like most major-league players, Ken wouldn't sign a new contract or report to spring training until team owners increased contributions to a new pension plan for the Players Association. An agreement was finally reached in late February 1969. Though he and several teammates were still unsigned, Dodgers owner Walter O'Malley invited them to work out with the rest of the team at Vero Beach, Florida, while negotiating their contracts. Boyer was among the last holdouts and didn't sign until the first week of March.[18]

Over the winter, Alston asked him to return as a player and unofficial coach. His limited role on the club was reflected in his infrequent play in the spring exhibitions. Boyer appeared in only 10 games—half of them as a pinch-hitter—though he batted .318 in 22 at-bats. One unique experience that spring was leaving the country to play the

Chicago White Sox on a cricket field in the Bahamas. In the March 14 contest, he played third base and singled in four at-bats, driving in a run.[19]

For the first time ever, both leagues were divided into two divisions with the four regular season winners squaring off in a best-of-five postseason playoff to determine the teams that would play in the World Series. In addition to the Dodgers, Giants, and Astros, the new National League West Division also featured the Reds, Braves, and expansion Padres. Los Angeles opened the season at Cincinnati on April 7, but Ken didn't play his first game until almost three weeks later. Behind 6-1 on April 26, the Dodgers rallied in the bottom of the ninth inning against Atlanta on two walks and three singles that plated three runs. Boyer pinch-hit with runners at first and third and two outs, but struck out looking. He made up for it two days later at San Diego, driving in the winning run in the ninth for a 4-3 victory. In late April, Ken went home after Kathleen broke her pelvis when a horse she was riding reared back and fell on her. When he returned, he was hitless in his next seven at-bats before delivering a two-out, pinch-hit RBI single that tied the game against the Padres in the ninth inning on June 16. At San Francisco on July 17, he smashed a two-run pinch-hit double off ex-Cardinals teammate Ray Sadecki in a wild 31-hit slugfest that ended in defeat, 14-13.[20]

It wasn't until first baseman Wes Parker missed three weeks after an unexpected appendectomy that Ken received his first start of the season. Batting fifth against the Chicago Cubs on July 24, he singled in four at-bats and reached base on an error by third baseman Ron Santo. He made four starts at first base in that time, the last being at St. Louis on August 1. He struck out twice and grounded into a double play against tough left-hander Steve Carlton before stroking a single to center in the ninth inning of a 7-2 loss. It was career hit 2,143, not only his last in St. Louis but the last of his major-league career. He pinch-hit the next evening when the Dodgers rallied for five runs in the seventh, but popped up in foul territory to third baseman Mike Shannon for the third out. The fans in St. Louis had not forgotten Boyer. As part of baseball's 100th anniversary celebration that year, they chose him as the third baseman on the "Greatest St.

Louis Team Ever," a mythical lineup that included former teammates Stan Musial, Bob Gibson, and Curt Flood.[21]

Ken's reserve role meant a lot of time on the bench, especially the last two months of the season. He readily shared his knowledge of the game and encouraged the next generation of Dodgers like Steve Garvey, Bill Buckner, Bill Russell, Bobby Valentine, and Don Sutton, who would take the franchise to greater success in the next decade. "Boyer helped me a lot…telling me what to expect from certain pitchers," said rookie infielder Ted Sizemore. Tommy John credited him for the six seasons he spent in Los Angeles where he won 87 games and appeared in two World Series. "They were looking for a pitcher, somebody that could keep the ball in the ballpark," he recalled. "[Boyer] said, 'There's a left-hander with the White Sox…You bring him out here with a good ballclub that has good defense and he'll pitch his fanny off for you.' They started scouting me. Then the next year, after the '71 season, I was traded from the White Sox to the Dodgers."[22]

Boyer downplayed his contributions from the bench. "I'm just showing up every day, keeping the kids loose with a few stories." But Alston saw much more. "Ken has not played much this year, but he has helped us beyond his bat." Like Ted Simmons earlier, he knew a good young hitter when he saw one. After Garvey singled for his first major-league hit at Houston on September 10, the twenty-year-old was surprised when he returned to the dugout and Boyer told him, "That's the first of 2,000." Garvey finished his nineteen-year career with 2,599 for the Dodgers and the San Diego Padres.[23]

Even when he wasn't on the field, Ken was still able to contribute to the team's success. He allowed veteran outfielder Willie Davis to borrow one of his 38-ounce Louisville Slugger U1 model bats when Davis was struggling at the plate. Ten ounces heavier than he was accustomed, Davis choked up four inches on the handle, stood farther back from the plate, and started hitting again. The result was a 31-game consecutive hit streak, the longest in Dodgers history. Boyer stopped using his own bats when his supply dwindled to two, saving them for his teammate. From August 1 to September 3, Davis increased his batting average fifty-eight points from .259 to .316 and Los Angeles won 18 of 31 games to climb from fourth to second place in the NL West, a game behind the front-running San Francisco Giants.[24]

What proved to be Ken's final major-league plate appearance took place at Dodger Stadium against the Chicago Cubs on August 9. He stepped to the plate and pinch-hit for pitcher Pete Mikkelsen in the ninth inning. With one out and Los Angeles trailing, 4-0, he faced right-hander Bill Hands, who would win 20 games that season. His last swing produced a grounder to short that Don Kessinger fielded and threw to first baseman Ernie Banks for the putout. Boyer couldn't recall the specifics of that milestone in retrospect, believing there would be more opportunities before the season was over. Exactly one month later, he announced his retirement at the end of the season. He watched from the bench over the final 50 games as the Dodgers closed the season in fourth place in the National League West Division with a record of 85-77, eight games behind the Atlanta Braves.[25]

In his final season, Ken batted .206 in 34 at-bats with two doubles and four RBIs in his final major-league campaign. "My legs pretty well made the choice for me," he said of his decision to retire. Specifically, his knees were in bad shape and would require surgery if he continued. He had "played longer than most people are entitled to," he reflected a few years later. "At the end, all I could do was hit."[26]

Boyer had no immediate plans after the season, but he wanted to stay in the game. He considered broadcasting at one time, but what he really wanted was to be a major-league manager.[27] "I have spent 20 years in baseball. I feel I owe it to the game to pass along what I know." He hoped to end his 15-year playing career with the St. Louis Cardinals. Instead, his old team did the next best thing, giving him the chance to start a new one.[28]

Ken Boyer with the New York Mets, 1966–67.
(*Author's Collection*)

A final pennant chase with the Chicago White Sox, 1967–68.
(*National Baseball Hall of Fame Library, Cooperstown NY*)

Closing out his playing career with the Los Angeles Dodgers, 1968–69.
(*National Baseball Hall of Fame Library, Cooperstown NY*)

Chapter Sixteen

Back to the Minors

Walter Alston and the Dodgers saw Ken Boyer's potential as a manager. They offered him the chance to pilot the Double-A Albuquerque, New Mexico, club in the Texas League in 1970. He was hesitant to accept the position, however, because it was a thousand miles from his family in Hermann, Missouri.

A more appealing opportunity came from the St. Louis Cardinals and Bing Devine, who had returned as general manager in 1968. Because Boyer was still under contract, Devine received permission from the Dodgers to speak with him about managing the Cardinals' Double-A club in Little Rock, Arkansas. "We had Ken in mind for the organization as soon as he was available after ending his playing career," he said. The choice wasn't a hard one for Ken to make. He accepted the Cardinals' offer and the Dodgers gave him his unconditional release on October 3, 1969.[1]

Once again, Devine played an influential role in Boyer's career. "Bing Devine made a commitment that if I wanted to stay in baseball, he'd try to get me to work in the Cardinals organization." He was excited to return to the organization. "There's a line of tradition here...When you put on a Cardinal uniform, you just seem to fall in step with people like Rogers Hornsby and Frank Frisch. Besides, I'm from Missouri."[2]

Boyer never considered managing seriously until he became friends with Dick Groat after the former Pittsburgh Pirates shortstop was traded to the Cardinals. At the time, both men were in their early thirties, yet Groat was already looking ahead and wanted to manage the Pirates someday. "We spent a lot of time in the car together talking," remembers Groat. "Both of us had some pretty good ideas about how to play the game of baseball." As Ken neared the end of his playing career in Los Angeles, he spent time with Alston discussing the strategies and complexities of managing. He reflected on the examples of those who had guided him throughout his professional career, from Hal Contini at Lebanon to Alston in LA. Boyer had been involved in baseball his entire adult life. Managing would be a way for him to stay in the game that he loved. It was what he knew best. "It just wouldn't seem right to leave it now," he said. "And more important, I've got to put food on my table."[3]

Approaching his thirty-ninth birthday, Ken was starting over. He would make significantly less than his major-league salary the previous year—$6,000 over six months—the same amount he received as a signing bonus from the Cardinals twenty-one years earlier.[4] Life in the minor leagues was far less glamorous, but the Little Rock position was a necessary stepping stone. Still, he couldn't help but feel he was ready to take over a major-league club. "I think it would be easier for me to manage in the majors right now than in the minors because I know the personnel and such things as how to position the defense. But the trend is that if you want to manage in the majors, you've got to manage a while in the minors."[5]

Ken joined the rest of the Cardinals minor-league staff for spring training in St. Petersburg in 1970. His impromptu participation in the annual March of Dimes benefit contest at Al Lang Field on February 21 confirmed he made the right decision retiring as an active player. After a single in four plate appearances and six innings at third base, one of his legs swelled from the fatigue. "They say your legs go first in baseball, and now I know what they're talking about."[6]

Boyer's inaugural season as a manager began with four straight losses and a miserable first month. But the Arkansas Travelers surged thereafter and took the Texas League's East Division lead from the Memphis Blues on June 8, holding it through the middle of August. The offense tied for third in the Texas League with a .261 average and was second with 92 home runs and third in RBIs, total bases, and slugging (.379). The best hitting prospect was twenty-two-year-old outfielder Jose Cruz, who batted .300 and led the club with 29 doubles, 21 homers, and 90 RBIs.

The fact that he was a recently-retired big-league star earned him instant credibility with his young players. "Basically, he had two rules—always be on time and if there was a fight, you better be out on the field," remembers pitcher Al Hrabosky. "He treated us all with a lot of respect. It was just fun being with him because he had a strong personality, but he was very fair and very real about it. He wasn't a big bully about it at all."[7]

Like many of his players, Ken had long sideburns, the style worn during the decade. But the old-school Cardinals director of player development, Bob Kennedy, disapproved of them. Before his arrival in Little Rock every six weeks, Boyer would tell Hrabosky, "Al, we've got to shave our sideburns because Kennedy is coming into town."[8]

Among the challenges he faced in his first season piloting a minor-league club was players leaving to fulfill their military obligations. It was the height of the Vietnam War and several on the Arkansas roster were serving in the Army Reserves and required to report for active duty on weekends. Coupled with injuries, he sometimes had as few as fourteen players available. He was forced to create makeshift lineups with players in irregular positions and needed every available man. After a hard slide by Danny Napoleon resulted in a large bruise on his leg, Boyer looked at the injury and determined, "I don't see no blood, and no bones are sticking out. You're in there to stay." A shortage of pitchers made him consider placing himself on the roster and returning to the mound for the first time in twenty years to pitch in hopelessly lopsided games.[9]

That season, Ken had the privilege of telling two players they were being promoted to the big-league club. The first was Hrabosky, who pitched 13 seasons for the Cardinals, Kansas City Royals, and Atlanta Braves. He was joined by Ed Crosby, a utility infielder for parts of six seasons with the Cardinals, Cincinnati Reds, and Cleveland Indians.

A more unpleasant chore was telling a player he was being demoted or released. It was even more difficult when the player in question was his youngest brother. Lenny Boyer was in his seventh season in the Cardinals organization, having received a $30,000 signing bonus in 1964. He had spent the past two seasons in Little Rock, where he batted .232 overall in 179 games, and was hitting only .230 at the time. "I had the talent and the ability, but I didn't push myself hard enough," he said in hindsight. The Travelers needed to add a right-handed hitter to the roster and Lenny was left-handed. Having made the decision to demote him and pitcher Danny Jaster to Class A Modesto, Kennedy met the club in Shreveport and wanted to spare Ken from an awkward situation. But Boyer wanted to give Lenny the news himself. "There was no need to run from it," he said. "I mean, I had accepted this job—and this was just a nasty part of it."[10]

Ken was rewarded for his club's first-place standing and named manager of the East Division team for the 30th annual Texas League All-Star Game in Albuquerque on August 18. His team led, 2-1, but the West squad piloted by Albuquerque skipper and former major-league catcher Del Crandall rallied to beat them, 8-2. Among the future big-leaguers in the contest were Cruz, Joe Ferguson of Albuquerque, and Mickey Rivers of El Paso, who knocked in three runs for the West team.[11]

When the regular season resumed, Arkansas and Memphis were tied for the division lead. With twelve games left in the season, the Travelers held a precarious half-game advantage over the Blues. An 8-3 lead disintegrated at San Antonio on August 27 and ended with a walk-off, two-run home run by Missions second baseman Bill Huisman. The 9-8 loss cost them first place. The Travelers dropped five of their next six games and were tied for second with San Antonio before the final series of the season at Memphis beginning September 4. A four-game sweep was crucial to overtake the Blues and clinch the title. In the opener, Arkansas scored ten runs in the sixth inning for the 13-9 victory. A four-run deficit the next evening proved too much to overcome and the Travs lost the game, 4-3, and the East Division flag to Memphis. The club finished the season with a 67-67 record and was third in the Texas League in attendance at 119,554, an improvement of 30,233 from the previous year. Outfielder Jose

Cruz and catcher Skip Jutze were named to the league's postseason All-Star team.[12]

Ken was surprised when St. Louis named him the major-league hitting coach for the 1971 season. After two consecutive pennant-winning seasons in 1967 and '68, the Cardinals had suffered back-to-back fourth-place finishes. The lowest team winning percentage (.469) in eleven years in 1970 led to the dismissals of hitting coach Dick Sisler and pitching coach Billy Muffett. Boyer was promoted along with former teammate and minor-league pitching instructor Barney Schultz. His instructional abilities and effectiveness with his minor-league players had made a positive impression during his short time in the organization. With the influx of young players in St. Louis, Red Schoendienst felt those same qualities would be beneficial at the major-league level. "The young players at Arkansas liked Boyer. He'll have the same authority with the hitters that Sisler had." Ken's goal was to build his managerial experience in the minors and eventually attain a position in the big leagues. Coaching in the majors wasn't in his plans. "However, I'm an organization man," he said, "and I'll do whatever the club wants."[13]

In addition to the artificial surface that replaced natural grass at Busch Memorial Stadium in 1970, another change since Ken's playing days was the team's new uniforms unveiled for the '71 season. The iconic birds-on-the-bat insignia remained across the front, but the button-down, lightweight wool jerseys were replaced by pullover, double-knit synthetic ones with beltless, tight-fitting pants. Though more durable and comfortable, the form-fitting nature of the new uniforms presented challenges for players, coaches, and managers who weren't in ideal physical shape. Queried one writer facetiously, "Could that be why trim Ken Boyer and Vern Benson and razor-thin Barney Schultz were added to the coaching staff?"[14]

Boyer spent the next two seasons as the first-base and hitting coach under Schoendienst. To be successful, he felt it was important for him to build relationships and cultivate trust with the players, an outlook that evolved during his own career. "He knew how to talk to the players," says Schoendienst. "If he saw a weakness and could help the hitter, that's what he talked about as far as hitting and trying to get a good strike. Swing at strikes, don't swing at the pitcher's pitch. He was a good hitting coach; he was very good." Boyer worked with highly-touted young catcher Ted Simmons and helped refine his batting stroke. He encouraged him not to crouch at the plate or give up switch-hitting when he struggled against right-handed pitching. In his first full major-league season, the twenty-one-year-old batted .304 with 32 doubles and 77 RBIs in 1971 on his way to becoming one of the greatest switch-hitters in baseball history. "Boyer helped me with things you can only learn from big-league experience," said Simmons.[15]

Meanwhile in Atlanta, brash younger brother Clete Boyer found himself in trouble over disparaging comments made about Braves general manager Paul Richards and manager Luman Harris. As a result, he was given his unconditional release and never played in the major leagues again. Ken, who had not spoken with him about the incident, declined comment except to offer some belated advice: "Silence is golden."[16]

Under Boyer's tutelage, St. Louis led the National League in batting average (.275), on-base percentage (.338), and tied for second in slugging (.385) in 1971. They finished in second place in the National League Eastern Division with a 90-72 record, seven games behind the Pittsburgh Pirates. A key contributor was Most Valuable Player Joe Torre, who won the batting title with a .363 average and paced the league with 230 hits and 137 RBIs (surpassing Ken's mark of 119 for Cardinals third basemen set in 1964). "For the first two months of the season, Joe Torre was as good a hitter as anyone I've watched," said Boyer. The offense slipped a year later despite a great season by Simmons (.303, 36 doubles, 16 homers, 96 RBIs) and the Redbirds dropped back to fourth place, 21 ½ games out of first.[17]

Ken suffered a personal loss when his mother passed away on November 24, 1971. Mabel Boyer had been in poor health for several years, suffering from liver and kidney ailments and mini strokes. When her sister Grace Heston died, Mabel's children were afraid for her to attend the funeral. She insisted but was so overwhelmed with grief that after kissing her sister goodbye, she suffered a fatal heart attack.[18]

BOYER RETURNED to the minors as manager of one of the Cardinals' two entries in the rookie-level Gulf Coast League in 1973. (The other team was managed by former St. Louis bullpen catcher and major-leaguer Lee Thomas.) Ten clubs played a short schedule of 56 games in Sarasota and Bradenton, Florida. In addition to managing the GCL Cardinals, Ken also had special scouting duties and served as hitting instructor for the Class A St. Petersburg Cardinals located thirty-six miles north of Sarasota. His objective was still a major-league managing position, he told a local writer, but insisted, "I'm not after Red's job though." The GCL Cardinals ended the season in sixth place with a record of 25-30, 15 ½ games behind the Texas Rangers club. He was named manager of the postseason All-Star team.[19]

In the minors, Boyer developed his personal philosophy of managing. "Ballplayers don't go for a lot of theories. They prefer guys with a practical nature." Flexibility, he believed, was "the sign of a good manager." He built trust with his players and didn't impose himself on them. If someone needed help to break out of a slump, they had to make the first move and ask for it. "That's the thing about Kenny," said Tulsa Oilers infielder Dan Radison. "[H]e doesn't force his theory on anybody. And that's the right way to do it. I needed help and he was there." Not far removed from his own career, Ken sympathized with his players "because I understand the problems that they all go through...[S]o many of us had to work very, very hard to get out of baseball what we did accomplish...it's a tremendously tough game."[20]

The Cardinals showed confidence in Boyer and named him manager of their Triple-A club in 1974. Over the next three seasons, he piloted the Tulsa Oilers to a winning record of 214-191 and a league championship. The teams featured several future major-leaguers such as Bob Forsch, Keith Hernandez, John Denny, Jerry Mumphrey, Tito Landrum, and Garry Templeton.

Tulsa dominated the Western Division and won the American Association title in 1974. The roster was a blend of young players and veterans, some with big-league experience. Pitching and defense were pivotal to their early success with five starters owning earned-run averages under 3.00 through the middle of June. The starting rotation included Forsch, Denny, Ray Bare, Ken Reynolds, Greg Terlecky, and Ken Crosby. A series of early-season rainouts dampened the offense, but it finally ignited behind first baseman Hernandez (.351, 14 homers, 63 RBIs), center fielder Hector Cruz (.255, 72 RBIs), shortstop

Ed Crosby (.313), catcher Marc Hill (.278, 14 homers, 58 RBIs), left fielder Jim Dwyer (.336), right fielder Ed Kurpiel (14 homers, 53 RBIs), and infielder Bob Heise (.326). On June 13, Hernandez's three-run blast enabled Tulsa to beat the St. Louis Cardinals in an exhibition contest at Oiler Park, 6-3.[21]

Ken made a trip to St. Louis on the first of June to watch his oldest son David work out with other high-school players eligible for the 1974 amateur free-agent draft. A recent graduate of Hermann High School, David batted .395 in his senior year and was drafted as a third baseman by the Cardinals in the 31st round (620th pick overall). He signed with the team on June 20 and reported to rookie ball at Sarasota, Florida, in the Gulf Coast League.[22]

A 13-4 triumph over the Omaha Royals that featured 21 hits boosted the Oilers' division lead to 16 games on the nineteenth. Animosity grew between the two clubs when Royals catcher Tom Harmon threw his shoulder into second baseman Heise after he completed a double play the next evening. At the time, Ken reportedly yelled from the visitors dugout, "We'll get him at Tulsa."

Back home on the twenty-fourth, both clubs knew what was coming. Each bullpen was empty and players stood in the dugout in anticipation. During Harmon's first plate appearance, Oilers hurler Ray Bare threw a brushback pitch at him, then plunked him on the wrist with his next offering. Harmon charged the mound and a wild melee ensued for sixteen minutes. "There were scrimmages all over the field," recalls former Oilers team trainer Lee Landers. "It was a good one." When order was restored, Harmon and Bare were both ejected from the game. Boyer defended his team afterward. "There are some things you have to do to protect your players in baseball. This isn't a Sunday School picnic." The Oilers were no-hit through eight innings by future big-leaguer Dennis Leonard and trailed, 1-0, before tying the game in the ninth and winning in the tenth, 2-1. Ironically, Harmon was traded to the Cardinals organization shortly after and sent to Tulsa. "It was interesting when he walked in the clubhouse," says Landers. "After initiation play, he got along good with everybody."[23]

With his team having the best record in the league, Ken was named manager of the All-Star team for an exhibition contest with the major-league Houston Astros in Oklahoma City on August 1. Among the dignitaries in attendance were Hall of Famers Warren Spahn, Lloyd Waner, Satchel Paige, Casey Stengel, Joe Medwick, and Bob Feller. The All-Stars tallied once in the seventh inning but former St. Louis Cardinals shortstop Ray Busse hit a three-run home run to beat them, 5-1.[24]

A series of big-league promotions over the summer took some of Tulsa's best players and diminished their sizable lead, but they clinched the division crown with a 2-1 victory over the Denver Bears on August 25. They ended with a 76-58 record, 9½ games ahead of the Wichita Aeros. Without the bats of Hernandez and Hill, who had been called up at the end of the regular season, Tulsa still prevailed in the seven-game championship series with the Indianapolis Indians, an affiliate of the Cincinnati Reds managed by Vern Rapp, to win the title. "This has to be a memorable season," said Ken amid the postgame celebration in the clubhouse. Before the season, a writer pointed out that Boyer had won a championship every ten years—first with the Houston Buffaloes in 1954, then with the St. Louis Cardinals in '64, and was due again with the Oilers in '74. "I hope I don't have to wait another 10 years for success," he remarked.[25]

Among Boyer's biggest supporters was Keith Hernandez. "He's a great guy to play for," the young first baseman said. "He really has rapport with the players and that makes it enjoyable. We just try to keep him happy." The son of a former Cardinals minor-leaguer, Hernandez remembered listening to Boyer's grand slam on the radio during the 1964 World Series. The twenty-year-old hit .351 with Tulsa to win the American Association batting title in 1974. His line-drive bat and fielding prowess at first base earned him a starting role in St. Louis the following season.[26]

A slow start in 1975 prompted Cardinals instructor Harry "The Hat" Walker to try remaking Hernandez into a strict opposite-field hitter. The lessons made things even worse; he was benched and eventually sent back to Triple-A with a .203 average through June 3. Ken empathized with him because Walker had tried doing the same thing to him during his rookie season in 1955. When Hernandez reached Tulsa, Boyer told him, "You're going to come out early every day. I'm going to throw to you and you're going to pull everything that I throw." He worked with Hernandez, who flourished with a .330 average in 85 games, second-best in the league. The young hitter closed the season back in St. Louis batting .350 in September. He reclaimed his starting position and enjoyed 17 years in the majors. "Kenny was one of the saviors of my career," says Hernandez.[27]

After guiding the Oilers to a second-place finish in 1975, Boyer spent four months managing the Ponce club in the Puerto Rico Winter League. Among his players were Hernandez, former Tulsa catcher Marc Hill (since traded to the San Francisco Giants), outfielder Ellis Valentine of the Montreal Expos, and pitcher Pete Vuckovich of the Chicago White Sox. Having pitched in only two pro seasons, Vuckovich appreciated his manager's wisdom and instruction. "Ken's the man who got me thinking like a big leaguer," he reflected years later. "He helped me learn how to cope with losing as well as winning. He'd say, 'Tomorrow is another day.'"[28]

Even though the Oilers were a good hitting club in 1976 (third-best in the American Association with a .271 batting average), the pitching was problematic with a 4.01 earned-run average. They finished in third place in the four-team Western Division and ended the season with a record of 65-70, 20½ games behind the Denver Bears. Outfielder Mike Easler, who had played parts of three seasons with the Houston Astros, led the team with a .352 average, 26 homers, and 77 RBIs. Jerry Mumphrey batted .338 in 19 games before being called up to St. Louis in May. But the most exciting young player was shortstop Garry Templeton, the Cardinals' first selection and 13th overall pick in the 1974 draft. The twenty-year-old streaked through the organization in two seasons while learning to switch-hit and play short. At Tulsa, he batted .321 with 25 doubles, 15 triples, six homers, and 38 RBIs in 106 games before his call-up to St. Louis in August. "Garry is as good a prospect as I've ever seen," praised Boyer. "He can run, throw, field, and hit, do everything you want a youngster to do except maybe hit with power...I've never seen a shortstop with more range." He remarked, "I'd like to have his future."[29]

MEANWHILE, Ken's own future looked promising, though at the expense of his good friend Red Schoendienst. The Cardinals finished the 1976 season in fifth place in the National League Eastern

Division at 72-90, the worst record since Boyer's rookie season in 1955. Schoendienst, the longest tenured manager in club history up to that time, was fired on October 5 after twelve years at the helm. For the past few years, Ken had been considered the favorite within the Cardinals organization to eventually take Red's place. Still, he took no chances and asked to meet with owner Gussie Busch and general manager Bing Devine the day after Schoendienst's dismissal. He made sure they knew his interest in the position. "I didn't want Mr. Busch to have the impression I was an easy-going, casual guy in uniform. I think he may have been startled that I asked, but I just wouldn't want to live with myself this winter if they went out and hired somebody else without my having asked."[30]

There were three candidates for the position, each a highly-regarded minor-league manager with no major-league experience—Boyer, Joe Altobelli of the Baltimore Orioles organization, and Vern Rapp, a St. Louis native and former Cardinals farmhand who led the Montreal Expos' Triple-A Denver club to the American Association title that season. Devine and Busch wanted a more forceful manager and disciplinarian to lead a talented but underachieving team. Boyer's relaxed style was too similar to that of Schoendienst's and Devine downplayed his chances. "Boyer is not in any better position than any of the others," he cautioned. "He is not the heir apparent."[31]

The search lasted only two days before Rapp, who had toiled as a minor-league manager for sixteen years, was offered the position on October 7. Altobelli was named manager of the San Francisco Giants the same day; Ken was the only one left without a major-league job. "Busch was impressed with him," offered Devine. "I think someday Boyer will be a big-league manager—and in the not-too-distant future."[32]

Naturally, Ken was disappointed. There wasn't even the solace of his Triple-A position to fall back on. Oilers owner A. Ray Smith moved his club from Tulsa to New Orleans in October. After three seasons and an American Association championship in 1974, Smith decided he wanted a new manager. In order for him to pilot a Triple-A club, Boyer had no choice but to leave the Cardinals organization.[33]

"It was an amiable parting," he later recalled about his decision. "I didn't burn my bridges when I left and had nothing bad to say about the organization. I didn't sound off...I pretty much agreed with what had been done. If they had to fire Red Schoendienst, the logical thing to do was to hire someone who was opposite Red's personality. That was Vern Rapp. And I figured if they hired Vern, I would have been better off if I got a fresh start with another team."[34]

The Baltimore Orioles hired Ken to manage the Triple-A Rochester Red Wings for 1977. Ironically, he took the position vacated by Altobelli when he left for San Francisco. The Red Wings were the defending International League champions and one of the most successful franchises in the minor leagues. Twenty-eight years earlier, an eighteen-year-old Boyer, fresh out of high school and just signed by the Cardinals, traveled to the city beside Lake Ontario in New York to await the start of his professional career.[35]

The Red Wings had a lot of power but were short on pitching. Many of their best young hurlers had moved up to Baltimore. They led the International League in home runs (133), finished second in OPS (.760), and third in hitting (.274). The pitching staff was first in strikeouts (732) but had the fourth-best ERA at 4.38. Thirty-year-old first baseman and major-league veteran Terry Crowley powered the offense with a league-leading 30 home runs and was named to the International League All-Star team. Center fielder Larry Harlow, demoted from the Orioles in early June, almost clinched the IL batting crown with a team-best .335 average. Right-hander Mike Parrott won Pitcher of the Year honors with a league-leading 146 strikeouts and tied for second with 15 victories.[36]

A four-game sweep of the front-running Pawtucket Red Sox the last week of June put Rochester in third place and 4½ games back. It proved to be the pinnacle of their season as the Red Wings tumbled back down in the standings and never challenged again. The Sox bludgeoned them in their subsequent series in the middle of August, scoring a multitude of runs in the initial frames of each contest. Ken lamented, "It's starting to look like an old movie—a bad old movie." The same could be said for the rest of the season. Rochester finished in sixth place with a record of 67-73, 13 games behind Pawtucket.[37]

BACK TO THE MINORS 315

Boyer and Warren Spahn were instructors during spring training with the St. Louis Cardinals in 1970. Boyer was slated to manage the Double-A Arkansas Travelers and Spahn the Triple-A Tulsa Oilers. Spahn used two canes while recovering from off-season surgery on both knees. (*Griva Family Collection*)

Boyer (middle row, center) managed the Double-A Arkansas Travelers to a second-place finish in 1970. His son David (bottom row, far left) was the batboy during summer vacation from school. (*Arkansas Travelers Baseball Club*)

In 1966, Ken purchased a Ford-Mercury dealership in Hermann, Missouri. (**Above**) Boyer stands with Arlene Griva and her son Darwin D. Griva outside the showroom. (*Griva Family Collection*). (**Right**) A hood ornament, license plate, and matchbook cover promoting his business (*Duane Kraettli*). Ken sold the dealership around 1978.

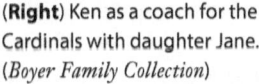

(**Above**) St. Louis Cardinals manager Red Schoendienst (center) surrounded by his coaching staff in spring training 1971. (Left to right) George Kissell, Vern Benson, Barney Schultz, and Ken Boyer. (*St. Louis Mercantile Library Collection*)

(**Right**) Ken as a coach for the Cardinals with daughter Jane. (*Boyer Family Collection*)

Ken managed the Tulsa Oilers, Triple-A club of the St. Louis Cardinals, for three seasons (1974–76). In 1974 (**left**), he guided Tulsa to an American Association title. After the 1976 season (**right**), the Cardinals rejected him in favor of fellow American Association manager Vern Rapp to succeed Red Schoendienst as St. Louis skipper. (*Tulsa Drillers Baseball Club*)

Boyer joined the Baltimore Orioles organization and managed their Triple-A club, the Rochester Red Wings, 1977–78. (*Author's Collection*)

Ken, Clete, and Cloyd Boyer during an Old Timer's Game at Atlanta-Fulton County Stadium in Atlanta on August 13, 1976. (*Cloyd Boyer*)

After six full seasons in the minor leagues (and two as a major-league coach), Boyer finally managed the St. Louis Cardinals from 1978–80.
(*St. Louis Mercantile Library Collection*)

Chapter Seventeen

Cardinals Manager

Six years in the minors had not abated Ken Boyer's ambition to become a major-league manager. Over the winter of 1977–78, he interviewed for vacancies with the Atlanta Braves and Milwaukee Brewers, both sub-.500 clubs for much of the decade. His meeting with the Braves began with brash young owner Ted Turner telling him front-runner Bobby Cox had already made a favorable impression. Undaunted, Ken made his case and elevated himself into strong consideration. The position still went to Cox, who named Cloyd Boyer as his pitching coach. Even though Ken was also runner-up to George Bamberger to manage the Brewers, Baltimore general manager Hank Peters was confident of his qualifications. "It's not a question if Boyer ever will manage in the majors—just when and where."[1]

Back home, Ken and Kathleen became grandparents for the first time when Gregory Ryan Hartwig, son of their oldest daughter Suzie, was born in December 1977. A second grandson followed two years later with the birth of Geoffrey Ross Hartwig. But after twenty-five years of marriage, they were divorced in 1978. An unfortunate aspect of life with a ballplayer—or one aspiring to be a major-league manager—is periods of separation. The lifestyle sometimes takes a toll on relationships. Like many baseball wives, Kathleen became self-reliant in her husband's absence. She was the sole caretaker and disciplinarian for six months or more during the season. Ken's inward personality also made it hard for him to express his feelings toward her. "Maybe you really don't need each other," Kathleen reflects. "You learn to make it on your own or learn to have your own life basically." The two remained on good terms and were together for high school graduations and other family events.[2]

THE BALTIMORE ORIOLES made changes to their organization in 1978 and the forty-six-year-old Boyer was the only pilot to return from the previous season, back at Triple-A Rochester, New York. The Red Wings opened on the road with five straight defeats beginning April 14 before shutting out the Richmond Braves in the home opener eight days later, 5-0. The victory sparked an identical five-game winning streak through the last week of the month. The roster featured several future big-leaguers such as Kevin Kennedy, Wayne Krenchicki, and Gary Roenicke. Among the veterans was Ray Bare, who pitched for parts of five seasons with St. Louis and Detroit and whom Ken had managed in his first minor-league season in 1970.[3]

Meanwhile, the Cardinals were looking for a new manager. Gussie Busch sought a firmer hand in charge when he selected Vern Rapp over Boyer eighteen months earlier. In a decade when long hair, large Afros, bushy mutton-chop sideburns, and facial hair were in style, the seventy-eight-year-old Busch wanted his players to look professional, clean shaven with short hair. Rapp vigorously enforced his boss's decree in spring training of 1977 much to the resentment of the players, particularly fleet outfielder Bake McBride and flamboyant reliever Al Hrabosky, who were eventually dealt away.

Over the course of the season, Rapp proved to be a strict and unyielding disciplinarian. Players had no respect for him and eventually lost confidence in his decision-making, mocking him behind his back. Veteran Lou Brock tried persuading him to ease his rules, but Rapp indignantly walked out of a team meeting declaring, "I'll never change." Despite the turmoil, the Redbirds improved their record to 83-79, a 14-game upturn from Red Schoendienst's last year, and finished third in the NL East Division.[4]

Relations between Rapp and the players were passable as the 1978 season began and St. Louis won four of their first six games. But defeats in nine of the next 10—the exception being a no-hitter by Bob Forsch against the Philadelphia Phillies on April 16—put the entire team on edge. Following a discouraging one-run loss in 10 innings to the Phillies the afternoon before Forsch's gem, veteran catcher Ted Simmons tried relieving the post-game tension by playing music in the clubhouse. Rapp took losses hard and was in no mood for it. He called Simmons into his office and the heated exchange was overheard through the slightly opened door. At one point, Rapp called him "a loser" before emotions cooled and both men shook hands, seemingly resolving the matter. But the players resented the remark and Simmons himself disclosed the incident inadvertently to Cardinals broadcaster Jack Buck two weeks later. Buck mentioned it on the radio as an example of the turmoil on the club. General manager Bing Devine felt the situation would not improve and Rapp was fired on April 25.[5]

Ken was considered the favorite to replace him. Having been turned down once by the Cardinals, he hesitated to raise his hopes again. "I'm not going to sit on any clouds because it's a long way to fall down if you don't get it." He was one of three candidates for the position along with St. Louis third-base coach and interim manager Jack Krol and Los Angeles Dodgers coach Preston Gomez, a former coach under Schoendienst with big-league managing experience.

Two days after Rapp's dismissal, Devine contacted the Baltimore Orioles and received a positive report on Boyer's performance and permission to talk with him. Ken was interviewed over the telephone that day and made a convincing presentation to Devine, Busch, and two other members of the search committee. "I think I've put in my time," he said. "But I thought it was my time when Rapp got the job."[6]

When a decision wasn't reached that evening, Boyer thought the job went to Gomez and he joined his team for a flight to Charleston, West Virginia, on the morning of April 29. Boyer had finished dinner at a local steakhouse and started writing a game report for the Orioles when Devine reached him with the news he had waited for almost ten years—he was the manager of the St. Louis Cardinals.[7]

"It was difficult to imagine the same people who had made the decision a year ago changing their minds and giving me another opportunity," said Ken. Though grateful they did, he curbed his enthusiasm with the knowledge that managers lived a precarious existence. He told his catcher, Kevin Kennedy, "I know I'm getting hired just so I can get fired." Kennedy remembered the candid statement when he managed the Texas Rangers and Boston Red Sox two decades later. "Strange thing to say before starting your first big-league managing job, and most guys don't want to admit it, but the reality is that getting canned is going to happen, sooner or later."[8]

From that moment, everything was at a frantic pace. Boyer asked Red Wings player/pitching coach Earl Stephenson to serve as temporary manager until a replacement arrived, then he addressed the players before their game. His mind was racing so fast that he broke out in a cold sweat while giving instructions to Stephenson and couldn't finish. That evening, he took a flight to St. Louis and was sequestered until a noon press conference at the Anheuser-Busch brewery offices the next day. "I really haven't been able to gather my thoughts yet," he told Joe Castellano of the *St. Louis Globe-Democrat*. "You think you're prepared to handle any kind of shock, but you're not. When one of my players goes to the big leagues, I always know what to say. But now that it happens to me, there are no words."[9]

IT WAS A HOMECOMING for Ken and the realization of a dream. "This is where I wanted to be. I started out with the Cardinals organization 30 years ago. They gave me my first chance to play, my first chance to manage in the minors, and now my first chance to manage in the big leagues." The Cardinals felt his relaxed personality and positive rapport with many of the young players were a perfect remedy for the contentious atmosphere created by his predecessor. Boyer would have simple rules of conduct, including professional clothes worn when the team traveled, but had no interest in restrictions on facial hair and grooming. "I want to treat men like men. All I'm interested in is how they play."[10]

At the press conference, he outlined his initial agenda for the team, including the possibility of a four-man starting rotation with nine pitchers on the roster, a consistent lineup, and returning Brock as a starting player batting leadoff. Ken hesitated to make predictions because of his unfamiliarity with the rest of the NL East contenders, but he liked the makeup of his club. "I think we have the ingredients to win: the ability to score runs and maintain a sustained attack, speed on defense as well as on offense, [and] good starting pitching." He retained Rapp's staff consisting of pitching coach Claude Osteen, hitting coach Mo Mozzali, third-base coach Krol, first-base coach Sonny Ruberto, and bullpen coach Dave Ricketts. Despite the change in leadership, the Cardinals had not given up on being competitive the remainder of the season. "Nobody, including the Philadelphia Phillies, has shown he'll run off in our division," said Devine.[11]

Reflecting on the eight years it took him to reach his goal, Boyer sighed, "I found out it's much more difficult to get to the majors as a manager than as a player."[12]

It was Ken's dream job, but his first season as a major-league manager proved to be a nightmare. He inherited a pair of excellent line-drive hitters in All-Star catcher Ted Simmons and first baseman Keith Hernandez, whom he had helped turn around at Tulsa three years earlier, as well as promising young hitter and defensive shortstop Garry Templeton. In addition to Hernandez and Templeton, there were a few other faces he recognized from his time in the Cardinals organization like starting pitchers Bob Forsch, Eric Rasmussen, and John Denny; outfielders Jim Dwyer and Jerry Mumphrey; and newly-acquired reliever Pete Vuckovich, whom he managed in the Puerto Rico Winter League. Brock, his old teammate with the Cardinals, was nearing the end of his eventual 19-year major-league career. He had eclipsed Ty Cobb as the all-time stolen base leader with 893 on August 29, 1977, and aspired for 3,000 career hits as his next Hall of Fame milestone. Like most St. Louis teams in the decade, the '78 club lacked long-ball power in cavernous Busch Stadium, with its 386-foot power alleys, and had finished next to last in the National League in home runs the year before.

When Boyer took over, the Cardinals were in last place in the National League Eastern Division but only four games behind the first-place Montreal Expos with a record of 7-12. He made his debut in St. Louis on April 29 against the NL West-leading Los Angeles Dodgers, who had won seven of their last eight games. The crowd of 20,596 fans applauded him as he trotted to home plate before the game wearing the familiar No. 14 with BOYER on the back of his uniform to turn in his first lineup card as manager. Among them were eighty friends from Hermann, Missouri, offering support. While home-plate umpire Bruce Froemming and the rest of the umpiring crew discussed the ground rules with him, Boyer doffed his cap to acknowledge the cheers.

Rasmussen dueled with Burt Hooton of the Dodgers over six scoreless innings. Hooton retired 18 of the first 20 batters he faced, yielding only a double to Simmons and a two-out walk to Mumphrey in the fifth. Hernandez led off the seventh with a single, went to second on a wild pitch, advanced to third on Simmons's groundout to second base, and scored on Ken Reitz's sacrifice fly to center field. Rasmussen pitched a complete game in one hour and 33 minutes, allowing only four hits for the 1-0 triumph. Boyer celebrated his first managerial victory at a post-game dinner with his children. The next afternoon, right-handers John Urrea and Vuckovich combined for another four-hitter to beat the Dodgers and future Hall of Famer Don Sutton, 4-0.[13]

The club rebounded from a 2-1 loss to the San Francisco Giants on May 1 for their third shutout in four games the next day. The offense exploded for 14 hits highlighted by six doubles and Forsch twirled a five-hitter to blank the Giants, 9-0. "If we keep giving up two runs every 36 innings, we'll get a big paycheck in October," said Boyer optimistically. A 16-hit assault against five hurlers in an 8-4 win over the San Diego Padres on the seventh was a happy sendoff as the fifth-place Redbirds embarked on a 13-game road trip to the West Coast and Chicago the second and third week of May. They won two of three from the Dodgers, including a three-hit, 2-0 shutout by Forsch on May 11, to boost their record to 14-16, just a game behind the Cubs and Pittsburgh Pirates, who were tied for third place.

From the beginning, Ken worked to improve relations between management and players fractured by the authoritative nature of Rapp. "That's the number one reason I was hired," he said. As a former player, it was natural for him to enjoy a beer with them in the clubhouse after a victory or join a game of cards on team flights. Serious discussions and discipline were handled behind his office door rather than in front of the whole team as his predecessor often did. Boyer later estimated there were "maybe half a dozen" issues he successfully dealt with over the course of the season. "I'll probably be criticized for it before the season's over," he suggested about his methods for fostering camaraderie. "But I think this standoff attitude between players and manager is so overrated. I don't know how it ever got started really. I've got to get to know these guys. We're together for 162 games a year. We have to know how each other thinks every minute. I don't see how there should be any communications gap. We're all in this together."[14] The players appreciated Boyer's efforts and he gained their respect. "I see nothing wrong with being friends with a man who I'm going to spend 180 days with," said Vuckovich. "I like being able to sit down with a man and talk to him and know it's not going through one ear and out the other."[15]

Boyer enjoyed a cordial relationship with the media. Some like Bob Broeg and Neal Russo of the *Post-Dispatch* and Bob Burnes and Jack Herman of the *Globe-Democrat* had been there during his playing career. The St. Louis media was less critical and abrasive than in larger cities and he enjoyed positive coverage, particularly in the aftermath of the Rapp debacle. Ken was articulate and kept his sharp sense of humor intact throughout his tenure. Though one writer remembered an occasion when he was "singed, ear-to-ear, with expletives" after questioning his strategy, such outbursts were uncommon. "You could ask him a question and he would give you an answer," recalls J.G. Taylor Spink Award winner Rick Hummel, who was the beat writer for the *Post-Dispatch*. "I think the guys appreciated that. I appreciated the directness maybe as much as anything, even though it might not always be the answer you were hoping for."[16]

Ken's managerial mettle was tested through a brutal stretch of 11 consecutive losses at San Francisco, San Diego, and Chicago, then returning home and falling to Montreal. They even dropped an exhibition game, 9-1, to their Triple-A club in Springfield, Illinois. The losing streak was the fifth-longest in club history and dropped them into the NL East cellar, trailing Philadelphia by eight games with a record of 14-27. Blame was fairly distributed as the offense batted a pitiful .228, pitchers had a collective 4.56 ERA, and fielders committed 14 errors. They were outscored 64 runs to 33 and lost five games by one run, including four straight May 13–15. It was a relief when Denny ended the skid with a two-hit, 2-0 shutout on the twenty-fourth. Boyer kept a calm demeanor throughout the ordeal, encouraging his players, pointing out fundamental mistakes, and trying different lineup combinations to break them out of the funk. "He just kept saying, 'The sun will rise tomorrow,'" said Denny. "I think Kenny telling us that we'd get 'em tomorrow really eased things." Despite the victory, Boyer cautioned, "We're not out of the woods yet. We still need consistent hitting. We can't expect a shutout every night...But it's a start."[17]

Unfortunately, the Cardinals stumbled through their next five games before winning the last three of a four-game series at New York. To bolster a lethargic offense, outfielder George Hendrick was acquired from the San Diego Padres in exchange for Rasmussen on May 26. In his debut during a May 29 doubleheader with the Mets, Hendrick made an outstanding throw from center field to nail Lee Mazzilli at the plate in the opener and went 3-for-5 in the second with a pair of doubles and two runs scored. St. Louis scored four runs in the tenth inning to take the finale, 6-2. Hendrick swatted a three-run homer the next evening and rookie Silvio Martinez, making his first major-league start, threw a one-hitter (his only mistake was giving up a homer to Steve Henderson in the seventh) to beat the Mets, 8-2. A 7-2 victory on May 31 gave them three in a row, their longest win streak of Ken's short tenure. The month ended with a horrendous 9-20 record, their worst of the season. One writer reminded him that he had seen better teams make worse mistakes during his playing career. Boyer replied, "I guess so, and I've also seen worse teams than this who didn't do some of the things this team does."[18]

The primary culprit was a languid offense that was fourth-worst in the NL in batting (.249) and slugging (.358) and last in on-base percentage (.303). All but one of the regulars batted well below their career averages. A big problem was an unproductive outfield led by veteran left fielder Brock, who was hitting a paltry .208 on his thirty-ninth birthday and benched toward the end of the season with a .221 average in 92 games. Hendrick was an initial disappointment in center field but rebounded in August and September to hit .288 with 17 home runs and 67 RBIs in 102 games. Jerry Morales was coming off an All-Star season and averaged 14 homers and 77 RBIs over the past four years with the Chicago Cubs when St. Louis acquired him over the winter. But the right fielder proved to be a bust in St. Louis, hitting .239 with four homers and 46 RBIs for the season. Reserve outfielders Jerry Mumphrey (.262) and Tony Scott (.228) offered no offensive alternatives.

Hernandez's average fell thirty-six points from the previous season to .255, though his outstanding defense at first base earned him his first Gold Glove Award. In his second full season in the majors, Templeton slumped at the plate and in the field for much of the season before heating up in July and August to finish at .280 while committing a major-league high 40 errors. The stalwart Simmons batted over .300 in the first-half before his own late-season slide reduced it to .287, though he paced the club with 22 homers, 80 RBIs, and 40 doubles, and slugged .512. To ensure the strain of catching every day wouldn't affect his hitting, Boyer began playing him in left field occasionally.[19]

Had it not been for starting pitchers Forsch, Denny, and Vuckovich, the wretched '78 campaign would have been even worse. Overall, the staff finished with a 3.58 ERA, an improvement of 23 points from the previous season with very little run support. Denny led the club with a 14-11 record, 234 innings pitched, and 11 complete games, while Forsch contributed 11 victories with a 3.70 ERA. Vuckovich rewarded Boyer's confidence in moving him from the bullpen to the rotation with 12 wins and a 2.54 ERA, third-best in the league, and led the staff with 149 strikeouts. The trio accounted for over half of the team's victories. Martinez, acquired over the winter from the Chicago White Sox, was a pleasant surprise in the rotation with a 9-8 record and a pair of complete-game one and two-hitters to his credit.

Losing seven straight on an eight-game road trip—including a no-hitter in Cincinnati by Tom Seaver on June 16—the players returned home on June 23 to find a scathing letter from Gussie Busch waiting for them in the Busch Stadium clubhouse. He was furious with the team's performance and indifferent attitudes and threatened wholesale changes in the future if they did not improve. Asked what their reaction would be, Boyer replied frankly, "Some will be moved and some will throw the statement in the trash can." He believed the team wasn't loafing but simply in a collective batting funk. "I'm satisfied in my mind that they're running everything out and playing hard.

When you're not hitting, it's hard to appear aggressive." The Cardinals showed signs of life afterward, taking three of four at Pittsburgh and Montreal before returning home and dropping five of seven to the Cubs and Pirates leading into the All-Star break the second week of July. They finished the first-half with a 34-53 record and trailed the division-leading Philadelphia Phillies by 16 games. St. Louis's only representative for the All-Star Game was starting catcher Simmons. Ken took advantage of the three-day break and traveled to Little Rock, Arkansas, to watch his son Dave play for the Arkansas Travelers, but the game was rained out.[20]

The Redbirds began the second-half with three victories in their first four games, then dropped seven of the next nine, all but one of them by two runs or less. On July 23, Vuckovich tossed a three-hit shutout at Los Angeles, 2-0, and Martinez sparkled with a two-hit, 2-1 victory at San Francisco three days later. A seven-game losing streak followed, the second-longest of the season, which included their twelfth straight losses in San Diego and against the Cubs. With a 40-68 record on August 4, an offense averaging a feeble 3.3 runs per game, and 54 games left in the season, a 100-loss season for the first time in 70 years seemed possible. Asked how he was maintaining his sanity, Boyer returned a faint smile. "Who says I have?"[21]

The Cardinals rallied and enjoyed their best month in August, albeit too late to salvage the season. They won five straight—even taking three of four from first-place Philadelphia—and used it as a springboard to win 18 of their next 24 games, the best record in the majors. Even though the team was hitting only eight points better, they were producing more often in the clutch, an ingredient missing most of the season. Their bats exploded for 23 hits with four-hit performances from Hendrick, Simmons, and Mumphrey in a 14-9 victory over the Cincinnati Reds on the twenty-first. A three-game sweep at Atlanta during the last weekend of August brought them six games closer to the Phillies and four games out of fourth place, though 12½ back of first. With a little over a month left in the schedule, Ken allowed himself to consider the possibility of a last-ditch run at the division title. "I've seen it happen before," he mused.[22]

That faint glimmer of hope vanished in September as the fifth-place Cardinals dropped 11 of their next 15 games and tumbled an additional

7 ½ games back. They took two of three at Wrigley Field the third weekend of the month to snap a 12-game losing streak against the Cubs and avoid the cellar the rest of the way. St. Louis finished with a 69-93 record, 21 games behind the NL East champion Philadelphia Phillies. Their .426 winning percentage was the worst in franchise history since 1924. "It took its toll mentally," recalled Hernandez. "It was such a long, grueling season." The players felt Boyer did a good job under the circumstances and morale on the team improved from what it had been before he took over. All but 11 losses occurred on his watch, yet blame wasn't placed on him. "This wasn't his team," remarked Vuckovich.[23]

Busch rewarded Boyer's patience and steadfastness taking over a difficult situation with a one-year contract to return for a fresh start in 1979. Ken had no expectations of security in a multi-year deal after such a miserable season. Players from the Cardinals past were reunited when Red Schoendienst (who spent the past two seasons coaching for the Oakland Athletics) and Dal Maxvill (coaching for ex-Cardinal Joe Torre with the New York Mets) returned to the organization as bench coach and first-base coach, respectively. Boyer wanted Schoendienst's experience as a major-league manager sitting with him in the dugout and Maxvill to emphasize defense with the infielders, particularly Templeton. Both lived in the St. Louis area and welcomed the chance to work close to home. "We're going to have fun putting a winner back together," said Schoendienst.[24]

Though Ken stayed, Bing Devine was gone. The sixty-one-year-old St. Louis native had worked his way up in the organization from part-time PR man to general manager. He was dismissed on October 18 for the second time as the Cardinals' general manager after guiding the club in that position for a combined 18 seasons. Busch wanted a younger man in charge and hired thirty-nine-year-old John Claiborne, who Devine had given his first job in major-league baseball.

For the first time ever, the team was aggressive in the free-agent market. Among those extended offers were left-handed pitcher Tommy John, right-handed closer Mike Marshall, and outfielder Pete Rose. Claiborne, Busch, and Boyer personally courting Rose in St. Louis and during baseball's winter meetings in Orlando, Florida. None signed with the Cardinals. "[W]e offered just as much or more money...

as the clubs they signed with," said Boyer. "We did everything we could." Two free agents— thirty-seven-year-old left-handed reliever Darold Knowles and reserve outfielder and former Redbird Bernie Carbo—did agree to two-year deals. Three young lefties were obtained in trades, including Bob Sykes from the Detroit Tigers as a fifth starter.[25]

In the off-season, Ken enjoyed the perks and responsibilities of being a major-league manager. He attended post-season dinners, promotional tours through Missouri and Illinois with the Cardinal Caravan, and even a roast in his honor. He also renewed his interest in charitable endeavors and served as chairman of the annual St. Louis area Cancer Crusade for the American Cancer Society. At the St. Louis baseball writers dinner in January 1979, he was recognized among the fifteen elite players during Anheuser-Busch's ownership of the Cardinals along with former teammates Stan Musial, Red Schoendienst, Bob Gibson, Curt Flood, Lou Brock, Tim McCarver, Mike Shannon, Lindy McDaniel, and Steve Carlton.[26]

THE CARDINALS entered the 1979 season with few substantial changes to a club that lost 93 games. Ken was confident in his starting rotation and believed the offense would live up to its potential. Off-season additions had strengthened the bullpen, giving him a left-right tandem in Knowles and Mark Littell as closers. "This is the nucleus of a heck of a club," he said. "We should win at least half of our games by everyone having his normal season."[27]

On a personal level, Boyer was disappointed when his son Dave was released by the Cardinals two weeks into minor-league spring training. The twenty-three-year-old had spent five seasons in the organization and played at Double-A Arkansas in 1978, hitting .227 in 78 games. Ken never had the chance to watch him play as a professional. As a manager, he understood the difficulty of releasing someone and seeing their dreams end. "There's no pleasant way to do it...I've been on this end of it. I have to do enough of it myself." Dave Boyer, a former linebacker at Hermann High School, went back to college and played football at the University of Missouri.[28]

The major-league campaign opened with three victories in the first four games (with one tie) and a half-game lead in the NL East, including a rare 8-1 victory over former Redbird lefty Steve Carlton and the Philadelphia Phillies on Opening Night at Busch Stadium. An embarrassing display of vandalism created a public relations headache as the club embarked on its first road trip. A ten-hour flight delay caused by bad weather kept the players grounded at St. Louis's Lambert Airport April 11–12. Three players reportedly went stir-crazy in a VIP waiting room. Conflicting reports claimed an accordion partition door was damaged, signage taken off the wall, and a telephone cord pulled out of the wall. Having had too much to drink, Reitz confessed to being the main culprit and paid $1,250 in fines and restitution. The team lost five of seven at Pittsburgh and Chicago, then returned home and dropped two more to Cincinnati, falling to fourth place in the NL East and 3 ½ games behind Philadelphia.[29]

Brock was 100 hits shy of the coveted 3,000-hit mark as the season began. Though he worked hard in spring training, Ken had reservations he could bounce back approaching forty years old. Still, he gave the veteran thirty days to prove he could produce in the starting lineup or else return to the bench. "Three thousand hits or no, if we can have somebody who can hit better and who can play better defense, we'll make a change," cautioned Boyer. Brock started slow and was hindered by a strained left thigh muscle. He was hitting .190 in his first 23 plate appearances when he officially announced on April 9 that he would retire at the end of the season. Brock caught fire at the plate the rest of April and May at a .381 clip (second-best in the NL) with 45 safeties toward his goal. Boyer rested him regularly to preserve his stamina. "He's 39, going on 23," said Ken with admiration.[30]

A 4-3 comeback victory over the Reds on April 22 sparked three wins in a row. Following a dramatic eleventh-inning, two-out walk-off grand slam by burly pinch-hitter Roger Freed against the Houston Astros on the first of May, the Redbirds won 11 of their next 16 games. Hernandez's RBI triple and Reitz's bases-loaded single on May 12 overcame a two-run deficit in the bottom of the ninth to beat the Atlanta Braves, 7-6, enabling St. Louis to climb to third place. Denny pitched a masterful two-hit, 1-0 shutout over Montreal on the fifteenth.

Boyer and his counterparts had to deal with minor-league and amateur replacements while major-league umpires were on strike the first seven weeks of the '79 season. He was uncertain about their competence initially. "I'd hate to lose a game and yet we haven't had any complaints," he said. That changed after a 3-2 defeat at Chicago on April 19 and several questionable calls, including a few in his own team's favor. In the first inning, Brock was called out on a stolen base attempt when shortstop Ivan De Jesus tagged Brock's loose batting helmet, a controversial ruling in what turned out to be a close game. Boyer insisted to second-base umpire Dick Cavenaugh that Brock's feet were on the bag to no avail. "Maybe he thought his feet were in the helmet," he cracked.[31]

With replacement umpires still in use, Ken received his first ejection as a big-league manager at Houston on May 9. The score was tied in the bottom of the ninth, 4-4, as Astros pinch-hitter Jimmy Sexton led off with an infield single against reliever Will McEnaney. The next batter, Terry Puhl, laid down a sacrifice bunt to advance the runner. Fielding the ball, McEnaney threw to Templeton for the force out at second. But substitute umpire Dave Pallone ruled the throw pulled Templeton off the bag and Sexton was safe. In the heated 10-minute exchange, Boyer was tossed along with Hernandez, who unintentionally bumped Pallone, and Simmons, who called him a "scab." When players in the Cardinals dugout threw towels onto the field in protest, Pallone ordered them off the bench and into the clubhouse or threatened to forfeit the game to Houston. Despite a five-hit performance by center fielder Tony Scott, St. Louis lost in 16 innings, 5-4. Boyer was one of four managers, five players, and one coach who were ejected from games in both leagues that evening. The strike was eventually settled and major-league umpires returned to work on May 18.[32]

After a sensational start to the season, Hernandez was struggling as his average dipped to .213 on May 2. On a team flight, Ken sat next to him and reassured him, "I got to see you in Triple-A. I know you can hit. I know you are an exceptional talent. And I know you're hurting right now…But I'll tell you right now—you're my first baseman, you are going to play every day, I don't care if you hit .170. I'll lose my job over my faith in you as a player." Boyer's confidence in him enabled Hernandez to finish the season at .344, winning the NL batting title, hitting 48 doubles (tops in the major leagues), scoring 116 runs, and tying with Willie Stargell of Pittsburgh for the MVP Award. "He saved my career twice," says Hernandez, remembering back to his 1975 season with him in Tulsa. "I went to the ballpark knowing that I could relax and I was going to play because of Ken Boyer."[33]

As a manager, Ken respected his players and treated them as he had wanted to be treated. He was even receptive to their suggestions to a certain extent. When Hendrick asked in late April to shift from center to right field, Boyer acquiesced by moving Scott to center. Templeton felt he was more productive in the leadoff spot and Boyer agreed, dropping Brock down to second in the order. But if players pressed too hard, he resisted and reasserted his authority. "I've never shrugged responsibility. I've kicked somebody's butt if I've had to."[34]

Still, Ken believed a happy player was a productive one and did his best to promote harmony on the club. He succeeded for the most part in 1979, though discontent at times was inevitable. Promised a starting berth in right field coming into the season, Mumphrey started slow and was injured in spring training. He lost the job to Scott and wanted to be traded. Boyer had to intervene in an argument between the temperamental Denny and a chattering Freed in the dugout. Carbo had seen little action off the bench halfway through the season despite a .375 average in 16 plate appearances. When he overslept and arrived in the clubhouse minutes before a game, Ken told him not to bother putting on his uniform. Carbo exploded with a barrage of expletives and Boyer fined him and suspended him for one game.[35]

Boyer's most problematic player was Templeton. His admiration for the stylish young shortstop began when he first managed him at Tulsa in 1976 and continued in St. Louis. A novice switch-hitter, Templeton was an exciting combination of speed, hitting prowess, and dazzling defense. At twenty-one years old, he batted .322 with 200 safeties, including a major-league leading 18 triples, 79 RBIs, and 28 stolen bases during his second season in 1977. His potential was compared to such legendary players as Stan Musial, Ernie Banks, and Hank Aaron. Boyer considered him as "perhaps the most exciting player I have ever seen, whether he's batting, fielding, or running the bases."[36] Templeton's average fell forty-two points to .280 a year later, but he still produced 31 doubles, an NL-best 13 triples, and stole 34 bases. Yet Claiborne played hardball during contract negotiations in the off-season. He offered him a ten percent pay cut and hard feelings continued into spring training in 1979. Templeton vowed he wouldn't do his best in order to force a salary increase or a trade. Boyer wanted him to focus on his defense and cut down on his major-league leading 40 errors the previous season. Both he and Maxvill tried convincing him to abandon his one-handed catches, but Templeton resisted their efforts. All the while, he erupted to the media. "I'm going to do my thing because it is my thing," he declared. "If they don't like it, then get me the hell out of here. Get me out of here where I can be more comfortable."[37]

The situation may have evoked memories for Ken when his own attitude and desire were questioned by Frank Lane, Fred Hutchinson, and the press early in his career. He defended his young player and blamed the media for inciting the controversy in the first place. "If you guys want to bury him, OK," he told them. "I'm not burying him. The kid is going to play ball here." Perhaps Boyer saw the same treatment he received in St. Louis from Harry Caray and some Cardinals fans. "Every time we get a good ballplayer, you want to run him out of town. Then when he's gone, you say it's our damn fault."[38]

A series of meetings between Templeton and his agent and Claiborne and Boyer led to a truce. Templeton apologized for his conduct, agreeing to play more aggressively. Management agreed not to alter his playing style. He "wants to play his way and I've given him the green light," conceded Ken, though he insisted, "We haven't tried to drive anything down his throat."[39]

Losing five of seven toward the end of May, the Cardinals won 10 of their next 12 games, including a season-high seven straight May 30–June 6. The offense outscored their opponents 89 runs to 67 and raised its batting average twenty-two points to a collective .290. Hendrick's 4-for-5 performance, three RBIs by Reitz, and two by Templeton sparked a 12-5 triumph over the Dodgers that pushed St. Louis into second place on June 2. On the tenth, a home run by Simmons was the difference in a 3-2 win over the San Diego Padres, tying them with the Montreal Expos for the division lead. He homered twice more from both sides of the plate—including a grand slam—the next evening at Los Angeles for the 9-7 victory.

It proved to be the pinnacle of the 1979 season for the Redbirds. They lost all but one of the next eight games on the West Coast and returned home in third place. On June 24, Simmons was struck by a foul tip while catching that broke a bone in his left wrist. He was a vital piece of the offense, enjoying the best start of his major-league career. He was second in the league in slugging (.645), tied for third in homers (18), and fourth in RBIs (52) with a .321 average. "We're not out of it, of course, but we're going to have to guard against letting down," cautioned Boyer in the wake of Simmons's injury. "Everyone just has to go out and do his job." Tied for second with Pittsburgh and 5 ½ back of Montreal, St. Louis had the chance to gain ground against the Expos at Busch Stadium June 25–27. Instead, they lost two of three and slid to fourth place despite a one-hit, 5-0 victory by Martinez in the finale.[40]

A 2-0 shutout by rookie John Fulgham over Pittsburgh and a twin-bill sweep highlighted by eight Redbird home runs in Atlanta on July 6 lifted them back to second place. Ten losses in their next 15 games before and after the All-Star break, however, dropped them to fifth place and eight back of Montreal. Four Cardinals were named as reserves to the National League All-Star team—Hernandez, Simmons, Templeton, and Brock—but only Hernandez and Brock appeared as pinch-hitters, the latter hitting a single in his final All-Star Game in Seattle on July 17. Templeton skipped the contest altogether because he wasn't elected a starter. "I'm sure he was hurt by not being voted in," offered Brock. "He's the best shortstop in the league."[41]

For the remainder of the season, the Cardinals exhibited a back-and-forth effort with clusters of wins and losses. The durable Simmons returned exactly a month after his injury and the club won six of seven, including five in a row the last week of July. A stretch of six defeats in seven games followed through the first weekend of August. Air travel continued to be a problem as the team dealt with mechanical difficulties, delayed early-morning arrivals, and striking airport employees during a 16-day road trip, their longest of the season. Nerves were frayed on a chartered flight from Pittsburgh to Chicago. Music from individual boomboxes became too loud and Ken ordered that headphones be used instead. Tempers flared and arguments broke out. Vuckovich—who admired and respected Boyer—reportedly had to be restrained by teammates. He later regretted what happened. "I know that Vuck felt very bad about it because Vuck really loved Kenny," recalls Hernandez. Boyer downplayed the incident. "It wasn't much of anything. Just an unfortunate happening. No rules were broken, no punches thrown. There were no real differences."[42]

In spite of the drama, the Redbirds enjoyed a five-game winning streak at the end of the trip, highlighted by Denny's two-hit, 4-0 shutout at New York on the ninth and a 17-hit attack in a 13-8 win over Chicago the next evening. The Cardinals swept the Cubs in the twin-bill for seven consecutive wins. The streak enabled St. Louis to climb to fourth place, five games behind the Pittsburgh Pirates.

Brock reached the 3,000-hit milestone in a 3-2 win at Busch Stadium on August 13. Two safeties short when the evening began, he singled to left in the first inning off right-hander Dennis Lamp. He was batting in the fourth when an inside fastball chin high sent him backward to avoid being hit. It got Brock's attention and he smoked the next pitch back to Lamp, deflecting off his right hand toward the third baseman, who had no play as Brock reached first. He became the fourteenth major-league player to reach the historic mark. "I've always wanted to leave baseball in a blaze of glory," he said. "I've always wanted to orchestrate my own exodus and I'm doing a pretty good job of it."[43]

On August 17, Fulgham blanked the San Francisco Giants with a two-hitter, 3-0, and snapped a three-game losing skid. The Cardinals won 14 of their next 17—including a rare 7-2 winning record on the last West Coast swing of the season—leading into a crucial 11-game stretch in September against the top two clubs in the NL East, Pittsburgh and Montreal. They split a two-game set with the front-running Pirates at Busch Stadium, losing the opener on September 5. Boyer signaled for a pickoff throw to first base by lefty reliever Knowles with two outs and the bases loaded in the eleventh inning of a 5-5 tie. The pitcher threw the ball out of Hernandez's reach and two runs scored in the 7-5 debacle. "I'm not much on trick plays," Ken confessed.[44]

St. Louis lost two of three to the Expos at home, then dropped two more at Pittsburgh before traveling to Montreal and splitting a four-game series there. It was a lost opportunity to gain ground in the division race: the league's best offense was outscored 35 runs to 16 in the last nine games and the bullpen lost two extra-inning contests to the Expos. The Redbirds fell 10 games behind the Pirates and Expos, who were tied for first with two weeks left in the season.

The switch-hitting Templeton learned he was 26 hits short of 100 from the right side and set a personal goal of 100 hits from each side of the plate. It was a feat never before accomplished in a single season in major-league history. He achieved it batting right-handed regardless of the pitcher in 34 plate appearances September 22–28. Templeton finished the campaign leading the NL with 211 safeties and 19 triples while tying for the fifth-best average at .314.[45]

Winning eight of their next 10 (including six in a row), the Cardinals were swept at home by the last-place New York Mets in the final four games of the season. Boyer allowed Simmons, Carbo, Freed, and another veteran the chance to manage the club during those games. St. Louis finished in third place with a record of 86-76, 12 games back of the NL East and eventual World champion Pittsburgh Pirates. Ken finished a distant fifth to Dick Williams of Montreal with two votes in the NL Manager of the Year balloting.[46]

Once again, the offense and pitching weren't in sync. The hitters bounced back from an abysmal '78 campaign and paced the National League in team batting average (.278), doubles (279), and triples (63) and tied for third with the Dodgers in on-base percentage (.331). Vuckovich and Martinez both delivered 15-win efforts in the starting rotation and rookie Fulgham was an unexpected surprise with 10 victories and a 2.53 ERA. But the stalwart Forsch (11-11) and Denny (8-11) had uncharacteristic downturns with ERAs of 3.83 and 4.85, respectively, and the staff finished a point above the league average with a collective 3.72 ERA. The bullpen tied for last in the NL in saves with 25 and lost 26 games in the opponent's final at-bat. Littell led the relievers with 13 saves, a 2.19 ERA, and over 82 innings pitched. His lefty counterpart, Knowles, was a disappointment with six saves and an inflated 4.07 ERA. Buddy Schultz endured tendinitis that limited him to 31 games, three saves, and a 4.46 ERA.[47]

An unproductive off-season failed to strengthen the bullpen. Instead, another bat was added to an already potent lineup with the acquisition of veteran outfielder Bobby Bonds from the Cleveland Indians. The thirty-four-year-old was coming off a season with 25 homers, 85 RBIs, and 34 stolen bases, but St. Louis was his sixth team in the past six years. With the retirement of Brock, Bonds was slated to play left field in 1980. It was hoped he would add speed and power to an offense lacking in both departments. After the trade, Bonds said, "If I just do what's average, it should be enough to win the pennant and get to the World Series."⁴⁸

ON OPENING DAY at Busch Stadium April 10, 1980, Vuckovich pitched a complete game and blanked the World champion Pittsburgh Pirates on three hits to win, 1-0. With no relief closer in the bullpen he trusted, Boyer nervously paced the dugout while the Pirates put runners at second and third with nobody out in the ninth inning. With 43,867 screaming fans on their feet, Vuckovich steadied himself and fanned Tim Foli, Dave Parker, and Willie Stargell in succession to preserve the victory. This contest was the first afternoon season opener in St. Louis in 26 years.

From that point, the season spiraled downward. St. Louis lost six of their first 10 games—including five to the Pirates—and found themselves in fifth place but just 2 ½ games behind Pittsburgh. Hendrick knocked in six runs in their 12-9 triumph over the division leaders on the afternoon of the seventeenth. Ten runs wasn't enough to beat the Pirates the next evening, 12-10.

The Cardinals had a similar experience in a wild contest against the Cubs at Wrigley Field on April 22. A 22-mile-per-hour wind played havoc with pop fouls, fly balls, and pitchers on both clubs. "In 20 years, I've never seen the wind blow like that," said Boyer. "I knew that on a day like today, whoever would bat last would win." In a game that featured six home runs, 12 hurlers, 28 runs, and 39 hits, St. Louis lost with two outs in the bottom of the ninth, the bases loaded, and the game tied at 12. Barry Foote belted closer Mark Littell's first pitch and the wind deposited it into the overhanging basket in right-center field for a dramatic, game-winning grand slam that beat the Redbirds, 16-12. The loss highlighted the team's alarming bullpen issues as St. Louis led 12-6 when the bottom half of the fifth inning started. "They have to go out and get a stopper," said Bonds about the front office. "You score 12 runs and don't win, that tells you something."

Desperate for bullpen help, the team acquired forty-one-year-old left-hander Jim Kaat off waivers from the New York Yankees and signed thirty-two-year-old free agent Pedro Borbon, who had been pitching batting practice for the club hoping they might take a chance on him.[49]

Despite a mediocre 8-10 record at the end of April, St. Louis was still within striking distance of Pittsburgh in third place and four games back. They lost two of three at home to the Houston Astros before winning four in a row over the San Francisco Giants and Los Angeles Dodgers the first week of May, their longest win streak so far. The offense exploded for double-digit victories of 10-7, 12-2, and 15-7, and the Redbirds rose to second place in the standings. But the team lost its second baseman and number-two hitter when Oberkfell was taken out by Steve Garvey of the Dodgers sliding into second to break up a double play on May 10. A torn knee ligament sidelined him for the next six weeks.

The loss of Oberkfell coincided with the start of a disastrous string of 13 losses in 14 games. When they embarked on a nine-game West Coast road trip through the middle of May, the Cardinals were the best offensive club in the National League. They had a collective .301 batting average with the best hitter in the league in Reitz (.406) and a robust quartet of Templeton (.361), Hendrick (.356), Simmons (.342), and Hernandez (.321). Yet they were ineffective in clutch situations despite the outstanding statistics and failed to drive in runs when needed. As a result, starting pitchers had little margin for error and were beaten in 10 of 13 games by two runs or less.

Each loss further demoralized the team and the clubhouse became known as the "St. Louis Morgue." The veterans became complacent, missing signals and not running out grounders and fly balls on the bases. There was little encouragement from teammates on the bench. The likelihood of a strike toward the end of the month also weighed on their minds, though Boyer couldn't see how it would affect his club more than any other. He was at a loss what to do to awaken them. "Maybe I should just come in and throw things around the clubhouse," he suggested.[50]

Ken reached the boiling point when he saw the carefree attitude of the players with music blasting in the clubhouse the morning of May 18 after a 4-2 defeat at San Francisco, their sixth in seven games, the previous evening. He called a meeting and gave them an overdue "butt-chewing," according to Hernandez, addressing their lackadaisical attitudes and efforts on and off the field. Boyer wouldn't offer details about the Sunday morning session except to say, "It wasn't chapel in there." Strict rules were established for the first time. Music was prohibited in the clubhouse before batting practice and after losses as well as on the team bus. Players were no longer allowed to drink in the hotel bars. Television was restricted in the Busch Stadium clubhouse. Curfews were implemented on the road. Fines and suspensions were threatened against those who violated them.[51]

Initially, the reactions were positive to Ken's candid remarks. But some players like Templeton had a different take. "Everyone knew our bullpen was the only major problem. The meeting got everybody down. Most of the guys felt it should have pertained only to baseball." Players soon resented the new edicts, particularly those restricting their music and access to the hotel bars. Boyer still allowed them to listen with headphones—"They can blow their heads off all they want," he said—but felt it was inappropriate to play loud music after losses. As for the hotel bars, he wanted to protect them from scrutiny by the writers who might see them drinking one night and having a poor performance the next day.[52]

Even though players hustled a little more, the losing streak continued unabated. "Every game is different, but yet they're all the same," Ken pondered. The Cardinals celebrated his forty-ninth birthday with their sixth straight loss, 4-3, on May 20. Another squandered lead given up by the bullpen the next evening in a 5-3 defeat—the third loss during the trip in their opponent's final at-bat—dropped them into the NL East basement. Meanwhile, the Players Association reached a last-minute agreement with team owners and prevented a work stoppage. "They should have struck nine days ago," said Boyer.[53]

He tried anything to break his club out of its collective funk. Defense was sacrificed for more offense and Simmons was put in left field in place of the injured Bonds for five games May 25–30. He committed only one error, a dropped fly ball, but had trouble catching up with line drives in the spacious Busch Stadium outfield. Decisions like playing Simmons in left and not using popular reserve catcher and pinch-hitter Steve Swisher were second-guessed by some players. Regarding Swisher, Boyer shot back, "They should have nothing to concern themselves except their own business. In fact, they have nothing else to be concerned about. The buddy-buddy stuff doesn't win ball games."[54]

The obvious remedy for the Redbirds' troubles was trading for an elite closer. Claiborne insisted there wasn't one available contrary to reports that Bruce Sutter of the Chicago Cubs—the reigning Cy Young Award winner with 95 saves over the past three seasons—might be available. "I don't think you could blast Bruce Sutter out of the Chicago Cubs organization with an atomic bomb," he insisted.[55]

The demoralized Cardinals returned home and lost three more to San Diego. The fifth-place New York Mets came to town on the twenty-sixth and ambushed Forsch for three runs in the first two innings. His teammates tied the game on Hendrick's solo home run in the fourth and went ahead, 6-3, on Simmons's RBI single and another round-tripper by Hendrick—a two-run shot—in the sixth. Forsch protected an 8-3 lead as New York tallied twice to reduce it to three runs in the ninth. It was at this point that St. Louis was often beaten. Thirteen of 25 defeats had come in the last three frames. With one out and a runner on second, Boyer went to the mound to check on his fatigued hurler. Forsch was determined to finish the game. "I could see in his eyes how he wanted to win so bad," he said of Boyer. "It just pumped me up. It made me feel so good to be out there." Forsch enticed a ground ball and struck out third-place hitter Joel Youngblood for the final out in the 8-5 triumph. The grueling 10-game losing streak was over—at least for the moment.[56]

Another loss the next evening made St. Louis the worst team in baseball with a record of 15-26. A 5-0 lead in the eighth inning with two outs was erased during the afternoon contest on May 28. Simmons misjudged a fly ball while playing left field, resulting in a bases-loaded double and a 6-5 defeat. Two days later, they were hammered, 10-4. The Cardinals received a clubhouse visit from Gussie Busch prior to the game against the Montreal Expos on May 31. Unhappy with their place in the standings beneath the Mets, he felt changes needed to be made "and I think we'll do it in the shortest time possible." That night, the Redbirds responded with a 15-hit effort as Forsch and Vuckovich (in the bullpen temporarily) combined for the 8-6 victory.[57]

Team morale was at an all-time low following a disastrous 7-6 loss in 12 innings on the first of June. St. Louis rallied from a 6-3 deficit to tie the score in the seventh inning, then relievers Vuckovich and Montreal's Woodie Fryman dueled for three subsequent scoreless frames. They gave way to recent minor-league call-up George Frazier and veteran Stan Bahnsen, who each retired the other side in order in the eleventh. But with two outs in the top of the twelfth and the go-ahead run on third, Frazier yielded a single to Warren Cromartie with two strikes that decided the contest. "You get so frustrated you want to kill people," said Vuckovich about the losses.[58]

Afterward, the Cardinals placed Littell and Martinez on the 21-day disabled list with elbow injuries and two new pitchers, John Littlefield and Kim Seaman, were called up from Triple-A Springfield. Martinez's injury returned Vuckovich to the rotation. Amid the chaotic roster moves, Boyer maintained his wry sense of humor. "I don't even know where my bullpen is right now," he deadpanned. "I'll have to go down and look at a scorecard to see who we've got. We're changing them faster that we can keep track of them."[59]

The Cardinals went back on the road and won two straight at New York, their longest win streak in a month. The forty-one-year-old Kaat pitched 10 shutout innings as an emergency starter on June 4 and Reitz smashed a leadoff home run in the tenth inning to beat the Mets, 1-0. It was the first time all season they won a game in their last at-bat. In three subsequent losses at New York and Montreal, St. Louis lost two in their opponents' final plate appearance, managing only four runs in 31 innings and stranding 18 runners. "We've had so many chances," lamented Boyer after a 13-inning, 2-1 defeat at Montreal on the seventh. "People say you ought to kick them in the butts and have a butt-chewing. But we've done that."[60]

Unbeknownst to him, Ken's fate as manager had been decided earlier that morning by Busch, Claiborne, and Lou Susman, Busch's attorney and influential adviser. The general manager boarded a plane for Montreal, but bad weather prevented him from arriving until the afternoon of June 8. That day, St. Louis was defeated in the first game of a Sunday doubleheader with the Expos, 6-4, their fourth loss in a row and twenty-first in the last 26 games.

Boyer sat at his desk in the visiting manager's office at Olympic Stadium working on the lineup card for the second game. He had penciled in Simmons batting fourth and Roy Thomas pitching and hitting ninth in the order when Claiborne walked into the room. Ken thought a trade had been made. Instead, Claiborne broke the news that he had been fired. Boyer spoke to the players before they took the field for the second game of the doubleheader. Afterward, he gathered his belongings and left the clubhouse.[61]

From the moment he accepted the position, Ken knew it could be taken away from him at any time. It was a reality every major-league manager faced. The team was mired at the bottom of the NL East standings with a disastrous record of 18-33 and a .353 winning percentage, still the worst in baseball. His initial reaction was unemotional as he made arrangements for a last-minute flight back home and hastily packed his belongings. Yet he couldn't help but feel blindsided and tried rationalizing the decision. "I worked hard to get here, and I don't think I screwed up," he said. He believed the players were doing their best under the circumstances. "I don't know what else I could have done." Rick Hummel of the *Post-Dispatch* noticed the "sadness etched on Boyer's face." For a third time, the Cardinals had broken his heart—first as a player when he was traded away after eleven seasons in St. Louis, then when he was passed over to manage the club after five years in the minors. Now they had crushed his dream to guide the Cardinals, the team of his childhood and adulthood, to a World championship.[62]

Meanwhile, back in St. Louis, Busch showcased his new manager for the media on the back porch of his south St. Louis County mansion. Forty-eight-year-old Dorrel "Whitey" Herzog, originally from nearby New Athens, Illinois, had guided the Kansas City Royals to three straight seasons of 90 wins or better and three American League Western Division championships from 1976–78. He was the third-base coach when Boyer was still a player with the Mets and both shared a New York apartment. "I'm a very good friend of Kenny Boyer," said Herzog. "These things happen. If you don't own the ball club or you don't die in the job, eventually you're going to get fired."[63]

For the players, it was just another chapter in a disappointing season. A few were genuinely upset, while others weren't surprised by the news. "Kenny Boyer is a winner," insisted Fulgham, who blamed his dismissal on a club that lacked his commitment to the game. Vuckovich, who respected and sometimes tested him during his tenure, was hurt by the decision. "Boyer became the victim of our lack of production. We stink, we lose—and he's gone. He's a kind man, a good man." "It's tough," said Hernandez. "Kenny's a real fine man and I hated to see him go. It's always the manager who has to go." Templeton admitted he "was a little shocked" at the timing. "They (management) figured they had to do something. They ought to ship out the entire bullpen. I'm as much to blame as anybody. We're not hitting in key situations." The most moving tribute was offered by Vuckovich: "I only hope I'm as mature and understanding as he is when I grow to be his age."[64]

ANOTHER DAY OF REFLECTION brought no clarity to the questions in Ken's mind. While reassuring Hummel that he "didn't jump off the top of the Arch," nonetheless he had no better explanation for his dismissal. "The whole thing is very, very difficult to figure out. It's probably going to be impossible for me. I'm never going to learn the things that led up to this." Claiborne offered no definitive answers except it was "a joint decision that we thought was for the good of the club. There are a lot of elements that go into that statement and I'm not going to go into those elements."[65]

The obvious reason was the team's uninspired performance in a season when the Cardinals were expected to contend for the NL Eastern Division title. Factors such as an insufficient bullpen and injuries to starting pitchers Fulgham and Martinez and key position players Bonds and Oberkfell were out of his control. Ken didn't think there were "internal problems" that could have cost him his job and Claiborne agreed. Asked what he could have done differently, Boyer replied, "I don't know. You'll have to ask the people that figured this out."[66]

Claiborne believed the Cardinals should have performed better than their record in spite of the injuries. The team's collapse coincided with the availability of Herzog, who had managed the Texas Rangers, California Angels, and Kansas City Royals. Claiborne had known Herzog since the late 1960s when they worked together in the New York Mets front office. He pursued Herzog for a consultant role in

St. Louis after he was fired by Kansas City at the end of the 1979 season. But Herzog wanted to manage again. Claiborne denied it had anything to do with Boyer's firing, but it was obvious Herzog would not be available much longer. Busch met with him at Grant's Farm on the morning of June 8. They agreed on a three-year, $300,000 contract, the longest and most expensive for a manager in club history. Boyer wished his successor good luck. "I hope they can turn it around."[67]

Managing had been Ken's way to stay connected with the game he loved. It gave him the opportunity to work with young players and help them realize their potential. He enjoyed the camaraderie of the clubhouse and wanted to foster close relationships with his players, giving them the same respect and sense of responsibility that his managers gave him. It was his intention to break down the barrier between player and management in the wake of Vern Rapp's uncompromising approach and inspire better teamwork. This philosophy worked well in his first two seasons, but fell apart during the abysmal 1980 campaign. "I think he probably got too close to the players early and then tried to distance himself too late," says Hummel.[68]

The makeup of the team wasn't compatible with his laid-back managing style. "Kenny inherited a bad team, and a team that was in a great deal of upheaval," recalled Schoendienst. "Kenny was a much more relaxed, player-oriented kind of manager, but he was just caught in the wrong place at the wrong time."[69] Perhaps the best explanation was offered by second baseman Tommy Herr, a late-season addition in 1979 who became a key contributor for the Cardinals during the 1980s:

> [O]ne of the things that struck me about the team was that there seemed to be a lot of rebels there, a lot of guys who had their own agenda and didn't have a lot of respect for authority. Ken wasn't real vocal. He was more of a stoic guy, but that type of manager needs players who have their own disciplinary values and can police themselves. That group of Cardinals didn't have that.[70]

After a few weeks at the helm, Herzog understood the personalities and challenges Boyer had to deal with in the clubhouse. "I've never seen such a bunch of misfits," he recalled in his autobiography. "Nobody would run out a ball. Nobody in the bullpen wanted the ball." He told Busch, "It's the first time I've ever been scared to walk through my own clubhouse. We've got drug problems, we've got ego problems, and we ain't ever going anywhere."[71]

Herzog's close relationship with Busch enabled him to name Schoendienst as the interim field manager and move temporarily into the front office to replace Claiborne, who was fired on August 18. This unexpected move, approved by the Cardinals owner, allowed the "White Rat" to clean house and build a team with speed, defense, and a solid bullpen. Amid a flurry of trades he made as general manager at the 1980 baseball winter meetings was one for Bruce Sutter, the big-name closer St. Louis needed the past three seasons. And it took less than an atomic bomb—as Claiborne insisted—to free him from the rival Chicago Cubs. Discussing the potential impact of Sutter for the Cardinals going into the '81 season, Herzog said, "If he was here last year, you'd be talking to Ken Boyer right now."[72]

Ken concluded his major-league managing career with a 166-190 record. After a year of reflection, he said, "I used to think managing would probably be an ego trip. It wasn't. Was it fun? I sure didn't see anything fun about it in my situation. There was nothing very rewarding in it for me."[73]

Chapter Eighteen

Heading for Home

For two weeks after his dismissal, Ken admitted he "didn't think about anything." It was too late in the season to find another major-league managing or coaching position. Unless he could pilot a club in the Pacific Coast League with the chance to visit cities he had never seen before, a return to the minor leagues didn't interest him. Boyer's options to stay in baseball were limited.

Then John Claiborne called him about the offer he had made him to stay in the Cardinals organization. At the time it was given, the general manager had just fired him and Ken's mind was far from the conversation at that point. He wasn't certain if the overture was sincere "or if he was just trying to appease me after they put the shock on me." It was a genuine offer to serve as a special assignment scout and Boyer accepted. Gussie Busch valued loyalty and recognized his importance to the Cardinals. It was an opportunity to stay in the organization that had not been afforded to his predecessors. "We are delighted that Kenny has chosen to stay with the club," said Busch. "We hope to keep Kenny in a Cardinal uniform for a long time."[1]

Boyer's responsibilities the rest of the 1980 season were vague, involving "team development and administration." He spent the summer visiting the minor-league affiliates at Springfield, Illinois; Little Rock, St. Petersburg, Gastonia, North Carolina; and Johnson City, Tennessee. It was a difficult transition from the hectic surroundings of a major-league manager to a nomadic and solitary occupation in the minors. "I don't have everybody around me like I did in St. Louis. Doing this job…you're always alone. You have a lot of time on your hands."[2]

Ken enjoyed a more active role in 1981. He scouted National League opponents in advance of the Cardinals playing them as well as six clubs in the American League. "I'm really excited about it," he said. "It really keeps you in touch with the right people." Sometimes he had the chance to work with individual players like Ken Oberkfell, who was transitioning from second to third base to make room on the infield for Tommy Herr. Oberkfell recalled Boyer "really helped me one-on-one, hands-on working at third base. He made me a pretty good third baseman." Scouting also gave him the opportunity to see his younger brother Clete, who was the third-base coach for the Oakland Athletics.[3]

When he was dismissed as Cardinals manager at Montreal in June 1980, Ken vowed he would manage again. A year later, however, he decided against seeking a position either in the majors or the minors. A coaching job was even less attractive. He did serve as interim manager of the Class A Gastonia Cardinals in the South Atlantic League on June 27 when their manager was suspended for bumping an umpire.

A. Ray Smith, who owned the Tulsa Oilers when Boyer managed them from 1974–76, convinced him to make a comeback. The wealthy construction magnate had transferred the Cardinals Triple-A club from Springfield, Illinois, to Louisville, Kentucky, and wanted him to be the manager for the upcoming 1982 season. The city had been without professional baseball for nine years and a groundswell of community support was financing the conversion of the University of Louisville's football stadium into a dual-purpose facility. Ken considered it "a great challenge" and accepted the position. At the press conference in Louisville on November 13, he wore a new white home Redbirds jersey over his shirt and tie. His hair was thick and dark though his sideburns were gray. The fifty-year-old Boyer spoke enthusiastically about the opportunity to manage again. He promised his team would "play the kind of game that's exciting to the fans." He added, "The Louisville Redbirds has a magical ring to me. The way this city has been presented to me, it's more like moving into a big league market than a minor league one."[4]

SADLY, a routine medical checkup that month changed his plans. There was concern about the results and a subsequent biopsy revealed he had inoperable cancer in both lungs, his heart, and his esophagus. He was given about a year to live. An examination during spring training eight months earlier showed no reason for concern. Ken had been a moderate smoker for many years. He smoked as a young man but stopped after returning home from the military in 1953. The pressure of the pennant race the last two weeks of the 1964 season led him to start again. By his own admission, he smoked "a lot" during that time and teammate Bob Gibson claimed Boyer had "the worst cigarette habit I've ever seen." His children insist he "wasn't a habitual smoker" but did so intermittently over the next seventeen years.[5]

Only they knew about his diagnosis. Because his father was in the final stages of intestinal cancer at the time, Ken thought it best not to tell his siblings. He was going through radiation treatments in St. Louis when Vern Boyer passed away on the first of December 1981. Ken's children went with him to the funeral burdened with a secret no one else in the family knew. His weight loss was noticeable to his brothers and sisters, yet he said nothing. "I remember sitting next to my dad at the funeral home," son Dan Boyer recalls. "All I could think about was what was going through his mind at that time. There was a point when I put my hand on his leg and he put his hand on top of mine." He described it as the most touching moment they ever shared as father and son. Ken's youngest child Jane later sat on his lap and cried. He asked her what was wrong but she couldn't tell him. He reassured her, "I'm not going anywhere."[6]

The Cardinals knew about Ken's illness, but he asked that it not be disclosed. On January 11, 1982, he attended the 25th anniversary of the St. Louis Baseball Writers' Dinner and was reunited with former teammates Gibson, Stan Musial, and Mike Shannon. It was a lively program and childhood heroes such as Marty Marion, Terry Moore, and other surviving members of the 1942 World Series club were recognized. Boyer was honored with the Dr. Robert F. Hyland Award for "Meritorious Service to Sports," sharing it with Gibson, publisher C.C. Johnson Spink of *The Sporting News*, and longtime St. Louis professional wrestling promoter Sam Muchnick.[7]

When he was unable to attend a promotional event in Louisville ten days after the Writers' Dinner, the Cardinals explained his absence as "personal." A. Ray Smith took it upon himself to reveal the illness for the first time publicly, explaining that Boyer was undergoing cancer treatment in St. Louis. The Redbirds owner was confident Ken would still manage the Redbirds. It became apparent a month later, however, that he would not be able to fulfill his responsibilities. Former St. Louis outfielder Joe Frazier, a teammate of Boyer during his first two big-league seasons, was named as his replacement. The *St. Louis Post-Dispatch* reported that the Cardinals would make Boyer "a special scout" instead.[8]

KEN'S PROGNOSIS was grim. Though radiation reduced the masses on his heart and esophagus, it proved ineffective for his lungs. Chemotherapy offered no guarantees for success. He learned about alternative forms of treatment that had reportedly helped others with terminal cancer at the Gerson Institute in San Diego. He went there in February. It promoted self-healing through the Gerson Therapy, a strict vegetarian diet of organic foods, raw juices, coffee enemas, and natural vitamin supplements that would purge the cancer-causing toxins from the body.

A controversial aspect of the treatment was the use of laetrile, a supplement derived from apricot seeds not approved by the U.S. Food and Drug Administration for treating the disease. It had been in the news two years earlier when motion picture actor Steve McQueen reportedly used it in his own cancer treatment. Boyer didn't consider laetrile the solution for his illness. "I don't think that alone is going to solve anybody's problem and I don't think anybody believes that it will," he said. "But it's a boost...I think it's a combination of a lot of things that eventually is going to whip the thing for me."[9]

Because of his use of laetrile, Ken had to cross the U.S.-Mexico border for treatment at the institute's clinic in Tijuana. He granted sports broadcaster Howard Cosell an exclusive interview there later that month. He had lost weight (and grown an uncharacteristic short gray and black beard) but remained optimistic about overcoming his illness. Confidence was a word he used throughout the interview. He intended to "stick with the program that I've been put on out here, and I have all the confidence in the world. I've seen too many other people come through it and no problems. I feel that if I can keep my head [up] on my shoulders, I'm going to do the same thing." Asked if he was bitter about his circumstances, he replied, "I don't feel victimized by anybody or anything except probably some of my own living habits and things that I've done myself."[10]

Because Ken didn't contribute to the health benefit program as part of the major-league players pension in 1974, his medical expenses were not covered. He was burdened with bills that reached upwards of $10,000. Each week of treatments added another $1,500. He was having financial struggles before his diagnosis and helping three of his four children with college-related expenses. Clete mentioned his brother's dilemma to his friend and manager Billy Martin of the Oakland Athletics. "Kenny's so proud, he won't ever tell anybody he can use help," he told Martin. "But he can. And I'm gonna try to help him. We don't want anybody feeling sorry for us, but the time comes when everybody needs a little help." Clete asked for his help to organize a charity dinner. Martin took charge, writing a heartfelt letter asking former major-league players, baseball officials, and entertainment personalities for donations and inviting them to the benefit dinner.[11]

The response was overwhelming. Between 700-750 attended the dinner at the Ramada Safari Resort in Scottsdale, Arizona, the spring training base of the Athletics, on March 28. The $50 a plate event raised $35,000 above expenses and exceeded Clete's expectations. "[Billy] didn't have to do it…He knows my brother, but not that well." Among the attendees were Mickey Mantle, Roger Maris, Harmon Killebrew, Frank Robinson, Eddie Mathews, Bill "Moose" Skowron, Reggie Jackson, Billy Williams, and Ferguson Jenkins, as well as managers Gene Mauch of the California Angels, Dick Williams of the San Diego Padres, Lee Elia of the Chicago Cubs, and Buck Rodgers of the Milwaukee Brewers. Others included Marvin Miller, executive director of the Major League Baseball Players Association; Hall of Fame umpire Jocko Conlan; and new Cubs broadcaster

Harry Caray. The emcee duties were shared by Ken's former teammate Bob Uecker and Joe Garagiola. Along with comedian Tom Dreesen, they helped make the event lighthearted. Howard Cosell gave the closing remarks. The evening took a more somber tone when Clete thanked everyone for their support. "From Ken Boyer and all the family, I thank you. I think I know now how Lou Gehrig felt. I feel the Boyer family is the luckiest family in the world."[12]

A similar tribute event was held in St. Louis and emceed by Cardinals radio broadcaster Jack Buck. Smaller fundraising efforts were organized with the help of former big-leaguers like Ralph Branca of the Brooklyn Dodgers and Sal Yvars of the New York Giants. Fifteen thousand dollars in gate receipts from a near-sellout spring training exhibition game between the Athletics and Angels on March 17 were offered. Generous donations were also made by Cosell, New York Yankees owner George Steinbrenner, former teammate Steve Carlton, the St. Louis Cardinals, and the Philadelphia Phillies. The Association of Professional Baseball Players of America, a non-profit organization that provided financial assistance to former major and minor-league players in need, gave $500 and offered the same amount monthly if needed. "Ken Boyer's situation is what our organization is all about," said APBPA secretary-treasurer Chuck Stevens. The largest single contribution of $5,000 was made by Ken's former manager Solly Hemus, who made him team captain in 1959. "I'd been fortunate to make some money in the oil business, and I contributed, and I was happy to do so," says Hemus. "I wish I could have given more than I did. He was a person that I respected."[13]

Ken wasn't able to attend the Scottsdale dinner, but nonetheless was grateful for the outpouring of support from baseball. "It's hard to say how he is," said Clete when asked about his brother. "He's keeping up with his treatment program, but we don't really know how he's doing. He's in great spirits. The idea of this dinner rally choked him up a couple of times." Ken wanted to thank Martin in person for everything he had done, but conflicting schedules prevented their meeting before he left the West Coast.[14]

AFTER THREE MONTHS of treatments in Tijuana, he flew home to St. Louis in April. His son Danny had not seen him in five months and was surprised at his father's physical appearance. "He left a pretty big guy and came back about 170 pounds," he recalls. "It was pretty shocking." His children knew Joseph and Georgana Linneman, owners of the Mari de Villa Retirement Center in the west St. Louis suburb of Town and Country, and secured an apartment for him there. The contributions helped make it possible. "I didn't know what to do until Billy came up with the idea for his dinner," said Clete. "The next two months are critical for him. If he can gain weight, he'll be okay. Mentally, he's fine, but he weighs 170 [pounds] and, at 6-[foot]-3, there isn't much on him."[15]

For the most part, Ken stayed at Mari de Villa and rarely left. His health improved somewhat. He spent time outdoors walking the manicured grounds and watching the construction projects on the property. On May 20, his children arranged a surprise party for him on his fifty-first birthday and close friends from St. Louis and Hermann were there. "It was a good day," son Dan remembers.

Ken kept up with the Cardinals, who were in first place in the NL East. Coaches Red Schoendienst and Hal Lanier and trainer Gene Geiselman were frequent visitors. He asked them about the team and how young players like Tommy Herr and Willie McGee were progressing. He even went to a game at Busch Stadium. His mind was sharp and back in the dugout even though he was sitting in the press box. When first baseman Keith Hernandez failed to make a play on a pop foul in front of the home dugout and allowed the catcher to make it instead, Ken chastised him, "Keith, don't let him take that ball."[16]

Family, friends, old teammates, and even visiting players and umpires saw him over the summer. His siblings made trips from southwest Missouri and brother Cloyd, now the pitching coach for the Kansas City Royals, stopped by as well. "He didn't really want too many people around," says his daughter Suzie (Boyer) Hartwig. "He had lost so much weight and he was very self-conscious about how he looked. He didn't want to have to spend a lot of time explaining things." Still, Joe Cunningham thought the number of visitors surprised Ken. "His ordeal, the way he faced it, may have been the first time in his life that Kenny Boyer realized how much affection so many people had for him."[17]

Don Blasingame had known him since they played together for the minor-league Houston Buffaloes in 1954. Both were teammates with the Cardinals for parts of five seasons. He was preparing to manage a professional team in Japan and had lunch with Boyer and Cunningham before leaving. "It was tough, but I knew this would be the last time," recalled Blasingame. "It was a sad time, but he never said anything. No one let on about what was going to happen. We laughed and joked through the whole lunch. He was that kind of guy."[18]

Veteran sports columnist Bob Burnes of the *St. Louis Globe-Democrat*, who covered Ken's eleven seasons with the Cardinals, was another visitor. He asked him about his most memorable career highlights. An obvious choice was the grand slam in Game 4 of the 1964 World Series. "I can't remember anything in my career that had more impact," he agreed. "But I felt happiest because it brought us back even in the series. If we had lost that game, we would have been down, three games to one." He was proud when the entire Cardinals infield of himself, shortstop Dick Groat, second baseman Julian Javier, and first baseman Bill White started for the National League in the 1963 All-Star Game in Cleveland. "I thought that was a pretty good tribute to the Cardinal organization. Besides, we won." The thought of his third choice brought a smile to his face. During the frenzied '64 pennant chase, the Redbirds beat the Chicago Cubs at Wrigley Field, 15-2, on September 13. St. Louis scored in all nine innings, the first time it had been done in the major leagues since 1923. "The thing that stood out was that everybody on the team did a perfect job that day." His last pick was his participation in Don Drysdale's streak of 58 $^{2}/_{3}$ consecutive scoreless innings May 14–June 8, 1968, as a member of the Los Angeles Dodgers. "When the streak got rolling and it was obvious that Drysdale had a shot at the record, Walt Alston told me one day that I'd be at third base every time Drysdale started, until the streak came to an end."[19]

Ken's health declined after he contracted shingles in June. Cancer eventually spread to his brain, causing him to lose most of his sight in one eye and blinding the other. His bedroom stayed dark because the sunlight hurt them. He could only speak softly because of the pain in his throat. As his condition worsened, he was moved from his apartment to a room under a nurse's supervision. He was in a great deal of pain, yet stoically declined medication. He slept most of the time. "He was wilting," says Schoendienst. "We'd go on the road for ten, twelve days, come back, and you'd see a different Boyer. That's how quick he was going. It was not good." Yet he never complained to his family, friends, or nurses and insisted he would recover. "Kenny was always so positive every time I visited with him," said brother Ron Boyer.[20]

Kathleen Boyer visited her former husband often. She found him to be just as determined to recuperate and leave the retirement center. "He never admitted he had cancer. He would say, 'My illness.'" She helped feed him and they enjoyed long conversations. "He still might have wanted to talk more in-depth about personal things," she said, "but that wasn't easy for him."[21]

If anyone could understand what Ken was going through, it was former teammate and Cardinals broadcaster Mike Shannon. In 1970, he had been diagnosed with glomerulonephritis (nephritis), an ailment that prevents the kidneys from filtering waste properly. The illness ended his playing career at the age of thirty and almost cost him his life. Shannon had a friend who worked at Mari de Villa and kept him updated on Boyer's condition. "Like all competitors, you fight," said Shannon. "Kenny fought like hell. Nobody ever fought harder." When the fight neared the end—when he felt he could offer the most help to his friend—he went to see him. "We talked honestly about dying. Dying is easy. I found that out, and Kenny felt that same way. It's the people you love—the people you will have to leave—that makes it so hard. We talked about that. I didn't bring him false hope, and he didn't want any...People will never know how beautifully he handled the end."[22]

Clete Boyer spent the Labor Day weekend with his brother and shared an adjoining room with Ken's oldest son David. "If I hadn't known him, I wouldn't have recognized him," he remarked. "He was down to 120 [pounds]. His mind was wandering so much. I'm not even sure he knew who I was at the end." His other siblings saw him that weekend as well. Schoendienst returned from a road trip and went to see his old teammate for the last time on Monday evening. "Kenny said...he believed he could come back from this. He went down fighting." The next morning, his nurse checked on him at 6:15. She spoke to him and he looked up at her for a moment. Then he was gone.[23]

KENTON LLOYD BOYER PASSED AWAY on Tuesday, September 7, 1982. His family believed he held on until his brother Clete's arrival. "Knowing all that Kenny went through these past few months, all the pain and suffering he endured without ever bitching or feeling sorry for himself, I'm relieved now," said Clete. "I feel good that at last Kenny is resting. I'm so proud of him, the type of player he was, the type of brother he was. He was a super brother and a super athlete. I idolized him so much."[24]

News spread throughout St. Louis and across the country of his death. "He was so much a part of this town," said Shannon. "When he died, this city went into shock." The Cardinals released a statement on behalf of Gussie Busch: "Ken Boyer gave the Cardinals and the baseball fans of St. Louis many great moments to remember, and we will remember him with admiration and respect. He was one of the truly outstanding players in the long history of the Cardinals. We share in his family's sorrow." The players wore a black armband on their left sleeve in his memory the remainder of the season.[25] Bob Forsch thought of him before taking the mound the next evening at Busch Stadium and blanking the Montreal Expos, 1-0. "I thought it would be nice to win for him," he said. "He was a nice man, a super guy."[26]

The first of two funeral services was held at Schrader Funeral Home in the southwest St. Louis suburb of Ballwin on September 9. Over two hundred mourners gathered in the chapel, where the closed casket was surrounded by beautiful floral arrangements with a handsome oil painting of Ken as manager of the Cardinals hanging above.[27] Among the mourners were Ken's children, his brothers and sisters, and many friends, former teammates, and players he led as manager. There was a private viewing for family members prior to the service. "The only outsider who was allowed—because he asked—was Jack Buck," says Suzie (Boyer) Hartwig. "He really, really liked Dad."[28]

Rev. John Long, a former pastor of the Alba Christian Church and friend of the Boyer family, officiated and gave the eulogy. He read from Psalms 23 and Romans 8, passages of the Bible he had shared with Ken during his visits. "Kenny fought a fight and he won...in that God drew him close to him." He had accepted Jesus Christ as his personal Lord and Savior, a source of strength and comfort for his grieving family. "Where there has been sickness, there's now joy,"

Rev. Long told them. "Where there has been pain, there's now relief. Where there's been dread and fear, there is now victory."²⁹

The next day, a second service was held at the Alba Christian Church in Ken's hometown nearly 300 miles southwest of St. Louis. Because the small white frame church couldn't contain all two hundred mourners, chairs were arranged outdoors under the trees and speakers for them to listen to the service. Afterward, the funeral procession drove two miles west to the nearby community of Purcell, where Ken was laid to rest in Friends Cemetery. Like the man himself, the gray granite marker placed there was modest and unpretentious, adorned with a pair of doves and a simple epitaph—"Dear Father." His children discussed a possible inscription acknowledging his playing career with the St. Louis Cardinals but decided against it. "It wasn't who he was," says Suzie (Boyer) Hartwig. "He wasn't showy. You have to respect who he was."³⁰

FOR THE FIRST TIME since Ken Boyer was still an active major-league player, St. Louis baseball fans were part of postseason baseball. The 1982 Cardinals clinched the NL East Division title on September 27 in Montreal. Fittingly, the last Expos' out started with Gary Carter hitting a ground ball to the third baseman. As Ken Oberkfell scooped up the ball and fired it across the diamond to Keith Hernandez, Jack Buck lit up the Cardinals' Radio Network describing the celebration on the infield of Stade Olympique (Olympic Stadium) with a franchise tribute that included Boyer.³¹

The Cardinals later faced the Atlanta Braves, winner of the NL West, in the then best-of-five-games National League Championship Series. Ken's memory was honored before the opening game of the NLCS at Busch Stadium on October 7 as Suzie, surrounded by siblings David, Dan, and Jane, threw out the ceremonial first pitch. St. Louis swept Atlanta in three games. On the brink of a 6-3 victory over the Milwaukee Brewers in Game 7 of the World Series on October 20, Buck took a moment during his broadcast in the ninth inning to mention the armbands on the players' sleeves and reflect on Boyer's passing. "[T]he thought of Kenny goes through your mind as the Cardinals enjoy this thrilling moment at the park. We haven't forgotten him." He later wrote, "I only wish he could have lived to see his club win the championship. And if general manager John Claiborne had picked up [relief pitcher] Bruce Sutter a year earlier, who knows? It might have been Kenny rather than Whitey Herzog being doused with the victory champagne."[32]

Ken Boyer's marker at Friends Cemetery in Purcell, Missouri.
(*Photo by the author*)

Chapter Nineteen

An Exceptional Ballplayer

Instead of sadness, longtime St. Louis sportswriter Bob Broeg's reaction to Ken Boyer's death was anger. It brought to mind his exclusion from the Baseball Hall of Fame—an honor that Broeg felt Boyer deserved—and the fact that he could not celebrate the achievement if he ever was enshrined. When he died, Ken was already excluded from the Baseball Writers Association of America (BBWAA) ballot because he had fallen one vote short of the five percent needed to stay on it in 1979. He received only meager support the previous five years while fellow third baseman Eddie Mathews scaled the ballot on his way to enshrinement a year earlier.[1]

Broeg championed Boyer's reinstatement over the next three years until the Hall finally acquiesced, bringing him back along with other discarded candidates like Dick "Richie" Allen, Curt Flood, Vada Pinson, and Ron Santo. His vote total more than tripled in his first year back on the ballot from 20 in 1979 to 68 in 1985. He enjoyed an upsurge over the next three years and reached a peak of 105 votes (25.5%) in 1988. The totals fluctuated after that, eventually falling to 54 in his final year of eligibility on the writers' ballot in 1994, despite the fact his lifetime statistics were unchanged.[2]

Once again ineligible for the BBWAA ballot, Ken's candidacy shifted to the Veterans Committee, made up of former players, front office executives, and writers. He never merited induction over the next fourteen years despite support from members like Broeg, Red Schoendienst, and Bill White. "There's no question I voted for him," says Schoendienst. "I think he deserved to be there." Beginning in 2010, the Hall of Fame Board of Directors split the Veterans Committee into three distinct 16-member groups based on the game's historical eras. Each committee met at the Baseball Winter Meetings on a rotating basis to consider ten candidates with 14 votes required for election. A screening committee placed Boyer on the ballot of the Golden Era Committee (covering the 1947–1972 era) in 2012 and 2015. Each time he garnered less than three votes, while fellow third baseman Ron Santo was elected posthumously in 2012.[3]

Ken Boyer was among the elite third baseman of his generation. For seven consecutive years, he was arguably the best overall at his position in the National League. Between 1958 and 1964, he batted .303 with a .372 on-base percentage, slugged .500, and averaged 25 doubles, 26 home runs, and 101 RBIs a season. He made eleven All-Star appearances (with six starts) during his 15-year career. He was deemed the best defensive third baseman by *The Sporting News* for five seasons, including four straight (1961–64), and received five Gold Glove Awards, four in a row (1958–61) and one in 1963. He finished in the top ten in the National League in Wins Above Replacement (WAR) five consecutive seasons (1958–62) and four times in the top five (1956, 1959–61). Three times he was in the top 10 for the National League Most Valuable Player before winning the award in 1964.[4]

When he retired in 1969, Boyer was sixth in WAR at 54.8 among third basemen and was second only to Eddie Mathews in career home runs (282). He and Mathews were the only ones with over 250 homers and 1,000 RBIs. Defensively, he had the fifth most assists all-time at the position and finished among the top three in that category during ten of his fifteen major-league seasons.[5]

"He was an exceptional ballplayer," says former teammate and manager Solly Hemus. "He had great range. He had a great arm. He could run like a deer, and he was just very, very fast, great agility, just covered a lot of ground (and) made great plays."[6]

"He was not only a good player, but he was a clutch player," Schoendienst points out. "He made great plays when you had to make them. A lot of guys make plays when you're getting beat by six or seven runs or winning by six runs, but he was always real consistent. No matter what the score was...he was always out there making the big plays."[7]

Hall of Fame pitcher Dizzy Dean had compared Boyer's abilities to Harold "Pie" Traynor, a career .320 hitter who was regarded as the premier third baseman in baseball history at the time. "Boyer can out-run, out-throw, and out-field [Fred] Lindstrom [another Hall of Fame third baseman], and hit with him, too," he added. Traynor himself agreed. "The best third baseman I've seen is Ken Boyer," he said in 1969. "For ten years before Boyer hurt his back, he was out of this world. He made all the plays, hit for power, and drove in big runs."[8] In 1965, Willie Mays assembled an all-opponent team made up of players he had faced at that point in his major-league career. He named Boyer and Mathews as the third basemen. Of those he selected, only two—Boyer and Gil Hodges—are not in the Hall of Fame.[9]

Ken achieved his greatest success in the Midwest, far from the national media spotlight. It was only in his declining years that he played in the larger markets of New York, Chicago, and Los Angeles. Broeg felt Boyer's diminished abilities and deadpan opinions contributed to the lack of support he received from writers in the Big Apple, who made up twenty-five percent of the BBWAA voting membership. "If we changed places," insisted his brother Clete Boyer, "and Ken played in New York, he'd be in the Hall of Fame today."[10]

The fact that Ken finished under 300 career home runs is often cited as a detriment to his Hall of Fame credentials. He played most of his 15-year career in a home ballpark unfavorable to right-handed hitters. A little more than half of his 255 home runs between 1955 and 1965 (130) were hit at Busch Stadium I (formerly Sportsman's Park), where the left-field wall was 351 feet from home plate, 379 feet to left-center (while increasing quickly to 400 feet), and 426 to center. "When I first came up, I was a pull-hitter, but the more a right-handed batter tries to pull for homers in our park, the more he beats his head against the wall," he remarked. A more mature and disciplined hitter in his prime, Boyer stroked outside pitches toward the 310-foot right-field pavilion roof.[11]

The cozier dimensions and daytime baseball of Wrigley Field certainly benefited Ron Santo's 342 career home runs, where 63% were swatted. By comparison, Ken averaged a home run in every 21 at-bats there (23 homers in 473 at-bats).[12] "For a long-ball hitter, Wrigley Field is the best in the league because you can reach the fence in left-center and right-center often," said Boyer. "You can hit a lot of ordinary flies that will go out of this park." It would be interesting to see his final career numbers had he played more games in the Friendly Confines rather than the first Busch Stadium.[13]

Another consideration in Ken's less robust lifetime statistics compared to Santo and Mathews is the loss of two years to military service (1952–53) in his early twenties. At least one of those seasons could have been spent in St. Louis. Had he made the same impression at Double-A Houston in 1953 as he did a year later, it's possible he would have been the starting third baseman instead of Ray Jablonski in 1954. (Boyer was a level above Jablonski in the minor-leagues in 1951.) An earlier start to his big-league career could have produced a season similar to his 1956 campaign in 1955—.306 with 26 home runs and 98 RBIs. Such a performance would have edged him into the 300-homer club with over 1,200 career RBIs.[14]

Both Santo and Boyer deserve to be enshrined. The fact that the Chicago Cubs third baseman has been elected should give credence to Ken's selection as well. Third base is the most inadequately represented position in the Hall. Baseball writer and author Jayson Stark pointed out that Boyer and Santo are the only major-league third basemen with seven consecutive seasons of 20 homers, 90 RBIs, and four or more Gold Gloves. "Boyer's underrated time has come," he concluded in his book *The Stark Truth*. "It has come because this guy was a great do-it-all player, and nobody remembers that."[15]

IN THE MEANTIME, Ken's accomplishments have been recognized by other sports institutions. In 1992, he was inducted into the Missouri Sports Hall of Fame. His high school athletic career was recognized when he joined the Webb City (Missouri) R-7 School District Hall of Fame in 2000. Eleven years later, he and his brothers Cloyd and Clete were added to the Joplin Sports Authority Hall of Fame. He was inducted into the St. Louis Sports Hall of Fame in 2012.

A weekend-long event celebrating the twentieth anniversary of the 1964 St. Louis Cardinals culminated in the retirement of Boyer's No. 14 on May 20, 1984. It became only the fifth number retired by the club, joining Dizzy Dean (17) and former teammates Stan Musial (6), Lou Brock (20), and Bob Gibson (45). On what would have been their father's fifty-third birthday, Suzie, David, Dan, and Jane accepted a pullover jersey with his name and number from Cardinals general manager Joe McDonald in a ceremony at Busch Stadium II. Broadcaster Jack Buck gave a tribute and highlights from Ken's career were shown on the scoreboard video screen. The jersey was later framed and given to Ken's friend Charlie Gitto, who displayed it on the wall of his Italian restaurant in downtown St. Louis.[16]

Boyer's contributions to St. Louis baseball history are acknowledged at present-day Busch Stadium III. A sidewalk plaque commemorates his grand slam in the 1964 World Series and his image and retired number are displayed along with other Cardinals on the left-field mural. Besides the retirement of his No. 14, the most special posthumous honor to date is Ken's induction into the Cardinals Hall of Fame in 2014. He was among the inaugural class that included former teammates Stan Musial, Bob Gibson, and Lou Brock, as well as the team's other Baseball Hall of Famers and those with retired numbers. "We felt strongly that those who had been inducted into Cooperstown and who already had their number retired by the Cardinals should be part of the Cardinals Hall of Fame on day one," explained Cardinals president Bill DeWitt III. Boyer and twenty-one Cardinals greats were officially inducted during a ceremony prior to the team's home opener on April 7. Plaques were displayed in the new 8,000 square foot Hall of Fame and Museum in Ballpark Village adjacent to Busch Stadium III.[17]

Boyer still holds a prominent place in team history. He is the sixth most valuable player with a Wins Above Replacement (WAR) rating of 58 and ranks in the top 10 in most career offensive categories. He is still considered their best third baseman ever. His position as the leading right-handed home run hitter and second on the all-time list, however, were eclipsed when Albert Pujols homered off Carlos Zambrano of the Chicago Cubs on April 28, 2007. As of 2015, his third-place standing in homers appears secure for the foreseeable future.[18]

AN EXCEPTIONAL BALLPLAYER

NOT MANY PEOPLE realize their childhood dreams; Ken Boyer was one of the lucky ones. "Ever since I was six years old," he said, "all I wanted to do was play ball for the Cardinals." He spent eleven of his fifteen major-league seasons with the birds-on-the-bat proudly across his chest. He was a credit to the storied franchise for his reliable production at the plate and solid defense at third base. His place in team history is such that every other St. Louis player at the position is compared against him.

Fans remember Boyer for the grand slam in Game 4 of the 1964 World Series that reversed the Cardinals' fortunes and contributed to a World championship for the first time in St. Louis since 1946. They think of his Most Valuable Player Award that season. What teammates remember about him is his leadership. He led not by force of will but by example and a firm, understanding demeanor. Teammates were treated with respect based on their character and not their skin color. He provided guidance and stability for a team with promising young players like Curt Flood, Julian Javier, and Tim McCarver, and future Hall of Famers Bob Gibson, Lou Brock, and Steve Carlton, who would win two more National League pennants and a World Series title after his departure. Asked how he wanted to be thought of, he said simply, "I just want it to be remembered that I was always fair."[19]

Regardless whether he is ever enshrined at Cooperstown, his memory endures with his family, friends, and teammates. His character and accomplishments are remembered by his fans. Ken Boyer will forever be The Captain.

Statistics

Minor League Statistics (Pitching)

Year	Team (Class)	G	CG	IP	ER	H	BB	SO	HB	BK	W	L	ERA
1949	Lebanon (D)	12	4	71	27	57	34	32	1	1	5	1	3.42
1950	Hamilton (D)	21	8	121	59	117	71	43	15	1	6	8	4.39
MiLB Career		G	CG	IP	ER	H	BB	SO	HB	BK	W	L	ERA
2 Years		33	12	192	86	174	105	75	16	2	11	9	4.03

Minor League Statistics (Batting)

Year	Team (Class)	G	AB	R	H	2B	3B	HR	RBI	SB	BB	SO	BA
1949	Lebanon (D)	16	33	10	15	1	1	3	9	—	4	8	.455
1950	Hamilton (D)	80	240	41	82	17	6	9	61	6	20	32	.342
1951	Omaha (A)	151	565	87	173	28	7	14	90	11	41	59	.306
1952	Military Service												
1953	Military Service												
1954	Houston (AA)	159	634	116	202	42	7	21	116	29	63	82	.319
MiLB Career		G	AB	R	H	2B	3B	HR	RBI	SB	BB	SO	BA
4 Years		406	1472	254	472	88	21	47	276	—	128	181	.321

Major League Statistics

Year	Team	G	AB	R	H	2B	3B	HR	RBI	SB	BB	SO	BA
1955	Cardinals	147	530	78	140	27	2	18	62	22	37	67	.264
1956	Cardinals	150	595	91	182	30	2	26	98	8	38	65	.306
1957	Cardinals	142	544	79	144	18	3	19	62	12	44	77	.265
1958	Cardinals	150	570	101	175	21	9	23	90	11	49	53	.307
1959	Cardinals	149	563	86	174	18	5	28	94	12	67	77	.309
1960	Cardinals	151	552	95	168	26	10	32	97	8	56	77	.304
1961	Cardinals	153	589	109	194	26	11	24	95	6	68	91	.329
1962	Cardinals	160	611	92	178	27	5	24	98	12	75	104	.291
1963	Cardinals	159	617	86	176	28	2	24	111	1	70	90	.285
1964	Cardinals	162	628	100	185	30	10	24	119	3	70	85	.295
1965	Cardinals	144	535	71	139	18	2	13	75	2	57	73	.260
1966	Mets	136	496	62	132	28	2	14	61	4	30	64	.266
1967	Mets	56	166	17	39	7	2	3	13	2	26	22	.235
	White Sox	57	180	17	47	5	1	4	21	0	7	25	.261
1968	White Sox	10	24	0	3	0	0	0	0	0	1	6	.125
	Dodgers	83	221	20	60	7	2	6	41	2	16	34	.271
1969	Dodgers	25	34	0	7	2	0	0	4	0	2	7	.206
MLB Career		G	AB	R	H	2B	3B	HR	RBI	SB	BB	SO	BA
15 Years		2034	7455	1104	2143	318	68	282	1141	105	713	1017	.287

All-Star Game Statistics

Year	Team	G	AB	R	H	2B	3B	HR	RBI	SB	BB	SO	BA
1956	NL	1	5	1	3	0	0	0	1	0	0	0	.600
1959	NL	1	1	1	1	0	0	0	0	0	0	0	1.000
	NL	1	2	0	0	0	0	0	0	0	1	0	.000
1960	NL	1	0	0	0	0	0	0	0	0	1	0	.000
	NL	1	1	1	1	0	0	1	2	0	0	0	1.000
1961	NL	1	2	0	0	0	0	0	0	0	1	2	.000
	NL	Reserve—Did not play											
1962	NL	1	2	0	0	0	0	0	0	0	0	1	.000
	NL	1	3	0	1	0	0	0	0	0	0	0	.200
1963	NL	1	3	0	0	0	0	0	0	0	0	0	.000
1964	NL	1	4	1	2	0	0	1	1	0	0	1	.500
All-Star Career		G	AB	R	H	2B	3B	HR	RBI	SB	BB	SO	BA
7 Years		10	23	4	8	0	0	2	4	0	3	4	.348

Acknowledgements

A book is a labor of love, but it's also a lot of labor. Thankfully, a baseball project, particularly a biography on a respected player like Ken Boyer, receives a lot of interest and encouragement from those who want to learn more about him. I'd like to acknowledge and thank everyone who has contributed in some way to this book.

The Boyer family has been gracious and supportive throughout its development. Ken's former wife Kathleen Boyer and children Suzie (Boyer) Hartwig, Dan Boyer, and Jane Boyer agreed to be interviewed, sharing personal memories that have added greatly to my understanding of him. Dan arranged for a discounted rate at the Renaissance Hotel Marriott in downtown St. Louis during my visits and Jane answered my emails and Facebook questions and helped track down various bits of family information. Thank you, Jane, for the wonderful present for my 44th birthday: a Mitchell & Ness reproduction Ken Boyer Cardinals jersey. I'll always treasure it.

Cloyd Boyer, Ken's oldest brother, spent a day driving with me around Alba and Jasper County, Missouri, pointing out significant places in his family's history. (By the way, if you ever drive through the small community of Purcell, be sure to watch the abrupt speed-limit change. It's not every day one is pulled over with a former big-league pitcher and pitching coach riding shotgun.) Mr. Cloyd also arranged for me to talk with his oldest sister, Juanita (Boyer) Woodshire, and his younger sister Pansy (Boyer) Schell. Another sister, Delores (Boyer) Webb, was kind enough to send me a copy of the family history she wrote.

During my research, Denise Griva contacted me and said her family was Ken's biggest fans. It wasn't until I met her and her family—father Darwin Griva, sister Debra (Griva) Shults, and niece Ashley Shults—that I fully appreciated how much they really were. The basement of her parent's home in Murfreesboro, Tennessee, held an impressive collection of Boyer memorabilia. The paneled walls were covered with personal photographs of Ken and various Griva family members as well as signed baseballs and bats and game-worn jerseys, caps, and spikes he had given them. Denise shared with me the scrapbooks her late mother, Arlene Griva, had compiled of newspaper and magazine clippings about Ken's career. These scrapbooks were invaluable in my research and included articles I never found anywhere else.

Thank you to everyone who agreed to be interviewed. Your memories of Ken made this book much more personal and insightful: Cloyd Boyer, Dan Boyer, Kathleen Boyer, Charlie Gitto, Darwin Griva, Dick Groat, Solly Hemus, Keith Hernandez, Al Hrabosky, Rick Hummel, Tommy John, Lee Landers, Hal Lanier, Tim McCarver, Robert Moscrey, Pansy (Boyer) Schell, Margaret Schmidt, Red Schoendienst, Bill Virdon, Delores (Boyer) Webb, and Juanita (Boyer) Woodshire. I would like to thank Tim McCarver in particular for his thoughtful memories of Ken and the Cardinals teams of the 1960s.

Thank you to those who supported my Kickstarter fundraiser and helped me with research and travel expenses. (Please see the list of contributors on page 377.) These funds enabled me to make a trip to St. Louis when it would have been difficult financially for me to do so. I'm also appreciative for the support of 570 (and growing) followers on my Facebook page (www.facebook.com/kenboyerbook) who've waited patiently for this book to be published.

The Society for American Baseball Research (SABR) provides its members with free access to *The Sporting News* digitized collection through Paper of Record, a tremendous resource for any baseball researcher. Thank you to fellow members Marty Friedrich, Maxwell Kates, Stephen Milman, Bill Nowlin, and Mark Aubrey for their assistance. Mark Armour, the director of SABR's Baseball Biography project, kindly sent me page scans from his personal copy of Bob Howsam's self-published, hard-to-find autobiography pertaining to Boyer's trade from the Cardinals to the Mets. Thomas Zocco scanned and emailed articles from his personal collection of *The Sporting News* when digital copies were missing. The late Ray Nemec sent me copies of Boyer's minor-league statistics. Thank you, Ray, for inspiring me to compile statistics for an obscure minor-league called the Kitty League, as you did for many other leagues. Your contributions to historical baseball research will be missed by all baseball researchers.

The Retrosheet.org website is an essential resource for any baseball researcher or writer. The daily box scores, team and player game logs, and personal batting and fielding data were indispensable tools for recreating Ken's major-league career. I'm grateful for the efforts of David W. Smith, Tom Ruane, and every volunteer who has contributed to Retrosheet since the project's inception in 1989. Similar praise to Sean Forman for his website Baseball-Reference.com, another valuable online research tool.

My baseball friend Dave Chase, general manager of the Sussex County Miners in the independent Can-Am League, tracked down an elusive box score for a 1957 Cardinals exhibition game in Memphis, Tennessee. He also suggested the title for this book.

Researchers Gord Brown, John Davis, and Art Spanjer provided invaluable research in the Hamilton, Omaha, and Houston newspapers, respectively. Their detective work enabled me to chronicle Boyer's formative years in the minor-leagues in 1950, 1951, and 1954. Bill Deane researched and made copies for me from Boyer's file at the National Baseball Hall of Fame Library in Cooperstown.

Bob Broeg, Neal Russo, Ed Wilks, and Rick Hummel of the *Post-Dispatch* and Bob Burnes and Jack Herman of the *Globe-Democrat*, were the stalwart writers who covered the Cardinals during Ken's playing and managerial careers. Thank you to each one for bringing the game to the fans.

Rob Rains, St. Louis sportswriter and prolific author of Cardinals history and biography, arranged interviews for me with Hall of Famers Rick Hummel and Red Schoendienst. Others who helped me obtain interviews include Kevin Sornatale with SportsNet New York and Larry Mago with Fox Sports Midwest.

John Vuch, Director of Baseball Administration for the St. Louis Cardinals, and Paula Homan, manager of the Cardinals Hall of Fame and Museum, were helpful in my inquiry about Ken's contract information with the team.

Thank you to helpful staff members at the main branch of the St. Louis Public Library, the St. Louis Mercantile Library at the University of Missouri-St. Louis, the Carthage (Missouri) Public Library, and the Waterfield Library at Murray State University. A few deserve special recognition: Charles Brown of the St. Louis Mercantile Library assisted me with newspaper clippings and photographic files in the library's collections, including files from the defunct *St. Louis Globe-Democrat*. Jennifer Stepp with the *St. Louis Post-Dispatch* provided me a list of articles mentioning Boyer that would have been more difficult to track down otherwise. Cheryl Smith, Reference Librarian at the Joplin Public Library in Joplin, Missouri, answered an email query seeking articles in the *Joplin Globe* for local coverage of Boyer's death and funeral. Jenifer Stepp, Licensing Administrator for the *Stars and Stripes* newspaper in Washington, D.C., gave permission to reproduce the photograph of Boyer playing ball in the Army.

Photographs are a pleasing addition to any book, especially those that give rare glimpses at the subject's life. Thank you to each person and institution for allowing me to use them in this book: the Boyer family; Cloyd Boyer; the Griva family; John Horne with the National Baseball Hall of Fame Library, Cooperstown, New York; the John Rogers Archive; the Houston (Texas) Municipal Research Center Photo Archives; the St. Louis Mercantile Library at the University of Missouri-St. Louis; the *Lebanon* (Pennsylvania) *Daily News*; the *Hamilton* (Ontario) *Spectator*; the Arkansas Travelers baseball club; the Tulsa Drillers baseball club; the Topps Company, Inc.; John Hall; Duane Kraettli; Kevin Noland; Nate Rider; and Dennis Smith, son of the late Hal Smith.

For any author, proofreaders and editors are essential contributors to the overall quality of their book. I'd like to thank the following individuals for taking time to read portions or the entire book and offering reassurances and suggestions for improvement: John Hall, Russ Lake, Mel Marmer, and Bill McCurdy. Russ, a fellow SABR member and Cardinals fan, has given his time and proofing skills for many baseball projects published by SABR. I'm grateful for his help with this one.

Finally, I want to thank my wife Cindy and my children, Braden and Brianna, for their love and support. They endure my obsession with time-consuming research and book projects; my children have never known a moment in their lives when I wasn't working on one. Cindy was especially helpful with the index. This book is dedicated to my father, Jerry McCann, with whom I share a passion for the St. Louis Cardinals. I wrote it for him because Ken Boyer was his favorite player. I hope you enjoy it, Dad!

Kickstarter Supporters

The following individuals contributed to the book's Kickstarter fundraiser
July–August 2013

Mark Aubrey	Suzie Hartwig
Greg and Karla Blackwell	John L. Hohlt
Donald Blau	Mark James
Brook Boyer	Kenneth Keller
Dan Boyer	Shannon Kelly
Jake Boyer	Mimi and Wes Kitashima
Jane Boyer	Mike Loechel
Johnny Brown	Mick McFadyen
Denny Campbell	Daniel McGregor
Cheryl Cantwell	Michael Miller
Chris Cary	Jack Morris
Christine Coleman	Sean Norton
Melissa Cook	Tim Perry
Ray DeRousse	Robert V. Pues
Joel Dinda	Scott Riley
Doug and Laurie Fredrick	Steve Schuerman
Wade Forrester	Debra Shults
Lendell Fullerton	Daniel Solzman
Joshua Gordon	Luci Valbuena
Geoff Hartwig	Mary Wood

Notes

Prologue

1. Ken Boyer to Mike Pisarkiewicz, undated letter, courtesy of Mike Pisarkiewicz and Jane Boyer. Based on the letter's content, it was written while Boyer was a minor-league manager for the St. Louis Cardinals in the early to mid 1970s.

Chapter 1: A Boy Who Always Delights in Sports

1. Boyer's parental grandparents, Lewis Winfield Boyer and Pansy (Powell) Boyer, lived at 143 South Leonard Street in Liberty. 1930 U.S. Census, Clay County, Missouri. Lewis W. Boyer Death Certificate, Missouri Death Certificates, Missouri Digital Heritage website, http://www.sos.mo.gov/images/archives/deathcerts/1945/1945_00013146.PDF. Boyer was delivered by Dr. Burton Maltby. Kenton Boyer Uniform Player's Contract for the Ban Johnson League, May 5, 1949. Boyer HOF file. The contract states the physician at Boyer's birth as "Dr. Maltby." Dr. Burton Maltby resided in Liberty, Missouri, at this time, according to the 1930 U.S. Census for Clay County, Missouri.

2. Schlett and Harris Families website owned by Christine Schlett Harris of Springfield, Missouri. http://schlett-harris.com/aqwg203.htm. Scotland County 1876 Plat Map, accessed January 4, 2013. http://www.rootsweb.ancestry.com/~moscotla/1876plat.html) Andrew Boyer died in Scotland County on November 27, 1889.

3. 1910 U.S. Census, Jasper County, Missouri. *The Jasper* (MO) *News*, December 4, 1919.

4. Marliene Erwin, ed., *Alba-Neck City-Purcell-Tri-City History, 1984*. Vol. 2 (Shawnee Mission, Kansas: Kes-Print, 1984), 207. Missouri Marriage Records, 1805-2002 <www.ancestry.com>

5. *Alba-Neck City-Purcell-Tri-City History* (Vol. 2), 207. Delores Boyer Webb, *Memories of My Life* (Self-published, no date), 4. Delores (Boyer) Webb believes Lila died from this disease.

6. Cloyd Boyer interview, January 5, 2013. 1930 U.S. Census, Clay County, Missouri. John Hall, "The KOM Flash Report for Week of March 22, 2015." David Lipman, *Ken Boyer* (New York: G.O. Putnam's Sons, 1967), 12–14. Roger Birtwell, "Meet the Boyers, No. 1 Baseball Family," *The Sporting News*, November 14, 1964, 6. (Note: *The Sporting News* hereafter referred to as *TSN*)

7. Webb, *Memories of My Life*, 4. Vern Boyer household, 1940 Census, Jasper County, Missouri. Cloyd Boyer interview. Webb, Memories: 1

8. Kathleen Boyer interview, August 30, 2013. Neal Russo, "Baseball in Blood of the Boyer Clan," *St. Louis Post-Dispatch*, May 24, 1978. St. Louis Mercantile Library Association Collections. Webb, *Memories*, 2.

9. Lipman, *Boyer*, 25. Myron Cope, "Ken Boyer: New Leader of the Cardinals," *Sport*, August 1961, 53.

10. Myron Cope, "Ken Boyer: New Leader of the Cardinals," *Sport*, August 1961, 53.

11. Mike Eisenbath, "In Search of...Cards' Kenny Boyer, A Heroic, Yet Private Man, Remains a Mystery," *St. Louis Post-Dispatch*, October 16, 1994. Cloyd Boyer interview, July 2011.

12. "Ken Boyer: New Leader of the Cardinals," *Sport*, August 1961, Mike Eisenbath, "In Search of...Cards' Kenny Boyer, A Heroic, Yet Private Man, Remains a Mystery," *St. Louis Post-Dispatch*, October 16, 1994.

13. Lipman, *Boyer*, 26, 32–33. *Joplin Globe*, August 14, 1945, 7. Neal Russo, "Wolves Howl, But Boyer Likes St. Louis," *St. Louis Post-Dispatch*, no date, Boyer HOF file.

14. Lipman, *Boyer*, 14–15.

15. *Alba-Neck City etc.* (Vol. 2), 88. John Hall, *The KOM League Remembered* (Charleston, SC: Arcadia Publishing, 2004), 32. Frank Young, "Ken Wore Overalls, Swung Big Bat in 2nd Grade, Prof Recalls," *TSN*, Nov. 14, 1964.

16. Undated article courtesy of Cloyd Boyer. Lipman, *Boyer*, 18–20.

17. Pansy (Boyer) Schell interview, January 9, 2013. Pansy told the author that Juanita remembered the date the family moved to Alba because it was on her birthday, November 3, 1940.

18. Four more children were born after the family's move to Alba: Ronald Dean in 1944; Leonard Eugene, 1946; Barbara Joan, 1948; and Marcella "Marcy" Kay, 1952. *Alba—Neck City—Purcell—Tri-City History*. (Vol. 2), 117.

19. Cloyd Boyer interview, July 2011. Webb, *Memories*, 4. Lipman, *Boyer*, 24.

20. Neal Russo, "Baseball in Blood of the Boyer Clan," *St. Louis Post-Dispatch*, May 24, 1978, St. Louis Mercantile Library Association Collection. Lipman, *Boyer*, 29. Tom Siler, "Baseball Youngsters are Overcoached, Says Boyer," *Chillicothe* (MO) *Constitution-Tribune*, March 28, 1964, 2. Robert L. Burnes, "Ken Boyer (1931–1982) Greatest Third Baseman in Cardinal History," *St. Louis Globe-Democrat*, September 8, 1982. Lipman, *Boyer*, 29.

21. The other grocery store owned by Buford Cooper was in Carterville, eleven miles south of Alba. Vern Boyer was an assistant coach on the Aces.

22. *Alba—Neck City—Purcell—Tri-City History*. (Vol. 2), 207. Cloyd Boyer interview, January 5, 2013. Lipman, *Boyer*, 30

23. John Hall email to the author, May 21, 2015. The following players from the 1940–1948 Cardinal Junior League were signed to pro contracts: Ted Atkinson, George Bogatie, Cloyd Boyer, Kenton Boyer, Wayne Boyer, Ray Coss, Royden Coss, Ben Craig, Joe Dean "Red" Crowder, Jack Dorrell, Don Fitzgerald, George Garrison, George Hosp, Willard "Billy" Johnson, Mickey Mantle, Raymond Dale Moore, George New, Wylie Pitts, and Max Rose.

24. *Joplin Globe*, April 5, 1946
25. *Joplin Globe*, June 5, 11, 17, 1941; July 29, 1942. Lipman, *Boyer*, 30-31.
26. "Card Junior League Adds Legion Team," *Joplin Globe*, January 9, 1948.
27. Lipman, *Boyer*, 9–11. Lipman attributes this game to the 1941 season, but Pittsburg did not join the Cardinal Junior League until 1942. Mike Eisenbath, "In Search of...Cards' Kenny Boyer, A Heroic, Yet Private Man, Remains a Mystery," *St. Louis Post-Dispatch*, October 16, 1994.
28. Lipman, *Boyer*, 38.
29. "Major Scouts Take District Athletes," *Joplin Globe*, March 11, 1945.
30. John Crittenden, "Boyer Boys Big in Baseball, Alba," *Miami* (FL) *News*, July 21, 1963. Lipman, *Boyer*, 38–40.
31. "Alba Team Winner Over Columbus, 9-4," *Joplin Globe*, June 12, 1945. *Ibid*, June 27, 1945; July 3, 8, 15, 1945.
32. *Joplin Globe*, July 31, August 14, 16, 21, 24, 1945. The Sunny Jims team was sponsored by Sunny Jim Walters, a Joplin candy maker, and played its home games over various seasons in Joplin and Carl Junction.
33. Lew Freedman, *The Boyer Brothers of Baseball* (Jefferson, NC: McFarland & Company, Inc., 2015), 30.
34. *Joplin Globe*, May 12, 1946. During the season, Kenton turned 16 on May 20 and Wayne 17 on July 13. *Ibid*, May 14, 21, 26, 30; June 5, 8, 11, 16, 18; July 2, 7, 19, 30; Aug 13, 1946. Lipman, *Boyer*, 35.
35. Mike Eisenbath, "In Search Of...Cards' Kenny Boyer, A Heroic, Yet Private Man, Remains A Mystery," *St. Louis Post-Dispatch*, October 16, 1994. Freedman, *Boyer Brothers*, 30. Lipman, *Boyer*, 33.
36. "Card Junior Teams Open Season Before 1,426 Paying Fans," *Joplin Globe*, May 20, 1947, 8. *Ibid*, July 30, 1947, August 3, 1947. Though he didn't start the game, Mickey Mantle had a single in two at-bats for Baxter Springs. Mantle played in only four games in 1947 and batted .169. He made his debut on July 20 against the Sunny Jims of Carl Junction. He spent much of the season in the hospital suffering from a leg infection that almost cost him his leg. It's not known how Ken Boyer did in the All-Star Game as no complete box score could be found. John Hall, *Mickey Mantle: Before the Glory* (Leawood, KS: Leathers Publishing, 2005), 71.
37. *Joplin Globe*, August 22, September 5, 12, 28, 1947. Mickey Mantle was not among the leading hitters in the 1947 Cardinal Junior League season.
38. John Hall email to the author, May 20, 2015. *Joplin Globe*, May 21; June 25, 27, 30; September 5; October 2, 1948. *Neosho* (MO) *Daily Democrat*, September 1, 1948. The age limit for the Ban Johnson League was twenty-one years old. "Whiz Kids to Compete in Ban Johnson League," *Joplin Globe*, March 27, 1949.
39. *The 1949 Albamo Yearbook*. <www.jaspercountyschools.org/id21.htm> Accessed January 5 and September 16, 2013. Zena (Allison) Williams email to the author, May 13, 2009. Neal Russo, "Wolves Howl, But Boyer Likes St. Louis." Undated *St. Louis Post-Dispatch*. Boyer HOF file. Lipman, *Boyer*, 25. The two-story Alba High School building was built in 1907 and is still standing in 2015.
40. Mike Eisenbath, "In Search Of...Cards' Kenny Boyer, A Heroic, Yet Private Man, Remains A Mystery," *St. Louis Post-Dispatch*, October 16, 1994.
41. Walter Bingham, "Dick Groat and His Hitting Machine," *Sports Illustrated*, July 22, 1963. Zena (Allison) Williams email to the author, May 13, 2009. Debby Woodlin, "Boyer Boys Were in a League of Their Own." *Joplin Globe*, June 11, 2007.

42. Lipman, *Boyer*, 22–23.

43. *1949 Albamo Yearbook.*

44. "Alba the Winner Over Webb City, 48 to 35, For 14th Win In Row," *Joplin Globe*, February 16, 1949. *Ibid*, February 20, 1949. "Warriors and Alba Clash Monday Night," *Ibid*, February 20, 1949. *Albamo Yearbook, 1949.* Wendell Redden, "Boyer: Class Athlete, Individual," *Joplin Globe*, September 8, 1982, 10A. The consecutive win streak was broken after a two-point loss to Carthage, 39-37. *1949 Albamo Yearbook.* The games used to calculate his average points per game were taken from the *Joplin Globe*: December 4, 11, 16, 17, 18, 19, 1948; January 5, 8, 19, 29; February 15, 16, 19, 22, 24, 26, 27; March 3, 4, 1949.

45. Cloyd Boyer interview, July 2011. Russ Kaminsky coached high school basketball for thirty-three years at Joplin High School and Parkwood High School (Joplin). His 591-222 record ranks him as one of the winningest coaches in high school basketball in the country. Kaminsky was inducted into the Missouri Sports Hall of Fame in 1998.

46. *Ibid.*

47. *The 1949 Albamo Yearbook.* <www.jaspercountyschools.org/id21.htm> Accessed January 5 and September 16, 2013. Lipman, *Boyer*, 41. Freedman, *Boyer Brothers*, 29. Greenfield was a school in Springfield, Missouri.

48. Lipman, *Boyer*, 41. Ralph Ray, "Boyer Rides Top Perch as Birds Build," *TSN*, May 11, 1960, 4. Neal Russo, "Wolves Howl, But Boyer Likes St. Louis." Undated *St. Louis Post-Dispatch*, Boyer HOF file. Klein, *Great Infielders of the Major Leagues* (New York: Random House, 1972), 106.

49. Red Smith, "Cards Happy They Got Boyer," *New York Herald Tribune* (reprinted in *Lawrence* [KS] *Daily Journal-World*, March 14, 1959, D-4.

50. *Burlington* (IA) *Hawk Eye Gazette*, April 22, 1954. "Retiring Runt Marr Says...' Scouts Nothing But Reporters Under Current Draft System," *Joplin Globe*, September 27, 1972, B1. "Players Rarely Remember First Big League Contract," *Annapolis* (MD) *Capital*, February 18, 1981, 22. Freedman, *Boyer Brothers*, 46. Lee Gray, "'Runt' Marr: 'Scout Is First Guy They Forget,'" *Nevada* (MO) *Daily Mail*, March 25, 1981.

51. Hall, *Mantle*, 134. Ray, "Boyer Rides Top Perch," *TSN*, May 11, 1960, 4.

52. Walter L. Johns, "Rookie Boyer Gets Chance As Regular On First Try," (Central Press story) *Hagerstown* (MD) *Morning Herald*, April 2, 1955, 14.

53. "St. Louis Cards Sign Kenton Boyer," *Joplin Globe*, May 28, 1949. "Cards Sign, Farm Youthful Pitcher," *Pacific Stars and Stripes*, June 1, 1949, 3. Kenton Lloyd Boyer Control Card, courtesy of John Vuch, Director of Baseball Administration for the St. Louis Cardinals. Neal Russo, "Wolves Howl, But Boyer Likes St. Louis," *St. Louis Post-Dispatch*, no date, Boyer HOF file. Jack Zanger claimed in his book *Ken Boyer: Guardian of the Hot Corner* that the workout at Sportsman's Park lasted three days. David Lipman in *Ken Boyer* doesn't state its duration. Jack Zanger, *Ken Boyer: Guardian of the Hot Corner* (New York: Rutledge Books, 1965), 36.

54. Kenton Lloyd Boyer Control Card, courtesy of John Vuch, Director of Baseball Administration for the St. Louis Cardinals. John Devaney, *The Greatest Cardinals of Them All* (New York: G.P. Putnam's Sons, 1968), 176–177. Lipman, *Boyer*, 45–46. Vern Boyer later recalled negotiations with the Cardinals for the bonus: "In Kenton's case, we thought he was good enough to demand a fair bonus, but we decided he'd do better to take the $6,000 and no more so he could be sent to the minors to get experience." Untitled clipping by Jack Rice, *St. Louis Post-Dispatch*, May 19, 1962, Ken Boyer file, St. Louis Mercantile Library Collection.

55. Boyer's first vehicle, Jane Boyer to the author, April 28, 2015. As the "bird dog" who first told the Cardinals about Kenton, Buford Cooper received $250 for his recommendation. Boyer Control Card, St. Louis Cardinals.

56. Mickey Mantle played in that game and two (possibly three) more games with Baxter Springs before reporting to the New York Yankees minor-league camp in Branson, Missouri. Sportswriters loved writing about he and Boyer's amateur matchups, though Ken downplayed their relationship at the time. "He was a shortstop and I was a shortstop," he told Red Smith in 1959, "and we played against each other but didn't pal around or anything." Hall, *Mantle*, 123. Red Smith, "Cards Happy They Got Boyer," *New York Herald Tribune* (reprinted in *Lawrence* [KS] *Daily Journal-World*), March 14, 1959, D-4.

57. "Alba Defeats Parsons in League Game, 16-15," *Joplin Globe*, June 1, 1949, 6. Mickey Mantle was hitless for the Whiz Kids in the May 29 game, but was told afterward that the New York Yankees would sign him to a contract. Hall, *Mantle*, 123. John Hall email to the author, May 20, 2015. Boyer's successor as shortstop of the Alba Aces was Bill Lewis. Fifteen years later, Lewis made his own appearance with the Cardinals—albeit just for a pre-game workout—when he was in St. Louis to perform in the play "Damn Yankees" at the Muny Opera. *TSN*, August 8, 1964, 10.

58. Lipman, *Boyer*, 35, 44–45. Ray, "Boyer Rides Top Perch," *TSN*, May 11, 1960, 4. Porter Wittich, "Globe Trotter," *Joplin Globe*, June 1, 1949, 6.

Chapter 2: A Cardinal Takes Flight

1. Lipman, *Boyer*, 46–48.

2. Kenton Lloyd Boyer Control Card, St. Louis Cardinals. To make room on the Lebanon roster, the Cardinals released right-handed pitcher Bob Wrightstone, who had a 1-5 record in six decisions. He was the son of former major-leaguer Russ Wrightstone. *Lebanon* (PA) *Daily News*, July 25, 1949.

3. Prior to Boyer's arrival, Contini was fined $50 by North Atlantic League president Ernest C. Landgraf for reportedly challenging two umpires in their dressing room after a rain-shortened game called against Lebanon.

4. *Lebanon Daily News*, April 8, 1960. Locally, the team was called the Lebanon College Hill Chix. Portions of Cole E. Grimes Stadium were still standing as of 2012. The Chix clubhouse building on the third-base line is now the Speedway Mart & Car Wash in Fredericksburg, and the grandstand still stands. <www.digitalballparks.com/NorthAtl/Lebanon.html> Accessed January 14, 2013.

5. *Lebanon Daily News*, July 27, 1949. Lipman, *Boyer*, 50.

6. *Lebanon Daily News*, August 1, 1949.

7. *Lebanon Daily News*, August 6, 1949.

8. *Lebanon Daily News*, August 8, 1949. The hit took place in the first game of a doubleheader at Cole E. Grimes Stadium.

9. *Lebanon Daily News*, August 13, 1949.

10. *Lebanon Daily News*, August 16, 17, 18, 22, 1949.

11. *Lebanon Daily News*, August 25, 1949.

12. *Lebanon Daily News*, September 6, 1949.

13. *Lebanon Daily News*, September 8, 1949.

14. *Lebanon Daily News*, September 9, 1949.

15. *Lebanon Daily News*, September 10, 12, 1949.

16. Lipman, *Boyer*, 51.

17. *Lebanon Daily News*, April 8, 1960.

18. Lipman, *Boyer*, 52–53. Kathleen Boyer interview, August 27, 2013.

19. Kathleen Boyer interview, August 27, 2013. Lucinda Herron, "Mrs. Ken Boyer: She Views Pennant Race from Home Plate," *St. Louis Globe-Democrat*, September 30, 1964. Neal Russo, "Boyer Was Right Number for Operator," undated *St. Louis Post-Dispatch* clipping, Griva Scrapbook Collection. Neal Russo, "Ken Boyer—Mr. All-Star at Hot Corner," *TSN*, September 26, 1964, 4.

20. "400 Card Farm Hirelings to Condition at Albany, Ga.," *TSN*, January 30, 1952, 27. "Set Up Cardinals School Lessons," *Ibid*, February 1, 1950, 26. "400 to Drill on Seven Fields at Card Farm Base," *Ibid*, February 20, 1952, 7. "Card Farmhands at Albany," *Ibid*, March 22, 1950, 30. "500 Farmhands Trying Out for 15 Card Affiliates," *Ibid*, April 5, 1950, 18. Mickelson, *Out of the Park*, 60. *Lebanon Daily News*, March 3, 1950.

21. Lipman, *Boyer*, 50

22. *Lebanon Daily News*, April 14, 1950. Kenton Lloyd Boyer Control Card. James Enright, "Players Hail Himsl's Return to Cubs," *TSN*, May 7, 1961, 8. Jerry Holtzman, "Himsl's 2-Week Cub Reign Ends; Craft Gets Baton," Ibid, May 3, 1961, 9.

23. *Hamilton* (Ont.) *Spectator*, May 1, 1950. Lipman, *Boyer*, 54, 55. *Hornell* (NY) *Evening Tribune*, May 6, 1950. 1950 Hamilton Cardinals Souvenir Program.

24. Steve Bitker, *The Original San Francisco Giants: The Giants of '58* (Champaign, IL: Sports Publishing Inc., 2001), 156.

25. *Hamilton Spectator*, May 27, 1950. "Gast Tagged with First Loss as Cards Score 2nd Straight Over Oilers, 11-7," *Olean* (NY) *Hearld*, May 12, 1950, 7. Johnny Nelson Jr., "Sports Corner," *Bradford* (PA) *Era*, May 19, 1950, 21.

26. "Cardinals Seek Stick Strength," *Hamilton Spectator*, June 6, 1950.

27. Joe Guido, "Sam McCain's Sensational 9th Inning Catch Aids Phils to Top Cards, 5-3," *Bradford Era*, June 6, 1950, 12.

28. *Hamilton Spectator*, undated clipping (June 1950). "Younger Boyer Hitting Hurler," *Charleston* (WV) *Daily Mail*, July 4, 1950. "Boyer is Pitcher, But Reluctantly," *Harrisburg* (IL) *Daily Register*, July 7, 1950. This article concluded: "Manager Vedie Himsl still lists young Boyer ninth in his regular lineup, at four-day intervals—but reluctantly." *Ibid*.

29. "Miller Tames Clippers with Great 4-0 Effort; Barnhart Cracks Homer," *Hamilton Spectator*, June 20, 1950. The story of the stray dog and Barnhart's second chance was also reported by the Associated Press. "Puppy Gets Assist in Pony League Tilt," *Troy* (NY) *Times Record*, June 20, 1950, 19.

30. "Phillies Rally in 9th Fails, Cards Win, 8-5," *Bradford* (PA) *Era*, June 22, 1950. "Phillies Again Lose One-Run Decision, Cardinals Win, 4-3," *Ibid*, June 23, 1950. "Olean Maintains PONY Loop Lead," *Hornell Evening Tribune*, June 24, 1950.

31. The story has been repeated that an injury to the club's third baseman and the failure of his replacement to report to the team gave Boyer the chance to transition from pitcher to full-time hitter. The injured player was actually first baseman Dick Barnhart. This mistake has been repeated in practically every profile of Boyer, including Lipman, *Boyer*, 54–55. In *Guardian of the Hot Corner*, Jack Zanger recounted a conversation between Himsl and Boyer in which the manager wanted him to replace the third baseman, who had been let go. Third baseman Hank Greifzu was indeed released, but it was catcher and future St. Louis teammate Hal Smith—and not Boyer—who replaced him initially. Boyer didn't shift across the diamond to third until catcher Joe Ossala was hurt and Smith had to catch again. Zanger, *Guardian of the Hot Corner*, 58–59.

32. "Lutz Hits Grand Slam Homer as Phillies Win," *Bradford Era*, June 27, 1950. "Phillies Beat Hamilton, 18-14; Locals 2 Games From 3rd Spot," *Ibid*, June 28, 1950. "Oilers Win 1,

Lose 2 Games Over Weekend; Hornell Narrows PONY Lead to 2 ½ Games," *Olean Times Herald*, July 3, 1950, 7.

33. "Hamilton Squad Expecting Help," *Hamilton Spectator*, July 5, 1950. "Dodgers-Cards Split Holiday Double Bill," *Hornell Evening Tribune*, July 5, 1950. The nine home-run barrage by both clubs broke the PONY League record of eight in one game set by London (Ontario) and Batavia in 1940 and Bradford (PA) and Hornell in 1948.

34. "Cardinals Top Reds in Tenth," *Hamilton Spectator*, July 17, 1950.

35. "Hornell Bats Boom in 16-6 Win," *Hamilton Spectator*, July 7, 1950. "Dodgers Slip Behind in Bow to Hamilton," *Hornell Evening Tribune*, July 8, 1950. "Three-Way Tie For 3rd Place PONY League," *Ibid*, July 12, 1950. *Ibid*, July 10, 1950. "PONY League," (Associated Press story) *Warren* (PA) *Times Mirror*, July 21, 1950. "Oilers Grab Two-Of-Three Weekend Games, But Lose Ground to Hornell," *Olean Times Herald*, July 29, 1950. "PONY Averages," *Ibid*.

36. "PONY League Averages," *Hornell Evening Tribune*, August 5, 1950. *Bradford Era*, August 7, 1950.

37. Dave Johnson, a native of Joplin, Missouri, was briefly Boyer's teammate with the Alba Aces in 1949 before both were signed by the St. Louis Cardinals. "Dave Johnson, Former J.H.S. Athlete Ace, Starring in Pro Ball," *Joplin Globe*, July 10, 1949, 16.

38. Bob Broeg, "Cards, Luke-Warm at Hot Sack, Boom Boyer as Best Ever," *TSN*, March 2, 1955, 9. Gord Brown's *Hamilton Spectator* research, email to the author. "Boyer Corks Two Homers in Rousing 12-0 Victory," *Hamilton Spectator*, August 31, 1950.

39. "Oilers Wipe Away McNamara," *Olean Times Herald*, September 8, 1950.

40. "Boyer's Wild Heave In Ninth Gives Oilers Deciding Play-Off Game, 3-1," *Hamilton Spectator*, September 12, 1950.

41. Boyer's teammate in Hamilton (and later in St. Louis), Hal Smith, recalled learning of the invasion when the team's bus stopped at a roadside café. Billy D. Higgins with Hal Smith, *The Barling Darling: Hal Smith in American Baseball* (Little Rock, AR: Butler Center Books, 2009), 42.

Chapter 3: Omaha and Overseas

1. "Card Kids Get Big Welcome at Albany," *TSN*, March 28, 1951, 17. *Salt Lake* (UT) *Tribune*, September 12, 1950. Ogden (UT) *Standard Examiner*, September 12, 1950.

2. *Omaha* (NE) *Evening World-Herald*, April 11, 1951. Robert Rausch player profile <baseball-reference.com/minors/player.cgi?id=rausch001rob> Joe Aliperto player profile <baseball-reference.com/minors/player.cgi?id=aliper001jos>

3. *Omaha Morning World-Herald*, April 10, 1951. *Omaha Evening World-Herald*, April 11, 1951.

4. Earl Weaver with Berry Stainback, *It's What You Learn After You Know It All That Counts: The Autobiography of Earl Weaver* (Garden City, NY: Doubleday & Company, Inc., 1982), 88.

5. *Omaha Evening World-Herald*, April 6, 1951

6. "Ken Boyer Remembered." Undated clipping from *Fowl Ball*, 19.

7. *Omaha Morning World-Herald*, April 24, 1951. *Omaha Sunday World-Herald*, April 29, 1951.

8. *Council Bluffs* (IA) *Nonpareil*, May 16-20, 1951. *Omaha Morning World-Herald*, May 21, 1951.

9. *Omaha Morning World-Herald*, May 23, 1951.

10. *Omaha Morning World-Herald*, May 24, 1951. *TSN*, June 6, 1951.

11. *Omaha Morning World-Herald*, May 26, 1951. *Council Bluffs Paralei*, May 29, 1951.

12. *Council Bluffs Nonpareil*, May 31, 1951. *Ibid*, June 4, 5, 7, 1951.

13. *Omaha Morning World-Herald*, June 10, 12, 16, 18, 1951. *Council Bluffs Nonpareil*, June 18, 1951.

14. *Omaha Morning World-Herald*, June 26, 1952. *Council Bluffs Nonpareil*, June 26, 1952.

15. Bruce Jacobs, "Hot Corner Hustler: Ken Boyer," *Baseball Stars of 1957* (New York: Lion Library Editions, 1957), 138. Barry Gottehrer, "The Million-Dolar Cardinal," 66. *Omaha Evening World-Herald*, August 18, 1951. *Omaha Morning World-Herald*, August 31, 1951. "Kissell has 49 Years of Card Memories." *Springfield (IL) State Journal-Register*, September 11, 1988.

16. *Omaha Morning World-Herald*, May 4, 8, 1951.

17. *Omaha Morning World-Herald*, June 28, 29; July 2, 1951. *Council Bluffs Nonpareil*, June 28, 29, 30, 1951. *Waterloo (IA) Daily Courier*, July 2, 1951.

18. *Omaha Morning World-Herald*, July 13, 1951

19. *Omaha Evening World-Herald*, July 26, 1951.

20. *Omaha Morning World-Herald*, July 23, 25, 1951. Boyer's bases-loaded triple contributed to Omaha's 15-0 victory over the Pueblo Dodgers on July 24. "Dickey's Corner" may refer to James Dickey, a left-handed hitter for Omaha who had four triples in 1949, presumably into the right-field corner of Municipal Stadium. Kevin Johnson to the author, February 4, 2013. James Shelton Dickey player page <www.baseball-reference.com/minors/player.cgi?id=dickey002jam> Accessed February 6, 2013.

21. *Omaha Evening World-Herald*, August 7, 8, 13, 1951.

22. *Omaha Evening World-Herald*, August 23, 25, 1951.

23. *Omaha Evening World-Herald*, July 26, 1951.

24. *Beatrice (NE) Daily Sun*, August 28, 1951. *Omaha Evening World-Herald*, September 1, 1951.

25. *Omaha Morning World-Herald*, August 31, 1951. *Ibid*, August 18, 1951. *Omaha Sunday World-Herald*, September 9, 1951.

26. *Omaha Morning World-Herald*, September 6, 1951. *Omaha Sunday World-Herald*, September 9, 1951.

27. *Omaha Evening World-Herald*, September 11, 1951. *Council Bluffs Nonpareil*, September 11, 1951.

28. *Omaha Evening World-Herald*, September 12, 1951.

29. *Omaha Evening World-Herald*, September 14, 1951. *Omaha Morning World-Herald*, September 15, 1951. *Omaha Sunday World-Herald*, September 16, 1951. *Omaha Morning World-Herald*, September 17, 1951.

30. "Kissell has 49 Years of Card Memories." *Springfield State Journal-Register*, September 11, 1988. *Omaha Morning World-Herald*, September 10, 11, 1951. *Council Bluffs Nonpareil*, September 9, 1951.

31. Clark Nealon, "Post Time," *Houston (TX) Post*, May 13, 1954. Jack Gallagher, "Boyer Boomed as Birds' New Golden Boy," *TSN*, January 19, 1955, 5. "Kissell Has 49 Years of Card Memories," *Springfield State Journal-Register*, September 11, 1988.

32. *Omaha Evening World-Herald*, February 1, 1952

33. *Omaha Morning World-Herald*, September 18, 1951. *Omaha Evening World-Herald*, October 6, 9, 1951. *TSN*, November 7, 1951, 6.

34. *Omaha Evening World-Herald*, October 9, 1951. Boyer had returned to Alba the first week of October, playing third base and brother Cloyd pitching for the Seneca Milnots in a game against the Tri-State Miners on October 7. *Joplin Globe*, October 7, 1951.

35. *Omaha Evening World-Herald*, April 5, 1952.

36. Kathleen Boyer interview, August 27, 2013. Kenton L. Boyer and Kathleen Oliver Marriage Certificate, Madison County, Arkansas, April 11, 1952, courtesy of Kathleen Boyer and Jane Boyer.
37. Kathleen Boyer interview, August 27, 2013.
38. Kathleen Boyer interview, August 27, 2013.
39. Kathleen Boyer interview, August 27, 2013.
40. Lipman, *Boyer*, 59. Kathleen Boyer interview, August 27, 2013. *El Paso* (NM) *Herald Post*, June 7, 1952, August 20, 21, 1952.
41. Kathleen Boyer interview, August 27, 2013. Mabel Boyer later gave birth to daughter Marcy, she and Vern's fourteenth and last child.
42. Lipman, *Boyer*, 59–60. Kenton Lloyd Boyer Report of Separation from the Armed Forces of the United States form, Boyer family collection.
43. *European Stars and Stripes*, May 4, June 10, 1952.
44. *European Stars and Stripes*, August 9, 11, 21, 24, 26, 1953.
45. Kenton Lloyd Boyer Report of Separation from the Armed Forces of the United States form, Boyer family collection. Kenton Boyer, U.S. Department of Veterans Affairs, BIRLS Death File, 1850-2010. Ancestry.com. PFC Kenton L. Boyer Honorable Discharge certificate, Boyer family collection. "Lynn Boyer Signs With The Cardinals," *Joplin Globe*, October 14, 1953, 2B.
46. *Joplin Globe*, October 11, 14, 18, 20, 1953. *TSN*, October 28, 1953, 17. Hall, *Mantle*, 188-189. John Hall, "KOM [League] Flash Update," March 9, 2015.
47. *Joplin Globe*, October 14, 23, 25, 1953. Lynn Boyer signed his contract on October 13, 1953. *Ibid*, October 14, 1953. A photo of Kenton and Cloyd in basketball referee attire may be found in the *Neosho* (MO) *News*, December 20, 1953.
48. "Houston Signs Rookie Infielders," *Dallas* (TX) *Morning News*, December 16, 1953. A.O. Camou, correspondent for *The Sporting News* who covered the Mexican Coast League, claimed the Guadalajara club "has released Marvin Williams to make room for Kent Boyer" in the December 2, 1953, issue. Boyer's daughter, Jane Boyer, refutes this claim. Jane Boyer to the author, Facebook message, June 8, 2015. A.O. Camou, "Hermosillo Closes on Pace-Makers in Mexican Coast," *TSN*, December 2, 1953, 35.

Chapter 4: Houston and Havana

1. Clark Nealon, "Post Time," *Houston Post*, May 13, 1954. Jack Gallagher, "Boyer Boomed as Birds' New Golden Boy," *TSN*, January 19, 1955, 5.
2. Peter Golenbock, *The Spirit of St. Louis: A History of The St. Louis Cardinals and Browns* (New York: HarperEntertainmnent, 2000), 405.
3. Bob Broeg, "Cards' Talent Scouts Beam at Early Camp," *TSN*, February 24, 1954, 16. Peter Hernon and Terry Ganey, *Under the Influence: The Unauthorized Story of the Anheuser-Busch Dynasty* (New York: Simon & Schuster, 1991), 212–213.
4. "Buffs Victim of Thieves," *TSN*, March 24, 1954, 30. "Buffs Make Up Theft Losses," *Ibid*, April 7, 1954, 30. The players were reimbursed for their losses by Houston Buffs general manager Art Routzong. *Ibid*. City Island Park is now called Jackie Robinson Ballpark, as Robinson played his first exhibition game with the Brooklyn Dodgers' Triple-A club, the Montreal Royals, against the Dodgers there on March 17, 1946. "City Island Ball Park" National Register of Historic Places website http://www.nps.gov/nr/feature/highlight/city_island_ball_park.htm (Accessed June 21, 2015).

5. Freedman, *Boyer Boyers*, 55–65.

6. Cloyd Boyer interview, July 2011. "Training in the Minors," *TSN*, April 7, 1954, 30. Lipman, *Boyer*, 63. Clark Nealon, "Early Help From Cardinals Boosts Morale at Houston," *Houston Post* (reprinted in *Dallas Morning News*), April 7, 1954, 15. Sonny Senerchia minor-league page, Baseball-Reference.com http://www.baseball-reference.com/minors/player.cgi?id=senerc001ema (Accessed June 20, 1954).

7. Clark Nealon, "Early Help From Cardinals Boosts Morale at Houston," *Houston Post* (reprinted in *Dallas Morning News*), April 7, 1954, 15. Nealon, "Buffs Clip Cards, 6-3," *Houston Post*, April 4, 1954.

8. Kathleen Boyer interview, August 30, 2013. Lipman, *Boyer*, 67. Ken Boyer Control Card, St. Louis Cardinals.

9. Clark Nealon, "The Plight of the Houston Buffs: Is This One for Better or Worse?" *Houston Post*, April 21, 1954.

10. Clark Nealon, "The Saga of Kenton L. Boyer, Young Man on His Way to the Majors." *Houston Post*, May 13, 1954. Healon, "Post Time," April 29, 1954.

11. Clark Nealon, "Buffs Edge OC, 2-1, Climb to 6th Place," *Houston Post*, April 28, 1954. Tom Davison, "Big Buff Hits Nick OC, 8-4," *Ibid*, May 1, 1954.

12. Clark Nealon, "Boyer Blasts Grand Slam and Schmidt Blanks Shippers, 5-0," *Houston Post*, May 12, 1954. "Fiscalini's Hit Nips Houston in Ninth, 4-3," *Ibid*, May 25, 1954. Nealon, "Houston Buys Chisox' Boyd," *Ibid*, May 25, 1954. Nealon, "Bob Boyd Sparkles in Debut As Buffs Wallop Sports, 11-4," *Ibid*, May 28, 1954.

13. Clark Nealon, "Buffs Defeat Cats Twice," *Houston Post*, June 2, 1954. Nealon, "Buffs Take 2 More Off Cats," *Ibid*, June 3, 1954.

14. Clark Nealon, "Buffs Take Fifth; Throttle Tulsa, 10-2," *Houston Post*, June 17, 1954. "Buffs Win 4th Straight, 4-2," *Ibid*, June 24, 1954. "Buff Bingles," *Ibid*, June 17, 1954. "Spooner Walks 14, But Halts Buffs, 7-2," *Ibid*, June 25, 1954. "Buffs Win, 10-2; Home Tonight," *Ibid*, June 26, 1954. Nealon, "Buffs Win, 6-3; Move Into First Division," *Ibid*, June 23, 1954.

15. "Piercy, Willis Stop Buffs on 7 Hits, 4-1," *Houston Post*, July 1, 1954. *Ibid*, July 3, 1954. Clark Nealon, "Buffs Blast Missions, 12-3," *Ibid*, July 4, 1954. L.E. Goldman, "Squeeze Wins For Herd, 3-2." *Ibid*, July 5, 1954. Nealon, "Padre Rallies Drop Houston," *Ibid*, July 6, 1954.

16. Clark Nealon, "Buffs Win, 4-3, in 10, Climb into 3rd Place," *Houston Post*, July 11, 1954. Nealon, "Mission Homers Beat Buff Twice," *Ibid*, July 14, 1954. Nealon, "Buffs Salvage Finale, Blast Missions, 11-1," *Ibid*, July 15, 1954. Nealon, "Boyer's Streak 5th in TL History," *Ibid*, August 11, 1954.

17. Clark Nealon, "Slugging Buffs Bop Cats, 18-4," *Houston Post*, July 17, 1954. Nealon, "Lefty Arroyo Strikes Out 15, Buffs Win, 5-2," *Ibid*, July 20, 1954. Nealon, "Lerchen's HR Wins for Buffs," *Ibid*, July 22, 1954. Nealon, "Buffs Win On Boyd's Homer," *Ibid*, July 23, 1954.

18. Ed Mickelson, *Out of the Park: Memoir of a Minor League Baseball All-Star* (Jefferson, NC: McFarland & Company, Inc., 2007), 130.

19. Clark Nealon, "North Homers Down South All-Stars, 9-8," *Houston Post*, July 24, 1954. "Eagles, in Last Place, Set Pace in All-Star Picks with Seven," *TSN*, July 28, 1954, 35.

20. "Buff Win, 3-1, Take Over 3rd," *Houston Post*, July 30, 1954. Clark Nealon, "Tulsa's Rally Nips Buffs, 7-4," *Ibid*, August 2, 1954. Rory Costello, "Willard Brown," SABR Baseball Biography Project, http://sabr.org/bioproj/person/49784799 (Accessed June 25, 2015). Brown was inducted to the Baseball Hall of Fame in 2006.

21. "3 Homers Help Buffs Humiliate Tulsa, 13-2," *Houston Post*, August 4, 1954. Clark Nealon, "Tribe Stops Buffs, Arroyo in 11th, 6-5," *Ibid*, August 7, 1954. "Tiefenauer Holds

Off Indians in Late Innings, Herd Wins, 4-2," *Ibid*, August 8, 1954. Statistics during Boyer's thirty-game hit streak were compiled from game box scores in the *Houston Post* and the *Dallas Morning News*.

22. "Arroyo's No-Hitter Chills Dallas, 3-0," *Houston Post*, August 12, 1954. Clark Nealon, "'Didn't Have My Strikeout Pitch' Says Happy Senor," *Ibid*. "Rac, Boyer Homer As Houston Wins, 7-2," *Ibid*, August 14, 1954. "Kenny Boyer Is Sidelined," *Ibid*, August 19, 1954. Nealon, "Houston Tops Missions, 7-6," *Ibid*, August 22, 1954.

23. "Buffs Plaster Shippers, 10-3," *Ibid*, August 29, 1954. John Hollis, "Buffs Crush Sports, 10-3," *Ibid*, August 27, 1954.

24. "Buffs Pound Ships For 8-4 Victory," *Ibid*, August 31, 1954.

25. "Texas League," *The Sporting News Baseball Guide and Record Book*, 205. Photocopies courtesy of Ray Nemec. "Buffs Punish Sports, Cinch Playoff Berth," *Houston Post*, September 2, 1954. "Buffs Explode For 5 in 8th and Win, 7-4," *Ibid*, September 3, 1954. "Brown's 3-Run Blast Paces Buff Win, 7-3," *Ibid*, September 4, 1954.

26. Clark Nealon, "Missions Turn Back Buffs, 8-3," *Houston Post*, September 5, 1954. Nealon, "Arroyo, Rac Spirit Houston Victory, 8-4," *Ibid*, September 6, 1954.

27. "Kellert, Andre Win TL Player Honors," *Houston Post*, August 26, 1954.

28. Robert Creamer, "Brilliant Enigma," *Sports Illustrated*, September 3, 1956. http://sportsillustrated.cnn.com/vault/article/magazine/MAG1131757/3/index.htm. Accessed September 15, 2013. "1954 Texas League," Baseball-Reference.com

29. "Boles' 3rd Homer Shades Buffs, 9-8," *Houston Post*, September 9, 1954.

30. "Buffs Even Playoff in Wild Battle, 5-4," *Houston Post*, September 10, 1954.

31. "Rand's Double Beats Indians in 10th, 6-3," *Houston Post*, September 11, 1954.

32. "Buffs Win On Smith's Blast," *Houston Post*, September 12, 1954. "Schmidt, Tiefenauer & Co Pitch Buffs into TL Finals," *Ibid*, September 13, 1954.

33. "Blasingame's Homer Beats Cats, 4-3, in 11th as 11,648 Pack Park," *Houston Post*, September 15, 1954.

34. "Buffs Edge Cats, 3-2, in 17 Innings to Take League Playoff Lead," *Houston Post*, September 17, 1954.

35. "Buffs Batter Cats, 11 to 2; Series if 3-1," *Houston Post*, September 18, 1954. "Buffs Storm to Dixie, 13-1," *Ibid*, September 19, 1954.

36. "Buffs Off to Dixie; Arroyo, Sooter Ready," *Houston Post*, September 20, 1954.

37. "Buffs Salt Atlanta's Crackers, 10-4, Take Lead in Dixie Series," *Houston Post*, September 22, 1954. "Schmidt's Nifty Two-Hitter Crumbles Crackers, 7-2," *Ibid*, September 23, 1954.

38. "Crackers Stall Buff March, 7-4," *Houston Post*, September 24, 1954.

39. "Buffs Explode in 6th to Grab 3rd Victory in Dixie Series, 5-2," *Houston Post*, September 25, 1954.

40. "Thompson's 3-Hitter Cools Off Buffs, 1-0," *Houston Post*, September 26, 1954.

41. "Crax Even Dixie with 6-2 Victory," Houston Post, September 28, 1954. Kenneth R. Fenster, "The 1954 Dixie Series," *The National Pastime: Baseball in the Peach State* (Cleveland, OH: Society for American Baseball Research, 2010), 78.

42. "Crax Roar Back, Win Dixie, 7-1," *Houston Post*, September 29, 1954. Fenster, "The 1954 Dixie Series," 80.

43. Jack Gallagher, "Boyer Boomed as Birds' New Golden Boy," *TSN*, January 19, 1955, 5. Bob Broeg, "Mancuso Sees Redbirds Rich in Hill Talent," *TSN*, September 8, 1954, 11.

44. Clifford Kachline, "Farm heads Pick Score as Top Rookie Prospect," *TSN*, November 3, 1954, 13. Bob Broeg, "Cards Coveted Rush and Cubs Shot for Moon," *Ibid*, October 13, 1954, 13. "Cards Will Trade 'Star-For-Star' To Improve Ball Club," *Lubbock* (TX) *Morning Avalanche*, October 7, 1954.

45. "Crackers Stall Buff March, 7-4," *Houston Post*, September 24, 1954.

46. Pedro Galiana, "Cuban Clubs Await Oct. 7 Starting Bell for Winter Season," *TSN*, October 6, 1954, 27. Galiana, "Almendares Gets Fast Start in Defense of Championship," *Ibid*, October 20, 1954, 23.

47. Lou Hernández, *Memories of Winter Ball: Interviews with Players in the Latin American Winter Leagues of the 1950s* (Jefferson, NC: McFarland & Company, Inc., 2013), 48, 63, 69, 73. Kathleen Boyer interview, August 30, 2013.

48. Hernández, *Memories of Winter Ball*, 64, 69, 73.

49. Galiana, "Cardinal Kids Catch Cuba's Fancy, Raise Havana Leones' Hopes," *TSN*, October 27, 1954, 25. Galiana, "Zeroes Stick Pin in Leones' Flag Bubble," *Ibid*, February 2, 1955, 24. Galiana, "Negray Gives Big Boost to Havana Leones," *Ibid*, December 15, 1954, 24.

50. Galiana, "Cardinal Kids Catch Cuba's Fancy, Raise Havana Leones' Hopes," *TSN*, October 27, 1954, 25. Galiana, "Connie Johnson Nips Almendares' 11-Win Skein in Cuban Loop," *Ibid*, November 24, 1954, 23. Galiana, "Mike Guerra Fired as Marianao Pilot; Reyes Takes Helm." *Ibid*, December 1, 1954, 32.

51. Harry Paxton, "The Beanball: Myth or Menace?" *Saturday Evening Post*, June 30, 1962, 44. Bill Virdon remembered Boyer spending a month in the hospital and not playing for three months. Actually, he left the hospital a week later and finished his recovery at his Havana apartment. He was back in the lineup about two weeks later when Gus Mancuso saw him in a game. Kenny Hand, "Batters Have to Learn How to Overcome Fear," *Baseball Digest*, August 1980, 72.

52. Galiana, "Negray Gives Big Boost to Havana Leones," *TSN*, December 15, 1954, 24. Lipman, *Boyer*, 70–71. Alfredo Ibanez player profile, http://baseball-reference.com. "Boyer Slightly Hurt," *Dallas* (TX) *Morning News*, December 7, 1954. J. Roy Stockton, "Doctor OK's Condition; Cards Play Camp Game," *St. Louis Post-Dispatch*, March 6, 1955, Ken Boyer HOF file. Biographer Jack Zanger claimed that Boyer was unconscious for five days rather than three as stated by David Lipman. Zanger, *Guardian of the Hot Corner*, 82. Ken's wife, Kathleen Boyer, remembered he was in the hospital "about a week or so." Kathleen Boyer interview, August 30, 2013. *TSN* correspondent Pedro Galiana gave no further reports about Boyer's condition and did not report exactly when he returned to the Habana lineup.

53. Bob Broeg, "Cards Trade Puts Kid Boyer on Spot, Along with F. Smith," *TSN*, December 15, 1954, 11. Ray Gillespie, "Stanky Stakes Off First-String Post for Boyer, Virdon," *Ibid*, January 19, 1955, 11.

54. Galiana, "Mancuso Labels Card Rookie Trio on Cuba 'Ready,'" *TSN*, December 29, 1954, 25.

55. Galiana, "New Year Defeats Slow Leones' Chase of Cuban Leaders," *TSN*, January 17, 1955, 22. Galiana, "Zeroes Stick Pin in Leones' Flag Bubble," *Ibid*, February 2, 1955, 24.

56. John J. Monteleone, ed. *Branch Rickey's Little Blue Book: Wit and Strategy From Baseball's Last Wise Man* (New York: Macmillan, 1995), 19.

57. Galiana, "Zeroes Stick Pin in Leones' Flag Bubble," *TSN*, February 2, 1955, 24. Galiana, "Almendares Plans Surprise in Caribbean Tournament," *Ibid*, February 9, 1955, 27.

58. Galiana, "Almendares Plans Surprise in Caribbean Tournament," *TSN*, February 9, 1955, 27. Kathleen Boyer interview, August 30, 2013.

NOTES   391

59. Viola (Clark) Oliver passed away at her home in Joplin, Missouri, on February 6, 1955. She was 52 years old. Viola Oliver Missouri Death Certificate No. 1452. http://www.sos.mo.gov/images/archives/deathcerts/1955/1955_00001452.PDF

60. Lipman, *Boyer*, 79.

61. Galiana, "Bragan's Blues Sweep Player Honors in Cuba," *TSN*, February 16, 1955, 27. Jorge S. Figuero, *Who's Who in Cuban Baseball 1878-1961* (Jefferson City, NC: McFarland & Company, 2003), 281. Both Jack Zanger and David Lipman in their respective biographies of Boyer state that dizzy spells forced him to return home early and not finish the Cuban Winter League season. This is inaccurate as Pedro Galiana, correspondent for *The Sporting News*, continued to report Boyer's presence in the Habana Leones lineup in January and February 1955, as well as his performance in the league All-Star Game on February 1. Zanger, *Guardian of the Hot Corner*, 82. Lipman, *Boyer*, 71.

Chapter 5: Great Expectations

1. Bob Broeg, "Cards, Luke-Warm at Hot Sack, Boom Boyer as Best Ever," *TSN*, March 2, 1955, Boyer HOF file.

2. Bob Broeg, "Brat Sees Platoons as Likely Cure for What Ails Redbirds," *TSN*, October 6, 1954, 15.

3. Ray Gillespie, "Cards See Clover Era in Talent Crop," *TSN*, February 23, 1955, 1–2.

4. Bob Broeg, "Cards, Luke-Warm at Hot Sack, Boom Boyer as Best Ever," *TSN*, March 2, 1955, Boyer HOF file.

5. Jack Herman, "Mgr. Boyer Recalls Boyer the Rookie," *St. Louis Globe-Democrat*, February 24, 1979

6. J. Roy Stockton, "Doctor OK's Condition; Cards Play Camp Game," *St. Louis Post-Dispatch*, March 6, 1955, Boyer HOF file. Red Byrd, "Some Winter Question-Marks for Cards Rounding Into the Right Spring Answers," *TSN*, March 16, 1955, 8. Byrd, "Ol' War Horse's No. 9 Now Carried by Card Colt Virdon," *Ibid*, March 9, 1955.

7. Bob Broeg, "Boyer Can Field, Run, Throw and Hit with Power." *TSN*, April 13, 1955, 2.

8. Arthur Daley, "Pie-in-the-Sky." *New York Times*, March 23, 1955.

9. Red Byrd, "Cardinals Like the Taste of Own Grapefruit Hurling," *TSN*, March 23, 1955, 9.

10. Arthur Daley, "Pie-in-the-Sky," *New York Times*, March 23, 1955. Shirley Povich, "Cards May Be Coming Up with Pennant Winner," *Washington Post*, March 24, 1955. Bob Broeg, "Cards, Luke-Warm at Hot Sack, Boom Boyer as Best Ever," *TSN*, March 2, 1955, Boyer HOF file. Red Byrd, "Cardinals Like the Taste of Own Grapefruit Hurling," *TSN*, March 23, 1955, 9. Jack Herman, "Mgr. Boyer Recalls Boyer the Rookie," *St. Louis Globe-Democrat*, February 24, 1979. Bob Broeg, "Pilot Boyer To Apply Tips—From Contini to Alston," *St. Louis Post-Dispatch*, March 2, 1970, 2B.

11. Dixie Walker, "Future Stars: Boyer, Spooner Cited by Dixie Walker," *Reading* (PA) *Eagle* (Associated Press story), February 28, 1955. Neal Russo, "Baseball in Blood of the Boyer Clan," *St. Louis Post-Dispatch*, May 24, 1978, St. Louis Mercantile Library Association Collection. C.C. Johnson Spink, "Score, Boyer Selected as No. 1 Rookies," *TSN*, April 13, 1955, 1.

12. Lipman, *Boyer*, 76

13. "Card in Hole—Break Up Double Play," photo caption, *Chicago Tribune*, April 13, 1955, 1-F. Edward Prell, "Cubs' 18-Hit Barrage Routs Cards, 14-4," *Ibid*, 6-F.

14. Retrosheet.org. Lipman, *Boyer*, 77. That same day in Liberal, Kansas, Boyer's younger brother Cletis played shortstop for the Alba High School team and hit a solo home run and struck out the side in an inning's work as a relief pitcher. *Joplin Globe*, April 13, 1955.

15. Milwaukee Braves 7, St. Louis Cardinals 8, April 14, 1955, box score, Retrosheet.org.
16. Bob Broeg, "Stanky Goes to Bat for Cards' Pitching—'Better Than in '54,'" *TSN*, May 18, 1955, 6. Myron Cope, "Ken Boyer: New Leader of the Cardinals," *Sport*, August 1961, 52.
17. "Cards Overcame Tigers by 10 to 9," *New York Times*, April 11, 1955. "Bunts and Boots," *TSN*, April 20, 1955, 39.
18. Dick Kaegel, "Boyer Brews Good Communications," *St. Louis Post-Dispatch*, May 9, 1978, 4C.
19. Bob Broeg, "Redbirds Leave Hopes of Streak on Bases on Trip," *TSN*, June 1, 1955, 9.
20. The clubhouse injury is discussed in the following works: Broeg and Vickery, *St. Louis Cardinals Encyclopedia*, 72. Broeg, *Redbirds*, 149. Bob Broeg, *Memories of a Hall of Fame Sportswriter* (Champaign IL: Sagamore Publishing, 1995), 232. "Brat Denies He Quit; Boasts 'Three Friends in St. Louis,'" *TSN*, June 8, 1955, 5. "Stanky Tabbed Firing Story as 'Another Wild Rumor,'" *TSN*, June 8, 1955, 8.
21. Bob Broeg, "Ken Boyer, Two-League Vet, Gives Edge to Cardinals," *St. Louis Post-Dispatch*, September 11, 1968, 2E. Broeg, "Pilot Boyer To Apply Tips—From Contini to Alston," *Ibid*, March 2, 1970, 2B.
22. "Hughes Just Jackpot Jim to Boyer—Three Swings and Three Homers," *TSN*, June 15, 1955.
23. Bob Broeg, "Road-Weary Cards Seeking Righty Power," *TSN*, June 22, 1955, 8.
24. Bob Broeg, "Pilots Lead Battle of Cincy, But Giles Gets in Last Licks," *TSN*, July 13, 1955, 19.
25. "Fans Name Only Five Repeaters in Balloting for Starting Lineup," *TSN*, July 13, 1955, 9.
26. Bob Broeg, "Lowest Card Finish Since '19 Looming," *TSN*, August 17, 1955, 11.
27. Bob Broeg, "'Don't's to Players Kill Spirit, Says Walker," *TSN*, August 17, 1955, 1.
28. Oscar Fraley, "Boyer Comes into Own," July 12, 1956, unidentified clipping in Boyer HOF file. Ellis Veech, "Hot Man at the Hot Corner," *Baseball Digest* (September 1956), 24. Joe Reichler, "Hands-Off Policy Taken Toward Kenny Boyer Pays Rich Dividends," *Las Cruces* (NM) *Sun-News*, June 28, 1956.
29. Bob Broeg, "Hitters Must Take Rap for Cardinal Skid," *TSN*, September 14, 1955, 8. "Dark's Batting Tips to Boyer Backfire in Win for Cards," *Ibid*, August 31, 1955, 38.
30. Broeg, *Memories*, 233–234. Harry Paxton, "The Beanball: Myth of Menace?" *Saturday Evening Post*, June 30, 1962, 42. Broeg incorrectly attributed the hit-by-pitch incident to Boyer's 1954 season at Houston rather than Havana, Cuba, that winter. Broeg, *Memories*, 234. In a roundtable discussion with other major-league players, Boyer stated that he was hit on the head with a pitch three times, the third being the one in Cuba. Paxton, "The Beanball," 44. Kathleen Boyer recalled Ken's brother Clete Boyer saying that "Ken had told him after that happened, he was always a little bit shy [at the plate]." Kathleen Boyer interview, August 27, 2013.
31. "The 1955 St. Louis Cardinals Regular Season Game Log," retrosheet.org.
32. Bob Broeg, "Fans Hear Harry Will Be Handed Hat in Cards' Shakeup," *TSN*, September 28, 1955, 21. Joe King, "Brooks' Bosses See Three Rivals in '56," *Ibid*, October 12, 1955, 9. O'Malley's entire statement reads: "We believe the Cards, for instance, are the best seventh-place club in either league any year. We have tremendous respect for them." Dodgers general manager Buzzie Bavasi added: "When you think of a club with Musial, Schoendienst, Virdon, Moon, Boyer and so many more good players finishing seventh, you have to realize the importance of pitching. We think they could come right up into the fight with a couple

of pitchers, and they are likely to get them." *Ibid*. Bob Broeg, ghostwriter for Stan Musial's autobiography, quoted O'Malley's pronouncement as the Cardinals being "the best seventh-place club in history." Stan Musial with Bob Broeg, *Stan Musial: "The Man's" Own Story* (New York: Doubleday & Company, 1964), 173.

33. Oscar Ruhl, "From the Ruhl Book," *TSN*, July 25, 1956, 13. "Score, Virdon Selected as Rookies of the Year," *New York Times*, October 2, 1955. Bob Broeg, "A.L. Places 8 of 11 on All-Rookie Team," *TSN*, October 26, 1955, 5–6.

34. "Mays and Newk to Lead Negro All-Star Junket," *TSN*, October 5, 1955, 10. "Ashburn, Boyer and Schmidt Wow 'Em in the West," *Ibid*, October 26, 1955, 23. Bob Phipps, "Late Arrival Fails to Slow Up Lane on Busy Visit to Omaha," *Ibid*, February 1, 1956, 24. Wally Moon with Tim Gregg, *Moonshots: Reflections on a Baseball Life* (San Antonio, TX: Moon Publishing, 2010), 118–119.

35. The minimum major-league salary figure was found in Graham Womack, "MLB Salaries Stayed Low Longer Than People May Think," Baseball: Past and Present blog, April 27, 2015 (Accessed June 11, 2015) http://baseballpastandpresent.com/2015/04/27/mlb-salaries-stayed-longer-people/ Kathleen Boyer interview, August 27, 2013. *St. Louis County Directory for 1959*, 135. Photocopy courtesy of the St. Louis Public Library. Lucinda Herron, "Mrs. Ken Boyer: She Views Pennant Race from Home Plate," *St. Louis Globe-Democrat*, September 30, 1964. Kathleen Boyer interview, August 27, 2013.

36. J.G. Taylor Spink, "Gashouse Gang Revival Due Under Lane," *TSN*, October 12, 1955, 1.

37. Richard C, Lindberg, *Total White Sox: The Definitive Encyclopedia of the World Champion Franchise* (Chicago: Triumph Books, 2006), 379.

38. Joe King, "Fans' Squawks, Richards' Rap Bring Stormy Night with Lane," *TSN*, June 13, 1956, 11. "Cardinals Enroll Boyer," *New York Times*, December 14, 1955. "Lane Signs Boyer," (Salt Lake City) *Desert News*, December 13, 1955. Tim Moriarty, "Four National League Stars Sign Contracts; Boyer Gets Pay Boost," *Reading* (PA) *Eagle* (United Press International story), January 4, 1957, 15.

39. "Sophomore Year No Jinx to Cardinals' Ken Boyer," *Dallas Morning News*, March 30, 1956. Bob Broeg, "Redbirds' Ken Boyer Gives Soph Jinx an Early Jolting," *TSN*, April 4, 1956, 28.

40. "Sophomore Year No Jinx to Cardinals' Ken Boyer," *Dallas Morning News*, March 30, 1956.

41. "Sophomore Year No Jinx to Cardinals' Ken Boyer," *Dallas Morning News*, March 30, 1956. Red Byrd, "Same Story Despite New Hands—Cards Still Weak in Clubs," *TSN*, March 28, 1956, 14. Bob Broeg, "Hats Off…Ken Boyer," *Ibid*, May 2, 1956, 21.

42. Ray Gillespie, "'Hair-Down' Party Gives Lane a Frank Run-Down on Cards by Own Staff," *TSN*, April 11, 1956, 9.

43. Rob Rains, *The St. Louis Cardinals: The 100th Anniversary History* (New York: St. Martin's Press, 1992), 137. "St. Louis Cardinals Uniform and Team History," Heritage Uniforms and Jerseys blog, http://blog.heritagesportsart.com/2010/08/st-louis-cardinals-uniform-and-team.html (Accessed November 8, 2103). Jerry Vickery and Bob Broeg, *The St. Louis Cardinals Encyclopedia* (Chicago: Masters Press, 1998), 90–91.

44. Robert Creamer, "The Gaudy Ones," *Sports Illustrated*, May 28, 1956, http://www.si.com/vault/1956/05/28/615532/the-gaudy-ones

45. Mike Eisenbath, *The Cardinals Encyclopedia* (Philadelphia: Temple University Press, 1999), 566. John Snyder, *Cardinals Journal: Year by Year & Day by Day with the St. Louis Cardinals*

Since 1882 (Cincinnati, OH: Emmis Books, 2006), 419–420. Neal Russo, "May Days Gay Days for Lane, Swapping Nine Players for Nine," *TSN*, May 23, 1956, 7. Frank Litsky, "Five Untouchables on Redbird Roster, Trader Lane Hints," *Ibid*, May 30, 1956, 8.

46. Joe King, "Fans' Squawks, Richards' Rap Bring Stormy Night with Lane," *TSN*, June 13, 1956, 11.

47. Bob Broeg, "Lane Tops Trade Swingers with Four-for-Four," *TSN*, June 20, 1956, 5–6. Eisenbath, *Cardinals Encyclopedia*, 566. "Fans Light Up Switchboard, Rap Schoendienst Departure," *TSN*, June 20, 1956, 5.

48. Broeg and Vickey, *St. Louis Cardinals Encyclopedia*, 74. Musial with Broeg, *Musial*, 177. James N. Giglio, *Musial: From Stash to Stan the Man* (Columbia, MO: University of Missouri Press, 2001), 185.

49. Bob Broeg, "Cards Still First Division 'Cinch' in Lane's Belief," *TSN*, July 4, 1956, 17.

50. Robert L. Burnes, "It's the 'Swish' in Those Swats by Long, Mantle," *TSN*, June 6, 1956, 12.

51. Bob Broeg, "Cardinals Squeeze Grapefruit Crown," *TSN*, April 11, 1956, 30. Broeg, "Ken's Homer Pace Threatens All-Time Highs for St. Louis," *Ibid*, June 13, 1956, 4.

52. Bob Broeg, "Fellow Stars Hail 'Player of Decade' Musial," *TSN*, July 18, 1956, 15.

53. Edgar Munzel, "Giles Told Smokey to Win, Rather than Parade Stars," *TSN*, July 18, 1956, 14.

54. Fred Lieb, "N.L. All-Stars Make Capital of Power," *TSN*, July 18, 1956, 13–14.

55. 1956 All-Star Game box score, http://retrosheet.org. Bob Broeg, "Fans Boo Removal of The Man Following Collision with Boyer," *St. Louis Post-Dispatch*, July 11, 1956. "Musial Took Spill in Field, But Escaped Serious Injury," *TSN*, July 18, 1956, 13.

56. Ellis Veach, "Hot Man at the Hot Corner," *Baseball Digest*, September 1956, 24.

57. Bob Broeg, "Fans Boo Removal of The Man Following Collision with Boyer," *St. Louis Post-Dispatch*, July 11, 1956.

58. Bob Broeg, "First Thumbing for Boyer Stirs Protest to Giles," *TSN*, August 1, 1956, 13. "Giles Was Ump Critic, Too, Lane Reminds Prexy," *Ibid*, August 8, 1956, 2. "Boyer Banished First Game," July 23, 1956, uncited clipping, Boyer HOF file. Frank Lane also said about the ejection: "Ken probably said, 'gee whiz, use your eyes,' or something like that, so Secory puts him out." *Ibid*.

59. Bob Broeg, "Herm's Kicks Open Door to Wins as Card," *TSN*, August 22, 1956, 6.

60. Robert Creamer, "Brilliant Engima," *Sports Illustrated*, September 3, 1956. http://sportsillustrated.cnn.com/vault/article/magazine/MAG1131757/index.htm

61. Lipman, *Boyer*, 92. Robert Creamer, "Brilliant Engima," *Sports Illustrated*, September 3, 1956. http://sportsillustrated.cnn.com/vault/article/magazine/MAG1131757/index.htm

62. Robert Creamer, "Brilliant Engima," *Sports Illustrated*, September 3, 1956. http://sportsillustrated.cnn.com/vault/article/magazine/MAG1131757/index.htm

63. Bob Broeg, "Hutch Says Hurling Will Help Cards to Keep Up Rise in '57," *TSN*, September 19, 1956, 9.

64. "St. Louis Cardinals 5, Milwaukee Braves, 4." Retrosheet.org. Red Thisted, "Cards Top Braves, 5-4, Trim Lead to ½ Game," *Milwaukee Sentinel*, September 29, 1956. Lou Chapman, "'We Gave Them the Runs That Beat Us,' Said Haney," *Ibid*, September 29, 1956.

65. "St. Louis Cardinals 2, Milwaukee Braves, 1." Retrosheet.org. Red Thisted, "Braves Lose, Hopes Fade as Bums Win," *Milwaukee Sentinel*, September 30, 1956. Lou Chapman, "Spahn Leaves in Tears; Tribe 'Dies' Hard," *Ibid*.

66. Jeffrey Neuman, *The Cardinals*. New York: Collier Books, 1983, 155.

67. C.C. Johnson Sprink, "A.L. Places Seven on '56 All-Star Team," *TSN*, October 17, 1956, 1. "Redlegs' Bailey Named N.L.'s Soph of Year," *Yonkers* (NY) *Herald Statesman* (Associated Press story), November 7, 1956. *TSN*, July 4, 1956, 23.

68. Tim Moriarty, "Four National League Stars Sign Contracts; Boyer Gets Pay Boost," *Reading* (PA) *Eagle* (United Press International story), January 4, 1957, 15.

Chapter 6: The Reluctant Dragon

1. Snyder, *Cardinals Journal*, 423–424.
2. "Busch Maps Cardinal Goal for Lane—Pennant by '58," *TSN*, February 20, 1957, 9.
3. *TSN*, January 18, 1957, 19, 25. "Spink Will Receive Citation from Elks as St. Louis Sports Personality of '56," *Ibid*, November 14, 1956, 17.
4. The A.B.C. Cap advertisement in *TSN*, April 17, 1957, 36. David Maraniss, "Roberto Clemente: The King of Beisbol," http://www.smithsonianmag.com/history-archaeology/Roberto-Clemente-The-King-of-Beisbol.html. Accessed November 18, 2013. Lee Lowenfish, *Branch Rickey: Baseball's Ferocious Gentleman* (Lincoln: University of Nebraska Press, 2007), 442.
5. "Boyer Shift to Garden Denied," *TSN*, September 12, 1956, 25.
6. Bob Broeg, "Weak Hammering Keeps Cards From Nailing Fourth Spot," *TSN*, August 29, 1956, 11. Snyder, *Cardinals Journal*, 423. Dan Daniel, "Over the Fence," *TSN*, April 17, 1957, 12.
7. Bob Broeg, "Confused Redbirds Reverse Their Old Win-Lose Pattern," *TSN*, May 22, 1957, 9. Ira Peck, "Ken Boyer: Cardinal in the Clutch" in Ray Robinson, ed., *Baseball Stars of 1965* (New York: Pyramid Books, 1965), 23.
8. Joe King, "Swap Talk Gives Redbirds Jitters, Flash Tells Lane," *TSN*, May 29, 1957, 4. "'You're Inconsistent,' Snorts Lane, Answering 'Jitters' Blast by Frisch," *Ibid*. "Boyer Status Card Puzzler," (Associated Press) *Hendersonville* (NC) *Times-News*, November 16, 1957, 8. Jim Van Valkenburg, "Ken Boyer Hottest Hitter in National," (Associated Press story) *Cortland* (NY) *Standard*, June 2, 1958. Perhaps the derogatory name was taken from a 1941 Walt Disney motion picture about a shy mythical creature entitled *The Reluctant Dragon*.
9. J.G. Taylor Spink, "Dark Does All His Knocking at Plate," *TSN*, May 15, 1957, 6. Barry Gottehrer, "The Million-Dollar Cardinal," *True Baseball Yearbook 1961*, 66.
10. "Hutch Told to Use Youths; Boyer Finally Goes to Center," *TSN*, May 20, 1957, 6. Musial and Broeg, *Musial*, 186. Jack Herman, "Cards to Start Kasko, Miksis," *St. Louis Globe-Democrat*, May 23, 1957.
11. "Boyer Wanted to Shift," *TSN*, August 21, 1957, 50.
12. Myron Cope, "Ken Boyer: New Leader of the Cardinals," *Sport*, August 1961, 55.
13. Bob Broeg, "Boyer Surprised—Gets Hike in Pay Instead of Swap," *TSN*, December 25, 1957, 8.
14. Robert L. Burnes, "Ken Boyer was Cardinals' Greatest Third Baseman!" *Baseball Digest*, January 1983, 64.
15. Bob Wolf, "Milwaukee Putting Its Chips on Red in '57 Pennant Whirl," *TSN*, June 26, 1957, 8. Les Biederman, "Bucs Balked in Bold Bid for Slugger," *Ibid*, 10.
16. *TSN*, July 9, 1957, 14. *Ibid*, July 17, 1957, 11.
17. Retrosheet.org
18. Bob Broeg, "Whirlwind Shrine Trip Leaves Cards Winded," *TSN*, July 31, 1957, 14. Edgar Munzel, "White Sox Clout Cardinals, 13-4, at Cooperstown," *Ibid*, 13–14.
19. Bob Broeg, "It's Rule-of-Thumb at Busch Stadium—Six Chased in Three Playing Dates," *TSN*, August 14, 1957, 21. Joe Garagiola, *Baseball is a Funny Game* (New York: Bantam Books, 1985), 37–38.

20. "Hutchinson Calls Off Curfew, 'Relaxed' Redbirds End Drop," *TSN*, August 28, 1957, 28. Bob Broeg, "Injury Halts Musial's Hot Bat Streak," *Ibid*, 19, 26.

21. Bob Broeg, "The Man Most Valuable? His Injury Proves It To Lane," *TSN*, September 4, 1957, 17.

22. Bob Broeg, "Squeaker Successes Buoy Cards' Hopes for Second," *TSN*, September 11, 1957, 19.

23. *TSN*, September 11, 1957, 32.

24. "Lynch's Pinch Homer Snaps Schmidt Win Streak at Ten," *TSN*, September 18, 1957, 30.

25. *TSN*, September 18, 1957, 32, 36. *Ibid*, September 25, 1957, 29, 30.

26. Hank Aaron with Lonnie Wheeler, *I Had A Hammer: The Hank Aaron Story* (New York: HarperCollins, 1991), 125–126. Cleon Walfoort, "Gladness, Madness Mark Celebration of Braves and City," *TSN*, October 2, 1957, 20. Bob Broeg, "Never-Say-Die Birds Whet Fan Appetites for Lively Fight in '58," *Ibid*, October 2, 1957, 22.

27. Bob Broeg, "Never-Say-Die Birds Whet Fan Appetites for Lively Fight in '58," *TSN*, October 2, 1957, 22.

28. "Musial Given Rest by Cards After Clinching Batting Title," *TSN*, October 2, 1957, 22.

29. "St. Louis Cardinals Attendance, Stadiums, and Park Factors," http://www.baseball-reference.com/teams/STL/attend.shtml. Accessed December 9, 2103. Dan Daniel, "Over the Fence," *TSN*, November 13, 1957, 10. Bob Burnes, "Ted, Lane, Hutch Majors' Top Men," *Ibid*, January 1, 1958, 1, 2.

30. Bob Broeg, "Boyer Signs, Indicates Slight Raise in Pay, No Cut in Morale," *St. Louis Post-Dispatch*, December 17, 1957, 4C.

31. Neal Russo, "Boyer was Right Number for Operator," *St. Louis Post-Dispatch*, undated clipping, Griva Scrapbooks.

32. Eisenbath, *Cardinals Encyclopedia*, 74.

33. Jack Herman, "Boyer Relaxes, Feels He Won't Be Traded Now That Lane's Gone," *St. Louis Globe-Democrat*, November 19, 1957. Ray Gillespie, "Rivals Aiming High on Trading Targets, Frantic Frank Finds," *TSN*, October 16, 1957, 8. "Cards, Bucs Discuss Deal, Boyer Involved," *Wilmington* (NC) *Star-News*, November 6, 1957.

34. Les Biederman, "Lane Shift Halted Pirates' Trade of Thomas to Cards," *TSN*, November 27, 1957, 42. Bob Broeg, "Busch Regime Seeks to Build on Farm Base," *Ibid*, November 20, 1957, 8. It was reported that Willard Schmidt was part of the package, but Lane denied it. "Cards, Bucs Discuss Deal, Boyer Involved," *Wilmington* (NC) *Star-News*, November 6, 1957. For some reason, Lane later claimed he had convinced Busch and Meyer that the Boyer trade with Pittsburgh would help the team. For his quote, see Biederman, 42. Pirates GM Joe Brown was upset Lane had publicly announced the players under consideration to be traded for Boyer. "I don't think it proper for Lane to talk about any of my players," he said. "I certainly haven't talked about any of his that we want. We have had several talks with the Cardinals, but we never mentioned any players." "Baseball Back in Business," *Spencer* (IA) *Daily Reporter*, November 6, 1957.

35. Hal Lebovitz, "Tribe Fans Whoop Over New Chief Lane," *TSN*, November 20, 1957, 6. Bob Broeg, "Bing Devine New G.M. Of Cardinals; Lane Takes Cleveland Job," *St. Louis Post-Dispatch*, November 12, 1957.

36. Hal Lebovitz, "Tribe Fans Whoop Over New Chief Lane," *TSN*, November 20, 1957, 6. Bob Broeg, "Bing Devine New G.M. Of Cardinals; Lane Takes Cleveland Job," *St.*

Louis Post-Dispatch, November 12, 1957. Hal Lebovitz, "Tribe Fans Whoop Over New Chief Lane," *TSN*, November 20, 1957, 3, 6.

37. Myron Cope, "Ken Boyer: New Leader of the Cardinals," *Sport*, August 1961, 52.

38. Jack Herman, "Boyer Relaxes, Feels He Won't Be Traded Now That Lane's Gone," *St. Louis Globe-Democrat*, November 19, 1957. Bob Broeg, "Fans Share Lane's Optimism in Cards, Advance Sale Shows," *TSN*, February 13, 1957, 22. Dick Schapp, "What They Say in the Dugouts About the St. Louis Cardinals," *Sport*, August 1958, 72. Lipman, *Boyer*, 97. Barry Gottehrer, "The Million-Dollar Cardinal," *True Baseball Yearbook 1961 Edition*, 59.

39. Associated Press, "Boyer, Given Reprieve, Looks for Good Year," *Daytona Beach* (FL) *Morning Journal*, March 11, 1958.

40. Jack Herman, "'Conservative' Bird Theme Under New G.M. Devine," *TSN*, November 20, 1957, 7. Bob Broeg, "Ken to Stay of Go? Cards Feeling Way," *Ibid*, November 27, 1957, 4.

41. Broeg, "Boyer Surprised—Gets Hike in Pay Instead of Swap," *TSN*, December 25, 1957, 8.

42. Dan Daniel, "Major Player Deals Left Hanging," *TSN*, December 18, 1957, 2. Bob Broeg, "Cardinals Will Hone for Race on Sharp Spring Competition," *Ibid*, 8. Broeg, "Boyer Surprised—Gets Hike in Pay Instead of Swap," *Ibid*, December 25, 1957, 8.

43. Bernard Fernandez, "Ashburn-Boyer Deal Just Wasn't in the Cards," *Philadelphia Inquirer*, July 26, 1995. Rains, *Cardinals*, 139.

44. "Boyer, Given Reprieve, Looks for Good Year," *Dayton Beach* (FL) *Morning Journal*, March 11, 1958.

45. Bob Broeg, "Cardinals Wishing Boyer Were Twins in Center, at Third," *TSN*, April 2, 1958, 20. "Ken Boyer, Off Trade Block, Happier With Job in Outfield," *Ibid*, March 12, 1958, 9. Broeg, "Bing Beats Drum Over Showing of Cardinal Hurlers," *Ibid*, 28. Gottehrer, "The Million-Dollar Cardinal," 66.

46. Unidentified *St. Louis Globe-Democrat* clipping, January 11, 1959, Boyer file, St. Louis Mercantile Library Association Collections.

47. Bob Broeg, "Cardinals Wishing Boyer Were Twins in Center, at Third," *TSN*, April 2, 1958, 20.

48. *TSN*, May 21, 1958, 23. Bob Broeg, "Redbirds Get Off Ground on Wings of Steadier Staff," *Ibid*, May 28, 1958, 10. Alvin Dark was traded to Chicago for pitcher Jim Brosnan on May 20.

49. Red Smith, "Cards Happy They Got Boyer," *Lawrence* (KS) *Journal-World* (Associated Press story). March 14, 1959.

50. Musial and Broeg, *Musial*, 202.

51. Bob Broeg, "Redbirds Get Off Ground on Wings of Steadier Staff," *TSN*, May 28, 1958, 10.

52. "Ken Boyer Has First Big Day of Season," (Associated Press story) *Gettysburg* (PA) *Times*, May 19, 1958. Bob Broeg, "Cardinals' Scoring Drouth Relieved by Base-Hit Showers," *TSN*, June 11, 1958, 16. Jim Van Valkenburg, "Ken Boyer Hottest Hitter in National," (Associated Press story) *Cortland* (NY) *Standard*, June 2, 1958. In the first-ever National League Player of the Month poll of baseball writers in May 1958, Boyer tied for second place with Frank Thomas of Pittsburgh and Daryl Spencer of San Francisco. Stan Musial and Willie Mays shared the honor. "Musial, Mays Tie in Player of Month Poll," *TSN*, June 11, 1958, 16. "Dodgers Victims of Boyer's Two Big Time Grand-Slams," *Ibid*, May 28, 1958, 10.

53. Bob Broeg, "Stonewall Jackson Helps Steady Cards in Stan's Dip," *TSN*, July 2, 1958, 17.

54. Bob Stevens, "Giants' Western Thrillers Beat '57 N.Y. Club on Draw," *TSN*, July 16, 1958, 14. Jack Herman, "Card Hurlers Kept Sweating by Lapse of Timely Swatting," *Ibid*, 27. Snyder, *Cardinals Journal*, 433.

55. The top three third basemen in the All-Star balloting were Frank Thomas of Pittsburgh, Eddie Mathews of Milwaukee, and Don Hoak of Cincinnati. Oscar Kahan, "Some of 'Big Names' Left Off List," *TSN*, July 2, 1958, 6. The on-base and hit streaks were found on Retrosheet "The 1958 STL N Regular Season Batting Log for Ken Boyer" http://www.retrosheet.org/boxesetc/1958/Iboyek1010041958.htm

56. Milwaukee at St. Louis, July 16, *TSN*, July 23, 1958, 32. Robert Markus, "Ex-Cub Larry Jackson Dies," *Chicago Tribune*, August 30, 1990, http://articles.chicagotribune.com/1990-08-30/sports/9003130130_1_idaho-legislature-cubs-wrigley-field (Accessed September 7, 2015).

57. St. Louis at Cincinnati, July 10, 1958, *TSN*, July 30, 1958, 24. Jack Herman, "Volley From Injury Jinx Keeps Redbirds Tumbling," *Ibid*, July 30, 1958, 8.

58. Bob Broeg, "Boyer's Hope For 2nd Half: A Feeling of Redbird Pride," *St. Louis Post-Dispatch*, July 10, 1978, 4B. Bob Burnes, "The Bench Warmer," *St. Louis Globe-Democrat*, May 3, 1978, 3C. Broeg, "Good-Pupil Boyer Has Own Ideas," *Ibid*, March 9, 1980, 2D.

59. Snyder, *Cardinals Journal*, 435. Devine, *Memoirs*, 89.

60. Red Smith, "Cards Happy They Got Boyer," *Lawrence (KS) Journal-World*, March 14, 1959. Neal Russo, "Boyer Showed Sharpest Power Gain on Cardinals," *TSN*, October 29, 1958, 18.

61. Oscar Kahan, "Players Pick N.L. All-Star Fielding Team of '58," *TSN*, November 5, 1958, 17.

62. Snyder, *Cardinals Journal*, 435. Devine, *Memoirs*, 89-90.

63. Lee Kavetski, "Thousands Cheer Cards' Arrival in Japan," *TSN*, October 29, 1958, 10.

64. Kathleen Boyer interview, August 27, 2013.

65. Lee Kavetski, "Cards' Japan Tour Real Good-Will Jaunt," *TSN*, November 12, 1958, 5, 10. Kavetski, "It's Party, Party After Party for Redbirds in Japan," *Ibid*, November 5, 1958, 9. Kavetski, "Hiroshima Visit Touching Highlight of Redbird Trip," *Ibid*, November 19, 1958, 5, 6. Kavetski, "All-Out Hustle Displayed by Redbirds Makes Big Hits With Nipponese Crowds," *Ibid*, 5. Kavetski, "Card Tour Ends in Tokyo Torch Parade," *Ibid*, November 26, 1958, 8.

66. Neal Russo, "Jaunt to Japan First, Then It's Work For Most Cards," *TSN*, October 8, 1958, 12. Oscar Kahan, "Broglio Bagged Hill Berth on Cards' Japanese Junket," *Ibid*, November 27, 1958, 6. Boyer's golf score is mentioned in Lipman, *Boyer*, 52. "Stan, Ken Tee Off On Ducks," *Ibid*, December 31, 1958, 27. Suzie (Boyer) Hartwig interview, July 22, 2011. Tim Renken, "'Batting Practice' in the Field at Nilo," *St. Louis Post-Dispatch*, November 8, 1964, 6F.

Chapter 7: The Captain

1. "Boyer Gets Award and Fat Raise," *St. Louis Globe-Democrat*, January 20, 1959. Ray Gillespie, "Boyer Rated Heir to Stan as Top Card," *TSN*, January 28, 1959, 15. Holmes, "Boyer Is Doing It Now," *Sport*, July 1959, 90. Regardless of his salary increase, Boyer still worked in the off-season to supplement his family's income. In the winter of 1958-59, he was employed at a St. Louis appliance and sporting goods store with teammates Hal Smith and Wally Shannon. Oscar Kahn, "Song-Writer Smitty Tunes Up for Card Catching Comeback," *TSN*, January 21, 1959, 14.

2. Oscar Kahan, "Broglio Bagged Hill Berth on Cards' Japanese Junket," *TSN*, November 26, 1958, 6. "Million-Dolar Tag, Solly's Estimate of Boyer's Value," *Ibid*, May 27, 1959, 15.

3. "St. Louis Cardinals," *Sports Illustrated*, April 13, 1959, http://www.si.com/vault/1959/04/13/616025/st-louis-cardinals

4. "An Unusual Musial," *TSN*, April 29, 1959, 23. Boyer's temporary replacement at third base was Ray Jablonski, whose trade four years earlier enabled him to break into the major leagues.

5. Ralph Ray, "Lo, The Poor Pilot! Hemus Finds Every Plan Can Go Wrong," *TSN*, May 6, 1959, 17.

6. A Sunday curfew suspended the game at the top of the seventh with the Redbirds leading, 2-1. It resumed on June 2 for a 3-1 victory. Ralph Ray, "Hemus Plunked, Lets Bat Sail in Fracas with Bucs," *TSN*, May 13, 1959, 23. *Ibid*, 20. Jim Brosnan, *The Long Season* (Chicago: Ivan R. Dee, 2002), 115–116. Ralph Ray, who covered the Cardinals for *The Sporting News*, speculated that Hemus purposely provoked a fight to light a fire under his lethargic club.

7. Curt Flood with Richard Carter, *The Way It Is* (New York: Trident Press, 1970), 70. Bob Gibson with Lonnie Wheeler, *Stranger to the Game: The Autobiography of Bob Gibson* (New York: Viking, 1994), 53.

8. Ralph Ray, "Coast Tannings Send Redbirds on Slab Search," *TSN*, June 10, 1959, 9. Frank Finch, "Whiff Kings Riding Title Trail Again," *Ibid*, June 10, 1959, 39.

9. Cincinnati Reds at St. Louis Cardinals box score, June 14, 1959, Baseball-Reference.com http://www.baseball-reference.com/boxes/SLN/SLN195906141.shtml (accessed June 15, 2015).

10. Jim Brosnan, "Businessmen Are Wrecking Baseball," *Saturday Evening Post*, May 30, 1964, 8. In response to Boyer's remark, Brosnan wrote, "Just what effective pitching had to do with observant reporting was not made clear." *Ibid*.

11. Ralph Ray, "Cards Look Ahead, Give Youth Its Fling as Hill Front-Liners," *TSN*, June 24, 1959, 15. "Father's Day Full of Bumps for Broglio, Boyer of Birds," *Ibid*, July 1, 1959, 11.

12. Joe King, "Lefty Hill Load Put Squeeze on Stengel," *TSN*, July 15, 1959, 13–14. Boyer and Stan Musial (both as pinch-hitters) were the only Cardinals who made it into the first All-Star Game. Though chosen for the team, Wilmer Mizell was sidelined with a back injury. *Ibid*, 18.

13. Jack Herman, "Pop-Gun Attack Puts Redbirds on Shaky Limb," *TSN*, August 12, 1959, 17. The wife of Boyer's teammate Wally Shannon gave birth to a girl at St. Mary's Hospital in St. Louis—the same facility and the same physician as Kathleen Boyer—a day later. *Ibid*.

14. Jack Herman, "Fluttering Redbirds Play Kissin' Cousins to Streaking Giants," *TSN*, August 19, 1959, 17. Jack Herman, "Solly Slapped with $100 Fine, Asked to Appear Before Giles," *Ibid*, August 26, 1959, 7. It was the third ejection of Ken's major-league career and the seventh of the season for Hemus, who also received a $100 fine and a meeting with National League president Warren Giles. Jack Herman, "Solly Hits 'Sawdust Trail' After Lengthy Visit to Giles 'Woodshed,'" *Ibid*, September 2, 1959, 8.

15. Cope, "Boyer," 50. Jack Herman, "Close-To-The-Vest Losses Toss Strait Jacket Over Cards," *TSN*, September 2, 1959, 8. "Boyer Named Team Captain by Red Birds," *St. Louis Globe-Democrat*, August 26, 1959. Neal Russo, "Cards Name Boyer Team Captain, First Since Schoendienst," *St. Louis Post-Dispatch*, August 25, 1959.

16. Solly Hemus interview, January 19, 2013.

17. Mike Eisenbath, "It Was The Game, Not Fame, That Boyer Sought," *St. Louis Post-Dispatch, October 16, 1994*, Boyer file, St. Louis Mercantile Library Collection. Halberstam, *October 1964*, 257–258. Tim McCarver interview, July 15, 2015.

18. Roy McHugh, "Patching Jobs Give Strength to Cards, Joe Garagiola Says," *Pittsburgh Press*, August 12, 1960, 23. "Bob Addie's Atoms," *TSN*, May 8, 1965, 16. In the same article, Addie thought Ken's younger brother Clete looked liked "[a] riverboat gambler fresh out of a Mark Twain story." *Ibid*. Tim McCarver interview, July 15, 2015.

19. Golenbock, *Spirit of St. Louis*, 425–426.

20. Tommy John interview, August 17, 2013.

21. Tim McCarver interview, July 15, 2015.

22. "Seven Pitchers Player Reps; Kuenn Only Outfield Choice," *TSN*, March 30, 1960, 20. Tim McCarver interview, July 15, 2015.

23. Stan Isle, "Young Could Join Banks and Wagner," *TSN*, September 13, 1982, 9. Tim McCarver email to the author, October 10, 2015.

24. George Vecsey, "Ken Boyer Gives Mets 'An Intangible Thing,'" *New York Times*, April 19, 1966, Boyer HOF file.

25. Tim McCarver interview, July 15, 2015.

26. "Ken Boyer Batting Gamelogs for Career Games 700 to 728," Baseball-Reference.com. http://www.baseball-reference.com/players/gl.cgi?t=b&id=boyerke01&year=1959&share=3.94#700-728-sum:batting_gamelogs OPS stands for on-base percentage plus slugging percentage.

27. In 2015, St. Louis outfielder Matt Holiday finished one game short of tying Boyer's 46-game on-base streak. (A list of the top 19 may be found on the Fungoes blog http://www.fungoes.net/2015/05/21/holliday-ascends-on-base-streak-list/ (Accessed June 6, 2015). During the on-base streak, Boyer batted .354 in 195 plate appearances with 63 hits, five doubles, two triples, 10 home runs, 30 RBIs, 16 base on balls, and one intentional walk. He had a .405 on-base percentage, .573 slugging, and .978 OPS. "Ken Boyer Batting Gamelogs for Career Games 683 to 728." Baseball-Reference.com. http://www.baseball-reference.com/players/gl.cgi?t=b&id=boyerke01&year=1959&share=2.30#683-728-sum:batting_gamelogs

28. "Ken Boyer's Streak Stopped as Hobbie Shuts Out Cardinals," *St. Louis Post-Dispatch*, September 14, 1959, Boyer HOF file. Chris Roewe, "Boyer 29-Game Hit Streak Longest in Big Time Since '50," *TSN*, Oct 28, 1959, 20.

29. Giglio, *Musial*, 240-243. "Musial, in Second Worst Start, Hints He May Hang Up His Bat After '59," *TSN*, June 17, 1959, 14. "Stan, on Part-Time Status, to Play Again Next Season," *Ibid*, August 19, 1959, 17.

30. Rory Costello, "Sam Jones." SABR BioProject http://sabr.org/bioproj/person/b2f99b7e. Accessed January 18, 2015.

31. Davenport and Neuman, *The Cardinals*, 161. Jack Herman, "Boyer's Bulging Bat Mark to Add Biceps to Cardinal Contract," *TSN*, October 28, 1959, 16.

32. Jack Herman, "Close-to-the-Vest Losses Toss Strait Jacket Over Cards," *TSN*, September 2, 1959, 8.

33. 1956 Ken Boyer signed Frank Scott representation contract, Hunt Actions Lot No. 852, http://www.huntauctions.com/phone/imageviewer.cfm?auction_num=131&lot_num=852 (Accessed November 4, 2015). Frank Litsky, "Frank Scott, 80, Baseball's First Player Agent," *New York Times*, June 30, 1998, http://www.nytimes.com/1998/06/30/sports/frank-scott-80-baseball-s-first-player-agent.html (Accessed November 4, 2015).

34. *TSN*, February 25, 1959, 23; April 15, 1959, 27. "Ken Boyer Appointed, Yoo-Hoo Drink Sales to Start," *St. Louis Globe-Democrat*, April 3, 1992, Boyer clippings file, *St. Louis Globe-Democrat* Collection, St. Louis Mercantile Library. Ken Boyer Vitalis Advertisement, http://www.vintageadbrowser.com/beauty-and-hygiene-ads-1960s/34 (Accessed October 10,

2015). Neal Russo, "Ken Boyer Signs Cardinal Pact, Takes Slight Cut to $45,000," *St. Louis Post-Dispatch*, January 30, 1963, 4B.

35. "Tuning In," *TSN*, October 14, 1959, 31. "Mantle's Star Club Cops Two on 3-Tilt Trip," *TSN*, October 21, 1959, 22. "Boyer 'Slams' in N.L. Win Before 4,500," *TSN*, October 28, 1959, 22. In the Oct. 18 exhibition at Houston, Solly Hemus managed the National League team and former Cardinals teammate Bill Virdon of the Pirates also homered. Proceeds from the contest went to a local youth baseball program. "Boyer 'Slams,'" *Ibid*, October 28, 1959, 22.

36. Jack Herman, "White Sets '60 Goal—King-Size Clouts for Cards," *TSN*, October 14, 1959, 16. "Ken Boyer Honored at Elks' Dinner as St. Louis Sports Figure of Year," *Ibid*, November 18, 1959, 14.

37. David Gough, "Home Run Derby." *The National Pastime: A Review of Baseball History*, No. 17 (1997), 111, 113.

38. *Home Run Derby*, Season 1, Episode 6.

39. *Home Run Derby*, Season 1, Episode 7. When they batted, Boyer and his opponents, Harmon Killebrew and Hank Aaron, all wore golf gloves—the precursor to modern-day batting gloves—likely because their hands were not sufficiently calloused after a winter of inactivity. Interestingly, for both episodes, Ken wore a Cardinals jersey with red piping on the front that resembled the style last worn by the club in his rookie season in 1955. It also had the number 7 on the back instead of his customary No. 14. He did, however, wear his current Cardinals navy blue cap. At the time, No. 7 was worn by Cardinals manager Solly Hemus. When the author interviewed Hemus, he could offer no explanation for Boyer wearing this mismatched jersey with his number for the show. Joe Hoppel email to the author, February 18, 2013. Solly Hemus interview, January 19, 2013.

40. Gough, Home Run Derby, 116. Don Zminda, "Home Run Derby: A Tale of Baseball and Hollywood." *The National Pastime: Endless Seasons—Baseball in Southern California*. Phoenix, AZ: Society for American Baseball Research, 2011. Unpaginated photocopy courtesy of Mark Aubrey.

41. "Redbirds Give Game Boost with Clinic in Church Gym," *TSN*, January 6, 1960, 8. Jack Herman, "Stan, Solly See Redbird Rise on Pickup in Power," *Ibid*, February 3, 1960, 13.

42. The baseball school operated under Boyer's name from 1958 to 1961. Among his assistant instructors were former and current major-leaguers Spud Chandler, Joe Nuxhall, teammate Hal Smith, Hoyt Wilhelm, and Frank Robinson. There was also a summer camp near Salem, Missouri, for boys ages eight to nineteen years old. *TSN*, March 12, 1958, 32; October 1, 1958, 60; October 22, 1958, 26; January 21, 1959, 23; February 11, 1959, 24; April 4, 1962, 44. "Ken Boyer's Missouri Baseball Camp" booklet in the author's personal collection.

43. Jack Rice, "Cards' Good Citizen Ken Boyer," *St. Louis Post-Dispatch*, July 10, 1960, Boyer HOF file.

44. "Kenny Boyer—Campaign Chairman—St. Louis Area Chapter, National Multiple Sclerosis Soc." Press release, Ken Boyer file, *St. Louis Post-Dispatch* Archives. "Ken Boyer To Head Sclerosis Drive," *St. Louis Post-Dispatch*, November 18, 1959, 3D. "Boyer Heading Drive For Sclerosis Fund," *Ibid*, January 19, 1964, 7H. "Ken Boyer Again To Head Multiple Sclerosis Drive," *Ibid*, January 16, 1967, 14A. Jack Rice, "Cards' Good Citizen Ken Boyer," *Ibid*, July 10, 1960, Boyer HOF file.

45. "No Yankee Deals, But Casey in Fine Fettle as Showman," *TSN*, December 16, 1959, 7. Roy Gillespie, "Diamond Facts and Facets," *Ibid*, September 7, 1960, 10.

46. "Slugger Signs After Getting Salary Hike," *St. Louis Globe-Democrat*, February 4, 1960. J. Roy Stockton, "Solly Sticks Glove Men's Fingers in Dikes on Defense," *TSN*, April 13, 1960, 18.

47. "Slugger Signs After Getting Salary Hike," *St. Louis Globe-Democrat*, February 4, 1960, St. Louis Mercantile Library Association Collection. United Press International photograph dated February 3, 1960.

48. Giglio, *Musial*, 244. "Quotes," *TSN*, March 30, 1960, 14.

49. Jack Herman, "Spencer Picking Up Drooping Redbirds with Lusty Clouting," *TSN*, May 25, 1960, 20.

50. "Cards' Fizzle on Cincy Trip, Began with Bus Breakdown," *TSN*, May 18, 1960, 15. Lowell Reidenbaugh, "Card Flip-Flops Peril Solly's Job," *Ibid*, May 25, 1960, 1, 8. Myron Cope, "Ken Boyer: New Leader of the Cardinals," *Sport*, August 1961, 56.

51. Jack Herman, "Spencer Picking Up Drooping Redbirds With Lusty Clouting," *TSN*, May 25, 1960, 20.

52. "Crowe Raps 11th Pinch-HR for New Major League Mark," *TSN*, June 1, 1960, 23. Crowe ended his major-league career with 16 pinch-hit home runs after the 1961 season with the Cardinals. As of 2015, the current record of 23 homers is held by Matt Stairs.

53. Lowell Reidenbaugh, "Card Flip-Flops Peril Solly's Job," *TSN*, May 25, 1960, 1, 8. Earl Lawson, "Roughed-Up Reds Compose New Words for 'St. Looie Blues,'" *Ibid*, June 1, 1960, 16.

54. Ralph Ray, "Alcatraz Cons Give Visiting Card Quartet Third Degree," *TSN*, June 15, 1960, 25. Neal Russo, "King of Cardinal Champions: MVP Prize Proved Ken Boyer's Greatness," *The Sporting News Baseball Dope Book 1965* (St. Louis, MO: The Sporting News, 1965), 100.

55. "Ken Didn't See Bullet—Nor Jim Bunning's Curve Ball," *TSN*, June 5, 1965, 4. An alternate version of this story claimed the girl was unharmed, with the spent bullet ending up inside her blouse instead. Neal Russo, "Million Memories—They're All That's Left in Cards' Old Park," *Ibid*, May 21, 1966, 25. During his career, Boyer was 12-for-46 against right-hander Jim Bunning with only two extra-base hits (including one home run) and 13 strikeouts. "Kenny Boyer didn't even want to hit when I pitched," Bunning remarked. "Selected Batter-Pitcher Matchups for Ken Boyer," Retrosheet website, http://www.retrosheet.org/boxesetc/B/MU0_boyek101.htm (Accessed October 31, 2015). Frank Dolson, *Jim Bunning: Baseball and Beyond*. Philadelphia: Temple University Press, 1998, 98.

56. Tim McCarver interview, July 15, 2015. Lee Landers interview, September 17, 2015.

57. Myron Cope, "Ken Boyer: New Leader of the Cardinals," *Sport*, August 1961, 51.

58. Lee Landers interview, September 17, 2015.

59. Walt Moryn hit 11 home runs and drove in 35 runs over 75 games for the Cardinals in 1960. Leon Wagner was batting .214 with four homers and 11 RBIs when he was sent down to Triple-A Rochester. St. Louis traded him after the 1960 season to the expansion Los Angeles Angels, where he excelled offensively and finished fourth in the 1962 American League MVP balloting. Ed O'Neil, "Gabe, Bing Beat Deadline With Last-Minute Trades," *TSN*, June 22, 1960, 25. "Wagner's Goal: '143 More Homers, to Prove I Belong,'" *Ibid*, 25.

60. Oscar Kahn, "Solly Continues Shuffling Cards in Search for Cluth Wallopers," *TSN*, July 6, 1960, 18.

61. Oscar Hahan, "Sadecki, Simmons Spice Cards' Staff in Kid-Vet Drama," *TSN*, June 29, 1960, 17. Giglio, *Musial*, 245-247.

62. Oscar Kahn, "Cards Ace Jackson Plays 20-Win Tune After Off-Key Notes," *TSN*, July 13, 1960, 19. Oscar Kahn, "Cocky Cardinals Hatch Big Plans for a Fast Finish," *Ibid*, July 20, 1960, 16.

63. "Batting-Fielding-Pitching," *TSN*, July 20, 1960, 27. Dick Young, "Young Ideas," *Ibid*, July 6, 1960, 28.

64. "New York Notebook," *TSN*, July 20, 1960, 9. "Senior Loop Swatters Sweep All-Star 'Series,'" *Ibid*, July 20, 1960, 7.

65. Oscar Kahan, "Geared-Up Cards Carry On Search For Fifth Starter," *TSN*, July 27, 1960, 10. Kahan, "Backstop Smith, Flyhawk Flood—Slick Glove Guys," *Ibid*, August 3, 1960, 16.

66. Oscar Kahan, "Geared-Up Cards Carry On Search for Fifth Starter," *TSN*, July 27, 1960, 10.

67. Lipman, *Boyer*, 121–122. Oscar Kahan, "Redbirds Feather Flag Nest with Two Fledgling Phenoms," *TSN*, August 10, 1960, 17. Jane Boyer to the author, February 14, 2015.

68. Lester J. Biederman, "'Young Card Deals Pirates 'Old' Trick, 3-2," *Pittsburgh Press*, August 12, 1960, 23. Ralph Ray, "Redbirds Take Nosedive on Field, Then Plan Motor Starts to Cough," *TSN*, August 24, 1960, 6. After losing the third game of the five-game series to the Pirates on August 13, Boyer and Musial traveled thirty miles south of Pittsburgh to Charleroi, Pennsylvania, where they took part in a home run hitting contest with Bob Skinner and Dick Stuart of the Pirates. The event benefited the efforts of the nearby town of Bentleyville in winning a prize of $20,000 to build a new baseball park there. Boyer and Musial easily won the friendly competition, each hitting seven home runs while Stuart hit one. Dick Groat of the Pirates pitched to both sides. "Cards Sluggers Win HR Contest," *TSN*, August 24, 1960, 27. Robert Inserra, "Bentleyville Kids Win Park in Kraft Contest," *Ibid*, October 26, 1960, 28.

69. Oscar Kahan, "Birds Chirp at Comeback by 'Washed-Up' Simmons," *TSN*, August 31, 1960, 6.

70. Ralph Ray, "Hats Off…! Ken Boyer," *TSN*, September 28, 1960, 25.

71. "Major Flashes," *TSN*, September 28, 1960, 27. Les Biederman, "Pirates Celebrate Clincher With a Champagne Shower," *Ibid*, October 5, 1960, 8.

72. Charles Maher, "Would Ken Boyer Crack Babe's Record in L.A.??" (Associated Press story) *High Point* (NC) *Enterprise*, June 2, 1960, 38.

Chapter 8: All This Integration

1. Neal Russo, "Boyer Given Two-Year Contact For About $100,000," *St. Louis Post-Dispatch*, February 9, 1961. Lipman, *Boyer*, 126–127. Myron Cope, "Ken Boyer: New Leader of the Cardinals," *Sport*, August 1961, 53.

2. Neal Russo, "Cards Racing Their Motors Over Control Artist Taylor," *TSN*, December 29, 1962, 28. Russo, "Ken Boyer Signs Cardinal Pact, Takes Slight Cut to $45,000," *St. Louis Post-Dispatch*, January 30, 1963, 4B. Ken Boyer's Travel Inn postcard. Ken Boyer's Travel Inn was located at 2601 North Glenstone Avenue. In 2015, the same motel is now the Ozark Inn.

3. Myron Cope, "Ken Boyer: New Leader of the Cardinals," *Sport*, August 1961, 53.

4. "Ball Players Will Sell Buildings," *Chicago Tribune*, May 23, 1962, Part 1-6, *Chicago Tribune* Archives, http://archives.chicagotribune.com/1962/05/23/page/6/article/ballplayers-will-sell-buildings (Accessed October 25, 2015). "Ball Players' Realty Firm is Penalized," *St. Louis Post-Dispatch*, April 27, 1962, 3A. "Ball Players' Firms May Be Complete Loss," *Chicago Tribune*, October 11, 1962, Part 4-5. Among the other major-league investors were Walt Dropo of the Chicago White Sox; Jimmie Dykes, coach for the Milwaukee Braves; Billy Pierce of the San Francisco Giants; and Bob Shaw of the Braves.

5. J. Roy Stockton, "Hemus High on Redbirds' Mound Kids," *TSN*, March 1, 1961, 16. J. Roy Stockton, "Jackson Injured By Bat—Twirler Out Four Weeks," *Ibid*, April 5, 1961, 17. Ray Gillespie, "Diamond Facts and Facets," *Ibid*, April 12, 1961, 12.

6. Bernie Livy, "750 Homers in 4 Seasons at Coliseum," *TSN*, April 18, 1962, 29. Remembering the team's struggles at the start of the 1960 season, Boyer deadpanned to writers after their 10-inning, 2-1 victory at Milwaukee on Opening Day: "Well, we're 13 games ahead of last year's pace. Excuse me, I have to go get a newspaper and find out who we're tied for first with." Myron Cope, "Ken Boyer: New Leader of the Cardinals," *Sport*, August 1961, 51.

7. Oscar Kahan, "Bing Sees Silver Lining in Cards' Sputtering Start," *TSN*, May 10, 1961, 30. Oscar Kahan, "Hats Off...! Ken Boyer" *Ibid*, September 27, 1961, Boyer HOF file.

8. Oscar Kahan, "Glaring Miscues Put Pressure on Cards' Slab Aces," *TSN*, May 31, 1961, 11. "Busch Backs Solly Hemus, Hopeful of First Division," *Ibid*.

9. "National League," *TSN*, June 14, 1961, 35.

10. Oscar Kahan, "Heart Condition Clouds Future of Cards' Hal Smith," *TSN*, June 28, 1961, 19, 22. Neal Russo, "Warwick, James Tote Top Guns in Redbird Arsenal," *Ibid*, June 21, 1961, 17. Oscar Kahan, "Graybeard Stan Stepping Lively in Swat Parade," *Ibid*, July 5, 1961, 21.

11. "Cards Fire Solly Hemus and Hire John Keane," *Daytona Beach* (FL) *Morning Journal* (Associated Press story), July 7, 1961, 17.

12. "Cards Fire Solly Hemus and Hire John Keane," *Daytona Beach* (FL) *Morning Journal* (Associated Press story), July 7, 1961, 17. Solly Hemus interview, January 19, 2013. "Hemus Takes It in Traditional Style," *Daytona Beach Morning Journal* (Associated Press story), July 7, 1961, 17.

13. Bob Broeg, "Pilot Boyer To Apply Tips—From Contini To Alston," *St. Louis Post-Dispatch*, March 2, 1970, 2B. Tim McCarver with Danny Peary, *Tim McCarver's Baseball for Brain Surgeons and Other Fans* (New York: Villard Books, 1998), 29.

14. John Harry Stahl, "Johnny Keane," in John Harry Stahl and Bill Nowlin, eds., *Drama and Pride in the Gateway City: The 1964 St. Louis Cardinals*. Lincoln, NE: University of Nebraska Press, 2013, 238–240.

15. "Cards Fire Solly Hemus and Hire John Keane," *Daytona Beach Morning Journal* (Associated Press story), July 7, 1961, 17. Oscar Kahan, "Redbirds Flash Dish Fireworks in Late Innings," *TSN*, July 19, 1961, 15.

16. Oscar Kahan, "Redbirds Flsh Dish Fireworks in Late Innings," *TSN*, July 19, 1961, 15.

17. "Stu Miller, All-Star Who Committed a Wind-Blown Balk, Dies at 87," *New York Times* (Associated Press story), January 6, 2015, http://www.nytimes.com/2015/01/07/sports/baseball/stu-miller-dies-at-87-blown-off-mound-in-all-star-game.html?_r=0. Accessed February 22, 2015. Jeff Faraudo, "An Ill Wind: Stu Miller Denies Being Blown Off Candlestick Park Mound at 1961 All-Star Game in San Francisco," *San Jose* (CA) *Mercury News*, July 9, 2011, http://www.mercurynews.com/portal/ci_18448327?_loopback=1. Accessed February 22, 2015. "Candlestick Gave All-Stars Stormy Footnote in 1961," *Sarasota* (FL) *Herald-Tribune* (Associated Press story), July 8, 1984, 6D. H.W. Siner, "When Roger Maris Was An All-Star," *McCook* (NE) *Daily Gazette*, July 8, 1988, 8. "Clemente Still Grinning After Nationals' Victory," *Chicago Daily Defender* (United Press International story), July 13, 1961, 23.

18. *TSN*, August 16, 1961, 27. Neal Russo, "Steady Socking by Javier Spurs Climbing Cards," *Ibid*, August 23, 1961, 8. Russo, "Boyer Sinks Reds, 6-5, With Two Out of Park," *St. Louis Post-Dispatch*, August 9, 1961, Boyer HOF file.

19. "N.L. Averages," *TSN*, September 6, 1961, 34.

20. "League Leaders on September 14, 1961," Retrosheet website. http://www.retrosheet.org/boxesetc/1961/DL09141961.htm. Accessed February 28, 2015. Mark Tomasik, "Ken Boyer added special twists to rare pair of cycles," Retrosimba blog, April 20, 2015. Accessed April 23, 2015. Oscar Kahan, "Hats Off...! Ken Boyer," *TSN*, September 27, 1961, Boyer HOF file.

21. Myron Cope, ""Ken Boyer: New Leader of the Cardinals," *Sport*, August 1961, 56.

22. Neal Russo, "Washburn Wows Redbirds with Dazzling Slab Debut," *TSN*, October 4, 1961, 30. Oscar Kahan, "Hats Off...! Ken Boyer," *Ibid*, September 27, 1961, Boyer HOF file. Clifford Kachline, "Mays Named Fifth Time on Glove All-Stars," *Ibid*, November 8, 1961, 11. Boyer received 90 votes for the Gold Glove at third base, finishing ahead of his nearest rival, Eddie Mathews of the Milwaukee Braves, who had 40 votes. *Ibid*.

23. Vickery and Broeg, *Cardinals Encyclopedia*, 296–297.

24. "Ken Boyer Goes to Hospital With Case of Pneumonia," *St. Louis Post-Dispatch*, January 3, 1962, 5C. Oscar Kahan, "Redbirds' Goals Wrapped Up in Broglio, Oliver," *TSN*, January 10, 1962, 17. Kahan, "Redbirds' Boyer Aims Bat at 100-RBI, 30-HR Goals," *Ibid*, January 24, 1962, 16.

25. Oscar Kahan, "Memories, Ditties and Digs Top Menu at St. Loo Feed," *TSN*, February 7, 1962, 8.

26. Halberstam, *October 1964*, 1994, 115. Bill White with Gordon Dillow, *Uppity: My Untold Story About the Games People Play*. New York: Grand Central Publishing, 2011, 65–66. Frederick G. Lieb, "Crowe Not 'Big Daddy' in Story About Negroes," *TSN*, March 23, 1960, 12.

27. White with Dillow, *Uppity*, 73–74. Stephen Nolgren, "Playing Pro Baseball While Black," *Tampa Bay* (FL) *Times*, April 7, 2011. http://www.tampabay.com/news/politics/playing-pro-baseball-while-black/1162358 (Accessed June 13, 2015). "Cards' White Raps 'Snub' in Florida," *Victoria* (TX) *Advocate* (Associated Press story), March 9, 1961. Jim Toomey, the Cardinals' public relations director, claimed the only players invited were those staying at the team's Vinoy Park hotel because of its close proximity to the St. Petersburg Yacht Club, where the breakfast would be held. Because Stan Musial, Lindy McDaniel, (presumably Boyer), and other players rented beachfront house with his families away from the team's hotel, none of them had been invited either. *Ibid*. Jim Patrick, "City Salutes Yanks, Cards—Color No Bar," *St. Petersburg* (FL) *Evening Independent*, March 9, 1961, 1-B.

28. White with Dillow, *Uppity*, 75.

29. White credited Cardinals general manager Bing Devine and Al Fleishman, who handled public relations for Anheuser-Busch, for the integration of the Cardinals' housing in 1962. Devine also recognized the efforts of Dick Meyer, also with Anheuser-Busch, in securing the hotels. Golenbock, *Spirit of St. Louis*, 440. The Boyers also spent several years during spring training at a hotel called the Sea Castle of Treasure Island. Suzie (Boyer) Hartwig email to the author, June 14, 2015.

30. Brad Snyder, *A Well-Paid Slave: Curt Flood's Fight for Free Agency in Professional Sports* (New York: Plume, 2007), 59. White with Dillow, *Uppity*, 78. Gibson with Wheeler, *Stranger to the Game*, 59. George Vecsey, *Stan Musial: An American Life* (New York: Ballantine Books, 2011), 248. "Musial Gets 'Concession'—Popcorn for Cardinals Kids," *TSN*, March 14, 1962, 13. "Time Meaningless to Minnie—Tagged 'Late Mr. Minoso," *Ibid*, March 21, 1962, 20. "Cardinals At Peak of Fla. Baseball Desegregation," *Baltimore Afro-American*, March 24, 1962, 15.

31. Tim McCarver interview, July 15, 2015.

32. Dick Groat interview, April 18, 2015. Halberstam, *October 1964*, 60.

33. Gibson with Wheeler, *Stranger to the Game*, 59. Bob Gibson and Reggie Jackson with Lonnie Wheeler, *Sixty Feet, Six Inches: A Hall of Fame Pitcher & A Hall of Fame Hitter Talk About How the Game is Played* (New York: Doubleday, 2009), 189–190. Dick Young, "Young Ideas," *TSN*, March 28, 1962, 31.

34. "Spring Standings," *TSN*, April 18, 1962, 40. J. Roy Stockton, "Redbird Curvers Rate Honor Roll in Keane's Book," *Ibid*, April 11, 1962, 38. C.C. Johnson Spink, "Yankees and Cards Picked to Cop Pennants," *Ibid*, 7–8.

35. Neal Russo, "Lindy and Broglio Pour Jet Fuel Into Redbird Express," *TSN*, April 25, 1962, 16. Clark Nealon, "Marathon Tie Marks Card, Colt 'Reunion,'" *Ibid*, May 2, 1962, 30. St. Louis at Houston game account, Ibid, 30. The game ended because of a 12:50 AM local curfew. The current major-league record (time wise) is eight hours and six minutes by the Milwaukee Brewers and Chicago White Sox, May 8–9, 1984. "Longest game in major league history," Baseball-Reference.com website http://www.baseball-reference.com/bullpen/Longest_game_in_major_league_history (Accessed April 21, 2015).

36. "Club Statistics," *TSN*, May 2, 1962, 26. Neal Russo, "Birds Gain Altitude on Fast Takeoff by Boyer, Jackson," *Ibid*, May 9, 1962, 10.

37. Neal Russo, "'Can't Remember Crashing Into Wall,' Minnie Reveals," *TSN*, May 23, 1962, 22. Russo, "Cards' Cuban Comet Plunges—Minoso Hit Again by Injury Jinx," *Ibid*, September 1, 1962, 6.

38. Neal Russo, "Stan Climbs Sock Peak, Pauses for Salute to Wagner," *TSN*, May 23, 1962, 22. Russo, "'I Never Worked So Hard for Two Hits,' Stan Says," *Ibid*, June 2, 1962, 11, 14.

39. "Reds Blow 9 to 1 Advantage, Lose to Cards in 11th Inning," *TSN*, June 23, 1962, 10. Neal Russo, "Cards Start to Fall Right as Keane Eyes Royal Flush," *Ibid*, 4.

40. "Five Repeaters Will Start," *TSN*, July 7, 1962, 6.

41. Neal Russo, "Keane Diagnoses Card Malady as Shocking Case of Gopheritis," *TSN*, August 4, 1962, 25.

42. "Boyer and Musial Give In—All Cards Wear Bat-Helmets," *TSN*, July 21, 1962, 31.

43. Neal Russo, "Cards' Cup of Kudos Overflows for Flossy Dish Work by Flood," *TSN*, August 11, 1962, 22.

44. "Chicago Star Dust," *TSN*, August 11, 1962, 10. Edward Prell, "American League Routs National, 9-4," *Chicago Tribune*, July 31, 1962, 2F. Regarding Luis Aparicio's catch of Boyer's potential line drive with the bases loaded in the first inning, Richie Ashburn remarked, "That's when your luck is going bad. Aparicio should have been over in the hole for Kenny. He plays him out of position and comes up with the great catch." "Chicago Star Dust," *TSN*, August 11, 1962, 10.

45. Ed Wilks, "Boyer Crowned Major's Player of Year," *TSN*, November 14, 1964, 2.

46. Fred Down, "Improved Infield Expected to Make Cards Contenders in '63," (United Press International story) *Hendersonville* (NC) *Times-News*, January 30, 1963, 12. "Boyer May Try Again in '67," (United Press International story) *Lima* (OH) *News*, September 22, 1965. "Ken Boyer Signs $50,000 Contract," *Los Angeles Times*, January 31, 1963, B4. Unidentified clipping, Griva Scrapbook Collection. Klein, *Great Infielders*, 107. Neal Russo, "Wolves Howl, But Boyer Likes St. Louis." undated *St. Louis Post-Dispatch* clipping, Boyer HOF file.

47. "Area Fans Hear Card Officials," *Joplin Globe*, February 21, 1964, 3B.

48. Curt Smith, *Voices of the Game: The First Full-Scale Overview of Baseball Broadcasting, 1921 to the Present* (South Bend, IN: Diamond Communications, 1987), 459.

49. Rich Wolfe and George Castle, eds. *I Remember Harry* (Champaign, IL: Sports Publishing, 1998), 161. Pat Hughes with Bruce Miles, *Harry Caray: Voice of the Fans* (Naperville,

IL: Sourcebooks MediaFusion, 2008), 20. Uecker added: "...[F]or some reason, he [Boyer] could never perform well enough to satisfy Harry Caray. Harry was as tough on Boyer as any announcer could be...Harry was powerful, and he knew it." *Ibid.*

50. Jack Buck with Rob Rains and Bob Broeg, *"That's A Winner!"* (Champaign, IL: Sagamore Publishing, 1997), 113–114. Bob Broeg, "Ken Boyer Deserving of the Hall," *Fowl Ball* (no date), 4. Wolfe and Castle, eds., *I Remember Harry*, 172. Tim McCarver with Danny Peary, *The Perfect Season: Why 1998 Was Baseball's Greatest Year* (New York: Villard Books, 1999), 33. Buck, Rains, and Broeg, *"That's A Winner!"* 114. Tim McCarver interview, July 15, 2015.

51. Buck, Rains, and Broeg, *"That's A Winner!"* 114. McCarver, *The Perfect Season*, 33. Luke Winn, "The Endless Summer of Bob Uecker," *Sports Illustrated*, July 1, 2013, 54. Myron Cope, "Harry Has His Own Ways," *Sports Illustrated*, October 7, 1968. sportsillustrated.cnn.com/vault

52. Myron Cope, "Harry Has His Own Ways," *Sports Illustrated*, October 7, 1968. sportsillustrated.cnn.com/vault.

53. Myron Cope, "Harry Has His Own Way," *Sports Illustrated*, October 7, 1968. sportsillustrated.cnn.com/vault.

54. David Halberstam, *October 1964* (New York: Villard Books, 1994), 259.

55. Jack Herman, "Stallard Says Caray Ridicules Red Birds," *St. Louis Globe-Democrat*, September 11, 1965. Harry Caray file, St. Louis Mercantile Library Collection.

56. McCarver with Peary, *The Perfect Season*, 33.

57. Kathleen Boyer interview, August 27, 2013. Milo Hamilton and Dan Schlossberg with Bob Ibach, *Making Waves: 60 Years at Milo's Microphone* (Champaign, IL: Sports Publishing, 2006), 39. Tommy John interview, August 17, 2013.

58. Tim McCarver interview, July 15, 2015. Wolfe and Castle, *I Remember Harry Caray*, 160–161.

59. Kathleen Boyer interview, August 27, 2013.

60. Lucinda Herron, "Mrs. Ken Boyer: She Views Pennant Race from Home Plate," *St. Louis Globe-Democrat*, September 30, 1964.

61. "Injury to Sideline Cards' Kenny Boyer," *Bridgeport* (CT) *Sunday Herald*, August 5, 1962, 37.

62. Neal Russo, "Roller-Coaster Hill Corps Upset Cardinal Flag Car," *TSN*, August 25, 1962, 8. Ed Wilks, "Busch Lowers Boom on Floppo Redbirds," *Ibid*, 9. "Players' Comments On Busch," *Nevada* (MO) *Daily Mail*, August 15, 1962.

63. Neal Russo, "Goat Horns? Boyer Rated Halo, Card Figures Show," *TSN*, December 22, 1962, 19. Russo, "White Whips Up Sock Storm—Wary of Late-Season Whammy," *Ibid*, September 15, 1962, 10.

64. Some Giants fans were so grateful to St. Louis catcher Gene Oliver for his decisive home run against the Dodgers on the last day of the season that they treated him to an all-expenses paid trip to watch the first two games of the World Series in San Francisco. "Cards' Oliver, Who Chilled LA, Gets Royal Treatment," *TSN*, October 20, 1962, 19.

65. Neal Russo, "Clutch Fizzles, Pay Slash Sting Boyer, Cards Big Clouter," *TSN*, February 9, 1963, 31.

66. Neal Russo, "Goat Horns? Boyer Rated Halo, Card Figures Show," *TSN*, December 22, 1962, 19.

Chapter 9: All-Star Infield

1. Neal Russo, "Hot Finisher Jackson No. 1 Pawn in Card Swap Talks," *TSN*, October 20, 1962, 17. Russo, "Cards Put Chill on Critics With Blazing Windup," *Ibid*, October 13, 1962, 16. Asked about the likelihood of a Boyer-for-Colavito trade, Cardinals general manager Bind Devine replied, "If we can't get the shortstop we want, we'll take a hard-hitting outfielder, but I don't think Detroit would be willing to let Colavito go." Russo, "Hot Finisher Jackson No. 1 Pawn in Card Swap Talks," *Ibid*.

2. Neal Russo, "Slugger Altman Sees Card Wall as Choice HR Target," *TSN*, October 27, 1962, 11. Russo, "Birds Hail Groat as Answer to Vexing Shortstop Puzzle," *Ibid*, December 1, 1962, 35.

3. Neal Russo, "Birds Toss Flag Eggs in B.R.'s Basket," *TSN*, November 10, 1962, 7. Bob Burnes, "B.R.'s Return Ruffles Redbird Feathers," *Ibid*, November 17, 1962, 7.

4. Devine with Wheatley, *Memoirs*, 16–17. Golenbock, *Spirit of St. Louis*, 448–449.

5. Halberstam, *October 1964*, 34.

6. John Devaney, "'Hey Dick, How Did You Do This?'" *Sport*, October 1963, 80-81. Dick Groat interview, April 18, 2015.

7. Neal Russo, "'Ken Boyer Signs Cardinal Pact, Takes Slight Cut to $45,000," *St. Louis Post-Dispatch*, January 30, 1963, 4B. Russo, "Goat Horns? Boyer Rated Halo, Card Figures Show," *TSN*, December 22, 1962, 19.

8. Dick Groat interview, April 18, 2015.

9. "Boyer's 2-Year Pact Ends; Cards Likely to Junk Plan," *TSN*, January 5, 1963, 14. Neal Russo, "Ken Boyer Signs Cardinal Pact, Takes Slight Cut to $45,000," *St. Louis Post-Dispatch*, January 30, 1963, 4B.

10. "Return of the Mahatma," *TSN*, March 9, 1963, 33. "'We Have An Outside Chance for Pennant,' Bing Believes," *Ibid*, April 13, 1963, 39. J. Roy Stockton, "Mahatma's Cloudy Forecast Kicks Up Storm of Bird Boos," *Ibid*, March 16, 1963, 33. Neal Russo, "Clutch Fizzles, Pay Slash Sting Boyer, Cards Big Clouter," *Ibid*, February 9, 1963, 31.

11. Neal Russo, "Redbird Big Three: 11-0 Mark in April," *TSN*, May 11, 1963, 9. Tom Pendergast, "Jackson to Face Cards with 'Mixed Emotions,'" *Joplin Globe*, May 2, 1963. "Selected Batter-Pitcher Matchups for Ken Boyer," http://www.retrosheet.org/boxesetc/B/MU0_boyek101.htm

12. Neal Russo, "Crippled Cards Get Quick Lift With Bench-Rider Burke's Bat," *TSN*, May 18, 1963, 11. "Edwards Spikes Boyer," *Cincinnati Post and Times-Star*, May 4, 1963, clipping in Boyer HOF file. "Boyer Spiked by Edwards; Wound Requires 13 Stitches," *Ibid*. "Ken Rates Himself as Lucky in Avoiding Serious Injury," *TSN*, undated clipping, Boyer HOF file. Russo, "King of Cardinal Champions: MVP Prize Proved Ken Boyer's Greatness," *The Sporting News Dope Book 1965 Edition* (St. Louis: The Sporting News, 1965), 101.

13. Retrosheet.org. Neal Russo, "Redbirds Preen Feathers Over 'Best Inner Cordon in League,'" *TSN*, June 8, 1963, 10.

14. Neal Russo, "Groat, Cards' Bat Magician, Sails Along at Merry Pace," *TSN*, June 22, 1963, 5.

15. Neal Russo, "Birds Feather Pitching Nest With Burdette," *TSN*, June 29, 1963, 7. Russo, "Gibson Leads Big Revival on Redbirds' Hill," *Ibid*, July 13, 1962, 24.

16. Neal Russo, "Gibson Leads Big Revival on Redbirds' Hill," *Ibid*, July 13, 1962, 24.

17. Walter Bingham, "Dick Groat and His Hitting Machine," *Sports Illustrated*, July 22, 1963.

18. Rains, *The St. Louis Cardinals*, 150–151.

19. Bill James, *The New Bill James Historical Baseball Abstract* (New York: The Free Press, 2001), 548, 552. James felt if the 1963 Cardinals had Joe Morgan at second base—then a late-season call-up with the Houston Colt .45s who later enjoyed a Hall of Fame career as a lifetime .271 hitter with 2,517 safeties and 268 home runs—rather than Julian Javier, "they would have been the greatest infield of all time, by far." *Ibid*, 552. Neal Russo, "Redbirds Preen Feathers Over 'Best Inner Cordon in League,'" *TSN*, June 8, 1963, 10.

20. "Why the N.L. Will Win: 'Great Pitching, Backed by Hefty Swings'—Dark," *TSN*, July 13, 1963, 11. Dick Groat interview, April 18, 2015.

21. Bob Broeg, "N.L.'s Swifties Scamper Past A.L. All-Stars," *TSN*, July 20, 1963, 5.

22. St. Louis Baseball Writers Association of America 1964 Cardinals 50th Anniversary Panel video. https://www.youtube.com/watch?t=80&v=1AkcrWkm_as Accessed April 30, 2015.

23. Neal Russo, "Shorty Shantz Mister Big of Cards' Bull-Pen Brigade," *TSN*, August 3, 1963, 9. Russo, "Flashy Flood's Soxk Shower Helps Whet Cards' Flag Appetite," *Ibid*, August 10, 1963, 8. Boyer batted .343 with 23 hits and 16 RBIs in 18 games against the expansion Colt .45s that season.

24. "Cards Slapped With Curfew Crackdown After Mets' Win," *TSN*, August 17, 1963, 11.

25. Neal Russo, "Discards Fatten Up on Punchless Cards," *TSN*, August 24, 1963, 7–8.

26. Neal Russo, "Even in Auld Lang Syne, The Man Hits Grand-Slam," *TSN*, August 24, 1963, 7. Giglio, *Musial*, 267.

27. Jack Herman, "Cardinals' Hero Will Remain With Club as Executive," *St. Louis Globe Democrat*, August 13, 1963.

28. Musial, *Stan Musial*, 237. "'Maybe Stan's Announcement Will Awaken Birds'—Groat," *TSN*, August 24, 1963, 7.

29. "Boyer Cracks Major Mark; No Putouts in Eight Games," *TSN*, August 24, 1963, 30. The eight-game streak began in the opener of an August 4 doubleheader with Philadelphia and carried through an August 11 game at Milwaukee. Boyer broke the record of seven straight games at third base set by Bobby Thompson of the New York Giants (May 4–13, 1952). Bobby Thompson 1952 Fielding Gamelog, Baseball-Reference.com, http://www.baseball-reference.com/players/gl.cgi?id=thomsbo01&t=f&year=1952&share=3.54#1377-1383-sum:fielding_gamelogs_5 (Accessed November 1, 2015). *The Sporting News* article makes two mistakes: Boyer's string did not begin on August 3 and Ray Jablonski of the Cardinals did not tie Thompson for the record. Instead, Jablonski went *six* consecutive games without a putout at third, July 1–5 (1st game). Ray Jablonski 1954 Fielding Gamelog, *Ibid*, http://www.baseball-reference.com/players/gl.cgi?id=jablora01&t=f&year=1954&share=2.87#227-232-sum:fielding_gamelogs_5 (Accessed November 1, 2015).

30. Neal Russo, "Boyer Joins White as Cardinals' Entry in 100-RBI Stakes," *TSN*, August 31, 1963, 9.

31. "Hats Off...! Ken Boyer," *TSN*, September 14, 1963, 25.

32. Peary, ed., *We Played the Game*, 565.

33. Musial with Broeg, *Musial*, 239. Dan O'Neill and Bernie Miklasz, *Stan Musial: Baseball's Perfect Knight* (St. Louis: St. Louis Post-Dispatch Books, 2010), 105. Gibson with Wheeler, *Stranger to the Game*, 78. Broeg and Vickery, *St. Louis Cardinals Encyclopedia*, 86–87.

34. Neal Russo, "Hats Off...! Ken Boyer," *TSN*, September 14, 1963, 25. Dick Groat interview, April 18, 2015.

35. "Yankees Clinch Pennant With Win Over Minnesota; Cardinals Cut Dodgers' Lead to 2 ½ Games," (Associated Press story) Oswego (NY) Palladium, September 14, 1963, 7. Tim McCarver interview, July 15, 2015.

36. Ed Wilks, "Keane: 'We Couldn't Be More Ready.'" *St. Louis Post-Dispatch*, September 16, 1963, 4C. Dick Groat interview, April 18, 2015.

37. Neal Russo, "Groat Yields Batting Lead to Clemente," *St. Louis Post-Dispatch*, September 18, 1963, 4C.

38. Neal Russo, "Burdette: 'Black Days At Black Rock,'" *St. Louis Post-Dispatch*, September 19, 1963, 2E.

39. Neal Russo, "Hit-Famished Redbirds Fall Off High Limb," *TSN*, October 5, 1963, 29.

40. Ed Wilks, "Day Was Long For Stan, Not Long Enough For Fans," *St. Louis Post-Dispatch, September 30, 1963*.

41. Musial with Broeg, *Musial*, 241. Neal Russo, "Shannon Shaping Up as Strong Candidate for Card Picket Post," *TSN*, October 19, 1963, 9. Neal Russo, "The Last Stan: Like the First, A Hero in a Cardinal Victory," *St. Louis Post-Dispatch*, September 30, 1963, 4B.

42. Neal Russo, "The Last Stan: Like the First, A Hero in a Cardinal Victory," *St. Louis Post-Dispatch*, September 30, 1963, 4B.

43. Tim McCarver interview, July 15, 2015. Kathleen Boyer interview, August 27, 2013. Red Schoendienst interview, February 15, 2013.

44. "Ken Boyer the Cards' Leader," *Lewiston* (MN) *Evening Journal*, May 15, 1961. "Major Flashes," *TSN*, December 31, 1958, 27. Ken Boyer (as told to Bob Broeg), "What It Means to be Stan Musial's Teammate," *Sport* (August 1962), 19, 88. "Ken Boyer Dies; Ex-Redbird Star," *St. Louis Post-Dispatch*, September 7, 1982, 5A.

45. "Bob Addie's Atoms," *TSN*, October 26, 1963, 14. "Splitting Swag," *Ibid*, October 26, 1963, 6.

46. Neal Russo, "Frisky Minnie Shapes Up as Dynamiting Card Spare," *TSN*, February 2, 1963, 20. Russo, "Groat Dubbed 'Dick Great' by Card Fans," *Ibid*, September 7, 1963, 3.

47. Altman suffered weakened eyesight over the winter of 1962–63 as a result of studying for his stockbroker's license in a dimly lit basement. George Altman with Lew Freedman, *George Altman: My Baseball Journey from the Negro Leagues to the Majors and Beyond* (Jefferson, NC: McFarland & Company, 2013), 99–100, 102.

48. Barney Kremenko, "Mets Give Roger 'A' for Effort, Plan Next House-Keeping Step," *TSN*, November 16, 1963, 9. Altman with Freedman, *Altman*, 99–100, 102. George Altman 1963 Batting Splits, Baseball-Reference.com http://www.baseball-reference.com/players/split.cgi?id=altmage01&year=1963&t=b (Accessed June 19, 2015).

Chapter 10: A Pennant Winner

1. "Musial's Locker at Shrine," *TSN*, May 9, 1964, 27. "Musial Is Honored At Party," *St. Louis Post-Dispatch*, September 30, 1963, 6B.

2. Ed Wilks, "Boyer Crowned Majors' Player of Year," *TSN*, November 14, 1964, 2.

3. Neal Russo, "Boyer Climbs Back to $50,000 Class," *St. Louis Post-Dispatch*, February 21, 1964, 4B.

4. Klein, *Great Infielders*, 108–109. "Lewis Led Spring Birds," *St. Louis Post-Dispatch*, April 13, 1964, 6C. "Rookie Lewis Paces Cards' Spring Swatters with .333," *TSN*, April 25, 1964,

35. Boyer batted .321 in 81 at-bats with 26 safeties—including five doubles, two triples, and one home run—along with seven RBIs. He played in all but three exhibition games. Snyder, *Cardinals Journal*, 470.

5. Neal Russo, "Redbird Batters Decorate Nest with Nifty Stickwork," *TSN*, May 16, 1964, 17.

6. Stan Isle, "Young Could Join Banks and Wagner," *TSN*, September 13, 1982, 9.

7. Lipman, *Boyer*, 169–170. Tim McCarver email to the author, October 10, 2015.

8. Neal Russo, "Cards Scamper for Plate Under Boyer Barrage," *TSN*, June 6, 1964. Boyer HOF file.

9. Neal Russo, "Redbirds Label Speedy Brock Hot Asset for Present, Future," *TSN*, June 27, 1964, 12. Edgar Munzel, "Cubs May Deal Top Youngster to Buttress Sagging Slab Staff," *Ibid*, June 6, 1964, 17. C.C. Johnson Spink, "Devine Explains Deal," *Ibid*, June 27, 1964, 14. Golenbock, *Spirit of St. Louis*, 454.

10. C.C. Johnson Spink, "Devine Explains Deal," *TSN*, June 27, 1964, 14.

11. "Bill White: We Thought Lou Brock Deal was Nuts," Retrosimba blog, March 29, 2011. Accessed May 11, 2015. Dan O'Neill, "Cards' 1964 Season Mirrors This One," St. Louis *Post-Dispatch*, October 9, 2011. Rains, *The St. Louis Cardinals*, 152. Neal Russo, "Redbirds Label Speedy Brock Hot Asset for Present, Future," *TSN*, June 27, 1964, 12.

12. "Cards Bomb Colts, Boyer Hits Cycle," *Pittsburgh Post-Gazette*, June 17, 1964. Mark Tomasik, "Ken Boyer Added Special Twists To Rare Pair of Cycles," Retrosimba blog, April 20, 2015. Accessed April 23, 2015. "Players Who Have Hit for the Cycle," History of the Game: Doubleday to Present Day, MLB Official Site http://mlb.mlb.com/mlb/history/rare_feats/index.jsp?feature=hit_for_cycle John Mabry became the second player in Cardinals history to hit for the natural cycle against the Colorado Rockies on May 18, 1996. Ibid.

13. Neal Russo, "Birds Flutter, Start Flirting with 9th Spot," *TSN*, July 11, 1964, 24. Ed Wilks, "Boyer Crowned Majors' Player of Year," *Ibid*, November 14, 1964, 2. Neal Russo, "Ken Boyer is Named MVP," *St. Louis Post-Dispatch*, November 24, 1964, 4B.

14. Once again, the All-Stars were selected not by the fans but the players, managers, and coaches.

15. Barney Kremenko, "Mick Lone A.L. Star Repeater; Five New Names in N.L. Lineup," *TSN*, July 4, 1964, 2.

16. Ken Boyer (as told to Neal Russo), "Redbird Flag in '64 Climaxed Boyer's Dream," *St. Louis Post-Dispatch*, February 12, 1967, Griva Scrapbooks.

17. David Vincent, Lyle Spatz, David W. Smith, *The Midsummer Classic: The Complete History of Baseball's All-Star Game* (Lincoln: University of Nebraska Press, 2001), 223. "Shea Shorts," *TSN*, July 18, 1964, 8.

18. Vincent, Spatz, Smith, *The Midsummer Classic*, 220–221.

19. Neal Russo, "Devine Examines Feeble Cards: 'Only Hot Streak Can Save You,'" *TSN*, July 18, 1964, 17.

20. Rookie Mike Shannon almost added the fourth home run in a row, but his drive hit off the top of the left-field wall for a double instead. "Three Successive Home Runs Match Feat of '44 Redbirds," *TSN*, August 1, 1964, 12.

21. "Busch 'Not Satisfied,' Hints Cards' Shuffle May Be Near," *TSN*, August 8, 1964, 10.

22. *St. Louis Globe-Democrat* photograph caption clipping dated August 28, 1964, Boyer file, St. Louis Mercantile Library Collection.

23. Neal Russo, "Busch Directs Cards' Exec Shakeup," *TSN*, August 29, 1964, 5.

24. Neal Russo, "All Relatives Gather 'Round as Sick Cards Sink in Coma," *TSN*, July 10, 1965, 20. Boyer's view had changed from what he told one writer in November 1964. Asked if Devine's firing was inspiration for their pennant chase, he replied, "That's really stretching the imagination." "Tim and Ken Reject Theory of Spur in Firing of Devine," *TSN*, November 28, 1964, 4. John Stahl, "Barney Schultz: A Cardinal's Baseball Odyssey," *Mound City Memories: Baseball in St. Louis* (Cleveland, OH: The Society for American Baseball Research, 2007), 107. Neal Russo, "Busch Directs Cards' Exec Shakeup," *TSN*, August 29, 1964, 5.

25. Unidentified clipping by Neal Russo, *St. Louis Post-Dispatch*, in Griva Scrapbook Collection.

26. "Ken Nearly Begged Off Sick—Then Collected 100th RBI," *TSN*, September 19, 1964, 8. *Ibid*, 22.

27. Ken Boyer and Neal Russo, "Redbird Flag in '64 Climaxed Boyer's Dream," *St. Louis Post-Dispatch*, February 12, 1967. Griva Scrapbook Collection.

28. Neal Russo, unidentified clipping from the *St. Louis Post-Dispatch*, September 11, 1964. Griva Scrapbook Collection.

29. "'Floor-Boarding' Cardinals Double-Clutch Milwaukee," *St. Louis Post-Dispatch*, September 16, 1964.

30. The first team to achieve the rare feat of scoring in every inning was the New York Giants, who beat the Philadelphia Phillies on June 1, 1923, by the score of 22-8. Robert E. Jones, "Scoring Every Inning," SABR Research Journals Archive, http://research.sabr.org/journals/scoring-every-inning (Accessed September 13, 2014).

31. Clifford J. Corcoran, "1964 National League: There is No Expedient to Which a Man Should Not Resort to Avoid the Real Labor of Thinking," in Steven Goldman, ed., *It Ain't Over 'Til It's Over: The Baseball Prospectus Pennant Race Book* (New York: Basic Books, 2007), 140.

32. "Cards Beat Pirates, 6-3; Trail Phils by 1 ½ Games," *St. Louis Post-Dispatch*, September 27, 1964, clipping from the Griva Scrapbook Collection.

33. Robert L. Burnes, "The Bench Warmer," *TSN*, October 31, 1964, 14. Ed Wilks, "Boyer Crowned Majors' Player of Year," *Ibid*, November 14, 1964, 2. Ken Boyer (as told to Neal Russo), "Redbird Flag in '64 Climaxed Boyer's Dream," *St. Louis Post-Dispatch*, February 12, 1967, clipping from Griva Scrapbook Collection.

34. Dick Groat interview, April 18, 2015.

35. Neal Russo, "Cards 1 ½ Back; Gibson Faces Phillies' Short," *St. Louis Post-Dispatch*, undated. Clipping from the Griva Scrapbook Collection.

36. Neal Russo, "Cards Late Bloomers Thorny to Phillies," *St. Louis Post-Dispatch*, September 29, 1964, 4C.

37. Eisenbath, *Cardinals Encyclopedia*, 82. Neal Russo, "Cards Late Bloomers Thorny to Phillies," *St. Louis Post-Dispatch*, September 29, 1964, 4C. Ed Wilks, "Phillies Subdued, But Defiant," *Ibid*, undated clipping from the Griva Scrapbook Collection. Halberstam, *October 1964*, 311.

38. "Bucs Tip Reds 2-0; Cards Win Again," unidentified and undated clipping from Griva Scrapbook Collection. Harry Caray, *St. Louis Cardinals World Champions 1964*. Narrated by Harry Caray and Jack Buck. St. Louis, MO: KMOX Radio, 1964.

39. William Leggert, "Miracle in St. Louis," *Sports Illustrated*, October 12, 1964. This sentiment was attributed to Boyer by other sportswriters. See also: Neal Russo, "Birds Get Relief in Climb to Top," *St. Louis Post-Dispatch*, September 30, 1964, 4C.

40. Bryan Burwell, "Years Roll Back as 1964 Cards Get Together," *St. Louis Post-Dispatch*, May 27, 2014.

41. "Cards Hand Phillies 10th Loss in Row," unidentified and undated clipping from Griva Scrapbook Collection. Ed Wilks, "Birds Pull for 'Little Alvin,'" Earl Lawson, "... Brings Back Memories of 1964 Pirate Game," *Cincinnati Post and Times-Star*, August 28, 1965, 9, clipping in Griva Scrapbook Collection. Undated *St. Louis Post-Dispatch* clipping in Griva Scrapbook Collection. *TSN*, October 17, 1964, 29. Mike Rathet, "Cards Listen to Reds: Ken Boyer Would Rather Be Playing," (Fredricksburg, VA) *Free-Lance Star* (Associated Press story), October 1, 1964, 8. Tim McCarver interview, July 15, 2015.

42. Neal Russo, "Birds Get Relief in Climb to Top," *St. Louis Post-Dispatch*, September 30, 1964, 4C.

43. Neal Russo, "Cards and Reds Lose; Birds Keep ½-Game Lead," *St. Louis Post-Dispatch*, October 3, 1964. Golenbock, *Spirit of St. Louis*, 462.

44. Unidentified clipping, Griva Scrapbook Collection. Golenbock, *Spirit of St. Louis*, 462–463.

45. Russell Lake, "A Three-Way Tie For The Pennant?" in Stahl and Nowlin, *Drama and Pride in the Gateway City*, 318.

46. "Cardinals' Boyer, Javier Set For Today's Opener," Undated United Press International clipping, Griva Scrapbooks.

47. Lipman, *Boyer*, 190.

48. Hernon and Ganey, *Under The Influence*, 219.

49. Ken Boyer (as told to Neal Russo), "Redbird Flag in '64 Climaxed Boyer's Dream," *St. Louis Post-Dispatch*, February 12, 1967, Griva Scrapbook Collection. Neal Russo, "'Bring On Yanks,' Keane Yells to Mob," unidentified clipping in Griva Scapbook Collection. "Boyer's Injury Worries Cardinals," unidentified clipping in Griva Scrapbook Collection. Lipman, *Boyer*, 193.

50. Neal Russo, "'Bring on Yanks,' Keane Yells to Mob," *St. Louis Post-Dispatch*, undated clipping, Griva Scrapbook Collection. Another version of this quote appears in an unidentified clipping in the Griva Scrapbooks: "With Philadelphia kicking the hell out of Cincinnati, we only had one game to worry about…ours. And our guys came through—everybody was hitting the ball today."

51. "Fans in Line All Night to get Pavilion Series Tickets," *St. Louis Post-Dispatch*, October 5, 1964, 1A.

52. Harry Caray, *St. Louis Cardinals World Champions 1964*. Narrated by Harry Caray and Jack Buck. St. Louis, MO: KMOX Radio, 1964.

53. Peter Golenbock, *Amazin': The Miraculous History of New York's Most Beloved Baseball Team* (New York: St. Martin's Griffin, 2002), 158.

54. *St. Louis Cardinals 1892–1992: A Century of Success*. VHS. Directed by Mike Kostel and Rich Domich (St. Louis, MO: St. Louis National League Baseball Club, Inc., and Major League Baseball Properties, Inc., 1992). "Fans in Line All Night to get Pavilion Series Tickets," *St. Louis Post-Dispatch*, October 5, 1964, 1A.

55. Roger D. Launius, *Seasons in the Sun: The Story of Big League Baseball in Missouri* (Columbia, MO: University of Missouri Press, 2002), 74. Ed Wilks, "Laughing Birds Open Door," *St. Louis Post-Dispatch*, undated clipping in Griva Scrapbook Collection.

56. *St. Louis Cardinals 1892–1992: A Century of Success*.

57. Neal Russo, "'Bring on Yanks,' Keane Yells to Mob," *St. Louis Post-Dispatch*, undated clipping, Griva Scrapbook Collection. After the game, Rod Kanehl of the New York Mets walked out of the shower in the visitor's clubhouse and saw Bing Devine sitting on a bench. "[I]n St. Louis, the Cards' locker room was right over our head, and I could hear corks popping

and the cheering," he recalled. "The Cards were going crazy upstairs...I turned to Bing and said, 'You know, that's your team. You should be up there.' And he looked at me and said, 'Thanks, Rod. I think I'll go up.'" Golenbock, *Amazin'*, 158.

58. Gibson and Pepe, *From Ghetto to Glory*, 73. Lipman, *Boyer*, 193.

59. William Leggett, "Miracle in St. Louis," *Sports Illustrated*, October 12, 1964, http://www.si.com/vault/1964/10/12/612594/miracle-in-st-louis

60. Ken Boyer (as told to Russo), "Redbird Flag in '64," *St. Louis Post-Dispatch*, undxated clipping in Griva Scrapbook Collection. Neal Russo, "'Bring on Yanks,' Keane Yells to Mob," *St. Louis Post-Dispatch*, October 5, 1964, 6B.

61. Ed Wilks, "Laughing Birds Open Door," *St. Louis Post-Dispatch*, October 5, 1964, clipping from the Griva Scrapbook Collection.

Chapter 11: A World Championship

1. J.G. Taylor Spink, "Characters You See at the World Series," *TSN*, October 19, 1960, 6. Larry Fox, "Oh, Brother! Boyers Dad on Hot Seat," *New York World-Telegram*, October 5, 1964, Boyer HOF File.

2. Freedman, *The Boyer Brothers*, 79, 131. Bob Broeg, "Ken Boyer on Brother Clete: 'He'll Swing in Dixie,'" *St. Louis Post-Dispatch*, April 2, 1967, 2B.

3. Unidentified clippings, October 7, 1964, Boyer HOF file. Unidentified and undated clipping, *Ibid*. Freedman, *Boyer Brothers*, 164. "Boyer's Home Folks Have Sweeter Story," *Dallas Morning News* (Associated Press story), October 12, 1964, 4. Tim McCarver with Phil Pepe, *Few and Chosen: Defining Cardinal Greatness Across the Eras* (Chicago: Triumph Books, 2003), 64.

4. Neal Russo, "Inter-Boyer Telegram Contains Hard Words," *St. Louis Post-Dispatch*, October 7, 1964, 1E.

5. Dave Anderson, "The Dinner for Ken Boyer," *New York Times*, March 2, 1982. McCarver with Pepe, *Few and Chosen*, 64.

6. Vern and Mabel Boyer had never flown before and did not attend the games in New York. Instead, they bought their first television to watch the games at home. Freedman, *Boyer Brothers*, 131. Joplin sportswriter Porter Wittich tried easing Mabel's concerns about flying. "I understand that," she replied, "but what if the plane goes down at some unscheduled place, all of a sudden like?" Porter Wittich, "Sideline Sports," *Joplin News-Herald*, October 6, 1964, 3B.

7. Neal Russo, "Boyer Makes Booers Boosters," *St. Louis Post-Dispatch*, November 20, 1964, 5C.

8. Bob Broeg, *St. Louis Post-Dispatch*, June 7, 1967, 5C, Griva Scrapbook Collection. Porter Wittich, "Sideline Sports," *Joplin News-Herald*, October 6, 1964, 3B. Mabel Boyer told Porter Wittich—who had covered the Boyer family since their days in the Cardinal Junior League in the 1940s—"In all fairness to both boys (Clete and Ken) I will have no favoriteness [sic], but when you think about it, Ken has never been in a world series [sic] before. Clete will be in his third. Clete is 26 and with the Yanks. Ken is 32 and with the Cards who are in their first series in 18 years, so maybe..." Wittich concluded: "And anybody can appreciate a mother's thoughts in that single word 'maybe.'" *Ibid*.

9. After retiring from the Locarni Quarry in nearby Carthage, Missouri, Vern Boyer became a community leader in Alba. He served on the school board and as mayor for four terms in the 1960s. He won his first election on April 7, 1964, defeating incumbent Fred Fox, 43 votes to 27. Mabel ran unopposed for the office of collector in the same election, win-

ning by 66 votes. "Father of Boyers Dies at 78," *Joplin Globe*, December 2, 1981, 8A. "Boyer Elected Mayor at Alba," *Miami* (FL) *News*, April 8, 1964, 9.

10. Tom Black, "50 Years Ago, World Series Placed Alba on the Map," *Joplin Globe*, October 26, 2014. www.joplinglobe.com (Accessed December 13, 2014). The radio station call letters are mentioned in John Crittenden, "Boyer Boys Big in Baseball, Alba," *Miami* (FL) *News*, July 21, 1963. *Joplin Globe*, October 7, 1964, 2B.

11. "Cardinals Boyer, Javier Set for Today's Opener," unidentified United Press International clipping, Griva Scrapbook Collection. Bob Broeg, "Boyer: Outcome, Not the Income," *St. Louis Post-Dispatch*, undated clipping. Griva Scrapbook Collection.

12. "Brought Back to Reality: Boyer's Injury Worries Cardinals," United Press Internation, unidentified clipping, Griva Scrapbook Collection.

13. Bob Broeg, "Boyer: Outcome, Not the Income," *St. Louis Post-Dispatch*, October 7, 1964, 2E.

14. Kevin D. McCann, "Mike Shannon," in John Harry Stahl and Bill Nowlin, eds., *Drama and Pride in the Gateway City: The 1964 St. Louis Cardinals* (Lincoln: University of Nebraska Press and the Society for American Baseball Research, 2013), 169.

15. "Stottlemyre Stifles Cards, Gives Bombers a Big Lift," *TSN*, October 24, 1964, 24–25.

16. *TSN*, October 24, 1964, 27. Dick Groat interview, April 18, 2015.

17. Dom Forker, *Sweet Seasons: Recollections of the 1955–64 New York Yankees* (Dallas, TX: Taylor Publishing Company, 1990), 68–69.

18. Forker, *Sweet Seasons*, 106.

19. Neal Russo, "Boyer Bomb, Blazing Bullpen," *St. Louis Post-Dispatch*, October 12, 1964, 2B.

20. Dick Groat interview, April 19, 2015. "Boyer's Home Folks Have Sweeter Story," *Dallas* (TX) *Morning News*, October 12, 1964. Halberstam, *October 1964*, 335–336. Frank Finch, "Boy, Oh Boyer! It's Even As Ken 'Slams' Yanks, 4-3," *Los Angeles Times*, October 12, 1964.

21. 1964 World Series Game 4 broadcast, The Milley Collection.

22. Frank Sargent, "Tale of Guy, His Gal, Her Dad and HR," *TSN*, October 24, 1964, 28. The article's writer was the father of Hession's fiancee, Mary Sargent, and had arranged for the couple to have tickets for the third and fourth games of the Series. "It must have been in the Cards," he added. *Ibid*.

23. Tim McCarver interview, July 15, 2015.

24. Ken Boyer's Grand-Slam HR Ties Up Series for Cardinals," *TSN*, October 24, 1964, 27. Dave Anderson, "The Dinner for Ken Boyer," *New York Times*, March 2, 1982. "Richardson Takes Blame for Muff," *Omaha* (NE) *World Herald*, October 12, 1964, 15. McCarver and Pepe, *Few and Chosen*, 64.

25. 1964 World Series. St. Louis Cardinals Vintage World Series Film. Major League Baseball Properties, 2005.

26. Dick Groat interview, April 18, 2015.

27. Dick Groat interview, April 18, 2015. Robert L. Burnes, "Team Success Came First for Ken Boyer," *St. Louis Globe-Democrat*, May 15, 1982. Gibson with Wheeler, *Stranger to the Game*, 96. Leonard Koppett, "Cards Top Yanks on 4-Run Homer by Boyer, 4 to 3," *New York Times*, October 12, 1964, 1. "One Big Souvenir is Worth Another," *Ibid*, October 12, 1964. "Youngster's Souvenir Signed by Ken Boyer," *Bridgeport* (CT) *Post*, October 12, 1964, 16.

28. "Advice for Reliefer Part of Boyer Feat," unidentified clipping, Griva Scrapbook Collection. "Richardson Takes Blame for Muff," *Omaha World Herald*, October 12, 1964,

15. "Ken Boyer Praises Relief Pitchers as Game Winners," (Associated Press story) *Buffalo Courier-Express*, October 12, 1964, 17.

29. Neal Russo, "Boyer Bomb, Blazing Bullpen," *St. Louis Post-Dispatch*, October 12, 1964, 2B. "Ken Boyer Praises Relief Pitchers as Game Winners," (Associated Press story) *Buffalo Courier-Express*, October 12, 1964, 17. "Advice for Reliefer Part of Boyer Feat," unidentified clipping, Griva Scrapbook Collection. "Richardson Takes Blame for Muff," *Omaha World Herald*, October 12, 1964, 15. An alternate version of Boyer's quote when asked if the grand slam was his greatest moment: "The top thrill was a week ago, the day we won the pennant. Nothing could surpass it, not even a second pennant." Russo, "Boyer Bomb," 2B.

30. Gibson would break Koufax's World Series strikeout record with seventeen in Game One of the 1968 Series against the Detroit Tigers on October 2, 1968.

31. "Ken Will Take Runs Any Time," *St. Louis Post-Dispatch*, October 13, 1964, 2C.

32. Earl Ruby, "Gibson Fans 13 for Series Victory on 3-Run Homer by McCarver," *Louisville Courier-Journal*, October 13, 1964, Griva Scrapbook Collection. Dave Anderson, "Ken Boyer: Hottest Ever at the Hot Corner," unidentified article, Griva Scrapbook Collection.

33. "10,000 Fans at Airport Welcome Cards Home," *TSN*, October 24, 1964, 30. "Cards Tell Crowd They'll Win Series," unidentified clipping, Griva Scrapbook Collection.

34. "Yanks Knot Series on Hrs by Maris, Mantle, Pepitone," *TSN*, October 24, 1964, 31.

35. Neal Russo, "Maxvill: Best of Scrubbinis," *St. Louis Post-Dispatch*, October 16, 1964, 3B.

36. "Free Ride to Series," unidentified clipping, Griva Scrapbook Collection. Roger Birtwell, "Meet the Boyers, No. 1 Baseball Family," *TSN*, November 11, 1964, 6.

37. Ed Wilks, "What Price Percentage?" *St. Louis Post-Dispatch*, October 16, 1964, 3B. Neal Russo, "Cards Are Great, Berra Tells Keane," *Ibid*, October 16, 1964, 1B. *TSN*, October 24, 1964, 34. Russo, "Thanks for the Memories: That 1964 Series—It Was Just the Most," *Ibid*, January 2, 1965, 34. "Weary Gibson and Redbird Belters Finish Off Yankees," *Ibid*, October 29, 1964, 23. "Cards New World Champions," *Lincoln* (NE) *Star*, October 16, 1964.

38. Neal Russo, "Cards Are Great, Berra Tells Keane," *St. Louis Post-Dispatch*, October 16, 1964, 1B.

39. 1964 World Series film.

40. Neal Russo, "Maxvill: Best of Scrubbinis," *St. Louis Post-Dispatch*, October 16, 1964, 3B. Eisenbath, *Cardinals Encyclopedia*, 497.

41. Neal Russo, "Keane Quits as Manager of Cardinals," *St. Louis Post-Dispatch*, October 16, 1964, 1–1B. Caray with Verdi, *Holy Cow!*, 157–159. Ed Wilks, "Busch Unsure on Keane," *St. Louis Post-Dispatch*, September 22, 1964, 4B. For particulars on Busch wanting to hire Durocher and Keane's clandestine meeting with the Yankees, see Caray with Verdi, *Holy Cow!*, 153–157.

42. "Keane Quits Cards, Yanks Fire Berra," *St. Louis Post-Dispatch*, October 16, 1964, 1B.

43. "Devine is 'Exec' of Year," *St. Louis Post-Dispatch*, October 16, 1964, 2B. Snyder, *Cardinals Journal*, 480. Neal Russo, "Redbird Office Discovers Olive Branch as Rickey Hits the Road," *TSN*, October 31, 1964, 6.

44. Ken Boyer (as told to Neal Russo), "Redbird Flag in '64 Climaxed Boyer's Dream," *St. Louis Post-Dispatch*, February 12, 1967," Griva Scrapbooks. Ed Wilks, "Boyer Crowned Majors' Player of Year," *TSN*, November 14, 1964, 2. Lassila, "Boyer," *Sarasota* (FL) *Journal*, July 7, 1973.

45. Ed Wilks, "Boyer Crowned Majors' Player of Year," *TSN*, November 14, 1964, 1. "After Years in Musial's Shadow, Boyer Supplies Extra Effort," *Ottawa* (KS) *Herald* (Associated Press story), November 25, 1964, 5.

46. Unidentified clipping, Griva Scrapbook Collection.

47. Neal Russo, "Boyer Driving to MVP," *St. Louis Post-Dispatch*, undated clipping, Griva Scrapbook Collection. Neal Russo, "Ken Boyer is Named MVP," *St. Louis Post-Dispatch*, November 24, 1964, 4B. George Vecsey, "Boyer in National League MVP," unidentified clipping, Boyer HOF file. Lipman, *Boyer*, 213. Neal Russo, "Ken Boyer is Named MVP," *St. Louis Post-Dispatch*, November 24, 1964, 4B. "Kenny Boyer Says Most Valuable Player Award Belongs to Teammates," *Neosho* (MO) *Daily News*, November 25, 1964, 10.

48. Ken Boyer 1964 Batting Splits, Baseball-Reference.com http://www.baseball-reference.com/players/split.cgi?id=boyerke01&year=1964&t=b (Accessed June 18, 2015).

49. Klein, *Great Infielders*, 109.

50. Bob Broeg, "Cardinal Testament: Last Day Shall Be First," *St. Louis Post-Dispatch*, October 16, 1964, 2B. Gibson with Wheeler, *Stranger to the Game*, 59, 101.

Chapter 12: All-Mixed Up

1. George Vecsey, "Boyer is National League MVP," unidentified clipping, Boyer HOF file. Mickey Herskowitz, "Houston Hails Winning Team at 'Busch U,'" *TSN*, January 30, 1965, 18. John Ferguson, "Rickey Speech Stirs Listeners at Tulsa Dinner," *Ibid*, February 20, 1965, 16. "Ken Honored as St. Louis Sports Personality of Year," *Ibid*, December 5, 1964, 17. Jack Herman, "MVP Title Has Boyer Racing Around Nation," *St. Louis Globe-Democrat*, January 23, 1965, St. Louis Mercantile Library Collection.

2. Bob Broeg, "They Produce for the Community," *St. Louis Post-Dispatch*, undated clipping, Griva Scrapbook Collection.

3. "Multiple Sclerosis Group to Honor Boyer," unidentified clipping, Griva Scrapbook Collection. Bob Broeg, "They Produce for the Community," *St. Louis Post-Dispatch*, undated clipping, Griva Scrapbook Collection.

4. Neal Russo, "Overjoyed Boyer Favors Staff of Four Starters," *St. Louis Post-Dispatch*, April 30, 1978, 4F. Halberstam, *October 1964*, 257.

5. Michael Wollscheidt comment on "Ken Boyer" page, The Ultimate Mets Database, http://ultimatemets.com/profile.php?PlayerCode=0108&tabno=7 (Accessed November 7, 2015).

6. Thomas Rogers, "Sports World Specials: Best Wishes," *New York Times*, March 15, 1982.

7. Neal Russo, "Boyer Was Right Number for Operator," *St. Louis Post-Dispatch*, undated clipping, Griva Scrapbook Collection. Suzie (Boyer) Hartwig interview, July 22, 2011.

8. Dan Boyer interview, July 22, 2011.

9. Cy Perkins, "Card Execs Roasted at Writers' Banquet," *TSN*, February 6, 1965, 9.

10. Neal Russo, "Give-and-Take Talk Lures Redbird Stars into Howsam's Fold," *TSN*, February 20, 1965, Boyer HOF file.

11. Dave Anderson, "Ken Boyer: Hottest Ever at the Hot Corner," unidentified article, Griva Scrapbook Collection. Neal Russo, "Ken Boyer is Named MVP," *St. Louis Post-Dispatch*, November 24, 1964, 4B.

12. Neal Russo, "Wings Clipped, Cardinals Start Off at Snail's Place," *TSN*, May 1, 1965, 22. Joseph Durso, "Life with Mets Begins for Boyer," *New York Times*, November 18,

1965, Boyer HOF file. Jack Herman, "Vet Unhappy at Inability to Find Self," *St. Louis Globe-Democrat*, September 21, 1965, Boyer file, St. Louis Mercantile Library Collection. Ken's statistics were compiled from spring exhibition box scores published in *The Sporting News*. In a March 30 game against the New York Yankees, a well-hit ball off the bat of Clete Boyer struck Ken in the face at third base. The blow wasn't serious enough to force him out of the game. *TSN*, April 17, 1965, 56. There are conflicting accounts exactly when Boyer's back injury took place. Because Jack Herman covered the team on a regular basis, the author has relied on his version rather than that of an Associated Press article. For the alternate version, see "Ken Boyer Relegated to the Bench," *Washington Post* (Associated Press story), June 16, 1965, D1.

13. Neal Russo, "Wings Clipped, Cardinals Start Off at Snail's Pace," *TSN*, May 1, 1965, 22. "Frick Repeats Task of '34, Presents Rings to Redbirds," *Ibid*, May 1, 1965, 22. *Ibid*, May 1, 1965, 30.

14. Neal Russo, "Redbirds Regroup, Cast Three Spear Carriers as Roman Legion," *TSN*, May 8, 1965, 13. "Boyer Given Good News—Back Ailment Called Minor," *Ibid*, May 8, 1965, 14. Mike Recht, "Something Familiar about Lefty Hurler," *Bowling Green* (KY) *Daily News*, April 27, 1965, 9. Ken was afraid his back pain might be a kidney stone as one had been surgically removed in 1950. "Boyer Given Good News," *TSN*, May 8, 1965, 14. Mike Recht, "Stan Musial Pitches to Ken Boyer During Special Batting Practice," *New London* (CT) *Day* (Associated Press story), April 27, 1965, 17. After playing two games beginning April 27, he sat out one more game on the 29th because of recurring pain. Neal Russo, "Swat Student Gagliano Passes Tough Test with Flying Colors," *TSN*, May 15, 1965, 18.

15. "Boyer Modest on His Big Day," *St. Louis Globe-Democrat*, May 3, 1965, Boyer file, St. Louis Mercantile Library Collection. Neal Russo of the *St. Louis Post-Dispatch* gives a slightly different version of Boyer's remarks that day: "About 15 years ago, I sat in those same stands when Stan Musial and Marty Marion were getting awards and I wished then that some day I'd be on the field receiving an award. I'm appreciative as much as I dreamed I would." Russo, "Red to Use Purkey 'to Save Games,'" *St. Louis Post-Dispatch*, May 3, 1965, 4C.

16. Neal Russo, "Swat Student Gagliano Passes Tough Test with Flying Colors," *TSN*, May 15, 1965, 18. Neal Russo, "Simmons Victim as Cards Strike Scoring Famine," *Ibid*, June 5, 1965, 3–4.

17. Philip J. Lowry, *Green Cathedrals: The Ultimate Celebration of Major League and Negro League Ballparks*. (New York: Walker Publishing Company, 2006), 102. "Astros' Scoreboard Tactics Off-Key," *TSN*, June 5, 1965, 14.

18. Gibson and Pepe, *From Ghetto to Glory*, 96.

19. Jack Herman, "Spezio Speaks Up As Card Clout Star," *TSN*, April 3, 1965, 12.

20. "Ken Boyer Relegated to Bench," *Washington Post* (Associated Press story), June 16, 1965, D1. "Inside Corner," *TSN*, June 26, 1965, 2. *Ibid*, June 26, 1965, 30. Neal Russo, "All Relatives Gather 'Round As Sick Cards Sink in Coma," *Ibid*, July 10, 1965, 20. Steve Jacobson, "Cards Talk Is Brave—It's Also in Private," *Newsday*, July 6, 1965, Boyer HOF file. Not long after the meeting, Boyer was picked off base when he forgot the count. "This has got to cost me money," he told his teammates when he got back to the dugout. *Ibid*.

21. Mark Armour, "Bob Howsam," in John Harry Stahl and Bill Nowlin, eds., *Drama and Pride in the Gateway City*, 278–279. White with Dillow, *Uppity*, 96, 98. Al Hirshberg, "Cards Stacked for New Deal," *Boston Traveler*, March 18, 1965, 38. Gibson with Wheeler, *Stranger to the Game*, 107.

22. Eisenbath, *Cardinals Encyclopedia*, 584.

23. Ed Wilks, "Ex-Bench Riders Gagliano, Buchek Use Spurs on Birds," *TSN*, July 31, 1965, 6. "Cardinal Hopes Laced in Girdle," *Victoria* (TX) *Advocate*, July 22, 1965, 7.

24. "Injury Jinx Works Overtime, 'Thumbs' Two Card Catchers," *TSN*, August 21, 1965, 18.

25. Bob Uecker and Mickey Herskowitz, *Catcher in the Wry: Outrageous But True Stories of Baseball*. (New York: Berkley Publishing Group, 1984), 61. Neal Russo, "Boyer Suggests Rest Plan to Assure Consistent Bats," *TSN*, September 11, 1965, 18.

26. Gibson with Wheeler, *Stranger to the Game*, 116. Jack Herman, "Vet Unhappy at Inability to Find Self," *St. Louis Globe-Democrat*, September 21, 1965, Boyer file, St. Louis Mercantile Library Collection. Lucinda Herron, "Mrs. Ken Boyer: She Views Pennant Race from Home Plate," *St. Louis Globe-Democrat*, September 30, 1964, Boyer file, St. Louis Mercantile Library Collection.

27. Neal Russo, "Card Clan Gathers to Finger Culprits; Vets See Ax Falling," *TSN*, October 2, 1965, 11.

28. *TSN*, October 9, 1965, 47.

29. John Patrick, "What Ken Boyer Must Prove to Himself," unidentified clipping, Griva Scrapbook Collection. Milton Gross, "The '66 Cards: A Cold Deck," unidentified clipping, Boyer HOF file. Gross claimed the clubhouse meeting took place in late July, but the Cardinals did not play in Cincinnati that month. If it occurred in that city, it may have been during the June 22–24 series instead.

30. Dick Groat interview, April 18, 2015.

31. Boyer batting splits for 1964 and 1965, Retrosheet.org. "At Last—Figures Verify Facts: Boyer N.L.'s Best at Hot Sack," *TSN*, December 18, 1965, Boyer HOF file. Steve Jacobson, "Boyer Could Lead, If Mets Can Follow," *Newsday*, March 10, 1966, 49c, Boyer HOF file.

32. Milton Gross, "The '66 Cards: A Cold Deck," *New York Post*, October 28, 1965, Boyer HOF file. Jack Herman, "Vet Unhappy at Inability to Find Self," *St. Louis Globe-Democrat*, September 21, 1965, Boyer file, St. Louis Mercantile Library Collection.

33. Milton Gross, "The '66 Cards: A Cold Deck," unidentified clipping dated October 28, 1965, Boyer HOF File. "'No Inkling,' Says Boyer," *TSN*, March 12, 1966, 28. Jack Herman, "Vet Unhappy at Inability to Find Self," *St. Louis Globe-Democrat*, September 21, 1965, Boyer file, St. Louis Mercantile Library Collection.

Chapter 13: But the Mets are in Last Place

1. As part of the Boyer trade, the Cardinals also agreed to send a player to be named later from their Triple-A club. It is uncertain whether this part of the deal was completed. Neal Russo of the *Post-Dispatch* quoted an alternate version of Boyer's reaction to the trade: "I'll be damned. You're kidding. After 17 years in the organization, it's a little hard to move on." Russo, "Boyer Goes as Redbirds Begin House-Cleaning on Top Floor," *TSN*, October 30, 1965, Boyer HOF file.

2. Bob Burnes, "Swapping Gate Idols an Old Cardinal Custom," *TSN*, November 6, 1965. Buck with Rains and Broeg, *"That's A Winner!"* 103. "Boy, 11, Petitions to Return Boyer," *St. Louis Globe-Democrat*, October 22, 1965, 2B. The fan was Robert Noel Sheets of nearby Florissant, Missouri, who had collected 370 signatures from fellow students and teachers at his school. While grateful for the effort, Kathleen Boyer doubted it would be successful. "But I think it's the cutest thing I ever heard of," she added. *Ibid*.

3. Bob Burnes, "Swapping Gate Idols an Old Cardinal Custom," *TSN*, November 6, 1965, Griva Scrapbook Collection. "Boyer 'Shook Up': 17 Years—Then a Phone Call," *St. Louis Post-Dispatch*, October 21, 1965, 4B, Boyer HOF file. Joseph Durso, "Life with Mets Begins for Boyer," *New York Times*, November 18, 1965, Boyer HOF file.

4. Ed Wilks, "Cards Deal Boyer, Now Seek Punch," *St. Louis Post-Dispatch*, October 21, 1965, 4B, Boyer HOF file. Neal Russo, "Boyer Goes as Redbirds Begin House-Cleaning on Top Floor," *TSN*, October 30, 1965, Boyer HOF file. Bob Burnes, "The Bench Warmer," *St. Louis Globe-Democrat*, October 22, 1964, 2B. Frank Finch, "Dodgers Passed Up Chance to Get Boyer," *Los Angeles Times*, November 8, 1965, B4.

5. Bob Broeg, "But Did the Redbirds Get Enough?" *St. Louis Post-Dispatch*, undated clipping, Boyer HOF file. Bob Burnes, "The Bench Warmer," *St. Louis Globe-Democrat*, October 22, 1965, 2B.

6. "Boyer 'Shook Up': 17 Years—Then a Phone Call," *St. Louis Post-Dispatch*, October 21, 1965, 4B, Boyer HOF file. "Ken Boyer Leading Five Lives From St. Louis to New York," *Pittsburgh Press*, January 9, 1966.

7. "Ken Boyer's Daughter Knows the Mets," October 21, 1965, unidentified clipping, Boyer HOF file.

8. Red Schoendienst interview, February 15, 2013.

9. "Ken Boyer Leading Five Lives From St. Louis to New York," *Pittsburgh Press*, January 9, 1966.

10. White with Dillow, *Uppity*, 99. "Boyer Can't Understand What Cards Saw in Trades," (Associated Press story) *Spokane* (WA) *Spokesman-Review*, November 19, 1965, 20. Lester J. Biederman, "Cardinal Trades Remain Puzzle," *Pittsburgh Press*, March 15, 1966, 41.

11. Bob Howsam with Bob Jones, *My Life in Sports* (Self-published, 1999), 77.

12. White with Dillow, *Uppity*, 99. Neal Russo, "Cards Seek Speed in Swapping White," *TSN*, November 6, 1965, 9. Asked what he thought of the trades, clubhouse comedian Bob Uecker remarked, "I don't know who made those deals. Maybe it was the clubhouse boy." Bob Wolf, "Mathews Gets Pal Joey Award; Praises Milwaukee's Support," *Ibid*, December 4, 1965, 32.

13. Joseph Durso, "Boyer Becomes an 'Early Bird' with Mets," *New York Times*, March 2, 1966. Boyer HOF file.

14. Red Foley, "Ken Boyer Comes to Mets In Deal for Jackson, Smith," *New York Daily News*, October 21, 1965, Boyer HOF file.

15. Barney Kremenko, "Met Gateway Post Could Go to Vet Boyer," *TSN*, January 8, 1966, 20. Kremenko, "Think Positive—That's the First Rule Pilot Wes Will Hand Mets," *Ibid*, December 4, 1965, 11.

16. Barney Kremenko, "Think Positive—That's the First Rule Pilot Wes Will Hand Mets," *TSN*, December 4, 1965, 18. Kremenko, "Long Island Fans Cheer Mets' Hot-Stove Express," *Ibid*, December 11, 1965, 17. Joseph Durso, "Second Baseman 13 Pounds Lighter," *New York Times*, February 8, 1967, 45. Kremenko, "Boyer Recovering from Horse Kick," *TSN*, February 5, 1966, 22.

17. Joe Krupinski, "Mets Dial Their Third Baseman," unidentified clipping, Boyer HOF file. The writers' curiosity even extended to the name of Boyer's horse and the one that kicked him. "My horse's name is 'Hawk,'" he told them. "I don't know the name of the other horse. The fellow riding the other horse wasn't familiar with it. He had just bought it and was riding him for the first time. Yes, I've been riding again since." *Ibid*.

18. At the 1964 All-Star Game in New York, Stengel approached Boyer's eight-year-old son David and offered to sign him to a contract with the Mets. "I belong to the Cardinals," he said. "Too bad," replied Stengel. "But I hear you got two sisters. Maybe I can sign them." Bob Addie, "Cream of Quotes in Writer's Notes," *TSN*, December 12, 1964, 2.

19. Jack Lang and Peter Simon, *The New York Mets: Twenty-Five Years of Baseball Magic*. New York: Henry Holt and Company, 1986, 58. Barney Kremenko, "Lengthy Slumps Killed Kranepool Bid for Bat Rise," *TSN*, December 11, 1965, 17.

20. Larry Fox, "In Spring Ken's the Weak-Hitting Boyer," *New York World-Telegram*, March 21, 1966, Boyer HOF file.

21. Steve Jacobson, "Boyer Could Lead, If Mets Can Follow," *Newsday*, March 10, 1966, 49C, Boyer HOF file.

22. George Vecsey, "Ken Boyer Gives Mets 'An Intangible Thing,'" *New York Times*, April 19, 1966, Boyer HOF file.

23. "Hats Off...! Ken Boyer," *TSN*, April 30, 1966, 29. "N.L. Averages (Batting)," *TSN*, May 14, 1966, 26.

24. Bob Hertzel, "Kenny Boyer—Now He's a Met," *Atlanta Journal*, April 23, 1966, Boyer HOF file. "Rain Dampens First Victory on Home Soil," *Chicago Tribune* (Associated Press story), April 23, 1966, E2.

25. "Schoendienst Lines Up New Lineup for Redbirds," *St. Louis Post-Dispatch*, May 4, 1966. Neal Russo, "Cards Bit by Hand They Once Fed," *Ibid*, May 5, 1966, 4E. Barney Kremenko, "Fast Ball 'Jumping' in Jack's One-Hitter," *TSN*, May 21, 1965, 28.

26. "Keane Goes Unnoticed at Game, Not Surprised with Yankee Surge," *Columbia (MO) Missourian* (United Press International story). May 11, 1966. "Musial Eulogizes Keane as Real Credit to Game," *TSN*, January 21, 1967, 36.

27. Barney Kremenko, "Mets Discover Key to Success with Hunt on Job at Keystone," *TSN*, May 28, 1966, 8.

28. Joseph Durso, "Three Errors in Sixth Inning lead to Third Defeat in Row," *New York Times*, May 28, 1966, 15.

29. Barney Kremenko, "A New Record for Mets—win 8 of 14 on the Road," *TSN*, July 9, 1966, 34.

30. Kathleen Boyer interview, August 27, 2013. Barney Kremenko, "Can Poor Mets Win 70? They're Sure Gonna Try!" *TSN*, December 18, 1965, 11. Whitey Herzog and Kevin Horrigan, *White Rat: A Life in Baseball* (New York: Harper & Row, 1987), 77. "'Brotherhood' Ends with Rent, Boyer Boys Learn," *TSN*, March 19, 1966, 17.

31. Tommy Holmes, "NL Has Another Topsy-Turvy Race," *Buffalo Courier-Express*, July 24, 1966, 3C. Don Lechman, *Los Angeles Dodgers Pitchers: Seven Decades of Diamond Dominance* (Charleston, SC: The History Press, 2012), 131.

32. "Mets Establish Club Mark with 18-14 Record in July," *TSN*, August 13, 1966, 17. *Ibid*, August 6, 1966, 24. Barney Kremenko, "'Togetherness' Aids Amazin' Mets' Push," *Ibid*, August 13, 1966, 17.

33. *TSN*, October 1, 1966, 26. "Boyer Signs '67 Contract with Mets," *Chicago Tribune* (United Press International story), December 28, 1966, B3. Barney Kremenko, "Boyer Signals He'll Return to Met Hot Sack," *TSN*, October 15, 1966, 19.

34. "Manager Westrum Tosses Champagne Party for Mets," *TSN*, October 22, 1966, 17.

35. Barney Kremenko, "Boyer Signals He'll Return to Met Hot Sack," *TSN*, October 15, 1966, 19. *Ibid*, October 1, 1966, 28. At the end of the season, Boyer, teammate Ron Hunt,

and manager Wes Westrum each received a new car either as a gift from fans or for winning a popularity contest. *Ibid.*

36. Deane McGowan, "Boyer Signs Mets' Pact for Reported $58,000," *New York Times*, December 28, 1966, 49. "Boyer Signs '67 Contract with Mets," *Chicago Tribune* (United Press International story), December 28, 1966, B3.

37. "Ken Prefers to Play," *TSN*, December 10, 1966, 42. Dave Darr, "Boyer Can't See Birds As Pennant Contenders," *St. Louis Post-Dispatch*, December 28, 1966, 3G. "Ken Boyer Signs, Mets Cut His Pay," *Ibid*, December 27, 1966, 5B. Joseph Durso, "1967 Looks Rosy to Mets' Boyer," *New York Times*, November 10, 1966, 68.

38. Dave Darr, "Boyer Can't See Birds As Pennant Contenders," *St. Louis Post-Dispatch*, December 28, 1966, 3G. Kathleen Boyer interview, August 27, 2013. Joyce Chancellor Facebook message to the author, April 19, May 11, 2015. As of 2015, a Ford dealership still occupies the former Ken Boyer Ford-Mercury building at 614 Market Street in Hermann, Missouri.

39. Bob Broeg, "Boyer Says Successor Smith Will Click for Cards," *St. Louis Post-Dispatch*, undated clipping. Joseph Durso, "Boyer Becomes an 'Early Bird' with Mets," *New York Times*, March 2, 1966, Boyer HOF file. Suzie (Boyer) Hartwig interview, July 22, 2011. Tommy John interview, August 17, 2013. Boyer's former home is now the Edelweiss Bed and Breakfast in Hermann. The business's website is http://edelweissbb.com/

40. Compiled spring training statistics from box scores in *The Sporting News. TSN*, April 15, 1967, 18. "Red Sox Top Mets, 23-18; Score Ten Times in Ninth," *TSN*, April 1, 1967, 33.

41. Martin Lader, "Reds Nip Los Angeles, 3-1; Rookie Misses Shutout," *Columbia* (MO) *Missourian* (United Press International story), April 21, 1967.

42. "K. Boyer First of Mets to Hit into Triple Play," *TSN*, May 20, 1967, 19. Barney Kremenko, "Ed and Ron, Met Platoon Pals, Critique Each Other's Bat Style," *TSN*, May 20, 1967, 19. Jack Lang, "Vacation for Boyer After 2,000th Hit," *Ibid*, May 27, 1967, Boyer HOF file.

43. Barney Kremenko, "Ed and Ron, Met Platoon Pals, Critique Each Other's Bat Style," *TSN*, May 20, 1967, 19. Jack Lang, "Vacation for Boyer After 2,000th Hit," *Ibid*, May 27, 1967. Boyer HOF file.

44. Jack Lang, "Wes Benches Bing's Pets, Charles Nabs Job at Third," *TSN*, May 27, 1967, 19. Barney Kremenko, "Met Uniform Puts Zing in Charles' Bat," Ibid, June 10, 1967, 16. *Ibid*, June 3, 1967, 29.

45. Milton Gross, "Boyer and Colavito: The Castoffs' Last Fling," *Sport*, November 1967, 41. Bob Rubin, "Ken Boyer: A Moment of Youth," unidentified clipping, June 27, 1967. Boyer HOF file.

46. Barney Kremenko, "Maz Raps Into Triple Play, But It's Only for Hollywood," *TSN*, July 15, 1967, 37. David Krell, "The Odd Couple's Triple Play at Shea Stadium," The Sports Post, August 31, 2013. http://thesportspost.com/blogs/view/the-odd-couple-triple-play-at-shea-stadium (accessed January 2, 2015). This part of the film may be viewed online at http://www.youtube.com/watch?v=-A2zB-e3mro

47. Bob Rubin, "Ken Boyer: A Moment of Youth," unidentified clipping, June 27, 1967. Boyer HOF file.

48. Barney Kremenko, "New Kranepool Adjusts, Beats Off Bat Slumps," *TSN*, August 5, 1967, 11. George Vecsey, "Ken Boyer Could Still Have a Met Future," July 24, 1967, unidentified clipping, Boyer HOF file. Ed Palladino, "Westrum Looks Toward Future," *Kingston* (NY) *Daily Freeman*, July 26, 1967, 32. "Ken Boyer Traded to the White Sox," *St. Louis Post-Dispatch*, July 23, 1967, Griva Scrapbook Collection. Bill Southworth was a cousin to future Hall of Fame manager Billy Southworth, who was the Cardinals' skipper in 1929 and 1940–1945

winning World Championships for St. Louis in 1942 and 1944. "Billy Southworth," National Baseball Hall of Fame website http://baseballhall.org/hof/southworth-billy

49. The Mets sent infielder Sandy Alomar to the White Sox on August 15 and Chicago sent catcher J.C. Martin to New York on November 27 to complete the trade. Ken Boyer page, Baseball-Reference.com. Boyer may have been dealing with shoulder pain for much of the season in New York, as well as an injured finger. "Ken Boyer Traded to the White Sox," *St. Louis Post-Dispatch*, July 23, 1967. Boyer HOF file. Milton Gross, "Boyer and Colavito: The Castoffs' Last Fling," *Sport*, November 1967, 42.

50. Milton Gross, "Boyer and Colavitio: The Castoffs' Last Fling," *Sport*, November 1967, 41.

Chapter 14: A Final Challenge

1. Jack Lang, "Shuffling Mets Someday May Rehire Boyer," *TSN*, August 12, 1967, 9. George Vecsey, "Ken Boyer Could Still Have a Met Future," July 24, 1967, unidentified clipping, Boyer HOF file.

2. "'I Can Help'—Boyer," *Chicago Tribune*, July 23, 1967, 2 (section 2). Milton Gross, "Boyer and Colavitio: The Castoffs' Last Fling," *Sport*, November 1967, 41.

3. Jerome Holtzman, "Chisox See Boyer as 'New Klu,'" *TSN*, August 5, 1967, 8.

4. Milton Gross, "Boyer and Colavitio: The Castoffs' Last Fling," *Sport*, November 1967, 41.

5. Edgar Munzel, "Chisox Need A Holler Guy, Says Stanky," *TSN*, May 13, 1967, 11. Milton Gross, "Boyer and Colavitio: The Castoffs' Last Fling," *Sport*, November 1967, 42.

6. Tommy John interview, August 17, 2013.

7. Milton Gross, "Boyer and Colavitio: The Castoffs' Last Fling," *Sport*, November 1967, 41, 90.

8. Milton Gross, "Boyer and Colavitio: The Castoffs' Last Fling," *Sport*, November 1967, 41, 90. "Boyer Adds Pep to Chicago Sox," *Pittsburgh Press* (United Press International story), August 6, 1967, 4-2.

9. Milton Gross, "Boyer and Colavitio: The Castoffs' Last Fling," *Sport*, November 1967, 41, 90. "Boyer Adds Pep to Chicago Sox," *Pittsburgh Press* (United Press International story), August 6, 1967, 4-2.

10. Jerome Holtzman, "Hats Off! Ken Boyer," *TSN*, August 12, 1967, 23.

11. "Chisox Pull Triple Play On Brooks' Ground Ball," *TSN*, August 26, 1967, 17. "Stanky Surprise: Boyer Delivers in Tigers' Park," *St. Petersburg* (FL) *Times* (Associated Press story), August 12, 1967, C1. Manager Eddie Stanky said one of the reasons Chicago traded for Boyer was to hit home runs at Tiger Stadium. "Stank Surprise," *St. Petersburg Times*, August 12, 1967, C1.

12. Jerome Holtzman, "'Chisox Need Lift, But Skipper Can't Give It to Them,'—Stanky," *TSN*, August 26, 1967, 6. Ira Berkow, "White Sox Hex Broken?" *New York Times* (reprinted in *Dallas Morning News*), August 15, 1983. Eddie Stanky and William Leggert, "Better from the Neck Up," *Sports Illustrated*, August 28, 1967. SI Vault, www.si.com/vault

13. "Peters Picks Up 13th Win 14-1," (Associated Press story), *Springfield* (MO) *Daily News*, August 17, 1967, 19, Griva Scrapbook Collection. "Injured Boyer Belts Long Single, Bats in Three Runs," *TSN*, September 2, 1967, 12.

14. Tommy John with Dan Velenti, *T.J.: My 26 Years in Baseball* (New York: Bantam Books, 1991), 104. Jerome Holtzman, "Slipping Sox Pin Hopes on Horlen," *TSN*, September 23, 1967, 5. There were no hard feelings between Boyer and Joe Horlen. After the game, they went to dinner together with a Chicago television broadcaster. "We were in a bar and Norm Cash and Eddie Mathews (with the Detroit Tigers) [were] there. They bought us a drink. To me, it was just another day." Joe Horlen interview with Mark Liptak, "Flashing Back with Joe Horlen," whitesoxinteractive.com (Accessed December 27, 2012).

15. Milton Gross, "Boyer and Colavitio: The Castoffs' Last Fling," *Sport*, November 1967, 41.

16. Jerome Holtzman, "A.L. Riddle: Who'll Play the Hot Hand?" *TSN*, September 30, 1967, 5.

17. "Major Flashes," *TSN*, August 12, 1967, 22. Tommy John interview, August 17, 2013.

18. Gary Peters interview with Mark Liptak, "Flashing Back with Gary Peters," http://www.whitesoxinteractive.com/rwas/index.php?category=11&id=2108 (Accessed December 27, 2012).

19. Jerome Holtzman, "Sox Stretch, Then Snap at 11th Hour," *TSN*, October 14, 1967, 9. John and Valenti, *T.J.*, 104–105. Joe Horlen interview with Mark Liptak, "Flashing Back with Joe Horlen," http://www.whitesoxinteractive.com/rwas/index.php?category=11&id=2755 (Accessed December 27, 2012).

20. Joe Horlen interview with Mark Liptak, "Flashing Back with Joe Horlen," whitesoxinteractive.com. (Accessed December 27, 2012).

21. Oscar Kahan, "Cards' Series Cuts of $8,314 Smallest for Winners Since '61," *TSN*, November 11, 1967, 30. Jerome Holtzman, "Short May Swap Chisox Hurler for Socker," *Ibid*, October 21, 1967, 20. The players pool was based on gate receipts from the first four games of the World Series and distributed to the top four National and American League clubs.

22. Edgar Munzel, "Sox Bosses Partly to Blame for Low Bat Marks—Boyer," *TSN*, June 1, 1968, Boyer HOF file. The watered-down infield in front of home plate was known as "Camp Swampy" in 1967. Lowry, *Green Cathedrals*, 54.

23. Tommy John interview, August 17, 2013.

Chapter 15: West Coast Finale

1. Lawrence Casey, "Sports Ledger," *Chicago Daily Defender*, January 15, 1968. Reliever and former Cardinals teammate Hoyt Wilhelm was the oldest overall player in the White Sox camp at forty-four years old.

2. "White Sox Drop Ken Boyer, Recall Rookie to Replace Him," *New York Times*, May 3, 1968, Boyer HOF file. "Chisox Drop Kenny Boyer From Roster," (United Press International story), *Logansport* (IN) *Pharus Tribune and Press*, May 3, 1968. "Boyer Not Finished, Waits for Phone Call," *Springfield* (MO) *Daily News*, May 4, 1968, Griva Scrapbook Collection.

3. "Ken Boyer Signed by Dodgers, Will Join Club Today," *Los Angeles Times*, May 11, 1968. Bob Hunter, "Ken Boyer Available to Dodgers," *Los Angeles Herald-Examiner*, September 2, 1964. Bob Broeg, "Ken Boyer, Two-League Vet, Gives Edge to Cardinals," *St. Louis Post-Dispatch*, September 11, 1968, 2E. James Enright, "Rocky, Boyer Cost Dodgers $95,000 Tab," *Chicago American*, May 15, 1968, Boyer HOF file. "We were very pleased when Ken told us, 'Frankly, that's $5,000 more than I figured you would offer me,'" one Dodgers official said. "That made it easy for us to sign Boyer." To make room for Boyer on the roster, the Dodgers optioned outfielder Cleo James to Triple-A Spokane in the Pacific Coast League. Enright, "Rocky, Boyer Cost Dodgers $95,000 Tab," *Chicago American*, May 15, 1968.

4. Walter Alston managed National League teams in the 1956, 1960 (twice), and 1964 All-Star Games. After Boyer's rookie season, Alston wrote, "I rate Boyer as one of the fine young ball players in the game." Walter Alston, "'It Won't Be A Cake Walk,' Says Alston," *TSN*, February 15, 1956, 7. "Boyer Starts for Dodgers," *St. Louis Post-Dispatch* undated clipping, Griva Scrapbook collection.

5. Retrosheet.org. *TSN*, June 1, 1968, 23. Ken did not start the May 22 game against the Cardinals, but pinch-hit for Len Gabrielson in the ninth inning and struck out.

6. A list for major-league pitchers with the most consecutive scoreless innings is given in Lyle Spatz, editor, *The SABR Baseball List & Record Book* (New York: Scribner, 2007), 270. Robert L. Burnes, "Team Success Came First for Ken Boyer," *St. Louis Globe-Democrat*, May 15, 1982.

7. Retrosheet.org. Tim Wendel, *The Summer of '68: The Season That Changed Baseball—and America—Forever* (New York: De Capo Press, 2013), 41.

8. Retrosheet.org. "Drysdale Sets New Record 1968," YouTube https://www.youtube.com/watch?v=RCgNVfQntVw Tony Ortega, "Pete Hamill's Eyewitness Account of Robert Kennedy's Assassination," The Village Voice, May 5, 2010 http://www.villagevoice.com/news/pete-hamills-eyewitness-account-of-robert-kennedys-assassination-6692381

9. Bob Hunter, "Drysdale's Feat in 'Untouchable' Class," *TSN*, June 22, 1968, 7. Retrosheet.org. Larry Schwartz, "Drysdale sets consecutive scoreless inning mark," ESPN Classic, http://espn.go.com/classic/s/moment010608drysdale-record.html (Accessed July 23, 2014). Robert L. Burnes, "Team Success Came First for Ken Boyer," *St. Louis Globe-Democrat*, May 15, 1982. According to *The Sporting News*, "Both Buzzie Bavasi and Ken Boyer called it their greatest thrills in baseball." "Don's Win No. 1 Thrill for Bavasi and Boyer," *TSN*, June 15, 1968, 13.

10. Bob Hunter, "Gabe Using Pull to Land Regular Dodger Post," *TSN*, July 13, 1968, 25. "Ken Boyer Just One of Long Line," unidentified clipping, Boyer HOF file.

11. Bob Broeg, "Ken Boyer, Two-League Vet, Gives Edge to Cardinals," *St. Louis Post-Dispatch*, September 11, 1968, 2E.

12. "Ken Boyer Shaken Up," *Milwaukee Sentinel*, July 30, 1968. *TSN*, August 10, 1968, 25.

13. Dan Hafner, "Champagne Flows as Aguirre Finally Wins One in 14th," *Los Angeles Times*, August 11, 1968, I1. Prior to the Dodgers' series against Philadelphia beginning August 9, Boyer's stiff neck had kept him out of the lineup for the last 11 games. *Ibid*.

14. Arthur Daley, "Cards' Simmons in Class with the Best," *New York Times*, reprinted in *Boston Herald*, March 19, 1973, Genealogybank.com. Retrosheet.org. Ted Simmons Statistics and History, baseball-reference.com. Simmons had struck out looking in his first at-bat.

15. Bob Broeg, "Ken Boyer, Two-League Vet, Gives Edge to Cardinals," *St. Louis Post-Dispatch*, September 11, 1968, 2E.

16. Bob Hunter, "Dodgers May Be Glad They Failed to Deal Haller, Big Gun in Arsenal," *TSN*, February 8, 1969, 41. Bob Hunter, "Boyer Adds a Clutch Bat to LA's Anemic Attack," *Ibid*, January 18, 1969, 34. Bob Broeg, "Ken Boyer, Two-League Vet, Gives Edge to Cardinals," *St. Louis Post-Dispatch*, September 11, 1968, 2E.

17. Bob Hunter, "Boyer Adds a Clutch Bat to LA's Anemic Attack," *TSN*, January 18, 1969, 34.

18. "Expansion of 1969," Baseball-Reference website http://www.baseball-reference.com/bullpen/Expansion_of_1969. Bob Hunter, "Boyer Adds a Clutch Bat to LA's Anemic Attack," *TSN*, January 18, 1969, 34. "3 Former MVPs May Go in Draft," *Washington Post*, October 13, 1968, C8. Bob Hunter, "'Be My Guest,' The O'Malley Tells Discontented Dodgers," *TSN*, March 15, 1969, 9. "Radatz Passes Test in Comeback Effort," *Columbia Missourian*, March

6, 1969. Mike Recht, "McMullen Ends Holdout, Signs For $30,000," (Associated Press story) *Oxnard* (CA) *Press-Courier*, March 6, 1969, 15. The terms of Boyer's 1969 contract were not reported.

19. The Dodgers played the White Sox at Nassua in the Bahamas on March 14 and 15. *TSN*, March 29, 1969, 35. Edgar Munzel, "White Sox Will Visit Bahamas and Mexico," *Ibid*, January 18, 1969, 33.

20. Bob Hunter, "Dodger Mod Squad Pushed Ahead with 'Grabby' at Short," *TSN*, May 10, 1969, 10. Neal Russo, "Boyer Returns, Sees Birds Walk Away," *St. Louis Post-Dispatch*, October 3, 1969, Griva Scrapbook. Jane Boyer email to the author, August 1, 2014.

21. "Parker Appendectomy Rocks Alston, Dodgers," *TSN*, August 9, 1969, 31. "Stan Voted Best in History For St. Louis; Gibson Cited," (Associated Press story) *Omaha* (NE) *World Herald*, June 3, 1969, 19. "It's How You Play The Game," *Columbia* (MO) *Missourian*, June 3, 1969.

22. Neal Russo, "Cards Give Fast Shuffle to Allen," *TSN*, October 17, 1970, 24. Tommy John interview, August 17, 2013.

23. Ross Newhan, "Boyer to Quit After Dodger Season Ends," *Los Angeles Times*, September 10, 1969, E-4. Neal Russo, "Cards Give Fast Shuffle to Allen," *TSN*, October 17, 1970, 24. Neal Russo, "Ken Boyer—Mr. All-Star at Hot Corner," *TSN*, September 26, 1964, 3. David Israel, "Hiring Boyer a Cardinal Sin," *Chicago Tribune*, May 12, 1978, E1. Neal Russo, "Overjoyed Boyer Favors Staff of Four Starters," *St. Louis Post-Dispatch*, April 30, 1978, 1F. Neal Russo, "Ex-Card Boyer Wary of 'Hot Weather' Birds," *Ibid*, May 14, 1969, Boyer HOF File. "Club 2,000 Induction to Garvey," *San Diego Union*, May 8, 1983.

24. Mark Tomasik, "Ken Boyer Aided Willie Davis' Hitting Streak," Retrosimba blog, May 6, 2011 (Accessed May 6, 2011). Tom Loomis, "Heavy Bat Helps Dodgers' Willie Davis Lift Light Average," *Toldeo Blade*, March 23, 1970.

25. Bob Broeg, "Boyer Returns, Sees Birds Walk Away," *St. Louis Post-Dispatch*, October 3, 1969, 1C, Griva Scrapbook Collection.

26. Larry Hug, "Boyer: A Cardinals Rule to Migrate East," *St. Petersburg* (FL) *Independent*, February 24, 1970, 2C.

27. Boyer was the sports director for KWK radio in St. Louis in the winter of 1961–62 and hosted a Sunday sports show on KMOX, the Cardinals' flagship station, in 1963 and 1964. *TSN*, January 24, 1962, 16; March 16, 1963, 35; February 15, 1964, 40.

28. "Boyer To Quit After Dodgers Season Ends," *Los Angeles Times*, September 10, 1969, E4. "17 Years—Then A Phone Call," *St. Louis Post-Dispatch*, October 21, 1965, 6B. Larry Hug, "Boyer: A Cardinals Rule to Migrate East," *St. Petersburg* (FL) *Independent*, February 24, 1970, 2C. "Ken Boyer...Greatest of a Baseball Clan," *Sarasota* (FL) *Journal*, July 5, 1973, D-1.

Chapter 16: Back to the Minors

1. Larry Hug, "Boyer: A Cardinal Rule to Migrate East," *St. Petersburg Times*, February 24, 1970, 2C. "Boyer to Manager Arkansas Club," (Associated Press story) Unidentified clipping, Griva Scrapbooks. Bob Harlan, St. Louis Cardinals Press Release, October 3, 1969, Boyer HOF file. Neal Russo, "'64 Hero Schultz Returns," *St. Louis Post-Dispatch*, October 1, 1970, 1E.

2. St. Louis Cardinals press release, October 3, 1969, Ken Boyer HOF file. Neal Russo, "Overjoyed Boyer Favors Staff of Four Starters," *St. Louis Post-Dispatch*, April 30, 1978, 1F. George Vecsey, "Ken Boyer Could Still Have a Met Future," *New York Times*, July 24, 1967.

Boyer HOF file. Neal Russo, "Boyer Returns, Sees Birds Walk Away," *St. Louis Post-Dispatch*, October 3, 1969, 1C.

3. Bob Broeg, "Pilot Boyer To Apply Tips—From Contini To Alston," *St. Louis Post-Dispatch*, March 2, 1970, 2B. Dick Groat with Frank Dascenzo, *Groat: I Hit And Ran* (Durham, NC: Moore Publishing Company, 1978), 97, 99, 101. Dick Groat interview, April 18, 2015. Rick Hummel, "Boyer's Credo: Keep 'Em Happy," *St. Louis Post-Dispatch*, April 26, 1979, 1D, 8D. Bill E. Burk, "Boyer Finds Pilot Must Think Ahead On Moves," *TSN*, May 9, 1970, 40.

4. Kenton Lloyd Boyer Control Card, St. Louis Cardinals.

5. Broeg, "Boyer Returns," *St. Louis Post-Dispatch*, October 3, 1969, 1C, Griva Scrapbook.

6. Frederick G. Lieb, "Kline's Donation Wins March of Dimes Game," *TSN*, March 7, 1970, 28. Larry Hug, "Ken Boyer: A Cardinal Rule To Migrate East," *St. Petersburg* (FL) *Independent*, February 24, 1970, 2C.

7. Al Hrabosky interview, July 17, 2015.

8. Al Hrabosky interview, July 17, 2015.

9. "Boyer's Balancing Act" in "Texas League," *TSN*, August 29, 1970, 36. "Game Off—Players in Army," *TSN*, May 30, 1970, 39. Bus Saidt, "Baseball Flows In Danny's Blood," *Trenton* (NJ) *Evening Times*, March 23, 1971, 32. "Texas League," *TSN*, July 11, 1970, 42.

10. "Boyer Demotes Brother" in "Texas League," *TSN*, June 6, 1970, 39. Ira Berkow, "'Ship Out,' Brother Tells His Brother," (Newspaper Enterprise Association story) *Blytheville* (AR) *Courier-News*, June 17, 1970, 14. Freedman, *Boyer Brothers*, 122–123, 125.

11. "Texas League," *TSN*, August 15, 1970. 42. Frank Maestas, "TL West Stars Belt East, 8-2, Before 6,047," *Albuquerque* (NM) *Journal*, August 19, 1970, F-1. Carlos Salazar, "River's Bat and West's Speed Decide Texas Star Game," *TSN*, September 5, 1970, 37. "West Wins Tex. League All-Star Game," (Associated Press story), *Hope* (AR) *Star*, August 19, 1970.

12. "Texas League," *TSN*, September 5, 1970. 37. Aurelio Rodriguez Jr., "Missions Whip Travs," *San Antonio* (TX) *Express*, August 28, 1970, 1-E. "10-Run Inning Sinks Memphis," *Northwest Arkansas Times*, September 5, 1970. "Blues Dodger Foes," *Albuquerque* (NM) *Journal*, September 6, 1970, F-1.

13. Neal Russo, "'64 Hero Schultz Returns," *St. Louis Post-Dispatch*, October 1, 1970, 1E. While managing at Arkansas, Boyer gave his reason for not wanting to be a major-league coach: "You get stereotyped and you get into a rut that is hard to get out of." Bill E. Burk, "Boyer Finds Pilot Must Think Ahead on Moves," *TSN*, May 9, 1970, 40.

14. Paul Stillwell, "Cards Try Pajamas After Sleepy Season," *Columbia* (MO) *Missourian*, January 22, 1971.

15. Red Schoendienst interview, February 15, 2013. *TSN*, June 10, 1972, 4. Ken Boyer (as told to Bob Broeg), "What It Means to be Stan Musial's Teammate," *Sport* (August 1962), 88. Jim Brosnan, "Power at the Plate," *Boys Life*, March 1975, 35–36. Jim Brosnan, *The Ted Simmons Story*. New York: G.P. Putnam's Sons, 1977, 84–85.

16. Ed Wilks, "Ken Keeps Quiet On Clete," *St. Louis Post-Dispatch*, May 30, 1971, 10D. Freedman, *The Boyer Brothers*, 192–193.

17. Neal Russo, "Torre's Bat Mark Soars as Waistline Shrinks," *TSN*, July 24, 1971, 3.

18. Webb, *Memories*, 2-3. "Mother of Seven Boyer Brothers Dies," *Joplin Globe*, November 25, 1971, 4A, 13.

19. Neal Russo, "Cards Turn to The Hat for Heads-Up Hitting," *TSN*, November 25, 1972, Boyer HOF file. "Birds Name Thomas as Rookie Pilot," *St. Louis Post-Dispatch*, February 21, 1973, 4C. Neal Russo, "Cards' Non-Roster Kids Cash In During Owner-Player Squabble," *TSN*, March 10, 1973, 44. Alan Lassila, "Ken Boyer: Greatest of a Baseball Clan," *Sarasota*

(FL) *Journal*, July 5, 1973, 1-D. Lloyd Johnson and Miles Wolff, eds. *Encyclopedia of Minor League Baseball*. 3rd ed. (Durham, NC: Baseball America, 2007), 563.

20. Alan Lassila, "Ken Boyer: Greatest of a Baseball Clan," *Sarasota* (FL) *Journal*, July 5, 1973, 1-D. John Ferguson, "Ice Cream Cone Enriches Radison's Taste," *Tulsa* (OK) *World*, undated clipping, Griva Scrapbook Collection. Ken Boyer interview by Ken Smith, March 1974, BL-1490.74, transcript in Boyer HOF file.

21. "Consistent Godby Leads Tulsa's 11-Game Streak," *TSN*, May 25, 1974, 33. "American Association Batting and Pitching Records," *Ibid*, June 29, 1974, 33. "Oilers Thump St. Louis, 6-3," *Tulsa* (OK) *World*, June 14, 1974, Griva Scrapbook Collection. "How They Stand," *Ibid*, July 13, 1974, 33. "Boyer Expects Hitting" in "American Assn.," *Ibid*, July 13, 1974, 34.

22. "Like Father, Like Son?" (photo caption) *St. Louis Post-Dispatch*, June 2, 1974, 2B. *Jefferson City* (MO) *News and Tribune*, June 23, 1974, 18. "1974 Baseball Draft," Baseball Almanac website, http://www.baseball-almanac.com/draft/baseball-draft.php?yr=1974 (Accessed September 3, 2015).

23. John Ferguson, "Royals Lose Bids For KO, No-Hitter," *Tulsa* (OK) *World*, Griva Scrapbook Collection. Lee Landers interview, September 17, 2015.

24. "Boyer All-Star Pilot" in "American Assn.," *TSN*, July 27, 1974, 50. "Godby Named To Association All-Star Squad," *Tulsa* (OK) *World*, undated clipping, Griva Scrapbook Collection. John Ferguson, "Astros Ax Stars With Busse's Bat," *Ibid*, August 2, 1974, Griva Scrapbook Collection.

25. John Ferguson, "It's Official: Oilers Best in the West," *Tulsa* (OK) *World*, August 26, 1974, Griva Scrapbook Collection. John Ferguson, "Thompson Gets Clincher Again With 3-Hitter," *Ibid*, September 10, 1974, Griva Scrapbook Collection.

26. Keith Hernandez and Matthew Silverman, Shea Good-Bye: The Untold Inside Story of the Historic 2008 Season. Chicago: Triumph Books, 2009, 200. John Ferguson, "Hernandez Is Right On Target Now That He's Hitting to Left," *Tulsa* (OK) *World*, July 7, 1974, Griva Scrapbook Collection. Keith Hernandez interview, July 8, 2015.

27. Keith Hernandez interview, July 8, 2015. Keith Hernandez and Mike Ryan, *If At First...* (New York: Penguin Books, 1987), 63–64. Walker explained his hitting philosophy: "'The secret is waiting. Stroke the ball, inside out. The only kind of guy who should try to pull the ball is a guy who can hit you 40 homers a year." Richard Goldstein, "Harry Walker, 80, is Dead; A Fidgeter With a Purpose," *New York Times*, August 10, 1999, http://www.nytimes.com/1999/08/10/sports/harry-walker-80-is-dead-a-fidgeter-with-a-purpose.html (Accessed September 3, 2015).

28. "Boyer Will Manage Winter League Club," *TSN*, June 28, 1975, Boyer HOF file. Neal Russo, "'Gimme the Ball, Often,' Vuchovich Tells Cards," *Ibid*, February 25, 1978, 54.

29. Pete Swanson, "Templeton, Dawson and Kemp Top A.A. Talent," *TSN*, October 2, 1976, 33. Neal Russo, "Cards' Templeton Quick to Fulfill Phenom Label," *Ibid*, September 4, 1976, 12.

30. Jack Herman, "Ken Boyer May Succeed Schoendienst," *St. Louis Globe-Democrat*, October 6, 1976, 1C. "Boyer Asks To Manager Cards," (Associated Press story) *Gallup* (NM) *Independent*, October 6, 1976, 5.

31. Jack Herman, "Ken Boyer May Succeed Schoendienst," *St. Louis Globe-Democrat*, October 6, 1976, 1C. Neal Russo, "Boyer's Chances For Redbirds' Job Reported Slim," *St. Louis Post-Dispatch*, October 6, 1970, 1D, 2D. Jack Herman, "Vern Rapp Named Cardinals' Manager," *St. Louis Globe-Democrat*, October 8, 1976, 4B. "Giants Hire Altobelli as New Manager," (Associated Press story) *Ibid*, October 8, 1976, 1B.

32. Jack Herman, "Vern Rapp Named Cardinals' Manager," *St. Louis Globe-Democrat*, October 8, 1976, 1B. *TSN*, September 25, 1976, 32.

33. "Boyer Was Rejected By New Owners," *St. Louis Post-Dispatch*, November 19, 1976, 7D.

34. Bob Chick, "But It Wasn't All Baseball," *St. Petersburg* (FL) *Evening Independent*, April 5, 1979, 3C.

35. "Boyer Reported Rochester Bound," *St. Louis Post-Dispatch*, November 18, 1976, 4E.

36. Johnson and Wolff, eds, *Encyclopedia of Minor League Baseball*, 577.

37. "Chapter 5: 1977-1982: Front Office Follies," "On A Silver Diamond: The Story of Rochester Community Baseball from 1956-1996," http://www.geneseo.edu/~bennettb/1977.html (Accessed December 10, 2011). "International League," *TSN*, September 3, 1977, 34.

Chapter 17: Cardinals Manager

1. "Kenny Boyer in Line For Braves' Position," (Associated Press story) *Joplin Globe*, November 15, 1977. "Boyer: 'Couldn't Turn It Down,'" *St. Louis Globe-Democrat*, April 26, 1978, 1E. Jack Herman, "Boyer Has Inside Track to Rejoin Cards as Pilot," *St. Louis Globe-Democrat*, April 28, 1978, 1B.

2. Suzie (Boyer) Hartwig email to the author, September 13, 2015.

3. "Caught On The Fly," *TSN*, December 31, 1977, 62. "Int. Items," *Ibid*, May 13, 1978, 37.

4. Jeff Meyers, "Cards' Brass Should Take the Rapp," *St. Louis Post-Dispatch*, April 27, 1978, 1D. "Krol On Interim Basis," *St. Louis Globe-Democrat*, April 26, 1978, 5E. Dick Kaegel, "Did 'Peter Principle' Do In Rapp?" *St. Louis Post-Dispatch*, April 26, 1978, 1E. Jack Herman, "Vern Rapp Is Fired As Cardinal Manager," *St. Louis Globe-Democrat*, April 26, 1978, 4A. Dick Kaegel, "Unrest, Turmoil Mark Start, End of Rapp Regime," *TSN*, May 13, 1978, 7.

5. Jack Herman, "Vern Rapp Is Fired As Cardinal Manager," *St. Louis Globe-Democrat*, April 26, 1978, 1A, 4A. Rapp claimed the "loser" remark made to Simmons was taken out of context: "I meant that he'd never played on a winner."

6. Joe Castellano, "Boyer—The Relaxed Approach," *St. Louis Globe-Democrat*, May 1, 1978, 8C. The other members of the search committee were Margaret M. Snyder (Busch's personal secretary, advisor, and soon his fourth wife) and Ben Kerner. *Ibid*.

7. "Boyer: 'Couldn't Turn It Down,'" *St. Louis Globe-Democrat*, April 26, 1978, 1E. Neal Russo, "Devine Won't 'Drag It Out' in Picking New Manager," *St. Louis Post-Dispatch*, April 28, 1978, 1D. Jack Herman, "Boyer Has Inside Track To Rejoin Cards as Pilot," *St. Louis Globe-Democrat*, April 28, 1979, 1B. Neal Russo, "Manager Boyer To Use Set Lineup," *St. Louis Post-Dispatch*, April 29, 1978, 5A. "International League," *TSN*, May 20, 1978, 36.

8. Neal Russo, "Manager Boyer To Use Set Lineup," *St. Louis Post-Dispatch*, April 29, 1978, 5A. Kevin Kennedy with Bill Gutman, *Twice Around the Bases: The Thinking Fan's Inside Look at Baseball* (New York: HarperCollins, 2006), 68.

9. Joe Castellano, "Boyer is Cardinals Manager," *St. Louis Globe-Democrat*, April 29, 1978, 1A. Brian A. Bennett, *On A Silver Diamond: The Story of Rochester Community Baseball from 1956-1996* (online edition). http://www.geneseo.edu/~bennettb/1978.html (Accessed December 10, 2011). Neal Russo, "Manager Boyer To Use Set Lineup," *St. Louis Post-Dispatch*, April 29, 1978, 5A.

10. Neal Russo, "Overjoyed Boyer Favors Staff of Four Starters," *St. Louis Post-Dispatch*, April 30, 1978, 4F. Russo, "Manager Boyer To Use Set Lineup," *Ibid*, April 29, 1978, 5A.

11. "Ken Boyer Takes Over Cardinals," (United Press International story) *Salina* (KS) *Journal*, April 30, 1978, 27. Neal Russo, "Manager Boyer To Use Set Lineup," *St. Louis Post-Dispatch*, April 29, 1978, 5A. Russo, "Overjoyed Boyer Favors Staff of Four Starters," *Ibid*, April 30, 1978, 1F. Jack Herman, "Boyer Has Inside Track To Rejoin Cards as Pilot," *St. Louis Globe-Democrat*, April 28, 1978, 1B.

12. Neal Russo, "Overjoyed Boyer Favors Staff of Four Starters," *St. Louis Post-Dispatch*, April 30, 1978, 4F.

13. Neal Russo, "Boyer Tags Templeton as Cards' Key," *TSN*, May 20, 1978, 35. Russo, "Rasmussem Blanks LA," *Ibid*, April 30, 1978, 5F. The one hour, 33-minute contest was not the shortest nine-inning game in major-league history. That distinction belonged to the first game of a September 28, 1919, doubleheader in which the New York Giants beat the Philadelphia Phillies, 6-1, in 51 minutes. "Cardinals Miss Mark," *TSN*, May 13, 1978, 30.

14. Dick Kaegel, "Boyer Brews Good Communications," *St. Louis Post-Dispatch*, May 9, 1978, 4C. Rick Hummel, "Boyer Assuming He Will Return," *Ibid*, September 29, 1978, 5D. Hummel, "Boyer Rehired; Coaches in Limbo," *Ibid*, October 1, 1978, 1F.

15. Rick Hummel, "Boyer Rehired; Coaches in Limbo," *St. Louis Post-Dispatch*, October 1, 1978, 1F.

16. Tom Barnidge, "The Sky Is Falling, So Cards Uphold Senseless Tradition," *St. Louis Post-Dispatch*, June 9, 1980, 2C. Rick Hummel interview, August 4, 2015. "As one who has followed the Cardinals since 1927, I can't recall any manager who was treated more gently than Boyer..." wrote Broeg. Bob Broeg, "Hurray For Garry's Change; Hogwash To Blaming Media," *Ibid*, March 30, 1979, 2B.

17. Neal Russo, "Cards End Agony at 11 in Row," *TSN*, June 10, 1978, 16. Dick Kaegel, "Phew!! Cards Finally Feel The Thrill Of Victory," *St. Louis Post-Dispatch*, May 25, 1978, 1B. Kaegel, "Boyer Stays Cool In Victory, Too," *Ibid*.

18. Neal Russo, "Ex-Padre Hendrick Answers Cardinals' Prayer," *TSN*, June 17, 1978, 22. Dick Young, "Young Ideas," *Ibid*, June 24, 1978, Boyer file, St. Louis Mercantile Library Collection.

19. Rick Hummel, "Failure to Play .500 Would Be Cardinal Sin," *TSN*, April 7, 1979, 32. "Cards Woeful at Plate," *Ibid*, July 1, 1978, 30. "N.L. Flashes," *Ibid*, June 24, 1978, 34. Neal Russo, "Tears—His Own—Mark Dwyer's Cardinal Exit," *Ibid*, July 1, 1978, 26.

20. Doug Grow, "Burning Busch Singes Cardinal Tail Feathers," *TSN*, July 8, 1978, 20. "Neal Russo, "Even Boyer Joins Boo-Bird Chorus," *Ibid*, July 29, 1978, 24.

21. "Boyer's Riding Bumpy Course with Limping Cards," Associated Press story, August 8, 1978, unidentified clipping in Boyer HOF file.

22. Neal Russo, "Cards Hot in August But It's Far Too Late," *TSN*, September 16, 1978, 12.

23. Neal Russo, "Hernandez Shakes Off cards' Bad Year," *TSN*, December 9, 1978, 39. Rick Hummel, "Boyer Rehired; Coaches in Limbo," *St. Louis Post-Dispatch*, October 1, 1978, 1F.

24. Joe Castellano, "Cardinals Hire Red, Maxvill as Coaches," *St. Louis Globe-Democrat*, October 10, 1978.

25. Neal Russo, "Bing Bids Birds Bye-Bye As Claiborne Moves In," *TSN*, November 4, 1978, 44. Russo, "Busch Okays Cards' Plunge Into Reentry Field," *Ibid*, November 25, 1978, 42. Loren Tate, "Cardinals Back in Market," *The Daily Herald*, February 2, 1979, 12. Russo, "Cards Need RBI Punch Over Home-Run Hitter," *TSN*, December 16, 1978, 46. Russo, "Redbirds Try to Right Ship with 3 Unproved Lefties," *Ibid*, December 23, 1978, 45. Rick Hummel, "Carbo Finds He's Wanted—By Cards," *Ibid*, March 24, 1979, 40.

26. Neal Russo, "Angry Templeton Cools Off—and Signs," *TSN*, February 24, 1979, 46. Russo, "Cards Make New Pitch For Reliever Marshall," *Ibid*, January 13, 1979, 35. "Ken Boyer to Kick Off Cancer Crusade," *St. Louis Globe-Democrat*, February 10, 1979, St. Louis Mercantile Library Collection.

27. "National League," *Sports Illustrated*, April 9, 1979. http://www.si.com/vault/1979/04/09/823510/national-league (Accessed July 27, 2015).

28. Rick Hummel, "Boyer's Sin Gets the Cards' Ax," *St. Louis Post-Dispatch*, April 4, 1979, 1B. Jeff Krupsaw, "Boyer Drops Baseball for Missouri Football," *Columbia (MO) Missourian*, August 11, 1979.

29. Rick Hummel, "Heads Throb Over Cardinal Pacts," *TSN*, November 10, 1979, 44. Neal Russo, "Champ Base Thief Brock Says 1979 Is His Swan Song," *Ibid*, April 28, 1979, 16. Hummel, "Some Cards Fly High—Even On Ground," *Ibid*, May 5, 1979, 7. John Sonderegger, "...And Birds Wreck Room At The Airport," *St. Louis Post-Dispatch*, April 15, 1979, 1F. Ed Wilks, "Players Fined For Redbird Airport Rumpus," *Ibid*, April 18, 1979, 3D. Initial reports claimed chairs had been damaged or broken and the accordian door ripped from its hinges. An official with Trans World Airlines claimed the incident was "blown out of proportion." He added, "I'm not trying to play the thing down at all. I just don't want them (the Cardinals players) to be blamed for something worse than what it really was." Joe Castellano, "Airline Says Damage By Cards Small," *St. Louis Globe-Democrat*, April 17, 1979, Boyer file, *St. Louis Globe Democrat* Collection, St. Louis Mercantile Library Association Collection.

30. "Boyer Tells Of Brock's 30-Day Test," *St. Louis Post-Dispatch*, October 25, 1979, 4F. Rick Hummel, "Brock of Ages Like Reborn Redbird at Plate," *TSN*, May 26, 1979, 15. Hummel, "Failure to Play .500 Would Be Cardinal Sin," *Ibid*, April 7, 1979, 32.

31. "Boyer Enraged Over Umpiring," (Associated Press story) *Nevada (MO) Daily Mail*, April 20, 1979, 8.

32. Rick Hummel, "Brock of Ages Like Reborn Redbird at Plate," *TSN*, May 26, 1978, 15. Stan Isle, "Substitute Umpires: Controversy and Chaos." *Ibid*, May 26, 1979, 36. "Blue, Ruthven Post Sixth Victories," (Associated Press story) *Lawrence (KS) Journal-World*, May 10, 1979, 18. "Umpires All Thumbs, Eject 10 in Disputes," (United Press International story), *Pittsburgh Press*, May 10, 1979, C-1. Boyer was fined $100 by the National League, while Hernandez was penalized $450 and Simmons $250. *TSN*, June 2, 1979, 20.

33. Keith Hernandez interview, July 8, 2015.

34. Bob Burnes, "Players Pulled Rug On Boyer," *St. Louis Globe-Democrat*, June 10, 1980, 2C. Rick Hummel, "Boyer's Credo: Keep 'Em Happy," *St. Louis Post-Dispatch*, April 26, 1979, 1D.

35. Rick Hummel, "Boyer Yields A Bit, Gains Lots of Happiness," *TSN*, May 12, 1979, 16. Hummel, "Mumphrey on Spot as Brock's Successor," *Ibid*, November 17, 1979, 55. Neal Russo, "Angry Templeton Cools Off—and Signs," *Ibid*, February 24, 1979, 46. Stan Isle, "Baseball Charters No Lark for Ozark," *Ibid*, October 20, 1979, 71. Hummel, "Fan Sentiment Against Templeton," *Ibid*, August 4, 1979, 24. Hummel, "Dejected Carbo Ponders His Future," *St. Louis Post-Dispatch*, May 28, 1980, 8F. Jim Kaplan, "The Week (July 8-14)," *Sports Illustrated*, July 23, 1979. SI Vault http://www.si.com/vault/1979/07/23/823809/the-week-july-8-14 (Accessed July 27, 2015).

36. Dan O'Neill, "Herzog and Templeton: No Grudges, No Regrets," *St. Louis Post-Dispatch*, July 22, 2010, http://www.stltoday.com/sports/baseball/professional/herzog-and-templeton-no-grudges-no-regrets/article_e2ebeb70-ce60-592f-a506-99c938347842.html

(Accessed August 9, 2015). "Templeton Excites Cards," (Associated Press story), *Spartanburg (SC) Herald-Journal*, September 2, 1976, C4.

37. Rick Hummel, "Peace Comes to Redbird Temple of Turmoil," *TSN*, April 14, 1979, 37.

38. Rick Hummel, "Templeton's Outbursts Are A Mystery To His Teammates," *St. Louis Post-Dispatch*, March 28, 1979, 1D. Bob Broeg, "Hurray For Garry's Change; Hogwash To Blaming Media," *Ibid*, March 30, 1979, 2B.

39. Rick Hummel, "Peace! Templeton Can Play Shortstop His Way," *St. Louis Post-Dispatch*, March 28, 1979, 1D.

40. Rick Hummel, "Simmons' Broken Wrist Jolts Cards," *TSN*, July 14, 1979, 16, 47.

41. Rick Hummel, "Redbirds Ring the Bell for Oberkfell," *TSN*, July 28, 1979, 11. Hummel, "Fan Sentiment Against Templeton," *Ibid*, August 4, 1979, 18.

42. Ed Wilks, "Cards Aren't Flying The Friendly Skies This Trip," *St. Louis Post-Dispatch*, August 6, 1979, 1C. "Redbird Notes," *Ibid*, August 4, 1979, 6A. Rick Hummel, "Cards Find Difficulty—and Success—On Road," *TSN*, August 25, 1979, 13. Stan Isle, "Baseball Charters No Lark for Ozark," *Ibid*, October 20, 1979, 71. Keith Hernandez interview, July 8, 2015.

43. Rick Hummel, "Theft King Brock Find 3,000-Karat Rock," *TSN*, September 1, 1979, 30. Hummel, "3,000 Hits: The Star In Lou's Crown," *St. Louis Post-Dispatch*, August 14, 1979, 1A, 4A. Showing no hard feelings, Brock checked on Lamp's condition after being taken out of the game. Ibid, 4A.

44. Rick Hummel, "Big Salute to 'St. Lou,'" *TSN*, September 22, 1979, 3.

45. "Temp Rips 100-100 Barrier," *TSN*, October 13, 1979, 50.

46. Rick Hummel, "'My Last Year With Cards'—Tyson," *TSN*, September 29, 1979, 15. Hummel, "Political Boo-Boo Irks Brock," *Ibid*, October 6, 1979, "Williams Top Manager," (Associated Press story) *Alton* (IL) *Telegram*, October 23, 1979, B-1. Milton Richman, "Too Much Legalese for Phillies," (United Press International story) *Clearfield* (PA) *Progress*, December 10, 1979, 15.

47. Rick Hummel, "Hendrick Ends Silence On Year With Cards," *TSN*, October 20, 1979, 27. Hummel, "Cards Resume Search for Lefty Pitchers," *Ibid*, October 27, 1979. 20.

48. Rick Hummel, "Bonds Reverses Field, Cottons Up to Cards," *TSN*, December 29, 1979, 33.

49. "Cubs Make Use of Wind," (United Press International story), *Roswell* (NM) *Daily Record*, April 23, 1980, 15. Richard Dozer, "Another Slam-Bang Cub Day," *Chicago Tribune*, April 23, 1980, 5-1, Chicago Tribune Archives http://archives.chicagotribune.com/1980/04/23/page/57/article/another-slam-bang-cub-day (Accessed August 13, 2015). Rick Hummel, "Redbirds Turn To Greybeards To Liven Up Their Bullpen," *TSN*, May 17, 1980, 35. "Borbon Gains Some Revenge," (Associated Press story) *Alton* (IL) *Telegram*, May 7, 1980, B-6.

50. Rick Hummel, "Lackadaisical Cardinals Beaten on Grand Slam," *St. Louis Post-Dispatch*, May 18, 1980, 1G. Joe Klein, "They Lost It On The Road," *Inside Sports*, July 31, 1980, 23–24. Robert L. Burnes, "Players Pulled Rug On Boyer," *St. Louis Globe-Democrat*, June 10, 1980, 2C. The Major League Baseball Players Association was prepared to start beginning May 23, 1980, over the owners' insistence on compensation for losing free agents. Both sides reached a temporary settlement before the deadline, though the players eventually did strike the following season.

51. Joe Klein, "They Lost It On The Road," *Inside Sports*, July 31, 1980, 24.

52. "Boyer's Laissez Faire Attitude Led Directly To His Undoing," (Associated Press story) *Cincinnati Enquirer*, June 10, 1980, Boyer HOF file. Rick Hummel, "More of the Same

For Puzzled Cards," *St. Louis Post-Dispatch*, May 20, 1980, 10A. Hummel, "Ken Boyer: 'The Whole Thing Is Difficult To Figure Out,'" *Ibid*, June 10, 1980, 12A.

53. Rick Hummel, "More of the Same for Puzzled Cards," *St. Louis Post-Dispatch*, May 20, 1980, 8A. Rick Hummel, "Last-Place Cards Now Face Strike," *St. Louis Post-Dispatch*, May 22, 1980, 5B. Neal Russo and Rick Hummel, "Settlement Is A Surprise To Simmons," *Ibid*, May 23, 1980, 1B.

54. Rick Hummel, "Bottom Line: Cards Worst in Majors," *St. Louis Post-Dispatch*, May 28, 1980, 8F. Hummel, "Trade: Cards' Last Resort?" *Ibid*, May 29, 1980, 1B, 5B. Cal Fussman, "Redbirds Sad, LeFlore Happy," *Ibid*, May 31, 1980, 6A. Rick Hummel, "New Attitude, Same Results For Cards," *Ibid*, May 19, 1980, 1B.

55. Bob Broeg, "Sutter Not Made Available By Cubs, Claiborne Insists," *St. Louis Post-Dispatch*, May 20, 1980, 10A. Cal Fussman, "Busch: 'We'll Have To Make Changes,'" *Ibid*, June 1, 1980, 1F.

56. Cal Fussman, "Forsch Takes Burden Off Redbirds' Shoulders," *St. Louis Post-Dispatch*, May 27, 1980, 9A.

57. Cal Fussman, "Busch: 'We'll Have To Make Changes,'" *St. Louis Post-Dispatch*, June 1, 1980, 1F.

58. Cal Fussman, "Vuckovich Rescues Cards With Save Against Expos," *St. Louis Post-Dispatch*, June 1, 1980, 1F.

59. Cal Fussman, "Bad Times Get Worse For Cards," *Ibid*, June 2, 1980, 1C. Fussman, "Tired of Stories About Bullpen? Then Don't Read This," *Ibid*, June 2, 1980, 2C.

60. Rick Hummel, "Almon's Blooper Beats Cardinals in 13th Inning," *St. Louis Post-Dispatch*, June 8, 1980, 1H.

61. Ed Wilks, "'Birds Will Bust Their Tails,' New Manager Herzog Says," *St. Louis Post-Dispatch*, June 9, 1980, 1A. Rick Hummel, "Boyer: 'No Emotion,'" *Ibid*, June 9, 1980, 1C.

62. Rick Hummel, "Boyer: 'No Emotion,'" *St. Louis Post-Dispatch*, June 9, 1980, 1C. Ed Wilks, "'Birds Will Bust Their Tails,' New Manager Herzog Says," *Ibid*, June 9, 1980, 1A. Jack Herman, "Firing Angers Some Red Birds," *St. Louis Globe-Democrat*, June 9, 1980, 1C.

63. Joe Castellano, "Boyer Out, Herzog In As Red Bird Manager," *St. Louis Globe-Democrat*, June 9, 1980, 1A.

64. Hummel, "Players Take Blame For Boyer's Firing," *St. Louis Post-Dispatch*, June 9, 1980, 1C. Jack Herman, "Firing Angers Some Red Birds," *St. Louis Globe-Democrat*, June 9, 1980, 1C. "Cardinals Fire Ken Boyer," (Associated Press story) *Toledo (OH) Blade*, June 9, 1980, 15.

65. Rick Hummel, "Ken Boyer: 'The Whole Thing Is Difficult To Figure Out,'" *St. Louis Post-Dispatch*, June 10, 1980, 12A.

66. Rick Hummel, "Boyer: 'No Emotion,'" *St. Louis Post-Dispatch*, June 9, 1980, 4C.

67. Rick Hummel, "Boyer: 'No Emotion,'" *St. Louis Post-Dispatch*, June 9, 1980, 4C. Rick Hummel, "Ken Boyer: 'The Whole Thing Is Difficult To Figure Out,'" *Ibid*, June 10, 1980, 12A. Hummel, "Boyer: 'No Emotion,'" *Ibid*, June 9, 1980, 4C. Ed Wilks, "'Birds Will Bust Their Tails,' New Manager Herzog Says," *Ibid*, June 9, 1980, 4A. Herzog with Horrigan, *White Rat*, 114–117. Jack Herman, "Herzog Gets $100,000 Contract," *St. Louis Globe-Democrat*, June 10, 1980, 2C.

68. Rick Hummel, "Boyer's Credo: Keep 'Em Happy," *St. Louis Post-Dispatch*, April 26, 1979, 8D. Rick Hummel interview, August 4, 2015.

69. Red Schoendienst with Rob Rains, *Red: A Baseball Life* (Champaign, IL: Sports Publishing, 1998), 172.

70. Golenbock, *Spirit of St. Louis*, 531.

71. Herzog with Horrigan, *White Rat*, 117.
72. "National League," *Sports Illustrated*, April 13, 1981. SI Vault http://si.com/vault/1981/04/13/825536/national-league (Accessed August 7, 2015).
73. "Boyer Blames Fate, Sore Arms," (Associated Press story) *Nevada* (MO) *Herald*, March 15, 1981, 8. "Class A Notes," *TSN*, July 25, 1981, 41.

Chapter 18: Heading for Home

1. Bill Plaschke, "Boyer Had Plenty of Company," *St. Petersburg* (FL) *Independent*, July 12, 1980, 3C. Rick Hummel, "Ken Boyer: 'The Whole Thing Is Difficult To Figure Out,'" *St. Louis Post-Dispatch*, June 10, 1980, 12A. *St. Louis Cardinals 1982 Media Guide*. St. Louis, MO: St. Louis Cardinals, 1982, 64. "Boyer Will Remain with Cardinals," (Associated Press story) *Alton* (IL) *Telegraph*, June 25, 1980, C4.
2. "Boyer Will Remain with Cardinals," (Associated Press story) *Alton* (IL) *Telegraph*, June 25, 1980, C4. Bill Plaschke, "Boyer Had Plenty of Company," *St. Petersburg* (FL) *Independent*, July 12, 1980, 3C.
3. "Boyer Blames Fate, Sore Arms," (Associated Press story) *Nevada* (MO) *Herald*, March 15, 1981, 8. Jim Henry, "Ken Oberkfell Relishes Managing Independent Baseball," *Joplin* (MO) *Globe*, July 5, 2015, Dave Anderson, "The Dinner For Ken Boyer," *New York Times*, March 2, 1982, A18, Boyer HOF file.
4. "Louisville Signs Ken Boyer," (United Press International story), *St. Louis Post-Dispatch*, November 14, 1981, 6A. "Ken Boyer Too Ill to Manage Redbirds," *Springfield* (IL) *State Journal-Register*, February 24, 1982, 33. Ken Boyer photograph and caption in the *St. Louis Globe-Democrat* Collection, Mercantile Library, St. Louis, Missouri.
5. Gibson with Wheeler, *Stranger to the Game*, 93. Suzie (Boyer) Hartwig, Dan Boyer, Jane Boyer interviews, July 22, 2011.
6. Dan Boyer interview, July 22, 2011. Jane Boyer interview, July 22, 2011.
7. Undated clipping, Griva Scrapbook Collection. "I hadn't smoked in 10 years until that [five-game] series in Pittsburgh the next to last weekend of the [1964] season," Boyer recalled. *Ibid*. Arnold Irish, "Menu at Writers' Dinner: Nostalgia, Needles," *St. Louis Post-Dispatch*, January 12, 1982, 1C, 3C.
8. "Boyer Receiving Cancer Treatments; Will Keep Job As Louisville Manager," (Associated Press story) *St. Louis Post-Dispatch*, January 23, 1982, 5A. "Cancer Strikes Ken Boyer," (Associated Press story) *Yonkers* (NY) *Herald Statesman*, January 24, 1982, D7. "Boyer Treated for Cancer," *TSN*, February 6, 1982, 46. "Boyer To Be A Cardinals Scout," *St. Louis Post-Dispatch*, February 23, 1982, 2C.
9. Suzie (Boyer) Hartwig, Dan Boyer, Jane Boyer interviews, July 22, 2011. Dave Anderson, "The Dinner For Ken Boyer," *New York Times*, March 2, 1982, A18, Boyer HOF file. "About Us," Gerson Institute website, http://gerson.org/gerpress/about-us/ (Accessed August 26, 2015). "The Gerson Therapy," *Ibid*, http://gerson.org/gerpress/the-gerson-therapy/ (Accessed August 26, 2015). Ken Boyer, interview by Howard Cosell, *Sportsbeat*, ABC, March 7, 1982.
10. Ken Boyer, interview by Howard Cosell, *Sportsbeat*, ABC, March 7, 1982.
11. Dave Anderson, "The Dinner For Ken Boyer," *New York Times*, March 2, 1982, A18, Boyer HOF file. Suzie (Boyer) Hartwig, Dan Boyer, Jane Boyer interviews, July 22, 2011. Milton Richman, "Billy Martin Helps One Boyer Prove Love to Another," (United Press International story) *Seattle* (WA) *Times*, March 1, 1982, D6.

12. John Sonderegger, "Martin Raises $35,000 at Boyer Benefit," *TSN*, April 17, 1982, 23. Harriet Hindman, "700 Attend Tribute for Ken Boyer," (United Press International story) *Clearfield* (PA) *Progress*, March 29, 1982. Dave Newhouse, "Bighearted Billy Hides Good Side," *TSN*, April 26, 1982, 13.

13. Jack Herman, "Devine Made Sure that Boyer's Career Here Was Not Short," *St. Louis Globe-Democrat*, September 9, 1982, 6C. Bob Glauber, "Area Residents Go to Bat for Ken Boyer," *Yonkers* (NY) *Herald Statesman*, March 30, 1982, C4. "Exhibition Raises $15,000 For Boyer Fund," unidentified clipping, Boyer HOF file. Dave Anderson, "$100,000 For Boyer," *New York Times*, March 29, 1982, C3, Boyer HOF file. Association of Professional Baseball Players of America website http://www.apbpa.org/ (Accessed August 19, 2015). Solly Hemus interview, January 9, 2013.

14. Harriet Hindman, "700 Attend Tribute for Ken Boyer," (United Press International story) *Clearfield* (PA) *Progress*, March 29, 1982. Dave Newhouse, "Bighearted Billy Hides Good Side," *TSN*, April 26, 1982, 13.

15. Jack Herman, "Devine Made Sure that Boyer's Career Here Was Not Short," *St. Louis Globe-Democrat*, September 9, 1982, 6C. Dave Newhouse, "Bighearted Billy Hides Good Side," *TSN*, April 26, 1982, 13. Dave Anderson, "$100,000 For Boyer," *New York Times*, March 29, 1982, C3, Boyer HOF file.

16. Dick Wagner, "Boyer Remembered in Services," *St. Louis Globe-Democrat*, September 10, 1982, 3C.

17. Suzie (Boyer) Hartwig, Dan Boyer, Jane Boyer interviews, July 22, 2011. Dick Wagner, "Boyer Remembered in Services," *St. Louis Globe-Democrat*, September 10, 1982, 1C, 3C. Freedman, *Boyer Brothers of Baseball*, 206. Robert L. Burnes, "Ken Boyer: His Measure Is In What We Remember," *St. Louis Globe-Democrat*, September 10, 1982, 2C.

18. David Craft and Tom Owens, *Redbirds Revisited: Great Memories and Stories from St. Louis Cardinals* (Chicago: Bonus Books, Inc., 1990), 21. Jerry Izenberg, "He Walked Final Mile of Boyer's Agony," (Newhouse News Service story), *St. Louis Globe-Democrat*, October 16, 1982, Ken Boyer file, St. Louis Mercantile Library Collection. Robert L. Burnes, "Team Success Came First for Ken Boyer," *St. Louis Globe-Democrat*, May 15, 1982.

19. Robert L. Burnes, "Team Success Came First for Ken Boyer," *St. Louis Globe-Democrat*, May 15, 1982.

20. Wendell Redden, "Boyer: Class Athlete, Individual," *Joplin* (MO) *Globe*, September 8, 1982, 7A. Kathleen Boyer interview, August 27, 2013. Red Schoendienst interview, February 15, 2013.

21. Kathleen Boyer interview, August 27, 2013. Mike Eisenbath, "In Search Of…Cards' Kenny Boyer, A Heroic, Yet Private Man, Remains a Mystery," *St. Louis Post-Dispatch*, October 16, 1994, Ken Boyer file, St. Louis Mercantile Library Association Collection.

22. Jerry Izenberg, "He Walked Final Mile of Boyer's Agony," (Newhouse News Service story), *St. Louis Globe-Democrat*, October 16, 1982, Ken Boyer file, St. Louis Mercantile Library Collection.

23. Milton Richman, "Undying Love Bound Boyers," *New York Post*, September 8, 1982, 59, Boyer HOF file. Jane Boyer and Kathleen Boyer interview, August 27, 2013.

24. Henry Hecht, "Ken Boyer Succumbs to Cancer at 51," *New York Post*, September 8, 1982, Boyer HOF file.

25. The black armbands were worn during the last 10 home games of the regular season, but time constraints prevented them from appearing on the sky blue road jerseys. They were added, however, for the National League Championship Series and the World Series. Jack

Herman, "Devine Made Sure That Boyer's Career Here Was Not Short," *St. Louis Globe-Democrat*, September 9, 1982, 6C.

26. Milton Richman, "Undying Love Bound Boyers," *New York Post*, September 8, 1982, 59, Boyer HOF file. Jerry Izenberg, "He Walked Final Mile of Boyer's Agony," (Newhouse News Service story), *St. Louis Globe-Democrat*, October 16, 1982, Ken Boyer file, St. Louis Mercantile Library Collection. "Ken Boyer Dies of Cancer at 51," *New York Post*, September 8, 1982, Boyer HOF file. "Cards Play With Boyer In Mind," (Associated Press story) *Daytona Beach* (FL) *Morning-Journal*, September 10, 1982, 9B.

27. The portrait of Boyer was commissioned by Joe Linneman, owner of the Mari de Villa Retirement Center, where Ken lived during his illness. It was painted by an artist with Tommy McDonald Enterprises, a Philadelphia portrait studio owned by the former pro football Hall of Fame quarterback. Wendell Redden, "Family Friends Gather in Tribute to Boyer," *Joplin* (MO) *Globe*, September 11, 1982. Phillip Lee, "Classic Catches Up With Tommy McDonald," ESPN Classic website, http://espn.go.com/classic/s/Where_now_mcdonald_tommy.html (Accessed August 26, 2015).

28. Dick Wagner, "Boyer Remembered in Services," *St. Louis Globe-Democrat*, September 10, 1982, 1C. Suzie (Boyer) Hartwig, Dan Boyer, Jane Boyer interviews, July 22, 2011.

29. "Funeral Service Conducted for Ken Boyer," *St. Louis Post-Dispatch*, September 10, 1982, 2C. Wendell Redden, "Family, Friends Gather in Tribute to Boyer," *Joplin* (MO) *Globe*, September 11, 1982. Among the mourners at Boyer's funeral in Ballwin were Cardinals coaches Red Schoendienst and Hal Lanier, general manager Joe McDonald, Director of Player Development Lee Thomas, Director of Administration Joe McShane, trainer Gene Gieselmann, equipment manager Butch Yatkeman, team physician Dr. Stan London, pitcher Bob Forsch, first baseman Keith Hernandez, former pitcher John Fulgham, and former General Manager Bing Devine. Wagner, "Boyer Remembered," *Globe-Democrat*, September 10, 1982, 1C, 3C.

30. Wendell Redden, "Family, Friends Gather in Tribute to Boyer," *Joplin* (MO) *Globe*, September 11, 1982. Suzie (Boyer) Hartwig, Dan Boyer, Jane Boyer interviews, July 22, 2011. The St. Louis Cardinals were represented at Boyer's funeral in Alba by coaches Red Schoendienst and Hal Lanier, Director of Player Development Lee Thomas, and pitcher Bob Forsch. Among the mourners were friends and former teammates Bill Virdon and Floyd Woodridge. Redden, "Family, Friends Gather," *Joplin Globe*, September 11, 1982.

31. Jack Buck, *Busch Beer Presents: Celebration! 1982 World Champion St. Louis Cardinals*. St. Louis National Baseball Club, 1982. https://www.youtube.com/watch?v=qyZUJiYRojE (Accessed September 10, 2015).

32. "Honor to Busch, Boyer's Children," (United Press International story) *Los Angeles Times*, October 5, 1982, D11. Jack Buck play-by-play, Game 7 of the 1982 World Series. http://www.youtube.com/watch?v=lOpRNY0Y0Rc (Accessed August 21, 2013). Jerry Izenberg, "He Walked Final Mile of Boyer's Agony," *St. Louis Globe-Democrat*, October 16, 1982, St. Louis Mercantile Library Collections. John Warner Davenport and Jeffrey Neuman, *The Cardinals: The Complete Record of Redbird Baseball* (New York: Collier Books, 1983), 4.

Chapter 19: An Exceptional Ballplayer

1. Bob Broeg, "Boyer Ranked Among Best," *St. Louis Post-Dispatch*, September 7, 1982, 1C.

2. Chicago Tribune, *Ron Santo: Heart and Soul of the Cubs* (Chicago: Triumph Books, 2010), 77. Baseball Hall of Fame Ballot and Voting Summaries (1975-1979), http://www.baseball-reference.com/awards/ (Accessed September 18, 2015).

3. Bill James, *Whatever Happened to the Hall of Fame? Baseball, Cooperstown, and the Politics of Glory* (New York: Simon & Schuster, 1995), 253. "Bill White: Cards Wanted Him As Manager," Retrosimba blog, http://retrosimba.com/2011/03/30/bill-white-cards-wanted-him-as-manager/ (Accessed September 13, 2013). Red Schoendienst interview, February 15, 2013.

4. Ken Boyer page, Baseball-Reference.com, http://www.baseball-reference.com/players/b/boyerke01.shtml. "The Sporting News All-Stars," Baseball Chronology site, http://www.baseballchronology.com/Baseball/Awards/TSN-AllStars.asp (Accessed October 24, 2015).

5. Bernie Miklasz, "Bernie: The Hall of Fame Case for Ken Boyer," *St. Louis Post-Dispatch*, November 1, 2014, http://www.stltoday.com/sports/columns/bernie-miklasz/bernie-the-hall-of-fame-case-for-ken-boyer/article_12a13e44-325b-516e-b033-ee7ab949e110.html (Accessed November 1, 2014). J.M. Catellier, "St. Louis Cardinals: Does Ken Boyer Belong in the Baseball Hall of Fame?" RantSports website, http://www.rantsports.com/mlb/2013/05/08/st-louis-cardinals-does-ken-boyer-belong-in-the-baseball-hall-of-fame/ (Accessed November 7, 2015).

6. Solly Hemus interview, January 19, 2013.

7. Red Schoendienst interview, February 15, 2013.

8. Bob Broeg, "Hot Corner? Traynor, No Argument." *TSN*, August 2, 1969, 29.

9. Bob Broeg, "Dean Compares Boyer to Traynor," *St. Louis Post-Dispatch*, June 2, 1964, Boyer HOF file. "Drysdale Picked by Mays as Hurler on All-Foe Club," *TSN*, August 28, 1965, 10. The players Mays chose were Gil Hodges, first base; Jackie Robinson, second; Ken Boyer and Eddie Matthews, third; Pee Wee Reese, shortstop; Stan Musial, Roberto Clemente, and Hank Aaron, outfield; Roy Campanella, catcher; and Don Drysdale, pitcher. *Ibid*.

10. Bob Broeg, "Ken Boyer—Deserving of the Hall," *Fowl Ball: A Collectible Newspaper Featuring St. Louis Baseball!*, undated article, 4, Boyer HOF file. McCarver with Pepe, *Few and Chosen*, 63.

11. Lowry, *Green Cathedrals*, 201. Oscar Kahan, "Redbirds' Boyer Aims Bat at 100-RBI, 30-HR Goals," *TSN*, January 24, 1962, 16. Fifty-one percent of Boyer's home runs were hit at Busch Stadium I. "The Batting Splits for Ken Boyer," Retrosheet site, http://www.retrosheet.org/boxesetc/B/Jboyek1010.htm (Accessed October 24, 2015).

12. Santo hit 216 of his 342 career home runs at Wrigley Field; Boyer had 130 of his 255 career home runs with the Cardinals at Busch Stadium I. Ron Santo and Ken Boyer player statistics, Retrosheet.org website.

13. "The Batting Splits for Ron Santo," Retrosheet site, http://www.retrosheet.org/boxesetc/S/Jsantr1020.htm (Accessed October 24, 2015). Lipman, Boyer, 146-147.

14. Boyer was at Class A Omaha when Jablonski was at Class B Winston-Salem in 1951. Ray Jablonski Minor-League Register, http://www.baseball-reference.com/register/player.cgi?id=jablon002ray (Accessed November 13, 2015).

15. Jayson Stark, *The Stark Truth: The Most Overrated and Underrated Players in Baseball History*. Chicago: Triumph Books, 2007, 124.

16. Jack Herman, "Memories of Ken Boyer, '64 MVP: Cards Salute the Retiring of No. 14," *St. Louis Globe-Democrat*, undated clipping, Boyer HOF file. In addition to Musial, Brock, and Gibson, the other retired number was No. 17 worn by Dizzy Dean. Ibid. Neal Russo, "Teammates Relieved As Shannon Misses HR," *St. Louis Post-Dispatch*, May 21, 1984, 1C. The framed jersey still hangs high over the entry area of Charlie Gitto's Pasta House at 207 North Sixth Street in St. Louis along with other sports and celebrity photographs and memorabilia.

17. "Cardinals Establish Hall of Fame & Detail Induction Process," St. Louis Cardinals Official Site, January 18, 2014, http://m.mlb.com/news/article/66822534/

cardinals-establish-hall-of-fame-detail-induction-process (Accessed October 24, 2015). The other inductees were Cardinals greats Jim Bottomley, Dizzy Dean, Frank Frisch, Chick Hafey, Jesse Haines, Rogers Hornsby, Joe Medwick, Johnny Mize, Enos Slaughter, Ozzie Smith, and Bruce Sutter; broadcaster Jack Buck; former owner August A. "Gussie" Busch Jr.; managers Whitey Herzog, Tony La Russa, and Billy Southworth, and general manager Branch Rickey. *Ibid.*

18. Albert Pujols Career Home Runs, Baseball-Reference.com, http://www.baseball-reference.com/players/event_hr.cgi?id=pujolal01&t=b (Accessed June 15, 2015).

19. Suzie (Boyer) Hartwig interview, July 22, 2011.

Bibliography

Aaron, Hank with Lonnie Wheeler. *I Had A Hammer: The Hank Aaron Story*. New York: HarperCollins, 1991.
Altman, George with Lew Freedman. *George Altman: My Baseball Journey from the Negro Leagues to the Majors and Beyond*. Jefferson, NC: McFarland & Company, 2013.
Bikter, Steve. *The Original San Francisco Giants: The Giants of '58*. Champaign, IL: Sports Publishing, Inc., 2001.
Boxerman, Burton A. and Benita W. Boxerman. *Ebbets to Veeck to Busch: Eight Owners Who Shaped Baseball*. Jefferson, NC: McFarland & Company, Inc., 2003.
Broeg, Bob and Jerry Vickery. *The St. Louis Cardinals Encyclopedia*. Lincolnwood, IL: Masters Press, 1998.
Broeg, Bob. *Memories of a Sportswriter*. Champaign, IL: Sagamore Publishing, 1995.
Brosnan, Jim. *The Long Season*. Chicago: Ivan R. Dee, 2002.
Brosnan, Jim. *The Ted Simmons Story*. New York: G.P. Putnam's Sons, 1977.
Buck, Jack with Rob Rains and Bob Broeg. *Jack Buck: "That's A Winner!"* Champaign, IL: Sagamore Publishing, 1997.

Caray, Harry with Bob Verdi. *Holy Cow!* New York: Villard Books, 1989.
Chicago Tribune. *Ron Santo: Heart and Soul of the Cubs.* Chicago: Triumph Books, 2010.
Cohen, Robert W. *The 50 Greatest Players in St. Louis Cardinals History.* Lanham, MD: The Scarecrow Press, Inc., 2013.
Craft, David and Tom Owens. *Redbirds Revisited: Great Memories and Stories from St. Louis Cardinals.* Chicago: Bonus Books, Inc., 1990.
Davenport, John Warner and Jeffrey Neuman. *The Cardinals: The Complete Record of Redbird Baseball.* New York: Collier Books, 1983.
Devaney, John. *The Greatest Cardinals of Them All.* New York: G.P. Putnam's Sons, 1968.
Devine, Bing with Tom Wheatley. *The Memoirs of Bing Devine: Stealing Lou Brock and Other Winning Moves by a Master GM.* Chicago: Sports Publishing LLC, 2004.
Dolson, Frank. *Jim Bunning: Baseball and Beyond.* Philadelphia: Temple University Press, 1998.
Eisenbath, Mike. *The Cardinals Encyclopedia.* Philadelphia, Temple University, 1999.
Erwin, Marliene, ed. *Alba-Neck City-Purcell-Tri-City History, 1984.* Shawnee Mission, Kansas: Kes-Print, 1984.
Figuero, Jorge S. *Who's Who in Cuban Baseball, 1878-1961.* Jefferson City, NC: McFarland & Company, Inc., 2003.
Flood, Curt with Richard Carter. *The Way It Is.* New York: Trident Press, 1970.
Forker, Dom. *Sweet Seasons: Recollections of the 1955–64 New York Yankees.* Dallas, TX: Taylor Publishing Company, 1990.
Freedman, Lew. *The Boyer Brothers of Baseball.* Jefferson City, NC: McFarland & Company, 2015.
Garagiola, Joe. *Baseball is a Funny Game.* New York: Bantam Books, 1985.
Gibson, Bob and Reggie Jackson with Lonnie Wheeler. *Sixty Feet, Six Inches: A Hall of Fame Pitcher & A Hall of Fame Hitter Talk About How the Game is Played.* New York: Doubleday, 2009.
Gibson, Bob with Lonnie Wheeler. *Stranger to the Game: The Autobiography of Bob Gibson.* New York: Viking, 1994.

Gibson, Bob with Phil Pepe. *From Ghetto to Glory: The Story of Bob Gibson*. Englewood Cliffs, NJ: Prentice-Hill, Inc., 1968.
Giglio, James N. *Musial: From Stash to Stan the Man*. Columbia: University of Missouri Press, 2001.
Golden, Steven, ed. *It Ain't Over 'Til It's Over: The Baseball Prospectus Pennant Race Book*. New York: Basic Books, 2007.
Golenbock, Peter. *Amazin': The Miraculous History of New York's Most Beloved Team*. New York: St. Martin's Griffin, 2002.
Golenbock, Peter. *The Spirit of St. Louis: A History of the St. Louis Cardinals and Browns*. New York: HarperEntertainment, 2001.
Groat, Dick with Frank Dascenzo. *Groat: I Hit and Ran*. Durham, NC: Moore Publishing Company, 1978.
Halberstam, David. *October 1964*. New York: Villard Books, 1994.
Hall, John. *Mickey Mantle: Before the Glory*. Leawood, KS: Leathers Publishing, 2005.
Hall, John. *The KOM League Remembered*. Charleston, SC: Arcadia Publishing, 2004.
Hamilton, Milo with Dan Schlossberg and Bob Ibach. *Makin' Waves: 60 Years at Milo's Microphone*. Champaign, IL: Sports Publishing, 2006.
Hernandez, Keith with Mike Ryan. *If At First...* New York: Penguin Books, 1987.
Hernández, Lou. *Memoirs of Winter Ball: Interviews with Players in the Latin America Winter Leagues of the 1950s*. Jefferson City, NC: McFarland & Company, Inc., 2013.
Hernon, Peter and Terry Ganey. *Under The Influence: The Unauthorized Story of the Anheuser-Busch Dynasty*. New York: Simon & Schuster, 1991.
Herzog, Whitey and Jonathan Pitts. *You're Missin' A Great Game: From Casey to Ozzie, the Magic of Baseball and How to Get It Back*. New York: Simon & Schuster, 1999.
Herzog, Whitey and Kevin Horrigan. *White Rat: A Life in Baseball*. New York: Harper & Row, 1987.
Higgins, Billy D. and Hal Smith. *The Barling Darling: Hal Smith in American Baseball*. Little Rock, AR: Butler Center Books, 2009.
Howsam, Bob with Bob Jones. *My Life in Sports*. Self-published, 1999.

Hughes, Pat with Bruce Miles. *Harry Caray: Voice of the Fans.* Naperville, IL: SourceBooks Media Fusion, 2008.

Jacobs, Bruce, ed. *Baseball Stars of 1957.* New York: Lion Library Editions, 1957.

James, Bill. *The New Bill James Historical Baseball Abstract.* New York: The Free Press, 2001.

James, Bill. *Whatever Happened to the Hall of Fame? Baseball, Cooperstown, and the Politics of Glory.* New York: Simon & Schuster, 1995.

John, Tommy with Dan Velenti. *T.J.: My My 26 Years in Baseball.* New York: Bantam Books, 1991.

Johnson, Lloyd and Miles Wolff, eds. *Encyclopedia of Minor League Baseball.* 3rd Edition. Durham, NC: Baseball America, 2007.

Kennedy, Kevin with Bill Gutman. *Twice Around the Bases: The Thinking Fan's Inside Look at Baseball.* New York: HarperCollins, 2006.

Klein, Dave. *Great Infielders of the Major Leagues.* New York: Random House, 1972.

Launius, Roger D. *Seasons in the Sun: The Story of Big League Baseball in Missouri.* Columbia: University of Missouri Press, 2002.

Lechman, Don. *Los Angeles Dodgers Pitchers: Seven Decades of Diamond Dominance.* Charleston, SC: The History Press, 2012.

Lindberg, Richard C. *Total White Sox: The Definitive Encyclopedia of the World Champion Franchise.* Chicago: Triumph Books, 2006.

Lipman, David. *Ken Boyer.* New York: G.P. Putnam Sons, 1967.

Lowenfish, Lee. *Branch Rickey: Baseball's Ferocious Gentleman.* Lincoln: University of Nebraska Press, 2007.

Lowry, Philip J. *Green Cathedrals: The Ultimate Celebration of Major League and Negro League Ballparks.* New York: Walker Publishing Company, 2006.

McCarver, Tim and Phil Pepe. *Few and Chosen: Defining Cardinal Greatness Across the Eras.* Chicago: Triumph Books, 2003.

McCarver, Tim with Danny Peary. *The Perfect Season: Why 1998 Was Baseball's Greatest Year.* New York: Villard Books, 1999.

McCarver, Tim with Danny Peary. *Tim McCarver's Baseball Book for Brain Surgeons and Other Fans.* New York: Villard Books, 1998.

Mickelson, Ed. *Out of the Park: Memoir of a Minor League Baseball All-Star.* Jefferson, NC: McFarland & Company, Inc., 2007.

Monteleone, John J., ed. *Branch Rickey's Little Blue Book: Wit and Strategy from Baseball's Last Wise Man*. New York: Mountain Lion, Inc., 1995.

Moon, Wally with Tim Gregg. *Moonshots: Reflections on a Baseball Life*. San Antonio, TX: Moon Publishing, 2010.

Musial, Stan and Bob Broeg. *Stan Musial: "The Man's" Own Story*. New York: Doubleday & Company, Inc., 1964.

O'Neill, Dan and Bernie Miklasz. *Stan Musial, Baseball's Perfect Knight: A Story Told from the Pages of the St. Louis Post-Dispatch*. St. Louis: St. Louis Post-Dispatch Books, 2010.

Peary, Danny, ed. *We Played the Game: 65 Players Remember Baseball's Greatest Era, 1947–1964*. New York: Hyperion, 1994.

Rains, Rob. *The St. Louis Cardinals: The 100th Anniversary History*. New York: St. Martin's Press, 1992.

Robinson, Ray, ed. *Baseball Stars of 1965*. New York: Pyramid Books, 1965.

Schoendienst, Red with Rob Rains. *Red: A Baseball Life*. Champaign, IL: Sports Publishing, 1998.

Smith, Curt. *Voices of the Game: The First Full-Scale Overview of Baseball Broadcasting, 1921 to the Present*. South Bend, IN: Diamond Communications, 1987.

Snyder, Brad. *A Well-Paid Slave: Curt Flood's Fight for Free Agency in Professional Baseball*. New York: Plume, 2007.

Snyder, John. *Cardinals Journal: Year by Year & Day by Day with the St. Louis Cardinals Since 1882*. Cincinnati, OH: Emmis Books, 2006.

Spatz, Lyle, ed. *The SABR Baseball List & Record Book*. New York: Scribner, 2007.

Stahl, John Harry and Bill Nowlin, eds. *Drama and Pride in the Gateway City: The 1964 St. Louis Cardinals*. University of Nebraska Press, 2013.

Stark, Jayson. *The Stark Truth: The Most Overrated and Underrated Players in Baseball History*. Chicago: Triumph Books, 2007.

The Sporting News Baseball Dope Book 1965. St. Louis: The Sporting News, 1965.

Uecker, Bob and Mickey Herskowitz. *Catcher in the Wry: Outrageous But True Stories of Baseball*. New York: Jove Books, 1984.

Vecsey, George. *Stan Musial: An American Life*. New York: Ballantine Books, 2011.

Vecsey, George. *Baseball's Most Valuable Players*. New York: Random House, 1966.

Vincent, David, Lyle Spatz, David W. Smith. *The Midsummer Classic: The Complete History of Baseball's All-Star Game*. Lincoln, NE: University of Nebraska Press, 2001.

Weaver, Earl with Berry Stainback. *It's What You Learn After You Know It All That Counts: The Autobiography of Earl Weaver*. Garden City, NY: Doubleday & Company, Inc., 1982.

Webb, Delores Boyer. *Memories of My Life*. Self-published, no date.

Wendel, Tim. *The Summer of '68: The Season That Changed Baseball—and America—Forever*. New York: De Capo Press, 2013.

White, Bill with Gordon Dillow. *Uppity: My Life in Baseball*. New York: Grand Central Publishing, 2011.

Wolfe, Rich and George Castle, eds. *I Remember Harry Caray*. Champaign, IL: Sports Publishing, 1998.

Zanger, Jack. *Ken Boyer: Guardian of the Hot Corner*. New York: Thomas Nelson & Sons, 1965.

Index

2nd Armored Division Travellers, 51
28th Division Artillery Redlegs, 50–51
28th Division Special Troops Troopers, 50, 51
172nd Regiment Indians, 50
899th Anti Aircraft Artillery AW Battalion, 50
4054th Army Service Unit baseball team, 50

Aaron, Hank, 96, 100, 113, 114, 132, 138, 142, 144, 197, 214, 335
Abernathy, Ted, 256
Adcock, Joe, 99
Agee, Tommie, 282
Al Lang Field (St. Petersburg, Florida), 80, 270, 277, 304
Alba Aces, 8, 9, 10, 11, 12, 16, 17, 32, 33, 249
Alba Christian Church, 359
Alba High School, 12, 14, 23, 31
Alba, Missouri, 4, 7, 8, 9, 12, 13, 15, 16, 23, 34, 35, 49, 50, 51, 89, 156, 233, 245

Albamo, The, 13
Albany, Georgia, 23, 39
Albuquerque (Double-A club), 303
Albuquerque, New Mexico, 306
Alcatraz Island Penitentiary, 149
Alemendares Blues, 70, 72
Aliperto, Joe, 39, 40
All-Star Games,
  1956, 95–96
  1957, 106–107
  1959 (1), 132–133
  1959 (2), 133
  1960 (1), 151–152
  1960 (2), 152
  1961 (1), 161–162
  1962 (2), 172–173
  1963, 187–189
  1964, 213–215
  1965, 260
Allen, Hank, 289
Allen, Richie (Dick), 223, 260, 362
Allentown, Pennsylvania, 28
Almendares, Pedro, 73
Alou, Felipe, 172
Alston, Tom, 105, 166

445

Alston, Walter, 96, 152, 293, 297, 299, 300, 303, 356
Altman, George, 182, 187, 190, 198
Altobelli, Joe, 313, 314
Ambassador Hotel (Los Angeles), 294
American Association, 9, 45, 103, 309, 312, 313
American Baseball Cap (A.B.C.) Company, 103
American Cancer Society, 332
American League, 96, 150, 152, 162, 166, 173, 189, 231, 233, 281, 283, 288, 290, 291
Amore, Vicente, 65
Amoros, Sandy, 70
Anderson, Bob, 138
Anderson, Ferrell (Andy), 51
Anderson, Harry, 109
Anheuser-Busch Brewery, 53, 54, 94, 167, 324, 332
Antiaircraft and Guided Missle Branch of the Artillery School (Fort Bliss, Texas), 50
Antonelli, Johnny, 107, 142
Aparicio, Luis, 173
Arbela, Missouri, 3
Arkansas Travelers, 305–307, 316, 330, 332
Arroyo, Luis, 60, 62, 63, 64, 67, 68, 86, 192
Ashburn, Richie, 89, 118, 246, 269
Associated Press, 167, 246
Association of Professional Baseball Players of America, 354
Astrodome (Houston, Texas), 258
Atchley, Jim, 66, 67
Atkinson, Dick, 65
Atlanta Braves, 271, 272, 273, 284, 293, 295, 298, 300, 308, 321, 330, 333, 334, 337, 359
Atlanta Crackers, 66-69
Atlanta-Fulton County Stadium, 320
Atlanta, Georgia, 66, 67, 272
Atlantic Coast Line, 80

Bad Kreuznach, Germany, 51
Bahnsen, Stan, 344

Bailey, Bob. 295
Bailey, Ed, 100
Bainbridge Hotel (St. Petersburg, Florida), 80
Baker, Bill, 109
Baldschun, Jack, 218
Ballpark Village (St. Louis), 366
Ballwin, Missouri, 358
Baltimore Orioles, 15, 43, 57, 75, 139, 142, 145, 214, 233, 284, 285, 313, 314, 319, 322, 323
Bamberger, George, 321
Ban Johnson League of Southeast Kansas, 12, 46, 249
Banks, Ernie, 256, 300, 335
Bare, Ray, 309, 310, 322
Barkley, Bob, 33
Barnhart, Dick, 27, 28, 29
Baseball Hall of Fame, *see National Baseball Hall of Fame*
Baseball Winter Meetings, 363
Baseball Writers Association of America (BBWAA), 100, 362, 363, 364
Batavia Clippers, 24, 27, 28, 29
Batavia, New York, 27
Batista, Fulgencio, 70
Bauman, Bob (Doc), 128, 149, 193, 234, 260
Bauta, Ed, 148
Baxter Springs Whiz Kids, 11–12, 16, 249
Baxter Springs, Kansas, 9, 12, 16
Beaumont Explorers, 57, 59, 61, 62, 63
Beaumont, Texas, 57
Bedell, Howie, 294
Bel Air Motel (St. Louis), 224
Bell, Gary, 152
Bell, Les, 244
Belmont, Missouri, 9
Benevolent & Protective Order of Elks (B.P.O.) Lodge No. 9 (St. Louis, Missouri), 103, 142, 253
Benson, Vern, 221, 307, 318
Berkeley, Missouri, 89
Berra, Yogi, 95, 96, 142, 152, 233, 244
Berry, Ken, 283, 290
Betebenner, Stanley, 33

Bilko, Steve, 55
Bird, Larry, 14
Black Wednesday, 288
Blades, Ray, 48
Blanchard, Johnny, 243
Blasingame, Don, 56, 59, 60, 61, 63, 64, 66, 67, 68, 69, 70, 77, 80, 85, 93, 99, 100, 108, 111, 123, 134, 356
Blaylock, Gary, 141, 203
Bloomington, Minnesota, 285
Boggess, Dusty, 129, 254
Boles, Howie, 64
Bonds, Bobby, 340, 341, 343, 346
Boone, Ike, 60
Boone, Ray, 95
Borbon, Pedro, 341
Boston Braves, 39, 41, 42
Boston Red Sox, 173, 214, 277, 281, 285, 286, 287, 288, 289, 324
Boston, Massachusetts, 162
Bottomley, Jim, 172
Bouchee, Ed, 134
Bouton, Jim, 234, 236
Boy's Life, 142
Boyd, Bob, 58, 60, 61, 62, 65, 66
Boyer, Andrew, 3
Boyer, Bobbie, 31
Boyer, Chester Vern, 3–7, 10, 16, 31, 36, 89, 233, 242, 252, 351
Boyer, Clarence, 3
Boyer, Cletis (Clete), 7, 31, 36, 56, 89, 146, 152, 229, 231–232, 236, 239, 240–241, 242, 243, 244, 245, 269, 274, 282, 284, 308, 320, 350, 353, 354, 355, 357, 358, 364, 365
Boyer, Cloyd, 5–12, 14, 15, 18, 26–27, 31, 32, 33, 36, 43, 49, 51, 53, 54–55, 89, 231–233, 320, 321, 355, 365
Boyer, Dan, 133, 156, 177, 205, 206, 255, 295, 351, 354–355, 359, 366
Boyer, David, 89, 125, 177, 196, 204, 205, 206, 295, 310, 316, 330, 332, 357, 359, 366

Boyer, Dewana (Suzie), *see Hartwig, Suzie (Boyer)*
Boyer, Jane, 153, 177, 205, 206, 318, 351, 359, 366
Boyer, Kathleen (Oliver), 4, 23, 49–50, 51, 56, 69, 70, 71, 73, 75, 89, 115, 125–126, 133, 147, 153, 161, 176–177, 178, 191, 204, 205, 207, 223, 229, 239, 245, 246, 255, 261, 264, 267, 274, 277, 295, 298, 321, 322, 357
Boyer, Lenny, 31, 306
Boyer, Lewis Lynn, 7, 31, 36, 52
Boyer, Lewis Winfield, 3
Boyer, Lila Thelma, 4
Boyer, Mabel (Means), 3–7, 31, 35, 50, 52, 89, 233, 242, 252, 308
Boyer, Marcy, 31, 232
Boyer, Milton Wayne, 4–7, 9, 11, 12, 14, 15, 31, 32, 33, 49, 80, 232
Boyer, Pansy (Powell), 3
Boyer, Pansy, 7, 31
Boyer, Ron, 31, 357
Boyer, Shirley, 7, 31
Bradenton, Florida, 309
Bradford Phillies, 25, 26, 27, 28, 29
Bradford, Buddy, 287
Bradford, Pennsylvania, 26
Bragan, Bobby, 272
Branca, Ralph, 354
Brandon, Bucky, 286
Brandt, Jackie, 93
Bressoud, Ed, 275
Brewer, Sam, 44
Brock, Lou, 137, 190, 211-212, 215, 216, 218, 219, 224, 225, 226, 227, 235, 237, 242, 246, 250, 259, 260, 263, 322, 325, 328, 332, 333, 334, 337, 338, 340, 366, 367
Broeg, Bob, 80, 81, 84, 85, 88, 89, 90, 97, 113, 119, 121, 157, 176, 247, 265, 266, 296, 327, 362, 364
Broglio, Ernie, 132, 141, 150, 152, 153, 154, 157, 159, 166, 178, 185, 187, 194, 212, 218

Bronze Hope Chest Award (Multiple Sclerosis Society), 254
Brooklyn Dodgers, 41, 42, 49, 51, 59, 83, 84, 86, 88, 91, 94, 96, 98, 99, 100, 106, 107, 108, 109, 110, 111, 112, 183, 188, 354
Brooklyn, New York, 94
Brosnan, Jim, 122, 131–132, 136
Broun, Heywood Hale, 279
Brown, Joe L., 115, 189
Brown, Leonard, 32
Brown, Prentice (Pidge), 28
Brown, Willard, 61, 62, 64, 66, 67
Bruton, Bill, 100
Buck, Jack, 175, 176, 227, 265, 323, 354, 358, 359–360, 366
Buckhart, Ken, 65
Buckner, Bill, 299
Buff Stadium (Houston, Texas), 59, 61, 62, 64, 65, 68, 119, 142
Buford, Don, 282, 284, 287, 289, 290
Buhl, Bob, 99, 135
Bunning, Jim, 149, 172, 218, 223
Burdette, Freddie, 218
Burdette, Lew, 111, 113, 158, 187, 188
Burnes, Bob, 266, 327, 356
Busch Gardens (Tampa, Florida), 168
Busch Memorial Stadium II, 272, 274, 293, 325, 355, 364, 365, 366
Busch Stadium (Houston, Texas), 142
  see also Buff Stadium
Busch Stadium I, 83, 84, 90, 104, 114, 119, 129, 130, 134, 135, 140, 148, 149, 152, 158, 164, 170, 171, 174, 176, 179, 187, 190, 191, 196, 198, 200, 208, 210, 223, 226, 227, 228, 232, 234, 242, 254, 257, 261 *see also Sportsman's Park*
Busch, August A. Jr. (Gussie), 53–54, 83, 90, 102, 105, 116, 125, 156, 160, 167, 178, 182, 183, 191, 216-217, 226, 228, 244–245, 264, 313, 322, 329, 331, 332, 343, 344, 345, 347, 348, 349, 358
Busse, Ray, 311
Byrd, Red, 81, 90

California Angels, 273, 281, 283, 286, 287, 346, 353, 354
Callison, Johnny, 215, 222, 245
Candlestick Park (San Francisco), 161, 171, 179, 210
Caray, Harry, 211, 223, 228, 261, 336, 354
  calls KB's World Series grand slam, 238–239
  on-air treatment of KB, 174–177
Carbo, Bernie, 333, 335, 339
Carbondale Pioneers, 19, 21
Carbondale, Pennsylvania, 21
Cardenas, Leo, 213
Cardinal Junior League, 8–12, 16, 33
Cardinals Caravan, 210, 333
Cardwell, Don, 147, 182
Caribbean Series, 73
Carl Junction, Missouri, 9, 12
Carlos, Cisco, 286
Carlton, Steve, 298, 332, 333, 354, 367
Carmichael, John P., 146
Carrigan, Sam, 65
Carter, Gary, 359
Carthage, Missouri, 10, 16
Cash, Norm, 116
Cassville All-Stars, 52
Castellano, Joe, 324
Castro, Fidel, 70
Cater, Danny, 285
Causey, Wayne, 282
Cavenaugh, Dick, 334
Ceccarelli, Art, 139
Central Park (New York), 274
Cepeda, Orlando, 214, 296
Chancellor, Raymond, 277
Charles, Ed, 278, 279, 280
Charleston, West Virginia, 323
Cheney, Tom, 145
Chicago Cubs, 24, 65, 82, 85, 88, 91, 97, 99, 102, 105, 106, 109, 110, 112, 114, 119, 120, 124, 130, 132, 133, 138, 139, 140, 150, 151, 152, 154, 155, 158, 159, 162, 164, 171, 172, 185, 187, 189, 190, 194, 196, 198, 211, 213, 214, 215, 216, 218, 219, 256, 257, 261, 263, 274, 275,

278, 293, 298, 300, 326, 327,
329, 330, 331, 340, 343, 348,
353, 356, 365, 366
Chicago Daily News, 146, 212
Chicago Tribune, 82
Chicago White Sox, 58, 90, 107, 119,
136, 142, 162, 166, 173, 177,
233, 280, 281–289, 291–292,
298, 299, 303, 312, 329
Chicago, Illinois, 82, 84, 157, 186, 253,
266, 364
Chuka, Joe, 44
Cienfuegos Elephants, 70, 71, 72, 73
Cimoni, Gino, 133, 145
Cincinnati Reds/Redlegs, 58, 67, 69,
71, 79, 85, 86, 88, 90, 91, 92,
94, 95, 98, 99, 100, 104, 105,
106, 110, 111, 112, 113, 121,
123, 131, 132, 133, 134, 135,
142, 143, 147, 148, 150, 153,
154, 157, 158, 159, 163, 164,
165, 170, 171, 172, 179, 186,
190, 191, 195, 196, 210, 213,
214, 215, 216, 218, 219, 220,
222, 223, 224, 225, 226, 227,
229, 245, 247, 257, 258, 259,
262, 273, 275, 278, 279, 292,
298, 311, 330, 333
Claiborne, John, 331, 332, 335–336,
343, 344, 345, 346, 347, 348,
349, 360
Cincinnati, Ohio, 84, 90
Cisco, Galen, 193
City Island Park (Daytona Beach,
Florida), 54
Civic Stadium (Hamilton, Ontario,
Canada), 24
Civic Theater (Webb City, Missouri),
6
Clarkson, James (Buzz), 61
Class D baseball, 20
Clay County, Missouri, 3, 4
Clemente, Roberto, 106, 152, 162, 164,
165, 214, 221
Clemons, Doug, 212
Clendenon, Donn, 220, 224

Cleveland Indians, 15, 19, 27, 41, 96,
116, 152, 161, 183, 283, 284,
286, 287, 292, 340, 356
Club Náutico (Havana, Cuba), 70
Cobb, Ty, 325
Coffman, Harold (Hal), 41, 42, 43,
46, 47
Colavito, Rocky, 116, 143, 161, 162,
173, 182, 284, 285, 287, 289,
292, 293
Cole E. Grimes Stadium
(Fredericksburg, Pennsylvania),
19, 22
Coleman, Ray, 66
College of Coaches, 24
Colorado Springs Sky Sox, 41, 42, 44,
45, 47
Colorado Springs, Colorado, 41, 44,
45
Columbia University, 254
Columbus Lions, 10
Columbus Red Birds, 40, 54
Columbus, Georgia, 60
Columbus, Kansas, 9, 10
Coma, Albert (Mike), 20
Comstock, Walter, 32
Cooper, Ramon, 33
Condrick, George, 58, 65, 66
Conlan, Jocko, 86, 353
Conley, Gene, 111
Connie Mack Stadium (Philadelphia),
219
Consolidated Investment Associates,
157
Contini, Harold (Hal), 19, 20, 21, 22,
24, 37, 304
Cook, Joe, 13
Cooper Grocery (Alba, Missouri), 8,
13
Cooper, Buford, 8, 9, 10, 11, 15, 16,
17, 33
Cooper, Cecil, 33
Cooper, Gary, 136
Cooperstown, New York, 209
Cope, Myron, 175
Corrales, Pat, 268
Cosell, Howard, 352–353, 354
Coss, Buford, 32

Coss, Ray, 32
Coss, Royden L., 32
Cossville, Missouri, 4, 9
County Stadium (Milwaukee), 113
Covington, Wes, 222
Cox, Billy, 188
Cox, Bobby, 321
Craig, Ben, 12
Craig, Roger, 92, 140, 158, 198, 221, 237, 240, 243
Crandell, Del, 99, 173, 306
Crawford, Sam, 107
Creamer, Robert, 98
Cristante, Leo, 67
Cromartie, Warren, 344
Crosby, Ed, 310
Crosby, Ken, 309
Crosley Field (Cincinnati), 84, 85, 110, 164
Crowder, Joe (Red), 51–52
Crowe, George, 130, 148, 166
Crowley, Terry, 314
Cruz, Hector, 309
Cruz, Jose, 305, 306, 307
Cuban Winter League, 69–74
Cuellar, Mike, 215, 216
Cullen, Tim, 288, 289
Cunningham, Joe, 105, 108, 111, 125, 129, 132, 133, 135, 138, 139, 141, 144, 149, 158, 159, 162, 166, 355
Cy Young Award, 343

Daley, Arthur, 81
Dallas Eagles, 59, 60, 61, 62
Damato, Joe, 62
Daniels, Bennie, 130
Dark, Alvin, 87, 93, 100, 104, 108, 109, 111, 112, 113, 120, 189
Davenport, Jim 122, 172
Davis, Jim, 102
Davis, Tommy, 173, 189, 279, 291
Davis, Willie, 299–300
Daytona Beach, Florida, 54
De Jesus, Ivan, 334
Dean, Jay (Dizzy), 364, 366
Decker, Vernon, 33

Del Greco, Bobby, 92, 99, 100, 103
Deland, Florida, 54
Denny, John, 309, 325, 327, 329, 333, 335, 338, 339
Denver Bears, 41, 44, 45, 46, 47, 311, 312, 313
Des Moines Bruins, 40, 42, 44, 47, 48
Des Moines, Iowa, 41, 44
Detroit Tigers, 15, 67, 84, 90, 95, 152, 161, 172, 270, 281, 283, 284, 286, 287, 288, 296, 322, 332
Detroit, Michigan, 253
Devine, Vaughan (Bing), 18, 117–118, 119, 123, 128, 131, 146, 156, 160, 182, 183, 184, 211, 215, 216-217, 228–229, 244, 245, 246, 259, 268, 276, 278–279, 280, 281, 303, 323, 325, 331
DeWitt, Bill III, 366
Dickson, Murry, 92, 102
Dietz, Dick, 294
DiMaggio, Joe, 139, 142
Diprima, Frank, 67
District of Columbia Stadium (Washington, D.C.), 172
Dixie Series, (1954) 66-69
Dodger Stadium, 171, 179, 185, 192, 210, 273, 293, 294, 295, 300
Donovan, Dick, 68
Downing, Al, 234, 237–238, 242–243
Dr. Robert F. Hyland Award, 352
Dreesen, Tom, 354
Drysdale, Don, 112, 138, 148, 155, 162, 179, 180, 210, 262, 273, 293-295, 297, 356
Dunn, J.C., 22
Duren, Ryne, 59
Durocher, Leo, 244
Duval community, Missouri, 4
Dwyer, Jim, 310, 325
Dyer, Eddie, 67

Easler, Mike, 312
Ebbets Field (Brooklyn, New York), 84, 85, 99, 106, 107, 110
Eberhardt, Walter C. (Doc), 256
Edwards, Johnny, 186, 214, 220

El Dorado Springs, Missouri, 15
El Paso Sun Kings, 60
El Paso, Texas, 49–50
Elia, Lee, 353
Ellsworth, Dick, 190, 257
Elston, Don, 164
Ennis, Del, 102, 108, 111, 112, 115, 174
Erskine, Carl, 99
European Stars and Stripes, 51
Eyrich, George, 41, 42

Face, Roy, 26, 48, 108, 142, 186
Fairley, Ron, 131
Felix, Cat, 66
Fenway Park (Boston), 162, 286, 288
Ferguson, Joe, 306
Fisher, Jack, 271
Fleishman, Al, 168
Fleming, Eugene, 26
Flood, Curt, 120, 130, 140, 147, 148, 162, 166, 169, 178, 179, 180, 186, 187, 190, 195, 197, 210, 212, 213, 214, 216, 218, 223, 224, 226, 235, 237, 239, 240, 250, 259, 263, 267, 299, 332, 362, 367
Flowers, Ben, 92
Foley, Doc, 66
Foli, Tim, 340
Fondy, Dee, 82
Foote, Barry, 340
Forbes Field (Pittsburgh), 132
Ford, Dale, 150
Ford, Whitey, 132, 234, 235
Forsch, Bob, 309, 323, 325, 326, 329, 339, 343, 358
Fort Bliss Baseball League, 50
Fort Bliss Falcons, 50
Fort Bliss, Texas, 49, 50
Fort Lauderdale, Florida, 167
Fort Worth Cats, 56, 58, 60, 61, 62, 65–66
Fort Worth, Texas, 59, 60, 66
Fox, Nellie, 96, 162
Frank Scott Associates, 141–142
Franks, Herman, 294

Frazier, George, 344
Frazier, Joe, 86, 92, 352
Fredricksburg, Pennsylvania, 19
Freed, Roger, 333, 335, 339
Freese, Gene, 48, 115
Fregosi, Jim, 214
Frene Valley, 277
Frick, Ford, 83, 257
Friend, Bob, 95, 153
Friends Cemetery (Purcell, Missouri), 359, 362
Frisch, Frankie, 104, 304
Froemming, Bruce, 326
Fryman, Woodie, 344
Fulgham, John, 337, 338, 346

Gabrielson, Len, 292, 293
Galena, Kansas, 11
Galiana, Pedro, 70
Garagiola, Joe, 109, 136, 354
Garagnani, Biggie, 94
Garvey, Steve, 299, 341
Gastonia, North Carolina, 350
Gazdik, Bill, 30
Gehrig, Lou, 354
Geiselman, Gene, 355
Georgia-Alabama League, 11
Gerson Institute, 352
Gerson Therapy, 352
Gibson, Bob, 129, 130, 133, 134, 139, 141, 148, 152, 162, 166, 168, 169, 174, 178, 179, 180, 184, 187, 188, 190, 193, 195, 212, 218, 219, 220, 222, 224, 225, 226, 227, 228, 236, 240, 241, 242, 243, 247, 250, 251, 256, 257, 258, 259, 261, 263, 279, 293, 296–297, 299, 332, 351, 352, 366, 367
Giles, Warren, 86, 95, 97, 241
Gillespie, Ray, 128
Gilliam, Junior, 96, 97
Gitto, Charlie, 366
Gohl, Victor, 47
Golden Era Committee (Baseball Hall of Fame), 363
Gomez, Preston, 323
Gonzáles, Miguel (Mike), 69, 73

Gotay, Julio, 182, 183
Governor's Cup (PONY League), 30
Gowdy, Curt, 238
Grammas, Alex, 80, 85, 92, 130, 147, 149
Gran Stadium de la Habana (Havana, Cuba), 70, 73
Grant's Farm (St. Louis), 191, 347
Grapefruit League, 146, 256
Gray, Dick, 148
Green, Gene, 120, 121, 122, 145
Greenwood, Missouri, 15
Greifzu, Hank, 26, 28
Griffith Stadium (Washington, D.C.), 95
Grit, 5
Griva, Arlene, 317
Griva, Darwin, 317
Groat, Dick, 132, 168, 182, 184, 186, 188, 189, 190, 191, 192, 193, 194, 195, 197, 213, 214, 216, 217, 219, 221, 222, 223, 227, 229, 236, 237, 238, 239, 241, 242, 243, 244, 246, 247, 257, 258, 262, 263, 267, 296, 304, 249, 356
Gross, Don, 111
Grove, Oklahoma, 15
Guiliano, Phil, 26
Gulf Coast League (GCL) Cardinals, 309
Gulf Coast League, 308, 310

Habana Leones (Lions), 69–73
Hack, Stan, 124
Haddix, Harvey, 86, 92, 93, 118, 163
Halberstam, David, 168
Hamilton Cardinals, 24–30, 38, 40, 55
Hamilton Spectator, 26
Hamilton, Jack, 179, 272, 273
Hamilton, Ontario, Canada, 24, 39
Hamilton, Steve, 243
Hands, Bill, 300
Hansen, Ron, 282
Harlow, Larry, 314
Harmon, Chuck, 92, 103
Harmon, Tom, 310

Harris, Luman, 308
Harris, Thomas L., 4
Hartwig, Geoffrey, 321
Hartwig, Gregory, 321
Hartwig, Suzie (Boyer), 127, 254, 255, 321, 355, 358, 359, 366
Hatten, Joe, 73
Hawaii, 126
Hazelton Mountaineers, 21, 22
Hazelton, Pennsylvania, 21
Hazle, Bob, 111
Heffner, Don, 61
Heise, Bob, 310
Hemus, Solly, 85, 86, 87, 92, 125, 128, 129, 130, 139, 140, 141, 146, 148, 150, 151, 153, 155, 158, 159, 160, 203, 354, 363
  makes KB team captain, 135
Henderson, Steve, 328
Hendrick, George, 328, 330, 335, 336, 340, 341, 343
Herbert, Ray, 84, 173
Herman, Jack, 105, 134, 265, 327
Hermann High School, 310, 332
Hermann, Missouri, 245, 277, 290, 292, 303, 326, 355
Hernandez, Keith, 309, 310, 311–312, 325, 326, 328, 331, 333, 335, 337, 338, 341, 342, 346, 355, 359
Herr, Tommy, 347, 350, 355
Herzog, Dorrel (Whitey), 274, 345, 346, 348, 360
Hession, Eddie, 239
Heston, Grace (Means), 125
High Noon, 136
Hill, Marc, 310, 311, 312
Hiller, Chuck, 275
Himsl, Avitus (Vedie), 24, 25, 26, 27, 29, 30
Hiroshima, Japan, 126
Hoak, Don, 188
Hobbie, Glen, 139, 155, 195
Hodges, Gil, 97, 131, 140, 142, 188, 364
Hoerner, Joe, 280
Holden, Danny, 42
Holland Park (Okahoma City), 65

Hollis, John, 62
Home Run Derby, 142–144
Hooton, Burt, 326
Horlen, Joe, 284, 285, 287, 288, 289
Hornell Dodgers, 25, 28–29
Hornsby, Rogers, 88, 139, 179, 304
Horton, Tony, 287
Hosp, George, 11
Hot Stove League Express, 269
Hotel Otesaga (Cooperstown, New York), 107
Houston Astros, 187, 190, 272, 274, 275, 278, 293, 295, 298, 310, 312, 333, 341
Houston Buffaloes (Buffs), 49, 52, 53–69, 77, 78, 160, 311, 356, 365
Houston Colt .45s, 166, 169, 170, 173, 178, 181, 185, 192, 210, 212, 260, 261, 262, 268
Houston Post, 56, 58, 61, 62, 67
Houston, Texas, 53, 56, 58, 61, 119, 169, 253
Howard, Elston, 69, 214, 233, 237–238
Howard, Frank, 195, 289
Howsam, Bob, 217, 255, 259–260, 264, 266, 268
Hrabosky, Al, 305, 322
Hubbell, Carl, 293, 294
Huggins-Stengel Field (St. Petersburg, Florida), 270
Hughes, Jim, 84, 85
Hughes, Tom, 139
Huisman, Bill, 306
Hummel, Rick, 327, 345, 346, 347
Humphreys, Bob, 219
Hunt, Ron, 269, 272, 273, 275
Hunter, Jim (Catfish), 280
Huntsville, Arkansas, 49
Hutchinson, Fred, 90, 91–92, 93, 94, 95, 98, 103, 105, 109, 110, 113, 114, 118, 119, 120, 121, 123, 124, 128, 165, 172, 214, 336

Ibanez, Alfredo, 71
Independent Meat Company, 89
Independent Packing Company, 102

Indianapolis Indians, 54, 311
International League, 314

J.G. Taylor Spink Award, 128, 255
Jablonski, Ray, 71, 79–80, 365
Jackson, Al, 187, 224, 225, 265–266
Jackson, Grant, 296
Jackson, Larry, 86, 100, 106, 108, 110, 113, 122-123, 126, 140, 141, 147, 151, 157, 159, 162, 163, 166, 172, 179, 180, 182, 185, 186, 189, 198, 256, 278, 294
Jackson, Reggie, 353
James, Bill, 189
James, Charlie, 161, 162, 170, 179, 180, 186, 210
Jamestown Falcons, 25
Japan tour (1958), 125–126
Jasper County, Missouri, 3, 4, 8, 9, 13
Jasper News, 4
Jaster, Danny, 306
Jaster, Larry, 272
Javier, Julian, 148, 158, 159, 170, 183, 188, 189, 190, 210, 221, 224, 226, 234, 235, 249, 259, 262, 268, 356, 367
Jeffcoat, Hal, 111, 131
Jenkins, Dan, 274
Jenkins, Ferguson, 353
John, Tommy, 136, 177, 277, 282, 286, 288, 289, 290, 299, 331
Johnson City, Tennessee, 10, 350
Johnson, Alex, 267
Johnson, Dave, 29
Johnson, Deron, 219
Johnson, Walter, 293
Jones, Charlie, 261
Jones, Cleon, 275
Jones, Sam, 93, 102, 107, 108, 110, 121, 123, 129, 140
Jones, Spike, 193
Jones, Willie (Puddin' Head), 148
Jones's Food Center (Alba, Missouri), 233
Joplin All-Stars, 51, 52
Joplin Globe, 10, 13, 14, 17, 52
Joplin High School, 14

Joplin Sports Authority Hall of Fame, 365
Joplin Sunny Jims, 10, 11
Joplin, Missouri, 9, 15, 23, 73, 80, 210, 232
Jordan, Michael, 14
Juarez, Mexico, 50
Jutze, Skip, 307

Kaat, Jim, 340, 344
Kaline, Al, 152, 161
Kaminsky, Russ, 14
Kanehl, Rod, 227
Kansas City Athletics, 15, 89, 214, 231, 256, 278, 282, 284, 285, 287, 280
Kansas City Blues, 9, 46–47
Kansas City Royals, 345, 346, 355
Kansas City, Missouri, 3, 49, 152, 253
Kansas, 8, 9, 89
Kasko, Eddie, 105, 112, 114, 196
Katt, Ray, 93
Keane, Johnny, 18, 67, 160, 162, 166, 167, 173, 191, 194, 196, 197, 209, 212, 217, 221, 222, 223, 224, 225–226, 227, 228, 232, 234, 236, 237, 240, 241, 242, 244–245, 272–273
Keating, Tom, 29
Keeler, Wee Willie, 139
Kellert, Frank, 63, 64
Kellner, Alex, 123
Ken Boyer Baseball School, 144–145
Ken Boyer Ford-Mercury, 277, 317
Ken Boyer TG 15 Trap-Eze Rawlings glove, 142
Ken Boyer TT20 Rawlings glove, 142
Ken Boyer's Travel Inn, 156–157
Kennedy, Bob, 305, 306
Kennedy, John F., 172
Kennedy, Kevin, 322, 324
Kennedy, Robert F., 294
Keough, Marty, 219
Kessinger, Don, 300
KFSB radio station (Joplin, Missouri), 233
Killebrew, Harmon, 143–144, 214, 353

King, Clyde, 59
King, Jim, 114
King, Martin Luther Jr., 291
Kirkland, Willie, 123
Kissell, George, 40, 42, 43, 45, 47, 48, 75, 318
Kline, Ron, 106, 145, 152
Kluszewski, Ted, 95, 282
KMOX radio station (St. Louis), 142, 144, 175, 224, 265, 283
Knights of the Cauliflower Ear, 102
Knowles, Darold, 332, 338, 339
Kolb, Gary, 193, 195
Koppett, Leonard, 239
Korean War, 30
Koufax, Sandy, 129, 131, 140, 161, 179, 194, 195, 210, 240, 262, 274–275, 297
Kranepool, Ed, 224, 228, 270, 271, 276, 277, 279, 280
Krenchicki, Wayne, 322
Krol, Jack, 323, 325
Kubiszyn, Jack, 183
Kuenn, Harvey, 95, 133, 142
Kurowski, Whitey, 100
Kyoto, Japan, 126

La Grave Field (Dallas, Texas), 60
La Palme, Paul, 86, 92
Labine, Clem, 134
Lambert Field (Airport), 107, 222, 241
Lamp, Dennis, 338
Landers, Lee, 149, 150, 310
Landrith, Hobie, 109, 113, 142
Landrum, Tito, 309
Lane, Frank, 89–90, 91, 92, 101, 102, 104, 106, 113, 114, 116–117, 201, 261, 336
  frustration with KB, 97–98
  tries to trade KB, 115–116
  tried to trade Stan Musial, 94
  trades Red Schoendienst, 93
Lanier, Hal, 355
Larsen, Don, 179
Law, Vern, 172
Lawry, Sylvia, 254

Lebanon Chix, 18, 19, 20, 21, 22, 23, 24, 37, 304
Lebanon Daily News, 18, 20, 23
Lebanon, Pennsylvania, 19
Lemmon, Jack, 279
Leonard, Dennis, 310
Lerchen, George, 58, 60, 64, 65, 66
Levine, Leo, 51
Lewis, Johnny, 210
Liberty, Missouri, 3, 4, 40
Liddle, Don, 93
Lieb, Fred, 95
Lincoln Athletics, 40, 43, 44, 46
Lincoln, Nebraska, 43, 44
Lindstrom, Fred, 364
Linneman, Georgana, 355
Linneman, Joseph, 355
Linz, Phil, 234, 236, 237, 238, 242
Littell, Mark, 332, 339, 340, 344
Little Rock, Arkansas, 303, 304, 330, 350
Littlefield, Dick, 93
Littlefield, John, 344
Locker, Bob, 286
Lockman, Whitey, 93
Lockport Reds, 26, 28
Logan, Johnny, 138
Long Beach, California, 294
Long Island, New York, 269
Long, Dale, 94, 95
Long, John, 358–359
Los Angeles Angels, 173, 189
Los Angeles Dodgers, 120, 121, 122, 124, 129, 131, 134, 138, 141, 146, 147, 148, 151, 154, 158, 159, 170, 172, 173, 179, 180, 185, 187, 188, 190, 192, 193, 194, 195, 197, 210, 216, 225, 229, 244, 254, 258, 266, 273, 275, 280, 292–300, 303, 323, 325, 330, 336, 337, 341, 356
Los Angeles Memorial Coliseum, 120, 122, 158, 175
Los Angeles, California, 110, 137, 142, 294, 364
Lou Gehrig Memorial Award, 254, 257
Louisville Colonels, 54
Louisville, Kentucky, 350

Lowell, Massachusetts, 239
Lowrey, Harry (Peanuts), 42, 56, 294
Luque, Dolph, 69–70
Lynch, Jerry, 112, 113
Lynchburg, Virginia, 10

Maas, Duke, 25
Maglie, Sal, 122
Mahaffey, Art, 268
Mahanoy City Brewers, 19, 20, 21
Major League Baseball Players Association, 137, 297, 353
Maloney, Jim, 196
Mancuso, Gus, 69, 72
Mantle, Mickey, 12, 15, 46, 51, 96, 101, 116, 142, 143, 214, 233, 234, 235, 236, 237, 241, 243, 249, 256, 353
Mapes, Cliff, 51
Maples, Tommy, 33
Mari de Villa Retirement Center, 355
Marianao Tigers, 70, 72
Marichal, Juan, 170, 171, 187, 297
Marion, Marty, 42, 48, 183, 351, 257, 272
Maris, Roger, 116, 234, 235, 237, 241, 243, 274, 296, 353
Marr, Clinton (Runt), 15, 52
Marshall, Mike, 284, 331
Martin, Billy, 353, 354, 355
Martin, Harold, 32
Martin, Pepper, 253
Mathes, Joe, 16, 40, 79
Mathews, Eddie, 100, 111, 113, 124, 129, 132, 152, 175, 189, 194, 217, 353, 362, 363, 364, 365
Matthau, Walter, 279
Mauch, Gene, 219, 353
Maxvill, Dal, 226, 227, 234, 242, 243, 244, 247, 296, 331, 336
May, Jerry, 221, 224
Mays, Willie, 79, 95, 96, 117, 132, 142, 162, 165, 189, 210, 213, 214, 255–256, 262, 364
Mazeroski, Bill, 142, 188, 189, 224, 279
Mazzilli, Lee, 328

McAlister, Fred, 60
McBride, Bake, 322
McCain, Sam, 26
McCarthy, Joe, 107
McCarver, Tim, 135, 136–137, 138, 149, 177, 168, 177, 193, 194, 210, 216, 218, 221, 223, 227, 228, 234, 235, 236, 239, 241, 242, 243, 247, 251, 254, 258, 332, 367
McCraw, Tom, 282, 287, 288, 289
McDaniel, Lindy, 99, 140, 141, 147, 151, 152, 157, 159, 172, 180, 182, 190, 198, 218, 332
McDaniel, Von, 106, 108, 109, 110
McDonald, Joe, 366
McEnaney, Will, 334
McGee, Willie, 355
McKinley, Bill, 235
McMahon, Don, 67, 111, 148, 283
McMillan, Roy, 113, 227, 275
McNertney, Jerry, 285
McQueen, Steve, 352
Means, Carrie (Dunlap), 4
Means, Willace F., 4
Medoc, Missouri, 9
Medwick, Joe, 260
Melton, Bill, 292
Memphis Blues, 305, 306
Memphis, Tennessee, 253, 291
Meusel, Bob, 232
Meusel, Emil, 232
Meyer, Dick, 69, 71, 116
Miami, Florida, 70
Mickelson, Ed, 24
Middleman, Dr. I.C., 80
Mikkelsen, Pete, 300
Miller, Bob, 134, 172
Miller, Marvin, 353
Miller, Stu, 24, 25, 27, 28, 30, 92, 161
Milwaukee Braves, 66, 83, 90, 91, 92, 93, 94, 97, 98, 99, 100, 105, 106, 107, 108, 109, 110, 111, 112, 113, 114, 121, 123, 124, 129, 130, 131, 132, 133, 134, 135, 138, 140, 141, 148, 150, 152, 153, 154, 155, 157, 158, 159, 164, 165, 170, 185, 189, 191, 194, 213, 215, 217, 219, 246, 247, 257, 259, 271
Milwaukee Brewers, 321, 353, 360
Milwaukee, Wisconsin, 53
Mindenmines, Missouri, 15
Minner, Paul, 82, 85, 88
Minnesota Twins, 172, 281, 285, 286, 287, 288, 289
Minoso, Minnie, 166, 169, 170
Missouri Sports Hall of Fame, 365
Mize, Johnny, 94
Mizell, Wilmer (Vinegar Bend), 84, 99, 108, 110, 111, 113, 133, 141, 144, 148
Mizuhara, Nobuyasu, 126
Modesto Reds, 306
Monahan, Joe, 16
Montag, Bob, 67, 68
Montana, 24
Montreal Expos, 297, 313, 325, 327, 330, 333, 337, 338, 339, 344, 350, 358, 359
Moon, Wally, 80, 81, 82, 83, 84, 89, 90, 92, 93, 97, 106, 107, 108, 109, 111, 112, 113, 114, 115, 120, 123
Moore, Dale, 32
Moore, Terry, 48, 105, 119, 351
Morales, Jerry, 328–329
Moran, Billy, 173
Morgan, Bobby, 92, 97, 102
Morgan, Vern, 48
Moryn, Walt (Moose), 150
Mozzali, Mo, 325
Muchnick, Sam, 352
Muffett, Billy, 113, 307
Mulberry, Kansas, 15
Multiple Sclerosis, 145, 254
Mumphrey, Jerry, 309, 312, 325, 329, 330, 335
Municipal Stadium (Cleveland), 189
Municipal Stadium (Kansas City), 152
Municipal Stadium (Omaha, Nebraska), 41, 42, 45, 47
Muny Stadium, *see Municipal Stadium, Omaha, Nebraska*
Murphy, Billy, 273
Murtaugh, Danny, 115–116

Musgraves, Dennis, 269
Musial, Dick, 110
Musial, Lillian, 161, 191, 207
Musial, Stan, 42, 48, 56, 71, 80, 81,
    83, 86, 87, 88, 90, 92, 93, 94,
    95, 96, 100, 102, 103, 106, 108,
    109, 110, 111, 114, 116, 118,
    121, 122, 124, 125, 126, 128,
    129, 130, 132, 133, 136–137,
    138, 139-140, 146, 147, 148,
    149–150, 151, 152, 153, 156,
    159, 161, 162, 163, 165, 167,
    168, 169, 171, 172, 173, 178,
    179, 183, 190, 191, 192, 193,
    194, 195, 196, 197, 207, 209,
    210, 240, 244, 246, 255, 256,
    257, 270, 272, 299, 332, 335,
    351, 366

Nagoya, Japan, 126
Napoleon, Danny, 305
Nashville, Tennessee, 253
National Baseball Hall of Fame, 107,
    209, 325, 362, 364
National Baseball Placement Bureau,
    144
National League (East Division), 308,
    323, 325, 331, 355, 359
National League (West Division), 298,
    300, 325, 359
National League, 49, 79, 82, 86, 87,
    88, 89, 90, 92, 96, 99, 100, 103,
    109, 110, 113, 114, 122, 123,
    124, 128, 130, 132, 133, 139,
    141, 143, 146, 147, 151, 152,
    154, 155, 157, 159, 161, 162,
    163, 164, 165, 166, 170, 171,
    172, 173, 175, 180, 183, 184,
    187, 189, 195, 197, 201, 210,
    211, 214, 223, 226, 228, 231,
    241, 246, 260, 262, 263, 268,
    269, 271, 275, 278, 282, 284,
    287, 292, 293, 294, 296, 297,
    308, 312, 363
Nazareth Barons, 21
Nealon, Clark, 56, 58, 61
Nebraska, 89

Neck City, Missouri, 9
Negro Leagues, 61
Nen, Dick, 195
New Athens, Illinois, 345
New Orleans, Louisiana, 313
New York Giants, 43, 44, 49, 86, 93,
    94, 96, 99, 102, 104, 106, 107,
    108, 110, 112, 142, 232, 293,
    354
New York Mets, 15, 166, 169, 172, 173,
    178, 185, 186, 187, 191, 193,
    198, 216, 224, 228, 229, 257,
    258, 265–280, 282, 284, 291,
    297, 302, 328, 331, 339, 343,
    344, 346
New York Times, 81, 239, 280
New York Yankees, 15, 46, 51, 54, 69,
    96, 141, 145, 152, 166, 197,
    214, 229, 231–245, 272, 285,
    340
New York, 253, 295, 364
Newcombe, Don, 106, 108, 142
Niekro, Phil, 271
Nieman, Bob, 142, 145, 151
North Atlantic League, 18, 19, 22, 37
Nuxhall, Joe, 88, 99, 111, 131, 220

O'Dell, Billy, 170
O'Malley, Walter, 88, 297
O'Toole, Jim, 133, 218
Oakland Athletics, 331, 350, 353, 354
Oberkfell, Ken, 341, 346, 350, 359
October 1964, 168
Oiler Park (Tulsa, Oklahoma), 310
Oklahoma City Indians, 57, 61, 62, 63,
    64, 65
Oklahoma City, Oklahoma, 56, 57, 61,
    65, 310
Oklahoma, 8
Olean Oilers, 25, 28, 29, 30
Olean, New York, 29, 30
Oliver, Clarence, 23, 49
Oliver, Gene, 169, 179, 186, 187
Oliver, Viola (Clark), 23
Olivo, Diomedes, 182
Olympic Stadium (Montreal), 345, 359

Omaha Cardinals, 40–49, 55, 75, 103, 193
Omaha Royals, 310
Omaha World-Herald, 43, 46, 48
Omaha, Nebraska, 39, 40, 53, 85
Opelika, Alabama, 11
Orlando, Florida, 331
Osaka, Japan, 126
Ossala, Joe, 28
Osteen, Claude, 254, 262, 273, 325
Outrigger Inn (St. Petersburg, Florida), 167
Owens, Jim, 134

Pacific Coast League, 143, 349
Pallone, Dave, 334
Paparella, Rudy, 26
Pappas, Milt, 278
Paramount Pictures, 279
Parker, Carl, 7, 32
Parker, Dave, 340
Parker, Wes, 294, 298
Parr, W.W. (Tiny), 20, 21, 23
Parrott, Mike, 314
Parsons, Kansas, 16
Pascual, Camilo, 172
Pass the Biscuits, Mirandy, 193
Patterson, Keith, 33
Pavletich, Don, 218
Pawloski, Stan, 120
Pawtucket Red Sox, 314
Peekskill Highlanders, 20, 22
Peekskill, New York, 20
Peete, Charlie, 103
Pena, Roberto, 294
Pennsylvania National Guard, 50
Pennsylvania-Ontario-New York (PONY) League, 27, 28, 24, 30, 37
Pepitone, Joe, 214, 241–242
Perranoski, Ron, 195
Perry, Gaylord, 278
Peters, Gary, 285, 286, 287, 288
Peters, Hank, 321
Phi Delta Theta, 254
Philadelphia Athletics, 39, 40

Philadelphia Phillies, 86, 89, 92, 94, 97, 99, 104, 106, 108, 109, 110, 112, 118, 123, 125, 130, 131, 132, 133, 134, 139, 147, 148, 149, 150, 152, 153, 158, 165, 178, 185, 187, 191, 192, 193, 194, 211, 212, 213, 215, 216, 218, 219, 220, 222, 223, 224, 225, 226, 227, 228, 229, 244, 245, 246, 247, 260, 267, 273, 275, 278, 294, 296, 323, 325, 327, 330, 331, 333, 354
Philadelphia, Pennsylvania, 142, 174
Philippines, The, 126
Phillips, Howie, 60, 61, 64, 65, 66, 68
Phipps, Robert, 43, 45, 46, 48
Pinson, Vada, 164, 165, 224, 362
Pioneer League, 39
Pittsburg Elks, 9
Pittsburg, Kansas, 9
Pittsburgh Pirates, 39, 55, 84, 91, 93, 94, 95, 98, 100, 106, 107, 108, 110, 112, 115–116, 121, 123, 129, 130, 131, 132, 133, 140, 142, 145, 146, 148, 150, 151, 152, 153, 154, 155, 159, 163, 164, 170, 171, 172, 173, 178, 182, 183, 184, 185, 186, 189, 193, 194, 215, 216, 220, 221, 222, 223, 224, 229, 232, 257, 258, 259, 260, 275, 279, 294, 304, 308, 326, 330, 334, 337, 338, 339, 340, 341
Pittsburgh, Pennsylvania, 83, 94, 184, 188
Pizarro, Juan, 111, 133
Pocatello Cardinals, 39
Podres, Johnny, 83, 120, 134, 147, 154, 155, 180, 194, 195
Poholsky, Tom, 92, 94, 102
Pollet, Howie, 168
Polo Grounds (New York), 87, 94, 99, 110, 169, 172, 178
Ponce de Leon Park (Atlanta), 68
Ponce, Puerto Rico, 312
Preston township, Missouri, 3
Pueblo Dodgers, 41, 42, 44, 45, 48
Pueblo, Colorado, 41

Puerto Rico Winter League, 312, 325
Puhl, Terry, 334
Pujols, Albert, 366
Purcell, Missouri, 12, 359
Purkey, Bob, 163, 179

Quintana, Patricio (Witty), 59–60

Rac, Russell, 41, 42, 46, 47, 63, 67, 68
Radatz, Dick, 214, 215
Radison, Dan, 309
Ramada Safari Resort (Scottsdale, Arizona), 353
Rand, Dick, 56, 58, 60, 65, 69
Rapp, Vern, 311, 313–314, 322, 323, 325, 326, 327, 347
Raschi, Vic, 54
Rasmussen, Eric, 325, 326, 328
Rausch, Bob, 39
Rawlings Baseball Advisory Board, 142
Rawlings Gold Glove Award, 125, 141, 155, 165, 202, 231, 263, 329, 363, 365
Rawlings Sporting Good Company, 125, 142
Rector, Marvin, 14
Reddington Beach (St. Petersburg, Florida), 168
Reese, Pee Wee, 96, 188
Reichler, Joe, 167
Reitz, Ken, 326, 333, 336, 341, 344
Repulski, Eldon (Rip), 88, 92, 99, 100, 102
Reynolds, Ken, 309
Rice, John, 47
Rice, Del, 111
Richards, Paul, 308
Richardson, Bobby, 237, 240, 235, 243,
Richardson, Gordon, 219, 223
Richmond Braves, 322
Ricketts, Dave, 325
Rickey, Branch, 72, 103, 183, 185, 188, 217, 245, 268
Rivers, Mickey, 306
Roberts, Claude, 28
Roberts, Robin, 94, 104, 112, 131, 134

Robinson, Brooks, 214, 284
Robinson, Frank, 82, 219, 220, 353
Robinson, Jackie, 183, 188
Rochester Red Wings, 17, 18, 19, 37, 39, 54, 55, 67, 85, 117, 118, 160, 314, 319, 322, 324
Rochester, New York, 18, 142
Rodgers, Buck, 353
Roenicke, Gary, 322
Rojas, Cookie, 223
Ronning, Al, 58
Rose, Dan, 33
Rose, Max, 33
Rose, Pete, 224, 331
Rosebank baseball team, 7, 31
Rosebank School, 7
Rosenblatt, Johnny, 44
Rothrock, Jack, 244
Routzong, Art, 57, 62, 69, 244
Ruberto, Sonny, 325
Ruiz, Chico, 220, 224
Runnels, Pete, 173
Russo, Neal, 92, 182, 221, 229, 260, 327
Ryan, Nolan, 275
Ryba, Mike, 48

Sadecki, Ray, 148, 153, 157, 166, 171, 172, 180, 184, 190, 193, 194, 220, 223, 225, 228, 235, 237, 243, 247, 259, 272, 298
Sadowski, Bob, 187
Saigh, Fred, 40, 53
San Antonio Bears, 60
San Antonio Missions, 57, 59, 60, 61, 62, 63, 64, 306
San Antonio, Texas, 63
San Diego Padres, 297, 298, 326, 327, 328, 330, 336, 343, 353
San Francisco Giants, 120, 121, 122, 123, 129, 132, 133, 134, 135, 138, 140, 141, 145, 146, 147, 148, 149, 151, 154, 158, 159, 161, 162, 163, 164, 165, 170, 172, 179, 180, 185, 186, 187, 188, 189, 192, 193, 210, 213, 214, 215, 216, 226, 232, 247,

258, 262, 269, 273, 274, 278,
  280, 293, 295, 298, 300, 312,
  314, 326, 327, 330, 341, 342
San Francisco, California, 110, 135,
  161
Sanford, Jack, 154
Santiago, Jose, 286
Santo, Ron, 189, 213, 263, 298, 362,
  363, 365
Sarasota, Florida, 291, 309, 310
Sarni, Bill, 86, 87, 93
Sawatski, Carl, 163, 190
Sayers, David, 44
Schaffer, Jimmie, 182, 190
Schell, Pansy (Boyer), 6
Schmidt, Willard, 41, 42, 43, 45, 48,
  49, 56, 58, 59, 60, 63, 65, 67,
  68, 86, 89, 108, 112
Schoendienst, Albert (Red), 42, 48,
  56, 79, 80, 81, 82, 83, 84, 87,
  88, 89, 92, 93, 94, 96, 102, 113,
  116, 187, 197, 135, 137, 157,
  171, 245, 256, 259, 262, 264,
  266, 267, 307, 312, 313, 314,
  318, 323, 331, 332, 348, 355,
  357, 363, 364
Schofield, Dick, 69, 105, 106, 120
Schrader Funeral Home (Ballwin,
  Missouri), 358
Schultz, Barney, 45, 137, 218, 220, 222,
  227, 228, 235, 236, 256, 259,
  307, 318
Schultz, Buddy, 339
Score, Herb, 96, 116
Scotland County, Missouri, 3
Scott, Frank, 141–142
Scott, Mark, 143–144
Scott, Tony, 329, 334, 335
Scottsdale, Arizona, 353-354
Seals Stadium (San Francisco), 120
Seaman, Kim, 344
Seaver, Tom, 278, 329
Secory, Frank, 96, 97, 238
Seneca Indians, 51
Seneca, Missouri, 51
Senerchia, Emanuel (Sonny), 55, 56
Seoul, South Korea, 126
Sexton, Jimmy, 334

Shannon, Mike, 135, 195, 216, 217,
  219, 220, 221, 222, 228, 234,
  235, 236, 242, 246–247, 259,
  296, 298, 332, 351, 358
Shannon, Walter, 16
Shantz, Bobby, 194, 195, 212
Shaw, Bob, 142
Shea Stadium (New York), 214, 220,
  271, 272, 273, 278, 279
Sheldon, Rollie, 243
Sherry, Larry, 134, 151
Shirley, Jack, 47
Short, Ed, 282, 290, 292
Shreveport Sports, 58, 59, 60, 61, 62,
  63, 65
Silvey, George, 16
Simmons, Curt, 185, 193, 194, 195
Simmons, Curt, 99, 148, 150, 165, 171,
  218, 223, 226, 236, 241, 247,
  259
Simmons, Ted, 296, 299, 308, 323, 325,
  326, 329, 330, 336, 337, 339,
  341, 343, 345
Simon, Neil, 279
Sioux City Soos, 40, 42, 44, 47
Sioux City, Iowa, 43, 46, 47
Sisler, Dick, 307
Sizemore, Ted, 299
Skinner, Bob, 219, 236
Skowron, Bill (Moose), 353
Skurski, Andy, 47
Skyline Motel (St. Petersburg,
  Florida), 167
Slaughter, Enos, 42, 48, 56, 247
Smith, A. Ray, 313, 350, 352
Smith, Bob, 212
Smith, Bobby Gene, 103, 105, 112, 120
Smith, Charley, 227, 265–267, 272
Smith, Frank, 71
Smith, Hal, 28, 55, 65, 106, 111, 133,
  140, 142, 144, 149, 159, 203
Smith, Mayo, 109, 284
Solt, Jim, 68–69
Sooter, Hugh, 61, 66, 67, 68
South Atlantic League, 350
Southern Association, 66, 67, 69
Southworth, Bill, 280

INDEX

Spahn, Warren, 90, 100, 114, 123, 131, 148, 150, 154, 194, 262, 269, 311, 316
Spanish Lake, Missouri, 145, 184, 265
Spencer, Darryl, 145, 147, 148, 158
Spink, C.C. Johnson, 352
Spink, J.G. Taylor, 89, 102, 255, 327
Spooner, Karl, 59, 66
Sporting News, see *The Sporting News*
Sports Illustrated, 98, 128, 175, 274
Sportsman's Park, 9, 16, 31, 82, 83, 177, 272, 364 *see also Busch Stadium I*
Spring, Jack, 212
Springfield, Illinois, 327, 344, 350
Springfield, Missouri, 49, 156
St. Louis Area Cancer Crusade, 333
St. Louis Baseball Writers Dinner, 255
St. Louis Browns, 9
St. Louis Cardinals Hall of Fame, 366
St. Louis Cardinals, 9, 10, 11, 13, 15, 16, 17, 18, 23, 24, 26, 31, 37, 39, 40, 42–43, 45, 48–49, 52, 53-54, 56, 67, 69, 71, 72, 74, 78, 79-264, 272, 278, 279, 280, 282, 284, 287, 293, 295, 296, 298–299, 300, 303–313, 321
St. Louis Globe-Democrat, 105, 134, 265, 266, 324, 327, 356
St. Louis Post-Dispatch, 79, 80, 90, 92, 113, 119, 121, 157, 221, 228, 229, 242, 260, 265, 266, 272, 296, 327, 345, 352
St. Louis Sports Hall of Fame, 365
St. Louis University, 256, 269
St. Louis, Missouri, 16, 48, 49, 54, 69, 80, 240, 253, 254, 267, 276, 277, 298, 310, 313
St. Petersburg Cardinals, 309
St. Petersburg Chamber of Commerce, 167
St. Petersburg Yacht Club, 167
St. Petersburg, Florida, 80, 102, 166, 256, 270, 277, 304, 350
Staley, Gerald, 71, 80
Stallard, Tracy, 176, 274
Stan & Biggie's Restaurant (St. Louis), 244

Staniland, Chuck, 145
Stanky, Eddie, 43, 54, 71, 79–80, 81, 82, 83, 84, 85, 124, 244, 282, 283, 284, 288, 289, 291
Stargell, Willie, 294, 334, 340
Stark, Jayson, 365
Steinbrenner, George, 354
Stengel, Casey, 96, 146, 269, 270, 311
Stenhouse, Dave, 173
Stephenson, Bobby, 93
Stephenson, Earl, 326
Stevens, Chuck, 354
Stockton, J. Roy, 79, 188, 242–243
Stottlemyre, Mel, 234, 236, 242
Stroudsburg Poconos, 19, 20, 21
Stroudsburg, Pennsylvania, 19
Sturdivant, Tom, 51
Sturm, Johnny, 15
Stuttgart, Germany, 50
Sudakis, Bill, 296
Susman, Lou, 344
Sutter, Bruce, 343, 348, 360
Sutton, Don, 299, 326
Swisher, Steve, 342
Swoboda, Ron, 270, 271, 274, 277
Sykes, Bob, 332
Syracuse, New York, 142

Tanner, Chuck, 68
Tatum, Tommy, 61, 65
Taylor, Ron, 183, 240
Taylor, Tony, 294
Tebbetts, Birdie, 86
Temple, Johnny, 95
Templeton, Garry, 309, 312, 325, 329, 331, 334, 335, 336, 337, 339, 341, 342, 346
Terlecky, Greg, 309
Terre Haute, Indiana, 283
Texas League, 49, 52, 53, 55, 56, 57, 58, 60, 62, 63, 64, 65, 67, 303, 305
  All-Star Game (1954) 60–61
  All-Star Game (1970) 306
Texas Rangers, 309, 324, 347
Thacker, Moe, 182
The Long Season, 131, 132

The Odd Couple, 279
The Sporting News, 82, 89, 90, 95, 100, 102, 114, 125, 128, 142, 151, 165, 182, 212, 245, 257, 352, 363
The Stark Truth, 365
Thomas, Frank, 115–116, 158
Thomas, Lee, 309
Thomas, Roy, 345
Thompson, Glenn, 68, 69
Tiefenauer, Bob, 64, 65, 66
Tiger Stadium (Detroit), 284, 296
Tijuana, Mexico, 352, 354
Tokyo, Japan, 126
Toomey, Jim, 149
Torre, Frank, 67, 68
Torre, Joe, 214, 308, 331
Toth, Paul, 212
Town and Country, Missouri, 355
Traynor, Harold (Pie), 79, 364
Treasure Island (St. Petersburg, Florida), 168
Tresh, Tom, 240, 241, 243
Trevino, Bobby, 60
Tri-County League, 13
Tri-State Miners, 51
Tris Speaker Award, 253
Tucker, Raymond R., 240
Tulsa Oilers, 57, 58, 61, 150, 309–312, 313, 318, 350
Tulsa, Oklahoma, 53, 253, 325, 335
Turner, Ted, 321

U.S. Army in Europe baseball tournament, 51
Uecker, Bob, 175, 176, 177, 258, 261, 267, 354
Umberger, Dick, 19, 20
Union Station (St. Louis), 121
United Fund of Greater St. Louis, 142
United Press International, 114
University of Arkansas, 15
University of Louisville, 350
University of Missouri, 15, 332
Urrea, John, 326

Valentine, Bobby, 299
Valentine, Ellis, 312
Valentine, Fred, 289
Valentinetti, Vito, 93
Valenzuela, Benny, 120
Veale, Bob, 193
Vecsey, George, 137, 280
Venzon, Tony, 173
Vernon, Mickey, 137
Vero Beach, Florida, 297
Veterans Committee (National Baseball Hall of Fame), 363
Veterans Hospital at Jefferson Barracks (St. Louis), 145
Vietnam War, 305
Vincent, Al, 58
Virdon, Bill, 69, 70, 71, 72, 73, 80, 81, 83, 84, 87, 89, 92, 103, 126, 184
Virdon, Shirley, 70
Vitalis hair tonic, 142
Vuckovich, Pete, 312, 325, 326, 327, 329, 330, 331, 337–338, 339, 340, 343, 346

Wade, Gale, 51
Wagner, Honus, 171
Wagner, Leon, 145, 148, 150, 189
Wagner, Patrick, 157
Wakefield, Bill, 190
Walker, Dixie, 55, 56–57, 58, 64, 68, 81
Walker, Harry (The Hat), 85, 86, 87, 88, 244, 311
Ward, Pete, 283, 291
Wares, Clyde (Buzzy), 48
Warwick, Carl, 210, 225, 235, 237, 239, 250
Washburn, Ray, 172, 180, 184, 185
Washingham, Bill, 71, 80
Washington Senators, 143, 173, 293
Washington Senators, 288, 289
Washington Touchdown Club, 95
Washington University (St. Louis), 80
Washington, D.C., 95, 172
Watson, Bob, 295
Wayne, John, 136
Weaver, Earl, 40, 42, 43, 48, 75
Webb Brothers, 4

Webb City R-7 School District Hall of Fame, 365
Webb City, Missouri, 4, 9, 56
Webb, Delores (Boyer), 4, 5, 7, 13, 31
Wehmeier, Herm, 92, 100, 111, 112
Weir, Missouri, 15
Weiss, George, 269, 276
Wellsville Senators, 25, 29
Wendlestedt, Harry, 294
Western League, 43, 44, 46, 47, 48
Westrum, Wes, 269, 271, 275, 276, 277, 278, 279, 280
Whinesenant, Pete, 68, 86
Whitaker, Bill, 21
White Sox Park, 283, 291
White, Bill, 129, 134, 139, 141, 147, 148, 151, 159, 160, 161, 162, 163, 165, 166, 178, 180, 185, 187, 188, 189, 190, 194, 195, 197, 210, 212, 214, 215, 216, 218, 220, 222–223, 225, 226, 227, 235, 239, 240. 241, 242, 243, 245, 246, 249, 250, 255, 257, 259, 262, 263, 267–268, 296, 356, 363,
   and segregation in St. Petersburg, 167–168
Whitfield, Fred, 183
Wichita Aeros, 311
Wichita Indians, 41, 42, 44, 45, 46
Wichita, Kansas, 41
Wilhelm, Hoyt, 86, 102, 142, 286
Wilks, Ed, 228
Williams, Billy, 214, 353
Williams, Dick, 339, 353
Williams, Stan, 158, 292
Williams, Ted, 96
Williams, Walt (No Neck), 282, 283, 285
Williams, Zena (Allison), 12, 13
Wills, Maury, 172, 194
Winston-Salem Cardinals, 40
Wittich, Porter, 14, 17
Woodmansee, Juanita (Boyer), 4, 7, 31, 49
Wooldridge, Floyd, 69
Works Progress Administration (WPA), 4

Wrigley Field (Chicago), 82, 88, 93, 99, 106, 109, 120, 121, 124, 147, 154, 171, 173, 258, 340, 356, 365
Wrigley Field (Los Angeles), 143
Wyatt, John, 214
Wyatt, Whitlow, 68
Wynn, Early, 116

Yankee Stadium, 152, 233, 237, 286
Yastrzemski, Carl, 286
Yatkeman, Butch, 80, 110
YMCA Industrial Athletic Association (St. Louis), 142
Yoo-Hoo chocolate drink, 142
Young, Dick, 151
Youngblood, Joel, 343
Yvars, Sal, 354

Zambrano, Carlos, 366
Zernia, Harvey, 47
Zimmer, Don, 28

www.ingramcontent.com/pod-product-compliance
Lightning Source LLC
Chambersburg PA
CBHW021954160426
43197CB00007B/129